Palgrave Studies in the History of Economic Thought

Palgrave Studies in the History of Economic Thought publishes contributions by leading scholars, illuminating key events, theories and individuals that have had a lasting impact on the development of modern-day economics. The topics covered include the development of economies, institutions and theories.

The series aims to highlight the academic importance of the history of economic thought, linking it with wider discussions within economics and society more generally. It contains a broad range of titles that illustrate the breath of discussions – from influential economists and schools of thought, through to historical and modern social trends and challenges – within the discipline.

All books in the series undergo a single-blind peer review at both the proposal and manuscript submission stages.

For further information on the series and to submit a proposal for consideration, please contact the Wyndham Hacket Pain (Economics Editor) wyndham.hacketpain@palgrave.com.

More information about this series at
http://www.palgrave.com/gp/series/14585

David Glasner

Studies in the History of Monetary Theory

Controversies and Clarifications

palgrave
macmillan

David Glasner
Washington, DC, USA

ISSN 2662-6578 ISSN 2662-6586 (electronic)
Palgrave Studies in the History of Economic Thought
ISBN 978-3-030-83425-8 ISBN 978-3-030-83426-5 (eBook)
https://doi.org/10.1007/978-3-030-83426-5

Cover credit: ilbusca

This Palgrave Macmillan imprint is published by the registered company Springer Nature Switzerland AG
The registered company address is: Gewerbestrasse 11, 6330 Cham, Switzerland

Preface

The studies in this volume, written over the course of four decades, are the result of my continuing interest in monetary theory and its historical development. The studies often reflect my own disappointment with that development, especially the long ascendancy of the quantity theory of money and the price-specie-flow mechanism as the lynchpins of monetary theory and policy.

The prolific writings of Ralph Hawtrey from 1913 through the mid-1930s provided a basis on which an improved monetary theory might have been constructed. But, working largely in isolation as a civil servant, with little opportunity, despite his early prominence, to educate younger economists who might have carried on his unique approach to monetary theory, his own contributions were gradually eclipsed during the Great Depression, when they were most needed, falling into undeserved semi-oblivion.

Hawtrey's friend, J. M. Keynes, whose early work was influenced by, and shared much in common with, Hawtrey's approach, eventually set the profession on a much different path from that followed by Hawtrey. A couple of decades after Keynes published his great work, Milton Friedman launched an anti-Keynesian Monetarist counter-revolution. In their monumental *Monetary History of the United States*, Friedman and Anna Schwartz seemed to provide historical and empirical support for his Monetarist doctrines with what seemed a more compelling monetary explanation of the Great Depression than either Keynesian or non-Keynesian economists had ever before articulated.

But there was an earlier monetary theory of the Great Depression that had been forgotten by the time the *Monetary History* was published: the explanation that Hawtrey and Gustav Cassel had both developed independently in warning—fully a decade before the onset of the Great Depression—of the danger of a catastrophic deflation unless the likely resumption of the prewar gold standard was managed in a way that minimized increases in the international monetary demand for gold.

The sad story of the collective amnesia suffered by the economics profession concerning the Hawtrey-Cassel explanation of the Great Depression is not widely known. Although our understanding of the causes Great Depression was greatly enhanced over the past 30 years by the work of Barry Eichengreen, Peter Temin, and others, the more recent work merely confirms and expands upon the fundamental early insights of Hawtrey and Cassel, and the immense contributions of those two great economists remain unrecognized or underrated.

That is not the only sad story told in this volume. We are still watching the latter story work itself out in real time, without knowing how, or when, it ends. Following its 1980s collapse as a guide for policy and a theoretical paradigm, Monetarism was superseded by a new paradigm in which expectations are formed rationally, and all agents make micro-founded optimal decisions. Yet again, the economics profession has, in my view, taken the wrong path.

Perhaps I will have occasion in the future to spell out more fully than I have in this volume the reasons for my dissatisfaction with the path taken by modern macroeconomic theory. But I have begun telling that story in my three final chapters about Hayek. Although his early work led him to offer horrendous policy advice, it also endowed him with profound insight, at least in the abstract, into the conditions for intertemporal equilibrium and macroeconomic stability.

That profound insight, developed almost simultaneously with Hayek by two young Swedish economists, Gunnar Myrdal and Erik Lindahl, helped lead Hayek's younger colleague at the London School of Economics, J. R. Hicks, to develop the idea of temporary equilibrium as an alternative to the pure Walrasian general-equilibrium approach, whose underlying assumption of perfect foresight renders it unsuitable for the analysis of involuntary unemployment and financial crises. And it is that analysis, after all, which is what justifies the existence of macroeconomics.

But neither Hayek nor Hicks was able to carry the temporary-equilibrium approach forward as an analytical tool for monetary and macroeconomic theorizing, which, instead, wandered into the dead-end known as the neoclassical synthesis.

Enthralled by rational expectations, macroeconomists sought escape from that dead-end by succumbing to the methodological imperatives of axiomatic mathematical formalism, devoting themselves for 40 years to a family of sterile micro-founded models that, obeying methodological fiat, assume away the vexing problems of uncertainty and imperfect foresight that are, or should be, at the heart of any useful macroeconomic theory. Modern macroeconomics has thus been reduced to a methodological approach by which it has been disabled from considering the very problems that macroeconomists and monetary theorists ought to be addressing.

Attentive readers of the essays in this volume will hardly conclude that I am hostile to the theory and practice of neoclassical economics in which I was trained at UCLA, and whose alien concepts have been instilled deeply in my mind by a half-century of repeated and varied iteration. But the version of neoclassical theory on which modern macroeconomics has been built is a vulgar and reductive neoclassicism that is rightly disparaged and mocked by its critics.

These pessimistic comments notwithstanding, I have not lost hope that the following essays may provide some hints and suggestions about finding alternative paths toward a more useful macroeconomics.

Washington, DC, USA David Glasner

Acknowledgments

The studies that follow were written over the course of four decades, and I fear that there are many deserving of thanks whose assistance I no longer recall, and whom I therefore cannot mention, much less adequately thank.

Thanks to those whom I do remember must start with my parents, Rabbi Juda and Deborah Glasner, Holocaust survivors who arrived in the United States with my brother, Moses, in time for me to become a natural-born citizen of the United States of America, thereby anchoring the residence and eventual citizenship of my parents and my brother in the United States. My parents raised their two sons lovingly, instilling in us reverence for, and attachment to, the cherished traditional Judaism in which we were raised and the liberal, democratic values of their adopted country. They encouraged the pursuit of our scholarly ambitions, even though those ambitions were not quite the ones that they would have chosen for us.

My scholarly debts, of course, begin with my teachers at UCLA, especially Armen Alchian, Harold Demsetz, Jack Hirshleifer, Benjamin Klein, Axel Leijonhufvud, and Earl Thompson. Only Klein, Leijonhufvud, and Thompson taught me about monetary theory and macroeconomics, but, at a deep level, my understanding of what economics is about and how it should be done was enriched immeasurably by what I learned from all of them. I also had the benefit of meeting, and briefly studying under, F. A. Hayek when he visited the UCLA philosophy department in the 1968–1969 academic year. Notwithstanding my criticism of some of his writings and policy recommendations, his work, as will be evident to readers of this volume, has been a continuing source of insight and inspiration for me.

In writing the studies in this volume, I have benefitted from comments, suggestions, and criticisms from among others James Ahiakpor, Armen Alchian, William Baumol, Mark Blaug, Meyer Burstein, Phillip Cagan, Robert Clower, Patrick Deutscher, Robert Dimand, Malcolm Fisher, June Flanders, Charles Goodhart, Harald Hagemann, Geoffrey Harcourt, Benjamin Klein, David Laidler, Axel Leijonhufvud, Richard Lipsey, Perry Mehrling, Donald Moggridge, Jürg Niehans, Denis O'Brien, Anna Schwartz, George Selgin, Rajiv Sethi, Neil Skaggs, Matthew Smith, Scott Sumner, Earl Thompson, Richard Trestrail, and Larry White. I deeply regret being unable to mention the names of others who also provided valuable assistance when I was writing these studies.

I was greatly impressed by the early papers of David Laidler on Thomas Tooke and Adam Smith, and they have served as a model for me to emulate. David has never disappointed me when I sought to draw on his wisdom and his insight into economic theory and its history, which he has always imparted to me with thoughtfulness and good humor. I am deeply grateful for the benefit of his friendship and counsel.

A paper on the foundations of national-income theory by another great Canadian economist, Richard Lipsey, also made a deep impression on me when I read it as a graduate student. It was also one of the first papers I read that discussed Ralph Hawtrey in detail. In recent years, after beginning my blog *Uneasy Money*, Dick and I began corresponding frequently, and I have benefitted greatly from his insight and advice on diverse topics, especially the Phillips Curve, monetary neutrality, and rational expectations.

Chapter 6 in this volume was originally a paper presented at a conference in Tokyo in 2011 commemorating the 200th anniversary of David Ricardo's first published work in economics. That conference was conducted along with another conference on Ricardo which was attended by Geoffrey Harcourt who presented a paper to a joint session of the two conferences. It was my good fortune to meet Geoff for the first time before his lecture, and we immediately took a liking to each other, finding out to our surprise that, despite the differences in our upbringings and our viewpoints on economics, we shared similar eastern European roots. Though we have not seen each other since, we have stayed in frequent touch, and I am honored by, and grateful for his friendship, as well as his close reading of, and editorial and substantive comments on, several chapters in this volume. His encouragement and assistance were instrumental in the publication of this volume.

In 2009, Scott Sumner began his blog *The Money Illusion*. He kindly mentioned my book *Free Banking and Monetary Reform* and its proposal, borrowed from Earl Thompson, to stabilize the average level of expected wages. I had previously met Scott only once or twice at conferences that we had both attended. His blog became an internet sensation and was among the most important and popular of the many economics blogs that sprang up after the 2008–2009 financial crisis. We began corresponding regularly and I frequently submitted comments on his blog. Inspired and encouraged by Scott, I launched my *Uneasy Money* blog, in July 2011, which achieved modest success of its own, especially when noticed by another blogger, named Paul Krugman. That success renewed my interest in monetary theory, which had flagged in the preceding decade, and eventually led me to write several blogposts that turned into chapters or sections of chapters included in this volume. Chapter 8, in particular, was written at Scott's invitation for a joint conference that he and the estimable George Selgin organized on behalf of the Mercatus Center and the Cato Institute. I shall always be grateful to Scott for his friendship and encouragement.

I owe special thanks to my co-authors, Ronald W. Batchelder and Paul Zimmerman, for collaborating with me on three of the essays included herein. I have learned much from our collaboration, and the papers are now far better than they would have or could have been had I written them alone. I very much look forward to collaborating with them again on future projects.

Special thanks are also due to an old friend, Grace Goldblatt, for wise advice on a problem that I was unprepared to address by myself. On short notice, she graciously stepped in and helped me navigate a tricky situation that required resolution before I could finish this project.

My daughters, Chaya and Shifra, have been the most precious gifts and the greatest blessings that my wife and I have ever received. We thank them for helping to keep us young and busy, for bringing their husbands, Eytan Storfer and Yair Gemara, into our family, and making us proud grandparents. I am also indebted to Yair for helping me reproduce the diagrams in Chapters 2–4 of this volume.

Finally, and most important, my thanks and my heart go out to my wife and dearest friend, Tovi. Without your love and support, patience and good humor, in good times and not so good times, very little of what follows could have been written. You raised our daughters to become the wonderful and accomplished young women that they are today. Your life's work continues, but you have already accomplished so much. "May the Lord reward your deeds, may you have full recompense from the Lord God of Israel" (*Ruth* 2:12). I love you dearly.

I also want to thank Rachel Sangster, Wyndham Hacket Pain, Lavanaya Devgun, Srishti Gupta, Shreenidhi Natrajan, and Zobaria Jidda of Palgrave Macmillan for their thoughtful and capable assistance in developing the proposal for this book, and carrying it forward to a successful conclusion. The task has not always been easy, but I hope that the end result will be satisfying and worthwhile for us all.

Finally, I gratefully acknowledge permission to republish the following studies in this volume.

Chapter 2, "A Reinterpretation of Classical Monetary Theory" was originally published in *The Southern Economic Journal*, Vol: 52:1, pp. 46–67 © 1985, Republished by permission. Southern Economic Association.
Chapter 3, "On Some Classical Monetary Controversies" was originally published in *History of Political Economy*, Vol 21:2, pp. 201–229. © 1989, Duke University Press. All rights reserved. Republished by permission. www.dukeupress.edu.
Chapter 4, "The Real-Bills Doctrine in the Light of the Law of Reflux" was originally published in *History of Political Economy*, Vol: 24:4, pp. 867–894. © 1992, Duke University Press. All rights reserved. Republished by permission. www.dukeupress.edu.
Chapter 5, "Classical Monetary Theory and the Quantity Theory" was originally published in *History of Political Economy*, Vol: 32:1, pp. 39–59. © 2000, Duke University Press. All rights reserved. Republished by permission. www.dukeupress.edu.
Chapter 6, "Monetary disequilibrium and the demand for money in Ricardo and Thornton" was originally published in *Ricardo on money and finance: a bicentenary reappraisal*, pp. 15–29. © 2013 [according to the front matter the copyright is held by the author].
Chapter 8, "Rules versus Discretion in Monetary Policy Historically Considered" was originally published in *The Journal of Macroeconomics* Vol: 54:4a, pp. 24–41. © 2017, Elsevier. All rights reserved. Republished by permission.

Chapter 11, "Ralph George Hawtrey" was originally published in *The Elgar Companion to John Maynard Keynes*, pp. 338–347 It appears in this volume under the title "Hawtrey and Keynes."
Chapter 12, "Where Keynes Went Wrong" was originally published in *Encounter*, December 1988.
Chapter 13, "Debt, Deflation, the Great Depression and the Gold Standard" was originally published in *Money and Banking: The American Experience*, pp. 277–310.
Chapter 16, "Hayek, Deflation, Gold and Nihilism" was originally published in *Hayek: A Collaborative Biography* Part XIII: 'Fascism' and Liberalism in the (Austrian) Classical Tradition, pp. 161–192
Chapter 17, "Hayek, Hicks, Radner and Four Equilibrium Concepts: Perfect Foresight, Sequential, Temporary and Rational Expectations" was originally published in *The Review of Austrian Economics*

Praise for *Studies in the History of Monetary Theory*

"Understanding the uses and limitations of monetary policy requires first understanding how economists think about money, past, present and future. That the history of monetary theory, like the history of economic thought generally, has fallen out of fashion in academia is all the more reason to value the important work of David Glasner and the insightful essays collected in this book."

—Barry Eichengreen, *University of California, Berkeley, USA*

"David Glasner has been pursuing fundamental questions in monetary theory in a deep way for over thirty years. This collection represents the distillation of his wisdom, and any economist interested in these issues will learn a great deal by reading these pieces. They are deep in the theoretical sense but practical as well."

—Tyler Cowen, *George Mason University, USA*

"David Glasner challenges much conventional wisdom about monetary history, and his essays are invariably provocative, well researched and clearly written. They are a pleasure to read. They deserve serious attention from anyone interested in how ideas about the monetary system have, and still do, interact with its evolution and operation."

—David Laidler, *University of Western Ontario, Canada*

"David Glasner has pulled together a lifetime of erudite work on the history of monetary thought in this collection of papers. It is divided into two main blocks, the first part revisiting the UK classical monetary debates of the early 19th century, and the second part primarily on the contribution of Hawtrey and Hayek to interwar monetary issues. All are well worth reading, but I especially liked the emphasis on Hawtrey's contribution."

—Charles Goodhart, *London School of Economics, UK*

"This collection of essays is both an engaging excursion into the history of monetary thought, and a powerful case for an approach to macroeconomics that allows for heterogeneity in beliefs and adjustments to disappointed expectations. It will be of value to students of modern macroeconomics who would like a clear-headed appraisal of the limitations of textbook models, by someone who thinks with exceptional clarity about these complex and contentious issues."

—Rajiv Sethi, *Barnard College, Columbia University, USA*

"This book will surely give the history of economic thought a good name. Its lucid and convincing analyses of the celebrated debates relating to monetary theory from Hume through to Cairnes, and to the twentieth-century contributions by Hawtrey, Keynes and Hayek render it ideal for advanced courses. The author's account of the influences governing his intellectual development provides an interesting case-study of the informal lines of communication at play in the academic context."

—Samuel Hollander, *University of Toronto, Canada*

"This delightful book reviews, from a modern perspective, some classic debates in monetary economics. Beyond their historical interest, these debates still appear in contemporary discussions, even if dressed in different clothes. Take the Real Bills Doctrine, but rewrite it in terms of shadow banks: if non-conventional financial institutions lend only on the security of real bills, can they create too much money? Anyone interested in macroeconomics will benefit much from reading Glasner's collection of essays."

—Jesus Fernandez-Villaverde, *University of Pennsylvania, USA*

"David Glasner is a well-known historian of monetary economics and editor of the widely-read *Business Cycles and Depressions: An Encyclopedia*. In this inspiring collection, he focuses on controversies in classical monetary theory and contributions by Keynes, Hayek and Glasner's real hero, Ralph Hawtrey, who significantly advanced the analysis of monetary factors in economic fluctuations. The underlying unity is Glasner's development of the implications of the monetary approach to the balance of payments and endogenous money."

—Harald Hagemann, *University of Hohenheim, Germany*

"David Glasner's book captures his lifetime exploration into the deeper longstanding questions of monetary and macroeconomic theory, questions like Say's Law, and the nature of macroeconomic equilibrium. Unlike most theorists, David's approach is to situate these questions in historical context. So this book is much more than a collection of carefully-crafted essays in the history of economic thought, though it is that too. Strongly recommended to all readers interested in monetary theory and macroeconomics."

—Nicholas Rowe, *University of Western Ontario, Canada*

"David Glasner's *Essays in the History of Monetary Theory: Controversies and Clarifications* examines the long sweep of monetary economics from the 18th to the 21st century in relation to changing monetary institutions. Anyone who wishes to better understand how money worked in the past and may work in the future will profit from reading Glasner's lucid and informative book."

—Kevin Hoover, *Duke University, USA*

"David Glasner's collection of papers, some published previously some new, constitute together an impressive and comprehensive set of original studies covering monetary and macro analysis from the mid-18th century to the 20th. It is an admirable lifework, presenting a refined perspective that will appeal to everyone interested in the history of human thinking dedicated to the study of whole economies. Old and new controversies come to life, elucidating why scholars reach different conclusions. Highly recommended."

—Arie Arnon, *Ben Gurion University, Israel*

"David Glasner provides a tour de force of the history of monetary thought. Along the way, he reminds us that everything old is new again when it comes to monetary theory."

—David Beckworth, *George Mason University, USA*

"David Glasner's studies into the history of monetary theory show how certain classical macroeconomic principles, properly understood, can clarify some of the macroeconomic debates that continue to divide the profession. Glasner is particularly good at explaining how overlooked thinkers such as Gustav Cassel, Ralph Hawtrey and Earl Thompson developed insights into the sources of business cycles that were in many ways superior to the approaches developed by more famous theorists such as Keynes and Friedman."

—Scott Sumner, *George Mason University, USA*

"David Glasner's *Studies in the History of Monetary Theory: Controversies and Clarifications* is a tour de force through classical monetary theory and policy from Hume and Smith, an examination of Say's Law, and the implications of these controversies for the critical debates of the 20th century. Glasner has an astute ability to provide clarity to critical debates on the complicated subject of monetary theory and policy and macroeconomic and economic performance through time. Highly recommended."

—Peter Boetke, *George Mason University, USA*

"A very much needed and welcome collection of essays on monetary and banking theories. David Glasner reminds us that there is much more to economics that the Chicago School and its strawmen. This is a true work of history of ideas, where explanations of current crises can be found in three centuries of the study of money and banking. This volume is a must read for anyone interested in money and banking."

—Maria Pia Paganelli, *Trinity University, USA*

"David Glasner's new book is a sensitive and erudite exposition and exploration of classical monetary theory, from Smith to Hume and their interpretations. It also excavates the work of Ralph Hawtrey, as well as the less appreciated insights of John Maynard Keynes and Friedrich Hayek. In doing so, it suggests a bold set of alternative starting points to study monetary macroeconomics and macroeconomic episodes, and a promising way to reverse the subject's retrogression."

—Arjun Jayadev, *Azim Premji University, India*

"This book is the product of decades of work by Glasner, and it shows. It reviews the thinking of major monetary economists, many of whom have been wrongly overlooked, especially Hawtrey and Cassel who presented an monetary interpretation of the Great Depression in contrast to Friedman's US-centric explanation. Glasner's book is a welcome addition to the literature, which has something for anyone interested in monetary economics, the history of economic thought, or the Great Depression."

—Gabriel Mathy, *American University, USA*

"It was watching, during the Great Recession, macroeconomists of note and reputation who knew none of the history of monetary economics repeatedly make mistake after mistake—often at an infantile level—because of their ignorance that made me realize how lucky I am to have been able to read and learn from David Glasner."

—Brad DeLong, *University of California, Berkeley, USA*

"David Glasner's *Essays in the History of Monetary Theory* collects and extends his scholarly, fascinating and readable work on classical monetary theory and on monetary interpretations of the Great Depression. Everyone interested in the history of monetary economics and macroeconomics, especially international adjustment under the gold standard and attempts to explain systemic coordination failure, should read this book. Scholars in these fields will long refer to these articles and assign them to their students."

—Robert Dimand, *Brock University, Canada*

Contents

About the Authors

David Glasner received his Ph.D. in economics from UCLA. He is the author of *Free Banking and Monetary Reform* and editor of *Business Cycles and Depressions: An Encyclopedia.*

Ronald W. Batchelder is Professor of economics at Pepperdine University. He has previously taught at Texas A&M, Tulane University, and UCLA. His research in applied economic theory, international financial institutions and the economic analysis of legal institutions has appeared in the *American Economic Review*, *Public Choice*, and *Explorations in Economic History*.

Paul R. Zimmerman received his doctorate from Florida State University. His research has appeared in the *American Economic Review*, *Journal of Law and Economics*, *Journal of Economic Behavior and Organization*, *Southern Economic Journal*, and other journals.

List of Figures

List of Tables

CHAPTER 1

Introduction

All of the studies in this volume, even the most recent one, are rooted in ideas that first entered my mind in what Joseph Schumpeter called the holy third decade of fertility in the life of a scientist, most of which I spent as a student (undergraduate and graduate) at UCLA where my interest in economics was kindled during the heyday of the storied UCLA economics department.

The principal recurring ideas in these studies are the following:

1. The standard neoclassical models of economics textbooks typically assume full information and perfect competition. But these assumptions are, or ought to be, just the starting point, not the end, of analysis. Recognizing when and why these assumptions need to be relaxed and what empirical implications follow from relaxing those assumptions is how economists gain practical insight into, and understanding of, complex economic phenomena.
2. Since the late eighteenth or early nineteenth century, much, if not most, of the financial instruments actually used as media of exchange (money) have been produced by private financial institutions (usually commercial banks); the amount of money that is privately produced is governed by the revenue generated and the cost incurred by creating money.

D. Glasner, *Studies in the History of Monetary Theory*, Palgrave Studies in the History of Economic Thought, https://doi.org/10.1007/978-3-030-83426-5_1

3. The standard textbook model of international monetary adjustment under the gold standard (or any fixed exchange rate system), the price-specie-flow mechanism, introduced by David Hume mischaracterized the adjustment mechanism by overlooking that the prices of tradable goods in any country are constrained by the prices of those tradable goods in other countries. That arbitrage constraint on the prices of tradable goods in any country prevents price levels in different currency areas from deviating, regardless of local changes in the quantity of money, from a common international level.
4. The Great Depression was caused by a rapid appreciation of gold resulting from the increasing monetary demand for gold occasioned by the restoration of the international gold standard in the 1920s after the demonetization of gold in World War I.
5. If the expected rate of deflation exceeds the real rate of interest, real-asset prices crash and economies collapse.
6. The primary concern of macroeconomics as a field of economics is to explain systemic failures of coordination that lead to significant lapses from full employment.
7. Lapses from full employment result from substantial and widespread disappointment of agents' expectations of future prices.
8. The only—or at least the best—systematic analytical approach to the study of such lapses is the temporary-equilibrium approach introduced by Hicks (1939).

The first idea was instilled by the intellectual leader of the UCLA economics department, Armen Alchian, whose output of publications, though not exceptional in quantity, was extraordinary in quality and profundity, asking, and at least suggesting answers to, fundamental questions in economics. Not the least important of those publications was the textbook, *University Economics*, coauthored with his colleague William Allen, and its posthumous sequel *Universal Economics*. It was a book devoted to teaching students the underlying intuition and logic of economic theory, not simply as a system of formal models, but as a way of thinking, a way of thinking enabling one to apply that intuition and logic flexibly in thinking through the implications of adjusting the underlying assumptions of standard neoclassical models.

Alchian's way of thinking was used by two of his younger colleagues, Ben Klein (1974) and Earl Thompson (1974), who independently developed the second idea: to analyze the production of money by profit-maximizing firms, i.e., banks, that create money only up to the point at which the marginal revenue from a unit of money equals its marginal cost. This way of thinking about how banks create money was radically different from the money-multiplier model, which had been the textbook approach to determining the quantity of money created by the banking system (the product of exogenously determined bank reserves multiplied by an exogenously given reserve ratio).

Thompson applied the second idea to derive a model of a competitive supply of a money convertible into gold, so that, under the gold standard, there is a uniform international price level across all gold-standard countries, thereby correcting the mistaken notion of the price-specie-flow mechanism (PSFM) that international monetary adjustment, under the gold standard, meant that price levels in countries gaining gold would rise while price levels in countries losing gold would fall, until their price levels were equalized and gold flows ceased. Contrary to PSFM, national price levels under the gold standard were positively, not negatively, correlated, while observed gold flows were uncorrelated with price-level changes. Thompson thus anticipated by several years the arguments of McCloskey and Zecher (1976) that demolished PSFM on theoretical and empirical grounds.

Thompson applied similar reasoning to explain the Great Depression as the consequence of gold appreciation in the late 1920s as the monetary demands for gold increased as countries sequentially restored the gold standard. It was only in the mid-1980s that I discovered that Thompson's conjecture that gold appreciation associated with restoration of the gold standard in the 1920s caused the Great Depression had been anticipated by Ralph Hawtrey and Gustav Cassel.

The fifth idea that when expected deflation exceeds the real rate of interest came to mind when Jack Hirshleifer, in his graduate course on the theory of capital and interest, derived the Fisher equation wherein the nominal interest rate equals (approximately) the real rate of interest plus expected deflation. Hirshleifer observed that in equilibrium the expected rate of deflation cannot exceed the real rate of interest. His observation prompted me to ask what would happen if a monetary shock caused the expected rate of deflation to increase? For the first, and perhaps the only time I can remember, Hirshleifer seemed at a loss. I never pursued the question with him, but it later occurred to me that if one assumes a parametric increase in the expected rate of deflation, then the only way that equilibrium could be restored would be for the real value of capital assets to fall until the real rate of interest rose to the parametrically determined rate of expected deflation. Presumably, the depreciation of capital assets would cause capital accumulation to slow or even turn negative until the real rate of interest rose to match the expected rate of appreciation of money, thereby restoring equilibrium. Once expected deflation exceeds the real rate of interest, asset prices begin to fall, because the expected return from holding money exceeds the expected return from real capital. If everyone tries to liquidate real capital, asset prices crash.

The sixth idea, impressed on me, when I was still an undergraduate, by Axel Leijonhufvud is that Keynes was trying to make a more fundamental point than that unemployment results from sticky wages, which is how his contribution came to be understood when the neoclassical synthesis of Walrasian general-equilibrium theory and the Hicksian IS-LM version of Keynesian theory still held sway. A Walrasian general equilibrium is a state of perfect coordination, and to attribute high unemployment to the stickiness of one price (the wage rate) trivializes what Keynes was trying to do. Keynes believed that high unemployment results from a systemic failure that prevents the state of coordination described by general equilibrium from being realized by market-price adjustments. The goal of macroeconomics was to identify the underlying systemic problem that leads to that systemic failure, a failure attributable not to mispricing in any single market, but to something deeper.

The seventh idea, from Hayek via Leijonhufvud and from Earl Thompson, is that the equilibrium in an intertemporal Walrasian model cannot be achieved via price adjustments in actual markets, because the consistency of plans that characterizes a Walrasian equilibrium depends not just on current prices but also on future prices. But future prices are, with few exceptions, unknown; they can only be anticipated. For a Walrasian equilibrium to obtain, future prices must be correctly anticipated (or at any rate not anticipated very incorrectly). Keynes also laid a great deal of stress on the importance of expectations, but Hayek's (1937) formulation of the problem framed the issue with greater depth and clarity than Keynes was able to do. Unfortunately, Hayek never managed to advance his analysis usefully beyond that point. Even more unfortunately, economists are still struggling to advance beyond that point.

The eighth idea, the importance of the Hicksian temporary-equilibrium method, came from Earl Thompson. The temporary-equilibrium method (Hicks, 1939) combines the analytical discipline of an equilibrium model with the recognition that economic agents are making decisions with imperfect and incomplete information, thereby allowing scope for the incorrect and conflicting expectations of future prices by heterogenous agents that result in the discoordination associated with an unceasing process of revision, and even abandonment, of plans. In such an environment, the potential non-existence of a temporary-equilibrium solution cannot be excluded, and chaotic breakdowns of economic activity, as occurred in the Great Depression, and seemed on the verge of occurring in the recent past, cannot be dismissed.

In intertemporal-equilibrium models, it is not only current prices that have to adjust to allow a state of economic equilibrium, expected future prices must also adjust to values consistent with equilibrium. But while there is a mechanism whereby current prices change in response to excess demands and excess supplies, there is no corresponding process whereby expectations of future prices change to become compatible with equilibrium. The existence of intertemporal equilibrium under plausible informational assumptions about agents remains an unproved proposition for which we have no plausible account of a process or algorithm that reaches that equilibrium state.

I have divided the following chapters into two parts. Part one is mainly concerned with aspects of classical monetary theory, a historical period of a little more than a century from David Hume and Adam Smith in the eighteenth century to J. S. Mill and J. E. Cairnes in the nineteenth. The second part consists of papers mainly focused on the work of three great twentieth-century economists: Ralph Hawtrey, J. M. Keynes, and F. A. Hayek.[1] My interest in classical monetary theory emerged early in my graduate studies owing to my exposure first to the work of Ben Klein on the competitive supply of money and somewhat later to the similar work of Earl Thompson. Thompson further explored the macroeconomic implications of competitive-money-supply theory, showing that standard results of general-equilibrium theory are inconsistent with the assumption of a fixed stock of non-interest-bearing money of the type assumed by Keynes (1936), Friedman (1956), and Patinkin (1965), but are consistent

[1] This is a bit overstated as the work of other economists, notably Gustav Cassel and Milton Friedman, Anna Schwartz and Piero Sraffa also receive significant attention.

with a competitively supplied money convertible into a real commodity like gold.

While Thompson alluded to the work of early classicals like Smith and Say and to the Banking School in its opposition to the Currency School and the Bank Charter Act of 1844, the model was his, not theirs, and, aside from suggestive references to their work, he did not show that his model was based on their work. My early papers, especially Chapters 2 and 3 were motivated by the conjecture that a careful reading of their writings on monetary theory would document sufficient similarity between their approach and Thompson's model to justify treating his model as capturing the intuition underlying a substantial body of classical monetary writings.

In Chapters 2 and 3, I lay out a simplified diagrammatic version of Thompson's model and show that many of the characteristics of that model were at least suggested by classical writers like Smith, Say, Mill, and Fullarton. In particular, I showed that the law of reflux of John Fullarton and the Banking School and at least one version of Say's Law (Identity) follow directly from Thompson's model. I also contrasted the sympathetic account of banking by Adam Smith with the hostility to banking of David Hume to suggest that the differences in attitude toward banks of these two great early classical writers might have been reflected in the opposing attitudes toward banking taken by the Currency and Banking Schools the Bank Charter Act and the fixed ceiling it imposed on the total quantity of banknotes circulating in Britain. I also explain why, the Humean price-specie-flow mechanism to the contrary notwithstanding, under the classical model of a competitive convertible money supply, arbitrage ensures that all countries with the same monetary standard share a common price level.[2]

After Chapter 2 was published, I received favorable comments on it from Jurg Niehans and Mark Blaug. Niehans and I exchanged further

[2] Chapters 2 and 3 were originally written as a single paper under the title "A Reinterpretation of Classical Monetary Theory." But, advised that it might be too long to be acceptable, I broke up the paper into two, including in the first section summarizing the extended discussion of the monetary controversies in the second paper (now Chapter 3), under the title "On Some Classical Monetary Controversies." I have dropped that summary section from Chapter 2, but have retained a summary presentation of the basic classical model in Chapter 3. I have also made some further editorial, corrections, changes and updates in the versions published in this volume.

correspondence about the relationship between the law of reflux and the real-bills doctrine that led to his inviting me to present a paper on the real-bills doctrine and the law of reflux to a session he organized at a meeting of the Western Economic Association. That paper is now Chapter 4. I attempted to distinguish between the real-bills doctrine as a monetary-policy rule, enunciated by Governors of the Bank of England during the Napoleonic Wars when their banknotes were inconvertible, and as a prudential rule for individual banks issuing convertible banknotes. I argued that, under Smith's understanding, banks were subject to the law reflux, so that they would not keep a larger quantity of their convertible liabilities outstanding for an extended period of time than the public wished to hold. To be able to meet demands for conversion of unwanted liabilities, banks would either have to keep sufficient reserves on hand, to borrow necessary funds, or to liquidate assets quickly enough to meet those demands. By lending on the security of real bills, banks, in the normal course of business, would be in a position to redeem their liabilities without having to exhaust reserves, liquidate assets, or borrow funds.

Although Blaug responded positively to my reinterpretation of classical monetary theory paper (Chapter 2), and included both that paper and the classical monetary controversies paper (Chapter 3) in a volume of readings (Blaug, 1991) he edited on *Pioneers in Economics*, he later (Blaug, 1995) wrote an article criticizing my paper in another volume that he edited, which also included an article critical of my papers by D. P. O'Brien (1995). The burden of those articles was that I had misrepresented classical monetary theory by arguing that the classical theory was an anti-quantity theory. The Blaug and O'Brien articles prompted me to write another paper, "Classical Monetary Theory and the Quantity Theory," which is now Chapter 5. The main point of Chapter 5 is that, although the quantity theory was certainly accepted by many classical theorists, there was another tradition, derived from Adam Smith, within classical economics that distinguished between the conditions that make the quantity theory relevant for monetary analysis and the conditions in which an alternative theory of a competitively supplied convertible money, whose value is fixed by convertibility and whose quantity adjusts to satisfy demand, is relevant. In Chapters 2–4, I assumed that all goods are tradable, making it possible to identify unambiguously an international price level. In responding to O'Brien's criticisms, I therefore explicitly allowed for a non-tradable-goods sector in which prices are not tightly constrained by international arbitrage. I argued that, even if the existence of non-tradable goods is taken into account, competitive banks have no inherent tendency to overissue their liabilities and threaten the maintenance of convertibility.

I did not publish again on classical monetary theory until invited to present a paper to a 2011 conference in Tokyo commemorating the 200th anniversary of Ricardo's first publication on money. The paper, first published in the volume of papers presented at the conference, "Monetary disequilibrium in Ricardo and Thornton" is Chapter 6. My discussion in that chapter considers two difficulties with how Ricardo and Thornton attempted to analyze monetary disequilibria and argues that the problems with their analyses can both be traced to the lack of a systematic theory of a demand to hold money, even though both Ricardo and Thornton, at times, showed an understanding that the demand for money can indeed play a role in monetary disturbances.

The following year Robert Dimand invited me to give a paper at the Southern Economic Association meeting commemorating the bicentennial of the publication of the *Bullion Report* (Cannan, 1925). In that paper, I chronicled the influence of issues raised in the *Bullion Report* on the subsequent development of monetary theory, and I drew connections between the analysis of the *Bullion Report* and those of later classical authors, especially those associated with the Currency-School/Banking-School debates and more recent monetary controversies. One topic I focused on was the role of competition in the supply of money, drawing explicit analogies between the analysis of the Smith and the Banking School and modern work by James Tobin (1963), Klein (1974), Thompson (1974), and, from a different perspective, Basil Moore (1988) and endogenous-money theorists. Another topic I discussed was the dispute between Smith and Hume over the price-specie-flow mechanism and its similarity to modern disputes about the theory of the balance of payments between supporters of PSFM and the monetary approach to the balance of payments. From my discussion of the real-bills doctrine and the law of reflux in Chapter 4, I also suggested that modern proposals for narrow banking and the separation of investment and commercial banking might be considered as echoing the Smithian version of the real-bills doctrine. Finally, I related the *Bullion Report* and the Bank Charter Act to subsequent discussions about the merits of rules versus discretion in monetary policy. I have subsequently revised and expanded the original paper, and it is published for the first time as Chapter 7. Instead of framing the discussion around the *Bullion Report*, I now call Chapter 7 "The Smithian and Humean Traditions in Monetary Theory."

In 2016, Scott Sumner asked me to present a paper at a conference that he and George Selgin organized on "Rules for a Post-Crisis World" for the Mercatus Institute of George Mason University. Extending the discussion of rules versus discretion in Chapter 7, I compared the discussions about monetary rules in the classical period, primarily the Bullionist Controversies about the 1797 suspension of convertibility of the pound sterling at start of the Napoleonic Wars until the 1821 resumption of convertibility, followed two decades later by the Banking-School/Currency-School debates over the 1844 Bank Charter Act. The two classical episodes exemplify the difference between price rules and quantity rules in monetary policy. The distinction between quantity rules and price rules lies at the heart of twentieth-century efforts to recreate or replace the international gold standard that collapsed in World War I and underlies the differing approaches to monetary rules taken by Henry C. Simons (1936) and his student Milton Friedman, the former favoring, albeit reluctantly, price rules over quantity rules, and the latter rejecting price rules as inadequate. The paper, originally published in 2017, is now Chapter 8.

Part one concludes with a paper originally written in 1998, "Say's Law and the Classical Theory of Depressions." It lay unfinished for many years, because I could not formulate the role of Say's Law in an updated version of the classical theory of depressions. It was not until after the financial crisis of 2008 and the subsequent Great Recession (aka Little Depression), and after I had further studied Ralph Hawtrey's (1913) model of financial crises (see Chapter 10) that I succeeded in formulating the role of Say's Law in terms of a temporary-equilibrium model in which neither Say's Law nor Walras's Law holds. The paper is published for the first time as Chapter 9.

The papers in part two focus on three great twentieth-century economists Hawtrey, Keynes, and Hayek. My interest in Keynes and Hayek began when I was an undergraduate at UCLA. Even at UCLA, Keynesian economics, in one form or another, was then the bedrock of introductory macroeconomics, and Hayek was a revered figure in the UCLA economics department. A highlight of my undergraduate years was Hayek's visit to UCLA for two quarters in the turbulent 1968–1969 academic year where he was a visiting professor in the department of philosophy, teaching an undergraduate course in the philosophy of the social sciences and conducting a graduate seminar on the first draft of *Law Legislation and Liberty* (Hayek, 1973–1976).

Hawtrey's name, however, was just one that I saw mentioned from time to time in the writings of other economists. I may have been aware that he was an older colleague of Keynes and had developed a monetary theory of the business cycle that at one time was considered important, but beyond that I had no specific knowledge about him or his work. I only became seriously interested in his work after having read the essay by Frenkel and Johnson (1976) on the origins of the monetary approach to the balance of payments and the important paper by McCloskey and Zecher (1976) which appeared in the same volume as the Frenkel and Johnson paper. Frenkel and Johnson cited Hawtrey more often than anyone else, especially in connection with the idea that, under the gold standard, there is an international price level shared by all countries, an idea of which I had already been persuaded by Earl Thompson.

But I did not begin to study Hawtrey's work carefully until after I published my first paper on classical monetary theory (Chapter 2) in 1985 when I was a fellow at the Manhattan Institute. After publishing that paper, I submitted a proposal to the Manhattan Institute for my book *Free Banking and Monetary Reform* (Glasner, 1989) in which I developed my ideas about classical monetary theory and suggested how those ideas could be implemented under free-banking system combined with a labor-standard implemented via indirect convertibility into gold, as had earlier been proposed by Earl Thompson (1982). The proposal was too arcane to have a realistic chance of being adopted, and the plan, though written about in *Forbes* and the *New York Times*, was little noticed and soon forgotten. But I tried to justify the plan by contrasting it with the disastrous attempt to restore the gold standard after World War I and the less disastrous, but still highly misguided attempt, of the Federal Reserve under Paul Volcker to control inflation by following Milton Friedman's advice to target the growth of the monetary aggregates.[3]

[3] To be clear, what was misguided was not the attempt to control inflation, but the notion that controlling inflation required adopting a Monetarist rule to control the growth of the monetary aggregates, which caused a deeper and longer recession than was needed to bring down the rate of inflation. Had the Fed adopted a strategy aiming to control not the growth in monetary aggregates but the rate of increase in nominal spending,

I had already learned from Thompson that the Great Depression was caused by the increasing demand for gold in the late 1920s as countries rejoined the gold standard, but, in reading further about the episode and the attempt to restore the gold standard, I picked up Hawtrey's (1948) *The Gold Standard in Theory and Practice*, and was amazed to find that, already in the 1920s, he had anticipated exactly the course of events described by Thompson. As I delved into other writings by Hawtrey, I was repeatedly struck by the acuity of his insight and the clarity of his analysis. I revised my discussion of the role of the gold standard in my book to credit Hawtrey with having foreseen the consequences of an uncoordinated restoration of the gold standard after World War I, and I know of no author before me that credited Hawtrey for having explained the Great Depression as the result of a failed attempt to restore the prewar gold standard.

The first five chapters in part two are all about Hawtrey, though Keynes shares the focus in Chapters 11 and 12. The primary focus shifts to Hayek in the final three chapters.

Chapter 10 is a paper written in 2013 as a series of posts on my blog, *Uneasy Money* <www.uneasymoney.com> commemorating the centenary of Hawtrey's (1913) first book, *Good and Bad Trade*. The book is an excellent introduction into Hawtrey's thought, providing a clear exposition of the main elements of his business-cycle theory, which, with one important exception, he consistently maintained throughout his long career.

The key idea in Hawtrey's model is that middlemen, traders and wholesalers, who hold inventories of finished and semi-finished goods, are the mechanism whereby final consumer demand for output is communicated to manufacturers. However, their role in transmitting information about consumer demands to manufacturers is not just passive, because their own holding of inventories is highly sensitive to the short-term interest rate, the key policy instrument of the monetary authority. Increases in Bank rate induce reductions in inventory holdings and increases in Bank rate cause inventory holdings to increase. Increases in desired inventories lead to increased orders to manufacturers which cause manufacturers to

inflation could have been reduced with a shorter and shallower recession. More than a decade before Volcker's failed Monetarist experiment, Hawtrey (1967) explained, in his final book, why the target of monetary policy should be the rate of growth in spending and income rather than the quantity of money.

increase output and hire additional workers. Decreases in desired inventories have the opposite effect. Thus, changes in Bank rate have substantial and rapidly transmitted effects on total output and employment, driving fluctuations in output, and are the primary source of cyclical fluctuations. The one important modification that Hawtrey subsequently made to his model was to recognize that, under the gold standard (or any system of fixed exchange rates), national monetary authorities can affect their local price levels only insofar as they affect a shared international price level to which they are linked by gold convertibility or fixed exchange rates.

Chapter 11, adapted from my book *Free Banking and Monetary Reform*, was originally published as an article in *Encounter*. The main idea of the article was that Hawtrey had already explained the cause of the Great Depression using a theory of the gold standard that Keynes, with some reservations to be sure, had largely shared with Hawtrey. Why Keynes felt it necessary to invent a completely new theory to solve a problem already solved by Hawtrey is the question I tried to answer in this article. The current version omits a number of paragraphs from the beginning and end of the original version that are not relevant to my main argument.

Chapter 12 was originally published as an entry on Hawtrey in the *Elgar Companion to John Maynard Keynes* edited by Robert Dimand and Harrald Hagemann. It is reprinted with only slight revision as "Hawtrey and Keynes" and focuses on their long, usually friendly, but sometime difficult, relationship from their days at Cambridge through the aftermath of the publication of the *General Theory*.

In 1987, after I had just finished the manuscript of *Free Banking and Monetary Reform*, I visited Los Angeles and spent an afternoon at UCLA looking up friends and teachers. One of those that I saw was Ronald W. Batchelder, who also was close to Earl Thompson; I mentioned to him that I had been reading a lot of Hawtrey's work and had found that Hawtrey had anticipated Thompson's explanation of the Great Depression, warning years in advance that restoring the gold standard would create a high risk of deflation and depression unless it was carefully managed to avoid a substantial increase in the monetary demand for gold. Ron's response to me was that he had been reading the work of Gustav Cassel, and that Cassel had made exactly the same warnings in the 1920s that Hawtrey had made. That was how our two papers about Hawtrey and Cassel, published here as Chapters 13 and 14, came to be written.

The first of the two papers, "Gold, Debt, Deflation and the Great Depression," was written when I was invited to present a paper to the Durrell Conference on Money and Banking: the American Experience in 1991 in Washington, DC, and I asked Ron to collaborate with me in writing the paper. The paper was included along with the other papers presented at the conference in a volume of the same name. Aside from presenting the main outlines of the Hawtrey-Cassel explanation of the Great Depression, the paper also explored the reasons why the United States, despite the catastrophic decline of output and employment from 1929 to 1932, took no action to halt the deflation, instead stubbornly maintaining the gold standard despite Congressional efforts to restore the US price level back to its 1926 level. We suggested that the massive shift of the US international position from being a net international debtor to a net creditor greatly increased the influence of creditor (in particular, banking) interests that believed that reversing the deflation of the previous three years would be harmful to their interests.

The second of the two papers, never previously published, "Pre-Keynesian Theories of the Great Depression: Whatever Happened to Hawtrey and Cassel?" was written soon after the previous paper and was originally presented at the 1991 meeting of the History of Economic Society at the University of Maryland. The problem posed by the paper was how to account for the almost complete silence in the subsequent literature about the explanation of the Great Depression offered by Hawtrey and Cassel, despite its clear and compelling explanation of the causes and the consequences of the Great Depression. In fact, as this and the preceding paper were being written, work by Peter Temin (1989), Barry Eichengreen (1992), and Kenneth Mouré (1991) was strongly confirming the Hawtrey-Cassel explanation of the Great Depression, which I had already credited to Hawtrey in my 1989 book. But only Mouré credited Hawtrey with having identified the chief cause of the catastrophe.

It might have been expected that, after the Keynesian Revolution distracted attention from monetary causes of the Great Depression, the renewed interest in monetary forces associated with Milton Friedman and the Monetarist Counterrevolution would have led to a rediscovery of Hawtrey and Cassel, but Friedman and his followers also ignored almost completely the earlier and more insightful work of Hawtrey and Cassel. Why was that? At best, it reflects a serious scholarly lapse on the part of Friedman, and an insular approach that looked only to Chicago for precursors and only to Keynes for a foil. Chapters 13 and 14 both show the inferiority of the treatment of the Great Depression in the *Monetary History* to the earlier work of Hawtrey and Cassel.

In Chapter 15, I turn to Hayek, whose work I have admired and studied closely and critically since I first became interested in economics. While there is much to be learned even from his early work on business cycles which first brought him fame, that work was seriously flawed in several respects. My work on Chapter 15 began as a post on my Uneasy Money blog about Sraffa's (1932) critique of Hayek's (1931) first English language book, *Prices and Production* in which he outlined his business-cycle theory. Keynes, whose *Treatise on Money* had just been harshly reviewed by Hayek (1931), asked Sraffa to review *Prices and Production* for the *Economic Journal*, of which Keynes was then the editor. Sraffa delivered a withering review disposing of Hayek's cycle theory, which, after a brief ascendancy in the economics profession, was quickly put aside, in no small part because of the damage done by Sraffa.

My blogpost and a subsequent paper (co-authored with Paul A. Zimmerman) here published for the first time considers just one part of Sraffa's attack on Hayek: the charge that Hayek's conception of the natural rate of interest, as the rate of interest that would prevail in a pure barter economy is incoherent. It is incoherent, according to Sraffa, because Hayek wanted it to serve as the policy rate adopted by the monetary authority. Sraffa charged that, in a barter economy, loans could be contracted in terms of real commodities and the rate of interest in terms of any commodity (the commodity rate or own rate of interest) might be different based on differences in the expected rate of appreciation or depreciation of those commodities. If so, there is no unique natural rate, and Hayek's idea of a natural rate is meaningless. Hayek's response to Sraffa's review was to admit that there might indeed be many own rates of interest, but that they would all be equilibrium rates. Sraffa ridiculed that response as either a non-sequitur or a concession, and the consensus following the exchange was that Hayek had been demolished by Sraffa and had failed to mount a credible defense.

The point of Chapter 15 is that Sraffa had overreached in charging that Hayek's conception of the natural rate was incoherent, because Hayek's understanding of the natural rate was the Fisherian real rate that was adjusted for the expected appreciation or depreciation of whichever commodity the loan was denominated in. In fact, it was precisely this conception of the own rate that Keynes, following Fisher, adopted in

Chapter 17 of the *General Theory*, and Hayek's conception was no less coherent than Fisher's and Keynes's conception. However, to have responded in this way would have forced Hayek to acknowledge that any money real rate could be validated by a corresponding and correctly anticipated rate of inflation. But this was a point that Hayek was unwilling to concede.

Chapter 16 continues in this vein to criticize Hayek's attachment to the gold standard and the deflationary policy that it entailed in the context of the Great Depression, even though Hayek's own analysis of the neutral-money policy that he had articulated implied not passively allowing deflation to rage during a downturn, but an active policy of monetary expansion to prevent a decline in total spending. The latter policy would cushion any reduction in output and employment by an offsetting inflation. Hayek later disavowed his puzzling support for continued deflation as a necessary price to pay for maintaining the gold standard, but the contradiction between his own rationale for neutral money and his inexplicable advocacy of deflation suggests that his policy choice was governed by a non-economic political rationale, which he himself suggested: to break the power of organized labor which he viewed as incompatible with the liberal economic system he favored. That judgment suggested a nihilistic willingness to use the Great Depression as a means to achieve a political end. But, Hayek at least was later willing to acknowledge the error and express regret for that wrong-headed advice.

Chapter 17 turns to Hayek's positive and lasting, if still underestimated, contribution to economic theory, the theory of intertemporal equilibrium. Hayek's innovation was to view intertemporal equilibrium as the mutual consistency of individually optimal plans, which, in an intertemporal context, requires that future prices either be known in advance or correctly anticipated. For prices to be known in advance, agents must either have perfect foresight, or, equally unrealistically, agree irrevocably in advance to all future trades to be executed at prices agreed upon in advance before trading starts. The latter, the Arrow-Debreu-McKenzie (ADM) model of Walrasian general equilibrium, has achieved canonical status. Hayek's version of intertemporal equilibrium, although practically unattainable, provides a theoretical benchmark that makes explicit, in a more realistic setting, the nearly unimaginable consensus of individual expectations about unknown future prices. But the assumption of consensus focuses attention on the problem of divergent expectations of the future as the inevitable source of disequilibrium. Because either in Hayek's version or in Radner's (1972) formalization of it as an equilibrium of plans, prices, and price expectations (EPPE), intertemporal equilibrium is contingent, and subject to change at any time, rather than perfect and perpetual, as it is in the perfect-foresight model or the ADM model, it rationalizes the introduction of a richer set of institutions, such as asset markets and money, than can be rationalized in a perfect-foresight model or the ADM model. Radner also formalized Hicks's conception of a temporary equilibrium in which current prices clear (so that excess demands in all current markets are zero) even though agents' expectations of future prices diverge from each other. As shown by Bliss (1976), a privately supplied medium of exchange produced by banks can be introduced into the temporary-equilibrium model, thereby allowing the possibility of financial crises resulting from substantially mistaken expected prices. Sufficiently great discoordination can even make it impossible to prove the existence of a temporary equilibrium. Finally, the rational-expectations equilibrium introduced by Lucas and real-business-cycle theorists, which has become the default model in modern macroeconomics, largely assumes away the potential for the coordination failures that result from the inevitable divergence of expectations by individual agents. By confining itself to the analysis of general-equilibrium states of coordination, modern macroeconomics, founded on the Lucasian rational-expectations axiom, therefore represents a scientific retrogression, not an advance.

References

Alchian, A. A., & Allen, W. R. (1972). *University economics* (3rd ed.). Wadsworth Publishing Co.

Alchian, A., & Allen, W. R. (2018). *Universal economics*. Liberty Fund.

Blaug, M. (1991). *Pioneers in economics: George Scrope, Thomas Attwood, Edwin Chadwick, John Cairnes* (Vol. 20). M. Blaug (ed.). Edward Elgar.

Blaug, M. (1995). Why is the quantity theory the oldest surviving theory in economics? In M. Blaug (Ed.), *The quantity theory of money: From Locke to Keynes and Friedman*. Edward Elgar.

Bliss, C. J. (1976). Capital theory in the short run. In M. Brown, K. Sato, & P. Zarembka (Eds.), *Essays in modern capital theory* (pp. 187–201). North-Holland.

Cannan, E. (Ed.). (1925). *The paper pound* (2nd ed.). P.S. King.

Eichengreen, B. (1992). *Golden fetters*. Oxford University Press.

Frenkel, J. A., & Johnson, H. G. (1976). The monetary approach to the balance of payments: Essential concepts and historical origins. In J. A. Frenkel & H.

G. Johnson (Eds.), *The monetary approach to the balance of payments* (pp. 21–45). University of Toronto Press.
Glasner, D. (1989). *Free banking and monetary reform*. Oxford University Press.
Hawtrey, R. G. (1913). *Good and bad trade*. Longmans.
Hawtrey, R. G. (1948). *The gold standard in theory and practice* (5th ed.). Longmans, Green, and Co.
Hawtrey, R. G. (1967). *Incomes and money*. Longmans.
Hayek, F. A. (1931). *Prices and production*. Routledge and Kegan Paul.
Hayek, F. A. (1937). Economics and knowledge. *Economica* n.s, *4*(1), 33–54.
Hicks, J. R. (1939). *Value and capital*. Oxford University Press.
Keynes, J. M. (1936). *The general theory of employment, interest and money*. Macmillan.
Klein, B. (1974). The competitive supply of money. *Journal of Money, Credit, and Banking*, *6*(4), 423–453.
McCloskey, D. N., & Zecher, J. R. (1976). How the gold standard worked, 1880–1913. In J. A. Frenkel & H. G. Johnson (Eds.), *The monetary approach to the balance of payments* (pp. 357–385). University of Toronto Press.
Moore, B. (1988). *Horizontalists and verticalists: The macroeconomics of credit money*. Cambridge University Press.
Mouré, K. (1991). *Managing the franc Poincaré*. Cambridge University Press.
O'Brien, D. P. (1995). Long-run equilibrium and cyclical disturbances: The currency and banking controversy over monetary control. In M. Blaug (Ed.), *The quantity theory of money: From Locke to Keynes and Friedman*. Edward Elgar.
Patinkin, D. (1965). *Money, interest, and prices* (2nd ed.). Harper and Row.
Radner, R. (1972). Existence of equilibrium of plans, prices, and price expectations in a sequence of markets. *Econometrica, 40*(2), 289–304.
Simons, H. C. (1936). Rules versus authorities in monetary policy. *Journal of Political Economy, 44*(1), 1–30.
Sraffa, P. (1932). Dr. Hayek on money and capital. *Economic Journal, 42*(1), 42–53.
Temin, P. (1989). *Lessons of the great depression*. MIT Press.
Thompson, E. A. (1974). The theory of money and income consistent with orthodox value theory. In G. Horwich & P. A. Samuelson (Eds.), *Trade, stability, and macroeconomics* (pp. 427–453). Academic Press.
Thompson, E. A. (1982, January 8). Free banking under a labor standard. Statement to the U.S. Gold Commission. https://drive.google.com/file/d/0B-AvoOmPTyGaY1ZhbnFzUXRwcGM/view.
Tobin, J. (1963). Commercial banks as creators of money. In D. Carson (Ed.), *Banking and monetary studies* (pp. 408–419). R. D. Irwin.

PART I

Classical Monetary Theory

CHAPTER 2

A Reinterpretation of Classical Monetary Theory

2.1 Introduction

Relevance to current policy issues is usually not the motivation for studying the history of economic theory. However, questions about the practicality of conducting monetary policy in a deregulated financial system by controlling the monetary aggregates are stimulating interest in convertibility as an alternative to our present monetary arrangements (Barro, 1979; Bordo & Schwartz, 1984). Since classical writers were mainly concerned with monetary theory and policy under a gold standard, it is to be expected that renewed attention will be devoted to classical monetary theory.

My aim in this chapter is to show that, contrary to received views about classical monetary theory, it was not based on the quantity theory of money. On the contrary, it was based on a theory of a convertible, competitively produced money supply that was fundamentally different from the quantity theory. Using the modern theory of a competitive money supply, we can now derive many of the basic propositions of classical monetary theory that were or misunderstood by subsequent theorists operating within the framework of the quantity theory.

Received views about classical monetary theory can be summarized by the following propositions:

D. Glasner, *Studies in the History of Monetary Theory*, Palgrave Studies in the History of Economic Thought,
https://doi.org/10.1007/978-3-030-83426-5_2

1. Classical monetary theory was based on the quantity theory (Blaug, 1985, 149–178; O'Brien, 1975, 143; Sowell, 1974, 59).
2. In classical theory, the role of convertibility was to impose a limit on the reserves against which the banking system could create nominal balances. Under convertibility, an excess supply of nominal balances that led to an increase in the price level would eventually be reversed by a loss of reserves and a consequent contraction of nominal balances (Barro, 1979, 13; O'Brien, 1975, 153).
3. For convertibility to be effective, the banking system had to maintain a stable ratio between their reserves and the nominal balances they created. Since the banking system would not necessarily do so of its own accord, the monetary authority had to impose the ratio on the banking system (O'Brien, 1975, 153–156; Robbins, 1976, 76; Viner, 1937, 221).
4. Though some, but not all, classical theorists did recognize the distinction between the expansion opportunities open to any single bank and those open to the entire banking system, classical theorists generally lacked an adequate theory of the process of money creation by a fractional-reserve banking system that properly took account of this distinction (Hayek, 1929 [1933], 152–153; Phillips, 1920, 32, 55, 730; Schumpeter, 1954, 239).
5. International monetary equilibrium was maintained, in the classical theory, by the Humean price-specie-flow mechanism **(PSFM)** that entails adjustments in the relative-price levels of countries experiencing balance-of-payments disequilibrium (Blaug, 1985, 208; O'Brien, 1975, 142; Viner, 1937, 293).
6. Classical theory incorrectly subscribed to Say's Law (Identity) and, thus, could not adequately explain the process of price-level adjustment implicit in the quantity theory. And lacking a real-balance effect, it illegitimately dichotomized the process of price determination between the real and the monetary sectors (Blaug, 1985, 149–178; O'Brien, 1975, 158–160).

Each of these propositions, at least in relation to a major group of classical monetary theorists, is incorrect. The critical mistake is the assumption that classical theorists used the quantity theory to explain price-level determination under convertibility. Most classical theorists used the quantity theory only to explain price-level determination for an inconvertible paper currency. But under the gold standard, the price level was determined by the value of gold, not the quantity of nominal balances.[1] A competitive process, sometimes described as the real-bills doctrine,[2] or the law of reflux, determined the quantity of nominal balances produced by the banking system under convertibility. No fixed relationship between gold reserves and nominal balances was, or needed to be, maintained because it was not possible, under convertibility, for the nominal quantity of money produced by the banking system to affect the price level. Instead, nominal balances fluctuated with "the needs of trade." And with the price level determined by convertibility, no monetary theory of price-level adjustment was necessary. There was no need for a real-balance effect and no inconsistency in maintaining Say's Identity. The law of reflux, in fact, is equivalent to Say's Identity.

Without relying on the balance-of-payments adjustment mechanism, the modern theory of a competitive money supply demonstrates the endogeneity of the nominal quantity of money produced by the banking system. As with any other competitively produced commodity, the output of nominal cash balances depends on the marginal costs and the marginal revenues of competitive producers. The money-multiplier analysis of deposit expansion, according to which the nominal money supply is (or can be made) an exogenously determined policy variable, has no role in the theory of a competitive money supply just as it had none for most classical theorists.[3]

The chapter is organized as follows. In the next section, I sketch a model of a competitively produced money and show the validity, within this model, of such allegedly invalid propositions often attributed to the classical theorists as the dichotomy between the real and the monetary

[1] "The value of a really convertible currency," Fullarton (1845, 69) wrote, "must always be identical with the value of the coin into which it is convertible. and can only vary with variations in the value of coin."

[2] When this chapter was originally written, I had not yet realized the distinction between the real-bills doctrine and the law of reflux, which is the subject of Chapter 4.

[3] Hicks (1977, 59–60) recognized, almost in passing, the distinction between the quantity theory and the classical theory of a convertible currency. In the latter, the money stock becomes endogenous while in the former it is exogenous.

sectors and Say's Law (Identity). In Sect. 2.3, I compare and contrast the quantity theory and my interpretation of the classical monetary model. I turn, in Sect. 2.4, to the role of competition in classical monetary theory. Next, I use the distinction between the quantity theory and the competitive money model to suggest an explanation of Adam Smith's neglect of **PSFM** and to offer a parallel explanation of the dispute between the Currency and Banking Schools. In Sect. 2.5, I compare my version of the classical theory with the modern restatements of the classical theory by Patinkin and others and show the formal equivalence between Say's Identity and the law of reflux. Finally, in Sect. 2.6, I discuss the implications of the classical model for contemporary monetary theory.

2.2 A Model of a Competitive Money Supply

The modern theory of a competitive money supply was developed independently and along somewhat different lines by Klein (1974), Thompson (1974), and Hayek (1978). Much of their work was foreshadowed in the "New View" of financial intermediaries, associated with, among others, Gurley and Shaw (1960) and Tobin (1963). The notion of a competitive money supply was also developed in a neglected article by Rueff (1947).

The truly novel contribution of Klein, Thompson, and Hayek was their argument that, even with costless creation of nominal cash balances, a legally unconstrained, competitive monetary system would not, as

Friedman,[4] Pesek and Saving[5] Johnson[6] and Patinkin[7] had asserted, generate an infinite, or indeterminate, price level. Klein (1974, 429–430) and Hayek (1978, 23) pointed out that only if competing money

[4] Friedman (1959, 7) wrote:

> This analysis, then, leads to the conclusion that some external limit must be placed on the volume of a fiduciary currency in order to maintain its value. Competition does not provide an effective limit, since the value of the promise to pay, if the currency is to remain fiduciary, must be kept higher than the cost of producing additional units. The production of a fiduciary currency is, as it were, a technical monopoly, and hence, there is no such presumption in favor of the private market as there is when competition is feasible.

Friedman did not explain why competition would not force competing issuers of fiduciary units to guarantee that they would not overissue. Without such a guarantee, their issues would not be acceptable to the public. The guarantee, of course, would likely take the form of a commitment to convert into gold. Friedman did not explicitly deny that competition is possible under a gold standard, but he did deny that the gold standard would arise spontaneously through competitive forces. As Klein (1974, 429) observed, he seems to assume that competing money producers cannot make their moneys distinguishable.

[5] Pesek and Saving (1967, 129) maintained:

> If we have a product, *any* product, the marginal cost of production of which is assumed to be zero, then the following propositions of value theory hold:
>
> a. Competition among producers of any good, monetary or non-monetary results in a determinate output and a zero price; a reciprocal of this price is, by definition, indeterminate …
> b. Output restrictions (outside restraint, monopoly, etc.) result in a determinate output and price, both positive …
>
> If a dominant money exists but the banking system is not restricted by two qualitative restraints, instant repurchase clause (convertibility) *and* a prohibition on the payment of interest on money] the banking industry will destroy itself as a money producer by being competitively driven to deteriorate the quality of its product: money will be converted into a moneydebt and, ultimately, into pure debt .

[6] Johnson (1967, 135) wrote:

> If deposits cost nothing to create and yet the assets held against them yield a positive return, banks subject to no restraint will be under competitive pressure to expand the nominal money supply until its purchasing power is reduced to zero: at best, the money supply so determined will be in neutral equilibrium.

producers were producing indistinguishable monies that did not bear the name or trademark of the issuer would competition generate an infinite price level. However, the violation of another money producer's trademark is not a requirement of competition, it is an infringement of property rights called counterfeiting. Thompson, however, differed from Klein and Hayek on one significant point. While Klein and Hayek maintained that competition between money producers would, even without convertibility, ensure the purchasing power of their monies, Thompson held that a finite price level would be achieved only if money producers committed themselves to convert their monies into a real asset at a stipulated rate of exchange. While conceding that money producers must resort to convertibility to ensure a finite price level, Thompson argued that, if property rights are enforced, convertibility results from competitive forces, not from a governmentally imposed obligation on the banking system.

I now give a brief account of Thompson's model as I regard it as closest in spirit to the classical money model.

The second part of this sentence is inconsistent with the first part. A neutral equilibrium without a determinate price level does not imply zero purchasing power. It means that the price level and the rate of inflation are not restricted to unique values. Changes in the rate of inflation would be matched by changes in the rate of interest paid on money, leaving money holders indifferent to changes in the rate of inflation. This is the kind of equilibrium envisioned by Gurley and Shaw (1960, 254–255) in a laissez-faire banking system. The price level and rate of inflation are also indeterminate in this sense in Klein's version of a competitive money model.

[7] Patinkin (1965b, 170) argued as follows:

> Note that under the assumption of zero costs it is essential to assume that the right to issue money is quantitatively restricted in some form or other. For otherwise individuals would continue producing money until the value of the marginal product was also zero: that is. they would issue an infinite quantity of money which would be valueless in terms of purchasing power over commodities.

Although of the authors I have quoted in this and the previous three footnotes, only Pesek and Saving categorically deny that a competitive money supply under convertibility would maintain a finite price level, all of them suggest that competition would lead to an infinite price level unless exogenously constrained (e.g., by a legal convertibility obligation).

Assume that a proper subset of individuals within an economy—let us call them bankers—can ascertain costlessly the probability of default by any borrower; suppose, too, that their costs of bookkeeping and enforcing payment are zero. Finally, assume that bankers are sufficiently numerous to make collusion prohibitively costly. Since bankers are the lowest-cost suppliers of credit, non-bankers borrow only from bankers. Non-bankers obtain credit by giving bankers IOUs that bear a competitive interest rate plus a risk premium. In exchange for these IOUs, the bankers give the non-bankers IOUs of their own which, because the credit of bankers is understood to be superior to that of non-bankers, are generally accepted as payment. If the credit of non-bankers were as good as that of bankers, non-bankers would issue their own debt when making payment rather than exchanging debt with bankers and using the bankers' debt for payment.

Since they can create debt costlessly, bankers earn the difference between the interest on IOUs they receive from non-bankers and the interest on IOUs they issue in exchange. But competition forces bankers to raise the interest on their debt as long as further profits would accrue from issuing additional debt, thereby dissipating any profit that would have accrued from the interest on IOUs obtained from non-bankers.

A delicate question arises here. It is the anticipated real interest rate that is the incentive for holding the bankers' IOUs. How can this real interest be paid? Unless bankers commit themselves to convert their IOUs into an asset which they cannot create costlessly, the prospect of real interest seems illusory. There is no reason to believe a promise to pay interest unless the value of the IOU is fixed in real terms by a contractual commitment to convert either on demand or at a specified redemption date. This is Thompson's (1974, 432–433) reason for arguing that competition would compel banks to commit themselves to convertibility. Ronald Coase (1972) made a similar argument in a different context.[8,9]

By giving holders of its IOUs the right of conversion into a real asset at a predetermined rate, a bank can guarantee a stipulated real rate of interest. A bank may do so by establishing convertibility into a real asset expected to appreciate at a rate equal to the real rate of interest, or by announcing that the conversion rate between its IOUs and a real asset of constant value will be periodically increased in the future.[10] The former arrangement bears some similarity to the classical gold standard. Apart from periods of rising prices following unanticipated gold discoveries, prices in terms of gold generally fell during the nineteenth century. Thus, money holders usually did receive some implicit interest. That money holders still bore some positive cost (given that real interest rates were generally greater than the rate of deflation) can be attributed to the real costs of producing money or to monopolistic elements in the banking structure of most countries. In Scotland, where a free-banking system evolved in the eighteenth century and continued until Peel's Act of 1844 subjected it to the regulations governing banking elsewhere in Great Britain, interest was paid on deposits, so that the cost of holding money

[8] Coase's argument is that a monopolist trying to maintain a monopoly price for a durable good by withholding part of its supply would be unable to do so without promising to buy back the good at the original price because prospective buyers would anticipate that the monopolist would later sell additional units originally withheld until the value of the good was reduced to the competitive level. Given such expectations, no buyer would pay more than the competitive price. To guarantee to buyers that he will not "cheat," the monopolist must make a commitment to preserve the value of the good, for example by promising to buy back at the original price at the buyer's demand. The problem of the monopolist is analogous to that of the money producer seeking to maintain a value for its money above the physical cost of producing it. Convertibility is the equivalent of a repurchase clause. I am indebted to Armen Alchian for drawing my attention to the analogy between Coase's example and a convertibility commitment by a money producer.

[9] For an alternative form of convertibility that would stabilize an index of wage rates and, thus, would be a kind of labor standard, see Thompson (1982).

[10] In the competitive model, however, the asset into which money is convertible does not necessarily function as a medium of exchange as did gold under the gold standard. The phenomenon of currency-switching in times of crisis when the public seeks to switch from holding bank monies (notes and deposits) to reserve money (gold) may have been a significant factor in nineteenth-century business cycles. This phenomenon is not possible in the purely competitive model outlined in this paper. For a discussion of the implications of this assumption of the competitive model, see below.

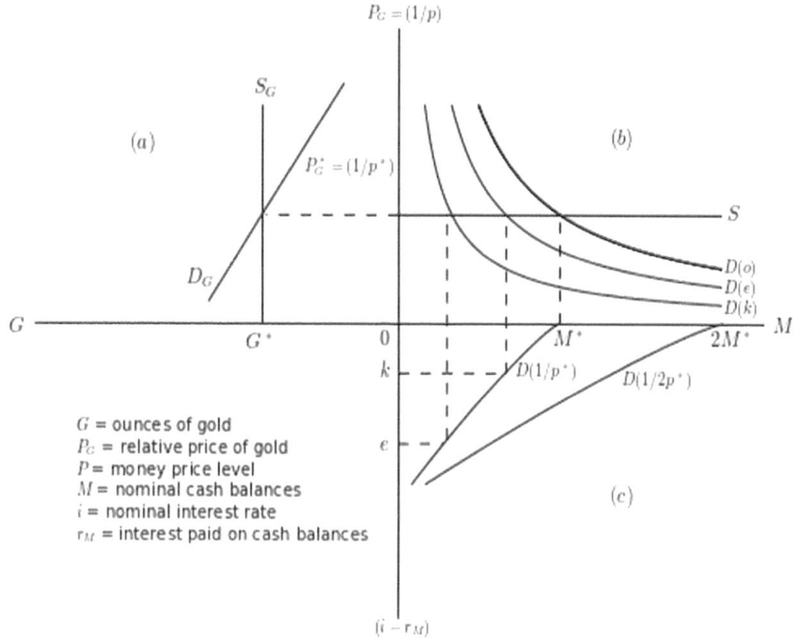

Fig. 2.1 Price-level determination under the gold standard

in Scotland was less than in England (Checkland, 1975, 68; Fullarton, 1845, 92).

The competitive money model I have outlined has the following properties:

1. The assumption that banks can produce cash balances costlessly implies that they bear no cost of holding reserves of the standard asset (gold). This would be possible if confidence in banks were such that they need hold no reserves regardless of their outstanding cash balances (liabilities). Such a situation would imply that banks have no demand to hold gold.[11]

[11] An alternative explanation would be that gold yields the competitive rate of interest, which could occur if gold were appreciating at a rate equal to the rate of interest. An asset can appreciate at a rate equal to the rate of interest in equilibrium only if it provides

Figure 2.1 shows the determination of the price level, P, and the spread between the interest rate on loans and the interest on money, $(i - r_M)$. In panel (a) the relative price of gold, P_G, is determined on the assumption that banks hold no gold reserves. Given the exogenously determined conversion rate, CR, P_G uniquely determines the price level, P. Their precise relationship is given by the equation:

$$CR/(1/P) = P_G.$$

Without loss of generality, we choose CR so that PG equals $1/P$; PG and $1/P$ can then be measured simultaneously along the vertical axis. In panel (b), a family of rectangular-hyperbolic demand curves depicts the relationship between the amount of nominal cash balances demanded, M and $1/P$. The demand for real cash balances along each demand curve is constant and depends on $(i - r_M)$. In panel (c), the demand for real cash balances as a function of $(i - r_M)$ is shown by a family of demand curves (each corresponding to a given price level). Competition ensures that $(i - r_M)$ equal the marginal cost of maintaining cash balances held by the public. If doing so is costless, the supply curve of cash balances in panel (c), indicating the total output of bank money as a function of $(i - r_M)$, coincides with the horizontal axis. Thus, the equilibrium amount of cash balances is represented by the point where the demand curve in panel (c) corresponding to the price level determined in panel (a) touches the horizontal axis.[12] Thus, the quantity-theoretic

no valuable current services. That would mean that the current demand for gold for monetary uses was small relative to the total stock. See discussion below in Sect. 2.6.

[12] If there were some positive, but constant, marginal cost of maintaining the cash balances held by the public, the supply curve would be perfectly elastic at ik, where k is the cost of permanently issuing one unit of money. If the marginal cost of producing cash balances increases with output, the supply curve is upward-sloping. In other words, $(i - r_M) = ik(M)$, where $k(M)$ is the marginal cost of permanently issuing cash balances held by the public as a function of the quantity of cash balances. Note, however, that even if the supply curve in panel (c) were upward-sloping, the supply curve in panel (b) would still be perfectly elastic with respect to $1/P$. The most explicit formulation of such a money model was by Laughlin (1903). See also Girton and Roper (1978). Although Laughlin recognized the similarity of this theory to Adam Smith's, he regarded the quantity theory as the dominant classical theory and sought to differentiate his own anti-quantity theory from the classical theory.

proposition that the price level depends on the exogenously fixed nominal quantity of money is reversed in the competitive model. Instead, the supply of cash balances is perfectly elastic with respect to the price level determined by convertibility, and also with respect to the spread between the nominal interest rate on loans and the nominal interest rate that banks pay on money.

2. Essentially similar conclusions follow even if we relax the assumption of costless production and assume instead that the demand for gold by the banking system of the country whose price level is being determined is small relative to the international market in which the price of gold is determined.

   Figure 2.2 illustrates the determination of P, $(i - r_M)$, and M, under these assumptions. In panel (a), determination of the relative price of gold for a small country is shown. Since the price of gold is determined internationally, the supply curve facing a small

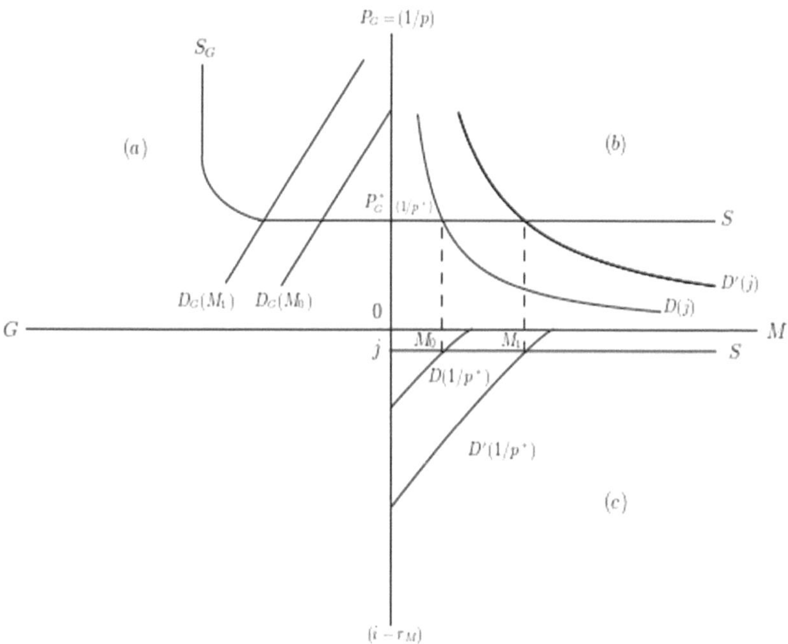

Fig. 2.2 Effect of increased demand for money in a small open economy

country is perfectly elastic at the prevailing world gold price unless the domestic demand for gold increases greatly. Hence, the supply curve is drawn with an L-shape. The demand of the banking system for gold is a function of its output of cash balances and each demand curve drawn in panel (a) corresponds to a different output of cash balances. M and $(i - r_M)$ are determined in panels (b) and (c) as they were in Fig. 2.1, except that the supply curve of cash balance with respect to $(i - r_M)$ is drawn below the horizontal axis in panel (c) to reflect the assumption that banks incur a positive cost of creating and maintaining cash balances in circulation. Thus, for a small country, the supply of money is perfectly elastic (at least in the neighborhood of equilibrium) at a price level determined by convertibility.

3. Even if the demand for gold is not insensitive to changes in the demand for money, the relative price of gold and the price level would be unaffected by domestic changes in the demand for money, provided that domestic changes in the demand for money are relatively small, or that they are correlated with changes in the opposite direction elsewhere. They would then affect only the quantity of money. Associated changes in the domestic gold stock would not imply any change in the price level.

In Figure 2.3, I illustrate two cases in which the demand for money changes. In one case, the demand shift (from D to D' in panels (b) and (c) is relatively small, so the corresponding shift in the demand for gold in panel (a) is small and does not alter the relative price of gold or the price level. In the other case, the demand shift (from D to D'') is sufficiently large to cause a shift in the demand for gold that does alter the relative price of gold and the price level. If the supply curve of cash balances in panel (c) were not horizontal, the spread between the rate of interest and the interest paid on money would also be affected. But as long as demand changes were not so great as to affect the relative price of gold, monetary equilibrium would be maintained through variations in r_M with no change in either P or i which, in the competitive model, are both invariant with respect to (small) changes in the supply of, and demand for, money.

In Figure 2.3, I illustrate two cases in which the demand for money changes. In one case, the demand shift (from D to D' in panels (b) and (c) is relatively small, so the corresponding shift in the

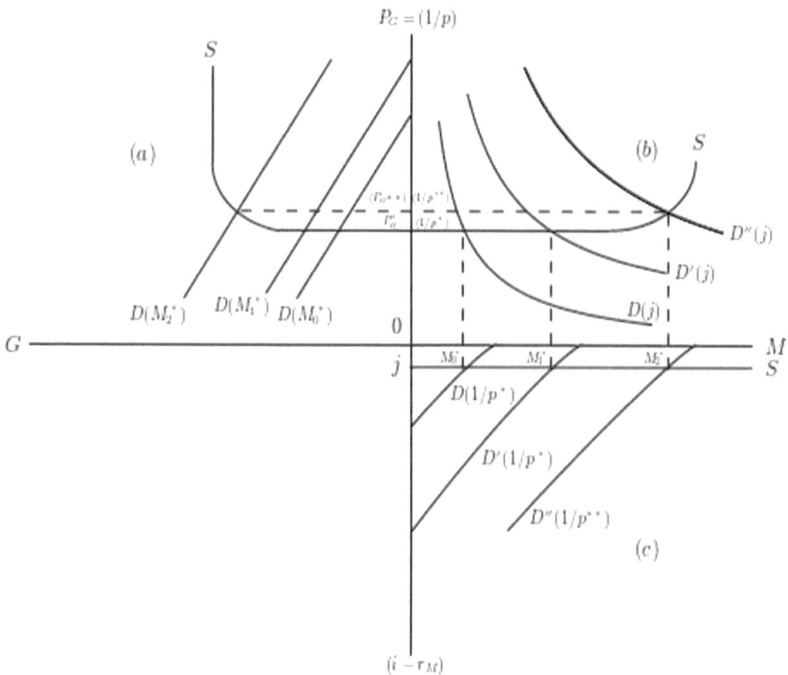

Fig. 2.3 Effect of increased demand for money in a large open economy

demand for gold in panel (a) is small and does not alter the relative price of gold or the price level. In the other case, the demand shift (from *D* to *D*″) is sufficiently large to cause a shift in the demand for gold that does alter the relative price of gold and the price level. If the supply curve of cash balances in panel (c) were not horizontal, the spread between the rate of interest and the interest paid on money would also be affected. But as long as demand changes were not so great as to affect the relative price of gold, monetary equilibrium would be maintained through variations in r_M with no change in either *P* or *i* which, in the competitive model, are both invariant with respect to (small) changes in the supply of, and demand for, money.

4. Because money yields competitive interest in this model, the optimum quantity of money in the sense of Bailey (1976),

Samuelson (1963, 1968), Friedman (1969), and others is automatically provided. Thus, the equilibrium of a model with a competitively produced money supply is Pareto-optimal. Because of the costliness of holding a non-interest-bearing, yet (by assumption) costlessly produced, money, the equilibrium of the standard general-equilibrium model with an exogenous money stock added, as in Patinkin (1965a) is not Pareto optimal.[13]

5. Furthermore, given that it is costlessly produced by a competitive banking system, and yields competitive interest, money is not a part of net wealth, so there is no real-balance effect. Excess demands in the real markets are functions of relative prices and resource endowments, not real cash balances.
6. Since money yields competitive interest, the demand for money is independent of the interest rate. Thus, the demand for money corresponds to the simple Cambridge equation and can be drawn as a rectangular hyperbola with respect to the inverse of the price level as in Fig. 2.1 (panel b). Such a demand for money was held by Patinkin (1965a, 162–195) to contradict Walras's Law. However, in the competitive model, the excess demand for money is not given by the negative value of the excess demands of the real sector, once the missing or suppressed market for "money-backing" services in which the public exchanges relatively illiquid IOUs (bonds) for the perfectly liquid IOUs (money) created by the banks is formally introduced into the model, as in Thompson (1974).[14] Such transactions, however, do not affect the market for bonds in the real sector where their price is determined; they affect only the spread between the return on bonds and the return on money. Thus, any excess demand for (supply of) money is offset not by an excess supply of (demand for) real goods but by an excess supply of (demand for) IOUs of the public to be held by the banks as backing for the

[13] Samuelson's contention (1963, 535; 1968, 9–10) that the amount of cash balances held under "laissez-faire" is not optimal is therefore incorrect. See Thompson (1974, 433–437) for a proof of Pareto-optimality.

[14] "Money backing" does not just refer to the reserves of the standard asset (e.g., gold) into which the bank promises to convert its liabilities. Any money created by a bank is "backed" by an asset the bank acquires in exchange, typically, the IOU the bank acquires from a member of the public when it creates the money in the process of lending. The IOU acquired by the bank provides the bank with "money-backing" service, generating a future cash flow to the bank.

IOUs they issue.[15] The law of reflux acknowledges the existence and operation of this "missing" market in the monetary sector.

7. Consequently, the absence of a real-balance effect implies that the real and the monetary sectors are validly dichotomized in a competitive money model.
8. Finally, Say's Law (Identity) holds[16] without implying indeterminacy of the price level, because the value of the excess demands for all real goods identically equals zero and the price level is fixed by convertibility.[16]

Thus, a number of supposedly invalid propositions attributed to classical economists turn out to be essential properties of a logically consistent model of a costlessly and competitively produced money. The relationship of a rather different theory—the quantity theory—to classical monetary theory is addressed in the following section.

2.3 The Classical Theory and the Quantity Theory

Three classical monetary theories can be distinguished: (a) the theory of a purely metallic currency, (b) the theory of an inconvertible paper currency, and (c) the theory of a competitive convertible paper currency. Only (b) corresponds to a strict quantity theory of money in which price-level changes are caused by, and proportional to, changes in nominal balances. Unfortunately, many classical theorists sometimes confused their theories by introducing quantity-theoretic propositions into arguments to

[15] Patinkin (1965a, 298), following Modigliani (1960, 183–184; 1963, 81–88), acknowledged the validity of a dichotomy for a pure inside-money economy. However, he maintained that the price level in such a system would be indeterminate unless the central bank arbitrarily determined some nominal variable. The argument in this section, which I believe would have been accepted by classical monetary theorists, is that a nominal variable is determined by the convertibility commitment imposed on banks by competition.

[16] However, as I explain in Chapter 9, the validity of Walras's Law and, therefore Say's Law (Identity), is contingent on all agents knowing in advance, or correctly anticipating, future prices.

which the quantity theory was not applicable. Such misplaced propositions have fostered the misconception that the quantity theory was the essential classical monetary theory (O'Brien, 1975, 143).[17]

Having already discussed the theory of a competitive convertible currency, I now turn to the theory of a purely metallic currency and the theory of an inconvertible paper currency.

The first point to note is that classical theorists recognized that the markets for metals such as gold are international. Since transportation costs for gold are relatively low, its value must, absent trade barriers, be approximately equal in all countries.[17] Moreover, uniformity of price levels is ensured not just by gold shipments, but also by the arbitrage of all tradable commodities (Frenkel and Johnson, 1976, 33–35).

Second, if gold can be produced at constant cost, the value of gold equals the cost of production. However, in the short run at least, costs rise rapidly as the rate of output increases, so the flow supply of gold is small relative to the stock. Since the stock is nearly fixed in the short run,

[17] J. S. Mill recognized the limited applicability of the quantity theory. He was, perhaps, in error in not distinguishing between a pure metallic and an inconvertible paper currency when he wrote (Mill 1909, 493), "It is to be remarked that this ratio would be precisely that in which the quantity of money had been increased. If the whole money in circulation was doubled, prices would be doubled. If it was only increased one-fourth, prices would rise one-fourth." But later Mill (528) wrote, "I apprehend that bank notes, bills or cheques. as such, do not act on prices at all. What does act on prices is Credit in whatever shape given, and whether it gives rise to any transferable instruments capable of passing into circulation or not." Mill went on to compare the effects on prices of a convertible with the effects of an inconvertible currency (544).

> Up to this point, the effects of a paper currency are substantially the same whether it is convertible into specie or not. It is when the metals have been completely superseded and driven from circulation. that the difference between convertible and inconvertible paper begins to be operative. When the gold or silver has all gone from circulation. and an equal quantity of paper has taken its place, suppose that a still further issue is superadded. The same series of phenomena recommences: prices rise, among the rest the price of gold and silver articles, and it becomes an object as before to procure coin in order to convert it into bullion. There is no longer any coin in circulation; but if paper currency is convertible, coin may still be obtained from the issuers, in exchange for notes. All additional notes, therefore, which are attempted to be forced into circulation after the metals have been completely superseded, will return up on the issuers in exchange for coin; and they will not be able to maintain in circulation such a quantity of convertible paper, as to sink its value below the metal which it represents.

short-run changes in the value of gold must be caused by demand, not supply, changes. Nor can anticipated changes in supply have much effect on the value of gold, because anticipated changes in supply would already be reflected in the current price.

Third, if the stock of gold were unexpectedly doubled, the value of gold would not, in general, fall by half. For a change in the stock of gold to cause an inversely proportional change in the price, the demand for gold must be unit-elastic in the relevant range. Although this may be presumed to be true of the monetary demand for gold, it need not be true of the non-monetary demand for gold.

Fourth, in any country, changes in the stock of gold do not affect the domestic price level. The independence of the domestic price level from the domestic stock of gold follows from the fact that the value of gold is determined in an international market. If the stock of gold in one country were doubled, gold would be exported until the amount of gold in the country fell to the original level. No change in price levels would be required. Only insofar as the increase in the domestic gold stock changed the world stock of gold enough to alter the world price level would a domestic price-level change be implied (Frenkel, 1976, 35).

Only under an inconvertible paper currency does the quantity theory become applicable. Since an inconvertible paper currency has no non-monetary use, the absence of money illusion implies that changes in the money stock lead to proportional change in the price level. If exchange rates fluctuate freely, the effects of a change in the money stock in one country are confined to that country and do not affect prices in other countries. The quantity theory applies within each country and exchange rates vary to ensure purchasing-power parity. With *truly* fixed exchange rates, the price levels in all countries are determined by the world supply and demand for currency. A doubling of the world's stock of currency doubles the price level in each country. And the international distribution of currency reflects the operation of the balance-of-payments mechanism (Frenkel, 1976, 35).

Among the leading figures in classical monetary theory, there was some confusion about these propositions. David Hume, in particular, was in error about all four propositions concerning a pure metallic standard. Hume (1752 [2006], 62–63) misapplied the quantity theory, which was relevant only to the case of an inconvertible paper currency, to the case of a pure gold money; he also gave an incorrect analysis of the case of a competitive convertible currency. Smith (1937) avoided Hume's incorrect application of the quantity theory to a metallic currency, and presented a substantially correct analysis of a competitive convertible paper currency and the mechanism of international adjustment. David Ricardo (1821 [1951]), however, may, at times, have lapsed into some of Hume's errors in analyzing the international adjustment mechanism under a gold standard and convertibility, perhaps because he was misled by his own quantity-theoretic analysis of the international adjustment mechanism under an inconvertible paper currency.[18] Henry Thornton (1802 [1939]) was essentially correct on all key points, as was J. S. Mill (1909), who explicitly limited application of the quantity theory to the case of an inconvertible currency (Hicks, 1977, 60 fn.). Nassau Senior (1960) was correct on all points except for failing to see that national price levels could not vary independently under a gold standard. And, on all these issues, the Banking School showed an understanding superior to that of the Currency School.

2.4 The Role of Competition in Classical Monetary Theory

Because the assumption of competition underlying much of classical monetary theory was overlooked, many classical monetary propositions have seemed puzzling or wrong. The key point to understand is that classical theorists regarded competition as a constraint on individual banks.[19]

[18] Some writers have defended Ricardo against the charge of inconsistency on this point. They maintain that Ricardo did distinguish between the quantity theory applicable to an inconvertible currency and a cost-of-production theory applicable to a convertible currency. See Girton and Roper (1978, 613) as well as references cited there. That interpretation of Ricardo is consistent with the view of classical theory I have presented in this chapter. One authority (Hegeland, 1951, 59–60) who maintains that Ricardo adhered to only one theory—the quantity theory—acknowledges that this did involve Ricardo in an inconsistency.

[19] As Smith (1937, 313) wrote:

> The late multiplication of banking companies in both parts of the United Kingdom instead of diminishing, increases the security of the public. It obliges all of them to be more circumspect in their conduct, and, by not extending their currency beyond its due proportion to their cash, to guard themselves against those malicious runs, which the rivalship of so many competitors is always ready to bring upon them. It restrains the circulation of each particular company within a narrower circle, and *reduces their circulation notes to a smaller number*. [my emphasis]

It was competition, not merely a legally imposed requirement to maintain convertibility into gold, that restrained banks in creating notes or deposits. Indeed, as Thompson (1974) has explained, and as many classical writers including Smith understood, since inconvertible money would not be held by the public when they could hold convertible money, competition would force convertibility on banks.[20]

The distinction first began to be made by members of the Currency School in arguing for a statutory limitation on the note issue of both the Bank of England and the country banks. I discuss the Currency-School and Banking-School positions in Chapter 3. What I would note here is that the Currency-School position was that the banking system is inherently, or at least on occasion, inclined toward expansion. Although convertibility provided an ultimate check on such expansion, the check would not operate until after the expansion was under way. Thus, unless the initial expansion could somehow be stopped early on, a cyclical pattern would be set in with a boom initiated by the overissue followed by a bust caused by the contraction required to protect convertibility (Viner, 1937, 239–241).

This line of argument, however, assumes that convertibility is simply an exogenous check imposed on the banking system to prevent overexpansion. In other words, a bank's marginal revenue from creating additional cash is presumed to exceed its marginal cost. Thus, unless constrained, all banks would tend to expand, in which case, no bank would be deterred from doing so by adverse clearings. Believing convertibility to be an inadequate brake on such expansion, the Currency School favored statutory limits on the power of the banking system to expand its note issue.[21]

Also see Fullarton (1845, 89–92). "But, far from contributing to the eventual enlargement of the aggregate mass of the banknote circulation, the effect of this competition was obviously to keep it down" (90).

[20] C. A. Phillips (1920, 32), who perfected the money-multiplier analysis, insisted, "[t]he accepted statements of banking theory, with scarcely an exception, have made no such distinction, with the result that confusion, obscurity, and error prevail with reference to the most fundamental principles of the subject." Also see Hayek (1933, 152–153). Viner (1937, 239–243) disputed Phillips's assertion, citing several authors who did make the distinction. Also see Schumpeter (1954, 730).

[21] Given its monopolistic quasi-central-bank position, the Bank of England probably could keep the borrowing rate for the entire banking system temporarily below the natural rate, thereby promoting an investment boom that could continue as long as the Bank of England was prepared to lose reserves. Neoclassical theories of the business cycle, starting

But convertibility is itself the result of competition among banks. It is the means by which competing banks guarantee that their monies maintain the stipulated purchasing power, and without which they could not induce the public to hold their monies. Each bank reaches an equilibrium in which the marginal revenue from producing additional balances equals the marginal cost of doing so, and beyond which there is, consequently, no tendency to expand. Convertibility is not an exogenous constraint imposed to prevent banks from expanding without limit, it is a commitment forced on banks by competition, because, without the commitment, no bank could achieve a profit-maximizing equilibrium.

To be sure, all banks could expand simultaneously more easily than any single bank, because, when expanding simultaneously, banks would not face adverse clearings. But it is also true that, acting together, all sellers of any product could raise its price more easily than any single seller could. All this means is that competition is less constraining if banks don't compete than if they do.[22] The assumption usually made by classical economists is that, in the absence of monopoly, banks, like other firms, banks do compete.

2.5 Modern Versions of Classical Monetary Theory

Modern versions of classical monetary theory have erroneously identified it with the quantity theory of money, taking for granted that the nominal money stock rather than the price level must be treated as the exogenous variable in the model. This error misled many writers, such as Viner (1937), Robbins (1958), Blaug (1985), and O'Brien (1975),

with Wicksell, were based on the Currency School's recognition of this possibility, which they incorrectly attributed to competitive forces.

[22] In Schumpeter's (1954, 730) words:

> First, we mention one [argument] that is perfectly true so long as we confine ourselves to considering the individual banking business in a competitive system of many banks. Credit expansion for the individual bank is, in fact, severely limited by the drain on reserves that it will eventually entail. Of course, this is no longer true for all banks taken together: but even for all of them, if the system be really competitive, that penalty on stepping out of line is a more effective brake upon expansion in line than critics of banking practice are usually prepared to recognize.

who have recounted the views of the classical monetary theorists and the controversies in which they took part.[28] Even Schumpeter, who, in some respects, had a more accurate understanding than other commentators, did not fully comprehend the issues that separated the Currency School and Banking School, describing (1954, 728) their differences as "minor disagreements as regards analysis." The extent of the difference had, however, been clear to Wicksell (1935, 169–175) who recognized that the two schools were arguing about the validity of the quantity theory as an explanation of prices.

Aside from accounts of the practical issues with which classical monetary theory dealt, there is also an imposing literature on the pure analytics of classical theory, addressing such topics as the dichotomization of the real and monetary sectors, the validity of Say's Law (Identity), the existence of a real-balance effect, and the neutrality of money. Patinkin has argued (1965a, 162–195) that classical monetary theory invalidly dichotomized the real and monetary sectors of the economy, incorrectly assumed the validity of Say's Law (Identity) for a monetary economy, and overlooked real-balance effects to explain price-level adjustments.

Patinkin's (1965a) widely admired exposition of the neoclassical synthesis was criticized for attributing to classical theorists positions with respect to dichotomization, Say's Law, and the real-balance effect that they did not hold. Such critics as Hickman (1950), Baumol and Becker (1952), Archibald and Lipsey (1958), and Niehans (1978) argued that the dichotomy, Say's Law (Equality), and the absence of real-balance effects must be understood as applying only to equilibrium states of economy and not, as Patinkin held, to disequilibrium states as well.

Such disputes can probably never be resolved, because the views of classical theorists on such questions were sufficiently vague to admit of numerous interpretations. Sowell (1972) has shown, for example, that a variety of propositions were subsumed by the classical theorists under the general heading of Say's Law. None of them seems to correspond precisely to Say's Law (Identity) in the sense of Lange (1942) and Patinkin (1965a). But many classical theorists, including Smith and Ricardo, did separate their analysis of relative-price determination from their analysis of price-level determination. They certainly believed that the factors accounting for the determination of relative prices were fundamentally different from those accounting for determination of the price level. It is the notion that a separation between the two sets of factors can be made that gives rise to the idea of a dichotomy and suggests Say's Law. It seems unlikely that this distinction was not in the minds of classical writers. The Lange-Patinkin version of Say's Law is, thus, not without foundation in the classical literature and has antecedents in earlier discussions of Say's Law.[23]

What I wish to take issue with in both the Lange-Patinkin formulation of the classical model and those of their critics is the introduction of an inconvertible money into the models and their discussion of the validity of the dichotomy and Say's Law within the context of such models. Although, when addressing practical problems to which it was relevant, classical theorists did work with a model of an inconvertible currency, they regarded such a currency as exceptional from a positive standpoint and opposed it from a normative one.

Two factors account for the misrepresentation of classical monetary theory in the modern literature. One is the interest of modern writers in the dichotomy and their desire to compare the classical model with the Keynesian model in which an exogenously determined supply of inconvertible money is an explicit, and perhaps, necessary assumption.[24] For

[23] Hayek (1933, 101–102) seems to have had something like the Lange-Patinkin interpretation of Say's Law in mind when he wrote:

> The automatic adjustment of supply and demand can only be disturbed when money is introduced into the economic system. This adjustment must be considered, according to the reasoning which is most clearly expressed in Say's *Theorie des Debouches,* as being always present in a state of natural economy. Every explanation of the Trade Cycle which uses the methods of economic theory... must, therefore, start by considering the influences which emanate from the use of money.

He also seems to have had it in mind in the following (1933, 107–108):

> In complete contrast to those economic changes conditioned by 'real' forces, influencing simultaneously total supply and total demand, changes in the volume of money have, so to speak, a one-sided influence which elicits no reciprocal adjustment in the economic activity of different individuals. By deflecting a single factor, without simultaneously eliciting corresponding changes in other part of the system, it dissolves its 'closedness', makes a breach in the rigid reaction mechanism of the system (which rests on the ultimate identity of supply and demand) and opens a way for tendencies leading away from the equilibrium position. As a theory of these one-sided influences. the theory of monetary economy should, therefore, be able to explain the occurrence of phenomena which would be inconceivable in the barter economy.

[24] See Rueff (1947). Also see Shackle (1967, 212–213), who draws attention to the fact that in the *Treatise* Keynes (1930) had assumed that the money stock is endogenous

the dichotomy to be free from patent violation, it must be assumed that money is created at no cost. Otherwise, the determination of equilibrium in the monetary sector cannot fail to have repercussions in the real sector. Thus, for the dichotomy issue to be raised at all, it had to be assumed that money could be costlessly created and yet retain a positive value. No real commodity, therefore, could serve as money. The other is the presumption that the classical theory of the relationship between the price level and nominal balances corresponded to some form of the quantity theory.

Since the assumption of competition in the supply of a costlessly producible asset seemed to make a positive value for that asset (or, at any rate, a determinate price level) impossible, it appeared, in the absence of a theory of a competitive money supply, necessary to compare the classical model with the Keynesian model in which an exogenously determined supply of inconvertible money was explicitly assumed.[25] For the dichotomy to be free from patent violation, one must assume that money is created costlessly; otherwise, the determination of equilibrium in the monetary sector could not fail to have repercussions in the real sector. Thus, to raise the dichotomy issue at all, one had to assume that money could be costlessly created and yet retain a positive value. No real commodity could serve as money. The second factor is the presumption that the classical theory of the relationship between the price level and nominal balances corresponded to some form of the quantity theory.

Since the assumption of competition in the supply of a costlessly producible asset seemed to make a positive value for that asset (or at any rate a determinate price level) impossible, it appeared, in the absence of a theory of a competitive money supply, necessary to assume that the nominal stock of the asset be exogenously, rather than endogenously, determined.[26] Nor, it must have appeared, would convertibility into some real asset at an exogenously determined conversion rate have solved the problem. Convertibility would have, *ipso facto,* destroyed the

while in the *General Theory* (1936), he assumed that it is exogenously determined, and Hicks (1977, 75–77), who contrasts the exogeneity of the money stock in the Keynesian model its endogeneity in classical and Wicksellian models.

[25] See footnotes 3–6 above.

[26] See Niehans (1978, 9) who argues that convertibility is inconsistent with neutrality as well as a dichotomy.

dichotomy by introducing monetary effects into the real sector because of the necessity of holding reserves of the asset into which money would be convertible. And since the price level was presumed to be determined by the quantity theory under a convertible as well as an inconvertible currency, the assumption of convertibility would not have altered fundamentally the model used to represent classical theory. But, as we have seen, an endogenously determined supply of costlessly produced money can be reconciled with a finite price level under convertibility. Costless production under competitive conditions does not imply an infinite price level, because competition itself compels the banks to maintain convertibility as well as to pay competitive real interest on the cash balances they produce. Nor would convertibility undermine the dichotomy between the real and the monetary sectors because, if banks can produce cash balances costlessly, they would incur no costs of holding reserves. If they incur no costs of holding reserves, then either (1) they are not holding any reserves because the confidence in the money produced by the banks is such that their commitment to convert suffices to maintain the value of the money they produce, thereby eliminating any demand for the real asset as a medium of exchange, or (2) the banks forego no interest on the reserves they hold because the reserve asset is, itself, appreciating at a rate equal to the rate of interest. An asset appreciating at a rate equal to the rate of interest cannot be providing any current real services. If it provides no current real services, then its being held by banks as a reserve withdraws it from no current use. The value of money being unaffected by its being used in the monetary sector, the dichotomy is preserved.

An exogenously determined stock of a costlessly produced inconvertible paper money is, thus, not essential to a model in which the classical assertions about Say's Identity and a dichotomy between the real and monetary sectors can be derived.[27] Indeed, the assertion of the Banking

[27] Fullarton (1845, 57–58) wrote:

> That soon after the discovery of the South American mines in the sixteenth century. a decline in the value of the precious metals was manifested all over the world by an universal rise of the money prices of commodities, is a fact which no one presumes to question. It is equally undenied and undeniable, that the inconvertible paper money issued by sovereign states may be, and in many instances has been. degraded by excess of quantity, until its value in exchange has been nearly extinguished altogether.

School that a convertible currency could not be redundant—the law of reflux—is precisely what is asserted by Say's Identity. The Banking School also recognized that this redundancy was possible in the case of a metallic or inconvertible currency.[28] Unlike inconvertible or metallic money, convertible bank money is not a "hot potato" that someone must hold. The public need not hold a larger amount of convertible bank money than it chooses to.[29] As required by Say's Identity, an excess supply

[28] Fullarton (1845, 57–58) wrote:

> That soon after the discovery of the South American mines in the sixteenth century. a decline in the value of the precious metals was manifested all over the world by an universal rise of the money prices of commodities, is a fact which no one presumes to question. It is equally undenied and undeniable, that the inconvertible paper money issued by sovereign states may be, and in many instances has been degraded by excess of quantity, until its value in exchange has been nearly extinguished altogether.

[29] Consider what Fullarton (1845, 64) wrote:

> Still more decidedly have the conventional issues of governments all the characteristics of a forced currency. [E]ven after the notes have become depreciated. the law compels the private creditor to accept them in satisfaction of his claim; and the government having no better money to offer, the only alternative left to its creditors and dependents is to take this or none. Bank-notes, on the other hand, are never issued but on the demand of the recipient parties. New gold coin and new conventional notes are introduced into the market by being made the medium of payments. Bank-notes on the contrary are never issued but on *loan,* and an equal amount of notes must be returned whenever the loan becomes due. Bank-notes never, therefore, can clog the market by their redundance, nor afford a motive to anyone to pay them away at a reduced value in order to get rid of them.

Compare Fullarton's statement to the following quote from Tobin (1963, 229):

> Once created printing press money cannot be extinguished. The community cannot get rid of this currency supply; the economy must adjust until it is willingly absorbed. The "hot potato" analogy truly applies. For bank-created money, however, there is an economic mechanism of extinction as well as creation, contraction as well as expansion. If bank deposits are excessive relative to public preferences, they will tend to decline. The burden of adaptation is not placed entirely on the rest of the economy.

of bank money has no impact on real markets, but instead prompts an exchange of assets between the public and the banks to retire the excess supply.[30]

2.6 Conclusion

I have been arguing that the modern approach to monetary analysis, which aggregates the liabilities created by the banking system with currency created by the government into a single measure of the money stock, supposedly under the control of the domestic monetary authority, has distorted our view of classical monetary theory. The aggregation of bank liabilities with the gold stock to determine the total money stock, and then applying the quantity theory to this aggregate is a misleading version of the classical model. The classical money model viewed bank liabilities as the output of a competitive industry operating under the same sorts of constraints, and influenced by the same kinds of incentives, as other industries. The supply of bank liabilities was, like the output of any other industry, determined by the cost and demand conditions relevant to the industry.

It was in this sense, I believe, that classical economists who spoke about the impossibility of overissue of banknotes were correct. At any time, there is some profit-maximizing output for a competitive industry. If the output deviates, in either direction, from that equilibrium output, economic forces tend to restore output to the equilibrium level. Because

[30] This point, too, was clearly expressed by Fullarton (1845, 64–65):

> However prone individuals may be to abuse at times the facility of borrowing, no merchant can ever desire to keep by him a larger sum in bank-notes than is indispensably necessary for his payments: and if anyone were disposed to indulge in so unprofitable a fancy, it would be a matter of not the slightest importance to any other than himself, for in as far as the public are concerned, notes which are not in use are the same as if they are not in existence. Those notes cannot be obtained from a banker, but by paying interest for the use of them, nor can they be obtained at all but for very short periods, at the expiration of which they must be replaced. Their circulation must always be strictly limited by the wants of those who have value or security to offer for them. And so limited, there can be no redundance; no holder of them can ever be placed in the same predicament with the importers of a double supply of bullion, or the recipients of a forced issue of government-paper, who have no means of turning their acquisitions to use by submitting to part with them at a reduced value.

of the distinction between nominal and real values for monetary units, a distinction not relevant for other industries, convertibility was a necessary anchor preventing changes in nominal units from changing the price level.

Nor have the effects of the modern money-supply paradigm been limited to causing a misunderstanding of classical monetary theory. Instead of seeking to apply more consistently the basic framework of economic analysis to a theory of the output of the banking industry, economists have been content to adopt a special theory of the money supply that, at best, is only indirectly influenced by the profit-maximization paradigm of standard marginal analysis.[31] Thus, for decades after after Hicks's (1935) classic article calling for the consistent application of the marginal utility theory to the demand for money, economists failed to apply the marginalist theory of the firm and the industry to their analysis of the supply of money. Though hardly marginalists, the classical theorists at least tried to apply the same theory of supply in monetary analysis that they used for other purposes. In this respect, I would argue, the classical theorists showed greater insight than their successors.

References

Archibald, G. C., & Lipsey, R. G. (1958). Monetary and value theory: A critique of Lange and Patinkin. *Review of Economic Studies, 4*, 1–22.

Bailey, M. J. (1976). The welfare cost of inflationary finance. *Journal of Political Economy, 2*, 93–110.

Barro, R. (1979). Money and the price level under the gold standard. *Economic Journal, 1*, 13–33.

Baumol, W. J., & Becker, G. S. (1952). The classical monetary theory: The outcome of the discussion. *Economica, 19*(76), 355–376.

Blaug, M. (1985). *Economic theory in retrospect* (4th ed.). Cambridge University Press.

Bordo, M. D., & Schwartz, A. J. (1984). *A retrospective on the classical gold standard, 1821–1931.* University of Chicago Press.

Checkland, S. G. (1975). *Scottish banking: A history, 1695-1973.* Collins.

Coase, R. H. (1972). Durability and monopoly. *Journal of Law and Economics, 16*(1), 143–149.

[31] In particular, the standard money-multiplier model involves a confusion of demand and supply concepts that is inconsistent with conventional supply-demand analysis, which requires the two concepts to be distinguished.

Frenkel, J. A. (1976). Adjustment mechanism and the monetary approach to the balance of payments: A doctrinal perspective. In E. Classen & P. Salin (Eds.), *Recent issues in international monetary economics* (pp. 29–48). North Holland.
Frenkel, J. A., & Johnson, H. G. (1976). The monetary approach to the balance of payments: Essential concepts and historical origins. In J. A. Frenkel & H. G. Johnson (Eds.), *The monetary approach to the balance of payments* (pp. 21–45). University of Toronto Press.
Friedman, M. (1959). *A program for monetary stability*. Fordham University Press.
Friedman, M. (1969). The optimum quantity of money. In *The optimum quantity of money and other essays* (pp. 1–60). Aldine Publishing Co.
Fullarton, J. (1845). *On the regulation of currencies* (2nd ed.). John Murray.
Girton, L., & Roper, D. (1978). J. Laurence Laughlin and the quantity theory of money. *Journal of Political Economy, 86*(3), 599–625.
Gurley, J. G., & Shaw, E. S. (1960). *Money in a theory of finance*. Brookings Institution.
Hayek, F. A. (1929 [1933]). *Monetary theory and the trade cycle*. Jonathan Cape.
Hayek, F. A. (1978). *Denationalization of money: An analysis of the theory and practice of concurrent currencies* (2nd ed.). Institute of Economic Affairs.
Hegeland, H. (1951). *The quantity theory of money*. Elanders Boktryckers Aktiebolag.
Hickman, W. B. (1950). The determinacy of absolute prices in classical economic theory. *Econometrica, 18*(1), 9–20.
Hicks, J. R. (1935). A suggestion for simplifying the theory of money. *Economica, 2*(5), 1–19.
Hicks, J. R. (1977). *Economic perspectives*. Oxford University Press.
Hume, D. (1752 [2006]). Of the balance of trade. In E. Rotwein (Ed.), *Writings on economics* (pp. 60–77). Routledge.
Johnson, H. G. (1967). *Further essays in monetary economics*. George Allen and Unwin.
Keynes, J. M. (1930). *A treatise on money* (2 vols.). Macmillan.
Keynes, J. M. (1936). *The general theory of employment, interest, and money*. Macmillan.
Klein, B. (1974). The competitive supply of money. *Journal of Money, Credit, and Banking, 6*(4), 423–453.
Lange, O. (1942). Say's law: A restatement and criticism. In O. Lange et al. (Eds.) *Studies in mathematical economics and econometrics* (pp. 49–68). University of Chicago Press.
Laughlin, J. L. (1903). *Principles of money*. Scribner.
Mill, J. S. (1909). *Principles of political economy*. W. Ashley (Ed.). Longmans, Green and Company.

Modigliani, F. (1960 [1982]). Liquidity preference and the theory of interest and money. In H. Hazlitt (Ed.), *Critics of Keynesian economics*, reprinted in *The Collected Papers of Franco Modigliani* (vol. 1, pp. 23–67). MIT Press.
Modigliani, F. (1963). The monetary mechanism and its interaction with real phenomena. *Review of Economics and Statistics, 45*(Supplement), 79–107.
Niehans, J. (1978). *The theory of money*. Johns Hopkins University Press.
O'Brien, D. P. (1975). *The classical economists*. Clarendon Press.
Patinkin, D. (1965a) *Money, interest and prices*. Harper and Row.
Patinkin, D. (1965b). *Studies in monetary economics*. Harper and Row.
Pesek, B. P., & Saving, T. R. (1967). *Money, wealth and economic theory*. Macmillan.
Phillips, C. A. (1920). *Bank credit*. Macmillan.
Ricardo, D. (1821 [1951]). The principles of political economy (Vol. I). In P. Sraffa (Ed.), *The works and correspondence of David Ricardo*. Cambridge University Press.
Robbins, L. (1958). *Robert Torrens and the evolution of classical economics*. Macmillan.
Robbins, L. (1976). *Political economy past and present*. Columbia University Press.
Rueff, J. (1947). The Fallacies of Lord Keynes' *General Theory*. *Quarterly Journal of Economics, 63*(2), 343–367.
Samuelson, P. A. (1963). D.H. Robertson (1890–1963). *Quarterly Journal of Economics, 79*(4), 517–536.
Samuelson, P. A. (1968). What classical and neo-classical monetary theory really was. *Canadian Journal of Economics, 1*(1), 1–15.
Schumpeter, J. A. (1954). *The history of economic analysis*. Oxford University Press.
Senior, N. (1960). *Three lectures on the value of money*, reprinted in *Selected writings on economic: A volume of pamphlets 1827–52 by N. Senior*. Augustus M. Kelley.
Shackle, G. L. S. (1967). *The years of high theory*. Cambridge University Press.
Smith, A. (1937). *The wealth of nations*. E. Cannan (Ed.). Modern Library.
Sowell, T. (1972). *Say's law: An historical analysis*. Princeton University Press.
Sowell, T. (1974). *Classical economics reconsidered*. Princeton University Press.
Thompson, E. A. (1974). The theory of money and income consistent with orthodox value theory. In G. Horwich & P. A. Samuelson (Eds.), *Trade, stability, and macroeconomics* (pp. 427–453). Academic Press.
Thompson, E. A. (1982, January 8). Free banking under a labor standard. Statement to the U.S. Gold Commission. https://drive.google.com/file/d/0B-AvoOmPTyGaY1ZhbnFzUXRwcGM/view.
Thornton, H. (1802 [1939]). *An enquiry into the nature and effects of the paper credit of Great Britain*. F. A. v. Hayek (Ed.). G. Allen & Unwin.

Tobin, J. (1963). Commercial banks as creators of money. In D. Carson (Ed.), *Banking and monetary studies*. R. D. Irwin.
Viner, J. (1937). *Studies in the theory of international trade*. Harper & Brothers.
Wicksell, K. (1935). *Lectures on political economy* (Vol. 2). G. Routledge and Sons.

CHAPTER 3

On Some Classical Monetary Controversies

3.1 Introduction

Most standard accounts of classical monetary theory (e.g., Blaug, 1985; O'Brien, 1975) emphasize its grounding in the quantity theory of money. In Chapter 2, I disputed the identification of classical monetary theory with the quantity theory, arguing that much of classical monetary theory can best be understood as a theory of a competitively produced convertible money in which the nominal quantity of inside money produced by the banking system has no effect on the exogenously fixed price level. For many classical economists, the quantity theory was strictly applicable only to an inconvertible fiat currency. Construed broadly as an extension of supply-demand analysis, the quantity theory could also account for the effects of gold discoveries—but only at the level of the closed world economy, not at the level of an open national economy. Moreover, by treating the quantity of money as the exogenous variable to which prices must adjust, the quantity theory could not cope analytically with the existence of a competitive banking system.

In Chapter 2, I argued that numerous supposed inconsistencies or errors in classical monetary theory—dichotomizing the determination of relative prices and the price level, ignoring the real-balance effect, and

D. Glasner, *Studies in the History of Monetary Theory*, Palgrave Studies in the History of Economic Thought, https://doi.org/10.1007/978-3-030-83426-5_3

belief in Say's Law[1] and the law of reflux—can be validly deduced from a model of a competitively produced convertible money. I also suggested that such a model could illuminate several classical monetary controversies that have puzzled later commentators who identified classical monetary theory with the quantity theory.

In this chapter, to support my reinterpretation of classical monetary theory, I examine those controversies in detail. To do so, I suggest some new readings of old texts. Obviously, those who are used to reading those texts from a quantity-theoretic perspective may find my interpretations forced. Demonstrating the correct reading of a text is a difficult, if not hopeless, task as literary critics and legal scholars well know. But if they are willing to postpone judgment on the basic issue, readers may find my interpretation of the texts no more forced than the more conventional ones.

The next section outlines a classical monetary model of a competitive convertible currency. In Sect. 3.3, I show how Adam Smith's adherence to something like this model accounts for his differences (including his omission of the price-specie-flow mechanism) with David Hume, a pure quantity theorist. Section 3.4 interprets the debate between the Banking and Currency Schools as an extension of the one between Smith and Hume and shows how the law of reflux advanced by the Banking School follows directly from the classical model. In Sect. 3.5, I show that Say's Law also follows from the classical model and, indeed, is equivalent to the law of reflux. I explore the reasons for abandonment of the classical theory in Sect. 3.6. In particular, I consider how Cairnes's quantity-theoretic analysis of the effects of the Australian gold discoveries helped establish the quantity theory and the price-specie-flow mechanism as the orthodox explanation of international prices. Section 3.7 contains some concluding observations about the relationship between the classical and the quantity theories of money.

3.2 A Classical Monetary Model

I begin by sketching a model developed by Thompson (1974) and described more fully in Chapter 2. Assume that banks can lend (estimate risk and collect repayment) costlessly, but that it is costly for non-banks to do so. As the least-cost providers of credit, banks issue IOUs that are instantly redeemable and, hence, more marketable than IOUs issued by

[1] Unless otherwise indicated, I use Say's Law in the strong sense of Say's Identity throughout the chapter.

others. Because bank IOUs are more readily accepted in payment than IOUs issued by other economic agents, non-banks exchange their own IOUs for those of the banks to use in making payments.

If banks compete with each other, they are obliged to pay interest on their IOUs, r_M, equal to the riskless rate of interest on loans, i. Otherwise, since banks operate costlessly, they would earn positive profits. To safeguard holders of its IOUs against its technical ability to issue liabilities without limit and render them worthless, a bank must commit itself to convert its IOUs at a stipulated rate into an asset whose value it cannot control.[2] Without offering some guarantee of convertibility into an "outside" asset, no bank could gain currency for its liabilities. Money holders would not necessarily insist on a promise of instant convertibility, but a commitment to convert eventually is essential.[3] Thus, a commodity (gold) standard is the outcome of a competitive process, not merely a legal requirement exogenously imposed on the banking system (Selgin & White, 1987; White, 1984b).

Except after unanticipated gold discoveries, prices measured in gold generally fell in the nineteenth century. Hence, holders of money convertible into gold usually did receive an implicit pecuniary return. Insofar as holding money required foregoing any interest, that implicit price reflected either real costs of producing money or monopoly power in the banking systems of most countries.

The determination of the price level, P, of the spread between the nominal interest rate on loans[4] and the interest banks pay on money, $(i - r_M)$ and of the nominal quantity of money, M, is shown in Fig. 3.1. Panel (a) shows the determination of the relative price of gold, P_G, on the assumption that banks hold no gold reserves. Unless gold is appreciating

[2] The asset into which convertibility is promised need not be a real commodity. An inconvertible fiat money issued by the government or a bank with monopolistic privileges like the Bank of England would also qualify.

[3] The Scottish banks, for example, had an option clause that allowed them to postpone converting notes into gold for six months after presented for redemption. Smith (1937, 309) condemned the option clause and favored legislation prohibiting its use. But K. Dowd (1988, 1989) reexamined the option clause and cast it in a more favorable light than did Smith.

[4] In this model, the nominal rate on loans corresponds to Wicksell's "natural rate." The competitive model assumes that banks charge the natural rate on loans. For a deviation between the natural rate and the market rate for loans to occur, some sort of market imperfection must be introduced. In Thornton, the sources of the imperfection were the 5% usury limit on interest, the monopoly power of the Bank of England, and the suspension of convertibility. See footnote 19.

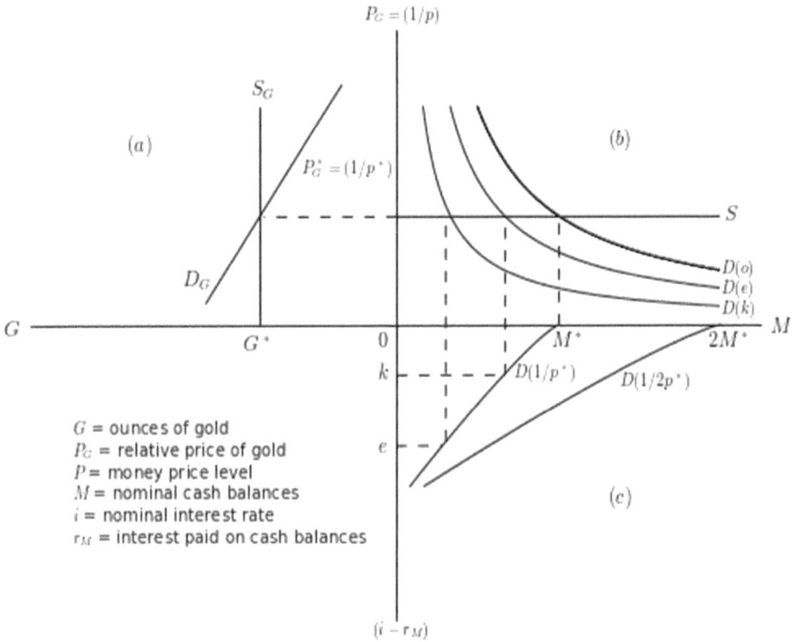

Fig. 3.1 Price-level determination under the gold standard

at a rate equal to *i*, this assumption is implied by the prior assumption of costless production. Given the exogenously determined conversion rate of currency into gold, *CR*, P_G uniquely determines *P* in accord with the equation $(CR)(1/P) = P_G$.

Without loss of generality, we can choose *CR* so that P_G equals *1/P*, allowing P_G and *1/P* to be measured simultaneously along the vertical axis. In panel (b), a family of rectangular-hyperbolic demand curves depicts the inverse relationship between the amount of nominal cash balances demanded, *M*, and 1/P. The demand for real cash balances along each demand curve is constant and depends on $(i - r_M)$. In panel (c), the demand for real cash balances as a function of $(i - r_M)$ is shown by a family of demand curves (each corresponding to a given price level). Competition requires that $(i - r_M)$ equal the marginal cost of maintaining cash balances held by the public. If that cost is zero, the supply curve of cash balances in panel (c), indicating the output of money by banks as a function of $(i - r_M)$, coincides with the horizontal axis. Thus, the equilibrium amount of money balances is represented by the point where the demand curve in panel (c) that corresponds to the price level determined in panel (a) touches the horizontal axis.[5]

In a standard quantity-theoretic analysis, the price level depends on an exogenously fixed nominal quantity of money. But in this model, the supply of money balances is perfectly elastic at a price level exogenously fixed by convertibility.

Even if banks cannot produce money costlessly, the same conclusions follow if the demand for gold by the banking system of the country whose price level is being determined is a small component of the international demand for gold (Chapter 2).[6]

I should also observe here that in the classical model an excess demand for inside money (in contrast to an excess demand for gold) does not correspond to an excess supply of goods in the real sector. The excess demand for inside money is offset, instead, by an excess supply of IOUs offered to the banking system in exchange for money. Nor does an excess supply of inside money correspond to an excess demand for goods in the real sector. It is offset by an excess demand for IOUs from the banking system, i.e., a desire by the public to reduce its indebtedness to the banking system. The classical proposition that an excess demand for money does not impinge on the real sector is known as Say's Law (Identity). The symmetric proposition that an excess supply of money does not impinge on the real sector is the law of reflux.

[5] If there were some positive, but constant, marginal cost of maintaining the money balances held by the public, the supply curve would be perfectly elastic at k, where k is the annual cost of issuing one unit of money. If the marginal cost of producing money balances increases with the quantity of money balances, the supply curve rises. In other words, $(i - r_M) = k(M)$ where $k(M)$ is the marginal annual cost of maintaining the money balances held by the public as a function of the quantity of money balances. Note, however, that even if the supply curve in panel (c) were upward-sloping, the supply curve in panel (b) would still be perfectly elastic with respect to $1/P$.

[6] Classical theorists were of different minds about the "smallness" of Great Britain in the early nineteenth century. Ricardo, as we shall see in Sect. 3.5, did not believe Britain was small after the Napoleonic Wars. He blamed the Bank of England for causing gold to appreciate by rapidly accumulating gold in anticipation of the resumption of convertibility. However, Senior (1830), explicitly addressing the smallness issue, concluded that the whole British gold coinage was a small fraction of the world gold stock. By the middle of the century, the smallness assumption was likely valid for Britain. That Britain was not small in relation to the markets for manufactured goods in the early nineteenth century is true, but not relevant to the properties of the model discussed in the text. Those properties depend on the relation between the demand for and supply of money and the relative price of gold. As I argue in the text, markets for real goods in this model are insulated from changes in the demand for, or supply of, money.

A further observation may be helpful. Neither Say's Identity nor the law of reflux asserts that the money market is always in equilibrium. An excess demand for, or excess supply of, money can occur. What the two propositions assert is that any excess demand for, or excess supply of, money is offset, not by a corresponding excess supply or excess demand in the real sector, but by an excess supply of, or excess demand for, IOUs that the banking system stands ready to exchange for money. Two markets are juxtaposed: a market for inside money and a market for IOUs that back money. The two markets are equilibrated by adjustments in the spread between the interest paid on money and the interest rate charged for loans (or paid on IOUs) or by adjustments in the quantity of money and IOUs. The equilibration occurs without directly impinging on the real sector of the economy, the proposition asserted by both Say's Identity and the law of reflux.

3.3 Hume and Smith on Banking and the Price-Specie-Flow Mechanism

The classical theory of a convertible, competitive money was first coherently expounded by Adam Smith (1937, 189, 313, 404–405). Smith recognized that the value of a metallic currency would be determined by the supply of, and demand for, the metal in international markets, so that the price level in any country was fixed by the internationally determined value of the metal.[7]

Working out a rudimentary theory of a competitive banking system to explain the market mechanism that constrains the note issues of such a system,[8] Smith was clearly responding to David Hume who maintained

[7] It is curious that in discussing the historical origins of the monetary approach to the balance of payments, neither Frenkel and Johnson (1976) nor Frenkel (1976) included Smith among the forerunners of the monetary approach who recognized the international determination of price levels under the gold standard, while including Hume despite recognizing that his analysis of international adjustment assumed that national price levels could deviate from the internationally determined value of gold. On this point, see Frenkel (1976, 41–42).

[8] Unfortunately, the contribution by Smith to banking theory usually singled out for attention (Mints 1945, 9, 25–27) is the real-bills doctrine (Smith 1937, 288–292). Since his discussion of the real-bills doctrine presumed convertibility, one should not assume that he, like some of its later advocates, believed that adherence to it would prevent depreciation of banknotes even without convertibility. Smith (1937, 309–313) explicitly

that banks were inherently inflationary. In his essay, "Of the Balance of Trade," Hume (1752 [2006]):

> I scarcely know any method of sinking money below its level, but those institutions of banks, funds, and paper credit which are so much practiced in this kingdom. These render paper equivalent to money, circulate it throughout the whole state, make it supply the place of gold and silver, raise proportionately the price of labour and commodities, and by that means either banish a great part of those precious metals, or prevent their farther encrease.

Smith (1937, 308) responded by observing that banks could not cause prices to rise as long as their notes were unquestionably convertible into gold.

> A paper money consisting in bank notes, issued by people of un doubted credit, payable upon demand without any condition, and in fact always readily paid as soon as presented is, in every respect, equal in value to gold and silver money; since gold and silver money can at any time be had for it. Whatever is either bought or sold for such paper, must necessarily be bought or sold as cheap as it could have been for gold and silver.

Understanding that, instead of promoting overissue as Hume alleged, competitive banking prevented it, Smith directly addressed (1937, 308–309) Hume's argument:

> The increase in paper money, it has been said, by augmenting the quantity, and consequently diminishing the value of the whole currency, necessarily augments the money price of commodities. But as the quantity of gold and silver, which is taken from the currency, is always equal to the quantity of paper which is added to it, paper money does not necessarily increase the quantity of the whole currency. From the beginning of the last century to the present time, provisions were never cheaper in Scotland than in 1759, though, from the circulation of ten and five shilling bank notes, there

recognized that inconvertible banknotes could be depreciated. For Smith, the real-bills doctrine was simply a rule of thumb for bankers to follow to maintain their liquidity and to permit their balance sheets to expand and contract in response to changes in the demand for money. See Smith (1937, 288–292), where he mentions the real-bills doctrine among other expedients for a bank to gauge how much money it could safely issue. This point is discussed at length in Chapter 4.

> was then more paper money in the country than at present. The proportion between the price of provisions in Scotland and that in England, is the same now as before the great multiplication of banking companies in Scotland. Corn is, upon most occasions, fully as cheap in England as in France; though there is a great deal of paper money in England, and scarce any in France. In 1751 and 1752, when Mr. Hume published his *Political Discourses*, and soon after the great multiplication of paper money in Scotland, there was a very sensible rise in the price of provisions, owing, probably, to the badness of the seasons, and not to the multiplication of paper money.

Introducing a convertible currency into a country does not raise prices; it frees up for productive use the capital formerly lying idle in specie and coin (Smith 1937, 275). Substituting paper for metallic money reduces the monetary demand for the metal, so that excess specie could be exported in payment for capital goods that promote economic growth. If the amount of coin and specie replaced were small compared to the world stock, the export of precious metals would not greatly affect their international values. With the value of precious metals unchanged, the price level, under a metallic standard, would not change either. And even if their value did fall, prices in the country into which the convertible paper currency was introduced would not rise above prices in other countries on that standard.

Smith maintained (1937, 277, 405) that a competitive banking system would supply as much money as the public needed to facilitate its transactions. This vague, though essentially correct, statement is at least superficially at odds with the assertion quoted above that the amount of paper currency produced by the banking system would displace an equal amount of precious metals. That, as Henry Thornton (1802 [1939]), 95–96) noted, would happen only if people wished to hold the same amount of money in notes that they held in coin or specie. Thornton saw that if people wanted to hold more notes in real terms than the real value of coin and specie they had been holding, the quantity of notes would increase by more than the metallic circulation declined. But Thornton never denied Smith's basic assertion that the introduction of paper currency by competing banks would not raise prices. Since the public willingly held the newly issued paper money, there was no tendency for prices to rise in a small open economy.

Thus, Smith may have meant no more than to deny that convertible notes would be issued to excess, thereby raising prices. Since Smith (1937,

405) believed that "a well-regulated paper money" could substitute for any shortage in the supply of gold and silver, he would not have denied that the reduction in the quantity of coin and specie did not have to match precisely the increase in the quantity of convertible paper.

A compelling reason for interpreting Smith's monetary theory as a theory of a competitive convertible currency is that doing so solves an apparent mystery in the history of economic thought (Viner, 1937, 87): Smith's disregard in *The Wealth of Nations* of the Humean price-specie-flow mechanism (PSFM) of international monetary adjustment, despite having reproduced Hume's analysis in his Glasgow lectures (1978, 507). Several solutions have been suggested to this puzzle (e.g., Eagly, 1960; Low, 1952; Petrella, 1968). But the simplest explanation is that Smith rejected PSFM, because it incorrectly applied the quantity theory to determine the price level of a country with a metallic currency. A national price level depends on the international value of the metal used as money, not the quantity of money in the country.[9] Schumpeter (1954, 367) rated Hume's analysis of international monetary adjustment above Smith's. Yet precisely because Smith did not invoke differences in national price levels that do not arise under an international metallic currency, that ranking should have been reversed.[10]

Recall Hume's famous account (1752 [2006], 62–63) of PSFM:

[9] Girton and Roper (1978, 615–618, especially fn. 53) suggested a similar solution to Viner's mystery. They also show that Laughlin (1903) had developed a sophisticated version of the classical monetary position. Also see Humphrey (1981), Laidler (1981) and Bloomfield (1975 [1994]) for similar solutions to the mystery. Although recognizing that PSFM is not applicable in Smith's model, these solutions to the mystery overlook the domestic mechanism that equilibrates the demand for, and supply of, money under a competitive banking system.

[10] Schumpeter (1954, 367) wrote:

> In *The Wealth of Nations*, Adam Smith did not advance beyond Hume but rather stayed below him. In fact it is not far from the truth to say that Hume's theory, including his overemphasis on price movements as the vehicle of adjustments, remained substantially unchallenged until the twenties of this century.

It is remarkable that Schumpeter could, in one breath, have dismissed Smith for not having reached Hume's level in analyzing international monetary adjustment, and in the next one praised Hume's analysis as remaining unchallenged until the 1920s when his overemphasis on price movements was corrected. It is remarkable, because it was on just this point that Smith rejected Hume's analysis.

> Suppose four-fifths of all the money in Great Britain to be annihilated in one night, and the nation reduced to the same condition, with regard to specie, as in the reigns of the HARRYs and EDWARDs, what would be the consequence? Must not the price of all labour and commodities sink in proportion, and everything be sold as they were in those ages? What nation could then dispute with us in any foreign market, or pretend to navigate or to sell manufactures at the same price, which to us would afford sufficient profit? In how little time, therefore, must this bring back the money we had lost, and raise us to the level of all the neighbouring nations? Where, after we have arrived, we immediately lose the advantage of the cheapness of labour and commodities; and the farther flowing in of money is stopped by our fullness and repletion.

Referring to a metallic currency, Hume used the quantity theory to show that prices would change in proportion to the quantity of money. But no effect on the price level—certainly not a proportionate one—follows from a change in the quantity of money in a country on an international metallic standard. The country whose stock of currency declines would exhibit an excess demand for money. The excess demand would be eliminated and the original quantity of money restored by a balance-of-payments surplus with no change in the country's price level.

Girton and Roper (1978), Humphrey (1981), and Laidler (1981) have all suggested that in place of PSFM Smith substituted (1937, 277–278) a primitive, but not incorrect, version of the stock-flow adjustment model of the international payments mechanism under fixed exchange rates that has been developed within the monetary approach to the balance of payments. Samuelson's (1980) demonstration that international monetary equilibrium is restored more rapidly in a model relying solely on money flows for equilibration (because prices for all goods are perfectly arbitraged across markets) than in a PSFM model that permits price-level differences confirms the astuteness of that omission.[11]

After expounding his celebrated conceptual experiment, Hume (1752 [2006], 67–68) did note a tendency toward equality among national price levels:

[11] Samuelson's argument shows that, contrary to an objection voiced by an anonymous referee, a non-PSFM model of international adjustment such as the one presented here can provide a causal explanation of the adjustment process and does not simply assert accounting identities or long-run equilibrium conditions.

> Now, it is evident, that the same causes, which would correct these exorbitant inequalities, were they to happen miraculously, must prevent their happening in the common course of nature, and must forever, in all neighbouring nations, preserve money nearly proportionable to the art and industry of each nation.

So it is not exactly clear how much Hume thought national price levels could deviate in the short run from the common international level. Nor did Hume indicate what, aside from price-level differences, would propel the adjustment to monetary disturbances. Developing Hume's analysis, later exponents of PSFM such as Viner (1937) insisted that some international price differences, if only in the non-tradable goods sector, were needed for international monetary adjustment. It is this contention which has been challenged by the monetary approach to the balance of payments (McCloskey & Zecher, 1976) and refuted by Samuelson (1980).

In describing PSFM, Hume assumed that a change in the quantity of money would immediately alter the price level, thereby initiating a long-run adjustment to the internationally determined price level. But in his famous discussion of the relation of the money supply to income and employment, Hume (1752 [2006], 37–38), not quite consistently, assumed that an increase in the quantity of money would not affect prices much in the short run, but would be fully reflected in prices in the long run.

> [W]e must consider that though the high price of commodities be a necessary consequence of the increase of gold and silver, yet it follows not immediately upon that increase; but some time is required before the money circulates through the whole state, and makes its effect be felt on all ranks of people. At first, no alteration is perceived; by degrees the price rises, first of one commodity, then of another; till the whole at last reaches a just proportion with the new quantity of specie in the kingdom.

Henry Thornton (1802 [1939], 238 note) saw the inconsistency Hume had fallen into and made the following comment:

> Mr. Hume, in observing that, when money encreases, "the price rises first of one commodity, then of another, till the whole, at last, reaches a just proportion with the new quantity of specie which is in the kingdom," appears to me not sufficiently to advert to the tendency of money to go

> abroad as soon as it shall have raised the gold price of articles above their level in other countries, allowing for the charges of transportation.

In another passage, Thornton (1802 [1939], 269–270) dismissed Hume's argument that paper money would increase the domestic price level with an argument that is scarcely different from that which Adam Smith would have given.

> [Hume] appears to forget, that, when the total circulating medium of a country, whether consisting of gold, or of paper, or of both, is rendered excessive; when it has thus lifted up the gold price of articles above the point at which they stand in adjacent countries, the gold is obliged, by the operation of the exchange, to transport itself to these other parts[12]; and that paper credit, therefore, enhances the prices not of that single spot in which it passes, but of the adjoining places, and of the whole world. The state which issues paper only in such quantity as to maintain its general exchanges, may be considered as substituting paper in the place of gold, and as gaining additional stock in return for whatever coin it may cause to be exported. It derives, therefore, from its own issue, the whole advantage of this augmentation of capital. It participates with other countries in that inconvenience of generally encreased price of commodities which its paper has contributed to produce.

The differences between Hume and Smith were to reemerge in several important monetary controversies of the nineteenth century. These controversies—the Banking-Currency Schools dispute, the argument about Say's Law, and the question of how the mid-century gold discoveries in California and Australia affected the general level of prices—will occupy us in the next three sections. Although not all classical theorists accepted the classical competitive monetary model—the debates were largely disputes between adherents of the competitive model and adherents of the quantity theory—subsequent misunderstanding of the competitive model has fostered the belief that the quantity theory was

[12] An anonymous reader suggests that this passage shows that Thornton acknowledged that price-level differences were necessary to international adjustment and that an over-issue of a mixed currency would depreciate the whole currency. However, this effect only arises because of the costs of transporting gold. If there were no such costs, the adjustment process would operate without the minor price-level deviations possible within the gold points.

the only (or, at least, the only respectable) monetary theory maintained by classical theorists. And it has made it seem as if those taking issue with the quantity theory lacked a coherent theory of money and prices.

3.4 The Currency School and the Banking School

In the first half of the nineteenth century, monetary questions were debated almost continually in Britain. The debates began shortly after the Bank of England suspended the convertibility of its notes into gold in 1797 when rumors of a French invasion triggered a run on its notes. Legal convertibility was not restored until 1821. During the suspension, the main issues were the policy of the Bank of England and its responsibility for the depreciation of the inconvertible pound in relation to gold. The debates of the suspension era are known as the Bullionist Controversies. I shall not discuss them here except to note that, although there was disagreement over the responsibility of the Bank of England for the depreciation of sterling, only John Wheatley (1807 [1822]),[13] following Hume, not Smith, assigned the country banks, whose notes remained convertible into Bank of England notes, any share of the blame for the depreciation.

For two decades after the Bank of England restored convertibility, the bank faced repeated crises in which convertibility was jeopardized. Because they seemed to initiate business-cycle depressions, these crises provoked further debate of the causes of the bank's difficulties and their relation to the business cycle.

The continuing monetary difficulties after the resumption raised the question whether the country banks and not just the Bank of England were disturbing the British monetary system. A group of writers, notably Joplin, McCulloch, Overstone, Pennington, and Torrens, maintained that business fluctuations and the threat to convertibility were caused by the failure of a convertible fractional-reserve currency to vary as a purely metallic currency would have under the same circumstances. In their view, a loss of gold was conclusive proof of an excess supply of currency. Under a pure metallic currency, the efflux of gold would reduce the domestic

[13] I am indebted to two anonymous referees for noting that Wheatley had held the country banks responsible for the depreciation.

stock of currency until the excess supply had been exported. But with a mixed currency, the Bank of England and the country banks could offset the export of gold by increasing their own issues. By maintaining an excess supply of money in the domestic market when a modest restriction could eliminate it, the banking system made a more severe restriction later inevitable.

Guided by this analysis, the Bank of England adopted the Palmer rule in 1827. The rule dictated that, at the lower gold point, the bank maintain a bullion reserve equal to one-third of its outstanding notes and deposits. As gold was exported, the bank was to retire notes or extinguish deposits by as much as the amount of gold exported. Thus, in contrast to the subsequent Bank Charter Act, the Palmer rule allowed a drain of metal to be met by a contraction of deposits instead of notes. But the bank was either unable or unwilling to follow the rule, while periodic crises, in which convertibility was endangered, continued to occur during the 1830s (Fetter, 1965, 32–33; Viner, 1937, 224–234).

Nor did the Palmer rule restrain the country banks, whose activities were a concern to many. Longfield (1840) and McCulloch (1831), for example, contended that the country banks, driven by competition, had expanded too rapidly, forcing the Bank of England to expand to protect its market share. Reflecting this critical attitude toward competition in banking, the Currency School began calling for legislation to force the quantity of banknotes to fluctuate with the import and export of gold.

Deeply influenced by the Currency School, Sir Robert Peel proposed, and Parliament enacted, the Bank Charter Act of 1844. The Bank Charter Act divided the Bank of England into two separate branches: a banking department and an issue department. Unlike the Palmer rule, the Act did not limit the creation of deposits: the banking department was expected to operate on strictly commercial criteria. Instead, the issue department was to be bound by a 100-percent marginal gold-reserve requirement on notes issued beyond the fiduciary limit of £14,000,000. To prevent the country banks from causing disturbances, the Act imposed an absolute limit on the total quantity of bank note issued by the country banks and authorized the government to bring about their eventual withdrawal from circulation.

Opposition to the Act was led by the Banking School. While both schools supported a convertible currency, the Currency School held that convertibility alone was an inadequate safeguard against overissue and that a 100-percent marginal gold-reserve requirement was needed to prevent overissue, to avoid cyclical fluctuations, and to ensure that convertibility would be maintained. The Banking School insisted that convertibility alone was an adequate safeguard against overissue and that the requirements of the Bank Charter Act were either unnecessary, futile, or harmful. Perhaps misled by the Ricardian doctrine of a redundant inconvertible currency, the Currency School assumed that, just as an excess issue of inconvertible banknotes would cause the currency to depreciate on the foreign exchanges, so an overissue of convertible banknotes would cause an outflow of gold.[14] And just as the depreciation of the inconvertible currency could be corrected only by its contraction, so an efflux of gold under convertibility could be corrected only by retiring convertible banknotes. In making this argument, the Currency School, guided by the quantity theory and PSFM, assumed that the outflow of gold indicated a disparity between domestic and foreign price levels.

The Currency-School argument betrayed an inadequate understanding of the domestic and the international adjustment processes for a competitive convertible currency. As I showed in Sect. 3.2, the price level, under a gold standard with a competitive supply of money, is fixed by the value of gold in relation to other commodities and the conversion rate of money into gold. Given the conversion rate, the nominal stock of money is determined by the cost of producing nominal balances and the demand for nominal balances of the public. The profit-maximizing behavior of the banks ensures that the quantity of money supplied equals the amount demanded. If either the public's demand for money, or the banks' cost of supplying it, changed, an automatic adjustment process would restore a stable equilibrium.

The Banking School had two explanations of this adjustment process.[15] One was that competition among banks would, through

[14] This argument should not be confused with the Smithian one concerning the export of gold that follows the introduction of banknotes into an economy without any notes. That efflux is part of an equilibrating adjustment by the banking system to what may be viewed as a parameter change: a reduction in banks' costs of creating notes. The new equilibrium entails a larger quantity of banknotes and a smaller quantity of coin. The efflux the Currency School had in mind is an equilibrating international adjustment to disequilibrating behavior by the banking system. According to the Currency School, the banking system was, except when undergoing a substantial loss of reserves, always inclined to create a domestic excess supply of money. In Smith's case, no contraction by the banking system is required in response to the efflux. According to the Currency School, an efflux always requires the note issue to be reduced.

[15] Both of these are traceable to Smith (1937, 284–286, 313).

clearing their mutual obligations, force any bank that created an excess supply of notes or deposits to contract.[16] The other explanation, the law of reflux, held that the public's demand for money limited the note issues of the banking system. Since banks only issue their moneys by making loans, any additional money supplied would be returned to the banks to extinguish previously incurred obligations. Unlike inconvertible fiat money issued by the government, money created by the banking system is not an exogenous variable—a "hot potato" that must be held by someone—to which the entire economy has to adjust; it is an endogenous variable driven by market forces toward its equilibrium level.

The usual reply is that these obstacles to overissue don't work if all banks are expanding together, with none of the expanding banks experiencing adverse clearings. But this argument implicitly assumes that, instead of competing against each other, banks act in concert. Obviously, like firms in any other industry, banks behave differently if they collude with each other than if they compete with each other (Chapter 2).[17]

[16] An early statement of this position dating back to the Bullionist period was that of Lord King (1804 [1844]) quoted in Viner (1937, 239).

> An excessive issue of notes by any particular banker is soon detected, if not by the public, at least by the interested vigilance of his rivals; an alarm is excited; and he is immediately called upon to exchange a very large portion of his notes in circulation for that currency in which they are payable.

[17] One could argue that if a single bank tried to increase its lending and were willing to tolerate diminished reserves, the rest of the banks would acquire excess reserves on which to base their own expansion. There are two points to note here. First, the bank in question would not in fact be expanding its asset portfolio by lending since, by assumption, there was no increased demand for its liabilities. It would simply be acquiring additional loans at the expense of reserves. Second, if the bank wishes to maintain the new composition of its portfolio, and if other banks in the system do not want to add to their reserves, then the total demand for reserves by the banking system has diminished and the excess supply of reserves must somehow be extinguished. In a small open economy with fixed exchange rates, this implies an export of the reserves by way of a temporary balance-of-payments deficit. In a closed economy or small economy with flexible exchange rates, either the domestic price level rises until the demand for reserves equals the supply, or the authority controlling the stock of reserves must retire the excess supply of reserves. In the case of a small open economy with fixed exchange rates, about which the Banking and Currency Schools were arguing, the adjustment exactly corresponds to the Banking-School version of adjustment since the export of specie is self-limiting, and is not evidence of an excess supply of money that requires a contraction of the banking system. I am indebted to an anonymous referee for bringing this issue to my attention.

A second objection to the law of reflux is that if banks maintain a lending rate below the Wicksellian natural rate, they will face an increasing demand for loans to finance investment projects. Thornton (1802 [1939]) elegantly stated this argument almost a century before Wicksell. Joplin (1832) and some members of the Currency School also stated it. However, the argument presupposes some kind of market imperfection or non-competitive behavior. Thornton identified the imperfection as the 5% usury ceiling on interest rates, or in the monopoly privileges of the Bank of England, which the suspension of convertibility enabled it to exploit. Although Thornton did not blame the country banks for the depreciation of sterling, the Currency School writers later did blame them (See also Chapter 6 for further discussion of Thornton's theory of the natural rate of interest.).[18]

John Fullarton (1845, 64–65) gave the most complete statement of the law of reflux:

> However prone individuals may be to abuse at times the facility of borrowing, no merchant can ever desire to keep by him a larger sum in bank-notes than is indispensably necessary for his payments; and if anyone were disposed to indulge so unprofitable a fancy, it would be a matter of not the slightest importance to anyone other than himself, for in as far as the public are concerned, notes which are not in use are the same as if they are not in existence. These notes cannot be obtained from a banker, but by paying interest for the use of them, nor can they be obtained at all but for very short periods, at the expiration of which they must be replaced. Their circulation must always be strictly limited by the wants of those who have value or security to offer for them. And so limited, there can be no redundance; no holder of them can ever be placed in the same predicament with the importer of a double supply of bullion, or the recipient of a forced issue of government-paper, who have no means of turning their acquisitions to use but by submitting to part with them at a reduced value.

[18] The nature of the imperfection the Currency School had in mind is not entirely clear. Joplin (1832) believed that it stemmed from the dual role of banks as suppliers of loanable funds and suppliers of currency. The latter function somehow kept them from adjusting their lending rates to match changes in the profitability of investment. Presumably this was because banks did not have to raise the funds they lent by offering interest but could simply create the currency they lent out. This, of course, ignores that banks must induce the public to hold their moneys, which they do by, among other things, paying competitive interest to holders of their moneys. So it is a misunderstanding to suppose that the power of producing money enables the producer to ignore changes in the market that dictate changes in the structure of interest rates.

What Fullarton ignored is that not everyone holding banknotes acquires them by borrowing from a bank; many people acquire them in exchange for goods or services. He also ignored that what the Currency School really wanted to avoid by limiting the quantity of banknotes was spending, not holding, notes. Moreover, if competition among banks led them to increase lending by keeping the lending rate below the Wicksellian natural rate, as the Currency School insisted it would, the interest rate would not deter borrowing for, and spending on, investment projects.

Yet Fullarton did recognize a fundamental point which, had he developed it fully, would have enabled him to dispose of the objections his critics raised against the law of reflux. For he understood that competition obliges banks to pay interest on the money they issue. Though paying interest on banknotes may, owing to high transactions costs, be too costly to be worthwhile, paying interest on deposits is not. Since banknotes are convertible into deposits, holders of banknotes bear an opportunity cost of holding money in the form of banknotes not deposits. The apparent profit margin on non-interest-bearing banknotes cannot lead banks to overissue notes, because excess notes are converted into interest-bearing deposits.

Moreover, since the size of a bank's asset portfolio depends on the willingness of the public to hold its liabilities, a bank cannot expand by reducing the interest rate it charges on loans; it can only alter the composition of its assets. When marginal revenue exceeds marginal cost, it cannot increase the size of its asset portfolio unless it can induce the public to hold more of its liabilities. To make its liabilities more attractive, it will usually increase the interest paid on deposits. Thus, banks compete for market share primarily by increasing rates paid on deposits, not by reducing rates charged on loans. Reducing its lending rate below the Wicksellian natural rate undermines the bank's ability to support the interest it must pay on deposits. Since they bear competitive interest, all deposits created are held willingly and affect neither spending nor prices. As Fullarton wrote (1845, 92–93):

> [T]he joint-stock banks have been far more successful in their efforts to promote and extend the use of banking accounts among all ranks throughout the kingdom, than in their attempts to engross or enlarge the circulation. This they have partly accomplished, by the facilities for that purpose which their numerous offices, dispersed over the country afford to every man, but chiefly the practice which they have borrowed from

> the Scotch bankers, of allowing interest to their depositors, and which, by the force of their example and competition, has become also, I believe, a very general practice among private bankers everywhere but in London. The inducement which such a system holds out to individuals to become depositors in banks, and to those who are already depositors to increase their deposits, are sufficiently obvious; and it is equally apparent that such circumstances must have a decided influence in reducing the circulation of bank-notes. The tradesman, instead of keeping by him an unproductive hoard of such notes for his daily disbursements, will prefer paying them into a bank which allows him interest for the amount, without any prejudice to his perfect command over the principal. He will make his payments thenceforth by cheque; and those cheques will, in the vast majority of cases, be adjusted by transfer or exchange, without any resort to money.
>
> The Scotch banks, among whom this practice of allowing interest to depositors has been coeval with their existence, are in themselves a standing refutation of the notion that bank-notes can be over-issued at the pleasure of the issuers.

Yet, for all his insight, Fullarton did overstate his case somewhat. He seemed to say that it was almost physically impossible for banks to over-issue notes—a proposition few have been willing to accept. He correctly observed that, while people could not reduce their holdings of precious metals or an inconvertible currency, they could reduce their holdings of banknotes and deposits. But he insisted that this mechanism would immediately overpower banks no matter how hard they all simultaneously tried to expand their issues of notes and creation of deposits. The point that would have clinched Fullarton's argument, but that he did not quite grasp, is that, by paying competitive interest on deposits, each bank reaches a profit-maximizing equilibrium at which the incentive, under given cost and demand conditions, to create additional notes and deposits is exhausted.[19]

[19] Nor did Fullarton accept the validity of Thornton's argument that a bank, like the Bank of England, with monopolistic powers could keep the loan rate below the natural rate long enough to stimulate investment and raise prices. White (1984a) has shown that there was a Free Banking School that accepted the validity of Thornton's analysis for the Bank of England while denying that it applied to the country banks. Like the Banking School, they opposed the Bank Charter Act of 1844, but also suggested abolishing the monopolistic privileges of the Bank of England and allowing free banking in England on the Scottish model. However, since by 1830, there was free banking in England in the creation of deposits, it is not obvious that the monopoly power of the Bank of England was very substantial.

The Currency-School argument that the banking system is under competitive pressure to overissue presumed that each bank could, at the margin, profit by lending additional banknotes. But if increased lending increases the quantity of interest-bearing deposits—as it must if the public can decide how much bank money to hold as notes and how much as deposits—the expansion of lending cannot be profitable.

Thus, the law of reflux can be understood as an explanation of the mechanism by which banks and the public jointly determine an equilibrium. Reflux enables banks to adjust the quantity of their outstanding liabilities to the amount that both they and the public wish to maintain. The equilibrium is such that banks have no incentive to create additional loans or issue more money and the public has no incentive to alter its indebtedness to the banking system or its holdings of bank money. Since the Banking School believed that this domestic mechanism equated the demand for, with the supply of, money, they denied that gold flows were caused by monetary disturbances. A gold outflow was not evidence, as the Currency School contended, of an overissue of banknotes. Rather, it was symptomatic of a real disturbance, for example, a poor harvest. Such a disturbance would reduce the demand to hold gold reserves, so that gold could be exported to finance food imports. The efflux would be temporary and might eventually be reversed. A monetary contraction to stem the outflow would simply aggravate the initial disturbance. The oft-repeated charge that the Banking School did not understand the monetary nature of the balance of payments is therefore unfounded.

The Banking School thus transmitted and enhanced an important tradition in classical monetary thought. The tradition begins with Adam Smith and was continued in large part, in the work of Thornton, Ricardo, and their contemporaries. Yet the conviction that Ricardo was a forerunner of the Currency School is so strong that a Parliamentary speech Sir Robert Peel gave acknowledging that the Bank Charter Act departed from the teachings of Smith and Ricardo is worth quoting.

> It has been contended by very eminent men that the only security you need against excessive issue of paper currency is immediate convertibility. This doctrine, indeed, appears to have the sanction of authorities no less eminent than Adam Smith and Ricardo. They assume that the paper engagement should always be liberally fulfilled – that there should be no postponement by means of paper; but they say also, that if you secure

practical immediate convertibility, then there will be no immediate apprehension of conversion. If that opinion be not well-founded, it would be no reflection on those eminent men. We are in a constant state of transition, and we are constantly making new discoveries as to the rules which regulate our paper currency. At the same time the House would no doubt be disposed to abandon an opinion sanctioned even by such men as Adam Smith and Ricardo, if from subsequent lights that been thrown on the subject they should become convinced that they were in error. Now, I shall contend, both upon reason and upon admissions of advocates of free competition - and this will be a most difficult and important part of the subject - that convertibility into gold, together with unlimited competition as to issue, does not give sufficient security. (*The Bankers' Magazine; and Journal of the Money Market*, Supplement. July 1844. "Sir Robert Peel's Speeches on the Currency," p. 186)

The Banking-School position in opposition to the Bank Charter Act was also endorsed by J. S. Mill (1857 [1967]) who explicitly denied that the overissue of a convertible currency is possible (1844b [1967]).

3.5 Say's Law

In the previous section, I showed that the law of reflux was advanced by John Fullarton and other members of the Banking School to show that an automatic mechanism equates the amount of money the banking system creates with the amount the public wants to hold. That mechanism ensured that the banking system could not maintain an excess supply of money (an overissue) in circulation long enough to raise prices and cause an outflow of gold. But, as I interpret it, what the mechanism really ensures is that the banking system has the appropriate incentives to allow the public to reduce its holdings of money to the desired level.

Although the connection between the two has almost never been made,[20] the law of reflux is analytically equivalent to Say's Law (Identity). The former denies that an excess supply of money implies an excess demand for goods in the real sector that would raise prices, while the

[20] Other than my 1985 article (Chapter 2) in which I made the point explicitly, the only hint of a such a connection occurs in Fetter (1965, 232). Fetter did recognize that the real-bills doctrine implied that the banking system would provide as much money as the public demanded, without seeing that this is also what was meant by Say's Law.

latter denies that an excess demand for money implies an excess supply of goods in the real sector that would depress prices. Both propositions follow equally from the theory of a competitive money supply introduced by Adam Smith.

The difficulty with Say's Law, as is well known, is that it seems to be valid only for a barter economy, because in a monetary economy an excess supply of all goods could be offset by an excess demand for money. Indeed, Say's Law is thought to be logically inconsistent with any mechanism for price-level adjustment since it seems to rule out either an excess demand for, or excess supply of, money. The modern solution (Becker & Baumol, 1952) has been to interpret Say's Law as an equilibrium condition (Say's Equality). The excess demand for money would tend to drive down the overall price level until the real value of nominal money balances increased to match the public's demand to hold money.

But this difficulty with Say's Law arises only when we interpret it within a quantity-theoretic framework. In that framework, an excess demand for, or excess supply of, money must be offset in real markets. But in the classical monetary model, in which it is the banking system, not the real economy, that adjusts to a difference between the amount of money the public holds and the amount it desires to hold, Say's Identity is perfectly valid.[21] Say (1880, 134) himself explicitly addressed the issue and denied that too little money could cause a general oversupply of goods:

> In the setting of the gold standard there were subliminal traces of the idea that if banks continued to loan on good assets the total means of payment would increase with the volume of business, and that hence, even though the gold supply did not increase as rapidly as production, there was no danger of price decline from an inadequate money supply.

[21] As an anonymous referee points out, Mill's famous discussion (1844a [1967]) of Say's Law interprets it in the weaker equality sense. However, Mill makes no reference to the operation of banks in that essay. That is legitimate if the excess demand is for outside money not inside money. In the classical model, an excess demand for outside money does impinge on the real sector, which is not surprising since the typical outside moneys—gold and silver—were also real commodities. But if the public does not lose confidence in banks, an excess demand for money is ordinarily an excess demand for inside money. And Mill does ascribe the excess demand for money to a "want of commercial confidence." So it should not be assumed that Mill, a supporter of the Banking School, would have rejected Say's Law as I have interpreted it.

> Sales cannot be said to be dull because money is scarce but because other products are so. There is always money enough to conduct the circulation and mutual interchange of other values, when those values really exist. Should the increase of traffic require more money to facilitate it, the want is easily supplied and is a strong indication of prosperity. . . . In such cases, merchants know well enough how to find substitutes for the product serving as a medium of exchange or money [by bills at sight, or after date, bank notes, running credits, write-offs, etc., as at London and Amsterdam][22]: and money itself soon pours in for this reason, that all produce naturally gravitates to that place where it is in most demand.

An even clearer statement of Say's Law was made by Ricardo in his 1819 testimony before the Parliamentary Commission investigating the resumption of the gold standard (1952a, 386).

> Q. When merchants have a want of confidence in each other, which disinclines them to deal on credit, is there not a greater demand for money?
>
> A. Undoubtedly.
>
> Q. Then, if this is a period when there is a greater demand for money on account of a want of confidence, does it not follow that it would be an inconvenient period for reducing the means of accommodation?
>
> A. It appears to me that that very circumstance would make a smaller reduction efficacious for that purpose; a demand for currency in consequence of a want of confidence, I should think a legitimate demand; it would enable the bank to keep their circulation at a higher level than they would be able to do, if there had not been a demand from such a cause.

Eight years earlier Ricardo observed in his letter to Tierney (1952b, 67–68) that a quantitative limit on the note issue of the banking system would prevent it from responding to an excess demand for money and that this failure could cause commercial distress.

> Depreciation cannot be effectually checked by any other means than by depriving the Bank [of England] of the power which they at present possess of adding indefinitely to the amount of their notes. This might be done in a direct manner by limiting the amount beyond which their paper should be issued; but it has been plausibly urged against such a measure that occasions may arise in which sound policy may require a temporary augmentation of bank paper, and to deprive the Bank of the power of

[22] The passage in brackets is a footnote in the original text.

increasing their notes at such periods might be the cause of considerable distress and difficulty to the mercantile class.[23]

Later in the same letter he observed that "if a greater circulation were required from the operation either of increased commerce, or of embarrassed credit, the bank might augment their issues without producing any effect whatever on the price of bullion, and consequently without exposing the Bank to any inconvenience, or depriving the merchants of that increased accommodation, which be essential for their operations."

While recognizing the significance of these and similar quotations for understanding Ricardo's views about monetary policy in general, Samuel Hollander concluded from a detailed discussion of Ricardo's position on Say's Law (1979, 474–539) that Ricardo held it only in the equality version. Hollander based his conclusion on other passages in which Ricardo acknowledged that an increase in the quantity of money or in the stock of gold would raise prices. But these passages referred either to increases in the quantity of inconvertible paper money or to increases in the quantity of gold, so that no mechanism existed for retiring the excess supply of money. Only in such cases did Ricardo concede that a price-level adjustment was necessary to eliminate the excess supply of money.

Hollander admitted that Ricardo did not use an excess demand for money to explain the post-Napoleonic War economic difficulties in Britain, which would be problematic if he believed only in Say's Equality. Ricardo did blame the Bank of England for accumulating too large a gold reserve, driving up the value of gold, and, thereby, causing deflation. But that was as far as he went in a monetary explanation of those difficulties. It is thus quite possible that Ricardo believed that the banking system would, on its own, adjust the quantity of money to whatever amount the public demanded at the prevailing price level; that is, he believed in Say's Identity for inside money. And that is why, except for the appreciation of gold, he did not rely on a monetary explanation for the postwar difficulties.

[23] Although Ricardo went on to write that he did not consider the objection to be as serious as those who raised it imagined, he did not reject the underlying rationale. Instead, Ricardo proposed a mechanism whereby the Bank could accommodate an increased demand for banknotes without causing them to depreciate further.

3.6 Cairnes on the Effects of the Australian Gold Discoveries

My discussion of the strengths of the classical theory leads to a further question: Why was such a good theory abandoned after the middle of the nineteenth century? Part of the answer lies in the doubts about competitive banking that the monetary difficulties in England created in the three decades after the resumption of convertibility. While Adam Smith[24] and J. B. Say[25] praised competition in banking, W. S. Jevons insisted (1875, 64) that "there is nothing less fit to be left to the action of competition than money."

Another reason the quantity theory displaced the classical theory was the apparent ability of the quantity theory and the price-specie-flow mechanism to account for the international response of prices to the gold discoveries in California and Australia in the late 1840s and early 1850s. According to the classical theory, prices should have risen after the gold discoveries because gold became cheaper. But there was no obvious reason for some prices to rise more than others if the value of gold fell. Nor,

[24] Smith (1937, 313) wrote:

> The late multiplication of banking companies in both parts of the United Kingdom, an event by which many people have been much alarmed, instead of diminishing, increases the security of the public. It obliges all of them to be more circumspect in their conduct, and, by not extending their currency beyond its due proportion to their cash, to guard themselves against those malicious runs, which the rivalship of so many competitors is ready to bring upon them. This free competition too obliges all bankers to more liberal in their dealings with their customers, lest their rivals should carry them away. In general, if any branch of trade, or any division of labour, be advantageous to the public, the freer and more general the competition, it will always be the more so.

To be sure, in an earlier passage, Smith (1937, 308) advocated suppressing small-denomination banknotes and the option clause. The restrictions were calculated to protect presumably ill-informed holders of small notes from losses when banks failed and to avoid even the slightest impairment of convertibility. Smith did not want mismanaged banks to shift their losses onto the rest of the community which is why he regarded them as no greater violations of natural liberty than the "obligation of building party walls, in order to prevent the communication of fire."

[25] Say (1880, 271): "The establishment of several banks, for the issue of convertible notes, is more beneficial than the investment of any single bank with the exclusive privilege; for the competition obliges each of them to court the public's favour by a rivalship of accommodation and security."

since gold is an internationally traded commodity, was there any reason for prices to rise more rapidly in some parts of the world than in others.

Quantity theorists attributed rising prices to the increase in the quantity of money triggered by the gold discoveries. The pattern of price increases would be determined by PSFM, so that the sequence of price increases would follow the movement of gold from the mines to the gold-importing countries.

In 1859, J. E. Cairnes (1873) published the first in a series of articles on the effects of the gold discoveries. He argued that the geographical pattern of increases in raw materials prices after the gold discoveries in Australia conformed to the one implied by PSFM. Prices increased first in Australia where gold discoveries quickly increased the quantity of money. As Australia exported gold to Britain, America, and Europe, money stocks and price levels increased as well. Since the banking systems in Britain, America, and, to a lesser extent, in Europe allowed money supplies to increase without a corresponding increase in holdings of gold, much of the new gold was reexported to the Orient where it went into existing hoards. Because PSFM implied that increased prices caused gold to be exported, prices must have risen a bit more in the United States and Britain than in Europe, and in Europe more than in the Orient where much of the gold was finally held.

Besides tracing the effects of gold flows on prices, Cairnes also analyzed the likely relative-price effects of the gold discoveries, considering technological factors as well as changes in income distribution and in spending habits. His microeconomic analysis of these effects—a model of rigorous economic reasoning independent of the quantity theory or PSFM—was largely borne out by the quantitative evidence he provided.

So skillful was Cairnes's theoretical argument and his presentation of supporting evidence that he seemed to confirm the quantity theory and PSFM to the satisfaction of most of his contemporaries and many later economists (Bordo, 1975). This impression was reinforced a few years later when, using more advanced statistical techniques than Cairnes had, W. S. Jevons (1884) arrived at broadly similar conclusions.

Only one adherent of the classical monetary theory, William Newmarch, systematically investigated (Tooke & Newmarch, 1857) the effects of the gold discoveries. Newmarch, however, was a more skillful statistician than a theorist and simply denied that gold discoveries had affected prices at all—a conclusion not implied by the classical theory. Yet Cairnes's criticism of Newmarch was so effective that he seemed to refute both Newmarch's position and the classical theory.

The interaction between Cairnes and Newmarch was problematic on both sides. While Newmarch's argument was inconsistent with the classical theory, Cairnes's evidence did not support the quantity theory and PSFM against the classical theory. The key point to Cairnes was that increases in the quantity of money—made possible by, but not identical to, the increase in gold stocks—had caused prices to rise. But his theoretical explanation did not entail the conclusion that an increase in the quantity of money had caused the increase in prices. Nor did his explanation imply that prices had risen most in parts of the world in which money stocks had increased the most.

Cairnes supported his conclusions with evidence that local increases in prices and local increases in money stocks were correlated. For internationally traded goods, Cairnes conceded that price increases were uniform everywhere. Thus, the geographic differences he found were differences in the increases of prices of non-traded goods. But those differences could have been caused not only by differences in the changes in local money stocks; they could, instead, have reflected changes, caused by the gold discoveries, in international relationships between tradable prices and non-tradable prices. Changes in money stocks, in the alternative interpretation, were merely incidental to those relative-price changes.

To understand this point, consider that, as Cairnes observed, the gold discoveries had quadrupled Australian wage rates for unskilled labor. Since the prices of exports and imports, which were determined in international markets, did not change, Australian non-gold exporters and import-competing producers could not absorb those wage increases. Workers previously employed in export or import-competing industries either went into the gold fields or shifted into the non-tradable-goods sector where prices could rise enough to allow employers profitably to pay the quadrupled wages.

The apparent inflation in Australia could, therefore, have reflected a drastic appreciation of non-tradable goods owing to the extraordinary increase in the marginal productivity of labor in gold mining. Monetary expansion following the gold discoveries did not cause that appreciation. The money stock grew passively in response to rising real income and to the increased internal price level implied by rising non-tradable prices with constant tradable prices. Precisely, the same effect would have been observed had comparable deposits of an unquestionably non-monetary exportable resource such as diamonds been found.

Cairnes (1873, 24) sought to buttress his case for the quantity theory by noting that for several months after gold had been discovered in Australia, prices rose comparatively slowly, owing to the absence of a local mint. Before the domestic money stock could increase, gold had to be shipped to Britain to be minted and then shipped back to Australia as gold coin. Prices in that interval rose much less than they did after new gold coins reached Australia. Cairnes concluded that only after the local money stock had increased was the full effect of the gold discoveries felt.

However, the facts recounted by Cairnes support a different interpretation of what happened. Even in the interval between discovery of gold and the arrival of gold coins from British mints, local prices rose somewhat. According to the quantity theory, an increase in the price level reflects an excess supply of money. Yet, during that interval, there was a shortage of money. The shortage of money was evidenced in the permission given to banks to issue token currency and in the fall in the price of gold from its mint price of 77.5 shillings to as little as 40 shillings. The nearly 100-percent premium on coins shows that the demand for money, owing both to rising incomes and significant economic dislocation caused by the gold discoveries, was increasing, while the short-run supply was practically fixed. Thus, the internal price level rose in the interval when gold could not be converted into coin even though there was an excess demand for money.

The subsequent importation of gold coins into Australia should therefore not be considered the cause of the increase in the Australian price level. With a fixed exchange rate, the discovery of gold in a small open economy such as Australia's required the internal price level to rise. At first, rising prices were moderated by an appreciation of the local currency against sterling.[26] But once exchange-rate parity was restored, the price level rose to the level consistent with parity. Monetary expansion was an automatic response to the demand at the original exchange rate, not the cause of the increase in prices.

Similarly, in countries that initially imported gold from Australia but which, given a limited internal demand for gold, re-exported gold to other countries, the prices of non-tradables also rose compared to those of tradables. But in countries where the final demand for gold was strong, non-tradable prices fell in relation to tradable prices. Thus, the pattern of price increases that Cairnes ascribed to the effects of different rates

[26] An anonymous referee suggests that the rise in prices before gold coins reached Australia could be attributed to an expectation that the quantity of gold coins would soon increase. This is a different argument from Cairnes's and does not account for the effects gold discoveries had on relative prices. But the relative-price effects alone do explain the behavior of the price level, so the quantity theory adds nothing to the explanation and may, therefore, be ignored.

of money growth really reflected changes in the price ratios of tradables to non-tradables caused by the gold discoveries and the international distribution of demand for gold.

The pattern was similar to what would be observed after any country began making large exports to the rest of the world. Countries with the greatest final demand for the products would have to finance their imports by increasing exports or reducing other imports. That would require a shift of resources from the production of non-tradables to tradables which would be reflected in a declining price ratio between non-tradables and tradables.

Indeed, at several points, Cairnes recognized that the pattern of price increases he observed had been determined by the requirements of international trade flows. But, seeking to confirm PSFM, he failed to distinguish between that effect and the supposed effect of increases in the quantity of money.[27]

3.7 Conclusion

My aim in this article has been to show that recognizing a classical theory of money distinct from the quantity theory helps us understand several classical monetary debates. It might be argued that I have exaggerated the differences between what I call the classical theory and the quantity theory. After all, just about everyone accepted the validity of the quantity theory for an inconvertible paper currency, and the one important classical figure who denied that the mid-century gold discoveries tended to raise prices, William Newmarch, seriously blundered in doing so.

Yet there was, I believe, a real, and still unresolved, disagreement among classical monetary theorists. Is a competitive banking system inherently disposed to overissue, and must it therefore be subject to an external quantitative constraint? Smith, Thornton, Ricardo, Mill, and the Banking

[27] To avoid confusion, let me repeat that I do not deny that the gold discoveries raised prices. My difference with Cairnes is that, in my interpretation, the gold discoveries depressed the value of gold. Under a gold standard, that meant a more or less uniform increase in nominal prices. However, aside from the general price-level effect, there were also relative-price effects which Cairnes ascribed to PSFM, but which can also be derived from an international-barter-trade model with both tradables and non-tradables. The increase in money supplies, as distinct from gold stocks, emphasized by Cairnes was, rather, a passive response to the relative-price and income effects of the gold discoveries.

School, the premier classical monetary theorists, denied that competitive banks would produce an excess supply of money as long as they were obligated to convert their obligations into an outside asset at a fixed exchange rate.[28] Hume, Wheatley, and the Currency School believed that, even under convertibility, a competitive banking system would inevitably overissue if not subjected to an external quantitative constraint.

Those whom I have called classical theorists excluded the convertible money created by the banking system from the quantity of money that could be said to have an independent effect on prices. From their point of view, the quantity of money produced by the banking system behaved passively. The quantity theorists, on the other hand, believed that the quantity of convertible money created by the banking system had no less impact on prices than did inconvertible fiat money or gold.

Thus, the significance of Cairnes's analysis in the history of monetary theory is his apparent demonstration that the quantity of money had been the active agent in transmitting price changes (Laidler, 1988). By doing so, he ensured the dominance of the quantity-theoretic view according to which a change in the price level is the effect of an exogenous change in the quantity of money. Unfortunately, the classical view that the price level is determined independently of the behavior of the banking system, which automatically responds to the public's demand for money and, thus, has no direct effect on the price level, was abandoned. Its abandonment, I would suggest, impoverished the subsequent development of monetary theory.

References

Becker, G. S. & Baumol, W. J. (1952). The classical monetary theory: The outcome of the discussion. *Economica, 19*(76), 355–376.

Blaug, M. (1985). *Economic theory in retrospect* (4th ed.). Cambridge University Press.

Bloomfield, A. I. (1975 [1994]). Adam Smith and the theory of International trade. In *Essays in the history of international trade* (pp. 109–144). Edward Elgar.

[28] Although they favored making convertibility a legal obligation of the banking system, they were not oblivious to the competitive pressures on banks to make their obligations convertible, even if not legally obligated to do so. But they felt so strongly about convertibility that they wanted to avoid even the slightest departures from instant convertibility on demand that might emerge in a fully competitive environment.

Bordo, M. D. (1975). John Cairnes on the effects of the Australian gold discoveries, 1851–73: An early application of the methodology of positive economics. *History of Political Economy, 7*(3), 337–359.
Cairnes, J. E. (1873). *Essays in political economy*. Macmillan.
Dowd, K. (1988). Option clauses and the stability of a Laisser Faire monetary system. *Journal of Financial Services Research, 1*, 318–333.
Dowd, K. (1989). *The state and the monetary system*. Philip Allan.
Eagly, R. V. (1960). Adam Smith and the specie-flow mechanism. *Scottish Journal of Political Economy, 17*, 61–68.
Fetter, F. W. (1965). *The development of British monetary orthodoxy 1797–1875*. Harvard University Press.
Frenkel, J. A. (1976). Adjustment mechanism and the monetary approach to the balance of payments: A doctrinal perspective. In E. Classen & P. Salin (Eds.), *Recent issues in international monetary economics* (pp. 29–48). North Holland.
Frenkel, J. A., & Johnson, H. G. (1976). The monetary approach to the balance of payments: Essential concepts and historical origins. In J. A. Frenkel & H. G. Johnson (Eds.), *The monetary approach to the balance of payments* (pp. 21–45). University of Toronto Press.
Fullarton, J. (1845). *On the regulation of currencies* (2nd ed.). John Murray.
Girton, L., & Roper, D. (1978). J. Laurence Laughlin and the quantity theory of money. *Journal of Political Economy, 88*(4), 599–625.
Hollander, J. (1979). *The economics of David Ricardo*. University of Toronto Press.
Hume, D. (1752 [2006]). Of the balance of trade. In E. Rotwein (Ed.), *Economic writings of David Hume* (pp. 60–77). Routledge.
Humphrey, T. R. (1981). Adam Smith and the monetary approach to the balance. *Federal Reserve Bank of Richmond Economic Review, 67*(6), 3–10.
Jevons, W. S. (1875). *Money and the mechanism of exchange*. D. Appleton.
Jevons, W. S. (1884). *Investigations in currency & finance*. H. S. Foxwell (Ed.). Macmillan.
Joplin, T. (1832). *An analysis and history of the currency question*. J. Ridgway.
King, L. P. (1804 [1844]). Thoughts on the restriction of payments in specie (2nd ed.). In E. Fortescue (Ed.), *A selection from the speeches and writings of the late Lord King*. Longman, Brown, Green, and Longmans.
Laidler, D. (1981). Adam Smith as a monetary economist. *Canadian Journal of Economics, 14*(2), 185–200.
Laidler, D. (1988). British monetary orthodoxy in the 1870s. *Oxford Economic Papers, 40*(1), 74–109.
Laughlin, J. L. (1903). *Principles of money*. Scribners.
Longfield, M. (1840). Banking and currency, II. *Dublin University Magazine, XV*, 218–19.
Low, J. M. (1952). An eighteenth century controversy: The theory of economic progress. *Manchester School, 20*(3), 311–330.

McCulloch, J. R. (1831). *Historical Sketch of the Bank of England*. Longman, Rees, Orme, Brown and Green.
McCloskey, D. N., & Zecher, J. R. (1976). How the gold standard worked, 1880–1913. In J. A. Frenkel & H. G. Johnson (Eds.), *The monetary approach to the balance of payments* (pp. 184–208). University of Toronto Press.
Mill, J. S. (1844a [1967]). Essays on some unsettled questions of political economy. In F. E. L. Priestly (Ed.), *The collected works of J. S. Mill* (pp. 229–340). University of Toronto Press.
Mill, J. S. (1844b [1967]). The currency question. In F. E. L. Priestly (Ed.), *The collected works of J. S. Mill* (vol. 4, pp. 341–362). University of Toronto Press.
Mill, J. S. (1857 [1967]). The bank acts. In F. E. L. Priestly (Ed.), *The collected works of John Stuart Mill* (vol. 4, pp. 499–548). The University of Toronto Press.
Mints, L. (1945). *A history of banking theory*. University of Chicago Press.
O'Brien, D. P. (1975). *The classical economists*. Clarendon Press.
Petrella, F. (1968). Adam Smith's rejection of Hume's price-specie-flow mechanism: A minor mystery resolved. *Southern Economic Journal, 34*(1), 365–374.
Ricardo, D. (1952a). *The works and correspondence of David Ricardo* (Vol. 5). P. Sraffa (Ed.). Cambridge University Press.
Ricardo, D. (1952b). *The works and correspondence of David Ricardo* (Vol. 9). P. Sraffa (Ed.). Cambridge University Press.
Samuelson, P. A. (1980). A corrected version of Hume's equilibrating mechanisms for international trade. In J. S. Chipman & C. F. Kindelberger (Eds.), *Flexible exchange rates and the balance of payments* (pp. 141–158). North Holland.
Say, J. B. (1880). *A treatise on political economy* (4th ed.). Philadelphia.
Schumpeter, J. (1954). *The history of economic analysis*. Oxford University Press.
Selgin, G., & White, L. H. (1987). The evolution of a free banking system. *Economic Inquiry, 25*(3), 439–457.
Senior, N. (1830). *Three lectures on the cost of obtaining money*. John Murray.
Smith, A. (1937). *The wealth of nations*. E. Cannan (Ed.). Modern Library.
Smith, A. (1978). *Lectures on jurisprudence*. Oxford University Press.
Thompson, E. A. (1974). The theory of money and income consistent with orthodox value theory. In G. Horwich & P. A. Samuelson (Eds.), *Trade, stability, and macroeconomics* (pp. 427–453). Academic Press.
Thornton, H. (1802 [1939]). *An enquiry into the nature and effects of the paper credit of Great Britain*. F. A. v. Hayek (Ed.). George Allen & Unwin.
Tooke, T., & Newmarch, W. (1857). *A history of prices and of the state of the circulation from 1792 to 1856* (Vol. 6). P.S. King & Sons.
Viner, J. (1937). *Studies in the theory of international trade*. Harper and Brothers.
Wheatley, J. (1807 [1822]). *An essay on the theory of money and principles of commerce* (Vols. I–II). T. Cadell and W. Davies.

White, L. H. (1984a). *Free banking in Britain: Theory, experience, debate* 1800-1845. Cambridge University Press.

White, L. H. (1984b). Competitive payments systems and the unit of account. *American Economic Review, 74*(3), 699–712.

CHAPTER 4

The Real-Bills Doctrine in the Light of the Law of Reflux

4.1 Introduction

Few propositions in monetary or banking theory have a longer history than the real-bills doctrine. Its sources have been traced back at least to John Law early in the eighteenth century, and it received the endorsement of Adam Smith in *The Wealth of Nations* (1937). The doctrine appears to have powerfully influenced the design of banking institutions and the conduct of monetary policy in Britain and even more so in the United States. Although subject to various interpretations, the doctrine is usually understood to assert that if banks lend only on the security of real bills representing actual goods in process, they cannot issue too much money. The point of ambiguity that accounts for differences in interpretation is whether the doctrine refers to a single bank or to an entire banking system.[1] If it applies only to an individual bank, the doctrine is a practical guide intended to help banks stay liquid and solvent. If it applies to the entire banking system, the doctrine becomes a prescription for monetary policy and controlling the price level. Yet, despite the endorsement

[1] I am indebted Jurg Niehans for emphasizing in private correspondence the importance of distinguishing between the real-bills doctrine at the level of an individual bank and at the level of the entire banking system.

D. Glasner, *Studies in the History of Monetary Theory*, Palgrave Studies in the History of Economic Thought, https://doi.org/10.1007/978-3-030-83426-5_4

of Adam Smith[2] and its considerable practical influence, the doctrine, in whatever form, has been judged by many economists (Bagehot, [1873] 1962; Blaug, 1985; Humphrey, 1982; Mints, 1945; O'Brien, 1975; Thornton, (1802 [1939]) to be fallacious, indeed, egregiously so.

Another monetary doctrine with which the real-bills doctrine has been identified is the law of reflux (Green, 1987; Mints, 1945; O'Brien, 1975; Perlman, 1989; Selgin, 1989).[3] The law of reflux is usually understood to assert that banks cannot overissue money, because any overissue would quickly flow back to them in debt repayments or as a demand for redemption. The history of the law of reflux is less ancient, its fame less widespread, its influence less far-reaching, and its standing among monetary economists no higher, than that of the real-bills doctrine. The disparity between the notoriety and influence of the two propositions reflects the general presumption that the law of reflux is an equivalent (or at most trivially different) formulation of the real-bills doctrine, so that the validity of the former depends on that of the latter.

My aim in this article is to offer a limited and qualified rehabilitation of the real-bills doctrine as applied to individual banks by showing that the law of reflux describes a problem to which this version of the doctrine was proposed as a practical remedy. That most discussions of the real-bills doctrine have focused on the version applicable to the entire banking

[2] Perlman (1989) denied that Smith espoused the real-bills doctrine. However, Perlman reached this conclusion by interpreting the real-bills doctrine in such a way that it applies to the entire banking system, not just a single bank. The difference between us hinges mainly on the semantic issue of what types of policy prescription may be subsumed under the heading of the real-bills doctrine (see Sect. 4.3).

[3] To my knowledge, only Laidler (1975), White (1984, 126), and Skaggs (1991) have clearly recognized that the law of reflux is conceptually distinct from the real-bills doctrine. However, despite distinguishing it from the real-bills doctrine, White, who ascribes validity to the law of reflux only insofar as it describes the constraint adverse clearings impose on bank expansion, criticizes Fullarton's version of the law of reflux, failing to see that it serves to elucidate the real-bills doctrine. While my interpretation of the law of reflux generally accords with that of Laidler and Skaggs, Laidler does not embed his discussion of the law within a competitive-money-supply model and does not use the law to explain the real-bills doctrine. Mints (1945, 88–95) is a somewhat more problematic case, recognizing that the real-bills doctrine asserted that lending on real bills would ensure that banks only issue as much money as required by the "needs of trade," while the law of reflux asserts that any issues in excess of the "needs of trade" would be returned to the banks. But misunderstanding how the law of reflux operates, he attached no significance to what seemed to him a trivial distinction.

system may be due to the fact that this version addresses a clearly specified problem: how to maintain a stable price level. The practical problem to which the narrow version of the real-bills doctrine offered a practical (though imperfect) solution is not so obvious. My contention is that, by understanding the law of reflux, we can gain insight into the underlying problem.

I have argued in the previous chapters (also see Glasner, 1989) that the law of reflux can be validly deduced from a model of a competitively supplied money. An important study (Skaggs, 1991) of its chief expositor, John Fullar ton, offered a similar interpretation. What the law of reflux asserts is that private banks cannot create an inflationary overissue, because there is a market mechanism that induces banks to supply just the amount of money that the public wants to hold. Thus, if the public holds either more or less money than it desires to, banks expand or contract their liabilities accordingly. What the real-bills doctrine meant to Adam Smith and others who applied it only to the individual bank is that, to withstand the fluctuations in their liabilities caused by changes in the public's demand to hold money, banks ought to hold assets that can be rapidly liquidated should the demand for their liabilities decrease. Otherwise, banks facing a declining demand for money would sustain losses in attempting to reduce their asset holdings as the public reduced its holdings of their liabilities. By holding their assets only, or at least mostly, as real, short-term, self-liquidating, collateralized bills, banks would avoid the need to sell illiquid assets at a loss or to borrow at penalty interest rates, because their asset portfolios would shrink automatically along with the demand for their liabilities.

In the next section, I discuss Adam Smith's understanding that the real-bills doctrine applies to an individual bank in contrast to later exponents of the doctrine who applied it to the entire banking system. In so doing, I show that, notwithstanding Perlman's (1989) claim to the contrary, there is a version of the doctrine whose paternity can rightly be ascribed to Smith. In Sect. 4.3, I turn to the law of reflux, showing (a) how it differs conceptually from the real-bills doctrine in whatever form, (b) the nature of the market mechanism that ensures its operation, and (c) the critical role of convertibility in that mechanism. In Sect. 4.4, I argue that the real-bills doctrine (applied to an individual bank) presumes that the law of reflux operates, so that unless one understands what the law of reflux meant, one cannot grasp the problem that the single-bank version of the real-bills doctrine addressed, or the remedy it proposed. I conclude in Sect. 4.5 by considering how well the remedy proposed by the single-bank version of the realbills doctrine handles the problem that it was meant to address.

4.2 The Real-Bills Doctrine Since Adam Smith

Although the origins of the real-bills doctrine may be traced back even further, there is no need, for my purposes, to look back further than Adam Smith. Smith seemed to support the real-bills doctrine by suggesting that banks could not go very far wrong by confining their lending to the financing of real bills. But his theory of banking embraced more than the real-bills doctrine.

Smith's banking theory starts from two premises: that banks can profitably issue notes to replace gold and silver, and that the creation of these notes is governed by the marginal revenue and marginal cost of issuing them (though his conceptual apparatus was not sophisticated enough to articulate explicitly the attention on incentives at the margin evident in the passage quoted below). The profitability, and social benefit, of note issue stem from the resources saved by substituting low-cost paper for precious metals. For Smith, overissue meant issuing more notes than would equate marginal revenue and marginal cost. The marginal revenue from issuing notes would correspond to the return on the IOUs a bank acquires in exchange for its notes; the marginal cost would reflect the amount of non-interest-bearing metallic reserves held to satisfy recurring demands for redemption. The quantity of metallic reserves held by banks would depend on the willingness of the public to hold the bank's notes. Here is how Smith (1937, 285–286) explained the bank's calculation:

> Let us suppose that all the paper of a particular bank, which the circulation of the country can easily absorb and employ, amounts exactly to forty thousand pounds; and that for answering occasional demands, this bank is obliged to keep at all times in its coffers ten thousand pounds in gold and silver. Should this bank attempt to circulate forty-four thousand pounds, the four thousand pounds which are over and above what the circulation can easily absorb and employ, will return upon it almost as fast as they are issued. For answering occasional demands, therefore, this bank ought to keep at all times in its coffers not ten thousand pounds only, but fourteen thousand pounds. It will thus gain nothing by the interest of the four thousand pounds excessive circulation; and it will lose the whole expence [sic] of continually collecting four thousand pounds in gold and silver,

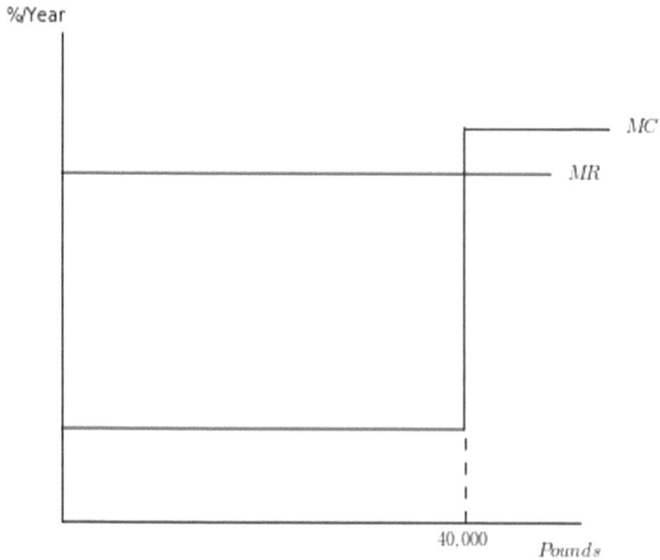

Fig. 4.1 Smith's model of equilibrium for an individual bank

which will be continually going out of its coffers as fast as they are brought into them.

The relationship described by Smith between marginal revenue and marginal cost is depicted in Fig. 4.1. The horizontal axis measures the quantity (expressed in pounds) of notes issued; the vertical axis measures an annual interest rate. Because notes are non-interest-bearing, the marginal revenue curve from issuing (and maintaining in circulation) notes can be represented by a horizontal line corresponding to the interest rate on the assets that the bank acquires in exchange for its notes. The marginal cost of issuing notes is the interest foregone on the non-interest-bearing metallic reserves that the bank holds against additional outstanding notes.[4] By assuming that £10,000 of metallic reserves must be held for £40,000 of notes, Smith seems to suggest that £1 of reserves must be held for each additional £4 of notes. Accordingly, up to a quantity

[4] Foregone interest is not the only cost the bank incurs by issuing notes, but the analysis is not altered significantly by abstracting from the other costs.

of £40,000, I draw the marginal cost curve as a horizontal line one-fourth of the distance between the horizontal axis and the marginal-revenue curve.[5] Smith assumed that the public was unwilling to hold more than £40,000 pounds of the bank's notes, so that if it issued more than this amount, the additional notes would be brought back for redemption. Thus, once its note issue exceeded £40,000, the bank would have to increase its metallic reserves pound-for-pound with increases in its note issue, which makes marginal cost at least equal marginal revenue. Since, the bank would have to incur costs of obtaining the additional reserves (286), marginal cost beyond £40,000 actually exceeds marginal revenue.

Figure 4.1 shows that profits reach a maximum when the note issue is £40,000. However, not knowing exactly how many of its notes the public wished to hold or at what quantity the marginal cost of issuing notes begins to exceed the marginal revenue from doing so, a bank might risk issuing even more than the profit-maximizing quantity of notes because of the high-profit-margin on the infra-marginal notes. Smith's version of the real-bills doctrine seems therefore to have been designed as an operational rule to help banks avoid issuing more notes than the profitmaximizing quantity identified in Fig. 4.1, or at least adjust quickly if too many notes had been issued.

Smith assumed that without special privileges freeing them of the necessity to do so, banks must commit themselves to maintain the convertibility of their notes into specie or coin.[6] So, the problem that

[5] In truth, however, such a relationship is inconsistent with the general inventory-theoretic proposition that a bank's demand for reserves increases in proportion to the square root of its liabilities. But since Smith is not explicit, the shape of the marginal cost curve he was thinking about cannot be inferred from his discussion.

[6] In book 2, Chapter 2 of *The Wealth of Nations* on money and banking, Smith never mentioned the possibility of inconvertible privately issued banknotes, though he does discuss (309–310) ways in which banks could attenuate their obligation to convert. They could, as the Scottish banks sometimes did, exercise an option clause allowing them to postpone redemption by exchanging their notes for a six-month, interest-bearing obligation, or by imposing costly conditions on the exercise of the right of redemption. Such conditions "must have degraded [the] currency below the value of gold and silver money" (310), but the value of the banknote clearly derives from the prospect that it can be redeemed at some cost. The only alternative source of value is for the government to accept paper currency in payment of taxes. "A prince, who should enact that a certain proportion of his taxes should be paid in a paper money of a certain kind, might thereby give a certain value to this paper money; even though the term of its final discharge and redemption should depend altogether upon the will of the prince" (312).

Smith was addressing was not an inflationary overissue by the entire banking system, but the loss of profit sustained by the overissuing bank.[7] The direct costs of overissue were borne by overissuing banks, not the public.[8] Thus, in discussing the consequences of overissue by the Bank of England and the Scotch banks (particularly the Ayr Bank whose history Smith recounted in some detail (297–301), which, after overissuing had been obliged to buy gold at a premium (often with borrowed funds) to meet demands to redeem their notes for gold, Smith referred only to the profits lost because of overissue. But, unlike instances of inconvertibility, these episodes did not cause the price level to rise.

Concluding his discussion of the Ayr Bank, Smith noted,

> At the first setting out of this bank, it was the opinion of some people, that how fast soever its coffers might be emptied, it might easily replenish them by raising money upon the securities of those to whom it had advanced its paper. Experience ... soon convinced them that this method of raising money was by much too slow to answer their purpose; and that coffers which originally were so ill filled, and which emptied themselves so very fast, could be replenished by no other expedient but the ruinous one of drawing bills upon London, and when they became due, paying them by other draughts upon the same place with accumulated interest and commission. But though they had been able by this method to raise money as fast as they wanted it; yet, instead of making a profit they must have suffered a loss by every such operation.... They could still have made nothing by the interest of the paper, which, being over and above what the circulation of the country could absorb and employ, returned upon them, in order to be exchanged for gold and silver, as fast as they issued it; and for the payment of which they were continually obliged to borrow money. On the

[7] While convertibility was maintained, inflation could result only from a depreciation of gold in relation to commodities. But since the value of gold is determined in an international market, no bank (and probably not even an entire national banking system) could (significantly) affect the international value of gold, although, in the aggregate, all banks can shift gold from monetary to nonmonetary uses, thereby tending to depreciate gold in relation to commodities (Chapter 2 and Glasner, 1989).

[8] However, Smith (300–301) felt that overexpanding banks were unlikely to lend money wisely and would thus tend to dissipate the capital stock. "The success of this operation, therefore, without increasing in the smallest degree the capital of the country, would only have transferred a great part of it from prudent and profitable, to imprudent and unprofitable undertakings" (301). Smith also thought banks imposed external costs on the public by issuing small-denominational notes, whose suppression he therefore favored (307).

> contrary, the whole expence [sic] of this borrowing, of employing agents to look out for people who had money to lend, of negociating [sic] with those people, and of drawing the proper bond or assignment, must have fallen upon them. (300)

However, even though "the circulation never could have been overstocked with paper money… if every particular banking company had always understood and attended to its particular interest," banking companies often failed to understand or attend to their interest, "and the circulation has frequently been overstocked with paper money" (286).[9] The point of Smith's version of the real-bills doctrine was therefore to help individual bankers estimate how much of their paper money "the circulation of the country could easily absorb and employ." Smith (1937, 288) observed:

> What a bank can with propriety advance to a merchant or undertaker of any kind is not either the whole capital with which he trades, or even any considerable part of that capital; but that part of it only, which he would otherwise be obliged to keep by him unemployed, and in ready money for answering occasional demands. If the paper money which the bank advances never exceeds this value, it can never exceed the value of the gold and silver, which would necessarily circulate in the country if there was no paper money; it can never exceed the quantity which the circulation of the country can easily absorb and employ.
>
> When a bank discounts to a merchant a real bill of exchange drawn by a real creditor upon a real debtor, and which, as soon as it becomes due, is really paid by that debtor; it only advances to him a part of the value which he would otherwise be obliged to keep by him unemployed and in ready money for answering occasional demands. The payment of the bill, when it becomes due, replaces to the bank the value of what it had advanced, together with the interest.

Smith offered two justifications for the real-bills doctrine. First, the sum advanced by a bank to customers borrowing on the security of real bills is unlikely to exceed the amount of "ready money" that the customer would have already been holding. A bank lending this much would thus

[9] At the risk of belaboring an obvious point, I point out again that in this context "overstocking" refers to the excessive redemption and transactions costs created by the overissue of a convertible currency, not to inflation.

be unlikely to issue more notes than the public would willingly hold. Second, the bill would, in the ordinary course of business, have to be repaid quickly, so that the bank would not have to wait long for repayment of whatever notes were issued (plus interest). To lend for longer terms would mean that "the whole of the returns is too distant from the whole of the outgoings, and the sum of his repayments could not equal the sum of its advances within such moderate periods as suit the conveniency of a bank" (291).

A problem with Smith's proposal is that, while calculated to prevent banks from overshooting the profit-maximizing quantity of notes, it represents only a lower bound for that quantity. A bank following the rule might issue less than the profit-maximizing quantity of notes. On the other hand, if the demand for notes is unstable, the proposal would at least enable a bank to liquidate its assets quickly when it had to contract its note issue. If the demand for its notes were shrinking, a bank holding long-term assets would either have to borrow (at penalty rates) or sell long-term assets (perhaps at a considerable loss) to meet noteholders' demands for redemption.

Analyzing Smith's discussion of banking, Perlman (1989) denies the paternity of the real-bills doctrine commonly ascribed to Smith. That position is unexceptionable if one understands the real-bills doctrine to apply to the banking system as a whole rather than to an individual bank, so the differences between Perlman and me are largely, though not entirely, semantic. For Smith certainly did not believe that, simply by lending on the security of real bills, an entire banking system could avoid an inflationary overissue. It was convertibility that prevented inflation. However, Smith took it for granted that, without special privileges conferred by the government, ordinary banks could operate only by committing themselves to convertibility. Although Smith did not advocate lending on real bills as an anti-inflation measure, he shared with subsequent supporters of the real-bills doctrine a concern for protecting banks' liquidity and solvency. And Mints, whose interpretation of the doctrine (though not of Smith's part in it) Perlman largely endorses, attacked not just the idea that the real-bills doctrine would prevent inflationary overissue, but also the idea that it would ensure the liquidity of individual banks (Mints, 1945, 29).

The notion that lending on real bills prevents inflationary overissue even without a convertibility commitment was not articulated until the directors of the Bank of England invoked it (about a decade after Smith's death) to rebut the allegation that the bank had caused the inflation that followed the government's suspension of the convertibility of Bank of England notes into specie in 1797. This argument transformed the real-bills doctrine from a practical guide for individual banks into a doctrine of monetary policy calculated to ensure that a monopolistic bank of issue or an entire banking system would avoid an inflationary overissue even if unconstrained by convertibility. It is this form of the argument (applied to an entire banking system) that Henry Thornton (1802 [1939]) refuted and Walter Bagehot (1873 [1962]) later described as classical in its nonsense, and it is this form of the argument that most critics have had in mind when attacking the real-bills doctrine, though Mints was at pains to discredit the doctrine in every conceivable form.

The doctrine reappeared in the Banking-School/Currency-School debates. However, the leading Banking-School figures, Fullarton (1845) and Tooke (1844), both subordinated it to the law of reflux, a fact overlooked by commentators who conflate the realbills doctrine with the law of reflux. Fullarton explicitly asserted (1845, 97) that the law of reflux could operate even if banks were lending on long-term mortgages. Thus, within the BankingSchool tradition, the law of reflux, not the real-bills doctrine, was the barrier to overissue.[10]

After Peel's Bank Charter Act was enacted in 1844, the Banking-School position and with it the law of reflux) lost prestige. Yet the real-bills doctrine, despite repeated attacks against it, remained influential. Indeed, the doctrine shaped the design of the U.S. Federal Reserve System, its chief architect, Representative (later Senator) Carter Glass, and his economic adviser, H. Parker Willis, having been adherents of the doctrine.[11] Moreover, the goal of limiting commercial banks to lending on real bills inspired Glass's efforts to separate commercial and investment banking, ultimately leading to the Glass-Steagall Act.

[10] Banking-School writers such as Fullarton and Mill also discussed the possibility that expectations of a higher price level could be self-fulfilling. Believing that the supply of money would adjust automatically to the increased demand for money accompanying an expectation of a rising price level, they viewed the increase in the quantity of money as the effect, not the cause, of rising prices.

[11] The example of Glass and Willis shows that the real-bills doctrine has not always been understood in the manner in which the directors of the Bank of England espoused it during the Napoleonic Wars. Glass and Willis, like another adherent of the doctrine, B. M. Anderson were unyielding supporters of the gold standard even at the depth of the Great Depression. Indeed, it was Glass who, aided by President Hoover's veto threat, scuttled the Goldsborough Bill after its passage by the House of Representatives, which would have obligated the Fed to pursue a policy of price-level stabilization, in effect forcing the United States off the gold standard (see Chapter 13).

4.3 The Law of Reflux

Identifications of the law of reflux with the real-bills doctrine abound in the literature (Blaug, 1985; Fetter, 1965; Green, 1987; O'Brien, 1975; Perlman, 1989; Selgin, 1989).[12] However, a careful reading of Fullarton's work shows that he recognized a distinction between the law of reflux and the real-bills doctrine. Indeed, as already noted, he clearly believed that the law of reflux holds even if banks do not observe the real-bills doc trine.

In Fullarton's formulation, the law of reflux asserts that any excess note issue of the banking system must necessarily either be returned to the banking system in exchange for assets held by the banking system, for example, securities and IOUs (1845, 64, 96–97) or gold (67), or be converted into equivalent liabilities such as deposits (67, 92–93). Although this formulation of the law of reflux is unrelated to the real-bills doctrine, the law of reflux is routinely described as an equivalent, or trivially different, version of the real-bills doctrine.

The difference between the propositions is evident from their concern with the opposite sides of a bank's balance sheet. The real-bills doctrine, in whatever form, asserts that in exchange for their demand liabilities, banks should acquire interest-earning assets of a particular class: real bills or their equivalent. As we have seen, supporters of the doctrine had various reasons for offering the prescription. Some, like Smith, applying it to individual banks, believed that holding only such assets would help a bank avoid issuing more than the profitmaximizing quantity of notes

[12] No one has yet traced the origins of the law of reflux. If my understanding of the law of reflux and the real-bills doctrine is correct, then Adam Smith would certainly have a claim to priority, even though the term "reflux" is not used in *The Wealth of Nations*. However, I have suggested (see Chapters 2 and 3, and Glasner, 1989) that the law of reflux is actually a symmetric version of Say's Law, addressing the case of an excess supply of money. An excess supply of money implies not an offsetting excess demand for real commodities, but an excess supply of cash to the banking system in exchange for assets held by the banking system. The term "reflux" is in fact used in the English translation of Say's *Treatise* (1880, 271) to describe the public's response to an excess supply of money.

> Should the paper issues of a bank at any time exceed the demands of circulation, and the credit enjoyed by the establishment, there follows a perpetual reflux of its notes, and it is put to the expense of collecting specie, which is absorbed as fast as collected.

and help it retire or redeem its notes economically should the demand for its notes decrease. Others, like the anti-Bullionists, applying it to the entire banking system, asserted that acquiring real bills only would allow a monopolistic bank of issue or an entire banking system, even if unconstrained by convertibility, to avoid issuing too many notes and causing inflation. However, the law of reflux is concerned with the liability side of banks' balance sheets, asserting that there is a market mechanism that determines the total quantity and composition of banks' liabilities.[13] Thus, the public can dispose of an excess supply of banknotes without spending them and driving up the price level. The mechanism operates (though at varying costs) regardless of what assets banks have acquired in exchange for their notes.

The law of reflux does bear a resemblance to the strong, and fallacious, form of the real-bills doctrine, which denies that banknotes issued in exchange for real bills can be overissued. But resemblance is not equivalence, and small distinctions can make a big difference. The anti-Bullionist version of the real-bills doctrine asserted that an inflationary overissue is impossible if banks lend only on the security of real bills, because the supply of real bills to the banks is perfectly correlated with the "needs of trade," that is, the demand for money. The law of reflux does not depend on conflating two distinct and incommensurate magnitudes (the stock demand to hold money and the flow demand for credit), or, as this conflation is often described, on a confusion between money and credit. What is the market mechanism that precludes an inflationary overissue of banknotes? Fullarton's argument was not entirely satisfactory, but he came closer to correctly describing the mechanism than is usually recognized (Chapter 3). In one sense, this argument is unassailable, simply making the obvious point that it is the public, not the banks, that determines the ratio between outstanding notes and deposits. The problem with the argument is that banks might overissue the total sum of their liabilities: notes and deposits. Although the Currency School could not take advantage of this weakness in Fullarton's argument, the unique status

[13] Laidler (1975) noted that the focus of the real-bills doctrine is on the asset side of the balance sheet while that of the law of reflux is on the liability side. He also noted that the law of reflux as formulated by Tooke (the same applies to Fullarton) explicitly addressed only the note liabilities of banks, implicitly assuming the overall quantity of liabilities to be fixed. However, as I point out below, Fullarton's discussion of the relationship between notes and deposits came close to demonstrating the proposition for all sight liabilities.

of banknotes as money and the unimportance of deposits being a basic tenet of the Currency School, the weakness appeared fatal to modern critics. But, in fact, all Fullarton had to (and very nearly did) show was that market forces make an overissue of deposits unprofitable for individual banks and would induce them to contract their outstanding notes and deposits before successive rounds of increased spending disposed of the excess liabilities via a balance-of-payments deficit or a rising price level.

The presumption motivating the Currency School and others, going back at least to David Hume, who feared that an overissue of banknotes would occur, is that banks are inherently biased toward overissue. The bias supposedly derives from the power of banks to issue noninterest-bearing notes in exchange for interest-bearing assets, so that, unless subject to a binding exogenous constraint, they always have an incentive to increase their note issue. While recognizing this incentive, Smith argued that the costs arising from the demands for redemption following an overissue render overissue a suboptimal strategy. Nevertheless, he believed that banks might err on the side of overissue. To counter this tendency, he proposed a version of the realbills doctrine as an operating rule. He also believed that competition among banks would discourage overissue by hastening and intensifying the negative clearing balance in relation to other banks that an overissuing bank would suffer. He therefore advocated strictly enforcing the convertibility commitments of banks to penalize overissuing banks and to deter other banks from following their example.

While generally subscribing to Smith's analysis, Fullarton went beyond Smith in explaining why banks could not overissue notes, and in suggesting (without quite fully explaining) why banks would not overissue their liabilities in general. Fullarton (1845, 84) explicitly recognized that banks enjoyed an excess of marginal revenue over marginal cost on issuing non-interest-bearing notes which they enjoyed on no other liabilities.

> Whether the banker's advances be large or small, whether the aspect of the times be cheerful or disheartening, it must be equally his policy to keep out as large a *circulation* as he can. What advances he does make, he will always be anxious to make in his own notes, because they yield him a profit such as no other form of issue yields.

But Fullarton pointed out that, despite the incentive of banks to increase their issue of notes indefinitely, it is the public, not the banks, that determines the composition of bank liabilities. "To suppose that, if issued in larger quantities," Fullarton (83) wrote, "[banknotes] could be kept in circulation, is to take it for granted, that the amount of notes in circulation depends, not on the wants of those who circulate them, but on the will of the issuer." Tactically, Fullarton had to go no further, since the Currency School, focusing exclusively on the potential overissue of notes, disregarded the creation of deposits.

Yet Fullarton (92–93) did go further, observing that the public has an incentive to convert non-interest-bearing notes into interestbearing deposits. Thus, since their customers determine how to divide their cash holdings between non-interest-bearing notes and interestbearing deposits, banks could not rely on earning the high-profit-margin generated by notes when those notes could instantaneously be converted into low-profit-margin, interest-bearing deposits. Fullarton could have clinched his argument by pointing out that since, at the margin, a bank can increase its outstanding liabilities only by increasing its deposits, competition among banks to induce the public to hold deposits would reduce the profit margin on deposits sufficiently to eliminate any incentive to create additional deposits. A bank would expand its balance sheet only to the point at which the spread between the return on the assets it acquires and the interest it pays on its liabilities just equals the marginal cost of such intermediation. Although he failed to make the point explicitly, the possibility that deposits might be overissued never having been raised by the Currency School, only a modest extension of his argument would have sufficed to do so.[14]

A diagram similar to the one used earlier to portray Smith's analysis of overissue may be helpful. We again measure the quantity of notes (and deposits) expressed in pounds along the horizontal axis and an annual interest rate along the vertical axis. The horizontal line labelled $\boldsymbol{MR_N}$ represents the [**author's note: the "16" is a remnant from a footnote in an earlier version that I can't delete**] apparent marginal revenue from issuing notes. However, the demand for notes is finite. Smith, writing before the great expansion of deposit banking in the nineteenth century, took account of this fact by assuming that a bank would bear reserve

[14] Of course, familiarity with the tools of marginal analysis may make the extension appear more modest to us a century and a half later than it would have appeared then.

and transactions costs on overissued notes exceeding the marginal revenue they generated.

Thus, in Fig. 4.2, marginal cost increases discontinuously when the amount of notes issued by a bank exceeds the amount the public is willing to hold. Writing more than a half century after Smith, Fullarton took account of the limited demand to hold notes by assuming that any unwanted non-interest-bearing notes would be exchanged for interest-bearing deposits. In Fullarton's analysis, $\boldsymbol{MR_N}$ is not the relevant marginal-revenue curve for the bank, because non-interest-bearing notes

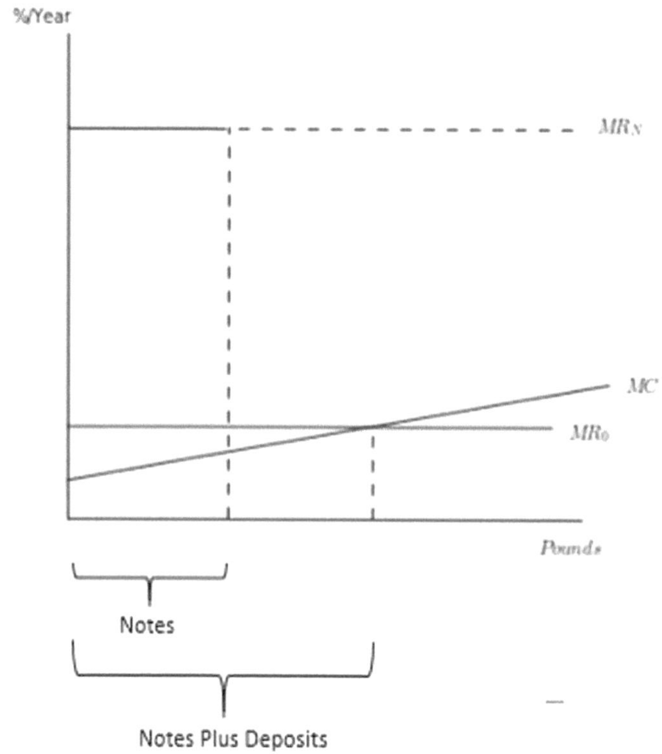

Fig. 4.2 Fullarton's model of equilibrium for an individual bank

can always be converted into interestbearing deposits.[15] Although the relevant marginal-revenue curve contains a segment coinciding with $\boldsymbol{MR_N}$ over a range corresponding to the quantity of the bank's notes that the public is willing to hold, marginal revenue, beyond that quantity, decreases discontinuously to coincide with $\boldsymbol{MR_D}$, the marginal-revenue curve for deposits. The height of the latter curve corresponds to the difference between the yield on IOUs acquired by banks in exchange for notes or deposits and the competitive interest that banks pay on deposits. The expansion of deposits being limited by the low-profit-margin on deposits, banks have no incentive to overissue notes. Profit maximization occurs not at the intersection of $\boldsymbol{MC}$ (representing the marginal cost of intermediation, exclusive of interest paid on deposits, which is reflected in $\boldsymbol{MR_D}$) with $\mathbf{MR}_N$, but at the intersection of $\boldsymbol{MC}$ with $\boldsymbol{MR_D}$.[16] Thus, unlike Smith, Fullarton did not need to rely on the high costs of redeeming excess banknotes to explain why overissue would not be a profit-maximizing strategy for banks.[17]

This analysis clears Fullarton and the Banking School of two serious charges. The first, raised by White (1984, 126), is that they disregarded the role of competition in preventing overissue. While it is true that Fullarton's attitude toward the monopoly of the Bank of England over

[15] Fullarton also emphasized the alternative of using unwanted notes to retire debt, but that choice is more appropriately considered at the margin between holding interest-bearing deposits and reducing indebtedness.

[16] I draw $\boldsymbol{MC}$ with an upward slope to make it possible to identify a unique equilibrium for each bank. If the marginal costs of intermediation are in fact constant, then individual banks would have no unique profit-maximizing quantity of deposits and notes. The equilibrium quantity of bank liabilities would be determinate only for the entire banking industry, but the equilibrium shares of individual banks would not. Alternatively (as an anonymous referee pointed out), one could assume that individual banks are somewhat differentiated, so that they would have to raise deposit rates to increase their market shares, which would imply a downward-sloping $\boldsymbol{MR_D}$.

[17] The high cost of converting excess notes and deposits into gold could be included within the model as it was in Fig. 4.1, except that the redemptions into gold would occur only when the sum of notes and deposits had been overissued. At that point, demands for redemption would arise and the cost of creating additional notes and deposits would, owing to the cost of the added holdings of non-interest-bearing gold reserves, begin to exceed the marginal revenue. However, it seems implausible that the marginal revenue from creating additional deposits would remain above the marginal cost until the public's demand lo hold deposits had been exhausted, causing a demand for gold redemption. Rather, one would expect that competition would cause the interest on deposits to increase until deposit expansion was no longer profitable.

the right of note issue was somewhat ambiguous,[18] the monopoly was of limited significance, because after 1833 competition from deposit-creating banks constrained the note issues of the Bank of England, despite its monopoly. The full import of the insistence by Fullarton and other Banking-School writers that deposits and banknotes are economically indistinguishable cannot be fully appreciated unless this competitive relationship is kept in mind.[19]

White maintains that the only valid channel of reflux is the unfavorable balance that an overissuing bank would face at the clearinghouse. Without the rivalry of other banks of issue, White argues, there is little constraint on the overissue of banknotes. But the overissue of banknotes is ruled out by the fact that the public, not the banking system, determines the composition of the stock of liabilities created by the banking system, while the size of this stock is determined by the marginal cost and marginal revenue of creating deposits, or, stated more generally, the size of the banking system's consolidated balance sheet is determined by the marginal revenue from acquiring interestearning

[18] Moreover, although Tooke's assertion that competition in note-issuing is equivalent to competition in smuggling is cited to show his hostility to free banking, Tooke subsequently renounced that opinion. By 1844, when Tooke attacked the Currency Principle, he had endorsed the notion of free banking, including freedom of issue.

[19] The usual interpretation of the Banking-School position on the equivalence of notes and deposits is that it made no sense for the Bank Charter Act to single out banknotes for quantitative control, but not deposits. However, when stated in this form, the objection could be understood to mean that the Bank Charter Act did not go far enough, which is not what the Banking School was arguing; they were pointing out that the market forces that limit the profit-maximizing creation of deposits by the banking system also limit the profit-maximizing creation of banknotes. However, since legal restrictions created a demand by commercial banks to hold Bank of England notes as reserves, the Bank of England might still have been able to overissue its notes, because an overissue of Bank of England notes that tended to raise the price level would tend to increase the demands of depositissuing banks to hold Bank of England notes as reserves. If so, only the check of an external drain would limit the note issues of the Bank of England. I am indebted to an anonymous reviewer for noting this qualification to the argument in the text. However, without an increase in the price level, deposit-creating banks would not willingly add to their holdings of non-interest-bearing Bank of England notes, so their status as legal reserves would not automatically induce banks to use any Bank of England notes coming into their possession as a basis for further deposit expansion in the manner supposed by the conventional moneymultiplier analysis.

assets and matching interest-earning liabilities and the marginal cost of intermediating between suppliers of assets and holders of liabilities.[20]

The charge of inconsistency[21] is buttressed by Fullarton's (1845, 207) apparent endorsement of the position of the directors of the Bank of England in the Bullionist debates and of the real-bills doctrine.

> Much as I fear I am disgracing myself by the avowal, I have no hesitation in professing my own adhesion to the decried doctrine of the old Bank Directors of 1810, "that so long as a bank issues its notes only in the discount of *good* bills, at not more than sixty days date, it cannot go wrong in issuing as many bills as the public will receive from it." In that maxim, simple as it is, I verily believe, there is a nearer approach to truth, and a more profound view of the principles which govern circulation, than in any rule on the subject which since that time has been promulgated.

[20] An anonymous referee argues that if banks can control the size of their own balance sheets, the Currency-School case stands, since the marginal costs and marginal revenues of the banks are not independent of the absolute price level. Presumably, this means that if enough banks expand together and increase the size of their balance sheets, the resulting increase in the price level would cause the marginal-revenue and marginal-cost curves to shift sufficiently to make the new quantity of notes and deposits consistent with equilibrium at the new higher price level. One reply to this argument is that, as Laidler (1975) observed, if we are considering a small open economy (which is not an obviously incorrect characterization of Britain in the mid-nineteenth century), convertibility under the gold standard pins down the domestic price level, so that an increase in prices would be unavailable to validate an overexpansion of the banking system. A second reply is that even if the domestic price level was not pinned down exogenously, the expansion by the banking system is inconsistent with the profit-maximizing behavior of each individual non-cooperating bank. Starting from a position of equilibrium, each bank must take the price level as exogenously determined, so the size of its balance sheet is strictly determined by the marginal-cost and marginal-revenue curves corresponding to the initial equilibrium price level. The point I am making in the text is not that an overexpansion could not possibly be sustained under any circumstances, but that competitive banks lack the supposed incentive to overexpansion that the Currency School attributed to them. Banks would expand their balance sheets beyond this level only if they believed that other banks would expand enough to raise the price level enough to validate their own expansion. But to assume this is to assume that banks are behaving cooperatively rather than competitively, which neither the Currency nor the Banking Schools did.

[21] Mints also criticizes Smith for the redundancy of his commitment to both convertibility and to the real-bills doctrine, which Perlman takes as evidence to support his denial that Smith espoused any form of the real-bills doctrine. The earlier discussion showed that demands to redeem excess note issues were in fact a key element of Smith's examination of overissue.

What role does convertibility play in the analysis of Fullarton and the Banking School and was their support for it inconsistent with a belief in the law of reflux? The key to understanding the role of convertibility in Fullarton's analysis is that, like Smith and Tooke, Fullarton could not conceive of an inconvertible currency circulating with a positive value without a special governmental enactment making it acceptable in the discharge of debts including tax liabilities (21). Without such government intervention, no bank could create a demand to hold an inconvertible currency that it issued. Banknotes are merely a species of credit, a promise by the issuer to pay the creditor metallic or "conventional" (fiat) money (36–37). This is the nub of Fullarton's distinction between a convertible currency and a forced currency (64).

Using modern terminology, one could paraphrase Fullarton as follows: outside money (in Fullarton's terms "money") must be either full-bodied commodity money or fiat money created by the government or its agent. Ordinary banks can create only inside money (in Fullarton's terms "credit"), which must ultimately be redeemable in terms of some asset whose value the bank cannot control (Glasner, 2000; Hoover, 1988). The value of inside money must then be identical to the outside money into which it is convertible, so that its value is fixed exogenously by convertibility (even if no actual redemptions for coin or specie occur), not by the quantity of inside money. At most, overissue of an inside money could cause a balance-of-payments disturbance,[22] but could never cause the value of the inside money to deviate from the value of the outside money, a value which must be invariant to the behavior of any single issuer of inside money.

Thus, to suggest that Fullarton or Smith could have dispensed with convertibility in analyzing the behavior of the banking system is to assume implicitly that banks were empowered by the state to issue outside money, as the Bank of England had been in 1797. But under the institutional arrangements that Fullarton and Smith were analyzing, banks clearly had no such power.

The general confusion of critics of the Banking School and the law of reflux is well exemplified by the comments of Mints (1945, 89–91) and Schumpeter (1954, 728). Mints questions why "in the light of their great reliance on the 'law' of the reflux as 'the great regulating principle

[22] However, the operation of the law of reflux rules out even a disturbance such as this.

of the internal currency,'" adherents of the banking principle "should have insisted upon the necessity of convertibility." After observing that J. S. Mill (a Banking-School sympathizer) "conceded that an inconvertible currency might be regulated quite satisfactorily by the price of bullion," Mints notes that "in this discussion Mill was considering the possibility of an inconvertible issue of government, not bank notes." Then, criticizing the Banking School, Mints asserts that "the tendency to shift to a consideration of government issues when they were discussing the question of inconvertibility [was] rather general." Mints concludes by observing that, although they advocated convertibility and recognized the redemption of notes as one mode of the operation of the reflux, "they minimized the significance of this aspect of the problem when they discussed the 'reflux' making the inference seemingly justifiable that they believed convertibility not necessary." Interestingly, Schumpeter (1954) used the same argument to reach the opposite conclusion, that the Banking School "did *not* hold that the circulating medium would regulate itself in the process of competitive banking." For if they believed that it would, "why," Schumpeter asked, "should they have insisted on convertibility at all…?" What Mints and Schumpeter failed to see was that convertibility could be a necessary precondition for the reflux to operate for private banks even if it was not the channel that was typically used. Unless contractually committed to convert their notes into an outside money, banks could not create a demand for their notes. That is why, understanding this necessity, Banking-School adherents always shifted to government issues when discussing inconvertibility. Rather than a gap in their theory, as Mints implied, this shift reflected their insight. Since excess banknotes are so easily convertible into deposits and since banks have no incentive to overissue interest-bearing depos its, the Banking School could safely disregard conversion into gold as a mechanism of reflux.

Fullarton's praise of the Bank of England directors during the re striction period, though certainly exaggerated (perhaps for rhetorical effect), involved him in no inconsistency.[23] The restriction converted Bank of England notes into outside money, so that they could circulate even

[23] Nor, as Skaggs (1991) argued, can Fullarton's statement be taken as an endorsement of the real-bills doctrine, because he never suggested that banks lend only on the security of real bills. His explicit advice to bankers was to "look after your securities; beware you never incur responsibilities out of proportion to your capital. These are the golden rules for the banker" (Fullarton, 1845, 195).

though they were inconvertible. Fullarton's point was that, al though the Bank of England notes had been transformed into an out side money, the position of the directors was that the bank, having met the government's fiscal requirements, should issue notes as if they were an inside money, that is only in exchange for real bills of exchange. While the value of sterling was no longer constrained by convertibility, the bank's creation of liabilities was still governed by the relationship between the marginal revenue and marginal cost of is suing those liabilities. As long as the bank remained independent and was not forced to lend excessively to the government, there was no reason to suppose that the bank would automatically engage in overissue.

Although Thornton, Bagehot, and critics of the directors' position correctly noted that the bank could theoretically have engineered an unlimited inflation while following the directors' version of the real bills doctrine and lending at too low an interest rate, they never showed that it was in the interest of the bank to have tolerated an unlimited increase in its liabilities. Lending at too low an interest rate was not obviously in the interest of the bank's shareholders, even if the result ing inflation depreciated the value of its liabilities. Beyond some point, the marginal cost of expansion would exceed the marginal revenue, so that the incentive to expand is not unlimited.

In fact, Fullarton criticized the suspension for cutting the contractual link with gold that otherwise tied down the value of sterling. When not fixed by convertibility, the value of sterling could fluctuate in response to a host of factors unrelated to overissue, such as temporary warinduced fluctuations in the demand for gold (1845, 22–23) or changes in the terms of trade between Britain and other countries.[24] But even though the value of sterling was not pinned down by convertibility, the Bank of England, as a commercial enterprise, had no incentive to create liabilities without limit, and neither the depreciation of sterling that followed the suspension nor subsequent fluctuations in its value are necessarily attributable to fluctuations in the quantity of Bank of England notes.

[24] Actually, the changes in the pound price of gold during the period in 1815 from Bonaparte's landing from Elba to Waterloo could perhaps more appropriately have been attributed to changing expectations of the likelihood that convertibility would be restored at the prewar parity. The pound fell on news suggesting an increased likelihood of a French victory and rose on news suggesting an increased likelihood of a British victory.

4.4 The Law of Reflux Creates the Problem That the Real-Bills Doctrine Tries to Solve

In the preceding section, I observed that the law of reflux is an assertion about how the liability side of a bank's balance sheet responds to the public's demand for its liabilities, while the real-bills doctrine is a prescription for the composition of the asset side of its balance sheet. The law of reflux asserts that there is an economic mechanism that allows the public, without increasing spending, to return excess issues to the banking system, while the real-bills doctrine, under the most common interpretation, suggests that by lending only on the security of real bills, banks will issue neither more nor less money than the public wants to hold, in which case, of course, no reflux would be necessary. Thus, in a certain sense, the law of reflux could even be said to conflict with the usual interpretation of the real-bills doctrine.

However, if the law of reflux does in fact hold, it is easy to see that it may create a problem for individual banks, which have to adjust to the public's demand for their money rather than the other way around. Money created by banks is not a hot potato that someone has to hold. The law of reflux shows that market forces induce a bank to accommodate a desire by members of the public to reduce their holdings of its money. How best to do so is the problem for which the realbills doctrine, applied to an individual bank, prescribes a solution, or at least a remedy. The remedy aims either to reduce the likelihood of inadvertent overissue, or to unwind an inadvertent overissue by reducing the cost of liquidating assets.

Adam Smith believed that following the doctrine would allow a bank to avoid overissuing its liabilities. Two goals of lending only on the security of real bills, as Perlman shows, were to enable banks to monitor the repayment records and creditworthiness of their customers and to prevent an inadvertent overissue. A third goal, which Perlman seems to overlook or to slight, though Mints did not, is that following the doctrine would reduce the cost to a bank of adjusting to a sudden decline in the demand for its notes, since the rapid turnover of bills would allow it to make the adjustment without having to sell illiquid assets at a loss. Thus, Perlman, focusing entirely on the price-level rationale of the real-bills doctrine, denies that Smith subscribed to it, whereas Mints recognized the liquidity rationale, and therefore did not hesitate to condemn Smith for helping to propagate the heresy.

Mints in fact paid considerable attention to the liquidity rationale for the real-bills doctrine, arguing that attempts by individual banks to increase their liquidity were futile, because all banks could not simultaneously liquidate their assets. However, this argument is relevant only to the special case in which the public tries to shift from holding inside to holding outside money. Lacking the power to create outside money, banks cannot possibly accommodate that demand.[25] Moreover, trying to meet the demand for outside money by liquidating assets and reducing lending to customers feeds a deflationary spiral, which erodes the value and liquidity of bank assets, reinforcing the desire of the public to shift from inside to outside money.

However, this is not the situation contemplated by the real-bills doctrine. The real-bills doctrine was supposed to protect a bank against either an inadvertent overissue, or a reduction in the public's demand for its money. The reduction in demand could be limited to that bank, or it could be part of a general shift in demand from bank money to alternative financial instruments (other than outside money) or to increased spending. All these contingencies would require banks to contract their balance sheets. Holding short-term assets, like real bills, would allow banks to avoid losses from having to dispose of long-term illiquid assets on short notice.

Thus, while Fullarton believed that the law of reflux would operate even if banks were lending on long-term assets like mortgages, he wanted banks to keep a large portion of their assets in the form of real bills or other short-term instruments. His apparent endorsement of the position of the directors of the Bank of England during the restriction period reflected (a) his belief that the Bank had not been unduly subservient to the fiscal demands of the government, and, therefore, neither discounted bills at too low an interest rate nor created more liabilities than the public wanted to hold, and (b) his belief that holding largely short-term bills would allow any bank to adjust its balance sheet quickly in response to

[25] To meet the demand, banks would already have to be holding enough outside money as reserves to redeem all the inside money the public tried to redeem, without also liquidating assets to replenish their holdings of outside money. Banks' demands for outside money would thus have to be both large and highly elastic. Selgin (1988) argues persuasively that often exceptional demands for outside money start as shifts from deposits to currency, which banks could not accommodate owing to restrictions on their powers to issue notes. The unsatisfied demand for banknotes is thereby transformed into a destabilizing demand for outside money.

changes in the demand to hold its liabilities or to correct an inadvertent overexpansion. It does not mean that Fullarton believed that a banking system empowered to issue inconvertible notes could guarantee a stable price level by lending only on the security of real bills. On the contrary, Fullarton (1845, 22) asserted that the value of an inconvertible paper currency "is entirely governed by its quantity, and we have no principle by which that quantity can be kept in exact proportion to the transactions which the currency has to perform."

4.5 The Validity of the Real-Bills Doctrine

My objectives in this chapter have been to distinguish between two principal versions of the real-bills doctrine (one applicable to individual banks and the other applicable to the banking system in general), to explain the logic of the law of reflux and how it differs from either version of the real-bills doctrine, and finally to suggest that the version of the real-bills doctrine that applies to individual banks is a response to the practical problems that banks face if the law of reflux works as I have suggested.

The question I wish to address briefly in conclusion is whether the real-bills doctrine as applied to individual banks really does solve the problem that the law of reflux raises for them. Unlike the question of whether the version of the real-bills doctrine that applies to an entire banking system is valid (to which the answer, of course, is no), this question does not admit of a straightforward, logically compelling answer. The question is a pragmatic one—actually several related pragmatic ones. Does this version of the real-bills doctrine enable a bank to alter the volume and composition of its liabilities quickly and at what cost? And are there alternative operating strategies that would work as well or better?

Let us approach these questions by considering the alternatives open to banks if the public can cause them (through the law of reflux) to contract their outstanding note and deposit liabilities. A bank can respond only by (a) contracting its assets by an equal amount and paying off the liabilities or (b) by incurring additional liabilities to pay off the ones that it has to redeem. Consider how it could contract its assets: First, it could simply sell them off. However, if they are illiquid, the losses from rapid realization could be very high. This presumably is what the real-bills doctrine was attempting to avoid. But could a bank hold liquid assets other than real bills that would serve the same purpose as holding real bills was designed to? At first glance, it appears that it could. A bank could hold marketable securities, including government debt, or it could hold fictitious bills which also mature in very short periods. Thus, it is not entirely clear what the rationale for holding only real bills would be.[26]

Nevertheless, one can at least suggest a few plausible reasons for preferring real bills to other assets. First, when the doctrine was originally articulated, there were few well-developed secondary markets for debt, especially for short-term instruments with high liquidity. Thus, to maintain a flexible asset portfolio, it was necessary for banks to lend short term to borrowers who would be likely to repay their loans at short intervals. The real bill may have been the most convenient instrument then available. Even Thornton (1802 [1939], 85–88) who dismissed most of the reasons in favor of lending on real bills, concluded that there might be some additional safety and liquidity attached (on average) to real bills not provided (on average) by fictitious bills. This may partially explain the preference for real over fictitious bills. Moreover, as Adam Smith pointed out, lending on real bills allows banks to monitor the creditworthiness of their borrowers more closely than they could by lending on fictitious bills. And although banks could seemingly achieve the liquidity objectives of the real-bills doctrine by investing in short-term government debt,[27] the experience of banks that had become heavy creditors of governments was probably sufficiently unhappy to make most students of banking doubt the prudence of investing in short-term government debt.[28] Holding other assets, for example, stocks that are readily marketable in secondary markets, could partially achieve the liquidity objectives of the doctrine, but the risk of capital loss in selling off substantial amounts of equities or long-term debt could be prohibitive.

By lending only or primarily on real bills, a bank could ensure that, under any foreseeable circumstances, a substantial fraction of its assets

[26] The rationale is clearer for the real-bills doctrine applied to an entire banking system, because then the supply of real bills is taken to be a good proxy for the "needs of trade" or the demand for money. Thus, one might conclude that this version of the real-bills doctrine establishes a more definite link between ends and means than does the version applied to individual banks.

[27] I am indebted to Larry White for bringing this point to my attention.

[28] The transformation of some types of short-term government debt from a risky to a safe debt instrument seems to be a fairly recent phenomenon and one that deserves further study.

would be rolled over within a short time, so that it would be able to liquidate its portfolio to meet a reflux of its liabilities. However, the question also arises whether a bank, holding just real bills, could contract its liabilities fast enough to contract its outstanding liabilities if the demand for them were contracting extremely rapidly. Perhaps not, but if bills mature every 60 days, a bank could retire about 10% of its outstanding note and deposit liabilities every week. This rate of contraction seems pretty rapid. A still faster one could be attained by lending on even shorter-term securities.

An alternative to contracting assets is to replace liabilities flowing back to the bank with new liabilities. By assumption, these new liabilities could not be note or deposit liabilities which the public is no longer willing to hold. Instead, the bank would have to issue some other form of debt on terms that were attractive enough to induce members of the public or other banks to hold the debt. If the bank faced a short-term problem, because it could not liquidate assets fast enough to enable it to redeem returning liabilities, the bank could seek to rediscount assets with other banks or to issue some other form of debt. To be able to do this, the bank would have to show a sound enough balance sheet and to offer attractive enough terms to make others willing to extend it credit to extinguish its excess liabilities. While holding real bills would not necessarily ensure that a bank would have access to such rediscounting facilities, the safety advantage that real bills provide might increase the probability of obtaining credit as the proportion of real bills on its balance sheet increased. But other assets might do as well.

Thus, the advantages of holding real-bills seem inadequate to demonstrate that, even at the level of the development of mid-nineteenthcentury financial markets, holding only real bills was a dominating operating strategy for banks. In fact, Fullarton's actual advice to bankers was simply to try to stay liquid, and he never suggested holding only real bills.

With continuing financial innovation and the development of a wide range of secondary markets for short-term and long-term instruments, modern banks can now achieve the safety and liquidity objectives of the real-bills doctrine by holding a much broader array of financial instruments than was contemplated by the early exponents of the doctrine. Well-developed secondary markets now exist for a variety of short-term instruments that are not real bills. Although no banker now would think of allowing his business to be governed by any form of the real-bills doctrine, a new type of financial intermediary, the moneymarket mutual fund, may be thought of as operating in the general spirit of the single-bank version of the real-bills doctrine.

Acknowledgements I wish to thank Jiirg Niehans, Neil Skaggs, Perry Mehrling, Larry White, and three anonymous referees for helpful comments and constructive criticisms that enabled me to formulate the ar guments of this article far more clearly than I could have otherwise. Responsibility for the remaining errors is of course mine alone.

References

Amon, A. (1984). The transformation in Thomas Tooke's monetary theory reconsidered. *History of Political Economy, 16*(2), 311–326.

Bagehot, W. (1873 [1962]). *Lombard Street: A description of the London money market*. Henry S. King.

Blaug, M. (1985). *Economic theory in retrospect* (4th ed.). Cambridge University Press.

Fetter, F. W. (1965). *The development of British monetary orthodoxy, 1797–1875*. Harvard University Press.

Fullarton, J. (1845). *On the regulation of currencies* (2d ed.). John Murray.

Glasner, D. (1989). *Free banking and monetary reform*. Cambridge University Press.

Glasner, D. (2000). *How natural is the state of monopoly over money*. SSRN: https://ssrn.com/abstract=2778253

Green, R. H. (1987). Real bills doctrine. In J. Eatwell, M. Milgate, & P. Newman (Eds.), *New Palgrave: A dictionary of economics*. Macmillan.

Hoover, K. (1988). Money, prices and finance in the new monetary economics. *Oxford Economic Papers, 40*(1), 150–167.

Humphrey, T. (1982). The Real-Bills Doctrine Federal Reserve Bank of Richmond. *Monthly Review, 68*(5), 3–13.

Laidler, D. (1975). Thomas Tooke on monetary reform. In *Essay on money and inflation*. University of Chicago Press.

Minis, L. (1945). *A history of banking theory*. University of Chicago Press.

O'Brien, D. P. (1975). *The classical economists revisited*. Oxford University Press.

Perlman, M. (1989). Adam Smith and the paternity of the real bills doctrine. *History of Political Economy, 21*(1), 77–90.

Say, J. B. (1880). *A treatise on political economy* (4th ed.). J. Grigg.

Schumpeter, J. A. (1954). *The history of economic analysis*. Oxford University Press.

Selgin, G. A. (1988). *The theory of free banking*. Rowman & Littlefield.

Selgin, G. A. (1989). The analytical framework of the real-bills doctrine. *Journal of Institutional and Theoretical Economics, 145*(3), 489–507.
Skaggs, N. T. (1991). John Fullarlon's law of reflux and Central Bank Policy. *History of Political Economy, 23*(3), 457–480.
Smith, A. (1937). *The wealth of nations*. Modern Library.
Thornton, W. H. (1802 [1939]). *An inquiry into the nature of effects of the paper credit of Great Britain* (F. A. v. Hayek, Ed. and Intro.). Frank Cass.
Tooke, T. (1844). *An inquiry into the currency principle*. Longman, Brown, Green, & Longmans.
White, L. H. (1984). *Free banking in Britain: Theory, experience, debate 1800–45*. Cambridge University Press.

CHAPTER 5

Classical Monetary Theory and the Quantity Theory

5.1 Introduction

When first offered, the interpretation of classical monetary theory presented in Chapters 2 and 3, the interpretation was considered novel, but it built on prior work by others. Relying on work by Laidler (1975, 1981), Thompson (1974), Frenkel and Johnson (1976), Girton and Roper (1978), and McCloskey and Zecher (1976), I suggested that notwithstanding the conventional identification of classical monetary theory with the quantity theory of money—and a rather crude version of the quantity theory, at that—many leading classical theorists espoused a monetary theory very different from the quantity theory. The difference between the two theories, I argued, is that the quantity theory treats the stock of money as an exogenous variable to which prices adjust, while the other (anti-quantity-theoretic) theory treats the absolute level of prices, fixed by the convertibility of money into a real commodity, as an exogenous variable to which the stock of money adjusts. I further argued that much of the history of classical monetary theory could be understood as a dialectic between these two clashing theories.

Until the early 1970s, the notion that the quantity theory was the dominant, if not the only, monetary paradigm in classical economics was not up for debate. The works cited above laid the foundation for my own challenge to the consensus. What role my 1985, 1989, and 1992 articles

D. Glasner, *Studies in the History of Monetary Theory*, Palgrave Studies in the History of Economic Thought,
https://doi.org/10.1007/978-3-030-83426-5_5

(Chapters 2, 3, and 4) and my book (Glasner, 1989) had in upsetting the consensus about the quantity theory in classical economics may be left to others to sort out (see Skaggs, 1999). But whatever its significance, my contribution to this reassessment of classical monetary theory did elicit critical responses from two very distinguished historians of economic thought: Mark Blaug (1995) and D. P. O'Brien (1995).

Blaug (1995, 32–33) charged that I misrepresented my anti-quantity-theoretic version of classical monetary theory as the exclusive classical monetary theory when, in fact, the quantity theory was integral to classical monetary theory, and that I mistakenly included David Ricardo, Henry Thornton, and J. S. Mill in the anti-quantity-theory camp. O'Brien (1995, 54) contended that the theory that I ascribed to classical monetary theorists bore no likeness to classical monetary theory, arguing that the model underlying my version of classical monetary theory is based on a series of untenable theoretical assumptions that the classical economists would have never entertained.

In responding to these issues, I first address the less fundamental, though hardly trivial, criticism of Blaug. Blaug actually acknowledges the anti-quantity-theoretic content of much of classical monetary theory, and, in doing so, he undercuts, at least in part, some of O'Brien's criticisms. In Sect. 5.2, I summarize the model that I used to explain the classical anti-quantity theory. O'Brien charges that the model, focused exclusively on long-run equilibrium conditions, not only ignores the short-run-adjustment problems that chiefly concerned the classical monetary theorists but also improperly assumes that purchasing-power-parity always obtains. I demonstrate that my model does *not* exclude the possibility of short-run disequilibria and that the only assumption of the model related to purchasing-power-parity is a routine one—that the law of one price obtains. I consider in Sect. 5.3, a model that explicitly allows for short-run variations in local price levels. It is only within such a model, according to O'Brien, that the issues that occupied the classical economists can be understood. In Sect. 5.4, I discuss the nature of monetary adjustment when the money stock consists of the liabilities (convertible on demand into gold) of a competitive banking system. In Sect. 5.5, I comment on the role of monetary policy in a model with an endogenous real business cycle, a circumstance that, in O'Brien's view, provides the rationale for the monetary regime proposed by the Currency School. Sect. 5.6 offers some concluding thoughts.

5.2 Blaug on Classical Monetary Theory

Blaug discusses classical monetary theory in the context of the question (which also provided the title of his paper): Why is the quantity theory of money the oldest surviving theory in economics? In sketching the history of this theory, Blaug represents the views of the classical economists in what seems to me an eminently reasonable fashion. Having identified the exogeneity of the money stock as the key factual prerequisite for the quantity theory, Blaug recognizes the tension between the theory and an adherence to the gold standard. Consequently, he remarks on the anomalous nature of David Hume's famous thought experiment about the adjustment process that would follow the destruction of four-fifths of Britain's domestic gold stock and why, notwithstanding the puzzlement of earlier commentators, notably Jacob Viner (1937), Adam Smith properly chose not to reproduce Hume's price-specie-flow analysis in his own account of international monetary adjustment. Only during the 1797 suspension of the convertibility of sterling into gold did the quantity theory come into its own as a policy-relevant analytical tool. With the British supply of money under the control of the Bank of England, and with fluctuating exchange rates in terms of gold and other currencies, the preconditions for the quantity theory to hold were more nearly satisfied during the suspension than they had been before, or, for a long time, would be again. After the resumption of convertibility, the Currency School derived their policy prescriptions from the quantity theory, whereas the Banking School reverted to a supposedly more general cost-of-production theory of the value of money.

This all seems to me to be on target, and Blaug (1995, 32) acknowledges that he is just reiterating what "has become almost a standard interpretation of classical monetary economics in recent years." However, Blaug concludes his account of the quantity theory in classical economics by alluding to "commentators who have taken historical revisionism one step further" and "argue that classical monetary theory has been misunderstood by just about everybody." Noting again that the Banking School denied that the monetary authorities could control the quantity of money produced by the banking system, Blaug attributes to me the thesis "that the victorious Currency School applied the quantity theory to a monetary regime for which it was, strictly speaking, inappropriate" (32). Quoting my assertion (Chapter 2) that misplaced quantity-theoretic propositions in the work of some classical economists "have fostered the misconception that the quantity theory was the essential classical monetary theory," Blaug comments (33) that if this indeed is a misconception, it was widely shared by the classical writers themselves.

Blaug's discussion here raises two questions. First, as a matter of positive economics, is the quantity theory really incompatible with a monetary regime based on convertibility? Second, as a matter of doctrinal history, did classical monetary theorists really consider the quantity theory incompatible with a monetary regime based on convertibility? On the first question, Blaug concludes that the key issue is the degree to which the money stock is exogenously or endogenously determined. On this question, I do not doubt that, for most of the classical period, the money stock was endogenously determined.[1] But the reasons for this endogeneity are more general than Blaug seems to recognize.

I return to this point in Sect. 5.3 and 5.4. The question of immediate interest is whether classical monetary theorists recognized the incompatibility of the quantity theory with a monetary regime based on convertibility. Blaug asserts that, in my 1985 and 1989 articles (Chapters 2 and 3), I said that the quantity theory was not the essential classical monetary theory; he takes exception to such a view. But I did not deny that the quantity theory was an important part of classical monetary theory. My point was that there was a coherent anti-quantity theory that was espoused by an important group of economists that belonged to the classical tradition. To be sure, I took the liberty of calling that anti-quantity-theoretic model "the classical monetary theory." Blaug calls my doing so a "trick," a way to confine "the label 'classical monetary theory' to those who either denied the exogeneity of the money supply, like the members of the Banking School, or who confined their arguments essentially to inconvertible paper money, like Ricardo and Thornton." But what Blaug disparages as a "trick," I conceived as a rhetorical device to underscore the theoretical coherence of a particular set of views that, unlike the quantity theory, were created by, and

[1] In fact, endogeneity is not quite enough to lay the quantity theory to rest. In a pure commodity money economy, for example, the stock of money is endogenous, but exhibits a nearly proportional relationship between the stock of money and prices. For an elegant discussion of this point, and Ricardo's recognition of it, see Cottrell (2017). Similarly, as an anonymous referee noted, the quantity theory could still hold if the money-supply function included endogenous variables as arguments and the money-supply function were independent of the demand for money.

found widespread support among, classical economists. In and of itself, employing such a rhetorical device did not deny that the quantity theory had a place in classical economics or even that it was often deployed to analyze convertible monetary regimes. Of course, the words Blaug used to disparage my use of the label "classical monetary theory" themselves constitute a rhetorical device to underscore his view that the quantity theory was an essential part of classical monetary theory—a judgment that I never disputed. So the issue between Blaug and me turns out to be rhetorical, not substantive.

However, Blaug (1995, 45 n. 9) does raise a substantive disagreement by challenging my contention that classical economists like Thornton, Ricardo, and Mill would have "excluded the convertible money created by the banking system from the quantity of money that could be said to have an independent effect on prices," or that "from their point of view, the quantity of money produced by the banking system behaved passively" (Chapter 3, p. 38). I continue to believe that my interpretation of Ricardo is well supported. Indeed, Arnon (1984, 1987, 1991) in discussing Ricardo's monetary theory and his monetary-policy views generally upholds my earlier (Chapters 2 and 3) and subsequent (Chapter 6) interpretations of Ricardo, as does the quotation from Sir Robert Peel's speech to Parliament quoted above in Chapter 3 (pp. 26–27). Blaug (1995, 31) seems even to concede as much in an earlier passage that also undercuts his rhetorical thrust against me.[2] Although Mill's tendency to be all-embracing in his theoretical discussions creates some ambiguities, his consistent espousal of Banking-School doctrines, a number of which he seems to have been the first to articulate, has been amply documented by Skaggs (1994). Nor can I understand how one who denied that banknotes could be overissued as long as any coin remained in circulation (Mill 1848 [1909], 634; see also 544, 654) could have believed that the quantity of money produced by the banking system did not, under convertibility, behave passively.

[2] Before criticizing my verbal "trick" of redefining classical monetary theory, Blaug (1995, 31) emphasis added) himself espoused a strikingly similar definition:

> When convertibility of paper money was restored in 1821, the members of what soon came to be known as the Currency School argued as if the quantity theory was relevant even for commodity money, while the members of the Banking School echoed the *truly classical*, pre-Ricardian cost-of-production theory.

Even Thornton, who, of the three mentioned by Blaug, may have held views furthest from my version of the classical monetary model, espoused many propositions consistent with that model. Thornton believed, for example, that the value of a convertible currency was determined by the value of gold, and that country banks passively supplied the quantity of paper money consistent with the price level determined either by convertibility or, during the suspension, by the Bank of England. To be sure, elements of his account of the adjustment by country banks to the lead of the Bank of England suggest that the country banks had a limited and transitory impact on local prices that triggered an interregional analogue of the price-specie-flow mechanism. But Thornton's own version of the price-specie-flow mechanism was sufficiently differentiated from Hume's to suggest that the adjustment process that he envisaged did not require a very long time to run its course. Indeed, Thornton (1802 [1939], 269–270) explicitly criticized Hume's price-specie-flow analysis precisely because it ignored the constraints of commodity-price arbitrage on spatial price differences.

However, Thornton's seminal articulation of the central-banking or lender-of-last-resort responsibilities of the Bank of England might be viewed as inconsistent with the spirit of the classical model that I described in earlier work, which emphasized the equilibrating role of competition in ensuring that banks supply just the amount of money demanded by the public, but no more. Although the classical model could provide a theoretical rationale for free banking and for withdrawing all monopoly privileges from the Bank of England, that policy conclusion, especially given the fragmented and undercapitalized character of the country banks, was not the only one consistent with the classical model. Even John Fullarton (1845) and Thomas Tooke (1844) and, a generation later, Walter Bagehot (1873 [1962]), although sympathetic to the idea of competition in banking, did not advocate stripping the Bank of England of its central-banking and lender-of-last-resort responsibilities.

In one of his important studies, Neil Skaggs (1995) showed that the widespread impression that during the nineteenth century, Thornton's teaching fell into obscurity only to be resurrected by Viner (1937) and by Hayek's introduction to Thornton (1802 [1939]) is belied by the extent to which his views and policy prescriptions were incorporated into the Banking-School doctrine and, through the Banking School, transmitted to Walter Bagehot, whose articulation of the central-banking and lender-of-last-resort responsibilities of the Bank of England defined British monetary orthodoxy toward the end of the nineteenth century (Laidler, 1988). It is entirely plausible that Thornton had less in common with the straightforward quantity-theoretic analysis of the Currency School than with the anti-quantity-theoretic tradition that inspired the Banking School.

One further reason for Thornton's particular relevance for this discussion is his concern with, and early contributions to, a theory of banking. The point of such a theory is to explain how the quantity of (bank-created) money is somehow determined by an interaction between the public's demand to hold bank-created money and the costs that banks incur in creating such money. Such a theory is totally absent from, and not easily reconcilable with, the quantity theory of money. In its cruder forms, the quantity theory takes the nominal quantity of money as an exogenous variable, and its analyses of the banking system, if any, rarely go beyond a more or less mechanical rendition of the money-multiplier concept.[3] In the classical period, the focus of the quantity-theoretic discussions of banking typified by, say, Robert Torrens (1858) was on a supposed propensity toward overissue and overexpansion, presumably requiring policy measures to constrain the fluctuations in some subset of bank-created monetary instruments to mirror those imputed to an imaginary, full-bodied, purely metallic currency. So Thornton's concern with how the quantity of bank-created money might respond to fluctuations in the demand for it is sufficient, by itself, to distinguish him from the quantity-theoretic tradition in classical economics.

[3] As mentioned in footnote 1, the quantity theory may be consistent with a functional relationship between the nominal quantity of money and other endogenous variables as long as the supply function is independent of the demand function. The theoretical point is that, in the quantity theory, differences between the quantity of money demanded and the quantity supplied do not, as they do in the classical model, trigger rapid adjustment in the quantity supplied. Instead, such discrepancies trigger adjustments in income and prices which, through a circuitous process, ultimately bring the quantity of money demanded and the quantity supplied back into equality.

5.3 O'Brien on the Law of One Price, Purchasing-Power-Parity, and the Quantity Theory in Classical Economics

O'Brien faults my account of classical monetary theory for two reasons. First, my model, in his view, applies only to long-run equilibrium, whereas the classical monetary theorists were concerned mostly with short-run monetary control. Second, my model improperly assumes that the law of one price holds continuously when, in fact, it holds, if at all, only in the long run. This assumption leads to the notion that convertibility entails a uniform international price level. Together, these assumptions "produce an account of classical monetary theory" that is "hard to recognize" (O'Brien, 1995, 51).

Interestingly, O'Brien holds up my model to illustrate a style of theorizing that, borrowing from Joseph Schumpeter, he calls the Ricardian Telescope. By this, O'Brien means an inappropriate Ricardian preoccupation with long-run equilibrium conditions that distracts us from the possibility that these conditions may not always be satisfied and that deviations from long-run equilibrium conditions could be cumulative. In making this charge against my model, O'Brien does not seem to have grasped it quite correctly. In addition, he seems insensible of the paradox latent in a charge that an account of classical monetary theory could be unfaithful to the original by following too closely the theoretical style of the premier theoretician of classical economics.

O'Brien characterizes long-run equilibrium in classical monetary theory as a set of international prices and a distribution of gold that would occasion no international flow of gold, that is, that entails equilibrium in the balance of payments. Thus, O'Brien considers the adjustment of relative prices to be integral to international monetary equilibration. My argument, that under the gold standard national price levels could not deviate from the uniform international level fixed by the value of gold, collides with O'Brien's understanding of the international adjustment mechanism.

What O'Brien does not address is that, quite apart from the international distribution of specie under the gold standard, profitable arbitrage opportunities should (in theory) constrain price differences in internationally traded commodities at different locations within limits set by the costs of transporting them between those locations. Moreover, the constraints on price differences between internationally traded commodities at different locations would (in theory) indirectly constrain price differences between untraded commodities at those locations, especially insofar as untraded commodities were supplied competitively. The arbitrage constraints on price differences between similar internationally traded commodities would not necessarily eliminate all price differences. The point is just that the error-correction mechanism driven by commodity arbitrage is more direct than the one driven by international specie flows. That long-run equilibrium in the balance of payments under the gold standard imposed the only relevant constraint on international price deviations is hardly as self-evident as it appears to O'Brien. As Samuelson (1980, 154–155) observed, "[Hume] made the mistake of supposing that the Quantity Theory of Money linked every price in a region to the money in that region alone. This overlooked the forces that keep the competitive prices of the same transportable good virtually the same in all regions."[4]

Indeed, O'Brien (1995, 54) explicitly commends the classical writers for not believing that the law of one price "holds *at all times*." In emphasizing the qualifier "at all times," O'Brien leaves it unclear over what time period he and the classical writers believe that the law of one price would not hold.[5] After appealing first to Nassau Senior and then to Adam Smith to support his contention that the classical economists rejected the law of one price and that national price levels could differ under the gold standard, even in the absence of balance-of-payments equilibrium, O'Brien (1995, 55) later concedes that Ricardo criticized Adam Smith for forgetting that the prices of internationally traded products like corn could not differ between countries. Having allowed the law of one price into classical economics through the back door, O'Brien shifts his focus

[4] Cesarano (1998) has argued that Hume did not make the mistake attributed to him by Samuelson and many others, including Thornton ([1802] 1939, 269–270). Cesarano makes a good case that Hume's analysis is not as misguided as it has been made to appear. But, even in Cesarano's interpretation, Hume's thought experiment is still problematical. At any rate, Samuelson's substantive analysis remains very much intact.

[5] O'Brien (1995, 54) seems to make a substantial concession to my position by stating that if the law of one price did hold, then all the positions that I attributed to the classical economists, such as the validity of the Banking School position and the validity of Say's Identity for a monetary economy, would follow. In fact, the law of one price is not a sufficient condition for these conclusions to follow. One must still assume that a competitive market mechanism governs the supply of money by the banking system.

to purchasing-power-parity, invoking the considerable authority of Jacob Viner against the doctrine even as he quotes Viner's explicit distinction between the law of one price and purchasing-power-parity.

O'Brien cites Viner as the authority for the proposition that a shift in the terms of trade between two countries can, even under the gold standard, cause their domestic price levels to diverge. Believing that this possibility refutes the following assertions of mine, O'Brien offers a detailed proof of the proposition. The fallacies (all drawn from Chapter 2) are as follows:

1. "The price level in any country was fixed by the internationally determined value of the metal" (205).
2. "With the value of precious metals unchanged, the price level, under a metallic standard, would not change either" (207).
3. Adam Smith rejected the Humean price-specie-flow mechanism "because it incorrectly applied the quantity theory to determine the price level of a country with a metallic currency. A national price level depends on the international value of the metal used as money, not the quantity of money in the country" (208).

The proof supplied by O'Brien consists in showing that in a two-good, two-country model, an increase in country **A**'s demand for country **B**'s export raises the relative price of **B**'s export compared to **A**'s export, that is, the terms of trade shift in favor of **B**. If both countries are specialized in the production of their own export, the domestic price level of **A** falls and the domestic price level of **B** rises. So much for the idea that domestic price levels are fixed by convertibility.

The difficulty with this proof is not with its logic, which is unassailable, but its relevance, for it uses the term *price level* in a sense different from the one I attached to it. O'Brien understands *price level* to mean the equivalent of the GDP price deflator. Thus, an increase in the price of the export of country **A** relative to the export of country **B** implies a corresponding increase in the GDP price deflator of **A** relative to that of **B**. But that is not what I meant. Rather, I had in mind a more comprehensive measure that includes all internationally traded goods.

Let the relative prices of the exports of the two countries change. Measured in terms of a common unit of account, their prices, even after the change, remain equal in both countries. Given this meaning, there is nothing wrong with saying that both countries share a uniform price level.[6] In fact, this equality of prices is inherent in the very diagrams that O'Brien uses to show that the GDP price deflators of the two countries diverge.[7]

O'Brien (1995, 59) concludes by attributing the "distinctly curious results" I reached to the combined confusion of assuming purchasing-power-parity and instantaneous adjustment to long-run equilibrium. However, the only confusions that I can detect are semantic: between the law of one price for similar tradable commodities and purchasing-power-parity and between two distinct meanings of the term *price level*. Moreover, the law of one price, as a staple of international-trade theory, is an assumption that O'Brien cannot avoid in his analysis, even though he argues as if it were a condition of long-run equilibrium. Referring to my citation of Samuelson's (1980) analysis of balance-of-payments adjustment under the assumption that "prices for all goods are perfectly arbitraged across all markets" (Chapter 3), O'Brien (1995, 59) observes that this "is, of course, something which would never occur during an adjustment period, if it ever occurred at all." Presumably, O'Brien is referring to the adjustment period during which balance-of-payments equilibrium is restored. But he neglects to explain how the arbitrage of price differences between internationally traded commodities depends on the balance of payments.[8]

[6] Viner (1937, 311–318) explicitly discusses the absence of any statistical concept of the price level in the writings of the classical theorists. Instead, they viewed the price level as a vector of all money prices for all goods.

[7] O'Brien (1995, 58–59) concludes that the "free-banking reinterpretation" of classical monetary theory is based on the proposition that, under all normal circumstances, the real exchange rate is constant. Since it is a commonplace of the pure barter theory of international trade that the terms of trade (to which the real exchange rate corresponds in a monetary model) can change, O'Brien appears to have inferred (incorrectly) from my assertion that a change in the quantity of money could not alter the real exchange rate that I deny that a real disturbance could do so.

[8] O'Brien relies on an article by Moosa (2001) to assert that, as a factual matter, the prices of goods were not equalized under the gold standard. Even accepting Moosa's study at face value, I do not see how it would affect an evaluation of the content of classical monetary theory. The law of one price was clearly accepted in some form by most classical economists. In some cases (e.g., Nassau Senior), they inconsistently framed quantity-theoretic arguments about international monetary equilibrium that were contradicted by the law of one price without explaining why the law of one price did not hold.

O'Brien (1995, 75–76 n) goes on to assert that "despite misconceptions to the contrary … it [is not] necessary for price equalization to exist for the gold standard mechanism to correct the balance of payments. Indeed … one would not expect purchasing-power-parity—merely the adjustment of relative price levels to the point at which reciprocal demand would bring payments into balance." O'Brien suggests here what he calls "price equalization" is brought about, if at all, only through the restoration of balance-of-payments equilibrium. He asserts that Samuelson "simply dismisses" the balance-of-payments adjustment mechanism advanced by Viner and Gottfried Haberler and "assumes price equality in order to put forward a version of the modern monetary theory of the balance of payments." "It should hardly be necessary to emphasize," O'Brien objects, "that one set of assumptions cannot invalidate an alternative set of assumptions" (1995, 76 n. 3). But Samuelson did not simply assume price equality any more than O'Brien simply assumed it in showing that the terms of trade could shift in a two-good/two-country model. They both assumed that competition would eliminate price differences between similar products, because intra-commodity arbitrage, derived from a deeper theoretical analysis than is the price-specie-flow mechanism, is woven into the very fabric of conventional economic analysis. A model of balance-of-payments adjustment cannot, in the absence of an explicit theoretical argument to the contrary, routinely proceed as if price differences subject to arbitrage are not eliminated.[9]

5.4 Local Price-Level Differences and the Gold Standard

I believe that I have shown that O'Brien's objections notwithstanding, my account of classical monetary theory is coherent and may even be true. Nevertheless, I would not summarily dismiss his objections as misguided. Something about my account clearly disturbs him. And he is too good

[9] O'Brien observes that Samuelson's model does allow for changes in the terms of trade between countries to induce departures from purchasing-power-parity. He suggests that this concession by Samuelson is somehow inconsistent with my account of classical monetary theory. As I have explained, such a shift in the terms of trade and the resulting violation of purchasing-power-parity does not contradict everything I have written, although it is true that I did not explicitly discuss this possibility in Chapter 2. On the other hand, I did discuss at length another possible departure from purchasing-power-parity in Chapter 3. See Sect. 5.4.

an economist and too careful a scholar for his concerns to be dismissed even if he has failed to identify adequately the basis for his misgivings. I therefore explore in this section another possible basis for those misgivings.

The nub of O'Brien's objections is my notion of a uniform international price level. Although he chose to criticize this property of my model by attacking the law of one price, he could also have done so by introducing various frictions or transaction costs or simply by postulating the existence of non-tradable goods. However, in challenging the idea of a uniform international price level, O'Brien focused exclusively on tradable goods, trying to prove that their domestic prices would not be tightly constrained under the gold standard. This approach was, I think, bound to fail. I should now like to consider how the analysis would have played out had O'Brien chosen to couch his criticism in terms of a model that included non-tradables.

Suppose that in addition to the two tradable goods (apart from gold) in our two-country model, each country has a third, non-tradable, one. Let the money stock in country **A** be increased exogenously. The resulting excess supply of money and excess demand for goods in **A** cannot initially raise the price of either of the two tradable goods, unless total world spending on both tradable goods rises, so that the relative price of gold falls and the world price level of tradable goods rises. Now suppose that the additional spending on the tradable goods in **A** is matched by a corresponding cutback on tradable-goods spending in **B**, with an unchanged division of spending between the two tradable goods. With the relative price between the tradable goods unchanged, there is no change, under the gold standard, in the price of either good. However, the additional spending on **A**'s non-tradable good raises its price (absolutely and therefore relative to the two tradable goods). The increased relative price of the non-tradable good draws resources from **A**'s export industry, reducing **A**'s exports, which, together with an increase in imports from **B**, creates a balance-of-payments deficit in, and an outflow of gold from, **A**. Gold flows out of **A** until the excess supply of money is eliminated and the price of the non-tradable good returns to its original equilibrium level.

Thus, if we allow for non-tradable goods, the potential for price-level disturbances that troubles O'Brien could indeed arise under a gold standard. If so, it is fair to ask whether my account of international adjustment under the gold standard can survive the inclusion of non-tradables in the analysis. In particular, is it possible that, under the gold standard, a banking expansion would increase the prices of non-tradables, triggering an unsustainable internal boom and a balance-of-payments deficit—the scenario that so preoccupied the Currency School? And if not forestalled or promptly reversed by appropriate policy measures, would such a boom increase the risk of a financial panic owing to a contraction belatedly initiated by a banking system whose commitment to convertibility was threatened by a continuing outflow of gold?

These issues cannot be considered strictly in terms of the theory of international monetary adjustment that chiefly concerned us in this and the previous section. They must also be viewed in light of the classical theory of banking to which I referred in Section one. This theory, which originated with Adam Smith, was further developed by John Fullarton (1845) in his contribution to the Banking-School/Currency-School debates and inspired his famous law of reflux (Chapter 4). Despite his explicit focus on the Banking-School/Currency-School debates and references to my enthusiasm for free banking, O'Brien is surprisingly reticent about this theory of banking.

5.5 The Classical Theory of Banking, the Law of Reflux, and the Quantity Theory

The key feature of what I call the classical theory of banking is the notion that there is an economic mechanism that induces profit-seeking bankers to supply an amount of banknotes (and deposits) that equals the amount demanded by the public. In contrast to David Hume (1752) who, perhaps prejudiced by the debacle of John Law's system a few decades earlier, believed that banks were inherently disposed to overissue, Adam Smith (1937) argued that the marginal cost of redeeming unwanted convertible notes would exceed the marginal revenue from issuing them, so that a private bank would never intentionally issue more of its notes than the public wanted to hold. Miscalculations might occur, but the resulting overissue would be unprofitable, and banks would try to avoid them. One way they could do so was to lend only on the security of real commercial bills. Hence the real-bills doctrine (Chapter 4).

Henry Thornton is often thought to have espoused a very different view of banking from that articulated by Adam Smith. Unlike Smith, Thornton emphasized the unique role of the Bank of England in the British monetary system and the need for the Bank of England to exercise judgment in discharging its special responsibilities. I do not wish to minimize these differences, which were perhaps insufficiently acknowledged in my earlier work. But notwithstanding his substantive differences with Smith, Thornton also believed that there was an automatic mechanism that equalized the quantity of paper credit supplied by the British banking system with the amount demanded. Thus, Thornton criticized Smith for asserting that banks, in displacing coin from circulation by issuing paper money, would issue no more paper than the amount of coin displaced. Thornton (1802 [1939], 95–96) observed that since the public would probably find it convenient to hold more paper money than they would have held in coin, banks would actually issue more paper than the quantity of coin displaced. But since they would not be issuing any more paper money than the public wanted to hold, banks would not thereby precipitate an inflationary overissue. Indeed, Thornton, in both his *Paper Credit* and in the *Bullion Report* (Cannan, 1925), absolved country banks of any responsibility for the inflation that occurred after the suspension of convertibility in 1797. Although no enthusiast for free banking, Thornton did not share the Humean prejudice that banks are inherently predisposed to inflationary overissue, a view that, though not widely held in the Bullionist controversies, became a basic tenet of the Currency School.

John Fullarton further developed the classical theory of the supply of bank money. Observing that banks could not prevent the public from converting banknotes into deposits and that competition obliges banks to pay sufficient interest on deposits to eliminate any profit from creating deposits at the margin, Fullarton (1845, 92–93) argued that banks would issue no more notes than the public demanded. Any unwanted notes would be converted into deposits, which generate no profit at the margin (Chapter 3). Bank incentives to expand were governed by the marginal profitability of creating additional deposits, not the infra-marginal profitability of notes.

In the previous section, I conceded that O'Brien could have grounds for concern about the potential for destabilizing monetary disturbances in a model with non-tradable goods whose prices, within some limits, could fluctuate in response to monetary disturbances. In the view of the Currency School and O'Brien, such disturbances are potentially destabilizing. If, in contrast to the simple case in which all goods are tradable, such disturbances do have price-level effects, is the Banking-School position that purely monetary disturbances are not a serious policy problem still defensible?

It will be useful first to recall that, for a monetary disturbance to be destabilizing under a gold standard, the disturbance must induce responses that entail a cumulative movement away from equilibrium, until more or less violently checked by some less immediate constraint, say, a loss of gold reserves. If such cumulative movements away from equilibrium are at all likely, then the concerns of the Currency School—the prevention or mitigation of potentially cumulative deviations from an equilibrium path caused by monetary disturbances—could plausibly determine the objectives of monetary policy.

However, even if domestic monetary disturbances, by affecting the prices of non-tradable goods, could affect domestic price levels under the gold standard, it does not follow that such disturbances would trigger cumulative deviations from equilibrium. A cumulative deviation requires a persistent monetary expansion. But if, as many classical economists believed, there is an automatic mechanism that equates the amount of money supplied by a competitive banking system with the amount demanded by the public, then a cumulative process would not automatically follow from an overissue of bank money, even an overissue that did raise the prices of non-tradables, unless that automatic mechanism ceases to operate.

Suppose that the banking system mistakenly overissued bank money and that the reflux mechanism did not withdraw the excess money from circulation rapidly enough (i.e., banks did not realize their mistake soon enough to allow the money they had created to be extinguished in the normal course of accepting repayment of outstanding loans) to prevent the prices of non-tradables from rising. If prices did rise, the nominal demand for money would increase accordingly to absorb the overissue so that, at least in the short term, the excess money would remain in circulation. The long-run outcome would depend on whether domestic banks, after the resulting balance-of-payments deficit causes an outflow of gold, choose to operate with a reduced level of gold reserves. If they do, then the world price level would adjust slightly as the relative price of gold fell and the earlier relative price ratio between tradables and non-tradables was restored. If domestic banks try to restore their reserves, they would tend to restrict their issue of money, and domestic non-tradables prices would recede toward their earlier levels. Thus, although an overissue by the banking system is possible, the effect would seem to be limited, not cumulative, in the short term and might well be reversed in the long term.

To account for a cumulative effect, one must show not just that overissue is possible, but that a competitive banking system, as David Hume and the Currency School believed, is predisposed to overissue. But if, as Adam Smith and the Banking School believed, a bank cannot profit from overissue, so that overissues are usually unintended, then episodes of overissue would not be serially correlated and would not lead to financial crises.

One way to rationalize a supposed propensity of competitive banks toward overissue would be to invoke the Thornton-Wicksell distinction between the natural and market rates. Because the natural rate is unobservable, competitive banks would typically not immediately adjust their lending rates upon an (unobservable) increase in the natural rate. The divergence between the natural rate and the lending rate encourages investors to resort to relatively cheap bank credit to finance their investment projects, fueling a rapid expansion in bank lending and deposit creation.

Although Thornton (1802 [1939], 253–256) not only recognized that, but explained how, such an expansion is possible, he qualified the argument by explicitly linking it to usury laws that prevented banks from raising their lending rates to match the market level. Thus, it is not clear how serious a problem Thornton, at any rate, would have considered deviations between the natural and market rates in the absence of legal constraints on bank lending rates. Certainly, profit-seeking banks have a strong incentive to raise their lending rates after a real increase in the demand for bank finance. The natural rate may be unobservable, but there are observable market indicators that do respond to changes in the natural rate.

It may be worthwhile at this point to observe that standard renditions of the cumulative process triggered by a divergence between the natural and market rates typically exclude an essential element from the analysis. Focusing on the relationship between the natural rate and the bank lending rate, they ignore entirely the bank borrowing or deposit rate. This might have made some sense in Thornton's time, when deposits did not account for the bulk of total bank liabilities; it did not make sense by the fourth and fifth decades of the nineteenth century at the height of the Banking-School/Currency-School debates. Unless deposit rates are somehow held even further below market levels than are lending rates, why would banks expand their balance sheets by issuing additional liabilities? They would be more likely simply to allow the composition of their assets to shift toward holding the IOUs of private investors and away from holding other, perhaps less risky, assets. Unless banks expand their balance sheets and increase the total volume of their liabilities, it is not so clear that the natural-rate/market- rate analysis would have strong implications for the behavior of the price level. Of course, the composition of the balance sheets of banks is not devoid of macroeconomic significance. As they become more heavily weighted toward business loans, balance sheets may become more risky and less liquid, which could have serious consequences at the end of the investment boom. And although such balance-sheet effects could serve as a rationale for providing the banking system with lender-of-last-resort protection, they have only a tenuous connection to the concerns that animated the Currency School.

Thus, even within a model that allows for short-run deviations in national price levels under the gold standard, of the kind O'Brien seems to envision, the endogenous mechanism tending to equate the amount of money supplied with the amount demanded would tend to limit, if not eliminate, the destabilizing effects of short-run deviations. However, in questioning the importance of such deviations, I do not necessarily dismiss the importance of all monetary disturbances.

5.6 Monetary Policy in an Endogenous Cycle

In discussing the Banking-School/Currency-School debates, O'Brien argued that the policy prescriptions of the Currency School were calculated to smooth out an endogenous real business cycle. Citing Lord Overstone's description of the inherent regularity of the business cycle, which monetary policy could, at best, only mitigate but never eliminate, O'Brien (1995, 68–75) tried to prove the superiority of the Currency-School regime to the non-interventionist policy of the Banking School. To do so, he deploys a mathematical model of an endogenous real cycle in which changes in the quantity of money positively affect prices and real income in the short run.

O'Brien's results follow straightforwardly from his assumptions. If there is an endogenous real cycle in real income and prices, and changes in the quantity of money cause corresponding short-run changes in real income and prices, it would be surprising indeed if reducing the quantity of money during the upswing, and increasing it during the downswing, did not reduce the amplitude of the cycle.

The Banking School shared the Currency School belief in an endogenous real cycle, though there were few who attributed to it the highly symmetrical character that Lord Overstone ([1857] 1972, 31) did. However, the Banking School held that underlying changes in economic activity—"the needs of trade"—elicited changes in the quantity of money. Banking-School theorists doubted that the underlying cycle responded to policy-induced changes in the quantity of money, believing that those instruments (banknotes) that the Currency School wanted and those (deposits and bills of exchange) that they did not want to control were readily substitutable for each other. Thus, a mildly restrictive stance during the upswing was unlikely to have much dampening effect. However, a strict quantitative limit on the total amount of banknotes could, and did, have a devastating psychological effect as soon as it was feared that the Bank of England would be statutorily barred from extending additional credit. Such fears, as Bagehot (1873 [1962]) described, proved to be self-fulfilling, and once they became widespread, the ensuing financial panic subsided only after the Bank Charter Act was suspended.

Thus, O'Brien's demonstration that the Currency-School policy regime produced a cycle of lesser amplitude than did that of the Banking School is contingent on assumptions about the demand for money that the Banking School would not have accepted. If we allow for empirically important kinds of disturbances to the demand for money, the Currency-School policy regime may well be a source of instability at least as dangerous as the passive Banking-School policy in the face of an endogenous real business cycle. No mathematical model can resolve the underlying dispute about the character of the demand for money.

5.7 Conclusion

In the previous chapters, I have offered what I believe is a coherent view of a certain tradition in monetary analysis that occupied an important place in classical economics. To provide such a view, I proposed a simplified model of a competitive supply of convertible banknotes and deposits. Although the abstract form of the model may, at first, have seemed strange to classical monetary theorists, I do not think that, having grasped its content, they would have found its conclusions at all shocking.

The tradition with which I have been concerned may be called anti-quantity-theoretic, because it recognizes that when the money stock largely consists of convertible paper produced by a competitive banking system, the quantity of money, even in the short run, is not an exogenous variable controllable by the monetary authority. Although the classical analysis of such a monetary regime was not wholly satisfactory, and though there were important analytical differences even among those classical writers who rejected a straightforward quantity-theoretic approach, this tradition seems worthy of continued interest and study. Such a judgment does not imply that the quantity theory was absent from classical economics or that its role was subsidiary to the anti-quantity theory. But it does, at least, require us to be more careful than we once were in specifying the theoretical presuppositions on which the propositions of classical monetary theory were based.

References

Arnon, A. (1984). The transformation of Thomas Tooke's monetary thought. *History of Political Economy, 16*(2), 311–326.

Arnon, A. (1987). Banking between the visible and invisible hands: A reinterpretation of Ricardo's place within the classical school. *Oxford Economic Papers, 39*(2), 268–281.

Arnon, A. (1991). *Thomas Tooke: Pioneer of monetary theory*. University of Michigan Press.

Bagehot, W. (1873 [1962]). *Lombard street*. Irwin.

Blaug, M. (1995). Why is the quantity theory the oldest surviving theory in economics? In M. Blaug (Ed.), *The quantity theory of money: From Locke to Keynes and Friedman*. Edward Elgar.

Cannan, E. (Ed.). (1925). *The paper pound* (2nd ed.). P. S. King.

Cesarano, F. (1998). Hume's specie-flow mechanism and classical monetary theory: An alternative interpretation. *Journal of International Economics, 45*(1), 173–186.

Cottrell, A. (2017). Monetary endogeneity and the quantity theory: The case of commodity money. In L.-P. Rochon & S. Rossi (Eds.), *Advances in endogenous money analysis* (Chapter 7). Edward Elgar.

Frenkel, J., & Johnson, H. G. (1976). The monetary approach to the balance of payments: Essential concepts and historical origins. In J. Frenkel & H. G. Johnson (Eds.), *The monetary approach to the balance of payments* (pp. 21–45). University of Toronto Press.

Fullarton, J. (1845). *On the regulation of currencies* (2nd ed.). J. Murray.

Girton, L., & Roper, D. (1978). J. Laurence laughlin and the quantity theory of Money. *Journal of Political Economy, 88*(4), 599–625.

Glasner, D. (1989). *Free banking and monetary reform*. Cambridge University Press.

Hume, D. (1752 [2006]). Of the balance of trade. In E. Rotwein (Ed.), *Economic writings of David Hume* (pp. 60–77). Routledge.

Laidler, D. (1975). Thomas Tooke on monetary reform. In *Essays on money and inflation* (pp. 211–227). University of Chicago Press.

Laidler, D. (1981). Adam Smith as a monetary economist. *Canadian Journal of Economics, 14*(2), 185–200.

Laidler, D. (1988). British monetary orthodoxy in the 1870s. *Oxford Economic Papers, 40*(1), 74–109.

McCloskey, D. N., & Zecher, J. R. (1976). How the gold standard worked. In J. Frenkel & H. G. Johnson (Eds.), *The monetary approach to the balance of payments* (pp. 21–45). University of Toronto Press.

Mill, J. S. (1848 [1909]). *Principles of political economy*. W. Ashley (Ed.). Longmans and Green.

Moosa, I. A. (2001). The classical gold standard: Miracle or myth? *Journal of International Economic Studies, 15*, 131–142.

O'Brien, D. P. (1995). Long-run equilibrium and cyclical disturbances: The currency and banking controversy over monetary control. In M. Blaug (Ed.), *The quantity theory of money: From Locke to Keynes and Friedman*. Edward Elgar.

Overstone (Lord). (1857 [1972]). *Tracts and other publications on metallic and paper currency*. A. M. Kelley.

Samuelson, P. A. (1980). A corrected version of Hume's equilibrating mechanism for international trade. In J. S. Chipman & C. F. Kindelberger (Eds.), *Flexible exchange rates and the balance of payments* (pp. 141–158). North-Holland.

Skaggs, N. (1994). The place of J.S. Mill in the development of British monetary orthodoxy. *History of Political Economy, 26*(4), 539–567.

Skaggs, N. (1995). Henry Thornton and the development of classical monetary economics. *Canadian Journal of Economics, 28*(4), 1212–1227.

Skaggs, N. (1999). Changing views: Twentieth-century opinion on the banking school– currency school controversy. *History of Political Economy, 31*(2), 361–391.

Smith, A. (1937). *The wealth of nations*. E. Cannan (Ed.). Modern Library.

Thompson, E. A. (1974). The theory of money and income consistent with orthodox value theory. In G. Horwich & P. A. Samuelson (Eds.), *Trade, stability, and macroeconomics* (pp. 427–453). Academic Press.

Thornton, H. (1802 [1939]). *An inquiry into the nature and effects of the paper credit of Great Britain*. F. A. Hayek (Ed.). George Allen & Unwin.

Tooke, T. (1844). *An inquiry into the currency principle*. Longman.

Torrens, R. (1858). *The principles and practical operation of Sir Robert Peel's act of 1844 explained and defended* (3rd ed.). Longmans, Paternoster.
Viner, J. (1937). *Studies in the theory of international trade*. Harper Brothers.

CHAPTER 6

Monetary Disequilibrium and the Demand for Money in Ricardo and Thornton

6.1 Introduction

I am grateful to have been invited to participate in a conference on the monetary theory of David Ricardo. Having left the academy many years ago to become a civil servant, I am honored to be in the company of so many distinguished Ricardian scholars, whose knowledge of, the vast output of the great man whose contributions to economic science we seek to perpetuate, undoubtedly far exceeds my own.

That I was asked to write a paper for the conference is presumably the result of four earlier papers on classical monetary theory (Chapters 2–5). Only in the first two of those papers did I explicitly discuss Ricardo's monetary theory, and then only to show that his monetary views were more or less in accord with a class of monetary models that I designated "classical monetary theory," in order to distinguish it from the more-familiar quantity theory of money. The quantity theory, in my view, is a pre-classical theory, which has been too freely ascribed to the classical economists who, in many ways, revised and expanded upon the monetary theory that they inherited from earlier sources.

My argument, in brief, was that the classical monetary theorists, starting with Adam Smith, advanced a theory of a privately produced and competitively supplied money, consisting of banknotes and deposits

D. Glasner, *Studies in the History of Monetary Theory*, Palgrave Studies in the History of Economic Thought, https://doi.org/10.1007/978-3-030-83426-5_6

convertible into a real asset (usually gold or silver).[1] In contrast to the quantity theory, in which the quantity of money is (at least in the short run) exogenously determined, in the classical theory the quantity of money is endogenous. Not only is the quantity of money endogenous, but there are two independent mechanisms in operation to make it so. First, the balance of payments ensured that an excess supply of money would cause specie to be sent abroad, and, second, if any bank did issue its banknotes to excess or created too many deposits, it would incur a loss of assets and profits owing to a negative balance at the clearing-house.[2] Quantity theorists in the Humean tradition would argue that the balance of payments operates only in the medium- to long-term. However, in the classical monetary tradition whose existence I attempted to document and to which, I believe, Ricardo clearly belonged, even a temporary overissue is ruled out by the integration of world markets, with prices of internationally traded articles always being tightly constrained by international competition and arbitrage. The Humean price-specie-flow mechanism (PSFM) is thus a carryover from pre-classical sources and had already been rejected by Adam Smith (see Humphrey, 1981, Chapters 2 and 3; Laidler, 1981; Samuelson, 1980; Viner, 1937). An excess supply of money would add to the local demand for tradable goods, causing a negative trade balance until the excess supply of money was eliminated, but, as implied by PSFM, without affecting domestic prices (at least for tradables).[3]

[1] Ricardo, in fact, favored limiting the convertibility of notes to gold bullion, which, except for a small class of international transactions, did not serve as a medium of exchange, only a standard of value (medium of account). So, Ricardo's objective was clearly to minimize the monetary demand for gold and to prevent a demand for gold for monetary purposes from having a destabilizing, i.e., deflationary, influence on the economy.

[2] Given the latter mechanism, gold flows reflected changes in the relative demands for gold for non-monetary uses, or to be held by the banking system as reserves or for coinage, not excess demands by the public for money to hold. The equilibration of the supply of money with the demand to hold money was achieved by a domestic monetary mechanism. As I observed in previous chapters, this mechanism has bearing on our understanding of how Say's Law could obtain even in a monetary economy.

[3] While the prices of tradables are tightly constrained by the forces of international commodity arbitrage to nearly continuous equality across space, non-tradables are constrained only indirectly by the tendency for profits to be equalized in all industries in all countries (Frenkel & Johnson, 1976). That equalization may occur only in the intermediate or long run.

That the Bank of England had a special, privileged position in the monetary framework of Great Britain might (or might not) be rationalized within such a theory, but doing so involved no rejection of the basic paradigm of an endogenous money supply and an exogenous price level (anchored by convertibility and international commodity arbitrage), nor did it render the quantity theory the appropriate theoretical model for analyzing the British monetary system under convertibility. The analysis is more complicated under inconvertibility than under convertibility, but, for the purposes of this quick overview, the complication need not detain us.

I would note in passing that my explorations into classical monetary theory were motivated not only by an interest in the history of monetary theory, but also by my realization, as a UCLA undergraduate taught by Ben Klein (see Klein, 1974), that traditional arguments against competition in the supply of money are logically defective. It was that conceptual insight, coupled with the explicit suggestion of another one of my teachers, the late, great, and sorely missed, Earl Thompson (1974), that the classical theorists had reasoned in terms of a competitive supply of money, which led me to explore the writings of the classical monetary economists to search for evidence of an understanding, on their part, of the conditions under which a privately produced, competitive supply of money could be workable.

Among the critical comments elicited by my earlier papers, a recurring theme was that I was trying to force the ideas of the classical economists into a theoretical framework that they would not have recognized, much less accepted. I have in mind especially the comments of two distinguished economists and historians of economics, whose contributions I greatly admire: Mark Blaug and D. P. O'Brien. I have previously attempted (Chapter 5) to respond to their specific criticisms, and I need not revisit that discussion here. But a general methodological point may nevertheless be in order: to do history of economic thought (or, indeed, the history of any science) correctly, it helps to have a more correct theory (or, rather, a more nearly correct theory) than the one employed by the economists or scientists under historical consideration. If we can see further than our predecessors, it is only because we stand on their shoulders. But just because we stand on their shoulders, and can see what they could not, we may also, if we make the effort, gain insights into the logic of their theories that they themselves did not have.

Rather than continue in this perhaps overly philosophical vein, let me briefly outline the basic idea that I am going to discuss. While my earlier work (Chapters 2–5) was mostly concerned with how the classical monetary theorists, to a greater or lesser extent, developed a theory of a competitive supply of money created by private banks, I believe that it is also worth paying attention to the classical theory of the demand for money, or, perhaps, to be more precise, to the absence of such a theory, and the consequences of the lack of an explicit theory of the demand for money in the treatment of monetary disequilibrium by Ricardo and Thornton. The classical theory of the money supply, although only partially developed, seems to me an important contribution inadequately transmitted to, and inadequately developed by, the successors of the great classical monetary theorists. However, the classical theory of the demand for money, despite perceptive observations by individual theorists, notably by both Ricardo and Thornton, offering sophisticated insights into the reasons for holding money in general—and especially for holding money in times of financial and economic distress—and for a preference for holding some monetary instruments instead of others, seems to me to have been fragmentary and unsystematic. Lacking a systematic theory of the demand to hold money as an asset—a theory that began to take shape only in the 1920s and 1930s, before Keynes made that theory the cornerstone of the *General Theory*—Ricardo, in attempting to prove that only an excess issue by the Bank of England could have caused a depreciation of sterling relative to bullion, could not formulate the theoretical problem that he was trying to solve in terms of the money-demand/money-supply framework that would have enabled him to offer a straightforward solution to the problem that he tried to solve. Similarly, Thornton's remarkable natural-rate theory, prefiguring subsequent theories of Wicksell, Marshall, and their many offspring, was incomplete at a crucial stage in the argument, i.e., the demand to hold money is missing from his model.

Ricardo and Thornton never seem to have engaged each other directly on the points of difference in their seminal contributions, although I conjecture that each was able to detect, or at least sense, weaknesses in the theory of the other. How each viewed the contribution of the other seems destined to remain one of the tantalizing unanswered questions in the history of economic thought. See Arnon (2010) for a more detailed analysis of the monetary theories of Thornton and Ricardo.

6.2 Ricardo on Depreciation and Overissue

David Ricardo's first contributions to economic theory were made in his letters to the *Morning Chronicle* in (1809 [1951]), later revised and published as *The High Price of Bullion*, (1810 [1951]). A fervent advocate of the gold standard, Ricardo, having missed the first round of the Bullionist debates after the Bank of England, with the approval of the government, suspended convertibility of its banknotes into gold, reopened the debates by arguing forcefully in his letters to the *Morning Chronicle* that the recent increase in the price of bullion had been caused by an overissue of Bank of England notes.

In attacking the policy of the Bank of England, Ricardo made an exceptionally strong claim. Not only did he attribute the rise in the price of bullion in 1809 to an overissue of notes by the Bank of England—an allegation previously advanced by others, notably Walter Boyd (1801), in the first round of debates, on which Henry Thornton had expounded at length in his great work of 1802—Ricardo went much further, contending that, as a matter of strict economic logic, an increase in the sterling price of bullion could not have been caused by anything but an increase in the quantity of Bank of England notes beyond that amount which could have circulated under convertibility. This proposition had not been advanced at all in the first round, and only John Wheatley (1807), writing during the period of relative calm between the first and second rounds, had ever previously advanced that proposition.

Thus, even those (again with the exception of Wheatley) who had held the Bank of England responsible for the depreciation of sterling had not argued that sterling could never depreciate relative to gold independently of an increased issue of Bank of England notes. Two contingencies were mentioned as possible exceptions to the presumption that a depreciation of sterling was caused by an overissue of banknotes: (1) a poor harvest requiring grain imports to replace domestic production; or (2) remittances to Continental allies in the war against Napoleon.

Because gold would have to be sent abroad to finance the payments for grain or for military supplies for continental allies, inconvertible banknotes being generally unacceptable outside of Britain, the necessary gold with which to effect the desired transactions could be obtained only by bidding up the price of gold in terms of sterling. This reasoning was sufficiently persuasive for Thornton to have accepted it, as did the first important Bullionist writer, Walter Boyd, and to have been endorsed by the Parliamentary Report recommending the restoration of convertibility, the famous *Bullion Report* (Cannan, 1925), co-authored by Thornton himself with Francis Horner and William Huskisson. However, Ricardo rejected it. Let us try to understand why.

Ricardo's general theoretical approach, as we know, was to work out a barter analysis, abstracting from money, and then to use the barter analysis as the benchmark to which his monetary analysis had to conform. In the barter theory of international trade, it is exports that constitute the demand for imports. Thus, if Britain had to import grain because of a domestic crop failure, the ultimate means of payment for the grain imports would be Britain's exports of other products. This reasoning seems to ignore the reality that a crop failure might occasion extraordinary purchases of grain that could not immediately be paid for by increased exports, but would, in the first instance, have to be paid for by gold shipments. But Ricardo believed that gold shipments would not be resorted to immediately to pay for increased grain imports. Rather, foreign lenders, anticipating increased British exports to finance additional grain imports, would lend short-term to cover the immediate demand for grain imports. The spot exchange rate for sterling might fall to the gold-export point, but the expectation of increased future British exports to finance the exceptional imports would drive the forward exchange rate above the spot rate, making borrowing gold or foreign currency today for future repayment cheaper than the costs of shipping gold. Meanwhile, because prices of internationally tradable products were constrained by international arbitrage from deviating from each other across countries by more than transportation costs, falling home demand for non-grain products to finance increased grain imports would cause their prices in Britain to fall to the point at which either exports from Britain would become profitable or imports to Britain would become unprofitable, thereby generating, with no export of specie, the expected export surplus required to finance the added imports of grain.

Let me observe in passing that Ricardo's reliance on tight integration of world markets for internationally traded goods shows clearly that, in contrast to the Humean PSFM, Ricardo reasoned in terms of a common international price level under a gold standard. "The exportation of the coin is caused by its cheapness, and is not the effect, but the cause, of an unfavourable balance: we should not export it, if we did not send it to a better market, or if we had any commodity which we could export more profitably" (Ricardo, 1810 [1951], 61). Commenting on Ricardo's rejection of "Thornton's assertion that an unfavourable balance of payments could cause an outflow of gold on the ground that it would first have to be explained why other countries were unwilling to accept the deficit in commodities rather than exclusively in gold," Hayek (1929 [1991], 200) defended Thornton, because "the only way payment for the extra imports can lead to an increase in exports is through the outflow of gold, which eventually produces a lowering of the domestic commodity prices."

Apparently presuming that adjustment to international monetary equilibrium is achievable only by way of the Humean PSFM, whereby differences between local price levels induce equilibrating commodity flows, Hayek failed to see that Ricardo conceived of an adjustment mechanism involving no difference between local price levels—an adjustment involving only commodity flows induced solely by arbitrage opportunities within the limits determined by the transport costs of individual commodities. Hayek based his defense of Thornton on the Humean PSFM that Ricardo explicitly rejected—a lapse on Hayek's part to be sure, but one characteristic of an interpretative approach to classical monetary theory in which classical monetary theory and the quantity theory of money are presumed to be one and the same.

Ricardo (1811 [1951]), however, had noted in his *Reply to Bosanquet* how arbitrage in the foreign-exchange and gold markets, constantly eliminating profit opportunities by buying in cheap markets and selling in dear ones, equalized the value of gold across all international centers. Considering commodity markets to be equally as efficient as the gold market in arbitraging local price differences for every tradable commodity across different locations, Ricardo believed that any slight decrease in commodity prices in Britain, owing to the reduced British demand for commodities in general occasioned by a bad harvest or foreign remittances, would cause British exports to increase. British purchases of grain abroad would create profitable opportunities for exporting British commodities regardless of whether it was profitable to ship gold.

The logic of Ricardo's argument that a bad harvest or foreign remittances could not cause a depreciation of sterling in terms of gold seems to me unassailable, as far as it goes. And yet, I do not think that Ricardo succeeded in his attempt to refute the proposition, a proposition accepted by Thornton and by most of the Bullionist writers, that a bad harvest or foreign remittances could cause a depreciation of sterling without an overissue by the Bank of England. What is wrong with Ricardo's argument?

The problem with Ricardo, as I suggested above, is a failure to tease out the implications for the demand for money of a bad harvest or of foreign remittances. We now take for granted that the demand for money to hold as an asset is a function of many variables, which would certainly include, among other items, the levels of income and wealth. But the demand for money was not part of Ricardo's basic theoretical repertoire, although he was able to recognize cases in which there was an exceptional demand for money, e.g., during a financial crisis. Unfortunately, the idea of a functional change in the demand for money lay just slightly beyond the limits of Ricardo's prodigious theoretical reach. Moreover, by reasoning in terms of a barter equilibrium, Ricardo was implicitly assuming that the excess demand for money was zero, thereby excluding changes in the demand for money from consideration.

How would a bad harvest affect income and wealth? And how would such a change in wealth affect the demand for money? Some members of the community would benefit from the increase in the prices of products that they were selling, provided that their own harvests had not been too greatly reduced. Although some members of the community would tend to gain from a bad harvest, in the absence of a substantial terms-of-trade effect in favor of domestic producers, it would seem that the net income and wealth of the community as a whole would be more likely to decline than to rise. Even so, it is still possible that the increase in income and wealth of those gaining from the bad harvest might increase their demand for cash by more than the rest of the community—those experiencing a reduction in their real income and wealth—would reduce their demand for cash. But, in theory, the effect could go in either direction. Whatever the overall effect on the demand for money (in Ricardo's case, the demand for inconvertible Bank of England notes), it is the sign of that overall effect, positive or negative, that determined whether sterling would appreciate or depreciate relative to bullion as a result of a bad harvest. Ricardo's failure to see this straightforward proposition was the result of the inadequacy of a theoretical apparatus that failed to assimilate the notion of a demand to hold money as an asset within a general analysis of the determination of the level of prices and the exchange rate.

Now I would acknowledge that one could defend Ricardo against the charge that he failed to take account of the fact that a bad harvest would likely reduce the demand for money by positing that Ricardo must have regarded a failure by the Bank of England to reduce its note issue, in the event of a reduced demand for Bank of England notes, to be equivalent to an increase in the note issue of the Bank of England. While such a defense is possible—and I leave it to others to decide whether it would be consistent with Ricardo's assertions that only an overissue of notes by the Bank of England could cause a depreciation of sterling relative to gold—I think that once we reach this point in the discussion about Ricardo's position, we have crossed the line from substance to semantics.

While on the subject of a falling demand for money as a possible cause of depreciation, I would observe that there was an entirely different reason why the demand for Bank of England notes might have fallen after the Restriction: that the Restriction could itself have engendered expectations that the future value of Bank of England notes would fall after the link between the value of the notes and the value of gold had been severed. In his classic treatment of the Bullionist Controversies, Jacob Viner (1937, 132) noted with surprise that the Bullionists made no such argument in criticizing the suspension of convertibility. Viner explained the absence of this argument from the Bullionist criticisms of the suspension by suggesting that to have made such an argument would have been risky in the charged political atmosphere while England was at war with France. To have called into question, even indirectly, the soundness of sterling by attributing a loss of its value to a lack of confidence in its future value would, Viner conjectured, have invited a charge that the critics were themselves bringing the national currency into "discredit" while England was at war. The argument seems plausible, but Viner, himself, acknowledged that it was only conjecture on his part. I would make the further observation that the Bullionists may not have attributed the depreciation of sterling against gold to the expectation of future inflation resulting from the suspension of convertibility simply because their analytical repertoire was not yet sophisticated enough to have drawn a connection between a decline in the demand for sterling induced by the suspension of convertibility and an expectation of future inflation.

6.3 Thornton on the Natural Rate of Interest and Inflation

Perhaps it is only fair that, after a century of relative obscurity, Henry Thornton now stands out as the premier monetary theorist of the classical period.[4] I have no interest in arguing about who was the greatest classical monetary theorist, and I have no quarrel with anyone who would award the laurels to Henry Thornton, especially inasmuch as he seems to have been an exceptionally admirable human being. However, I do propose to argue in this section that what is generally considered to have been Thornton's greatest contribution, his essentially full anticipation of Wicksell's natural-rate model almost a century before Wicksell expounded it, was logically incomplete and possibly invalid (as indeed was Wicksell's own model). Here again, the sources of the problem turn out to have been an inadequately developed theory of the demand for money and lack of attention to international commodity arbitrage. After explaining what I think is wrong with the Thornton-Wicksell natural-rate model, I will offer some thoughts on why Ricardo seems not to have been persuaded by Thornton's model even though he must have been acquainted with it.

The natural-rate model is well-enough known for a very brief verbal summary of the model to suffice as an introduction to the discussion. At any moment, there is a range of potential investment opportunities open to entrepreneurs. The minimum rate that entrepreneurs regard as sufficient to warrant undertaking any of the prospective investment projects under consideration may be described as the natural rate of interest, or what Thornton called the rate of profit, and what Keynes called the marginal efficiency of capital. If the banking system offers to lend at a rate below the rate of profit or the natural rate of interest, entrepreneurs will seek to borrow funds from banks on favorable terms, and, as a result, the banks will create increasing amounts of money (either notes or deposits) in lending to eager borrowers. The additional money created will force

[4] Skaggs (1995) showed that assertions about Thornton's obscurity for most of the nineteenth and the early part of the twentieth centuries were overstated, and that Thornton actually was neither forgotten by, nor without influence on, the likes of Mill and Bagehot and others who helped to formulate what constituted British monetary orthodoxy at the end of the nineteenth and early twentieth centuries.

up prices, and, if interest rates are not raised, the process will continue without limit.[5]

Thomas Humphrey (1997), relying on David Laidler's (1975) encapsulation of the Wicksellian model, summarized the Thornton–Wicksell model in a system of five equations. Borrowing Humphrey's notation, I will write the system in terms of the following variables: real investment, I; savings, S; the rate of interest charged by banks on loans, i; the natural rate of interest (the profit rate on investment), r; excess aggregate demand, E; the change in the money stock, dM/dT; and the change in the price level, dP/dT. The five equations describing the dynamics of the system are the following:

$$I - S = a(r - i), a > 0; \tag{6.1}$$

$$I - S \equiv dM/dT \tag{6.2}$$

$$I - S \equiv E \tag{6.3}$$

$$dP/dT = kE, k > 0 \tag{6.4}$$

$$di/dT = b(dP/dT), b > 0 \tag{6.5}$$

Equation (6.1) indicates that the difference between investment and saving is proportional to the difference between the natural rate and the banks' lending rate. Equation (6.2) shows that money that is newly created by the banks finances that portion of business investment for which there is no corresponding amount of voluntary private savings. Equation (6.3) says that the gap between investment and savings is identically equal to excess aggregate demand. Equation (6.4) shows that the

[5] Actually, although Thornton held that there was no limit to the amount that a bank could lend if it offered to do so at a lending rate below the natural rate, that conclusion presumes that there are unlimited seemingly profitable investment projects available at the interest rate at which banks are prepared to lend. But there is nothing that guarantees that the number of such available projects is unlimited. There may in fact be a finite number of such projects, and even if the number is, for practical purposes, unlimited, an attempt to realize them all simultaneously would drive up factor costs, thereby reducing what Keynes called the marginal efficiency of investment below the marginal efficiency of capital.

rate of inflation is proportional to excess demand. Finally, Eq. (6.5) indicates that if banks set their lending rate below the natural rate, then the pressure of excess demand eventually forces banks to raise the lending rate to match the natural rate, thereby restoring an equilibrium with a stable price level and no excess demand.

A few substitutions lead to the following relationships:

$$dP/dT = ka(r-i) \tag{6.6}$$

and,

$$dM/dT = a(r-i). \tag{6.7}$$

Equations (6.6) and (6.7) relate the rate of monetary growth and the rate of inflation to the difference between the natural rate of interest and the lending rate set by banks. Because Eq. (6.5) says that the lending rate converges to the natural rate, the rate of monetary expansion and the rate of inflation also converge to zero, at which point the equality between savings and investment, and, hence, macroeconomic equilibrium, is restored.

What seems puzzling to me about this system is that while it contains a variable representing the quantity of money supplied, it has no variable for the quantity of money demanded, so that what purports to be a theory of monetary disequilibrium lacks an equilibrium condition requiring the quantity of money demanded to equal the quantity supplied. The missing demand-for-money variable and the missing equilibrium condition were not left out, owing to an oversight by Laidler and Humphrey. They were accurately representing the Thornton–Wicksell model in which the demand to hold money plays no explicit role, or, perhaps, on an alternative interpretation, is implicitly assumed to adjust passively to whatever quantity of money is supplied.

One way to understand the system may be to assume that the real demand to hold money is a constant, implying that the increase in the price level following an increase in the quantity of nominal money is the rise in prices necessary to keep the real quantity of money constant.[6] This assumption would still leave the real quantity of money demanded

[6] In his own unique version of the Thornton-Wicksell model, R. G. Hawtrey (1913, 1919) derived the effect of a reduced Bank Rate from its effect on the incentives of traders to add to their stocks of goods in process, and, by doing so, to increase consumers'

invariant to changes in the interest rate, a version of the demand for money not very congenial to modern sensibilities, but often attributed—mistakenly in my view—to classical monetary theorists. This difficulty could presumably be overcome by making *k* in Eq. (6.6) a function of the rate (or rates) of interest. So, if the amount of money supplied were to increase owing to an increased natural rate, gradually raising (as specified in Eq. [6.5]) the market interest rate, then the quantity of money demanded would fall, owing to the increased interest rate. Because the quantity of money demanded falls, restoration of equilibrium between the demand for money and the supply of money would require a price-level increase more than proportional to the increase in the nominal quantity of money.

While it would be possible to add an equation for the demand for money and an equilibrium condition to the Thornton–Wicksell model in the way that I just outlined, doing so would still leave another—and I think deeper—problem with the model unresolved. The other problem that I have with the natural-rate/market-rate paradigm is that the cumulative process it describes—banks increasing lending to businesses and entrepreneurs in response to an increase in the profit rate expected by entrepreneurs—involves an essentially mechanical response by the banks to the increasing demand for bank loans, a response not grounded securely in the self-interest of the engines of the process: the individual banks themselves. With no increase in the demand to hold money, increased lending by any single bank would cause interbank clearings to turn against that bank unless it simultaneously took steps to induce the public to increase their holdings of its liabilities. The most direct,

incomes and outlays, not by creating an excess supply of money that would raise prices. Hawtrey later (1938, 37) succinctly described the difference of perspective:

> The intention [of the Bank of England] was, by varying the discount rate, to regulate the amount of bills brought to the Bank of England, and so to control the volume of currency against which those bills were held. But the policy was by no means dependent on the quantity theory. In fact the discount rate modified the quantity of currency by modifying activity; the latter was cause and the former was effect. The link between the quantity of currency and the price level existed (though not in so rigid a form as was then supposed). But the variations in the quantity of money and the price level were effects of a common cause, the variations in the consumers' income, and it was these latter that were influenced by the discount rate.

although not the only, way to induce the public to hold additional liabilities of the bank would be to raise the interest paid on deposit balances held at the bank.

Now it is true that increased lending by other banks would tend to offset the adverse clearings against any single expanding bank occasioned by its own increase in lending, but there would still be net leakages out of the banking system, either internally, via demand for coin, or externally, via a demand for bullion, so that parallel expansion by the whole banking system would not fully insulate individual banks against pressure on their reserve positions when simultaneously increasing their liabilities with no equivalent increase in the amount of those liabilities demanded by the public. Banks would therefore feel pressure to raise their deposit rates to maintain or replenish their reserves, and, before long, to raise their lending rates as well, thereby limiting the increase in their lending as rates rose toward the expected entrepreneurial profit rate. In the Thornton-Wicksell model, the only pressure to increase the lending rate comes from the tendency for prices to rise in response to the monetary expansion fueled by the banks. But consideration of the incentives of the banking system suggests that the pressure to raise interest rates would be felt even before any price-level effects were evident.[7]

Another problematic aspect of the Thornton-Wicksell model is the unspecified and ambiguous relation between domestic prices, external prices, and the exchange rate. Such ambiguity was absent from Ricardo's discussion, because he emphasized the constraint on domestic prices imposed by international commodity arbitrage under the gold standard, limiting the extent to which increased bank lending in any one country could raise the price level in that country. The inflationary effects in one

[7] The discussion in this paragraph does not dispute that banks can expand to some degree if they do so in concert. Expansion in concert is certainly possible, but it is a less-compelling argument than conventional banking theory seems to take for granted. What is it about banking that allows one to assume, with little supporting argument, that an individual bank would expand conditional on the assumption that all other banks will also do so, irrespective of, for example, the number of other banks in the system? Would one casually assume that individual non-banking firms would raise their prices conditional on the assumption that every competing firm will also raise its price, irrespective of the number of other competitors in the market? What accounts for the difference in the conventional assumption about how competitive firms and competitive banks make their decisions? I am unaware of any discussion of this issue in the literature on banking theory.

country, as Adam Smith (1937) had earlier observed about the substitution of banknotes for coin, are exported, and dissipated, via commodity arbitrage, and the effects of reserve drains on private banking positions are, via the processes mentioned in the preceding paragraph, likely to limit increases in lending, driving up both deposit and lending rates before significant inflationary effects appeared.

One might also observe in this connection that Thornton's discussion was, at least in one important respect, superior to Wicksell's: Thornton offered his analysis in the course of a discussion of an inconvertible currency with a binding constraint on bank lending rates, owing to the 5-percent usury limit on the interest rate that banks charged borrowers. Wicksell, on the other hand, explicitly argued that, irrespective of whether bank liabilities were directly or indirectly convertible into gold, movements in the price level were governed solely by the relation between the bank lending rates and the profit rate expected by entrepreneurs.

It is also noteworthy that Thornton, in expounding his version of the natural-rate theory, was mainly concerned with showing that simply following the real-bills doctrine, as the directors of the Bank of England claimed to have been doing, provided no guarantee against inflation and the depreciation of sterling. Thornton had explained earlier in his volume that rising prices and a premium on bullion might be caused either by an overissue by the Bank of England or by a balance-of-payments deficit resulting from a bad harvest or overseas remittances. Defenders of the Bank of England had argued that if the Bank of England abided by the real-bills doctrine, overissue would be impossible, so that any observed inflation or depreciation of sterling must have resulted from an unfavorable balance of payments, not overissue. Thornton advanced his natural-rate theory to refute this anti-Bullionist argument, showing that even if the Bank had restricted itself to lending on the security of real bills, the 5-percent ceiling on the interest rate that the Bank could charge for loans would induce entrepreneurs to borrow in unlimited quantities from the Bank if the expected profit rate exceeded 5 percent. The point was that even if an unfavorable balance of payments might cause a depreciation of sterling, merely abiding by the real-bills doctrine would not—anti-Bullionists' claims to the contrary notwithstanding—necessarily prevent an overissue by the Bank of England.

For Ricardo, the whole exercise was unnecessary. Believing that he had shown that a depreciation of sterling was impossible except as a result of overissue, he had no reason to refute the real-bills doctrine. Refuting the real-bills doctrine was necessary only if one conceded that a premium on bullion might be caused by something other than an overissue. Ricardo never made that concession. Ricardo must also have objected to the substance of Thornton's treatment. As Ricardo relied on international commodity arbitrage to obviate financing overseas purchases with bullion, he could not have agreed with Thornton that a bank-lending rate pegged below the profit rate would lead to an increase in domestic prices, and then, as a result, an outflow of gold and a depreciation of sterling. As long as the pound was convertible into gold, international commodity arbitrage would keep British prices equal to those abroad in terms of gold equivalents. If the convertibility of Bank of England notes were suspended, then the depreciation of sterling would measure the extent of overissue. From Ricardo's perspective, the distinction between the natural rate and the market rate was entirely redundant.

6.4 Conclusion

In this chapter, I have explored some of the differences that separate the two premier theoreticians of classical monetary theory after Adam Smith, and the reasons for their different positions. A critical reason for their differences has turned out to be Ricardo's consistent adherence to the principle that international commodity arbitrage would equalize commodity prices across all countries operating on the gold standard. Despite Thornton's recognition of this principle at some points in his great work, he did not maintain that position consistently, lapsing into arguments that relied on the Humean PSFM that Ricardo rejected. This was especially true of Thornton's rendition of the natural-rate/market-rate theory, in which the proposition that overissue could result in a depreciation of sterling was established by way of a variation on the Humean adjustment process that Ricardo considered fallacious.

While Ricardo may have had valid reasons for rejecting Thornton's most celebrated contribution to monetary theory, his own analysis of the possible causes of a depreciated inconvertible currency was not without flaws of its own. That error, I suggested, would have been evident to Ricardo if he had been working with a more clearly articulated conception of the demand for money to hold. It similarly appears that Thornton's exposition of his natural-rate theory was marred by a faulty, or at least incomplete, understanding of the demand for money to hold.

Before bringing this discussion to a close, let me offer one further observation on the relation between Ricardo's and Thornton's monetary theories. In Ricardo's account, the value of money can be said to be determined by the value of gold as a commodity, for which there is a demand encompassing both monetary and non-monetary uses. Arbitrage between monetary and non-monetary uses equalizes the value of gold across all uses. Banks affect the value of money only insofar as they reduce the total demand for gold by allowing gold to be withdrawn from some monetary uses and to be devoted instead to non-monetary uses of lower value than was otherwise possible. Thornton's analysis is less straightforward than Ricardo's. By increasing the quantity of money, banks, under a gold standard, can raise prices, in the short term, even without causing a reduction in the monetary demand for gold.

A similar analytical difference can be discerned today between those who argue that the value of money is determined essentially by the supply of, and demand for, high-powered money—defined as non-interest-bearing currency and reserves—and those who argue that the value of money is determined by the supply of all kinds of money and near-moneys and the demand for all such instruments, regardless of whether those instruments bear interest. The first approach might be called Ricardian and the second Thorntonian.

An interesting parallel between the Ricardian and Thorntonian approaches may be found in the more recent controversy (now, to my amazement, almost 50 years old) between what was then called the New View of banks and financial intermediaries and the Old View. Advocates of the Old View generally thought that they were defending the notion that monetary policy could affect aggregate demand and the price level through changes in the Bank Rate charged directly by central banks to commercial banks or set indirectly through open-market operations, while advocates of the New View argued that, in a proper general-equilibrium model, there is no meaningful distinction between the monetary liabilities of banks and the non-monetary liabilities of other financial intermediaries. Advocates of the New View were therefore supposed to be arguing—indeed, apparently supposed themselves to be arguing—that monetary policy does not matter. But if I am right in suggesting that the New View was really Ricardian (treating the financial sector, including banks, as irrelevant to the determination of the price level) and the Old View was Thorntonian (treating movements in the price level as the result of expansion or contraction by the banking system), then the crux of the argument was whether the effects of monetary policy can be analytically reduced to the supply of, and demand for, high-powered money (what we now call the monetary base), or whether some aggregate measure of all monetary instruments (of varying degrees of "moneyness") must be juxtaposed against some aggregate measure of the demand to hold such instruments. Whether monetary policy is effective, or not, is orthogonal to this issue. But, at the time, everyone involved seemed to think that the dispute mattered only because of its policy implications.

Having disposed of the bogus policy issue, I think that a dispassionate assessment of the analytical arguments would show that the New View clearly had the better analytical grasp of the role of banks and financial intermediaries in the economy. The subsequent policy success of Monetarism (though short-lived) unfortunately cut short the promising analytical progress that the New View had started to make. But this is a story that will have to be told on some other occasion (touched on in the following chapter).

References

Arnon, A. (2010). *Monetary theory and policy from Hume and Smith to Wicksell*. Cambridge University Press.

Boyd, W. (1801). *A letter to the right honourable William Pitt, on the influence of the stoppage of issues in specie at the Bank of England, on the prices of provisions, and other commodities*. J. Wright.

Cannan, E. (1925). *The paper pound* (2nd ed.). P. S. King & Son.

Frenkel, J. A., & Johnson, H. G. (1976). The monetary approach to the balance of payments: Essential concepts and historical origins. In J. A. Frenkel & H. G. Johnson (Eds.), *The monetary approach to the balance of payments* (pp. 21–45). University of Toronto Press.

Hawtrey, R. G. (1913). *Good and bad trade*. Longmans, Green & Co.

Hawtrey, R. G. (1919). *Currency and credit*. Longmans, Green & Co.

Hawtrey, R. G. (1938). *A century of bank rate*. Longmans, Green & Co.

Hayek, F. A. (1929 [1991]). The period of restrictions, 1797–1821. In W. W. Bartley III & S. Kreges (Eds.), *The trend of economic thinking: Essays on political economists and economic history* (The Collected Works of F. A. Hayek), Vol. 11, pp. 177–215. The Liberty Fund.

Humphrey, T. R. (1981). Adam Smith and the monetary approach to the balance of payments. *Federal Reserve Bank of Richmond Economic Review, 67*(Nov.), 3–10.

Humphrey, T. (1997). Natural rate of interest. In D. Glasner (Ed.), *Business cycles and depressions: An encyclopaedia* (pp. 476–479). Taylor & Francis.
Klein, B. (1974). The competitive supply of money. *Journal of Money, Credit and Banking, 6*(4), 423–453.
Laidler, D. (1975). On Wicksell's theory of price level dynamics. *Essays on money and inflation* (pp. 101–119). University of Chicago Press.
Laidler, D. (1981). Adam Smith as a monetary economist. *Canadian Journal of Economics, 14*(2), 185–200.
Ricardo, D. (1809 [1951]). The price of gold: Three contributions to the Morning Chronicle. In P. Sraffa (Ed.), *The works and correspondence of David Ricardo* (pp. 13–46). Cambridge University Press.
Ricardo, D. (1810 [1951]) The high price of bullion. In P. Sraffa (Ed.), *The works and correspondence of David Ricardo* (pp. 47–127). Cambridge University Press.
Ricardo, D. (1811 [1951]). Reply to Mr. Bosanquet. In P. Sraffa (Ed.), *The works and correspondence of David Ricardo* (pp. 155–256). Cambridge University Press.
Samuelson, P. A. (1980). A corrected version of Hume's equilibrating mechanism for international trade. In J. S. Chipman & C. F. Kinleberger (Eds.), *Flexible exchange rates and the balance of payments* (pp. 141–158). North Holland.
Skaggs, N. (1995). Henry Thornton and the development of classical monetary economics. *Canadian Journal of Economics, 28*, 1212–1227.
Smith, A. (1937). *The wealth of nations*. E. Cannan (Ed.). Modern Library.
Thompson, E. A. (1974). The theory of money and income consistent with orthodox value theory. In G. Horwich & P. A. Samuelson (Eds.), *Trade* (pp. 427–453). Academic Press.
Thornton, H. (1802 [1939]). *An inquiry into the nature and effects of the paper credit of the Bank of England*. F. A. v. Hayek (Ed.). George Allen & Unwin.
Viner, J. (1937). *Studies in the theory of international trade*. Harper Bros.
Wheatley, J. (1807). *An essay on the theory of money and the principles of commerce* (Vol. I). Cadell & Davies.

CHAPTER 7

The Humean and Smithian Traditions in Monetary Theory

7.1 Introduction

Our understanding of classical monetary theory has changed substantially over the past four decades. The old view, reflected in classic works by Viner (1937) and Fetter (1965) and upheld more recently by O'Brien (1995), emphasized the centrality in classical monetary economics of the quantity theory of money. However, the quantity theory is not easily applicable to a monetary system based on a metallic standard, a system regarded by most classical economists not only as normal, but as socially desirable, perhaps even morally imperative. The more recent understanding of classical monetary theory reflected in work by Laidler (1975, 1981), Skaggs (1991, 1995, 1999) and in Chapters 2–5 above applied a theoretical framework in which competing private banks supply banknotes and deposits with a value fixed by convertibility into a metallic monetary standard.

Predating the classical period by centuries, the quantity theory was equipped to handle analysis of neither a purely metallic currency nor a mixed currency containing both circulating metallic coins and convertible banknotes and deposits. The strict quantity theory does not apply to a metallic currency, because the principle of monetary neutrality, under which changes in the nominal quantity of money result in proportional changes in money prices, presumes that money serves as a pure medium

D. Glasner, *Studies in the History of Monetary Theory*, Palgrave Studies in the History of Economic Thought,
https://doi.org/10.1007/978-3-030-83426-5_7

of exchange, providing no real (non-monetary) services and satisfying no non-monetary demand. Nor can the quantity theory apply to the quantity of banknotes or deposits issued by banks, because the issue of bank money, being convertible into the standard commodity, cannot reduce the value of the standard commodity into which it is convertible unless it causes a proportional reduction in the demand for the standard commodity.

At the cusp of the classical period, the quantity theory was elegantly summed up in several seminal essays by Adam Smith's friend David Hume, especially his articulation of what became known as the price-specie flow mechanism (PSFM). However, Hume's analysis, abstracting from any real services provided by metallic money, was not strictly correct even for a purely metallic currency. Nor was Hume's reasoning clear on how prices adjust after the hypothesized changes in the quantity of gold in just one country. However, a straightforward reading of Hume suggests that he believed prices in that country would change proportionately to the change in the gold stock in that country even though prices in that country would be constrained by tradable-goods prices in all the countries in which the quantity of gold did not change.

Perhaps this was why Adam Smith (1937) avoided reproducing, or even referring to, Hume's earlier analysis, despite having reproduced it in his *Lectures* (Smith, 1978), a seeming oversight characterized by Viner (1937) as one of the great mysteries of classical economics. The upshot of this distinction between the pre-classical quantity theory endorsed by Hume and the classical theory traceable to Smith is not that the quantity theory was rejected by, or absent from, classical monetary theory, that claim being clearly at odds with the facts. Rather, the upshot is that the core monetary analysis of the classical economists (Smith, Ricardo, Thornton, Say, Tooke, Fullarton, and J. S. Mill) pertains to a privately produced money convertible into a metallic standard that does not fit within the four corners of the quantity theory.

The quantity theory of money still has its place in explaining the value of an inconvertible money. Indeed, contributors to the Bullionist controversies relied on an inverse relation between the quantity of an inconvertible money and its purchasing power as an analytical principle. The possibility that a monetary disturbance emanating from the banking system was largely dismissed in the Bullionist controversies, such a disturbance having been assumed to come only from a bank, like the Bank of England, granted monopolistic legal-tender privileges for its notes. But in subsequent discussions from the mid-1820s through the 1840s, whether disturbances from the private banking system could affect the price level and exchange rates became a controversial issue. The almost continuous controversies about monetary policy beginning with the suspension of convertibility in 1797 until enactment of the Bank Charter Act in 1844 provoked a varied collection of ideas that have undergone interpretation and reinterpretation, analysis and reanalysis, informing and guiding the subsequent development of monetary theory.

In this retrospective view of the influence of Hume and Smith on current monetary theory, I shall consider five areas of monetary theory and policy in which the classical monetary debates have echoed and reverberated in monetary debates from the nineteenth century to the present. I have already alluded to two of these: first, whether competitive banks can, by increasing their issue of liabilities (either banknotes or deposits), create an inflationary disturbance leading either to an increase in the local price level, or to a subsequent contraction necessary to avoid a permanent or temporary breach of the monetary standard, and, second, the nature of the adjustment process whereby a monetary disturbance in one country is transmitted to other countries under a metallic standard or a system of fixed exchange rates.

In the next two sections, I consider these closely related issues in turn, focusing first on the opposing Humean and Smithian attitudes toward competitive banking and second on the opposing Humean and Smithian theories of international monetary adjustment. The Humean theory of banking viewed competitive banks as inherently predisposed toward inflationary overissue owing to a presumed incentive toward overissue created by the difference between the face value of banknotes and deposits and the negligible cost of printing banknotes or creating deposit entries, while the Smithian theory recognized costs and constraints on the issue of banknotes or deposits by competing banks ignored by the Humean theory. Moreover, accepting the quantity theory, the Humean theory presumed that bank overissue would cause localized inflation, at least in the short term, with the resulting international price differences eliminated only via PSFM while the Smithian theory maintained that international monetary equilibrium is assured by international arbitrage that equalizes local prices in terms of the common monetary standard.

While the Humean tradition views the overissue of bank liabilities as the source of monetary disturbances, in the Smithian tradition, the source of instability is the danger that bank assets may lose value, impairing the liquidity, or the solvency, of those banks. The possibility that shocks affecting the value of bank assets and the potential for such shocks to endanger the liquidity, or solvency, of banking institutions led Henry Thornton to argue that the Bank of England should act as a lender of last resort when banks, owing to liquidity or solvency concerns, limit the extension of credit, thereby exacerbating a cumulative contraction of credit and spending. Fullarton, amplifying Thornton's doctrine, cited the need for a lender of last resort in arguing against the 100-percent marginal reserve requirement imposed on the Bank of England by the Bank Charter Act, thereby making it impossible for the Bank of England to discharge its responsibility. It was from both Thornton and Fullarton that Bagehot (1873 [1962]) derived the lender-of-last-resort doctrine of which he provided the orthodox version. Smith himself offered an alternative approach to the problem of illiquidity and insolvency owing to a negative shock to the value of bank assets. To guard against this risk, Smith espoused a version of the real-bills doctrine, advising banks to lend by issuing their liabilities only on the security of valid short-term commercial (not financial) loans. Adam Smith's discussion of the real-bills doctrine suggests that not only may it be legitimate to restrict the types of assets held by banks, but also to restrict the types of activities in which they engage. Such an argument might rationalize legislation like the Glass-Steagall Act prohibiting the combination of investment- and commercial-banking activities within a single institution. I discuss these questions in Sect. 7.4.

Finally, the Smithian and Humean traditions have developed differing attitudes toward the role of specific rules governing the conduct of monetary authorities. During the Bullionist debates, the question was whether the Bank of England should be bound by an obligation to convert its notes into gold on demand, or whether it should be freed from that obligation and allowed to set policy using its best judgment at any time. Mainstream opinion strongly favored convertibility into gold. Although Thornton (1802 [1939]) gave a favorable account of the conduct of the Bank of England after convertibility was suspended, he was one of the authors of the 1810 Bullion Report (Cannan, 1925) that recommended rapid resumption of convertibility. In the Banking-School/Currency-School debates, the issue was not convertibility but whether the total quantity of banknotes should be constrained by law to fluctuate along with gold flows. In other words, was it necessary to supplement the gold standard with a set of rules beyond the obligation to convert banknotes into gold at a fixed parity? The consensus favoring the gold standard continued until its collapse in the Great Depression. Since then, economists and statesmen and policymakers have tried with mixed success to formulate rules governing the conduct of monetary authorities in a world of fiat currencies. The Humean preference for quantity rules has largely been abandoned after the failure of the Monetarist experiment of 1981–1982. However, the more eclectic Smithian tradition favoring some generalized version of the gold-standard price rule continues as an ongoing search for a workable rule that is not vulnerable to shocks unforeseen, or not taken seriously, when the rule was formulated. The question then arises whether any rule could work under all conditions, and if not, whether an imperfect rule is preferable to no rule at all.

7.2 Overissue by Private Banks

In his essays on money, expounding and extracting the implications of the quantity theory of money, David Hume asserted that prices in any country rise or fall in proportion to the quantity of gold or other precious metals circulating in the country. He also asserted that, by adding to the monetary circulation in any country, banks cause inflation and currency debasement. There is reason to believe that Adam Smith, having cited Hume's account of the price-specie-flow mechanism (PSFM) in his *Lectures on Jurisprudence*, disagreed with Hume and therefore did not refer to the PSFM in the *Wealth of Nations* (Laidler, 1981; Bloomfield 1975 [1994]; Smith, 1937; Viner, 1937). Perhaps reluctant to criticize his closest friend in print, Smith expounded his own theory of banking and international monetary adjustment without mentioning Hume.[1]

[1] Ahiakpor (2004) maintains that in discussions elsewhere in the *Wealth of Nations*, Smith did recognize and adopt the Humean PSFM. However, I would suggest that the passages cited by Ahiakpor refer to exports and imports of gold as a commodity with a variable nominal price in terms of local currencies that are not denominated in gold. In the Humean PSFM and in Smith's monetary discussions, gold, or silver, is treated as a numeraire so that its nominal price is fixed at one and imports and exports of gold reflect monetary forces that differ from those described by Smith in the non-monetary discussions of gold imports and exports. Such a misapplication of the pure barter analysis of a real commodity used as a medium of exchange to monetary analysis is similar to Cairnes's (1873) analysis of the effects of the Australian gold discoveries discussed above in Chapter 3.

Smith's generally benign view of banks was largely accepted in the Bullionist debates, only the Bank of England, whose notes were granted legal-tender status, being assigned responsibility for inflation after the suspension of convertibility of banknotes into gold. The country banks, still obligated to redeem their notes and deposits into Bank of England notes, were held blameless for the depreciation of sterling, blame being attributed exclusively to overissue by the Bank of England.[2]

Not until after convertibility was restored in 1821 were private banking institutions identified as sources of instability.[3] Subsequent monetary disturbances led some to argue that the country banks, not just the Bank of England, were increasing money and credit excessively, causing an outflow of specie, eventually requiring credit, and note issue, to be restricted to prevent a suspension of convertibility. This negative view of banking evolved into the Currency Principle, which inspired the Bank Charter Act of 1844, precipitating the famous debate between the Currency School (which favored) and the Banking School (which opposed) the Act.

Upholding the Smithian tradition, the Banking School rejected the argument that banks, obligated to make their sight liabilities convertible into an asset not under their control, could overissue their liabilities. A variant of the Smithian view was advanced by the Free-Banking School (White, 1984), which held that, unlike other banks, the Bank of England, alone shielded by monopolistic privileges from the competitive constraints

[2] The meaning of "overissue" in this context is ambiguous inasmuch as there is no clear, i.e., observable, criterion by which to judge what constitutes the "correct" quantity. When there is convertibility into an external standard of value, such as gold, the quantity of convertible liabilities into the standard is that quantity which the public wishes to hold. As long as convertibility is maintained, the existing quantity held by the public is presumptively the correct quantity given the value of those convertible liabilities. When convertibility is suspended, it is not clear whether a fall in the value of those liabilities is the result of there having been an overissue, or, given the reduced value attached to inconvertible notes, the result of an increased nominal quantity of notes demanded by the public. Failure to make this distinction has been a persistent flaw in the reasoning of monetary theorists, especially, though not exclusively, in the Humean tradition. Fullarton clearly did grasp the distinction.

[3] In fact, Hume had argued that commercial banking was destabilizing and inherently inflationary more than a half-century before Robert Torrens and Lord Overstone, who pioneered the Currency Principle, resurrected his argument and made it a cardinal tenet of the Currency School.

on its note issue, could engage in overissue, at least temporarily, until an external drain forced it to contract its issues, precipitating a crisis.

The Currency School adopted Hume's view that, owing to the gap between the face value of banknotes and their cost of production, banks have an unlimited incentive to increase their note issues. Thus, without a quantitative limit on the note issues of both the Bank of England *and* the country banks, the British economy would suffer continuing cycles of credit expansion and contraction caused by the banking system. Overissue would continue until the resulting outflow of gold depleted the reserves of the Bank of England sufficiently to compel the Bank to restrict lending and curtail credit, precipitating a crisis followed by economic dislocation and stagnation.

The dispute between the Smithean and Humean traditions turns on whether a stable equilibrium for a single banking firm can be determined. According to Hume, there is none, because the market value of a banknote exceeds the trivial cost of printing the note. On this view, later echoed by Thomas Tooke before defecting from the Currency School to the Banking School (Arnon, 1991), free banking is akin to swindling.

According to Smith, banks expand their lending and money creation until the incentive for further expansion is exhausted. But that incentive is not unlimited. Expansion is constrained by the willingness of the public to hold additional banknotes or deposits created by the bank and the costs incurred by the bank to expand its operations, costs that exceed the mere cost of ink and paper on which banknotes are printed. Each bank eventually reaches an equilibrium at which it perceives no further opportunity for profitable expansion, given its costs and the willingness of the public to hold additional liabilities issued by the bank.[4] As shown above in Chapter 3, this argument, sketched by Smith in the *Wealth of Nations*, was refined and further elaborated by John Fullarton (1845).

Taking the presumed behavior of a purely metallic currency as the model to which a convertible currency supplied by a competitive banking system should conform, the Currency School proposed a 100-percent

[4] An important subsidiary assumption is that the liabilities of individual banks (either banknotes or deposits) are distinguishable from one another. If those liabilities were not distinguishable, clearly each issuing institution would have no reason not to increase its issue without limit. Indeed, before changing his mind and opposing the Currency Principle, Thomas Tooke famously compared free trade in banking to free trade in swindling.

marginal gold-reserve requirement on banknotes over and above a fixed fiduciary issue that would be allowed to the banking system, thereby providing sufficient profit to existing banks to elicit their acquiescence to a ceiling on their note issues and a 100-percent marginal gold-reserve requirement.[5]

The Humean view of banking was later formalized, in what is called the money multiplier, by C. A. Phillips (1920). In the simplest model of the money multiplier, all money is held as bank deposits, and banks "lend" all the reserves that they hold beyond the minimum percentage of their deposits that they are required to hold in reserve. If the quantity of reserves is R and the required reserve ratio is rr, then the quantity of deposits, Q, equals R/rr. If rr equals zero, then the quantity of deposits is infinite, and hyperinflation is the result. To prevent this catastrophic outcome, rr must be set greater than zero.

The money multiplier was an invaluable tool whereby the quantity theory of money could make to accommodate, though far from seamlessly, the behavior of the banking system within its purview.[6] The accommodation involved defining a monetary base, B, consisting of currency, C, and bank reserves, R, and a money multiplier, m, reflecting the ratio between the total quantity of money (currency plus deposits) and reserves (gold or fiat) held by the monetary authority. The product of the monetary base and the money multiplier ($B \times m$) was then identified as the quantity of money, M, in the quantity-theoretic equation of exchange determining the price level, in either the Fisherian form $MV = PQ$, where V is the velocity of circulation, Q is output or income, and P

[5] Deposits were not covered by the Bank Charter Act, a lacuna repeatedly noted by the Banking School, so the use of deposits became increasingly widespread—a development not unrelated to the ceiling imposed on the total quantity of banknotes by the Bank Charter Act—the effect of the Bank Charter Act steadily declined over the course of the nineteenth century.

[6] The textbook form of the money multiplier$m$ is $(1 + c)/(c + rr + er)$ was c is the ratio of currency to deposits held by the public, rr is the legally required percentage of the deposits that they have created that banks must hold in the form of reserves and er is the ratio of excess reserves held by banks to the deposits that they have created. The multiplier implicitly assumes that banks and the public make decisions about desired *ratios* rather than *quantities*, as if households made consumption decisions about how much fish and meat and bread to purchase in terms of proportions between different items consumed rather than adjusting those quantities based on circumstances and preferences without regard to the ratios in which the items are consumed. Underlying assumptions about how agents behave are thus determined by algebraic convenience not economic theory.

is the price level, or the Cambridge form $M = kPQ$, where k $(= 1/V)$ represents the fraction of total income held by the public in the form of money.

The problem for the quantity theory is that M consists mostly of liabilities created by fractional-reserve banks, not by the monetary authority. The problem was supposedly solved by the money multiplier, whereby any change in B is transformed into a corresponding change in M. But the money multiplier itself depends on decisions made not by the monetary authority: decisions by the public about how much currency to hold, and decisions by the banks about how much reserves to hold. Those decisions can cause the money multiplier to change. Even worse, far from representing a structural *supply* relationship between the monetary base and the quantity of money, the money multiplier is a reduced form, dependent on both the *demand* of the public to hold currency and the derived *demand* of the banking system to hold reserves. To import a reduced form of demand relationships into a purported money-supply function is an elementary analytical blunder,[7] but it went unnoticed, because it allowed an aggregate quantity of money consisting of disparate components (currency and deposits) to be defined as if there were no analytical distinction between them, to operationalize a simplified quantity theory purporting to explain the price level and nominal income.

The problematic nature of the money multiplier was never explicitly addressed until it was attacked in the 1960s by what was then called the New View. Tobin's 1963 paper "Commercial Banks as Creators of Money" served as a definitive criticism of the money multiplier. His key analytical insight was to view commercial banks as profit-maximizing firms, deciding how much money (deposits) to create based on their marginal costs and marginal revenues. In this approach, there is no inherent tendency for banks to create more money than the public, at any moment, wish to hold. Bank money created in this fashion is not a "hot potato" transferred from one holder to another until other economic variables have adjusted to accommodate it. On the contrary, just as there is an economic mechanism for banks to create money balances (deposits), derived from a comparison of revenues and costs, there is a corresponding

[7] Of course, such a device was a violation of what later came to be known as the Lucas Critique, wherein a reduced form derived from deeper, but unspecified, structural equations is treated as if it were itself a structural relationship embodying at least qualitatively a definite relationship between the variables in the reduced form.

mechanism to extinguish those balances. Voilá, Fullarton's law of reflux rediscovered after more than a century!

Tobin's argument elicited fierce responses from Monetarists (Brunner, 1971; Yeager, 1968), and even Harry Johnson (1971a) responded dismissively. In part, the negative reaction reflected a misunderstanding of what Tobin's argument actually proved, a misunderstanding perhaps even shared by Tobin himself. The presumption seems to have been that, if a direct market mechanism tends to keep the nominal quantity of deposits supplied by banks equal the nominal amount demanded by the public, then banks could not be a source of monetary disequilibrium, and the friction that provides monetary policy the traction with which to affect economic activity would be eliminated. Tobin's analysis seemed to imply that, contrary to Monetarist and quantity-theoretic reasoning, monetary policy is ineffectual. But this inference was unwarranted, inasmuch as it presumed an illegitimate conflation of currency issued by the monetary authority (what was called outside money) with deposits (inside money) created by commercial banks. But even if the quantity of deposits created by the banking system is a distinct variable with a determinate equilibrium solution, and powerful economic forces propel the nominal quantity of deposits toward that amount, the control of the monetary authority over the monetary base enables the monetary authority to control the nominal GDP and the price level.

By analogy, the law of reflux did not prevent Fullarton from acknowledging that, given convertibility into gold, the price level was governed by the real value of gold, determined at any moment by the global stock of gold and the real and monetary demands to hold or use gold. Given that real value of gold, banks would supply whatever quantities of banknotes and deposits the public wished to hold. A similar analysis applies to a fiat-money system except that the price level is determined by the stock of, and demand for, the fiat currency instead of the stock of, and demand for, gold. Given the price level determined by the supply of, and demand for, the fiat currency, banks produce whatever quantity of deposits the public demands. But that quantity itself depends on the price level.

Fullarton's Smithian idea that the creation of liquid liabilities exchanged for illiquid liabilities of the public is subject to equilibrating forces that tend to equate the quantity of bank liabilities in the hands of the public with the amount that the public wishes to hold was clearly ripe for rediscovery in the 1960s. And Tobin's contribution was followed by a number of other contributions including by one of Friedman's own students Benjamin Klein (1974) as well by Fischer Black (1970 [2010]) and Earl Thompson (1974), developing the idea of a competitive supply of money, and refuting Friedman's (1960) Humean claim that competition among banks to supply money is inherently inflationary and self-destructive.

The endogeneity of money has also figured prominently in the work of many post-Keynesian theorists, notably Basil Moore (1988). Although Moore cited Tobin's work extensively, he does not mention Fullarton or other classical antecedents to his position. But other authors have commented on the connection and that the ideas of the Banking School have left their imprint or been rediscovered by a variety of authors who are otherwise not usually considered to be of like mind. More recently Perry Mehrling (1996, 2020) has further extended the application of the law of reflux to modern monetary arrangements.

Although the monetary approach to the balance of payments of which Harry Johnson was probably the most important figure, is of more direct relevance to the next section than to this section, Johnson also came round to the view that the quantity of money at least to countries with fixed exchange rates is an endogenous rather than a policy variable under the control of the monetary authorities. But it also possible that Johnson came to accept that the endogeneity of the money supply may not be under the control of the monetary authority even when the monetary authority does not maintain a fixed exchange rate. Johnson (1971b, 1971c) evidenced an increasing interest in how competitive forces in banking could work themselves out in the form of interest payments on deposits (of the sort emphasized by Tobin and also hinted at by Fullarton and earlier classical writers) without the destabilizing effects that Hume, the Currency School and their followers attributed to competitive banking.

7.3 Price-Specie-Flow Mechanism

The tortured intellectual history of the price-specie-flow mechanism (PSFM) necessarily begins with a still classic exposition in a Hume (1752 [2006]) essay, which has remained a staple of the theory of international adjustment under the gold standard or any international system of fixed exchange rates. Regrettably, the two-and-a-half-century life span of PSFM provides no ground for optimism about the prospects for progress in what some are pleased to call, without irony, economic science.

PSFM describes how, under a gold standard, national price levels tend to be equalized, with deviations between the national price levels in any two countries inducing gold to be shipped from the country with higher prices to the one with lower prices until prices are equalized. Premised on a version of the quantity theory of money in which (1) the price level in each country on the gold standard is determined by the quantity of money in that country, and (2) money consists entirely in gold coin or bullion, Hume elegantly articulated a model of disturbance and equilibration after an exogenous change in the stock of gold in one country.

Viewing banks as inflationary engines of financial disorder, Hume disregarded banks and their convertible monetary liabilities in his account of PSFM, leaving to others the task of describing the international adjustment process under a gold standard with fractional-reserve banking. The task of devising an institutional framework, within which PSFM could operate, for a system of fractional-reserve banking proved to be problematic and ultimately unsuccessful.

For three-quarters of a century, PSFM served a purely theoretical function. During the Bullionist debates of the first two decades of the nineteenth century, triggered by the suspension of the convertibility of the pound sterling into gold in 1797, PSFM served as a theoretical benchmark, not a guide for policy, it being generally assumed that, when convertibility was resumed, international monetary equilibrium would be restored automatically.

However, the 1821 resumption was followed by severe and recurring monetary disorders, leading some economists, who formed what became known as the Currency School, to view PSFM as a normative criterion for ensuring smooth adjustment to international gold flows. That criterion, the Currency Principle, stated that the total currency in circulation in Britain should increase or decrease by exactly as much as the amount of gold flowing into or out of Britain.[8] In practice, the criterion was understood to mean that, given an existing fiduciary note issue against which no gold reserves were held, banknotes beyond that fiduciary issue should be issued only upon a corresponding gold inflow into Britain, while any gold outflow should occasion an equal reduction in the quantity of outstanding banknotes.

[8] In principle, both banknotes and (at least checkable) deposits should have been included in the definition of money. However, the Currency Principle was usually formulated in terms of banknotes, with deposits excluded from the definition of currency. The anomalous treatment of deposits was criticized effectively by opponents of the Currency Principle, but supporters of the Currency Principle, with rare exceptions, defended the distinction.

The Currency Principle, codified by the Bank Charter Act of 1844, sought to mimic the Humean mechanism, through a variety of restrictions on the right of disparate note-issuing banks in the United Kingdom, in England and Wales, Scotland and Ireland, and the imposition of a 100-marginal gold-reserve requirement on any newly created banknotes. The opposition to the Bank Charter Act was led by the Banking School, which flatly rejected the quantitative limits of the Bank Charter Act as both unnecessary and counterproductive, because banks, obligated to redeem their liabilities directly or indirectly in gold, would issue liabilities only insofar as they expected those liabilities to be willingly held by the public, or, if not, to be capable to redeem any excess liabilities whenever redemption was demanded.

Rejecting the Humean view that banks issue banknotes or create deposits without constraint, the Banking School accepted Smith's view that banks issue money in a form more convenient to hold, and to transact with, than metallic money, so that bank money allows an equivalent amount of gold to be shifted from monetary to real (non-monetary) uses, providing a net social savings. For a small open economy, the diversion (and likely export) of gold bullion from monetary to non-monetary uses has negligible effect on prices (which are internationally, not locally, determined).

The quarter-century following enactment of the Bank Charter Act showed that the Act had not eliminated monetary disturbances, the government having been compelled to suspend the Act in 1847, 1857, and 1866 to prevent incipient crises from causing financial collapse. Indeed, it was precisely the fear that liquidity might not be forthcoming that precipitated increased demands for liquidity that the Act made it impossible to accommodate. Suspending the Act was sufficient to end the crises with limited intervention by the Bank.

Surprisingly, the disappointing results of the Bank Charter Act provided little vindication to the Banking School. Instead, a partial, uneasy, and not entirely coherent, accommodation seemed to emerge between PSFM doctrine and the reality of a monetary system in which the money stock consists mostly of banknotes and bank deposits issued by fractional-reserve banks. But despite the failure of the Bank Charter Act, PSFM achieved almost canonical status in expert opinion, continuing, albeit with some notable exceptions, to serve as the textbook model of the gold standard.

The requirement that gold flows induce equal changes in the quantity of money within a country into (or from) which gold is flowing was replaced by an admonition that gold flows lead to "appropriate" changes in the central-bank discount rate, or in an alternative monetary instrument, to cause the quantity of money to change in the same direction as the gold flow. While such vague maxims, sometimes described as "the rules of the game," gave only directional guidance about how to respond to change in gold reserves, their hortatory character, and avoidance of quantitative guidance, allowed monetary authorities latitude to avoid the self-inflicted crises induced by the quantitative limits of the Bank Charter Act.

Nevertheless, the myth of rules relating the quantity of money in a country to fluctuations in its gold reserves, whose observance ensured the smooth functioning of the international gold standard, enshrined PSFM as the theoretical paradigm for international monetary adjustment under the gold standard.

That paradigm was misconceived in four ways that can be briefly summarized.

1. Contrary to PSFM, changes in the quantity of money in a gold-standard country cannot change local prices proportionately, because prices of tradable goods in that country are constrained by arbitrage to equal the prices of those goods in other countries.
2. Contrary to PSFM, changes in local gold reserves are not necessarily caused either by non-monetary disturbances such as shifts in the terms of trade between countries or by local monetary disturbances (e.g., overissue by local banks) that must be reversed or counteracted by central-bank policy.
3. Contrary to PSFM, changes in the national price levels of gold-standard countries were uncorrelated with gold flows, and changes in national price levels were positively, not negatively, correlated.
4. Contrary to PSFM, local banks and monetary authorities exhibit their own demands for gold reserves, demands exhibited by law (i.e., by legal requirements to hold gold reseres equal to some fraction of banknotes issued by banks or monetary authorities) or by choice (i.e., independent of legally required gold holdings). Such changes in gold reserves may be caused by changes in the local demands for gold by local banks and the monetary authorities in one or more countries.

Many of the misconceptions underlying PSFM were identified by Fullarton's criticism of the Currency School. In articulating the classical law of reflux, he established the logical independence of the quantity of convertible money in a country from the quantity of gold reserves held by the monetary authority. The gold reserves held by individual banks, or their deposits with the Bank of England, are not the raw material from which banks create money, either banknotes or deposits. Rather, it is their creation of banknotes or deposits when extending credit to customers that generates a derived demand to hold liquid assets (i.e., gold) to allow them to accommodate the demands of customers and other banks to redeem banknotes and deposits. Causality runs from creating banknotes and deposits to holding reserves, not vice versa.

The misconceptions inherent in PSFM and the resulting misunderstanding of gold flows under the gold standard led to a further misconception known as sterilization: the idea that central banks, violating the obligations imposed by "the rules of the game," do not allow, or deliberately prevent, local money stocks from changing as their gold holdings change. The misconception is the presumption that gold inflows ought necessarily to cause increases in local money stocks. The mechanisms causing local money stocks to change are different from those causing gold flows. And insofar as those mechanisms are related, causality flows from the local money stock to gold reserves, not vice versa.

Gold flows also result when monetary authorities transform their own asset holdings into gold. Notable examples of such transformations occurred in the 1870s when many countries abandoned their de jure bimetallic (and de facto silver) standards to the gold standard. Monetary authorities in those countries transformed silver holdings into gold, driving the value of gold up and silver down. Similarly, but with more catastrophic consequences, the Bank of France, in 1928 after France restored the gold standard, began redeeming holdings of foreign-exchange reserves (financial claims on the United States or Britain, payable in gold) into gold. Following the French example, other countries rejoining the gold standard redeemed foreign exchange for gold, causing gold appreciation and deflation that led to the Great Depression (see Chapters 13 and 14).

The Bank of France has been widely criticized by both contemporary (e.g., Hawtrey, 1932) and subsequent (e.g., Eichengreen, 1992; Friedman, 1991; Johnson, 1997; Mouré, 1991, 2002) critics. But many critics, misled by the sterilization misconception, argued that the fault of the Bank of France lay in not increasing the quantity of francs, as required by the "rules of the game," along with the huge gold inflow. Acknowledging that his earlier treatment of the Great Depression (Friedman & Schwartz, 1963) had not adequately taken into account its international causes, focusing exclusively on the monetary mismanagement of the Federal Reserve, Friedman (1991) in a forward to the memoir of Emile Moreau, Governor of the Bank of France in the 1920s and 1930s, described the problem as follows.

> Rereading the memoirs of this splendid translation ... has impressed me with important subtleties that I missed when I read the memoirs in a language not my own and in which I am far from completely fluent. Had I fully appreciated those subtleties when Anna Schwartz and I were writing our *A Monetary History of the United States*, we would likely have assessed responsibility for the international character of the Great Depression somewhat differently. We attributed responsibility for the initiation of a worldwide contraction to the United States and I would not alter that judgment now. However, we also remarked, "The international effects were severe and the transmission rapid, not only because the gold-exchange standard had rendered the international financial system more vulnerable to disturbances, but also because the United States did not follow gold-standard rules." Were I writing that sentence today, I would say "because the United States and France did not follow gold-standard rules."

Let us pause to note Friedman's assertion that the United States and France did not follow "gold-standard rules." Warming up to the idea, he accused them of sterilization.

> Benjamin Strong and Emile Moreau were admirable characters of personal force and integrity. But ... the common policies they followed were misguided and contributed to the severity and rapidity of transmission of the U.S. shock to the international community. We stressed that the U.S. "did not permit the inflow of gold to expand the U.S. money stock. We not only sterilized it, we went much further. Our money stock moved perversely, going down as the gold stock went up" from 1929 to 1931.
>
> Strong and Moreau tried to reconcile two ultimately incompatible objectives: fixed exchange rates and internal price stability. Thanks to the level at which Britain returned to gold in 1925, the U.S. dollar was undervalued, and thanks to the level at which France returned to gold at the end of 1926, so was the French franc. Both countries as a result experienced substantial gold inflows. Gold-standard rules called for letting the stock

> of money rise in response to the gold inflows and for price inflation in the U.S. and France, and deflation in Britain, to end the over-and under-valuations. But both Strong and Moreau were determined to prevent inflation and accordingly both sterilized the gold inflows, preventing them from providing the required increase in the quantity of money.

Friedman's discussion of sterilization is at odds with basic theory. Working with a naïve version of PSFM, he imagines that gold flows passively respond to trade balances independent of monetary forces and that the monetary authority under a gold standard is supposed to ensure that the domestic money stock varies roughly in proportion to its gold reserves. Ignoring the international deflationary dynamic, he asserts that the US money stock perversely declined from 1929 to 1931, while its gold stock increased. With a faltering banking system, the public shifted from holding demand deposits to currency. Gold reserves were legally required against currency, but not against demand deposits, so the shift from deposits to currency entailed an increase gold reserves.

At first, the increase in gold reserves had been the consequence of tightened monetary policy by the Fed, causing an influx of gold as a means of satisfying the unsatisfied demand for cash by the public. Later, after deflation set in, falling asset values and bankruptcies undermined the US banking system, causing the bank failures that led the public to shift from deposits to currency that amplified the inflow of gold. The United States and France together initiated a vicious cycle of increasing demand for gold and deflation for which the gold standard provided no automatic self-correction mechanism. (See Chapters 13 and 14).

Friedman also erred in stating "the common policies they followed were misguided and contributed to the severity and rapidity of transmission of the U.S. shock to the international community." The shock to the international community originated not in the United States but in France. The Fed could have absorbed and mitigated the shock by allowing an outflow of its huge gold reserves, but instead amplified the shock by raising interest rates to nearly unprecedented levels, drawing gold into the United States.

After correctly noting the incompatibility between fixed exchange rates and internal price stability, Friedman contradicts himself by asserting that, in seeking to stabilize their internal price levels, Strong and Moreau violated the gold-standard "rules," as if it were the rules, not arbitrage, that constrained national price under a gold standard to converge toward a common level.

Friedman's assertion that, after 1925, the dollar was undervalued and sterling overvalued was not wrong. But he misunderstood the consequences of currency undervaluation and overvaluation under the gold standard, a confusion stemming from an underlying misconception, derived from PSFM, that foreign-exchange rates adjust to balance trade flows, so that, in equilibrium, no country runs a trade deficit or surplus.

Thus, in Friedman's view, dollar undervaluation and sterling overvaluation implied a US trade surplus and a British trade deficit, causing gold to flow from Britain to the United States. Under gold-standard "rules," the US money stock and US prices were supposed to rise while the British money stock and prices were supposed to fall until undervaluation and overvaluation were eliminated. Friedman therefore blamed sterilization of gold inflows by the Fed for preventing the necessary increase in the US money stock and price level to restore equilibrium. But, in fact, from 1925 through 1928, prices in the United States were roughly stable and prices in Britain fell slightly. Violating gold-standard "rules" did not prevent the US and British price levels from converging, a convergence driven by market forces, not "rules."

The stance of monetary policy in a gold-standard country had minimal effect on either the quantity of money or the price level in that country, which were mainly determined by the internationally determined value of gold. What the stance of national monetary policy determines under the gold standard is whether the quantity of money in the country adjusts to the quantity demanded by the creation or withdrawal of money through the domestic monetary system or by an inflow or outflow of gold. Sufficiently tight domestic monetary policy restricting the quantify of domestic money causes a compensatory gold inflow increasing the domestic money stock, while sufficiently easy money causes a compensatory outflow of gold reducing the domestic money stock. Tightness or ease of domestic monetary policy under the gold standard mainly affected gold and foreign-exchange reserves, and, only minimally, the quantity of domestic money and the domestic price level.

However, the combined effects of many countries simultaneously tightening monetary policy in a deliberate, or even inadvertent, attempt to accumulate—or at least prevent the loss—of gold reserves could indeed drive up the international value of gold through a deflationary process affecting prices in all gold-standard countries. Even while admitting that, in his *Monetary History*, he had understated the effect of the Bank of France on the Great Depression, Friedman referred only to the overvaluation of sterling and undervaluation of the dollar and franc as causes of the Great Depression, remaining oblivious to the deflationary effects of gold accumulation and appreciation.

It was thus nonsensical for Friedman to argue that the mistake of the Bank of France during the Great Depression was not to increase the quantity of francs in proportion to the increase of its gold reserves. The problem was not that the quantity of francs was too low; it was that the Bank of France allowed the French public no means of increasing the quantity of francs that they held other than to import gold.

Unlike Friedman, F. A. Hayek (1932 [1984]) actually defended the policy of the Bank of France, denying that the Bank of France had "systematically hoarded gold" by nearly quadrupling its gold reserves between 1928 and 1932.

> France did pursue an extremely cautious foreign policy after the franc stabilized at a level which considerably undervalued it with respect to its domestic purchasing power, and prevented an expansion of credit proportional to the amount of gold coming in. Nevertheless, France did not prevent her monetary circulation from increasing by the very same amount as that of the gold inflow – and this alone is necessary for the gold standard to function.

Thus, for Hayek to absolve the Bank of France for its policies, it was necessary for the Bank to have done no more than to discharge its minimum legal obligation under the gold standard to buy gold with francs at the legal price of gold in terms of francs, notwithstanding the effects of the enormous gold accumulation by the Bank on the international value of gold and, consequently, on international deflation.

That economists as eminent as Hayek and Friedman could either defend or criticize, the conduct of the Bank of France during the Great Depression, because the Bank either did, or did not, follow "the rules of the game" under which the gold standard supposedly operated, shows the uselessness and irrelevance of the "rules of the game" for policy guidance. For that reason alone, the failure of empirical studies to find evidence that "the rules of the game" were followed during the heyday of the gold standard is unsurprising. But the deeper reason for that lack of evidence is that PSFM, whose implementation "the rules of the game" were supposed to guarantee, was based on a misunderstanding of the international adjustment mechanism under either the gold standard or any fixed-exchange-rates system.

Despite the grip of PSFM over most of the profession, a few economists did show a deeper understanding of the adjustment mechanism. The idea that the price level in terms of gold directly constrained the movements of national price levels across countries was indeed recognized by writers as diverse as Keynes (1913), Mises (1912 [1934]), and Hawtrey (1913) who all pointed out that the prices of internationally traded commodities were constrained by arbitrage and that the free movement of capital across countries would limit discrepancies in interest rates across countries attached to the gold standard, points that could already be traced back to Smith, Thornton, Ricardo, Fullarton and Mill in the classical period. But, until the monetary approach to the balance of payments became popular in the 1970s, only Hawtrey consistently and systematically deduced the implications of those insights in analyzing both the Great Depression and the Bretton Woods system of fixed, but adjustable, exchange rates following World War II.

The inconsistencies and internal contradictions of PSFM were sometimes recognized, but usually overlooked, by business-cycle theorists when focusing on the disturbing influence of central banks, perpetuating mistakes of the Humean Currency School doctrine that attributed cyclical disturbances to the misbehavior of local banking systems that were inherently disposed to overissue their liabilities.

7.4 The Real-Bills Doctrine, the Scope of Banking and Lender of Last Resort

In the two previous sections, I contrasted the Humean and Smithian views of fractional-reserve banking and its role in providing the public with the desired quantity of money (banknotes and deposits) and promoting international adjustment. The cash created by banks consists of liabilities on themselves that they exchange for liabilities on the public. Liabilities on the public accepted by banks are bank assets, generating revenue streams whereby banks cover their outlays including obligations to creditors and stockholders.

The preceding discussion focused on the liability side of bank balance sheets, and whether any economic forces limit the size of those balance sheets, implying a point of equilibrium bank expansion. Believing that banks have an unlimited incentive to issue liabilities, their face value exceeding their cost of production, Hume regarded banks as dangerous and inflationary. Smith disagreed, arguing that, although bank money is a less costly alternative to the full-bodied money preferred by Hume, banks cannot create liabilities without limit, because, unless they exchange their liabilities for assets generating corresponding revenue streams, they will be unable to redeem those liabilities, which their creditors, at will, are entitled to do. To enhance the attractiveness of those liabilities and increase the demand to hold them, competitive banks promise to convert those liabilities, at a fixed rate, into an asset whose value they cannot control. Banks, therefore, have neither the capacity nor the incentive to cause inflation.

I turn now to another topic: whether the Smithian rejection of the idea that banks are systematically biased toward overissuing liabilities implies that banks require no external control or intervention. I begin by briefly referring to Smith's support of the real-bills doctrine, discussed in Chapter 4, and extend that discussion to two other issues: the lender of last resort and the scope of banking.

A. Real-Bills Doctrine

I argued in Chapter 4 that, besides sketching the outlines of Fullarton's argument for the law of reflux, Adam Smith recommended that banks observe a form of the real-bills doctrine, namely that banks issue sight liabilities only in exchange for real commercial bills of short (usually 90-days) duration. Increases in the demand for money cause bank balance sheets to expand; decreases cause them to contract. Unlike Mints (1945), who identified the law of reflux with the real-bills doctrine, I suggested that Smith viewed the real-bills doctrine as a pragmatic policy to facilitate contractions in banks' balance sheets as required by the reflux of their liabilities. By issuing sight liabilities only in exchange for short-term bills, thereby limiting the duration mismatch between liabilities and assets, banks would facilitate the contraction of balance sheets when demand for their liabilities decreased, thereby minimizing, or rendering unnecessary, liquidation of longer-term assets at depressed prices.

On this reading, Smith recognized that banking policy ought to take account of the composition of bank balance sheets, in particular, the assets that banks accept in exchange for their sight liabilities. I would also emphasize that, on this reading, Smith did not believe, as did many later advocates of the doctrine, that lending on the security of real bills is sufficient to prevent a change in the price level. Even if banks have no systematic incentive to overissue their liabilities, unless those liabilities are made convertible into an asset whose value is not controlled by the banks, the value of bank liabilities is undetermined. Convertibility into a real asset anchors the value of bank liabilities, thereby increasing the attractiveness of those liabilities to the public and the public's willingness to accept and hold them.

But Smith's support for the real-bills doctrine indicates that, while understanding the equilibrating tendencies of competition on bank operations, he also recognized the inherent instability of banking caused by fluctuations in the value and liquidity of their assets. Smith's support for the real-bills doctrine addressed one type of instability: the maturity mismatch between banks' assets and liabilities. But there are other sources of instability, which may require further institutional or policy measures beyond the general laws of property and contract whose application and enforcement, in Smith's view, usually sufficed for the self-interested conduct of private firms to lead to socially benign outcomes.

In the remainder of this section, I consider two other methods of addressing the vulnerability of bank assets to sudden losses of value: (1) the creation or empowerment of a lender of last resort capable of lending to illiquid, but solvent, banks possessing good security (valuable assets) as collateral against which to borrow, and (2) limits beyond the real-bills doctrine over the permissible activities undertaken by commercial banks.

B. Lender of Last Resort

Although the real-bills doctrine limits the exposure of bank balance sheets to adverse shocks to the value of long-term assets, even banks whose liabilities were issued in exchange for short-term real bills of exchange may be unable to meet all demands for redemption in periods of extreme financial distress, when debtors cannot sell their products at the prices they expected and cannot discharge their own obligations to creditors. If banks are called upon to redeem their liabilities, banks may be faced with a choice of depleting their cash reserves when they are most needed, or liquidating other assets at substantial, if not catastrophic, losses.

Smith's version of the real-bills doctrine addressed one aspect of balance-sheet risk, but the underlying problem is deeper and more complicated than the liquidity issue that concerned Smith. The claims accepted by banks in exchange for their liabilities are typically not easily marketable, so if assets must be shed quickly to satisfy demands for payment, banks' solvency may be jeopardized by consequent capital losses. Limiting portfolios to short-term assets limits exposure to such losses, but only when the disturbances requiring rapid asset liquidation affect only a relatively small number of banks. As the number of affected banks increases, their ability to counter the disturbance is impaired, as the interbank market for credit starts to freeze up, leaving all banks unable to offer short-term relief to, or receive it from, other momentarily illiquid banks. It is then that emergency lending by a lender of last resort to illiquid, but possibly still solvent,[9] banks are necessary.

What causes a cluster of expectational errors by banks in exchanging their liabilities for claims supplied by their customers that suddenly become less valuable than they were upon acceptance? Are financial crises that result in, or are caused by, asset write-downs by banks caused by random clusters of errors by banks, or are there systematic causes of such errors? Does the danger lie in the magnitude of the errors or in the transmission mechanism?

Here, too, the Humean and Smithian traditions seem to be at odds, offering different answers to problems, or, if not answers, at least different approaches to problems. Focusing on the liability side of bank balance sheets, the Humean tradition emphasizes the expansion of bank lending and the consequent creation of banknotes or deposits as the main impulse to macroeconomic fluctuations, a boom-bust or credit cycle triggered by banks' lending to finance either business investment or consumer spending. Despite their theoretical differences, both Austrian business-cycle theory and Friedmanite Monetarism share a common intellectual ancestry, traceable by way of the Currency School to Hume, identifying the source of business-cycle fluctuations in excessive growth in the quantity of money.

[9] In a crisis, the distinction between illiquidity and insolvency is no longer relevant, because the solvency of all banks is systemically endangered. The distinction between illiquidity and insolvency is relevant under normal conditions, not when, to adapt Lavington's (1922) phrase, the insolvency of each is the result of the insolvency of all.

The eclectic Smithian tradition accommodates both monetary and non-monetary business-cycle theories, but balance-sheet effects on banks are more naturally accommodated within the Smithian tradition than the Humean tradition with its focus on the liabilities rather than the assets of banks.

The current state of our knowledge provides no clear answers to whether serious financial disturbances result from big expectational errors, whether random or systematic, or tell us much about the relative importance of the initial errors versus transmission effects. However, in later chapters, I will be arguing that the Great Depression was caused by one big error. After the steep deflation and depression of 1920–1922, followed by a gradual restoration of the gold standard, fears of further deflation were dispelled and steady economic expansion, especially in the United States, resulted. Suddenly in 1929, as France and other countries rejoined the gold standard, the fears voiced by Hawtrey and Cassel that restoring the gold standard could have serious deflationary consequences appeared increasingly likely to be realized. Real signs of deflation began to appear in the summer of 1929, and a few months later, the stock market collapsed. Rather than use monetary policy to counter incipient deflation, policy makers and many economists mistakenly argued that deflation was the solution not the problem. And the Depression came.

It is generally agreed that the 2008 financial crisis that triggered the Little Depression (aka Great Recession) was largely the result of a housing bubble fueled by unsound mortgage lending by banks and questionable underwriting practices in packaging and marketing of mortgage-backed securities. However, the housing bubble seems to have burst in the spring of 2007, yet the crisis did not start until September 2008.

It is at least possible, as I have argued (Glasner, 2018) that, despite the financial fragility caused by the housing bubble and unsound lending practices that fueled the bubble, the crisis would have been avoided but for a reflexive policy tightening by the Federal Reserve starting in 2007 that caused a recession that started in December 2007 and deteriorated rapidly in the summer of 2008. Distracted by rising headline inflation owing to rising oil prices that summer, the Fed, instead of easing monetary policy to counter a deepening recession, kept its interest-rate target steady from May until October of 2008. If my interpretation is correct, the financial crisis of 2008 and the subsequent Little Depression (aka Great Recession) were at least as much caused by mistaken monetary-policy decisions as by the unsound lending practices and mistaken expectations of lenders.

It is when all agents are cash-constrained that a lender of last resort that can provide the liquidity unavailable from the usual suppliers is necessary to avoid a systemic breakdown. In 2008, the Fed was unwilling to satisfy demands for liquidity until the crisis had deteriorated to the point of a worldwide collapse. In the nineteenth century, Thornton and Fullarton understood that the Bank of England was uniquely able to provide liquidity in such circumstances, recommending that it lend freely in periods of financial stress.

That policy was not viewed favorably either by Humean supporters of the Currency Principle, opposed to all forms of fractional-reserve banking, or by Smithian supporters of free banking, who distrusted the privileged central-banking position granted to the Bank of England. Although the Fed in 2008 acknowledged that it was both a national and international lender of last resort, it was tragically slow in taking the necessary actions to end the crisis after allowing it to spiral nearly out of control.

While cogent arguments have been made that a free-banking alternative to the lender-of-last-resort services of the Bank of England might have been possible in the nineteenth century, even a free-banking system would require a mechanism for handling periods of financial stress. Free-banking supporters argue that bank clearinghouses have emerged spontaneously without central banks, and could provide the lender-of-last-resort services provided by central banks. But, insofar as bank clearinghouses would take on the lender-of-last-resort function, which involves some intervention and supervision of bank activities by either the clearinghouse or the central bank, the same anticompetitive or cartelistic objections to the provision of lender-of-last-resort services by central banks also would apply to the provision of those services by clearinghouses. So, the tension between libertarian, free-market principles and lender-of-last-resort services would not necessarily be eliminated if bank clearinghouses replaced central banks to provide those services.

This is an appropriate place to consider Walter Bagehot's contribution to the lender-of-last-resort doctrine. Building on the work of Thornton and Fullarton, Bagehot formulated the classic principle that, during times of financial distress, the Bank of England should lend freely at a penalty rate to banks on good security. Bagehot, himself, admitted to a certain unease in offering this advice, opining that it was regrettable that the Bank of England achieved a pre-eminent position in the British banking system, so that a decentralized banking system, along the lines of the Scottish free-banking system, could have evolved. But given the historical development of British banking, including the 1844 Bank Charter Act, Bagehot, an eminently practical man, had no desire to recommend radical reform, only to help the existing system operate as smoothly as it could be made to operate.

But the soundness of Bagehot's advice to lend freely at a penalty rate is dubious. In a financial crisis, the market rate of interest primarily reflects a liquidity premium not an expected real return on capital, the latter typically being depressed in a crisis. Charging a penalty rate to distressed borrowers in a crisis only raises the liquidity premium. Monetary policy ought to aim to reduce, not to increase, that premium. So Bagehot's advice, derived from a misplaced sense of what is practical and prudent and financially sound, rather than from sound analysis, was far from sound either analytically or financially.

Under the gold standard, or under any fixed-exchange-rate regime, a single country has an incentive to raise interest rates above the rates of other countries to prevent a gold outflow or attract an inflow. Under these circumstances, a failure of international cooperation can lead to competitive rate increases as monetary authorities scramble to maintain or increase their gold reserves. In testimony to the Macmillan Committee in 1930, Ralph Hawtrey masterfully described the obligation of a central bank in a crisis. Here is his exchange with the Chairman of the Committee, Hugh Macmillan:

> *Macmillan*: Suppose … without restricting credit … that gold had gone out to a very considerable extent, would that not have had very serious consequences on the international position of London?
> *Hawtrey*: I do not think the credit of London depends on any particular figure of gold holding. … The harm began to be done in March and April of 1925 [when] the fall in American prices started. There was no reason why the Bank of England should have taken any action at that time so far as the question of loss of gold is concerned. … I believed at the time and I still think that the right treatment would have been to restore the gold standard de facto before it was restored de jure. That is what all the other countries have done. … I would have suggested that we should have adopted the practice of always selling gold to a sufficient extent to prevent the exchange depreciating. There would have been no legal obligation to continue convertibility into gold … If that course had

been adopted, the Bank of England would never have been anxious about the gold holding, they would have been able to see it ebb away to quite a considerable extent with perfect equanimity, . . and might have continued with a 4 percent Bank Rate.

Macmillan: ... the course you suggest would not have been consistent with what one may call orthodox Central Banking, would it?

Hawtrey: I do not know what orthodox Central Banking is.

Macmillan: ... when gold ebbs away you must restrict credit as a general principle?

Hawtrey: ... that kind of orthodoxy is like conventions at bridge; you have to break them when the circumstances call for it. I think that a gold reserve exists to be used. ... Perhaps once in a century the time comes when you can use your gold reserve for the governing purpose, provided you have the courage to use practically all of it.

Hawtrey here was echoing Fullarton's insight that there is no rigid relationship between the gold reserves held by the Bank of England and the total quantity of sight liabilities created by the British banking system. Rather, he argued, the Bank should hold an ample reserve sufficient to satisfy the demand for gold in a crisis when a sudden and temporary demand for gold had to be accommodated. That was Hawtrey's advice, but not Bagehot's, whose concern was about banks' moral hazard and imprudent lending in the expectation of being rescued by the Bank of England in a crisis. Indeed, moral hazard is a problem, but, in a crisis, it is a secondary problem, when, as Hawtrey explained, alleviating the crisis, not discouraging moral hazard, must be the primary concern of the lender of last resort.

C. Scope of Banking

Inclined to find remedies for financial distress in structural reforms limiting the types of assets banks accept in exchange for their sight liabilities, Smith did not recommend a lender of last resort.[10] Another method of reducing risk, perhaps more in tune than a lender of last resort with

[10] See Laidler (1988) and Skaggs (1995) for discussions of the links between Thornton, Tooke, and Fullarton and, in turn, between them and Bagehot.

the Smithian real-bills doctrine, is to restrict the activities of banks that issue sight liabilities.

In Anglophone countries, commercial banking generally evolved as separate and distinct from investment banking. But it was only during the Great Depression and the resulting wave of bank failures that the combination of commercial and investment banking was legally prohibited by the Glass-Steagall Act, eventually repealed in 1999. On the Continent, where commercial banking penetrated less deeply into the fabric of economic and commercial life than in Anglophone countries, commercial banking developed more or less jointly with investment banking in what are called universal banks.

Whether the earlier, and more widespread, adoption of commercial banking in Anglophone countries than on the Continent contributed to the idea that no banking institution should provide both commercial- and investment-banking services is not a question about which I offer a conjecture, but it seems a topic worthy of study. The Glass-Steagall Act, which enforced that separation after being breached early in the twentieth century, a breach thought by some to have contributed to US bank failures in the Great Depression, was based on the presumption against combining commercial and investment banking in a single institution. But even apart from the concerns that led to enactment of Glass-Steagall, limiting the exposure of commercial banks, which supply most of the cash held by the public, to the balance-sheet risk associated with investment-banking activities seems reasonable. Moreover, the adoption of government deposit insurance after the Great Depression as well as banks' access to the discount window of the central bank may augment the moral hazard induced by deposit insurance and a lender of last resort, offsetting potential economies of scope associated with combining commercial and investment banking.

Although legal barriers to the combination of commercial and investment banking have long been eliminated, proposals for "narrow banking" that would restrict the activities undertaken by commercial banks continue to be made. Two different interpretations of narrow banking—one Humean and one Smithian—are possible.

While the Humean concern about banking was that banks are inherently disposed to overissue their liabilities, that concern was dismissed by the Smithian tradition, recognizing that banks, even if unconstrained by reserve requirements, would not issue liabilities beyond some optimal level. The Humean response to this concern has been to propose 100-percent-reserve banking, a comprehensive extension of the marginal reserve requirement on the issue of banknotes imposed by the Bank Charter Act. Such measures could succeed, as some supporters (Simons, 1936) came to realize, only if accompanied by a radical change in the financial practices and arrangements on which all current debt contracts are conducted. It is difficult to imagine that the necessary restructuring of economic activity would ever be implemented or tolerated.

The Humean concern was dismissed by the Smithian tradition, recognizing that banks, even if unconstrained by reserve requirements, have no incentive to issue liabilities without limit. The Smithian concern was whether banks could cope with balance-sheet risks after unexpected losses in the value of their assets. Although narrow-banking proposals are a legitimate and possibly worthwhile response to that concern, the acceptance by central banks of responsibility to act as a lender of last resort and widespread adoption of government deposit insurance to dampen contagion effects have taken the question of narrowing or restricting the functions of money-creating banks off the table. Whether we would be better served by another strategy for addressing the systemic risks associated with banks' creation of money than relying solely on deposit insurance and a lender of last resort is a question that still deserves thoughtful attention.

7.5 Rules Versus Discretion in Monetary Policy

The Bullion Report (Cannan, 1925), issued to Parliament in 1810, is an appropriate starting point from which to consider how the nature of monetary institutions and the role of monetary policy has been viewed within the Humean and Smithian traditions. The Report discussed several important theoretical issues, but its main purpose was to recommend an early resumption of the convertibility (suspended in 1797 early in the Napoleonic Wars) of banknotes issued by the Bank of England into gold, the gold standard then being regarded as a safe, workable, and largely self-regulating, monetary regime.

One might well identify the Bullion Report and the preceding debates as the first installment in a two-century-long series of discussions about the monetary institutions and the rules under which monetary policy should be implemented. Since the seminal contribution of Henry Simons (1936), these debates have been focused on the question whether monetary policy should be conducted according to explicit rules or at the discretion of the monetary authorities.[11] A detailed historical account of these debates will be presented in Chapter 8; my concern in this section is with how the presuppositions of the two traditions have informed the debates about rules versus discretion in monetary policy.

The Bullion Report acknowledged that gold was not an invariable standard of value. One of the authors of the Report, Henry Thornton (1802 [1939]), had defended the policy of the Bank of England not long after the suspension, arguing that a wisely crafted policy by the Bank of England had achieved a better outcome than would have occurred under convertibility. But the subsequent experience of monetary policy untethered to convertibility evidently persuaded Thornton that, over the long term, unconstrained policy was unlikely to result in better outcomes than would result if convertibility into gold was restored.

Despite the rejection by Parliament of the Report's recommendation to quickly restore the gold standard while the Napoleonic Wars were ongoing, the argument of the Report in favor of the gold standard undoubtedly influenced, even compelled, the decision to restore the gold standard after Napoleon's defeat. But formal restoration of gold standard in 1821 did not produce the anticipated monetary stability, with frequent monetary disturbances punctuated by financial crises occurring about once a decade until 1866. The disturbances led Parliament, under the influence of the Currency School, to pass the Bank Charter Act of 1844. As explained above, the Currency School viewed monetary disturbances as symptomatic of the failure of a mixed (gold and paper) currency to fluctuate exactly as a pure metallic currency would have.

Thus, in the Humean tradition, which became ascendant only after the Bullion Report confidently predicted monetary stability after its restoration, the gold standard is not considered to be a self-sustaining monetary system. Rather, it must be supplemented and constrained by quantitative rules governing the creation of bank liabilities to prevent cycles of overissue and monetary contraction from leading to financial crisis, insolvency and collapse. The Smithian tradition, while not dismissing the

[11] The original framing by Simons (1936) was between rules and authorities. I am not sure when the choice shifted from rule and authorities to rules and discretion. I suspect, but have not confirmed, that it was Friedman who reframed the discussion. In Chapter 8, relying on the seminal article by Dworkin (1967), I explain why the legal and philosophical meaning of "discretion" is very different from the sense in which Friedman and subsequent writers have used the term.

possibility of financial disorders, rejected the Humean diagnosis of cycles of overissue and contraction, boom and bust.

The functional identity between bank deposits and banknotes having been ignored by the quantitative rules imposed by the Bank Charter Act, the steady displacement of banknotes by bank deposits as the primary means of payment over the course of the nineteenth century eventually rendered the quantitative limits imposed by the Bank Charter Act on the creation of banknotes largely, if not entirely, irrelevant, thereby mitigating its harmful effects. Thus, by the last third of the nineteenth century, when the gold standard evolved into a truly international monetary system, an uneasy, and somewhat confused, compromise emerged in which, though the underlying rationale for quantitative rules was not discarded, rules were interpreted with sufficient vagueness to allow the system to function with the "rules of the game" that supposedly guided operation of the gold standard more honored in the breach than the observance (McCloskey & Zecher, 1976).

More than three decades of relative tranquility, financial and monetary order, and rapid growth under the international gold standard created a consensus, at least in elite opinion, that the gold standard was, and should remain, the pillar of sound national and international finance. Far from shaking faith in the gold standard, its breakdown at the start of World War I and the ensuing catastrophe reinforced the elite consensus in its favor, so that few, Fisher (1920) and Keynes (1923) being notable exceptions, questioned the objective of restoring it after the war. However, there was an understanding by some observers that the classical presumption that the gold standard was the reliable and secure arrangement by which to achieve a stable value of money was unlikely to be validated in the postwar environment without major reforms in its operation.

Ralph Hawtrey and Gustav Cassel,[12] in particular, forthrightly warned of the deflationary dangers of restoring the international gold standard without international cooperation to limit increases in the monetary demand for gold as countries rejoined the gold standard. The orthodox supporters of the gold standard criticized not only those who would abandon the gold standard, but also those, like Hawtrey and Cassel, who proposed international cooperation—disparagingly characterized as "monetary management"—to stabilize the value of gold and the international price level.

[12] The following discussion of the account of the Great Depression offered by Hawtrey and Cassel draws on Chapters 13 and 14 and Irwin (2012, 2014).

While conducting policy to avoid significant price-level fluctuations provoked the disapproval of the orthodox supporters of the gold standard, those supporters were untroubled by either the quantitative restraints of the Bank Charter Act or by the supposed constraints of "the rules of the game." Why the orthodox supporters of the gold standard rejected the goal of price-level stability as inconsistent with the gold standard while seeing no inconsistency between the gold standard and either the vague quantitative "rules of the game," or even the strict constraints of the Bank Charter Act is unclear, the underlying inconsistency never having even been noticed. Like the goal of price-level stability, those quantity rules may or may not have been justified in their own right; they may or may not have contributed to the smooth working of the gold standard, but in no sense were they essential to its operation.

These quantitative rules governing operation of the gold standard were the residue of the Humean analysis of a purely metallic currency, not a mixed currency consisting largely of the liabilities of a private banking system. While concern for price-level stability was never an explicit goal of the gold standard, the presumption that gold would normally serve as a stable measure of value was indeed a principal justification advanced in its favor.

Within the Smithian tradition, concern for price-level stability was as plausible a rule for the gold standard as "the rules of the game" so often invoked by orthodox supporters of the gold standard. Indeed, a century earlier David Ricardo (1816 [2015]) proposed his ingot plan for the postwar resumption of the gold standard precisely to limit the increase in the demand for gold after resumption for the express purpose of moderating its deflationary effects. Thus, impeccable classical precedent supported Hawtrey and Cassel in seeking to limit the increase in the monetary demand for gold following the postwar restoration of the gold standard.[13]

In Chapters 13 and 14, I discuss in detail the contributions of Hawtrey and Cassel and their diagnoses and accounts of the Great Depression. My concern here is to trace the influence of Hume and Smith on how

[13] Ludwig von Mises and F. A. Hayek, two leading supporters of the orthodox gold standard in the 1920s, opposed Britain's restoration of the gold standard in 1925 at the prewar parity, relying on Ricardo's somewhat obscure statement that he would never advise a country whose currency had depreciated by more than five percent against gold to restore a gold standard at the old parity. However, Mises and Hayek ignored Ricardo's ingot plan, whose express purpose was to limit the monetary demand for gold during a restoration to avoid an appreciation of gold and consequent deflation.

economists have thought about the monetary regimes and how they should be governed. Because the Humean tradition suffered from a dual misunderstanding of banking and the international adjustment mechanism, its chief nineteenth-century legacy was a misguided emphasis on quantitative rules governing the gold standard that were irrelevant or unworkable, at best, and disruptive and crisis-prone, at worst. In contrast, the Smithian tradition, generally endorsing the nineteenth-century consensus favoring the gold standard, developed no specific monetary rules other than the direct or indirect convertibility of bank liabilities into gold at a fixed parity, leaving the quantity of gold reserves held by banks and monetary authorities to the discretion of bankers and monetary authorities. But after the collapse of the gold standard during World War I, at least some within the Smithian tradition were seeking a new monetary regime, within or outside the framework of the gold standard, that would control and stabilize the price level.

After the international gold standard collapsed for the second time in less than twenty years, in the Great Depression, the search for a monetary regime to replace the gold standard took on an added urgency. Some economists retained their faith in the gold standard, others welcomed an absence of legal constraints that would empower monetary authorities to conduct policy as appropriate under the circumstances of the moment, and there were others who sought a new regime governed by clear rules.

An alternative policy rule more in line with the Humean tradition than earlier managed-money proposals with or without attachment to the gold standard was advanced in the early 1930s by a group of economists, most of whom were connected with the University of Chicago, a proposal that therefore came to be called the Chicago Plan. Requiring all banks to hold cash reserves equal to 100 percent of their deposits, the plan was clearly inspired by the quantitative limits on banknotes of the Bank Charter Act.

Although endorsed by many politicians and economists, most notably Irving Fisher (1935) who abandoned his own earlier plan for price-level stabilization in its favor, the program was not enacted. Moreover, a classic article by Simons (1936), which framed the issue of rules versus discretion in monetary policy, argued that the 100-percent banking proposal could not be implemented without a radical restructuring of modern economic institutions, particularly reliance on debt finance. Simons regretfully concluded that, without such comprehensive reform, the only practical rule was to stabilize the price level.

Notwithstanding Simons's retreat from 100-percent banking and advocacy of price-level targeting instead, his student Milton Friedman continued to advocate 100-percent banking in his early writings on monetary policy (Friedman, 1960). Although he later abandoned the 100-percent banking proposal as impractical and unnecessary, Friedman, unlike Simons, replaced 100-percent banking not with a price-level rule, but with another quantity: increasing the money stock at a constant rate between 3 and 5% annually (Friedman, 1962).[14] Justifying his preference for a quantity rule over a price-level rule, Friedman asserted that the discretion of the monetary authority could be limited only by a quantity rule, because the monetary authority has direct control only over the quantity of money, not over the price level. The monetary authority would, therefore, be less accountable for failing to meet its target (the price level) than for failing to control its instrument (the quantity of money).[15]

In 1981–1982, the Federal Reserve pursued an anti-inflation strategy explicitly based on Friedman's idea that reducing inflation to below four percent required reducing the growth rates of the monetary aggregates supposedly directly controlled by the Fed. Although the Fed did succeed in reducing inflation from ten percent to less than four percent, after the US economy endured its worst recession since 1937–1938, the Fed consistently failed to meet its targets for reducing the growth rates in the monetary aggregates, even as the economy was contracting rapidly and inflation was falling, though not to the less than four-percent target. By finally abandoning its futile attempt to control the monetary aggregates in the summer of 1982, the Fed enabled a recovery to begin. Only after abandonment of the targets for the monetary aggregates and the

[14] See Friedman (1967) for his criticism of Simons for abandoning his support of a quantity rule in favor of a price-level rule, a shift that Friedman implausibly attributed to the influence of Keynesian ideas about the instability of the demand for money.

[15] Friedman's premise was clearly wrong, because the quantity of money is not an instrument under the control of the Fed. It, too, is a target. The Fed has direct control over the monetary base (currency plus demand deposits) not the quantity of deposits created by the banking system. Friedman tacitly assumed that the money multiplier (the ratio of bank deposits to reserves) is a constant or nearly a constant, but that is clearly not the case, as Friedman's own research showed. The money multiplier is a reduced form not a structural relationship, and is therefore sensitive to decisions taken by the public and the banks. The attempt to control any particular aggregate would itself tend to alter the empirical relationships upon which the monetary authority would have to rely in attempting to achieve its quantitative target for its chosen aggregate.

beginning of a recovery did the rate of inflation fall below the four-percent inflation target, the sharply reduced rate of nominal income growth having been initially reflected in negative output growth with inflation falling below the four-percent target only after the resumption of output growth.

The episode definitively refuted both of Friedman's key assertions: (a) that the quantity of money is an instrument under the direct control of the Fed and (b) that the Fed, therefore, has more control over the monetary aggregates than over the price level and inflation.

Nevertheless, long after inflation subsided, Friedman continued to decry the Fed's rejection of his strategy rather than the strategy itself, predicting a resurgence of double-digit inflation, even as inflation consistently remained below four percent. Friedman's repeated predictions of resurgent inflation marked the end of targeting the monetary aggregates and, more generally, of Humean quantity rules.

The decline, if not demise, of the Humean monetary tradition—a continuing source of misunderstanding, confusion, and bad policy—is hardly a cause for sorrow. As for the Smithian monetary tradition, it would be a stretch to claim that current thinking about monetary policy owes very much to Smith. But Smith's support for a monetary system mostly consisting of convertible bank liabilities with a reasonably stable and predictable price level at least foreshadows the current monetary system in which bank liabilities remain the primary medium of exchange under a monetary regime that aims for an annual rate of inflation of about two percent. While a vague monetary-policy rule aiming at a stable price level or rate of inflation would not pass muster in the Humean tradition, such a rule would not obviously be rejected within the eclectic Smithian tradition.

Recently the attention of monetary reformers has been drawn to a new kind of rule formulated in terms of nominal expenditure or nominal (NGDP).[16] Because nominal gross domestic product reflects both the price level and the level of output, stabilizing NGDP automatically bounds the potential fluctuations in both inflation and real output. Reductions in real output induce stimulative increases, instead of contractionary decreases, in prices while the expansion of real output automatically reduces inflation, thereby limiting any tendency for cumulative destabilizing booms.

[16] Although interest in targeting national income has increased in recent years, its roots can be discerned in the work of such diverse economists as Hawtrey, Hayek, Meade, and Tobin.

The problem, for which we are unlikely ever to find a solution, with formulating any monetary rule is that, without a fully adequate theory of how an economy works, it is risky to specify a monetary-policy rule for that economy. Since the nineteenth century, monetary reformers have been proposing policy rules whose effects they have grossly misunderstood. The Currency School erroneously believed that monetary and financial crises were caused by the failure of a mixed metallic and fiduciary currency to fluctuate exactly as a purely metallic currency would have. Owing to, more or less random, fluctuations in the value of gold, the attempt to impose that rule exacerbated the crises to which the gold standard is always susceptible. More than three-quarters of a century later, the Great Depression was caused by a mismanaged, and perhaps misconceived, attempt to restore the collapsed prewar gold standard without considering how its restoration would affect the value of gold and the international price level. More than half a century later, a misguided Monetarist rule for a constant rate of growth in the money stock, stubbornly based on a false belief in the inherent stability of the demand for money, proved incapable of implementation, only to be abandoned just in time to avert another catastrophe.

The best we can realistically hope for is a rule that does not induce destabilizing inconsistencies between policy and expectations. Quantity rules that arbitrarily limit the quantity of money create expectations that liquidity will not be available as happened under the Bank Charter Act and as happened in the ill-fated Monetarist experiment of 1981–1982. Inflation targeting can also cause inconsistencies between policy and expectations, as happened in 2008, when temporary negative supply shocks increased the price of oil and other commodities in the summer of 2008 and deterred the Fed from easing credit during a worsening recession for fear that inflation expectations were becoming unanchored. The implicit tightening of policy associated with not continuing to reduce the Fed funds rate as economic conditions deteriorated caused a rising liquidity premium and an increasing demand for credit that was not accommodated, producing a financial crisis in September 2008 followed by the worst downturn since the Great Depression. For the time being at least, no realistic rule for monetary policy seems more likely to maintain consistency between policy and expectations than a rule targeting a steady rate of growth in NGDP of about five percent.

7.6 Conclusion

Classical monetary theory is rich in theoretical insights and in practical lessons. My own view is that classical monetary theory teaches us that the monetary authority can control the price level by controlling the monetary base without concerning itself about any of the other monetary aggregates. It also suggests to me that we need to think carefully about ways to confine commercial banks, especially if the liabilities that they create are insured by the government, to a fairly restricted set of activities. Finally, before we adopt any monetary rule we ought to be able to satisfy ourselves that the rule will not have the perverse expectational implications that have resulted from earlier attempts to follow monetary rules.

References

Ahiakpor, J. (2004). *Classical macroeconomics: Some modern variations and distortions*. Routledge.

Arnon, A. (1991). *Thomas Tooke: Pioneer of monetary theory*. University of Michigan Press.

Bagehot, W. (1873 [1962]). *Lombard street: A description of the London money market*. Irwin.

Black, F. (1970 [2010]). Banking and interest rates in a world without money: The effects of uncontrolled banking. In *Business cycles and equilibrium: Updated edition* (pp. 1–22). John Wiley.

Bloomfield, A. I. (1975 [1994]). Adam Smith and the theory of international trade. In *Essays in the history of international trade theory* (pp. 109–144). Edward Elgar.

Brunner, K. (1971). Yale and money. *Journal of Finance, 26*(1), 165–175.

Cairnes, J. E. (1873). *Essays in political economy*. Macmillan.

Cannan, E. (Ed.). (1925). *The paper pound* (2nd ed.). P.S. King.

Dworkin, R. M. (1967). The model of rules. *University of Chicago Law Review, 35*(1), 14–46.

Eichengreen, B. (1992). *Golden Fetters*. Oxford University Press.

Fetter, F. W. (1965). *The evolution of British monetary orthodoxy*. Harvard University Press.

Fisher, I. (1920). *Stabilizing the dollar*. Macmillan.

Fisher, I. (1935). *100% money and the public debt*. Adelphi.

Friedman, M. (1960). *A program for monetary stability*. Fordham University Press.

Friedman, M. (1962). *Capitalism and freedom*. University of Chicago Press.

Friedman, M. (1967). The monetary theory and policy of Henry Simons. *Journal of Law and Economics, 10*(1), 1–13.
Friedman, M. (1991). Preface in E. Moreau. *The golden franc: Memoirs of a governor of the bank of France: The stabilization of the franc*. Westview Press.
Friedman, M., & Schwartz, A. J. (1963). *A monetary history of the United States, 1867–1960*. Princeton University Press.
Fullarton, J. (1845). *On the regulation of currencies* (2nd ed.). J. Murray.
Glasner, D. (2018). *The Fisher effect and the financial crisis of 2008*. https://papers.ssrn.com/sol3/papers.cfm?abstract_id=3247795.
Hawtrey, R. G. (1913). *Good and bad trade*. Longmans.
Hawtrey, R. G. (1932). *The art of central banking*. Longmans.
Hayek, F. A. (1932 [1984]). The fate of the gold standard. In R. McCloughry (Ed.), *Money, capital and fluctuations* (pp. 118–135). University of Chicago Press.
Hume, D. (1752 [2006]). Of the balance of trade. In E. Rotwein (Ed.), *Writings on economics* (pp. 60–77). Routledge.
Irwin, D. (2012). The French Gold sink and the great deflation of 1929–32. *Cato Papers on Public Policy, 2*, 3–41.
Irwin, D. (2014). Who anticipated the great depression? Gustav Cassel versus Keynes and Hayek on the interwar gold standard. *Journal of Money, Credit and Banking, 46*(1), 197–228.
Johnson, H. G. (1971a). Recent developments in monetary theory. In *Further essays in monetary theory* (pp. 21–49). George Allen & Unwin.
Johnson, H. G. (1971b). A comment on Pesek and savings's theory of money and wealth. In *Further essays in monetary theory* (pp. 133–136). George Allen & Unwin.
Johnson, H. G. (1971c). Is there an optimal money supply. In *Further essays in monetary theory* (pp. 137–147). George Allen & Unwin.
Johnson, H. C. (1997). *Gold, France, and the great depression, 1919–1932*. Yale University Press.
Keynes, J. M. (1913). *Indian currency and finance*. Macmillan.
Keynes, J. M. (1923). *A tract on monetary reform*. Macmillan.
Klein, B. (1974). The competitive supply of money. *Journal of Money, Credit and Banking, 5*(4), 423–453.
Laidler, D. (1975). Thomas Tooke on monetary reform. In *Essays on money and inflation* (pp. 211–227). University of Chicago Press.
Laidler, D. (1981). Adam Smith as a monetary economist. *Canadian Journal of Economics and Political Science, 14*(2), 185–200.
Laidler, D. (1988). British monetary orthodoxy in the 1870s. *Oxford Economic Papers, 40*(1), 74–109.
Lavington, F. (1922). *The trade cycle: An account of the causes producing rhythmical changes in the activity of business*. P.S. King.

McCloskey, D. N., & Zecher, J. R. (1976). How the gold standard worked, 1880–1913. In J. A. Frenkel & H. G. Johnson (Eds.), *The monetary approach to the balance of payments* (pp. 357–385). University of Toronto Press.

Mehrling, P. (1996). The relevance to modern economics of the banking school view. In G. Deleplace & E. J. Nell (Eds.), *Money in motion: The post Keynesian and circulation approaches* (pp. 330–340). St. Martin's Press.

Mehrling, P. (2020, January 28). *Payment versus funding: The law of reflux for today* (Institute for New Economic Thinking Working Paper no. 113). https://www.ineteconomics.org/uploads/papers/WP_113-Mehrling-Payment-vs-Funding.pdf.

Mints, L. W. (1945). *A history of banking theory*. University of Chicago Press.

Mises, L. v. (1912 [1934]). *The theory of money and credit*. Jonathan Cape.

Moore, B. (1988). *Horizontalists and verticalists: The macroeconomics of credit money*. Cambridge University Press.

Mouré. K. (1991). *Managing the franc Poincaré*. Cambridge University Press.

Mouré, K. (2002). *The gold standard illusion: France, the Bank of France, and the international gold standard, 1914–1939*. Oxford University Press.

O'Brien, D. P. (1995). Long-run equilibrium and cyclical disturbances: The currency and banking controversy over monetary control. In *The quantity theory of money: From Locke to Keynes and Friedman*. Edward Elgar.

Phillips, C. A. (1920). *Bank credit*. Macmillan.

Ricardo, D. (1816 [2015]). *Proposals for an economical and secure currency*. Cambridge University Press.

Simons, H. C. (1936). Rules versus authorities in monetary policy. *Journal of Political Economy, 44*(1), 1–30.

Skaggs, N. T. (1991). John Fullarton's law of reflux and central bank policy. *History of Political Economy, 23*(3), 457–480.

Skaggs, N. T. (1995). Thomas Tooke, Henry Thornton and the development of British monetary orthodoxy. *Canadian Journal of Economics, 28*(4b), 1212–1227.

Skaggs, N. T. (1999). Changing views: Twentieth century opinion on the banking school-currency school controversy. *History of Political Economy, 31*(2), 361–391.

Smith, A. (1937). *The wealth of nations* (E. Cannan, Ed.). Modern Library.

Smith, A. (1978). *Lectures on jurisprudence*. Oxford University Press.

Thompson, E. A. (1974). The theory of money and income consistent with orthodox value theory. In G. Horwich & P. A. Samuelson (Eds.), *Trade stability and macroeconomics: Essays in honor of Lloyd Metzler* (pp. 427–453). Academic Press.

Thornton, W. H. (1802 [1939]). *An inquiry into the nature and effects of the paper credit of Great Britain* (F. A. v. Hayek, Ed.). George Allen & Unwin

Tobin, J. (1963). Commercial banks as creators of money. In D. Carson (Ed.), *Banking and monetary studies* (pp. 408–419). R. D. Irwin.
Viner, J. (1937). *Studies in the theory of international trade*. Harper and Brothers.
White, L. H. (1984). *Free banking in Britain*. Cambridge University Press.
Yeager, L. (1968). The essential properties of a medium of exchange. *Kyklos, 21*(1), 45–69.

CHAPTER 8

Rules Versus Discretion in Monetary Policy Historically Contemplated

No monetary rule would be necessary, or even make sense, in a world in which all money was commodity money. It would be pointless to have a monetary rule if the value of money did not exceed its cost of production. Although we have come to expect monetary rules to have additional desirable properties, monetary rules originated in the early attempts to cope with the dangers of using a medium of exchange whose quantity could be profitably (opportunistically) increased to the disadvantage of those already holding either the medium of exchange or claims to fixed amounts of the medium of exchange.[1]

So the idea of a monetary rule to govern the operation of a monetary system did not emerge until after banks began issuing banknotes. Having a negligible cost of production, banknotes represent a value far greater than the minimal cost of printing them. A value greater than the cost of issuing banknotes could be imparted to those otherwise worthless

[1] To a limited extent, the problem of monetary rules arose even in the age of metallic currencies minted by a sovereign entity, inasmuch as debts were being contracted in terms of the currency unit, corresponding to a fixed weight of gold or silver, of a particular sovereign entity. Until they were severely worn or clipped, coins would circulate at face value, but when the debasement of coins was sufficiently large, Gresham's Law would begin to operate, causing the value of the coinage to sink to its debased value. On rules against debasement see Bisson (1979).

D. Glasner, *Studies in the History of Monetary Theory*, Palgrave Studies in the History of Economic Thought, https://doi.org/10.1007/978-3-030-83426-5_8

pieces of paper by means of a legally binding obligation undertaken by the bank to redeem its notes, at the bearer's option, for a fixed weight of gold or silver or some other valuable commodity whose supply—and, hence, value—was beyond the control of the bank. While this convertibility commitment has been, and still is, thought of as a kind of rule, it was not originally adopted as a rule of public monetary policy, but as a business necessity or expedient; convertibility was the means by which banks, seeking to advance their profitable engagement in the business of money-lending, could create a demand for the banknotes that they issued to borrowers, thereby avoiding or reducing their costs of holding coin or bullion.

It was not until the first two decades of the nineteenth century, after the wartime suspension of the gold convertibility of banknotes issued by the Bank of England, that a long series of debates over the conduct of the Bank of England during the period of restriction led to the first self-conscious reflections by policy makers about what rules ought to govern the issue of banknotes. Although these debates led to a consensus that the convertibility of banknotes into gold should be restored after the war against France, recurring monetary disruptions followed the restoration of convertibility in 1821, leading to renewed debates about whether convertibility alone was a sufficient or adequate rule by which to govern the British monetary system. The latter series of debates led to the enactment in 1844 of the landmark legislation known as the Bank Charter Act.

Despite the monetary rule promulgated by the Bank Charter Act, monetary disturbances did not cease, and the gradual evolution of banking practices transformed the British monetary system in ways that, by 1870, reduced the monetary rule of the Bank Charter Act to virtual irrelevancy. At just about the same time, a period of transformative change in the international monetary system was beginning, as the United States and many Continental countries abandoned their silver or bimetallic standards, and shifted to gold convertibility, so that, by 1880, the gold standard was no longer a peculiarly British institution but an international system, remaining in force until the outbreak of World War I. Brought into existence by a succession of independent decisions taken by individual countries, the international gold standard was not governed by a set of agreed-upon binding rules. Although lip service was occasionally paid to a vague set of unwritten "rules of the game," those rules were more honored in the breach than in the observance.[2] By describing the gold standard in this way, I render no judgment about whether the international gold standard functioned well or badly, I am just observing that the classical gold standard was not necessarily what is now called a "rules-based" monetary system (Bloomfield, 1959; McCloskey & Zecher, 1976).

What did emerge from the evolution of monetary institutions and the associated discussions in the nineteenth century were two kinds of monetary rules: price rules and quantity rules. The simplest price rule, of course, is the legal requirement that banknotes be convertible into a single commodity, e.g., gold, or silver. The first[3] legislated quantity rule was that imposed by the Bank Charter Act, requiring that no banknotes beyond a fixed minimum threshold be issued except upon the physical deposit of an equal value of gold to be held in the vaults of the Bank of England.[4] However, such was the prestige of the gold standard that the quantity rule was considered subordinate to the gold standard, a mechanism whereby the gold standard could be constrained to operate as it would under supposedly ideal conditions.

Mistaking the quantity rule superadded to the gold standard for the gold standard itself, many subsequent writers have thought of the gold standard as an arrangement whereby the total quantity of money would be limited by the amount of gold held in reserve or as "backing" for banknotes or paper currency. The reserve requirement was mistaken for

[2] Bloomfield (1959) was the first of many studies to show that the rules of the game were not generally followed during the heyday of the international gold standard, McCloskey and Zecher (1976) clarified the conceptual confusions giving rise to the rules-of-the-game doctrine.

[3] In the 1830s, before the Bank Charter Act was enacted, the Bank of England was, at least informally, guided by what was called the Palmer rule during the 1830s.

[4] Strictly speaking, the rule did not specify the quantity of banknotes to be issued, though it did the maximum fiduciary issue of the Bank of England and of the country banks. The total quantity of banknotes issued by the Bank of England was constrained by a 100-percent marginal reserve requirement. I consider the rule to be a quantity rule, because it was intended to constrain the total issue of banknotes to fluctuate in a particular fashion rather than allow the quantity of banknotes to be determined by the decisions of profit-seeking bankers. Although the Currency School conceded that the quantity of banknotes issued could not permanently exceed the quantity consistent with the operation of the price-specie-flow mechanism, the 100-percent marginal reserve requirement was supposed to prevent the temporary and destabilizing excess issues of banknotes were thought to be the cause of financial disturbances.

the essential property of the gold standard. An ancillary rule adopted to repair a perceived defect in how the gold standard had operated was mistaken for the mechanism by which the value of the medium of exchange is made identical to the value of a specified amount of gold.

Introduced as an ancillary rule to ensure that the gold standard functioned in the desired fashion, the quantity rule was logically independent of the gold standard. But it took almost a century after the Bank Charter Act was passed before a quantity rule was proposed as a stand-alone rule for monetary policy. When it was proposed as an alternative, rather than as adjunct, to the gold standard, it was necessary to explain why a quantity rule is superior to the gold standard or to any other price rule, i.e., why a rule specifying a policy instrument is superior to a rule specifying the policy target. It was Simons (1936) who provided such an explanation three years after he and ten of his colleagues at the University of Chicago proposed a rule for 100-percent reserve banking as an adjunct to a price-level target. The 1936 argument made by Simons relied on a newly articulated distinction between rules and authorities, or, as it has come to be described, between rules and discretion, discretion being the prerogative of an independent, and presumably unconstrained, decision-maker empowered to make decisions about policy. Simons contended that the gold standard or any other price rule granted the monetary authority excessive scope for independent decision-making. Even under a gold standard or some other price rule, too many decisions—e.g., the level and composition of reserves held, the interest rate at which the central bank would lend to banks seeking liquidity—were ceded to the discretion of the monetary authority. Only a mechanical quantity rule such as the 100-percent-reserve banking scheme proposed by Simons and his colleagues and a numerical limitation on the total quantity of money in circulation would eliminate the exercise of discretion.[5]

Simons regarded such discretionary authority as inherently undesirable, but at least as much for political as for economic reasons. Although

[5] Simons (1936) did not discuss the possibility of a private banking system operating without a gold standard. So the possibility that a competitive banking system under a metallic standard could obviate the grant of discretionary powers to a monetary authority was not addressed by Simons. However, until the late stages of his career, Milton Friedman (e.g., 1948, 1959, 1961) held to the view that the supply of money could not be competitively determined. In this opinion, he was echoing the widely held opinions of Chicago quantity theorists like Simons and Lloyd Mints.

Simons did mention increased uncertainty as a harmful effect of discretion, establishing that connection would have required a more careful analysis of the meaning of discretionary monetary policy than Simons provided.[6] Thus, Simons was making a political judgment that the discretion vested in a monetary authority instructed to achieve a price rule, was less consistent with the liberal—in the nineteenth-century sense—political values to which he appealed than the minimal discretion vested in a monetary authority governed by a rule setting the instrument under its control.

Notwithstanding his preference for a quantity rule in principle, Simons withdrew his support for the quantity rule that he had earlier proposed, because he concluded that such a rule could not be implemented unless centuries-old financial practices and institutions were scrapped and replaced by an entirely new set of practices and institutions. Recognizing that the chances of enacting such reforms were nil, Simons reluctantly endorsed a price rule to stabilize a broad index of commodity and product prices as the best feasible rule under then prevailing conditions.

Although Simons retreated from the quantity rule that he had earlier proposed, his argument against discretion was adopted by his student Milton Friedman who became an equally eloquent opponent of discretion and, in his own way, a more steadfast supporter of a quantity rule than was Simons. Friedman (1967) later justified his support for a quantity rule by dismissing Simons's insistence on scrapping existing financial practices and institutions and by relaxing the strict numerical simplicity of Simons's constant-quantity-of-money rule. Whether the anti-discretion arguments that Friedman borrowed from Simons survived the adjustments that Friedman made in the quantity rule turned out to be less obvious than Friedman assumed.

8.1 The Bullionist Debates

In the early stages of the British-French wars after the French Revolution, the exaggerated rumor of a French invasion having led to a run on the Bank of England, the British government in 1797 made banknotes issued

[6] Simons favored mechanical rules for setting the instruments of monetary policy over rules that merely specified the targets of monetary policy, without explaining why a rule setting the instrument would necessarily result in a less uncertain decision-making environment for economic agents than a rule specifying the policy target.

by the Bank of England legal tender, and prohibited the Bank of England from redeeming its banknotes for gold. A premium on gold in terms of sterling subsequently emerged in Continental commodity markets. Over the course of decade and a half, a series of debates ensued, involving some of the finest economic minds in Great Britain, over the causes and consequences of what was called high price of bullion, and what, if anything, ought to be done about it.

Especially notable were two pamphlets by David Ricardo (1810 [1951], 1811 [1951]), his first publications on economics, and a book Henry Thornton (1802 [1939]). Ricardo argued that the existence of a premium on bullion was conclusive evidence that the Bank of England had issued too many banknotes, so that the high price of bullion reflected a debasement of the pound caused by the Bank of England. Taking a less categorical position than Ricardo, Thornton acknowledged that an overissue of banknotes by the Bank of England could have caused the high price of bullion, while also arguing that the premium on gold could have had causes other than overissue, such as a bad harvest requiring extraordinary levels of grain imports, or foreign remittances to British allies in the war against France.

But the key point for purposes of this discussion is that although the possibility of overissue by the Bank of England was understood in the Bullionist debates, that understanding did not lead anyone to propose a quantitative limit on the issue of banknotes once convertibility was restored. It was presumed that restoring the legal obligation to convert banknotes into gold would suffice to prevent overissue.

Much has been written on the many-sided Bullionist debates, as they are now called, but I need mention only their final outcome: the appointment of a Parliamentary Commission, including Henry Thornton and two less renowned colleagues, William Huskisson and Francis Horner, who together wrote a report published in 1810 (Cannan, 1925) recommending the speedy resumption of the convertibility of Bank of England notes. Although the British government and Parliament were unwilling to follow the recommendation while the war with France was ongoing, the report rallied public opinion to favor a restoration of convertibility once the war was over.

After Napoleon's defeat in 1815, the process of restoring convertibility was begun with the intention of restoring the prewar conversion rate between banknotes and gold. In 1819 Parliament enacted a statute (The Resumption of Cash Payments Act) defining the pound sterling as a fixed weight of gold, and requiring that the convertibility of Bank of England notes be resumed no later than 1823. With markets anticipating the restoration of convertibility, the premium on gold gradually diminished, so that convertibility was restored ahead of schedule in 1821. The restoration of gold convertibility was not simply a commercial decision made by a private institution; it was a deliberate and carefully considered political decision taken by Parliament codified as a statute legally defining the pound sterling as a fixed weight of gold creating a de jure gold standard instead of the previous bimetallic standard and de facto gold standard that had prevailed for most of the eighteenth century.

The general presumption when the de jure gold standard was enacted was that, with the conditions for monetary and financial stability restored, the economy could take care of itself.[7] However, within a few years, the widely shared expectation that the resumption of the gold standard would lead to financial and economic stability was disappointed first by financial crisis and depression in 1825 and then by a series of further disturbances, including financial crises in each of the next four decades (1836, 1847, 1857 and 1866).

8.2 The Currency-School-Banking-School Debates

To explain why the anticipated financial and economic stability did not follow from the resumption of convertibility, some monetary theorists adapted David Hume's (1752 [2006]) discussion of what later became known as the price-specie-flow mechanism (PSFM) to serve as a theory of economic fluctuations. In that discussion, Hume described the automatic tendency toward equilibrium in the balance of trade and the distribution of gold among nations. The key equilibrating factor was that any country experiencing a balance-of-trade surplus would receive a corresponding influx of gold as payment while any country experiencing a balance-of-trade deficit would undergo a corresponding efflux of gold to finance the

[7] Not everyone agreed that the conditions for economic stability had been restored. There were those who disagreed with the decision to restore convertibility including Attwood (1817) and the Birmingham School, who opposed convertibility on principle, while others, notably Boyd (1801) and Lord King (1804 [1844]), opposed the monopolistic privileges of the Bank of England as the sole issuer of banknotes within a 65-mile radius of London.

deficit. According to the quantity theory of money, prices in the countries gaining gold would tend to rise, and prices in the countries losing gold would tend to fall; the adjustment in relative price levels of countries gaining gold and those losing gold would tend to eliminate the balance-of-payments imbalances and the need for gold shipments to finance those imbalances. The adjustment would continue until an equilibrium distribution of gold, and an equality of price levels and trade balances was achieved.

Couched in terms of a pure gold currency, Hume's account of the equilibrating mechanism gave no insight into the adjustment process for a medium of exchange consisting of both gold coins and convertible banknotes, and especially, into how the tendency toward equilibrium would—or would not—operate. In other writings, however, Hume's references to the inflationary tendencies of banks at least suggested that the effect of introducing convertible banknotes into the circulating medium would not be altogether benign.

In the Humean tradition, sudden changes in the demand for money are either ignored or viewed as aberrational, and should such demand shifts occur, they are attributed to uncertainty caused by the policy mistakes of the monetary authorities.[8] The ideal policy would be to keep the quantity of money fixed, or nearly fixed, allowing changes in the quantity of money only in a manner consistent with the operation of PSFM as described by Hume in which the quantity of money in a country changed by exactly as much as the quantity of gold imported into, or exported from, the country. Gold, being durable with a rapidly rising marginal cost with respect to the rate of production, implying that gold production in any short period of time is small relative to the total stock of gold, the primary virtue of the gold standard in this tradition is to constrain the quantity of money in the short to medium term. Banks, being able to create paper money at negligible cost in exchange for debt, are therefore viewed as potentially, if not inherently, destabilizing and inflationary.

Believing that the Humean adjustment process would not work smoothly unless all gold shipments into, or out of, Britain were matched by an equivalent increase or decrease in the total quantity of banknotes

[8] I do not assert that Hume and other quantity theorists denied that the demand for money could ever increase or that such increases could be deflationary. Rather such increases in demand were treated as one-off shocks and were not systematically incorporated into their conceptual framework.

circulating within Britain, the Humean monetary theorists who formed what became known as the Currency School argued that the unconstrained issue of banknotes by competing banks, including the Bank of England, had obstructed the PSFM described by Hume. They therefore attributed the financial distress and economic disruption following restoration of the gold standard to the failure of the Bank of England and the other British banks to expand or contract the total quantity of banknotes in exact correspondence with inflows and outflows of specie.

They did not deny that eventually the Humean adjustment process would constrain the inherent tendency of banks to expand their note issues. Rather, they believed, it was the belated and sudden contraction of bank lending after an extended drain of gold reserves that caused financial distress and crisis. It was the ability of banks to short-circuit the adjustment mechanism by maintaining—if only temporarily—a greater quantity of banknotes in circulation than was consistent with international equilibrium that led to a more severe crisis than the relatively mild contraction or slowdown that would result if banks had not delayed restricting the supply of credit until their solvency was threatened.

To avoid the abrupt reductions in the extension of bank credit that cause financial crisis and economic distress, the Currency School proposed immediately linking changes in the total quantity of banknotes to the amount of gold flowing into, or out of, the country. Under the Currency Principle, banks would be obliged to increase or decrease the quantity of banknotes in circulation by exactly as much as the gold reserve held by the Bank of England increased or decreased, thereby ensuring the automatic operation of the Humean adjustment mechanism and avoiding the crisis-prone adjustments characterizing the post-resumption period.

In 1844, the British Prime Minister, Sir Robert Peel, and his government enacted legislation enforcing the Currency Principle on the Bank of England and other note-issuing British banks. The Act capped the note issue of all British banks other than the Bank of England at existing levels while allowing the Bank of England a fixed fiduciary issue of £14 million banknotes against which no gold reserves were required to be held. However, all banknotes issued by the Bank of England beyond its fixed fiduciary issue required the Bank of England to hold an equivalent amount of gold in reserve. With a 100-percent marginal gold-reserve requirement imposed on the note issue of the Bank of England, the total quantity of banknotes circulating in Britain could not increase unless an equal quantity of gold bullion was deposited at the Bank of England.

The case against Peel's Bank Charter Act and the underlying Currency-School doctrine was advanced by a group known as the Banking School.[9] Rejecting the skeptical attitude toward banks and banking derived from Hume, they viewed the banking system as a stabilizing, not a destabilizing, influence, capable of accommodating fluctuations in the demand for money by creating convertible banknotes or deposits, thereby moderating the fluctuations in income and employment that the Currency School attributed to bank misbehavior. The theory of banking underlying the Banking School doctrine was first advanced by Adam Smith (1937), who subscribed neither to Hume's theory of international adjustment nor to his antipathy toward banking (Chapters 2 and 3). The Smithian theory was further developed by a leading figure of the Banking School, John Fullarton (1845), who coined the term "law of reflux" to convey the idea that banks have an incentive to supply as much—but only as much—money as the public demands.[10] Fullarton argued that, once an increased demand for liquidity was satisfied, excess banknotes would be returned to the banks as loans came due, and, unless an increased demand for liquidity from some other source allowed banks to keep them in circulation, the notes would be withdrawn from circulation.[11] The Humean analysis, abstracting from any notion of a demand

[9] As documented by White (1984) and Schwartz (2008), a third school of thought, the Free-Banking School, participated in the debate over the Bank Charter Act of 1844. Although the Free-Banking School made notable contributions, those contributions had less influence on the subsequent development of monetary doctrines and rules than of the Currency and Banking Schools. Largely owing to the contribution of White (1984) and Selgin (1988), a revival of interest in the contributions of the Free-Banking School began in the last decade and a half of the twentieth century.

[10] An anonymous referee questions whether Fullarton was in fact developing the Smithian theory of banking, contending that Smith relied on adverse clearings or international gold flows to discipline the note-issuing propensities of private banks. Although they are not the same mechanisms, adverse clearings and reflux are not inconsistent or incompatible, both tending to bring the quantity of money supplied by competitive banks into equality with the amount demanded by the public. See Chapter 4.

[11] Under convertibility, the value (purchasing power) of banknotes was pinned down by commodity arbitrage. Thus, excess banknotes would not increase the demand for commodities as long as the convertibility commitment remained credible, the expectation of continued convertibility precluding the inflationary expectations that might cause the demand for commodities to increase. According to this reasoning, excess banknotes would simply be held as long as the convertibility commitment remained credible. A version of this reasoning was developed by Paul Krugman (1998) in the context of a fiat-money regime; the reasoning had previously been articulated by Hirshleifer (1970, 135–137).

for liquidity, was therefore irrelevant to understanding how the quantity of banknotes ought to fluctuate.[12] By imposing a 100-percent marginal reserve requirement on banknotes, the Bank Charter Act would increase the costs borne by traders and dealers in obtaining liquidity, exacerbating financial disturbance and disorder.[13]

Supporters of the Bank Charter Act looked forward to an era of financial tranquility and economic stability after its enactment, but another financial crisis occurred in 1847. And the 1847 crisis was not quelled until the government suspended the Bank Charter Act, thereby allowing the Bank of England to lend to dealers and traders to satisfy their liquidity demands. Crises occurred again in 1857 and 1866, and, like the 1847 crisis, those crises were not brought under control until the Bank Charter Act was suspended.

[12] Although PSFM does assume that there is a determinate demand for gold, which serves as a numeraire and medium of exchange, it does not explain what factors affect the demand to hold gold for liquidity purposes, as opposed to the demand for non-monetary purposes. More important, PSFM takes no account of changes in the demand for liquidity and the possibility that such changes could be accommodated by domestic sources without affecting the demand for gold. Taking the demand for liquidity as given, the Humean analysis, upon which the Currency School based its proposal for a 100% marginal reserve requirement, failed to recognize that an increase in the quantity of notes could accommodate an increase in the demand for liquidity with no need for a corresponding influx of gold, and that an outflow of gold could reflect a change in desired domestic holdings of gold that required no corresponding reduction in the total quantity of banknotes.

[13] For the Banking School, however, the gold standard was, indeed, a necessary and sufficient condition for the efficient operation of the monetary system. By fixing the value of the currency, the gold standard ensured that the quantity of money within Great Britain would adjust automatically to the amount the public wished to hold, with the value of gold being determined primarily by real forces independent of the operation of a competitive banking system. That adjustment could operate either through the law of reflux or the balance of payments, or both simultaneously. Thus, in the Banking School view, no quantitative rule beyond a simple commitment to maintaining the convertibility of sterling into gold was necessary.

So nineteenth-century Britain provides two paradigms of monetary rules.[14] The first is a price rule in which the value of a monetary instrument is maintained at a level above its cost of production by way of a legal convertibility obligation. Given convertibility, the actual quantity of the monetary instrument created by banks is supposed to be whatever quantity the public wishes to hold. That, at any rate, was the theory of the gold standard, as it was understood by Adam Smith, by most of the Bullionist writers, and by the Banking School.

There were—and are—at least two basic problems with that theory. First, making the value of money equal to the value of gold does not stabilize the value of money unless the value of gold is stable, and there is no necessary reason for the value of gold to be stable.[15] Second, the banking system that produces a low-cost medium of exchange may exacerbate instabilities in the value of, gold, e.g., if the demand of the banking system for gold is highly unstable.[16] For example, in periods of financial distress when the public loses confidence in the solvency of banks, banks may feel constrained to increase precautionary gold holdings. The

[14] The monetary orthodoxy of the late nineteenth and early twentieth centuries reflected an uneasy practical compromise between the Currency-School and Banking-School positions (Fetter, 1965; Laidler, 1988). However, the presumption engendered by the Humean price-specie-flow analysis that the international adjustment process under the gold standard requires that the quantity of money in any country be changed by roughly the same proportion as the change in the gold reserves of that country was a principle that supposedly governed the working of the gold standard during its heyday from 1880 to 1913. The substantial evidence that the behavior of the gold reserves and money stocks in countries on the gold standard often fluctuated in the direction opposite from that required by the "rules of the game" was regarded as a puzzling anomaly by most international monetary specialists.

[15] Stability in the value of gold can have two possible meanings: (a) no fluctuations and (b) long-run stability despite short-term fluctuations. A third possible meaning could be a stable long-run trend with or without short-term fluctuations about the trend. In asserting that the value of gold is not necessarily stable, I had in mind the possibility of short-run fluctuations of sufficient magnitude to have macroeconomic consequences. Although there are plausible reasons why one could project that the value of gold would tend toward some long-run value over time, any such tendency would be very slow given steeply rising short-run costs of extraction and the small ratio of current output to the existing stock.

[16] As pointed out by an anonymous referee, a disturbance to the banking system of a small open economy would be unlikely to affect the internationally determined value of gold. However, if banking disturbances in one country are contagious, or if they are caused by disturbances affecting a number of countries, the increase in the monetary demand for gold could be large enough to affect the international value of gold, thereby triggering

resulting increase in the monetary demand for gold drives up the value of gold, triggering a vicious cycle in which the attempt by each to increase his own liquidity impairs the solvency of all.[17]

The second paradigm is a quantity rule under which the quantity of convertible banknotes is required to vary in a prescribed way, by exactly as much as the quantity of gold reserves held by the central bank. The quantity of banknotes could not increase unless gold was deposited at the Bank of England in exchange for banknotes. So, aside from the direct conversion of gold into banknotes, there were no mechanisms for accommodating increases in the demand to hold banknotes other than a gold inflow induced by a trade surplus, and a decline in the price level, neither of which would likely occur in the short to medium term. By foreclosing an immediate quantity response to an increase in the demand for banknotes, the quantity rule enacted by the Bank Charter Act necessarily led to financial distress when the demand to hold banknotes increased significantly.

In proposing a quantity rule, the Currency School aimed to make the gold standard operate as if the circulating medium consisted entirely of full-bodied gold coins. Regardless of whether that aim was desirable, the gold standard—the convertibility of banknotes into a fixed weight of gold on demand—could not achieve that aim without additional constraints. The idea that the gold standard ought to operate as if the circulating medium were a full-bodied gold coinage was not entailed by any logical or legal necessity rendering the gold standard unworkable unless it operated that way; it was simply the implication of a particular economic theory, according to which a full-bodied gold currency would automatically adjust to a hypothetical shock in the international distribution of gold. Abstracting from any complications relating to the demand to hold money, that economic theory was a remarkably ill-suited to serve as a guide in modifying the gold standard or prescribing a monetary rule.

Although originally intended to be ancillary to the gold-standard price rule, the quantity rule had no organic connection to the gold standard.

an international deflation. As McCloskey and Zecher (1976) show, local price-level movements under the gold standard were highly correlated, contrary to the implication of the naïve price-specie-flow analysis.

[17] Additionally, banks may, themselves, through miscalculation or undue optimism, lend to customers that turn out to be unable to repay their loans or, more generally, may acquire assets whose value falls, impairing bank solvency.

When a quantity rule was first proposed by the Currency School, the gold standard was an accepted—and virtually unchallenged—part of the institutional landscape of Britain, so it was natural for a quantity rule to be framed as an adjunct, not an alternative, to the gold standard. But it was entirely possible for a quantity rule to be formulated independently of a gold standard, or of any price rule.[18] Even so, it was almost a century after the Bank Charter Act was enacted until a quantity rule was proposed as an alternative to the gold standard, or to any other price rule.

8.3 The Undoing of the First Quantity Rule

The necessity of suspending the Bank Charter Act three times in the 22 years following its enactment to enable the Bank of England to issue additional banknotes to satisfy extraordinary demands for liquidity by the public led Walter Bagehot (1873) to observe, in an early anticipation of the Lucas Critique, that it was precisely the fear that liquidity might not be forthcoming in the future that itself precipitated an immediate demand

[18] In other words, given a private banking system operating with fractional reserves, the automatic operation of the gold standard could not, according to the Currency-School doctrine, ensure monetary stability. Rather than the gold standard, it was the statutory 100-percent marginal reserve requirement for the banking system as a whole that guaranteed monetary stability. But if a statute could prescribe a mechanical rule for the behavior of the quantity of money under a gold standard, a statute could also prescribe a mechanical rule for the behavior of the quantity of money under an inconvertible currency. The gold standard became just a piece of excess baggage that could be discarded once the appropriate statutory rule was enacted, for example, a rule prescribing a constant quantity of the national currency, with inflows or outflows of currency being reflected in the exchange rate of the currency in terms of foreign currencies rather than, as under the gold standard, in the quantity of the currency. The Currency-School theorists either failed, or refused, to follow the logic of their theory to its ultimate conclusion, but it was there waiting in plain sight.

for liquidity.[19] Thus, the absence of financial crises in Britain in the half-century between the crisis of 1866 and the outbreak of World War I suggests that the financial community came to expect, based on the experience of the crises of 1847, 1857, and 1866, that the Bank Charter Act would be suspended in a crisis, thereby obviating a precautionary demand for liquidity in anticipation of a crisis that itself brings on the crisis.[20]

But the Bank Charter Act had a deeper, more enduring, but unforeseen, effect on the British monetary system than the financial crises it caused or intensified. In 1844, when the Bank Charter Act became law, most British banks extended credit by issuing banknotes to borrowers (usually commercial enterprises) who in turn exchanged the banknotes for goods and services from their suppliers. Banks also lent by crediting depositor accounts, but chequeable bank deposits were not yet widely held even by businesses, and with a limited infrastructure for check-clearing, payment by cash was usually easier than payment by check. So bank deposits played a relatively minor role in the British financial system when the Bank Charter Act was enacted. Opponents of the Bank Charter Act did point out that the legislation was inconsistent in imposing a

[19] An anonymous referee questions whether Bagehot anticipated the Lucas Critique, asserting that the fact that the financial community came to expect liquidity injections after they had been provided in successive financial crises was just the expectation that the policy was meant to induce. But Bagehot's point was that the constraint imposed by the Bank Charter Act initially created a perverse expectation that there would be no liquidity injection, and the perverse expectation induced by the statutory limit which gave rise to repeated financial crises was eliminated only after repeated suspensions of the act demonstrated that the quantity rule imposed by the statute would be overridden by the discretionary action of the government. Another anonymous referee asks for evidence that an increase in the demand to hold banknotes triggered any of the crises after 1844. The best evidence that an increase in the demand for money triggered the crises is that the crises could only be resolved after the government suspended the provision of the Act that prohibited an increase in the quantity of banknotes that would satisfy the increased demand for banknotes.

Hawtrey (1932, 125) writes:

> The object of the Government's intervention was to induce the Bank "to enlarge the amount of their discounts and advances on approved security." The discounting facilities were the root of the matter. The panic was attributed to the Act of 1844 because the limit placed upon the fiduciary issue was the obstacle to free lending by the Bank, and relief was given by suspending the limit. That once done, the panic subsided and it was not found necessary actually to exceed the limit.

[20] An alternative explanation for the absence of crises after 1866 is suggested below.

quantity rule on banknotes while leaving bank deposits unconstrained. But, given the importance of banknotes, supporters of the Act either ignored the criticism or invoked a dubious distinction between banknotes and bank deposits, arguing that only the former were a true medium of exchange, the latter being just a way of economizing on holding the former.

However, by imposing what became a nearly prohibitive tax on the creation of new banknotes, the Bank Charter Act created a powerful incentive to expand the use of bank deposits, helping speed the expansion of joint-stock banks which, with the single exception of the Bank of England itself, has previously been prohibited from issuing notes. Over the next three decades, the quantity of bank deposits held in Great Britain increased rapidly while the aggregate quantity of banknotes remained almost constant. Thus, by about 1870, as Bagehot (1873) recognized, the Bank Charter Act had, or was about to, become irrelevant to the day-to-day functioning of the British monetary system, because the capacity of the Bank of England to extend credit, and to serve as a lender of last resort, no longer constrained by the 100-percent marginal reserve requirement of the Bank Charter Act, was effectively restored, as it could supply credit to financial markets through its normal lending operations.

8.4 An International Gold Standard

Just as the British monetary system was escaping the legal constraints of the Bank Charter Act, the international monetary system was starting to undergo a radical transformation of its own. Between about 1870 and 1880, the gold standard was rapidly transformed from a mainly British institution into the dominant international standard, a dominance lasting until the start of World War I when the gold standard ceased to function. Although the 100% marginal reserve requirement was being reduced to irrelevance, monetary orthodoxy reflected an uneasy compromise between the opposing views of the Currency and Banking Schools. The Currency-School doctrines retained a residual influence by way of what were known as the "rules of the game," which central banks supposedly were obligated to follow if they adopted the gold standard, although the empirical and historical evidence that the "rules of the game" were systematically followed is, at best, weak and possibly nonexistent (McCloskey & Zecher, 1976). The main requirement of the "rules of the game" was that central banks increase their liabilities when gold flowed into their vaults and reduce their liabilities when gold flowed out of their vaults. Such responses by central banks were thought to be at least directionally consistent with the Humean PSFM even though a strict correspondence between the quantity of gold reserves and the quantity of money in circulation was no longer insisted upon.

The Bank Charter Act having been reduced to irrelevance, the classical gold standard functioned tolerably well for about three and a half decades until belligerent governments prevented the normal execution of international and domestic monetary transactions at the outbreak of World War I. In retrospect, the gold-standard era stands out as an exemplary period of peace, progress, and prosperity for which the gold standard may deserve at least partial credit. So it is hardly surprising that a primary goal of postwar reconstruction was restoration of the gold standard.

Despite the widespread sentiment favoring resumption of the gold standard after World War I, there was no consensus among those supporting its resumption about how the gold standard should work. One group, whom I shall call the gold-standard fundamentalists, sought to recreate as faithfully as possible the prewar gold standard, which they viewed with more or less unqualified admiration, but largely through Currency-School glasses. The most fervent representatives of this view included the Austrian economists Ludwig von Mises and F. A. Hayek and such followers as the young Lionel Robbins, along with such French economists as Charles Rist and Jacques Rueff. But the view was also largely reflected in mainstream sources such as the famous report (principally written by A. C. Pigou) of the Cunliffe Committee (Gregory 1918 [1964]) representing what might be considered the financial orthodoxy of Great Britain in the aftermath of World War I. The Cunliffe report recommended restoring the gold standard in a form as close as possible to that which had existed—or was thought to have existed—before the Great War. The job of central banks was to be confined to maintaining convertibility of the national currency unit into gold while observing "the rules of the game," so that the process of international adjustment would at least directionally correspond to the Humean PSFM.

An alternative strategy for recreating the gold standard—advocated by R. G. Hawtrey (1919 [1923]) and Gustav Cassel (1923) and embodied in the Resolutions of the 1922 Genoa Monetary Conference—was that the leading central banks (the US Federal Reserve, and the Bank of England) maintain convertibility of the dollar and sterling into gold, acting in concert to stabilize the value of gold near its postwar level rather than allow gold to appreciate back to its prewar value.[21] The key to accomplishing this goal was to limit the monetary demand for gold reserves by having central banks other than the Fed and the Bank of England hold dollar- or sterling-denominated foreign-exchange reserves instead of gold, thereby preventing an appreciation of gold as countries rejoined the gold standard. Moreover, the Federal Reserve System, which had accumulated 40% of the world's monetary gold reserves, was expected to adopt a mildly expansionary policy accommodating a limited increase in the monetary demand for gold if countries chose to hold some gold reserves once they did rejoin the gold standard.

Notwithstanding differences about how a restored gold standard would operate in practice, expert opinion overwhelmingly favored a return to the gold standard. There were, to be sure, important dissenters from the majority view, notably Irving Fisher (1920) and J. M. Keynes (1923) who both argued that monetary policy should aim to stabilize domestic price levels while allowing exchange rates to adjust to accommodate changes in the underlying terms of trade between countries rather than forcing those changes to be reflected in falling prices and wages in countries against which the terms of trade were deteriorating.

But even these two exceptions are telling because both Fisher and especially Keynes were very clear that they wished to replace the traditional gold standard not to promote inflation but to ensure that prices would be stable. Indeed, Keynes's argument in 1923 was precisely that the Federal Reserve, holding 40 percent of the world's monetary gold stock, could not be trusted to continue holding an unproductive asset and would succumb to the temptation to sell off its holdings of gold, thereby precipitating an inflationary surge. So, from the perspective of this chapter, the relevant point is that in the aftermath of World War I, a consensus formed in favor of adopting some sort of price rule to govern policy. The differences were about the nature of the price rule. One group favored a price rule strictly limited to stabilizing the value of

[21] For further discussion of the views of Hawtrey and Cassel see Chapters 13 and 14 and Irwin (2014). Mazumdar and Wood (2013) argue that Genoa Resolutions aiming to depress the value of gold would discourage gold production, eventually causing the value of gold to rise more rapidly than it otherwise would have, so that deflation was inevitable. The argument is directionally correct, but there is a very big difference between the effects of gradual deflation, such as characterized the 1870s and 1880s, and the sudden steep deflation of 1929–1933. Gradual deflation might have been tolerable; steep deflation was disastrous.

all currencies in terms of gold, while allowing the value of gold to find its own level; a second group favored a price rule stabilizing the value of currencies in terms of gold, while central banks cooperated to stabilize the value of gold relative to other goods; a third group favored stabilizing the domestic value of each currency, while allowing the value of gold and the foreign-exchange value of currencies to be adjusted as necessary to maintain domestic price-level stability. The idea of a formal quantity rule was not even up for discussion, though it continued to exert influence through the notion that the operation of the gold standard required specific rules of the game to be observed.

For a while, especially after Britain restored the convertibility of the sterling at the prewar parity in 1925, the restoration of the gold standard seemed to be successfully on course, with many other countries stabilizing their currencies in terms of gold. Another important milestone was the successful 1926 stabilization of the French franc, albeit at a sharply devalued level, in terms of gold. But with no clear consensus about what objectives policy makers should aim for, and with policy makers lacking a coherent theory of how the gold standard was operating, the economic expansion of the 1920s came to a catastrophic halt late in 1929 as the international economy entered a sharp downturn that turned into the Great Depression.

Elaborating on the work of Hawtrey and Cassel, Ronald W. Batchelder and I (Chapters 13 and 14), Eichengreen (1992), Irwin (2014), Johnson (1997), Mouré (1991, 2002), and Sumner (2015) have argued that the 1929 downturn was triggered by the rapid gold accumulation of the Bank of France after 1928 when France formally restored the convertibility of the franc into gold, and when the Federal Reserve, seeking to quell stock-market speculation, started tightening monetary policy, causing an inflow of gold into the United States, just as France was also accumulating large amounts of gold. The accumulation of gold in turn triggered a rapid deflation, the central characteristic and primary cause of the economic contraction and financial crises of the early 1930s.[22]

[22] An anonymous referee argues that US deflation in the Great Depression was proximately caused by the M2 collapse resulting from the banking crises, not from the trend Cassel warned about (inadequate global gold output relative to secularly growing demand to hold gold). Cassel made two arguments about gold; one was that there would likely be a long-run tendency for the output of gold to fall short of the amount needed to prevent deflation. Cassel was indeed concerned by this secular trend, but he and Hawtrey attributed the deflation of 1929–1933 not to that secular trend, but to the

Although[23] both Hawtrey (1919 [1923]) and Cassel (1923), when proposing central-bank cooperation to limit the accumulation of gold reserves, had warned of the danger of a deflationary collapse almost a decade before it occurred, their explanation of the economic catastrophe was largely ignored amid the welter of competing explanations being offered. In the next section, I focus on one of these explanations: an explanation offered by a group of economists at the University of Chicago in 1933 in proposing a new version of the quantity rule that had been the centerpiece of the Bank Charter Act of 1844.

8.5 The Quantity Rule Redux: Inventing the Rules Versus Discretion Dichotomy

In March 1933, at the bottom of the Great Depression immediately after the bank holiday imposed by the newly inaugurated President Franklin Roosevelt, 11 economists (including Frank Knight, Lloyd Mints, Henry Simons, Aaron Director, Paul Douglas, Albert Hart) at the University of Chicago circulated a memorandum proposing a series of comprehensive reforms of the American banking and financial system including a proposal for liquidating all existing commercial banks and replacing them with (a) deposit-taking institutions holding 100-percent reserves against deposits and (b) legally separate investment trusts issuing credit to businesses using funds provided by private investors.[24] Federal Reserve notes

rapidly increasing monetary demand for gold by both the Federal Reserve and especially the Bank of France starting in 1928. The M2 collapse was the effect, not the cause, of a worldwide deflation precipitated by the sudden and massive increase in the world's monetary demand for gold.

[23] An anonymous referee suggests that Hawtrey and Cassel were themselves culpable for having supported a return to the gold standard that was almost certain to self-destruct, because France would never agree to restrain its demand for gold reserves as Hawtrey and Cassel had naively assumed it would. There may be some merit in this charge, but their failure to accurately assess the political forces that would ensure the collapse of the gold standard is a failure different in kind from the analytical errors made by most other economists at the time, and subsequently by Friedman, in misdiagnosing the economic and monetary forces that caused the Great Depression.

[24] The plan mentioned in the text was outlined in the March 1933 memorandum authored by the 11 Chicago economists and described in more detail in a November 1933 memorandum (Simons et al., 1933 [1990]) of which Simons was the principal author. The narrative concerning the genesis of and the political reception of the Chicago Plan draws heavily on Phillips (1995).

would replace all other forms of hand-to-hand currency, and the quantity of such notes would be under the direct control of the Fed, which would be instructed to aim for an increase of 15% in the wholesale price level, and, upon achieving that increase, to stabilize the price level thereafter. Echoing the Humean hostility to banks that had informed the earlier quantity rule proposed by the Currency School in the 1840s, the authors of the plan believed that the Depression had been caused by inherent weaknesses of fractional-reserve banking system. The existence of fractional-reserve banks constituted both a source of instability and an obstacle to increasing the quantity of money to promote economic recovery. The Chicago plan was quickly endorsed by Irving Fisher (1935) who, within a year, wrote a short book supporting what soon became known as the Chicago Plan.

The Chicago Plan differed from the monetary regime of the Bank Charter Act in three important respects. First, the Chicago Plan entailed the complete elimination of all privately created bank money (either notes or deposits), a full—rather than marginal—100-percent-reserve requirement, effectively abolishing all privately created money. Second, the Chicago Plan explicitly rejected the gold standard, basing the system on inconvertible fiat currency—banknotes or reserves created by the Federal Reserve—whose quantity would be completely determined by the monetary authorities. Third, the Chicago Plan replaced the gold-standard price rule with a price-level rule. A precise rule governing the quantity of money created by the monetary authorities was not specified by the Chicago Plan, but the possibility of controlling the quantity of money through fiscal policy and open-market operations was acknowledged.

Aside from the favorable reception the plan received from academic economists like Irving Fisher, and from economists and other officials of the Roosevelt administration such as Gardiner Means, Rexford Tugwell, and Secretary of Agriculture Henry Wallace, the proposal also drew support from a number of Senators and Representatives, including Senator Bronson Cutting of New Mexico, a Republican Progressive who became the leading Congressional sponsor of the plan and began drafting legislation to enact the plan into law.[25]

Despite the interest and support of various members of the Roosevelt administration, the administration never endorsed the plan. While the

[25] Senator Cutting's efforts to advance the plan came to an untimely end when he was killed in an airplane crash in May 1935.

success of early New Deal reforms, such as deposit insurance, in restoring a semblance of stability to the financial system, lessened the appetite for reforms as drastic as the Chicago Plan, the banking and financial industries, fearing the disastrous effects the plan would have on their interests, mobilized opposition to prevent its passage. Unwilling to adopt the radical proposals of the Chicago plan, the administration proposed a set of milder reforms centralizing and enlarging the powers of the Federal Reserve System to control the monetary aggregates, separating commercial from investment banking, and establishing a permanent system of deposit insurance, which were enacted by Congress in 1935. Although the banking and financial industries and their supporters actually opposed many of the provisions of the administration legislation, they either supported or tempered their opposition to the legislation, lest failure to pass the administration's bill lead to enactment of the Chicago Plan.[26]

It was against this backdrop that Henry Simons, the principal author of the November 1933 memoranda outlining the Chicago Plan, wrote his famous 1936 paper "Rules Versus Authorities in Monetary Policy." In that paper, Simons suggested even more far-reaching reforms than those contained in the Chicago Plan, proposing an outright ban on all forms of short-term lending for fixed monetary obligations. The only fixed monetary obligations that Simons was willing to permit were very long-term or perpetual debts (consols). All shorter-term fixed obligations were, in Simons view, inherently unstable and potentially illiquid, so that their values were subject to sudden fluctuations whenever doubts about the solvency of debtors arose, leading to self-reinforcing declines in the value of such assets and financial panics. In addition, Simons proposed that, rather than aim at a stable price level, the Federal Reserve should be instructed to maintain a constant quantity of money (Federal Reserve notes plus demand deposits) in circulation.

But more noteworthy than the specifics reforms Simons proposed is the monetary theory and political philosophy that inspired Simons. "Rules versus Authorities in Monetary Policy" is a passionate, and at times almost despairing, expression of liberal idealism and reformist zeal tempered by a

[26] See article in the *New York Herald Tribune* "Many Withhold Opposition to Present Banking Bill Lest Legislators Put Forward Measure Requiring 100% Reserves for Demand Deposits" (February 25, 1935, p. 41) quoted in Phillips (1995). I do not mean to suggest that there was no principled basis on which to oppose the Chicago Plan.

realistic understanding of the practical obstacles to achieving his reformist goals. Simons devoted roughly equal attention to two separate topics which he tried to resolve into a comprehensive proposal for reform of the US financial system.

Starting from the strict quantity-theoretic position articulated by Hume and the Currency School that changes in the quantity of money have no effect on an economy in which relative prices smoothly adjust to equilibrium values, but do provide a temporary stimulus if price adjustment is impeded by monopolistic practices, regulation or other obstacles, Simons acknowledged the short-term benefit of inflation in diluting administered or monopolistically determined prices., Nevertheless, he opposed inflation as a temporary expedient and a distraction from fundamental structural reforms promoting competition and price flexibility. Believing a competitive economy to be inherently stable, Simons assumed that normal technical progress and economic growth would lead to secularly falling prices consistent with stable nominal factor prices and money incomes, so he saw no reason for the nominal quantity of money to increase over time. A fixed nominal quantity of money therefore seemed to him to be the optimal monetary rule for a liberal economic system, because that rule would render policy decisions by the monetary authority unnecessary, which, from his point of view, was an optimal state. The simplest possible monetary rule—holding the nominal quantity of money constant—was likely also the best rule, both from the standpoint of monetary policy and from the standpoint of liberal values, inasmuch as it would eliminate any exercise of discretion regarded by Simons (1936, 5) as "arbitrary" and "dictatorial."[27]

But the quantity of money in circulation could not be kept constant unless the power to create money was taken from private banks. As long as private banks retained the power, by creating deposits, to create money, the quantity of money, was beyond the control of the monetary authority. A 100-percent-reserve requirement on deposits would make bank deposits equivalent to government currency by forcing banks to hold an amount of government-issued currency or reserves equal to the amount of deposits created. In principle, this was the system advocated

[27] Simons conceded that sufficiently large fluctuations in the demand for money could make a constant-quantity-of-money rule destabilizing, but, given sufficiently competitive and flexible price system, Simons assumed that the deflationary effects of a large increase in the demand for money would not lead to a cumulative economic contraction.

by the Currency School in the Bank Charter Act, except that the Bank Charter Act grandfathered in a fixed fiduciary issue of private banknotes by the banking system while the creation of deposits by private banks was considered unproblematic by authors of the Act.

However, Simons identified a fatal flaw in the system created by the Bank Charter Act: the tendency of financial innovation to circumvent any attempt to limit the private creation of financial instruments to replace higher-cost government supplied media of exchange. The inevitable creation of near moneys or money substitutes, enabling the public to shift from holding the controlled forms of money to holding higher-yielding near moneys or money substitutes would render attempts to control the quantity of money futile unless all forms of financial innovation could be suppressed. And, barring a comprehensive reform of the legal system prohibiting the creation of short-term private debts—a reform Simons regarded as desirable but politically infeasible—no policy aimed at holding the quantity of money constant would succeed in the long run. As Simons recognized, it was just such a process of shifting from holding banknotes to holding deposits that caused the Bank Charter Act to sink into irrelevancy within three decades of its enactment. Thus, Simons concluded—unhappily—that enacting a requirement of 100-percent-reserve banking and enacting a quantity rule holding the quantity of money constant would ultimately be undone by the same forces that undermined the Bank Charter Act.

Acknowledging the futility of enacting the ideal, no-discretion, monetary rule of a constant money stock, Simons regretfully accepted a policy—stabilizing a price index—he had rejected in principle for allowing the monetary authority to exercise discretion to choose both the price index to be stabilized and the specific methods and procedures for stabilizing that index. Simons harshly condemned the exercise of such discretion as illiberal and an unnecessary addition to the uncertainty borne by private decision-makers forced to anticipate the policy decisions of the monetary authority.

Although presaged in the Bank Charter Act, the notion that monetary policy should be confined to implementing, with no exercise of discretion, mechanical rules, does not seem to have ever been advanced until Simons made it the central idea of his 1936 essay. In contrast to the Currency School, whose proposal of a 100-percent marginal reserve requirement was deduced from a technical analysis of the monetary-adjustment mechanism, Simons, having characterized the exercise of discretion by monetary authorities as “dictatorial” and “arbitrary,” based on his case for a mechanical rule on political-philosophical, not merely, technical grounds. Nevertheless, despite his preference for a 100-percent-reserve currency with a fixed quantity of money, Simons, concluding that the 100-percent-reserve system could not be successfully implemented, reluctantly settled on what he considered a more discretionary, and therefore less satisfactory, rule for the monetary authority to stabilize a price-level index number.

Despite Simons's reluctant advocacy of price-level stabilization as the best feasible rule for monetary policy, his student Milton Friedman (1960) long remained steadfast in supporting the Chicago plan for 100-percent-reserve banking and a mechanical rule governing changes in the quantity of money. Eventually, Friedman also abandoned his support for 100-percent-reserve banking, while shifting his support from a quantity rule based on 100-percent-reserve banking to his *k*-percent rule for the overall growth in the money stock consisting of both government-issued currency and privately created bank deposits. Friedman (1967) argued that this shift in the quantity rule that he supported was more consistent with Simons's original objective of eliminating any exercise of discretion by the monetary authority and was based on a more accurate understanding of the causes of the breakdown in the banking system than was the 1936 shift by Simons from supporting a constant-quantity-of-money rule to a constant price-level rule. However, Friedman's own analysis of the causes of the banking collapse is itself seriously flawed[28] and his assumption that a *k*-percent rule would require no exercise of discretion by the monetary authority is theoretically unjustified and clearly runs afoul of the Lucas Critique.

[28] The main flaw in Friedman's account of the banking collapse is that he overstated its causal significance as a precipitating factor of the Great Depression, arguing as if the Great Depression were a purely domestic US shock transmitted from the United States to the rest of the world, when, the shock was actually international, reflecting a sharp appreciation in the real value of gold owing to a massive increase in the monetary demand for gold that began in 1928 when the Bank of France started redeeming its growing foreign-exchange holdings for gold and was augmented, subsequently, by the tightening of Federal Reserve policy to puncture a perceived stock-market bubble. Friedman (1991) himself conceded that he had underestimated the role of the Bank of France in causing the Great Depression. The general tenor of the narrative in Friedman and Schwartz (1963) minimized the role of the gold standard as an international institution and the extent to which the domestic price levels of gold-standard countries were highly correlated, focusing instead on the correlation between domestic US monetary aggregates and US prices and income levels (see Chapters 13 and 14).

8.6 Friedman, from 100-Percent-Reserve Banking to the *k*-Percent Rule

Milton Friedman had been a student of Henry Simons at the University of Chicago before going to Columbia to finish his graduate education. Upon returning to Chicago as an assistant professor in the fall of 1946, he would have become Simons's colleague, but Simons died (an apparent suicide) that summer. In one of his first publications on monetary policy, Friedman (1948) listed as his first proposal:

> *A reform of the monetary and banking system to eliminate both the private creation or destruction of money and discretionary control of the quantity of money by central-bank authorities.* [Friedman's emphasis] – The private creation of money can perhaps best be eliminated by adopting the 100-percent reserve proposal, thereby separating the depository from the lending function of the banking system.

In a footnote, Friedman credited Simons with authorship of the proposal citing two publications (Simons, 1936; Simons et al. 1933 [1990]). It is also noteworthy that the idea of separating the depository from the lending functions of banks was presaged by the legal separation mandated by the Bank Charter Act between the banking department of the Bank of England, which engaged in lending and deposit creation, and the issue department which was authorized to issue additional notes only up the limit of its gold reserves.[29]

Friedman (1951, 211) subsequently explained why he believed that the supply of money was an exception to the rule that competitive forces would operate to determine the optimal allocation of resources devoted to any commodity.

> The introduction of fiat elements into the monetary stock immediately raises the question, Who is to create the fiat currency and control its

[29] It is in the larger context of Friedman's position on 100% reserve banking, of which he remained an advocate until he shifted to the *k*-percent rule in the early 1960s, that his anomalous description of the classical gold standard of late nineteenth century till World War I as a pseudo-gold standard can be understood. What Friedman (1961) described as a real gold standard was a system in which only physical gold and banknotes and deposits representing corresponding holdings of physical gold circulate as media of exchange. But this is not a gold standard that has ever existed, so what Friedman called a real gold standard was merely the gold standard of his hyperactive imagination.

> issuance? Fiat currency is practically costless, whereas commodity currency is not. Under competition there will be a tendency for each kind to be produced up to the point at which its value equals its costs. This sets definite limits to the quantity of a commodity currency; it means indefinite increase in the quantity of a fiat currency and indefinite decrease in its value. There is no stable competitive equilibrium except when the fiat currency declines so much in value that it becomes a commodity currency, the commodity being the paper and services used in producing the currency. Competition is therefore inappropriate for determining the amount of a fiat currency. The production of fiat currency is, as it were, a natural monopoly, which explains why a measure of control has typically been exercised by government, why the privilege of issuing currency has been fought for so vigorously, and why proponents of a private competitive order, like Henry Simons, have held the view – which I share – that the creation of fiat currency should be a government monopoly. This problem of control is seen clearly and faced openly when the fiat element is introduced through a fiduciary issue, as in Peel's Act of 1844.

This passage is notable for (1) its erroneous reasoning in arguing that competition in the supply of a fiat money (i.e., non-commodity money regardless of whether the "fiat" money is made contractually convertible into an outside asset) is unworkable, (2) its explicit acknowledgment of Simons's view about the necessity for a government monopoly over the creation of fiat money, i.e., a 100-percent-reserve requirement, and (3) its acknowledgment of the influence of the Currency School (via Peel's Act of 1844).

Eventually, Friedman modified his views on monetary policy and monetary rules significantly. In *A Program for Monetary Stability*, Friedman (1960) still supported, or at least paid lip service to, 100-percent-reserve banking. But by 1962 in *Capitalism and Freedom*, and just before his *Monetary History of the US* was published, Friedman had already switched to his *k*-percent rule, arguing that it would be sufficient for monetary stability if the Federal Reserve kept the total quantity of money growing at a steady rate of growth of *k*-percent a year where *k* was some small number usually chosen between 2 and 4. In a 1967 lecture at the University of Chicago Law School, where Simons had long held a non-tenured appointment, Friedman explained why he had changed his mind about 100-percent-reserve banking and why he believed a rule governing the rate of growth in the quantity of money was preferable to the price-level rule that Simons had ultimately—albeit reluctantly and with grave misgivings—come to favor over the simple rule of a constant quantity of money. The tenor of Friedman's assessment was signaled in his third paragraph.

> On re-reading Henry Simons' work in preparation for this lecture. I was struck by the contrast between my reaction to his discussion of monetary theory, on the one hand, and to his proposals for monetary reform, on the other. The monetary theory impressed me as sophisticated and correct; the proposals for monetary reform as largely irrelevant and wrong.

Friedman's main point was that Simons had misunderstood the factual background to the Great Depression, a cataclysm that inspired most of Simons's proposals for reform. Friedman argued that Simons had mistakenly assumed that the collapse of income and employment was caused by a deep instability in the demand for money by the public. The growing demand for liquidity, especially currency, led the public to try to increase their holdings of cash and to convert deposits into currency, thereby precipitating a contraction of spending income and employment. Friedman believed that Simons's view of the Great Depression was very close to Keynes's view in which it was an inherently unstable private sector, displaying in particular an unstable demand for money, that caused the Great Depression. It was this belief in an unstable demand for money, Friedman argued, that led Simons to doubt that a mechanical rule for the behavior of the money supply could be formulated. Simons feared that shifts between the demand for money and the demand for near moneys and money substitutes would undermine the constant-quantity-of-money rule that Simons, but for his concerns about an unstable demand for money, would have preferred.

Friedman then asserted that his empirical research had shown that, contrary to what Keynes and Simons believed, the Great Depression had not been caused by a sudden drastic increase in the demand for money caused by a sudden change in profit expectations ("animal spirits"). Rather, in Friedman's telling, a tight-money policy by the Federal Reserve in 1928 and 1929 had caused a normal business-cycle contraction, which only began to spiral rapidly downwards in late 1930 when the Federal Reserve refused to extend credit to the Bank of United States, allowing it to fail, thereby causing a loss of confidence in the banking system and triggering a wave of bank failures around the country. Another wave of bank failures followed in March 1931, when the Fed again refused to provide aid to other troubled banks, thereby defaulting on its obligation to act as a lender of last resort to ensure the stability of the banking system. Finally in September 1931, the Fed, responding to Britain's suspension of sterling convertibility and fearing a speculative attack on the dollar in anticipation of a suspension of dollar convertibility or a dollar devaluation, sharply tightened its policy to preempt such a speculative attack, triggering another contraction of spending, income and employment.

Friedman focused his criticism of Simons's rejection of the constant-quantity-of-money rule in favor of a price-level rule in the following passage.

> With all its merits, however, this rule cannot now be recommended as a basis for monetary reform. The obvious weakness of a fixed quantity, as a sole rule of monetary policy, lies in the danger of sharp changes on the velocity side, for no monetary system can function effectively or survive politically in the face of extreme alternations of hoarding and dishoarding. It is easy to argue that something would be gained in any event if perverse changes were prevented merely as to quantity, but the argument is unconvincing. The fixing of the quantity of circulating media might merely serve to increase the perverse variability in the amounts of "near-moneys" and in the degree of their general acceptability, just as restrictions on the issue of bank notes presumably served to hasten the development of deposit (checking-account) banking. (Simons, 1936, 5)

In Friedman's narrative of the Great Depression, it was a policy failure by the Fed that caused a loss of confidence in private banks that precipitated the Great Depression. Based on that narrative, he concluded that the potential changes in the velocity of money that so troubled Simons would not be a serious concern if the Fed ensured that the quantity of money grew at a steady rate. But Friedman's response avoided—or rather evaded—the other point that Simons was making: that a constant quantity-of-money rule, a rule that—with a single exception—had never actually been imposed, would likely cause monetary changes tending to defeat the objective of the rule. Thus, when a similar rule was implemented by the Bank Charter Act, imposing a 100-percent marginal reserve requirement on the note issue of the Bank of England, British banks began to shift their business models away from issuing banknotes, whose quantity was constrained by the Bank Charter Act, toward creating deposits, which were free from legal reserve requirement. While the quantity of banknotes remained within the limits set by the Bank Charter Act, the quantity of deposits in Britain increased rapidly during the second half of the nineteenth century.[30]

It is unclear to me whether Friedman stopped advocating 100-percent-reserve banking in the early 1960s because he regarded the idea as politically unrealistic, though Friedman was certainly not averse to support causes with little or no chance of success, or because he was persuaded that 100-percent-reserve banking was not really necessary. But, evidently, he believed that the Fed was fully capable of achieving whatever rate of growth in the quantity of money that a legislated rule prescribed. This was actually a point that Friedman emphasized frequently: To eliminate the exercise of discretion by the Fed, it was necessary to adopt a rule that could be mechanically implemented by the Fed. Friedman rejected a price-level rule precisely because it could not be implemented without an exercise of discretion—i.e., judgment—by the Fed. According to Friedman, the quantity of money is directly controlled by—an instrument of—the monetary authority while the price level is just a policy target—not an instrument—of the monetary authority.[31]

[30] Friedman's response, emphasizing Simons's failure to understand the nature of the monetary forces that led to the Great Depression, applies at least equally, if not more so, to Friedman himself, inasmuch as he paid scant attention to the critical role of the gold standard, and especially the gold-accumulation policy of the Bank of France, in causing the deflation that had been foreseen by many economists, most notably Hawtrey and Cassel, in their proposals for restoring the gold standard after World War I. See Chapters 13 and 14.

[31] See Friedman (1962b, 242):

> If a rule is to be legislated, what rule should it be? The rule that has most frequently been suggested by people of a generally 'new liberal' persuasion is a price-level rule; namely, a legislative direction to the monetary authorities that they maintain a stable price level. I think this is the wrong kind of rule. It is the wrong kind of rule because the objectives it specifies are ones that the monetary authorities do not have the clear and direct power to achieve by their own actions.... There is unquestionably a close connection between monetary actions and the price level. But the connection is not so close, so invariable, or so direct that the objective of achieving a stable price level is an appropriate guide to the day-to-day activities of the authorities.

One may infer that Friedman believed that the connection between the monetary actions of the monetary authority and the quantity of money is so close, so invariable, and so direct that the monetary authority could be reliably expected to achieve it.

But the quantity of money (i.e., currency plus deposits) is not an instrument of the Fed, because it is banks not the Fed that create deposits; the Fed creates only the monetary base (i.e., currency plus reserves) not deposits. Because the quantity of money includes deposits, which, under a private fractional-reserve banking system, are privately created, the Fed cannot control the quantity of money without taking into consideration the behavioral responses of private agents whose decisions the Fed cannot directly control. Friedman was not unaware that the quantity of money depends not just on the decisions of the Fed, but also on the decision of the non-bank public, reflecting their preferences for holding currency and the various alternative forms of deposits and other similar monetary instruments and on the decisions of the banks to about how much reserves to hold against their outstanding deposit liabilities. The various choices made by the public between holding currency, deposits or other instruments and the choices made by banks to hold reserves are all incorporated into the so-called money multiplier, reflecting a relationship between the quantity of base money and the total quantity of money in the hands of the public that can be statistically estimated. Friedman believed that this empirical relationship between base money and the total money stock could be estimated with sufficient precision to enable the Fed to determine the exact amount of reserves required by the banking system to ensure that the quantity of money is exactly the amount selected by the Fed.[32]

But the assumption that the measured statistical relationships embodied in the money multiplier would remain stable if those relationships were being used to control the quantity of money is subject to the same sort of criticism that Simons had raised against formulating a

[32] A further problem with the use of the statistical relationships embodied in the money multiplier is that these relationships are expressed as ratios of aggregates such as a currency/deposit ratio reflecting a ratio between the amount of currency the public wishes to hold and the amount of deposits the public wishes to hold at any time. But there is no basis for assuming that this is a ratio that individuals have a desire to maintain at a particular level. That the ratio at any moment has a particular value does not mean that in responding to a change in the monetary base the public wants to maintain just the ratio of currency to deposits that obtained prior to the increase in the monetary base. In other words, at the margin, people may choose to hold increasingly large shares of additional cash in the form of deposits relative to currency. Or expressed differently, the currency/deposit and reserve/deposit ratios are themselves reduced forms, not structural relationships, so there is no warrant for treating them as constants when attempting to predict the effects of policy changes.

rule to hold the quantity of money constant. The criticism was succinctly summarized in 1975 by the Bank of England economic advisor Charles Goodhart in his famous dictum: "Any observed statistical regularity will tend to collapse once pressure is placed upon it for control purposes," a dictum that came to be known as Goodhart's Law.

Goodhart's Law is also an application of the Lucas Critique (Lucas, 1976). Although conventionally treated as a component of the money supply, the money multiplier does not describe a structural relationship; it is a reduced form embodying deeper supply and demand relationships sensitive to the expectations of both demanders and suppliers of money. If an econometric estimate of the money multiplier is stable enough to be relied on for empirical purposes, it would have to reflect ongoing equilibrium relationships. However, those equilibrium relationships would be conditional on a set of expectations embedded in the underlying structural relationships from which the reduced form is derived and estimated. Friedman's assumption that the money-multiplier relationship estimated when monetary policy was not governed by the *k*-percent rule would remain constant after the *k*-percent rule was adopted was hardly self-evidently justified.[33]

[33] Perhaps the most penetrating critique of Friedman's*k*-percent rule was offered by his ideological soulmate, F. A. Hayek (1978).

> As regards Professor Friedman's proposal of a legal limit on the rate at which a monopolistic issuer of money was to be allowed to increase the quantity in circulation, I can only say that I would not like to see what would happen if it ever became known that the amount of cash in circulation was approaching the upper limit and that therefore a need for increased liquidity could not be met.

In a footnote, Hayek added the following:

> To such a situation the classic account of Walter Bagehot... would apply: "In a sensitive state of the English money market the near approach to the legal limit of reserve would be a sure incentive to panic; if one-third were fixed by law, the moment the banks were close to one-third, alarm would begin and would run like magic.

Two anonymous referees challenge Hayek's remark about what might happen when the quantity of money reached the upper limit of the permissible range, suggesting incorrectly that Hayek was confusing quantity of money rule with a monetary-base rule. Hayek was simply saying that the anticipation of a future tightening of monetary policy would induce an immediate increase in the demand for money. The resulting monetary disequilibrium arises because the public's demand for money exceeds the amount that the monetary

This does not mean that a skillful policy maker could not successfully target the quantity of money if that was the chosen policy target. But success would be very unlikely if the policy maker followed a mechanical rule. To target the quantity of money successfully would require the exercise of judgment (aka discretion). In claiming that his *k*-percent rule could be implemented with no exercise of discretion, Friedman mistakenly treated the quantity of money as an instrument, when in fact it is a target. The quantity of money could be treated as a policy instrument only under the 100-percent-reserve banking regime favored by Simons, which Friedman abandoned without realizing that, in doing so, he had compromised his own argument against the exercise of discretion. Moreover, by formulating his monetary policy rule in terms of a target rather than an instrument, Friedman also undercut his own case against targeting the price level, which was precisely that a rule merely specifying a target rather than an instrument confers too much discretion on the monetary authority in deciding how to achieve its target.[34]

8.7 Rules Versus Discretion or Rules and Discretion

As noted above, the dichotomy between rules and discretion in discussions of monetary policy was first explicitly formulated by Henry Simons. Although his formulation juxtaposed rules and authorities, he denounced the "dictatorial" and "arbitrary" discretion exercised by authorities. So the juxtaposition of rules and discretion clearly addresses the same dichotomy to which Simons referred in his article. However, the meaning that Simons attached to the term "discretion"—an arbitrary and unconstrained exercise of will—is not the only possible, or even the most plausible, meaning to attach to the term in the context of formulating

authority is allowed to accommodate; there is no hidden assumption about a monetary-base rule. See footnote 36 below for a discussion of how the dynamic described by Hayek was actually manifested in the 1981–1982 attempt by the Volcker Fed to target the monetary aggregates.

[34] One might argue that the claim that the relationship between the monetary base and the quantity of money is easier to estimate than the relationship between the monetary base and the price level seems fairly plausible. But the experience of the Volcker Fed in the 1980s when inflation was stabilized while the quantity of money behaved erratically suggests that the claim is hardly self-evident, or even valid under all circumstances. See the following footnote.

a monetary rule. If we adopt a more plausible meaning of "discretion," the sharp and irreconcilable dichotomy between rules and discretion that so troubled Simons and Friedman dissolves.

F. A. Hayek (1960) addressed the concept of discretion from a number of angles in his articulation of the foundations of political liberalism. In one context, discretion relates to the task of a judge deciding a case in which the specific facts do not clearly correspond to any specific legal rule whose application would determine his decision. In such cases, when an explicit legal rule is not clearly applicable, the judge is often said to exercise discretion in deciding the case. To Hayek, however, the discretion exercised by the judge does not mean that the judge is free to decide the case arbitrarily. Rather, "the task of the judge," wrote Hayek, "is to discover the implications contained in the spirit of the whole system of valid rules of law or to express as a general rule, when necessary, what was not explicitly stated previously in a court of law or by the legislator." Judicial discretion does not empower the judge to make an unconstrained choice. "A particular interpretation of the law may be subject to dispute..." Hayek conceded, "but this does not alter the fact that the dispute must be settled by an appeal to the rules and not by a simple act of will."

A similar analysis of what discretion means was provided at about the same time by a liberal of a different stripe, Ronald Dworkin (1967). Like Hayek, Dworkin discussed the meaning of discretion in the context of a judge deciding a "hard case," a case in which conflicting rules of law seem to be applicable, or a case in which none of the relevant rules seems to fit the facts of the case. Such a judge is said to exercise discretion, because his decision is not straightforwardly determined by the existing set of legal rules. Legal positivists, against whom Dworkin was arguing, would say that the judge is able, and called upon, to exercise discretion in deciding the case, meaning (or so positivists argue), that by deciding the case, the judge does impose his will. It is something like the positivist view that underlies the Simons-Friedman hostility to discretion.

To elucidate the concept of discretion, Dworkin considers the example of a sergeant ordered by his lieutenant to take his five most experienced soldiers on patrol, and reflects on how to interpret an observer's statement: "the orders left the sergeant a great deal of discretion." It is clear that, to carry out his orders, the sergeant is expected to exercise his judgment, because he is given no metric for measuring the experience of his soldiers. But that does not mean that, when choosing five soldiers for the patrol, he is just exercising his will. The decision can be carried out with good, or with bad, judgment, but it is judgment that is exercised, not will, just as a judge, in deciding a hard case, is exercising his judgment—on a more sophisticated level to be sure than the sergeant choosing soldiers—not just indulging his preferences.[35]

In his discussion of discretion, Hayek made another point overlooked by Simons and Friedman: The exercise of discretion by government officials becomes inconsistent with liberal values only insofar as that exercise of discretion impinges on the personal or property rights of private individuals. Discretion may be abused, but the exercise of discretion is not inherently abusive. Monetary authorities in implementing their monetary policies—setting lending rates to banks, engaging in open-market transactions—neither exercise coercive powers over individuals nor infringe on their personal or property rights; they are merely entrusted with administrative control over resources that they are empowered to use in executing voluntary transactions with members of the public.

Insofar as government officials, including monetary authorities, exercise discretion over resources that have been legally entrusted to them, their discretionary control over those resources may raise questions about how much administrative oversight is needed to ensure that their decisions are consistent with the public-policy objectives they are directed to advance. But such questions require an assessment of whether the actions taken are appropriate to the ends that officials are instructed to achieve, not whether the actions were carried out mechanically as prescribed by an explicit set of rules. What makes discretionary monetary policy problematic is not an arbitrary infringement of personal rights. As Hayek explained:

> Even if the control of money is in the hands of a monopoly, its exercise does not necessarily involve coercion of private individuals. The argument against discretion in monetary policy rests on the view that monetary policy and its effects should be as predictable as possible.

But if the case against discretion in monetary policy rests on its unpredictability, it is not clear that a mechanical quantity rule that prevents the

[35] If it were shown that a judge, simply indulging his preferences, made a decision in bad faith, offering pretextual arguments to justify his decision, he would be said to have *abused his discretion*.

monetary authority from exercising any judgment would make monetary policy more predictable than would, say, a price rule specifying a policy objective or target, but allowing discretion to be exercised over the means whereby the objective is achieved.

As I showed in Section five, Simons himself acknowledged that, at least under our present system of financial and banking institutions and practice, a mechanical rule would probably make policy less, rather than more, predictable. Friedman disagreed and tried to show that Simons was wrong in that judgment, arguing that Simons had a faulty understanding of the causes of the Great Depression. In fact, it was Friedman's understanding of the causes of the Great Depression that was faulty in a number of important respects, failing in particular to understand the international nature of the monetary shock to the world economy associated with the massive increase in the monetary demand for gold starting in 1928. Friedman also misunderstood Simons's argument about why a mechanical quantity rule, if not coupled with a radical restructuring of our entire financial and banking systems, was likely to be self-defeating, and he failed to grasp how severely his assumption that the monetary authorities could easily control the overall quantity of money was compromised by both Goodhart's Law and the Lucas Critique.[36]

[36] As I have explained elsewhere (Glasner, 1989, 219), the Fed, by targeting the monetary aggregates in carrying out its anti-inflationary monetary policy in the early 1980s, created a perverse positive feedback loop in which the release of weekly data showing that monetary growth was above target, would immediately cause expectations of future tightening, thereby inducing attempts to increase holdings of cash in advance of monetary tightening and causing the rate of increase in the monetary aggregates to accelerate, further reinforcing fears of still further tightening to achieve monetary targets. While Friedman attributed the consistent failure of the Fed to achieve its monetary targets during the course of what was then steepest postwar downturn to Fed incompetence or irresolution, the obvious reason for the failure was the perverse expectations of future monetary tightening occasioned by the attempt to implement the Monetarist strategy. The beginning of the recovery from the 1982 recession followed soon after Volcker's July testimony to Congress that monetary growth at the upper end of the Fed's target range would be acceptable, thereby easing precautionary demands for liquidity triggered by an expected drop in the rates of growth of the monetary aggregates. By mid-August, an extended stock-market rally was under way, presaging the start of a sustained economic expansion.

8.8 Conclusion

Although recognition of a need for some rule to govern the conduct of the monetary authority originated in the perceived incentive of the authority to opportunistically abuse its privileged position, the expectations of the public (including that small, but modestly influential, segment consisting of amateur and professional economists) about what monetary rules might actually accomplish have evolved and expanded over the course of the past two centuries. As Laidler (2017) argued, that evolution has been driven by both the evolution of economic and monetary institutions and the evolution of economic and monetary doctrines about how those institutions work.

I have distinguished between two types of rules: price rules and quantity rules. The simplest price rule involved setting the price of a commodity—usually gold or silver—in terms of a monetary unit whose supply was controlled by the monetary authority or defining a monetary unit as a specific quantity of a particular commodity. Under the classical gold standard, for example, the monetary authority stood ready to buy or sell gold on demand at a legally determined price of gold in terms of the monetary unit. Thus, a fixed price of gold under the gold standard was originally thought to serve as both the policy target of the rule and the operational instrument for implementing the rule.

However, as monetary institutions and theories evolved, it became apparent that there are policy objectives other than simply maintaining the convertibility of the monetary unit into the standard commodity that require the attention of the monetary authorities. The first attempt to impose an additional policy goal on a monetary authority was the Bank Charter Act of 1844, specifying quantity target—the aggregate of banknotes in circulation in Britain—which the Bank of England was required to reach by following a mechanical rule. By imposing a 100-percent marginal gold-reserve requirement on the notes issued by the Bank of England, the Bank Charter Act made the quantity of banknotes issued by the Bank of England both the target of the quantity rule and the instrument by which the rule was implemented.

Owing to deficiencies in the monetary theory on the basis of which the Act was designed and to the evolution of British monetary practices and institution, the conceptual elegance of the Bank Charter Act was not matched by its practical efficacy. Despite, but, more likely, because of, the ultimate failure of Bank Charter Act, the gold standard, surviving recurring financial crises in Great Britain in the middle third of the nineteenth century, was eventually adopted by many other countries in the 1870s, becoming the de facto international monetary system from the late 1870s until the start of World War I. Ultimately, operation of the gold standard was defined by, and depended on, the observance of a single price rule in which the value of a currency was defined by its legal gold content, so that, corresponding to each gold-standard currency, there was an official gold price at which the monetary authority was obligated to buy or sell gold on demand.

The value—purchasing power—of gold was relatively stable in the roughly 35 years of the gold standard era, but that stability could not survive World War I, and so the problem of reconstructing the postwar monetary system was what kind of monetary rule to adopt. Was it enough to restore the old currency parities—perhaps adjusted for differences in the extent of wartime and postwar currency depreciation—that governed the classical gold standard, or did other factors, e.g., the purchasing power of gold, in restoring the gold standard have to be considered? This conundrum was never satisfactorily answered, and the failure to do so led to the economic collapse that started in 1929 and resulted in the demise of the gold standard.

Seeking a new monetary regime to replace the gold standard, Henry Simons and ten other economists proposed a new system based on 100-percent-reserve banking. The original Chicago plan for 100-percent-reserve banking specified a monetary rule for stabilizing the purchasing power of fiat money. The 100-percent-reserve banking plan also provided the monetary authority with complete control over the quantity of money, thereby enhancing the power of the monetary authority to achieve its price-level target. The plan was thus inspired by a desire to increase the likelihood that the monetary authority could successfully implement the desired price rule. The price level was the target, and the quantity of money was the instrument. But, as long as fractional-reserve banks remained in operation, the monetary authority would lack effective control over the instrument. Ensuring that the monetary authority had such control was one rationale for replacing fractional-reserve banks with 100-percent-reserve banks.

Simons soon concluded that, in principle, a price-level target is undesirable, because allowing the monetary authority to choose which price level to stabilize, thereby favoring some groups at the expense of others, would grant too much discretion to the monetary authority. Rejecting price-level stabilization as a monetary rule, Simons argued that the exercise of discretion could be avoided only if the quantity of money was both the target and the instrument of a monetary rule. Simons therefore favored keeping the quantity of money in the economy constant—forever. But after choosing the ideal rule, Simons rejected it, realizing that the reforms in the financial and monetary systems necessary to make the rule viable over the long run would never be adopted. So, reluctantly and regretfully, he reverted to the price-level stabilization rule that he and his colleagues proposed in 1933.

Milton Friedman continued to espouse Simons's opposition to discretion, and as late as 1960 he proposed a system of 100-percent-reserve banking. But eventually, he adopted a *k*-percent rule instead of 100-percent-reserve banking. After abandoning 100-percent-reserve banking, Friedman argued that the *k*-percent rule was less discretionary than the gold standard or a price-level rule, because neither the gold standard nor a price-level rule eliminated the exercise of discretion by the monetary authority in implementing policy, failing to acknowledge that, under any of the definitions that he used (usually M1 and sometimes M2), the quantity of money is just a target, not an instrument. But, unlike the target of a stable price level, the rate of growth in the quantity of money is a target for whose stabilization there is no independent rationale.

It is now, I think, generally understood that a monetary authority has available to it four primary instruments in conducting monetary policy, the quantity of base money, the lending rate it charges to banks, the deposit rate it pays banks on reserves, and an exchange rate in terms of some other currency or some asset. A variety of goals remain available as well, nominal goals like inflation, the price level, or nominal income, or even an index of stock prices (Farmer, 2016), as well as real goals like real GDP and employment.

Ever since Friedman (1968) and Phelps (1967) argued that the long-run Phillips Curve is vertical, a consensus has developed that countercyclical monetary policy is basically ineffectual, because the effects of countercyclical policy will be anticipated, so that the only long-run effect of countercyclical policy is to raise the average rate of inflation without affecting output and employment in the long run. Because the reasoning that generates this result is essentially that money is neutral in the long run, the reasoning is less compelling than the professional consensus in its favor might suggest. The monetary-neutrality result applies only under the very special assumptions of a comparative-statics exercise comparing an initial with a final equilibrium (Lipsey, 2017). But the whole point of countercyclical policy is to speed the adjustment from a disequilbrium with high-unemployment back to a low-unemployment equilibrium. A comparative-statics exercise provides no theoretical, much less empirical, support for the proposition that anticipated monetary policy cannot have real effects.

The range of possible targets and possible instruments now provide considerable latitude to recommend alternative monetary rules incorporating many different combinations of alternative instruments and targets. As of now, we have arrived at few solid theoretical conclusions about the relative effectiveness of alternative rules, and little empirical evidence about their effectiveness. But at least we know that, to be viable, a monetary rule must be expressed in terms of one or more targets while allowing the monetary authority at least some discretion to adjust its control over its chosen instruments in order to achieve its target (McCallum, 1987, 1988). That does not seem like a great deal of progress to have made in the two centuries since economists began puzzling over how to construct an appropriate rule to govern the decisions of the monetary authority. But it is progress nonetheless. And, if we are so inclined, we may at least take some comfort in knowing that earlier generations have left us a lot of room for improvement.

References

Attwood, T. (1817). *A letter to the right honourable Nicholas Vansittart, on the creation of money, and on its action on national prosperity*. Birmingham.

Bagehot, W. (1873 [1962]). *Lombard street: A description of the money market*. Irwin.

Bisson, T. N. (1979). *Conservation of coinage: Monetary exploitation and its restraint in France, Catalonia, and Aragon*. Oxford University Press.

Bloomfield, A. I. (1959). *Monetary policy under the international gold standard, 1880–1914*. Federal Reserve Bank of New York.

Boyd, W. (1801). *Letter to the right honourable William Pitt on the influence of the stoppage of issues in specie at the Bank of England on the prices of provisions and other commodities*. London. J. Wright.

Cannan, E. (1925). *The paper pound of 1797–1821* (2nd ed.). Routledge.

Cassel, G. (1923, November). The restoration of the gold standard. *Economica, 9*, 171–85.

Dworkin, R. (1967). The model of rules. *University of Chicago Law Review, 35*, 14–46.

Eichengreen, B. (1992). *Golden Fetters*. Oxford University Press.

Farmer, R. (2016). *Prosperity for all*. Oxford University Press.

Fetter, F. W. (1965). *The development of British monetary orthodoxy, 1797–1875*. Harvard University Press.

Fisher, I. (1920). *Stabilizing the dollar*. Macmillan.

Fisher, I. (1935). *100% Mony* Rev. ed. Adelphi.

Friedman, M. (1948). A monetary and fiscal framework for economic stability. *American Economic Review., 38*(3), 245–264.

Friedman, M. (1951). Commodity reserve currency. *Journal of Political Economy, 59*(3), 203–232.

Friedman, M. (1960). *A program for monetary stability*. Fordham University Press.

Friedman, M. (1961). Real and pseudo gold standards. *Journal of Law and Economics, 4*(2), 66–79.

Friedman, M. (1962a). *Capitalism and freedom*. University of Chicago Press.

Friedman, M. (1962b). Should there be an independent monetary authority? In L. Yeager (Ed.), *In search of a monetary constitution* (pp. 219–243). Harvard University Press.

Friedman, M. (1967). The monetary theory and policy of Henry Simons. *Journal of Law and Economics, 10*(2), 1–13.

Friedman, M. (1968). The role of monetary policy. *American Economic Review, 58*(1), 1–17.

Friedman, M. (1991). Foreward. *The Golden Franc: Memoirs of a governor of the Bank of France: The stabilization of the Franc (1926–1928)* by Emile Morreau. Westview Press.

Friedman, M., & Schwartz, A. J. (1963). *A monetary history of the United States, 1867–1960*. Princeton University Press.

Fullarton, J. (1845). *The regulation of currencies* (2nd ed.). John Murray.

Glasner, D. (1989). *Free banking and monetary reform*. Cambridge University Press.

Gregory, T. (1918 [1964]). *First Interim Report of the Cunliffe Committee on currency and foreign exchanges*. In T. Gregory (Ed.), *Select statutes, documents and reports relating to British banking, 1832–1928*. Routledge.

Hawtrey, R. G. (1919 [1923]). The gold standard. *Economic Journal, 29*(116), 428–442, in Hawtrey, *Monetary reconstruction* (pp. 48–65). Longmans, Green and Co.

Hawtrey, R. G. (1932). *The art of central banking*. Longmans, Green.

Hayek, F. A. (1960). *The constitution of liberty*. University of Chicago Press.

Hayek, F. A. (1978). *The denationalization of money* (2nd ed.). Institute of Economic Affairs.

Hirshleifer, J. (1970). *Investment, interest, and capital*. Prentice-Hall.
Hume, D. (1752 [2006]). Of the balance of trade. In E. Rotwein (Ed.), *Writings on economics* (pp. 60–77). Routledge.
Irwin, D. A. (2014). Who anticipated the Great Depression? Gustav Cassel versus Keynes and Hayek on the interwar gold standard. *Journal of Money, Credit and Banking, 46*(1), 197–228.
Johnson, H. C. (1997). *Gold, France and the Great Depression, 1919–1932*. Yale University Press.
Keynes, J. M. (1923). *A tract on monetary reform*. Macmillan.
King (Lord). (1804 [1844]). Thoughts on the effects of the bank restrictions, 2nd edition. In E. Fortescue (Ed.), *A selection from the speeches and writings of the late Lord King*. Longman, Brown, Green, and Longmans.
Krugman, P. (1998). It's Baaack: Japan's slump and the return of the liquidity trap. *Brookings Papers on Economic Activity, 1998*(2), 137–205.
Kydland, F., & Prescott, E. C. (1977). Rules rather than discretion. *Journal of Political Economy, 85*(3), 473–491.
Laidler, D. (1988). British monetary orthodoxy in the 1870s. *Oxford Economic Papers, 40*(1), 74–109.
Laidler, D. (2017). Economic ideas, the monetary order and the uneasy case for policy rules. *Journal of Macroeconomics, 54*(PA), 12–23.
Lipsey, R. G. (2017). Is money ever neutral? The neutrality of money reconsidered. Simon Fraser University Department of Economics Discussion paper.
Lucas, R. (1976). Econometric policy evaluation: A critique. *Carnegie-Rochester Conference Series on Public Policy, 1*, 19–46.
Mazumder, S., & Wood, J. H. (2013). The Great Deflation of 1929–33: It almost had to happen. *Journal of Economic History, 66*(1), 156–177.
McCallum, B. T. (1987). The case for rules in the conduct of monetary policy: A concrete example. *Weltwirtshaftliches Archiv, 123*(3), 415–429.
McCallum, B. T. (1988). Robustness properties of a rule for monetary policy. *Carnegie-Rochester Conference Series on Public Policy, 29*, 173–204.
McCloskey, D. N., & Zecher, J. R. (1976). How the gold standard worked: 1880–1913. In J. A. Frenkel & H. G. Johnson (Eds.), *The monetary approach to the balance of payments*. University of Toronto Press.
Mouré, K. (1991). *Managing the Franc Poincaré*. Cambridge University Press.
Mouré, K. (2002). *The gold standard illusion*. Oxford University Press.
Phelps, E. S. (1967). Phillips curves, expectations of inflation and optimal unemployment over time. *Economica, 34*(135), 254–281.
Phillips, R. J. (1995). *The Chicago plan and new deal banking reform*. Routledge.
Ricardo, D. (1810 [1951]). The high price of bullion. In P. Sraffa (Ed.), *The works and correspondence of David Ricardo* (pp. 47–127). Cambridge University Press.

Ricardo, D. (1811 [1951]). Reply to Mr. Bosanquet. In P. Sraffa (Ed.), *The works and correspondence of David Ricardo* (pp. 155–256). Cambridge University Press.

Schwartz, A. J. (2008). Banking school, currency school, free banking school. In S. N. Durlauf & L. E. Blume (Eds.), *The new Palgrave dictionary of economics* (2nd ed.) Macmillan.

Selgin, G. (1988). *The theory of free banking*. Rowman & Littlefield.

Simons, H. C. et al. (1933). Banking and currency reform. Manuscript, reprinted *in Research in the history of economic thought and methodology* (Vol. 8). W. Samuels (Ed.). JAI Press.

Simons, H. C. (1936). Rules versus authorities in monetary policy. *Journal of Political Economy, 44*(1), 1–30.

Smith, A. (1937). *The wealth of nations*. E. Cannan (Ed.). Modern Library.

Sumner, S. (2015). *The Midas Paradox: Financial markets, government policy shocks, and the Great Depression*. Independent Institute.

Thornton, H. (1802 [1939]). *An enquiry into the nature and effects of the paper credit of Great Britain*. F. A. Hayek (Ed.). George Allen & Unwin.

White, L. H. (1984). *Free banking in Great Britain: Theory, experience and debate*. Cambridge University Press.

CHAPTER 9

Say's Law and the Classical Theory of Depressions

9.1 Introduction

Say's Law occupies a prominent, but uncertain, position in the history of economics, having been the object of repeated controversies since the early nineteenth century. Despite a formidable secondary literature, the recurring controversies still demand a clear resolution. Say's Law has been variously defined, and arguments about its meaning and validity have not reached a consensus about what is being attacked or defended. So, I propose in this chapter to reconsider Say's Law in a way faithful in spirit to how it was understood by its principal architects, J. B. Say, James Mill, and David Ricardo and to their contemporary critics, while providing a conceptual framework within which to assess the views of both the original participants and subsequent commentators.

In doing so, I hope to dispel perhaps the oldest and certainly the most enduring misunderstanding about Say's Law: that it somehow was meant to assert that depressions cannot occur, or that they are self-correcting if market forces are allowed to operate freely. As I have tried to suggest with the title of this paper, Say's Law was actually one of the insights into the causes of depressions imparted by the classical economists. Indeed, a version of the idea underlying Say's Law also underlies those modern explanations of depressions that emphasize coordination failures, though

D. Glasner, *Studies in the History of Monetary Theory*,
Palgrave Studies in the History of Economic Thought,
https://doi.org/10.1007/978-3-030-83426-5_9

Say's Law conveys an additional insight missing from most modern explanations.

The conception of Say's Law articulated in this paper bears a resemblance to what Clower and Leijonhufvud (1981) called Say's Principle. However, their distinction between Say's Law and Say's Principle suggests a narrower conception and application of Say's Principle than is warranted. And their endorsement of the idea that the validity of Say's Law critically depends on the absence of money implies the straightforward misinterpretation of Say's Law earlier propounded by, among others, Hayek, Lange, and Patinkin in which only what became known as Walras's Law, and not Say's Law, is a logically necessary property of a general-equilibrium system. Finally, it is appropriate to note at the outset that, in most respects, the conception of Say's Law for which I shall be arguing was anticipated in a quirky, but unjustly neglected, work by Hutt (1975) and by the important, and similarly neglected, work of Earl Thompson (1974).

In the next section, I offer a restatement of the Classical conception of Say's Law. That conception was indeed based on the insight that, in the now familiar formulation, supply creates its own demand. But to grasp how this insight was originally understood, one must first understand the problem for which Say's Law was the proposed solution. The problem concerns the relationship between a depression and a general glut of all goods, but has two aspects. First, is there any sense in which it could be said that a depression is caused by a general glut of all goods? Second, in a market economy is it logically conceivable that there could be a general glut of *all* goods? In Section 9.3, I consider the early objections to Say's Law and the responses to those objections offered by the originators of the doctrine. In Sect. 9.4, I discuss the modern objections offered to Say's Law, their relation to the earlier objections, and the validity of those modern objections. In Sect. 9.5, I re-examine the Classical doctrine, relating it explicitly to a theory of depressions characterized by insufficient aggregate demand. I also elaborate on the important, but subtle, differences between my understanding of Say's Law and what Clower and Leijonhufvud called Say's Principle. In Sect. 9.6, I show that, when considered in the context of a temporary-equilibrium model, in which there is an incomplete set of forward and state-contingent markets, not even Walras's Law, let alone Say's Law, is a necessary property of the model. An understanding of the conditions in which neither Walras's

Law nor Say's Law is satisfied provides an important insight into financial crises and the systemic coordination failures characteristic of the deep depressions to which they lead.

9.2 The Classical Conception of Say's Law

Say's Law was originally advanced to refute a perennially popular explanation of recurrent depressions: that they are symptomatic of a general glut of unsold commodities caused by overproduction. This notion has been a staple of the literature on business cycles and crises since the eighteenth century. A corollary of the general-glut theory of depressions, or at least it seemed so to early exponents of the theory, is that, by eliminating the glut that had caused it, restricting output and supply could alleviate, or even cure, an ongoing depression.

The early classical economists strove to refute this idea, and it was J. B. Say (1803) who provided the most famous statement of their position, which came to be known as The Law of the Markets, or simply Say's Law. The Law expresses the simple insight that all exchanges are reciprocal, so that there can be no demand without supply, and the offer to supply constitutes a corresponding demand. Hence, a state of depression in which workers cannot find employment reflects neither a general oversupply of all goods nor insufficient aggregate demand. "Products," Say (1803, 2:179) insisted, "can never be too abundant, since some provide the means of purchasing the others."

What must be occurring in a state of depression is rather some disproportionality or misalignment between supply and demand, some commodities being in excess supply and others in correspondingly excess demand. Far from eliminating the glut, restrictions of output cause demand to shrink further. The cure for a depression is to shift productive resources from producing outputs in oversupply relative to demand to producing outputs in undersupply relative to demand.

To understand the meaning and significance of the proposition that supply creates its own demand, one must understand the conceptual problem that the classical exponents of Say's Law wished to solve: how to understand what happens in a depression, when businesses have unsold stocks of goods and workers cannot find employment. The commonsense interpretation of such events is that the aggregate desire to produce and to sell exceeds the aggregate desire to consume and to buy. The apparently reasonable inference that follows from that interpretation is that suppliers could more easily dispose of their goods and services if only they reduced output. If so, restricting output would seem like a reasonable response to a depression.

Classical supporters of Say's Law like David Ricardo challenged that interpretation. Lack of "adaptation" to "the wants and tastes of society" was, according to Ricardo (1951, 415), "the only cause of the stagnation which commerce at different times experiences." The Classical economists therefore denied the apparently commonsense observation that the failure of everyone to sell as much as he wanted to sell signaled overproduction. Restricting output to eliminate the glut, in their view, only exacerbates the shrinkage of demand. While this is all that Say's Law was intended to show, the attacks by critics and the responses of its proponents drew the debate into discussions of related issues. Those discussions, concerning which the contributions of the proponents of Say's Law were often less lucid than they were on the central question, led to confusion about the meaning, significance and validity of Say's Law. I turn now to these related questions.

9.3 The Classical Objections to Say's Law

Attempting to refute Say's Law, the general-glut theorists, of whom the most prominent were Malthus and Sismondi, advanced a variety of objections and counterexamples intended to show that Say's Law need not hold under all circumstances and that a general-glut theory of depressions is indeed logically tenable. Classical supporters of Say's Law rejected those objections completely. However, Say (1826) himself eventually conceded that certain exceptions to his law might be found, leading some to conclude that Say eventually modified his original denial of the possibility of a general glut of commodities. But I am going to suggest that Say's concessions that a general glut might be possible under some circumstances did not substantively modify his denial that a general glut could cause a depression. I now consider individually the objections raised against Say's Law in the Classical period.

The Supply of Commodities May Reflect a Demand to Hold Money Rather than a Demand for Other Commodities

The fundamental idea expressed by Say's Law, that, to be effective, demands must be financed by corresponding supplies of other commodities, has widely been understood to hold only in a barter economy. Indeed, at least since Patinkin's (1948, 1951, 1965) exhaustive treatment of the subject, this has been the standard, and seemingly conclusive, objection to Say's Law. In a money economy, it is argued, a supply of goods need not represent a demand for real goods, only a demand to increase holdings of cash. In that case, supplying real commodities need not entail a corresponding demand for other commodities. An overall excess supply, or glut, of commodities may therefore be offset merely by an excess demand to hold (or, in the term used by the classical economists "hoard') money. I return to this objection in Sect. 9.4.

Though they worked without a formal general-equilibrium model, the classical proponents of Say's Law took notice of this objection and understood its import. They responded in two ways, one straightforward and one subtle. The straightforward response was to the formal question of what, as a matter of accounting, corresponds to an excess demand to hold money. The subtle one responds to the causal question whether restricting the supply of commodities would indeed eliminate an excess supply of commodities. Unfortunately, neither response has been well understood by the literature, which, as often happens, fails to distinguish between accounting identities and equilibrium conditions.

I have already discussed the straightforward response in Chapter 2 (also see Glasner, 1989). The upshot of the response is that, given a convertible, competitively supplied, money (the institutional norm for most of the classical period), the early mainstream classical economists, (including Smith, Say, James Mill, and Ricardo), as well as the later classical economists associated with, or sympathetic to, the Banking School, (such as Tooke, Fullarton, and J. S Mill) believed that market forces would induce competitive banks to supply as much money as the public demanded at a price level determined not by the quantity of money, but by convertibility. In such a monetary environment, an excess demand for money is not offset by an excess supply of commodities. Instead, the excess demand for money corresponds to an offsetting excess supply of assets offered to the banking system in exchange for monetary liabilities issued by the banking system. An excess demand for money need cause no offsetting excess supply of real commodities. Rather, the disturbance is confined, at least in theory, to the monetary sector, inducing a purely monetary adjustment to the monetary disturbance.[1]

The subtle response is that, even if there is an aggregate excess supply of commodities, reducing output would not restore equilibrium, because reducing output would inevitably reduce demand, so that the excess supply of commodities would not be eliminated.

The secondary literature on Say's Law has therefore doubly misunderstood the response of classical proponents of Say's Law to the objection that the Law does not hold when an excess demand for money is offset by an excess supply of commodities. First, much of the secondary literature has identified Say's Law with the proposition that the aggregate excess demand for real commodities is always zero. However, this proposition is different from Say's Law as a denial of the general-glut theoryof depressions and underlies the distinction made by Becker and Baumol (1952) between Say's Identity and Say's Law.

However, the latter distinction merely contrasts the proposition that the sum of all excess demands for real commodities identically equals zero (Say's Identity), which is valid for a barter economy, but (supposedly) not for a money economy, with the proposition that in a general equilibrium the sum of all excess demands for real commodities equals zero (Say's Law), which is an uninteresting implication of the definition of a general equilibrium. What the straightforward response discussed above shows is that, when a competitive banking system supplies a convertible money, Say's Identity does hold, just as it would under a barter economy, thereby collapsing the distinction between Say's Law and Say's Identity. The latter distinction failed to recognize the existence, first noticed formally by Thompson (1974), of a second market in the monetary sector of an economy with a privately supplied money, a market for money-backing services in which private agents exchange their IOUs with banks for bank IOUs that are generally accepted media of exchange. Excess demands and supplies in these two markets are offsetting, so that the excess demands in the real sector of the economy satisfy Say's Identity.

But the subtle response is concerned with the causes of, and remedies for, business cycles, not with a mere accounting identity. Under

[1] I should note that a formally analogous mechanism operates when there is an excess supply of money. The mechanism was described and analyzed at length by Fullarton (1845) under the heading of the law of reflux. See Chapters 2–4.

the interpretation advanced in this chapter, Say's Law asserts (1) that a state of depression cannot be caused by a general glut of commodities, and (2) that a depression or a general excess supply of commodities cannot be remedied by reducing output. But Say's Identity means that an excess demand for money does not imply an offsetting excess supply of commodities and is therefore closely related—perhaps even necessary for—but not equivalent, to Say's Law as a proposition about causality. For although the causal version of Say's Law also implies that an excess demand for money is not offset by an excess supply of commodities, the causal version of Say's Law has the added implication that restricting the supply of goods causes the aggregate demand for commodities to contract. This version of Say's Law implies that a depression can result from cumulative restrictions of output in multiple markets for goods, providing the germ of a theory of the mechanism whereby an output restriction in one market is transmitted, and even amplified, from one market to another and another, and so on. This point below will bear further attention below.

A related objection to Say's Law is that supplies of commodities in the present may reflect demands for future commodities rather than present ones, so that a current general glut of commodities could result from a general increase in the desire to save for the future. But since the Classical economists, including general-glut theorists, generally assumed that savings would be directly transformed into investment, I consider this objection to Say's Law in the next section on modern objections to Say's Law.

Entrepreneurial Error Can Cause Temporary Levels of Unsustainably High Output and Employment

In attempting to refute the reasoning, articulated by Say's Law, that denies that depressions are a manifestation of, or caused by, a general glut of commodities, critics of Say's Law (Malthus, 1836; Sismondi, 1827) subtly shifted the terms of the debate, seeking to demonstrate the abstract theoretical possibility of a general glut of commodities (Sowell, 1972). They did so by supposing that capitalists with overly optimistic price expectations might invest so heavily and offer so much employment that the resulting output could be sold only at prices below those that had been expected. Optimistic entrepreneurial price expectations having been disappointed, the realized level of output produced would be unsustainable, and therefore could, in that sense, be construed as a general glut of output.

On this point, the reasoning of critics of Say's Law was fundamentally sound, presaging a theory of intertemporal equilibrium in which current production decisions affecting future output are based not on observed current prices, but on expected future prices. Such problems of intertemporal inconsistency provide an important insight into the origins and character of financial crises. But the insights were not systematically developed and remained in the background in the classical discussions of Say's Law. Indeed, its full import and significance remain largely unrecognized.[2]

In contrast, the defenders of Say's Law, with the notable exception of Say (1826) himself, who ultimately conceded the possibility of a general glut under the assumed circumstances, mistakenly sought to refute this argument of their critics. However, since the whole point of Say's Law was to deny that a general glut could be the cause of a depression, the demonstration that a state of overproduction and overemployment (i.e., the exact opposite of a depression) was possible hardly undermined the essential validity of the doctrine. On the contrary, the hypothetical situation in which the glut occurs is at the peak of the cycle, not, as commonly supposed, at its trough.

Of course, it could be argued that a state of overproduction and overemployment is a necessary prelude to a depression (as in overinvestment theories of the business cycle, like that of the Austrian School). The sequel to such a state need not be a smooth asymptotic return to a sustainable long-run equilibrium growth path; it may be a cyclical adjustment in which output and employment first fall below their long-run path. But such an argument would require a more elaborate chain of reasoning than any provided by the general-glut theorists who attacked Say's Law. Nor could such a chain of reasoning proceed without, at least implicitly, relying on the basic insight of Say's Law to explain how withdrawals of supply, previously offered under overly optimistic expectations, might

[2] I draw attention, in Chapter 17, to the insights of the intertemporal-equilibrium framework in which, owing to the incomplete array of markets, expected prices must be viewed as equilibrating variables rather than as parameters, or as definitionally rational, so that expected prices are always assumed to be equal to their future equilibrium values.

lead to a cumulative contraction of demand. To explain how an unsustainable level of output leads not just to a reversion to the long-run growth path, but to a decline of output below that path, one has to account for a contraction of aggregate demand that prevents rapid reversion to that path. Such an explanation would likely rely on arguments about the cumulative impact of non-clearing markets and a resulting (perhaps involuntary[3]) withholding of supply. In other words, it would rely on arguments bearing at least a family resemblance to Say's Law.

Say's Law Is Inconsistent with the Observed Existence of States of Depression

The charge that Say's Law implies that states of depression cannot occur, and that it is therefore refuted by recurring observations of such states, is a familiar, but not well-founded, argument. Say's Law was advanced to dispute a particular theory about the cause of the periodic depressions or commercial crises of the eighteenth and early nineteenth centuries. The intention of its originators was therefore obviously not to deny that such states could occur, but to deny that the cause of those disturbances was a general glut of commodities. The argument was that mismatches between supply and demand cause reductions of realized supply in some markets, thereby triggering a cumulative contraction of demand for commodities in general. Although Say's Law may be satisfied, in a strictly accounting sense, both in a state of depression and in a state of full employment, it also says something important about the dynamic process leading from a state of full employment to a state of depression.

The almost directly opposite criticism of Say's Law, that it is consistent with any level of aggregate income, was raised by Keynes and his followers in attempting to highlight the absence of a theory of aggregate income in classical economics. I consider this criticism at length in the next section.

[3] By "involuntary," I mean a failure of the optimizing choices of independent agents to be mutually consistent, so that some or all of those optimizing choices cannot be executed as intended. I discuss the point about the inability of agents to execute their optimizing plans at length in Chapter 17 and more briefly in Sect. 9.6 of this chapter.

9.4 Modern Objections to Say's Law

In discussions of Say's Law since Keynes (1936) attacked the doctrine, two further criticisms of the doctrine, to which I have already alluded briefly, have been raised. One is that the current supply of commodities may reflect a demand for future rather than present commodities; the other is that Say's Law implies that any level of income is consistent with equilibrium. I turn first to the intertemporal objection.

The Supply of Commodities May Reflect a Demand for Future Commodities Rather than a Demand for Current Commodities

Most Classical theorists regarded it as a truism that savings would, more or less automatically, be transformed into investment. They did not, therefore, seriously entertain the possibility that attempts to increase future consumption by increasing current savings would reduce current expenditure. However, the separation of saving from investment decisions is a crucial feature of the Keynesian theory of aggregate demand and of the possibility of an underemployment equilibrium. That separation means that an increase in ex ante saving does not necessarily induce a corresponding increase in ex ante investment. In the Keynesian model, the difference between ex ante saving and ex ante investment is eliminated by a contraction of total spending and income. What prevents ex ante investment from increasing to match an increase in ex ante savings in the Keynesian theory is that the rate of interest does not fall sufficiently to induce an increase in ex ante investment sufficient to absorb the added saving, because liquidity preference induces people to try to add to their cash balances when the rate of interest falls.

But with the stock of money exogenously fixed, as Keynes (1936, 174) assumed it to be, the collective attempt to increase aggregate cash holdings is futile, causing instead aggregate expenditure and income to decline. Rather than stimulate investment by reducing the rate of interest sufficiently to maintain the original equilibrium level of expenditure and income, the attempt to increase saving causes reduced expenditure and income to fall, the gap between ex ante saving and ex ante investment being closed by a decline in ex ante saving induced by a decline in income.

Say's Law and Walras's Law

Thus, in the Keynesian version of this criticism, it is because saving can be held as cash and withdrawn from the income-expenditure flow, that an act of saving need not be transformed into a corresponding investment expenditure that would prevent spending from falling below the level consistent with full employment. This objection to Say's Law is therefore just an alternative articulation of an objection already made by nineteenth-century critics (considered above in Sect. 9.3) that an increased demand to hold money can cause aggregate expenditure and income to contract.

As already noted, the argument did not go without response, but the nature and import of the response were not well, or widely, understood, and the criticism was widely credited. Thus, in his early writings on business-cycle theory, F. A. Hayek (1929 [1933]), making no claim to originality, maintained, matter of factly, that money involves a disconnect between aggregate supply and aggregate demand, describing money as a "loose joint" in the theory of general equilibrium.

Oskar Lange (1942) subsequently provided a formal statement of the problem, introducing a distinction between Say's Law and Walras's Law. Lange defined Walras's Law as the proposition that the sum of excess demands, corresponding to any price vector announced by a Walrasian auctioneer, must identically equal zero.[4] In a barter model, individual optimization subject to the budget constraint corresponding to a given price vector implies that the value of the planned purchases and planned sales by each agent are exactly equal; the sum of all individual excess demands must therefore equal zero. In a barter model, Walras's Law and Say's Law are equivalent.

But in a model in which agents hold cash to be used when transacting, they may supply real goods in order to add to their cash holdings. Because individual agents may seek to change their cash holdings, Lange argued that the equivalence between Walras's Law and Say's Law in a barter model does not carry over to a monetary-exchange model. Say's Law is invalid in such model unless excess demands in the markets for real goods sum to zero. But if agents all wish to add to their holdings of cash, their excess demands for cash are offset by an excess supply of goods, which is precisely what Say's Law (in the accounting sense) denies. It is only when an equilibrium price vector is found at which excess demands in

[4] Excess supplies are recorded as negative excess demands.

each market are zero that Say's Law is satisfied. Say's Law, then, becomes a contingent property of general equilibrium, not, as Say and his contemporaries and followers had supposed, a necessary accounting relationship characterizing rational economic conduct.

When our analysis is extended from a barter to a monetary setting, Say's Law must be restated in the generalized form of Walras's Law. But, unlike Say's Law, Walras's Law does not exclude the possibility of an aggregate excess supply of all goods. Aggregate demand can be deficient, and result in involuntary unemployment.

At bottom, this critique of Say's Law depends on the assumption that the quantity of money is exogenously fixed, so that individuals can increase or decrease their holdings of money only by spending either less or more than their incomes. However, as noted above in Sect. 9.3, if there is a market mechanism whereby an increased demand for cash balances elicits the desired increased in cash balances, so that the public need not reduce expenditures to finance additions to their holdings of cash, Lange's critique loses its force.

A competitive monetary system based on convertibility into gold or some other asset[5] has, at least potentially, this self-adjusting property. When money is privately supplied, additional cash is created when a bank accepts the money-backing asset (IOU) offered by a customer in exchange for issuing its liability (a banknote or a deposit) that is generally accepted as a medium of exchange. As first pointed out by Thompson (1974) Lange's analytical oversight was to assume that in a Walrasian model with n real goods and money, there are only $(n + 1)$ goods or assets. However, there are really $(n + 2)$ goods or assets; there are n real goods and two monetary assets (i.e., the money issued by the bank and the money-backing asset in exchange for which the money is issued). Thus, an excess demand for money need not be associated with, or offset by, an excess supply of real commodities, as Lange assumed; it may be offset by a supply of money-backing assets offered by agents seeking to increase their cash holdings.[6]

[5] The classical economists generally regarded gold or silver as the appropriate underlying asset into which privately issued monies would be convertible, but the possibility of a fiat standard was not rejected on analytical principle.

[6] Following Thompson (1977), I made this point in Glasner (1989). The point had been made previously by Rueff (1947) and Shackle (1967).

Say's Law Implies that any Level of Aggregate Income Is Consistent with Macroeconomic Equilibrium

Say's Law asserts that the source of the demand for commodities in general is the supply of commodities offered in exchange. This idea was interpreted by Keynes to mean that aggregate demand and aggregate supply are identical concepts, meaning that any level of aggregate demand corresponds to an identical level of aggregate supply, so that any level of aggregate demand, regardless of unemployment associated with that level of aggregate demand, is an equilibrium. In Keynes's terminology, Say's Law implies that the aggregate-expenditure (demand) curve in the naive Keynesian cross diagram coincides with the 45° line (the aggregate-supply curve) at every income level.

At a Keynesian level of aggregation, this argument has some plausibility. But even at that level of aggregation, not every level of income corresponds to an equilibrium in both the labor market and the commodity market unless the labor-supply curve is perfectly elastic at some real wage up to the point of absolute labor exhaustion (at which point, the curve becomes perfectly inelastic). As the level of aggregation is reduced, comparing the level of total income between states corresponding to different degrees of disequilibrium in individual markets is no longer straightforward. In a dynamic disaggregated model, the connection between the macroanalysis of aggregate income and expenditure and the microanalysis of equilibrium in individual markets dissolves, and the dynamic properties of the two models are incommensurable. At best, the insights of either may inform the choice of exogenous factors introduced ad hoc into the dynamic analysis of the other.

The insight that Say's Law offers into the contraction of expenditure and output in a depression is that restricting supply or output is more apt to reinforce than to dampen those contractionary forces. Nor does Say's Law imply that macro-equilibrium is consistent with any level of aggregate demand and aggregate income. Rather, it asserts that the level of aggregate demand is affected by the magnitude of notional excess demands in individual markets. It is therefore worth exploring how Say's Law may provide a conceptual bridge between the analysis of disequilibria at the micro level of individual markets and at the macro-level of aggregate income.

9.5 Say's Law in a Theory of Depression

The burden of my argument has been that Say's Law, as conceived by its Classical expounders, has been imperfectly understood by most critics, and that most of the criticisms leveled against it have been either incorrect, beside the point, or, at best, correct under a set of assumptions different from those posited by those expounders. In making this argument, I have tried to proceed at a level of abstraction not too different from that at which it was originally expounded. I believe that it will be helpful now to restate the argument at a somewhat higher level of abstraction.

Modern macroanalysis is, for better or worse, generally based on some variant of the Walrasian general-equilibrium model. A general equilibrium is defined as an allocation of resources and commodities and a price vector such that excess demands in all markets are less than or equal to zero and the value of any strictly negative excess demand is zero (because the corresponding price is zero). In the standard Walrasian model, no trading occurs at a disequilibrium price vector. The equilibrium price vector is found via a *tâtonnement* process in which an "auctioneer" calculates planned excess demands at a sequence of provisional price vectors, with no trading allowed at any provisional price vector until an equilibrium price vector is discovered by trial and error.[7] Within this paradigm, Walras's Law is a straightforward result given the standard Arrow-Debreu assumptions of a complete set of markets for present, future, and contingent delivery.

In the non-Walrasian world that we inhabit, with no auctioneer to compute planned demands and supplies at a provisional price vector, the planned excess demand for, or planned excess supply of, a particular good at any moment is neither registered nor observed. Instead, trading of any commodity at a disequilibrium price vector[8] is limited to the lesser of the amount of that commodity notionally demanded and the amount notionally supplied. An excess notional supply of any commodity at a given price

[7] For analytical convenience and other reasons, but without strong analytical justification or plausibility, the equilibrium price vector is typically assumed to be unique.

[8] I refer to a price vector, because the amounts demanded and supplied of almost any good depend not just on the price of that particular good, but on the entire array of prices for substitutes and complements to that particular good. However, price adjustments for any particular good are generally responsive, in the first instance, to the state of excess demand for that particular good.

vector normally[9] implies that the amount actually supplied is less than the amount that would have been supplied at the equilibrium price vector.[10] In this case, the amount actually supplied equals not the amount that would have been supplied at the equilibrium price vector, but the (lesser) amount actually demanded at the actual (disequilibrium) price vector at which trading occurs.

However, the effects of disequilibrium cannot be confined to a single market. If we abstract from the existence of durable assets and the possibility of borrowing or lending, then the value of total actual purchases of every individual in any time period cannot exceed the value of that individual's total actual sales in that period. If an agent's realized sales are constrained by demand at a disequilibrium price vector, the agent's actual purchases (effective demand) must be correspondingly limited. Disequilibrium in one market, by reducing realized sales (from which purchases are financed) relative to sales that would have been realized at the equilibrium price vector, necessarily reduces the overall demand for other goods.[11]

Thus, modern interpretations of Say's Law, hewing to the Walrasian general-equilibrium paradigm, miss the central message that Say's Law tried to convey: that a restriction of supply, whether deliberate or unplanned, in any market reduces demand in other markets. Moreover, insofar as a disequilibrium in one market reduces demand in other markets, the absence of an auctioneer to ensure that a new general-equilibrium price vector is reestablished before trading resumes causes disequilibria in other markets, possibly triggering a cumulative contraction in realized sales and, hence, in total demand, via what Hutt (1975)

[9] By "normally," I mean that suppliers cannot compel unwilling buyers to purchase their unsold wares.

[10] This statement is not strictly correct inasmuch as it is at least theoretically possible that, at the equilibrium price vector, the amount of a particular commodity that is actually supplied would be less than the notional supply at the disequilibrium price vector owing to changes in the prices and quantities of other commodities that cause a contraction in the equilibrium amount demanded and supplied of any particular commodity.

[11] Demands for goods that are close substitutes might actually increase since the above-equilibrium price for any particular good might increase the demand for goods that are close substitutes.

called a "supply-side multiplier." If trading contracts before an equilibrium price vector is restored, a downward spiral of prices and output may result.[12]

If transactors do not supply as much as they had planned to at prevailing prices, then, depending on the soundness of their balance-sheets, and the resilience of credit markets, transactors may curtail their demands in subsequent periods; a failure to supply as much as had been planned in the previous period tends to reduce demand in this period. If the "distance" from equilibrium is large enough, the demand failure may be amplified, rather than damped, in subsequent periods. Thus, Clower and Leijonhufvud (1981) showed that the Keynesian multiplier was, at bottom, just another way of articulating the insight embodied in Say's Law (or, if one insists on distinguishing what Say meant from Lange's reformulation of it, Say's Principle).

The foregoing argument relies on both Hutt (1975) and Clower and Leijonhufvud (1981). However, it differs from Clower and Leijonhufvud in two respects. Adopting Clower's (1967) distinction between money and barter, Clower and Leijonhufvud argued that that distinction is critical to understanding the effective-demand failure that concerned Keynes. The existence of a medium of exchange that is demanded not only to be used in exchange, but to be held as an asset is what can cause total spending to fall and unemployment to rise. But the money-barter distinction seems artificial, because what gives rise to a medium of exchange is the variety and heterogeneity of goods that are being traded. And it is that variety and complexity in the exchange process that increases the vulnerability of that process to destabilizing disturbances and possible breakdowns.

Consider a model with just two goods, say labor and corn, there is only one relative price to be determined, and a planned excess supply of labor would be offset by a corresponding planned excess demand for corn. A disequilibrium will be restored by adjustment of the single relative price. A cumulative contraction of demand caused by an excess supply of labor

[12] The point is not whether prices (and wages) are "sticky"; it is whether flexibility leads to the restoration of an equilibrium. The flexibility of prices is irrelevant; what matters is whether the price vector is at an equilibrium. Prices in each market, responding to the excess demand or supply in that market, will not necessarily arrive at an equilibrium, because the equilibrium price in each market depends not just on the price in that market, but on prices in all other markets. The Walrasian price-adjustment algorithm need not reach the equilibrium price vector in a finite number of iterations.

occurs only if an equilibrium price vector is not restored. It is not the absence of money that rules out the possibility of a cumulative contraction of demand implicit in Say's Law; it is the level of aggregation in which a single homogeneous output excludes the possibility of a disequilibrium relative price vector.

If an additional good, say, wine, is added to the economy, a cumulative contraction becomes possible when a disequilibrium relative price of wine in terms of corn creates a planned excess supply of corn and an excess demand for wine. Because less wine is produced than demanded and corn suppliers can't sell as much as they would like to, total output (and, hence, total income) is less than its potential. Workers work fewer hours than they would be willing to work, or some workers who would like to work can't get jobs. In this simple three-good example, it is easy to see what adjustments are needed, but as the number of goods and the number of relative prices that need to be equilibrated increases, the chances increase that prices in some markets will be misaligned, and resources misallocated, increase. With each misalignment and misallocation, the potential for those disturbances to be transmitted from market to market, and from sector to sector, increase. The magnitude of these potentially cumulative contractions depends on the size of the initial disequilibrium, on the speed with which a new equilibrium relative-price vector is restored, and on the extent of interdependence among the markets.

The upshot of this simple example is twofold: first to refocus attention on the idea of disproportionality that the originators of Say's Law emphasized in attempting to explain how depressions occur, and, second, to cast doubt on the role of highly aggregated models that, even before Keynes, have characterized macroeconomic theory. Highly aggregated models have provoked a certain unease among critics of macroeconomic analysis, but the general argument that aggregation involves not just simplification, but abstracts from some fundamental characteristics of economic interactions (e.g., Hayek, 1967, 30) has received less attention than it deserves. Indeed, the widespread, and largely uncritical, adoption of representative-agent one-sector or two-sector models in macroeconomics has, in my view, taken macroeconomics in exactly the wrong direction.

9.6 Say's Law Violated

I have argued that Clower and Leijonhufvud and Hutt explained how the insight underlying Say's Law provides a basis for a theory of the mechanism that can propagate and amplify a disequilibrating disturbance in one market or sector into a broader macroeconomic disturbance and disequilibrium. I now want to extend the argument by relaxing the strict Walrasian framework within which Lange formalized both Walras's Law and Say's Law. It can then be shown that, under plausible conditions, neither Walras's Law nor Say's Law is satisfied.

Following Radner (1972), I relax the Walrasian framework by assuming that there is an incomplete set of forward and state-contingent markets within which to undertake future transactions in the present (see Chapter 17). Without a complete set of markets in which future prices are determined and visible to all agents, agents must formulate their intertemporal plans for production and consumption relying only on observed current prices and their expectations of, currently unobservable, future prices. As already noted, the standard proofs of Walras's Law and of Say's Law (or Identity) are premised on the assumption that all agents make decisions about purchases and sales based on their common knowledge of all current and future prices.

In the temporary-equilibrium framework introduced by Hicks (1939), economic agents make their production and consumption decisions based not on their common knowledge of all current and future market prices, but on their own conjectural expectations of future prices, expectations that may—or may not—be correct, and may—or may not—be aligned with the expectations of other agents. Unless the agents' expectations of future prices are aligned, the expectations of some, or all, agents must be disappointed, and the plans to buy and sell, formulated based on those expectations, will have to be revised, or abandoned, once agents realize that their expectations were incorrect.

Consider a simple two-person, two-good, two-period model in which agents make plans based on current prices observed in period 1 and their expectations of what prices will be in period 2. Given price expectations for period 2, period-1 prices are determined in a *tâtonnement* process, so that no trading occurs until a temporary-equilibrium price vector for period 1 is found. Assume, further, that price expectations for period 2 do not change in the course of the *tâtonnement*. Once a period-1 equilibrium price vector is found, the two budget constraints subject to which the agents make their optimal decisions, need not have the same values for expected prices in period 2, because it is not assumed that the period-2 price expectations of the two agents are aligned. Because the proof of Walras's Law posits that agents base their decisions to buy and sell each commodity on prices for each commodity in each period that are common to all agents, Walras's Law cannot be proved unless the period-2 price expectations of all agents are aligned.

The implication of the potential violation of Walras's Law is that when actual prices turn out to be different from those that had been expected, economic agents, who previously assumed obligations that are about to come due, may be unable to discharge those obligations. In standard general-equilibrium models, the *tâtonnement* process assures that no trading takes place unless equilibrium prices have been identified. But in a temporary-equilibrium model, when decisions to purchase and sell are based not on equilibrium prices, but on actual prices that may not have been expected, the discharge of commitments is not certain.

But if Walras's Law does not hold, neither does Say's Law. Supply cannot create demand when the insolvency of economic agents obstructs mutually advantageous transactions between agents when some agents have negative net worth. The negative net worth of some agents can be transmitted to other agents holding obligations undertaken by agents whose net worth has become negative. Moreover, because the private supply of a medium of exchange by banks depends on the value of money-backing assets held by banks, the monetary system may cease to function in an economy in which the net worth of those agents whose obligations are held by banks becomes negative. Thus, the argument made in Sect. 9.4 for the validity of Say's Law in the Identity sense breaks down once a sufficient number of agents no longer have positive net worth.

9.7 Conclusion

My aim in this chapter has been to explain and clarify different ways in which Say's Law has been understood and misunderstood. A fair reading of the primary and secondary literature leads to the conclusion that many criticisms of Say's Law have misunderstood the argument that Say's Law either was intended, or could reasonably have been interpreted, to make. But I think a stronger conclusion can be defended: properly understood, Say's Law provides an insight into the cumulative process of economic contraction whose existence, in the eyes of critics, supposedly proved its invalidity. Finally, I have also shown that, under plausible conditions, the disappointment of expectations—the primary cause of financial crises and breakdowns—may entail losses of net worth and contagious insolvency and bankruptcy, when even Walras's Law, and *a fortiori* Say's Law, no longer hold. Understanding how Say's Law may be violated may thus help us understand the dynamics of financial crises and the cumulative systemic coordination failures characteristic of deep depressions.

References

Becker, G. S., & Baumol, W. J. (1952). The classical monetary theory: The outcome of the discussion. *Economica, 19*(76), 355–376.

Clower, R. (1967). A reconsideration of the foundations of monetary theory. *Western Economic Journal, 6*(1), 1–9.

Clower, R., & Leijonhufvud, A. (1981). Say's principle: What it means and what it doesn't mean, in Leijonhufvud, Information and coordination: Essays on macroeconomic theory, (pp. 79–102). Oxford University Press.

Glasner, D. (1989). *Free banking and monetary reform*. Cambridge University Press.

Hayek, F. A. (1929 [1933]). *Monetary theory and the trade cycle*. Jonathan Cape.

Hayek, F. A. (1967). The theory of complex phenomena. In *Studies in philosophy, politics, and economics* (pp. 22–42). University of Chicago Press.

Hicks, J. R. (1939). *Value and capital*. Clarendon Press.

Hutt, W. H. (1975). *A rehabilitation of Say's law*. Ohio University Press.

Keynes, J. M. (1936). *The general theory of employment, interest and money*. Macmillan.

Lange, O. (1942). Say's law: A restatement and criticism. In O. Lange, F. McIntyre, & T. O. Yntema (Eds.), *Studies in mathematical economics and econometrics* (pp. 49-68). University of Chicago Press.

Malthus, T. R. (1836). *Principles of political* economy (2nd ed.). W. Pickering.

Patinkin, D. (1948). Relative prices, Say's law, and the demand for money. *Econometrica, 16*, 135–154.

Patinkin, D. (1951). The invalidity of classical monetary theory. *Econometrica, 19*(2), 134–151.

Patinkin, D. (1965). *Money, interest, and prices* (2nd ed.). Harper and Row.

Radner, R. (1972). Existence of equilibrium of plans, prices, and price expectations. *Econometrica, 40*(2), 289–303.

Ricardo, D. (1951). Notes on Malthus. In P. Sraffa (Ed.), *The works and correspondence of David Ricardo* (Vol. 2). Cambridge University Press.

Rueff, J. (1947). The fallacies of Lord Keynes' *General Theory*. *Quarterly Journal of Economics, 51*(2), 343–367.

Say, J. B. (1803). *Traité d'économie politique* (1st ed.). Paris.

Say, J. B. (1826). *Traité d'économie politique* (5th ed.). Paris.

Shackle, G. L. S. (1967). *Years of high theory*. Cambridge University Press.

Sismondi, J. C. L. (1827). *Nouveaux Principes d'économie politique* (2d ed.). Paris.

Sowell, T. (1972). *Say's law*. Princeton University Press.

Thompson, E. A. (1974). The theory of money and income consistent with orthodox value theory. In G. Horwich & P.A. Samuelson *Trade, stability and macroeconomics: Essays in honor of Lloyd Metzler* (pp. 427–453). Academic Press.

Thompson, E. A. (1977). *A reformulation of macroeconomic theory* (UCLA Discussion Paper Number 91. Unpublished manuscript). http://www.econ.ucla.edu/workingpapers/wp091.pdf

PART II

Hawtrey, Keynes, and Hayek

CHAPTER 10

Hawtrey's *Good and Bad Trade*: A Centenary Retrospective

10.1 Introduction

Over a career spanning almost 60 years, Ralph George Hawtrey produced a steady stream of publications, at least twenty books, over a hundred articles, mostly in professional journals, and perhaps an equal number of book reviews, becoming one of the best-known and most frequently cited economists of the interwar period. A Cambridge man, and an Apostle who recommended Keynes, four years his junior, for membership in the Apostles, Hawtrey, like Keynes, belonged to the Bloomsbury Group and remained close to Keynes, though not part of his inner circle. Despite his irritation at Hawtrey's persistent criticisms of early drafts of the *General Theory*, Keynes more than once acknowledged Hawtrey's influence on his thinking, famously describing Hawtrey as his "grandparent in the paths of errancy" (Keynes, 1937, 241n.).

Good and Bad Trade, Hawtrey's first work in economics, was published in 1913 when Hawtrey was 34 years old, and had worked at the Treasury for almost a decade. It was only Hawtrey's second publication, the first having been an article on naval strategy, written before his arrival at Cambridge. Perhaps on the strength of that youthful publication, Hawtrey began his civil-service career in the Admiralty, before transferring shortly thereafter to the Treasury, where he remained till 1947.

D. Glasner, *Studies in the History of Monetary Theory*, Palgrave Studies in the History of Economic Thought, https://doi.org/10.1007/978-3-030-83426-5_10

At Cambridge, Hawtrey studied mathematics and philosophy. He was deeply influenced by the Cambridge philosopher G. E. Moore, an influence apparent in *The Economic Problem* (1926), one of Hawtrey's few publications not mainly concerned with monetary theory and policy. Hawtrey's mathematical interests led him to a correspondence with another Cambridge man Bertrand Russell, a correspondence cited in the *Principia Mathematica* and acknowledged in the preface. Surprisingly, Hawtrey seems to have had no contact with Alfred Marshall or any other Cambridge economists while at Cambridge. Indeed, the only economist mentioned by Hawtrey in *Good and Bad Trade* is Irving Fisher, whose distinction between the real and nominal rates of interest is mentioned in Chapter 5, and whose proposal to stabilize the purchasing power of the dollar by altering its gold is discussed in Chapter 20.

An autodidact in economics, Hawtrey probably began his self-education while studying for the civil-service entrance examination. In his forward to the 1962 edition of *Good and Bad Trade*, Hawtrey (1913 [1962], vii) recounted being informed, in 1909, by an unidentified economist friend that the principle he was relying on to explain the business cycle—the fall of prices below those that producers had expected when borrowing to finance their productive activities—had been anticipated by Fisher in his *Theory of Interest* (1907). Hawtrey added that his cycle theory consisted in a new development and elaboration of Fisher's insight.

Hawtrey's self-education was evidently continuing even as he was writing *Good and Bad Trade*, acknowledging in the forward to the second edition (p. ix) inaccuracies in his account of the functions of bill-brokers. Despite some gaps in his self-education, Hawtrey's exceptional analytical skill, his attention to detail, and his meticulously logical exposition were already manifest in his first work. Referring to Hawtrey's 1937 exchange with Keynes about the theory of interest in the *General Theory*, G. L. S. Shackle (1967, 243) described the effect that Hawtrey's expository style had on readers, already likely felt by readers of his first work:

> Sir Ralph's patient, exact and unimpassioned formulations steadily build up in his reader a solid trust in Sir Ralph's logic, and a disposition to look a second and a third time at any proposition which seems at first sight to endanger his faith.

At the outset (p. 3), Hawtrey laid out the following description of his method and his goal:

> My present purpose is to examine certain elements in the modern economic organization of the world, which appear to be intimately connected with the fluctuations. I shall not attempt to work back from a precise statistical analysis of the fluctuations which the world has experienced to the causes of all the phenomena disclosed by such analysis. But I shall endeavor to show what the effects of certain assumed economic causes would be, and it will, I think, be found that these calculated effects correspond very closely with the observed features of the fluctuations.
>
> The general result up to which I hope to work is that the fluctuations are due to disturbances in the available stock of "money" – the term "money" being taken to cover every species of purchasing power available for immediate use, both legal tender money and credit money, whether in the form of coin, notes, or deposits at banks.

The chief problem with the business cycle, Hawtrey explained, is that unemployed workers cannot earn an income with which to sustain themselves during business-cycle contractions. Although, when analyzed in the context of an equilibrium, money might seem unimportant, inasmuch as any set of absolute prices is consistent with equilibrium, provided that relative prices are consistent with equilibrium, Hawtrey attributed the problem to a malfunction of the monetary system.

For perhaps 25 years after Hawtrey published *Good and Bad Trade*, the basic model described in his first work on the business cycle was considered the definitive articulation of a purely monetary theory of the business cycle. In his classic survey of business-cycle theories, Gottfried Haberler (1937) undertook an extensive summary Hawtrey's work as the representative treatment of a purely monetary cycle theory. Even another decade later, Schumpeter (1954) still credited Hawtrey with having advanced the most comprehensive monetary theory of the cycle.

When Schumpeter wrote, monetary theories of the cycle, having failed to account for the Great Depression and then having been eclipsed by the Keynesian ascendancy, had already fallen out of fashion. But just as Schumpeter was writing about Hawtrey, Milton Friedman was beginning his long collaboration with Anna Schwartz, later to be joined by many dedicated students and colleagues, in attempting to show that monetary forces really did play the central role in the Great Depression. Unaware of, or uninterested in, Hawtrey's contributions, Friedman, advancing his own version of a monetary theory of the Great Depression, acknowledged only a largely invented Chicago oral tradition as a forerunner of his own monetary theory, thereby contributing to, and hastening, Hawtrey's passage into obscurity.

A milestone in both the history of monetary theory and the history of business-cycle theory, *Good and Bad Trade* undoubtedly deserves renewed attention and reconsideration. Aside from its general importance as a path-breaking work of monetary theory, *Good and Bad Trade* is also noteworthy for at least seven specific contributions: (1) the concept of effective demand, (2) the concept of purchasing-power parity, (3) the concept of a multiplier, (4) the pathological implications of an expected deflation greater than the real rate of interest, (5) the "Treasury view" he subsequently articulated in Hawtrey (1925), (6) the positive historical correlation between price levels and interest rates (Gibson Paradox), and (7) a theoretical account of the dynamics of financial crises and their relationship to cyclical fluctuations.

Finally, notwithstanding the remarkable continuity in Hawtrey's theoretical approach and basic model throughout his long career, Hawtrey did, in subsequent works, change one important feature of the model presented in *Good and Bad Trade*: his reliance on the price-specie-flow mechanism (PSFM) to explain the process of international adjustment in prices, interest rates, and gold reserves under the gold standard.

The chapter is organized as follows. In the next section, I sketch the logical structure of the book, highlighting the main elements of Hawtrey's theoretical schema. In Sect. 10.3, I discuss the abovementioned innovations or advances made by Hawtrey in *Good and Bad Trade*. In Sect. 10.4, I consider his explanations for financial crises. And in Sect. 10.5, I discuss his revision in later works of the price-specie-flow mechanism described in *Good and Bad Trade*. I conclude in Sect. 10.6.

10.2 The Structure and Argument of *Good and Bad Trade*

A. An Overview of *Good and Bad Trade*

Hawtrey's explanatory strategy was to start from what he regarded as the simplest possible assumptions, derive a useful result, and then to gradually modify the assumptions to make the analysis correspond increasingly closely to conditions in the real world. Hawtrey's objective in *Good and Bad Trade* was to derive from his theoretical model a pattern of cyclical fluctuations resembling those actually observed. After a brief introductory chapter, Hawtrey, in Chapter 2, introduced the idea of a demand to hold money such that people aim to hold, on average, a certain percentage of their total money income in the form of money as a working balance with which to carry out transactions. Given such a demand to hold money, and a fixed amount of inconvertible paper money, the absolute level of total income in nominal terms and the absolute level of prices would be determined, money income being a multiple (corresponding to the inverse of the percentage of total income that people wish to hold as money) of the fixed quantity of money. In Chapter 3, Hawtrey extended his analysis to encompass credit money created by banks.

In Chapter 4, Hawtrey discussed the organization of production, the accumulation of capital, and the employment of labor, explaining the matching circular flows: expenditure on goods and services, the output of goods and services, and the incomes accruing from that output and expenditure.

Having introduced the basic elements of a simple isolated economy, Hawtrey, in Chapter 5, described how an isolated economy using just fiat money would adjust to a change in the quantity of fiat money, and, in Chapter 6, how such an economy would adjust to a monetary disturbance affected a banking system supplying credit money convertible into fiat money. In Chapter 7, Hawtrey discussed how monetary disturbances affecting the banking system might arise in an isolated community.

In Chapter 8, Hawtrey extended the discussion of the previous three chapters to an open economy connected to an international system in which each country uses its own fiat money. Hawtrey explained the exchange rates of the various national currencies in such an interconnected international system by formulating the principle of purchasing-power parity. In Chapter 9, Hawtrey dropped the assumption of inconvertible paper moneys and introduced an international metallic system (corresponding to the international gold standard then in operation).

Having described his working model of multiple economies using credit (i.e., bank-created) moneys convertible into gold, Hawtrey, in Chapter 10, discussed other sources of change, e.g., population growth and technological progress, and changes in the supply of gold. In Chapter 11, Hawtrey dropped the assumption of the previous chapters that there are no forces leading to changes in relative prices among commodities, showing that such changes, unlike changes in monetary conditions, give rise to no cumulative changes in income and expenditure, and therefore have only transitory effects.

In Chapter 12, Hawtrey began a deep analysis of money, credit, and banking, largely focusing on the differences between deposits and banknotes, and, in Chapter 13, he described international differences in money and banking institutions. In Chapters 14 and 15, Hawtrey undertook an explanation of how monetary instability can produce a recurring cycle, not just a cumulative expansion or contraction that leads directly to a new equilibrium state. In Chapter 16, Hawtrey explained that financial crises are the result of a severe monetary contraction when banks respond to the drain on their reserves characteristic of the late stages of a business-cycle expansion, the crisis being triggered if the monetary contraction is unusually sharp.

The final four chapters discuss the effect of government policies on the business cycle. Chapter 17 considers how the business cycle had been affected by changes in monetary arrangements during the second half of the nineteenth century, primarily the shift from bimetallic standards to the gold standard in the 1870s. Chapter 18 considers the effects of tariff policy on the cycle, and Chapter 19 discusses whether the requirements of the government for banking services in receiving payments from, and in disbursing payments to, the public have repercussions on the cycle. Finally, in Chapter 20, Hawtrey considered proposals for moderating the severity of the cycle, the two proposals of interest being Irving Fisher's proposal for stabilizing the price level by altering the gold content of the currency to reflect changes in a general index of prices and the proposal of the Minority Report of the Poor Law Commission to increase government spending during recessions to mitigate unemployment.

B. The Basic Model of *Good and Bad Trade*

Hawtrey aimed to explain recurrent cyclical fluctuations, believing that only monetary disturbances could account for (a) cumulative expansions and contractions and (b) for the transformation of a contraction into an expansion and vice versa, rather than a direct reversion to an equilibrium state. To explain cumulative expansions and contractions, Hawtrey focused on the sensitivity of middlemen, wholesalers, and merchants who finance their inventories mainly with short-term bank loans. Hawtrey held that the desired levels of such inventories would vary directly with the costs of financing the inventories. Changes in desired inventories would in turn cause middlemen to make similar changes in the size of their orders to manufacturers, thereby causing similar variations in manufacturing output. Changes in output would lead to changes in workers' incomes as manufacturers changed payrolls more or less in proportion with output changes, while workers changed their purchases of finished goods in rough proportion with income changes. The process of adjusting inventories, orders, and output would continue, because changes in consumer demand would cause additional, though progressively smaller, changes in desired inventories, and, consequently, in output and income as the adjustment process continued.

Hawtrey's recognition of the connection between income and expenditure was the germ of the multiplier analysis, which Hawtrey actually worked out for Keynes a decade and a half later in his comments on the draft of the *Treatise on Money* that Keynes sent to Hawtrey before publication. The key difference between the Hawtreyan multiplier and the Keynesian multiplier was that Hawtrey believed that the multiplier effect was triggered by changes in bank lending rates, while Keynes believed that they were triggered by changes in spending plans of households, business, or government.

The tendency for changes in bank lending rates to generate cumulative expansions or contractions was not sufficient to account for the observed cyclical pattern of those fluctuations. Hawtrey therefore had to explain how the expansion or contraction itself could give rise to a change in monetary conditions that would reverse the initial cumulative expansion or contraction once it had gotten underway.

Hawtrey identified the banking system as the transforming agent required for a theory of recurring cycles. The key behavioral relationship for Hawtrey was that banks demand reserves—either gold or currency or reserves held with the central bank—into which their own liabilities (banknotes or deposits) are convertible. Given their demand for reserves, banks set interest rates with a view to maintaining their reserves at the level desired, given their outstanding liabilities (deposits and banknotes). Accordingly, they raise interest rates when they consider reserves to be inadequate, and reduce rates when reserves seem excessive. Whether total spending increases or decreases depends on whether the lending rate set by banks is less than or greater than the profit rate of businesses. If the bank rate is less than the profit rate, borrowing from the banks increases;

if the profit rate is greater than bank rate, borrowing decreases. The profit rate corresponds to the real or natural rate plus expected inflation.

Hawtrey combined this behavioral relationship with two key empirical relationships: (1) that workers and other lower-income groups generally make little use of banknotes (limited in Britain to denominations above £5, roughly the equivalent of $200 at today's prices) and almost none of bank deposits; (2) that the labor share of total income is countercyclical. Hawtrey began his story at the upper turning point, when a combination of rising inflation and diminishing reserves causes banks to raise their interest rates to stem outflows of reserves.[1]

At the peak of the cycle when employment is close to—perhaps beyond—being full, with expenditure increasing and inflation rising, the bank rate is presumably below the profit rate. When banks increase their lending rates to stem a reserve outflow, the initial effect is to reduce spending. Despite a slowdown in spending, the loss of reserves may not stop, because workers increase their desired holdings of cash as their wages rise, causing a further drain on bank reserves. The rate banks charge borrowers may therefore continue to increase for a time even after it already exceeds the profit rate. Meanwhile, the increased bank rate causes middlemen and traders to reduce desired stock levels; their orders to manufacturers begin to diminish, causing manufacturers to curtail output and employment. This reaction starts a downturn, triggering a vicious downward cycle of declining orders, output, employment, and spending. Falling wages and employment cause workers to reduce their demand for cash. All these effects of the downturn improve the reserve position of the banks, while also tending to reduce the quantity of reserves that banks want to hold, their liabilities having fallen owing to the reduced business demand for bank credit. As their reserve positions improve, banks begin reducing their lending rates, but that adjustment tends to lag behind the reduction in the profit rate. Eventually, the excess reserves held by banks

[1] There are two possible causes of a loss of reserves for the banking system as a whole. First, an increase in the share of wages would cause businesses to withdraw increasing amounts of currency from the banks in order to pay their workers, labor in Hawtrey's time still receiving payment in banknotes rather than deposits in their bank accounts. Second, if a monetary expansion in one country was proceeding more rapidly than in other countries, that country would tend be acquiring fewer financial claims on other countries than other countries were acquiring on it, so that there would be a tendency for the net deficit to be discharged by gold shipments, thereby reducing the total reserves held by the banking system.

increases sufficiently that they reduce their lending rates below the profit rate. When lending rates fall below the profit rate, businesses again find it profitable to increase their borrowing, and for middlemen and traders to add to, rather than decrease, their inventories, creating the conditions for a turnaround and a new expansion of stocks, output, and employment.

Although both employment and wages fall in the downturn, Hawtrey maintained that profits fall more sharply than wages, so that the share of labor in total income actually increases in the downturn. The full passage is worth quoting, because it also constitutes an implicit criticism of the Austrian theory of the downturn, although it is doubtful that Hawtrey was yet acquainted with the Austrian theory of the business cycles, its primary text, Mises's *Theory of Money and Credit*, having been published in German in 1913 at about the same time as *Good and Bad Trade*. The key difference between Hawtrey's monetary theory of the cycle and the Austrian theory is that the Austrian theory presumes that business investment in fixed capital is highly sensitive to short-term bank lending rates while Hawtrey believed short-term lending rates primarily affect the holding of working capital and inventories. Hawtrey considered the Austrian focus on long-term capital investment a factually incorrect premise and their focus on the capital structure of the economy as an important causal factor in the cycle to be misplaced, inasmuch as long-term capital investment is financed mainly by retained earnings, or by the issue of new stock and bonds, not by short-term borrowing from banks.[2]

> [R]ather than let their plant lie idle, manufacturers will sacrifice part or even the whole of their profits, and that in this way the restriction of output is mitigated. If all producers insisted on stopping work unless they could obtain a normal rate of profit, there would be a greater restriction of output and more workmen would be discharged, and in that case the proceeds of the diminished output would be divided (approximately) in the same proportion between the capitalists and the workmen as before.

[2] Hawtrey (1939) offered a detailed critique of Hayek's business-cycle theory, introducing the distinction between capital-widening investment to expand productive capacity to match increased output and capital-deepening to increase the capital intensity of a given output. Hawtrey considered most fixed investment to be of the former not the latter type, while in Austrian theory it is the latter not the former type that is critical. Interestingly, as Hicks (1969) observed, a similar disagreement about the channel through which changes in bank rate affect investment emerged between Hawtrey and Keynes when Hawtrey (1932, Chapter 6) reviewed Keynes's *Treatise on Money*.

> But in consequence of the sacrifice of profits to output which actually occurs, the number of workmen in employment and therefore also the aggregate of working-class earnings will not be so severely diminished as they would otherwise be. Thus the capitalists will get a smaller proportion and the workmen a greater proportion of the gross proceeds than before. But anything which tends to increase or maintain working-class earnings tends to increase or maintain the amount of cash in the hands of the working classes. If the banks have succeeded in reducing the outstanding amount of credit money by 10 percent, they will probably have reduced the incomes of the people with bank accounts by 10 percent, but the earnings of the working classes will have been reduced in a much smaller proportion – say, 5 percent. (pp. 189–190)

The reduced quantity of the liabilities of the banking system in the hands of the public will relieve the pressure felt by banks to increase their reserves, diminishing their need to raise interest rates.

> Here is the process at work which is likely enough to produce fluctuations. For the bankers will thereupon be ready to *increase* the stock of credit money again, and once they have embarked on this course they may find it very difficult to stop short of a dangerous inflation…
>
> Instead of ending up, therefore, with the establishment of a golden mean of prosperity, unbroken by any deviation towards less or more, the depression will be marked in its later stages by a new complication. At the time when the reduction of wages is beginning to be accompanied not merely by an increase of employment, but also by an increase of profits, the banks will find that cash is beginning to accumulate in their vaults. They will ease off the rate of interest to something a little below the profit rate, and dealers will take advantage of the low rate to add to their stocks. The manufacturers will become aware of an increase in orders, and they will find that they can occupy their plant more fully. And now that stocks and output are both increased, borrowing will be increased and the bankers will have gained their end. But then the new accession to the amount of credit money means a corresponding increase of purchasing power. At existing prices the dealers find that their stocks are being depleted by the growing demand from the consumer. The prospect of rising prices is an inducement to add to their stocks as much as they can at existing prices, and so their orders to the manufacturers grow, wholesale prices go up; and as the consumers' demands on the dealers' stocks grow, retail prices go up; and as prices go up, the money needed to finance a given quantity of goods grows greater and greater, and both dealers and manufacturers borrow

> more and more from their bankers. In fact here are all the characteristics of a period of trade expansion in full swing. (pp. 190–192)

How far such a cumulative process of credit expansion can proceed before it reaches its upper turning point depends on the willingness of the banks to continue supplying credit as the margin of their reserves relative to liabilities steadily diminishes. But as the expansion proceeds, and businesses begin to expect to profit from selling their products at rising prices, businesses, short of workers with which to increase output, will start bidding up wages. As costs rise relative to prices, the incentive for further expansion will dissipate.

> Production having been stimulated to great activity there is a scarcity of labour, or at any rate of properly trained and competent labour, and employers are so anxious to get the benefit of the high profits that they are more ready than usual to make concessions in preference to facing strikes which would leave their workers idle. There follows a period of full employment and rising wages. But this means growing cash requirements, and sooner or later the banks must take action to prevent their reserves being depleted. If they act in time they may manage to relieve the inflation of credit money gradually and an actual financial crisis may be avoided. But in either case there must ensue a period of slack trade. Here, therefore, we have proved that there is an inherent tendency toward fluctuations in the banking institutions which prevail in the world as it is. (p. 199)

10.3 Innovations in *Good and Bad Trade*

I indicated above that at least seven different conceptual or theoretical innovations could be identified in *Good and Bad Trade*. I consider each of them in turn.

A. The term "Effective Demand".[3]

At very outset (p. 4) of *Good and Bad Trade*, the reader encounters the following passage.

> The producers of commodities depend, for their profits and for the means of paying wages and other expenses, upon the money which they receive

[3] I am indebted to David Laidler for drawing my attention to the fact that, in using the term "effective demand" in *Good and Bad Trade*, Hawtrey anticipated Keynes's usage of the term.

> for the finished commodities. They supply in response to a demand, but only to an *effective demand*. A want becomes an *effective demand* when the person who experiences the want possesses (and can spare) the purchasing power necessary to meet the price of the thing which will satisfy it. A man may want a hat, but if he has no money [i.e., income or wealth] he cannot buy it, and his want does not contribute to the *effective demand* for hats. (p. 4, emphasis added)

Almost immediately thereafter, at the beginning of Chapter 2 (p. 6, emphasis added), Hawtrey continues:

> The total *effective demand* for all finished commodities in any community is simply the aggregate of all money incomes. The same aggregate represents also the total cost of production of all finished commodities.

Again, in Chapter 4 (pp. 32–33, emphasis added), Hawtrey the concept of effective demand:

> It was laid down that the total *effective demand* for all commodities is simply the aggregate of all incomes, and that the same aggregate represents the total cost of production of all commodities.

Hawtrey attributed fluctuations in employment to fluctuations in effective demand, because wages and prices would not adjust immediately to a change in total spending. Here is how Keynes defined effective demand (1936, 55).

> [T]he *effective demand* is simply the aggregate income or (proceeds) which the entrepreneurs expect to receive, inclusive of the income which they will hand on to the other factors of production, from the amount of current employment which they decide to give. The aggregate demand function relates various hypothetical quantities of employment to the proceeds which their outputs are expected to yield; and the effective demand is the point on the aggregate demand function which becomes effective because, taken in conjunction with the conditions of supply, it corresponds to the level of employment which maximizes the entrepreneur's expectation of profit. (emphasis added)

So the conception of effective demand presented by Keynes in the *General Theory* is essentially the same as that which Hawtrey had presented two decades earlier. Keynes's conception is, to be sure, more sophisticated than Hawtrey's, being expressed in terms of entrepreneurial expectations of income and expenditure and specifying a general functional relationship (aggregate demand) between employment and expected income. But the basic idea still bears a close resemblance to Hawtrey's usage of the same term. Interestingly, Hawtrey never asserted a claim of priority on the concept, whether because of an innate diffidence,[4] or because of some disagreement with how Keynes used the idea, I cannot venture to say. Perhaps others may be able to suggest reasons for Hawtrey's silence on this point.

B. Purchasing-Power Parity

In Chapter 7, Hawtrey analyzed an international system of fiat currencies, each issued and used within a single country in which that currency alone (or credit money convertible into that currency) is routinely accepted as payment. Hawtrey set out to explain the exchange rates between pairs of such currencies and the corresponding price levels in those countries. In summing up his discussion (pp. 90–93) of what determines the rate of exchange between any two currencies, Hawtrey made the following observation:

> Practically, it may be said that the rate of exchange equates the general level of prices of commodities in one country with that in the other. This is of course only approximately true, since the rate of exchange is affected only by those commodities which are or might be transported between the two countries. If one of the two countries is at a disadvantage in the production of commodities which cannot be imported, or indeed in those which can only be imported at a specially heavy cost, the general level of prices, calculated fairly over all commodities, will be higher in that country than in the other. But, subject to this important qualification, the rate of exchange under stable conditions does represent that ratio between the units of currency which makes the price-levels and therefore the *purchasing powers* of the two units equal. (pp. 92–93, emphasis added)

That is a terse, and precise, statement of the purchasing-power-parity doctrine. What makes it interesting, and possibly noteworthy, is that Hawtrey made it 100 years ago, in 1913, three years before Hawtrey's

[4] A diffidence noted by Clarke (1988) in Hawtrey's having not made any claim of priority to the Keynesian multiplier analysis. See footnote 8 below.

older contemporary Gustav Cassel (1916, 1918), often credited with having originated the doctrine, gave his formulation of the doctrine. Here is how Cassel put it:

> According to the theory of international exchanges which I have tried to develop during the course of the war, the rate of exchange between two countries is primarily determined by the quotient between the internal purchasing power against goods of the money of each country. The general inflation which has taken place during the war has lowered this purchasing power in all countries, though in a very different degree, and the rates of exchanges should accordingly be expected to deviate from their old parity in proportion to the inflation in each country.
>
> At every moment the real parity between two countries is represented by this quotient between the purchasing power of the money in the one country and the other. I propose to call this parity "*the purchasing power parity.*" As long as anything like free movement of merchandise and a somewhat comprehensive trade between two countries takes place, the actual rate of exchange cannot deviate very much from this purchasing power parity. (1918, 413)

Of course, as documented by Humphrey (1979), the purchasing-power-parity doctrine has a long pedigree extending back to Henry Thornton (1802 [1939]) and was understood by many classical economists before it was articulated by Cassel and Hawtrey.[5]

Hawtrey went on to explain how international relationships would be affected by a contraction in the currency of one country. The immediate effects would be the same as those described in the case of a single closed economy. However, in an international system, the effects of a contraction in one country would create opportunities for international transactions, both real and financial, that would involve both countries in the adjustment to the initial monetary disturbance originating in one country. Hawtrey sums up his discussion about the adjustment to a contraction of the currency of one country as follows:

> From the above description, which is necessarily rather complicated, it will be seen that the mutual influence of two areas with independent currency

[5] Mises (1913 [1934]) also anticipated Cassel's articulation of the purchasing-power-parity doctrine.

> systems is on the whole not very great. Indeed, the only important consequence to either of a contraction of currency in the other, is the tendency for the first to lend money to the second in order to get the benefit of the high rate of interest. This hastens the movement towards ultimate equilibrium in the area of stringency. At the same time it would raise the rate of interest slightly in the other country. But as this rise in the rate of interest is due to an enhanced *demand* for loans, it will not have the effect of diminishing the total stock of bankers' money. (p. 99)

He concludes the chapter with a refinement of the purchasing-power-parity doctrine.

> It is important to notice that as soon as the assumption of stable conditions is abandoned the rate of exchange ceases to represent the ratio of the purchasing powers of the two units of currency which it relates. A difference between the rates of interest in the two countries concerned displaces the rate of exchange from its normal position of equality with this ratio, in the same direction as if the purchasing power of the currency with the higher rate of interest had been increased. Such a divergence between the rates of interest would only occur in case of some financial disturbance, and though such disturbances, great or small, are bound to be frequent, the ratio of purchasing powers may still be taken (subject to the qualification previously explained) to be the normal significance of the rate of exchange. (p. 101)

Thus, according to Hawtrey, interest-rate differentials between countries could prevent equalization of the purchasing powers of the two currencies, the higher interest rate in one country depressing the purchasing power of the currency of that country relative to the other. Hawtrey's reasoning was not fully spelled out, but it might be rationalized as having intuitively grasped a tendency explained 70 years later by Max Corden (1985) in his theory of exchange-rate protection in which a country depreciates its exchange rate to favor its tradable-goods sector. Exchange-rate depreciation enhances the profitability of the country's tradable-good sector only if exchange-rate depreciation does not lead to equiproportionate increases in wages and prices. To prevent equiproportionate increases in wages and prices, the monetary authority must create an excess demand for money, so that households and firms reduce their spending in order to build up their cash holdings. Given the depreciated exchange rate and reduced domestic spending, imports will decrease and exports will increase, causing resources to be shifted from the non-tradable-goods sector to the tradable-good sector.

In Hawtrey's example, the monetary disturbance in one country causes an excess demand for cash in that country, raising interest rates and reducing prices, thereby causing currency appreciation. As interest rates in that country rise, borrowers will seek to borrow from lenders in the other country, thereby redistributing cash balances between the two countries and reducing the interest-rate differential between them. But the indebtedness of one country to the other will require a reduction of spending in that country, causing a shift of resources from its non-tradable- to its tradable-goods sector. That shift implies that the prices of non-tradable goods in the debtor country will fall, while, in the other creditor country, the prices of non-tradables will rise. Thus, purchasing power of the currency in terms of both tradables and non-tradables will increase in the debtor country and will fall in the creditor country.

C. Income and Expenditure

In explaining the cumulative processes of expansion and contraction, Hawtrey recognized that an increase (decrease) in orders from traders to manufacturers causes the total output of manufacturers, along with total employment and income, to increase (decrease). The increase (decrease) in income induces a further increase (decrease) in spending by workers, leading to a further increase (decrease) in orders. Increased (decreased) spending by consumers causes a drawdown (buildup) of inventories and further increases (decreases) in the orders of traders and middlemen trying to restock (reduce) their inventories to desired levels, triggering further increases (decrease) in output, income and employment, and so on. Although Hawtrey did not explicitly assume that the ratio of the change in consumption to the change in income was less than one, that assumption was clearly made implicitly.

In his next book on business cycles, *Currency and Credit* (1919), Hawtrey was more explicit in spelling out the relationship between income and expenditure, introducing the concepts of "consumers income" and "consumers outlay" to represent the ideas of income and expenditure.[6] So it was no accident that Hawtrey was an early discoverer of the multiplier (Cain, 1982; Davis, 1980; Deutscher, 1990; Dimand, 1997), for which he presented an algebraic exposition in a memorandum originally written to supplement his critical comments on Keynes's *Treatise on Money*, later included in (Hawtrey, 1932, Chapter 6).[7]

Despite being articulated more explicitly in later works, the key elements of his analysis were already identified in *Good and Bad Trade*. The multiplier analysis provided the basis of Hawtrey's theory cyclical theory, making Hawtrey's role in developing the multiplier a natural development of his earlier work rather than, as Clarke (1988) suggested, an accidental aberration unrelated to the body of Hawtrey's work.[8]

In particular, Clarke considered Hawtrey's derivation of the multiplier to be at odds with his subsequent well-known (if not notorious) articulation (Hawtrey, 1925) of the "Treasury view" that government spending cannot increase output and employment. But that supposed inconsistency arises from a misunderstanding of Hawtrey's reasoning in support of the Treasury view. Hawtrey argued that additional government spending, whether financed by taxation or by borrowing, must diminish private spending by an equivalent amount, without changing

[6] As noted by Cain (1982) and Davis (1980), Hawtrey, in the revised (1928) edition of *Currency and Credit*, provided a verbal exposition of the multiplier relationship.

[7] Whether Hawtrey should be credited as the discover of the multiplier analysis is controversial. Deutscher (1990) suggests that his treatment was not meant as a serious discovery but only was offered as an informal example for Keynes's benefit, which may explain why Hawtrey never claimed priority. I do not necessarily disagree with Deutscher, but it is at least worth noting that, given his understanding of the income-consumption relationship and his reliance on that relationship in the exposition of his own cycle theory, it was entirely natural and unsurprising that he would have been able to provide Keynes with an algebraic treatment of a relationship that he had long been thinking carefully about.

[8] Clarke (1988, 242–243) wrote:

> The self-effacing Hawtrey may, as Davis (1980) claims, deserve a more prominent place in the literature on the coming of the multiplier – but notably as the one who, having stumbled upon it, painstakingly suppressed news of its discovery in his subsequent publications.

It was not the analysis per se that Hawtrey did not embrace in his publications. Rather, Hawtrey believed—rightly or wrongly—the analysis to be inapplicable to changes in government spending.

total spending (effective demand). The multiplier analysis becomes applicable when there is a net increment to total spending. If an increase in government spending were offset by an equal reduction in private spending, as Hawtrey argued, there would be no basis upon which the multiplier could take effect. The issue is not the multiplier but the "crowding out." The issues are related but not the same.

Hawtrey's premise may have been incorrect, because taxation and borrowing may reduce not just private spending, but also private saving. Depending on the circumstances, reduced private saving entails either reduced private investment or reduced cash holdings. If increased government spending is partly financed by reduced cash holding, then increased government spending would indeed lead to an increase in total spending. Hawtrey (1939) eventually conceded the point in his review of the *General Theory*. Hawtrey's argument for the Treasury view was not premised on the non-existence of a multiplier effect, but on its inapplicability.

D. Deflationary Expectations

In Chapter 14, explaining a business-cycle downturn, when, a rising rate of interest reduces total spending triggering an inflow of gold to the banks, Hawtrey digressed to consider what he called "a special case."

> What if the rate of depreciation of prices is actually *greater* than the natural rate of interest? If that is so, nothing that the bankers can do will make borrowing sufficiently attractive. Business will be revolving in a vicious circle; the dealers unwilling to buy in a falling market, the manufacturers unable to maintain their output in face of ever-diminishing orders, dealers and manufacturers alike cutting down their borrowings in proportion to the decline of business, demand falling in proportion to the shrinkage in credit money, and with the falling demand, the dealers more unwilling to buy than ever. This, which may be called "stagnation" of trade, is of course exceptional, but it deserves our attention in passing
>
> From the apparent impasse there is one way out – a drastic reduction of money wages. If at any time this step is taken the spell will be broken. Wholesale prices will fall abruptly, the *expectation* of a further fall will cease, dealers will begin to replenish their stocks, manufacturers to increase their output, dealers and manufacturers alike will borrow again, and the stock of credit money will grow. In fact the profit rate will recover, and will again equal or indeed exceed the natural rate. The market rate, however, will be

> kept *below* the profit rate, since in the preceding period of stagnation the bankers' reserves will have been swollen beyond the necessary proportions, and the bankers will desire to develop their loan and discount business. (pp. 186–187)

Although Hawtrey, in Chapter 4, referred to the Fisher equation relating the real and the nominal rates of interest by way of the expected rate of inflation, in this context, despite its obvious relevance, he overlooked the Fisher equation. The problematic nature of the Fisher equation when the expected rate of deflation exceeds the real rate of interest so that it cannot be satisfied at a non-negative nominal rate of interest is an anomaly rarely mentioned in the literature,[9] Hawtrey's discussion being the earliest discussion that I am aware of. Though he correctly understood the pathology associated with the situation, he did not fully describe the pathology or provide a complete account of how a new equilibrium might be established or of the nature of a new equilibrium if it were to be reached.

Instead, Hawtrey simply assumed that a sufficiently large reduction in nominal wages would cause price expectations to turn positive rather than remaining negative, or, worse become even more negative. Nor did Hawtrey reckon with the possibility that a downward spiral of output and prices might not, even with steep nominal wage reductions, lead to a new equilibrium but continue indefinitely unless countered by a deliberately expansionary countercyclical policy.[10]

E. The Treasury View

Perhaps Hawtrey's most famous paper is his 1925 paper "Public Expenditure and the Demand for Labour" in which he argued that government spending in a depression would not reduce unemployment, because any spending by the government would displace an equal amount of spending

[9] See Glasner (2018) for a discussion of the implications of the Fisher equation for such a situation and their role in accounting for the 2008–2009 financial crisis and its aftermath.

[10] The last comment should not be construed to mean that Hawtrey did not favor a countercyclical policy, which he certainly did; it is directed only as Hawtrey's belief (reflected in the passage quoted in the text) that in theory a sufficient wage reduction accepted by all workers could reverse a downturn.

by the private sector. His argument was invoked several years later in 1929 by Winston Churchill, then Chancellor of the Exchequer, in responding to the proposals, supported by Keynes and other economists, of the Liberal opposition, an argument he described as the "orthodox Treasury view."

Especially after the *General Theory* was published, the Treasury view has been considered a fallacy, and Hawtrey's role in articulating it has been considered a blemish on his reputation.[11] Although Hawtrey's reasoning was not beyond reproach, as he himself later acknowledged, it was not entirely wrong either.[12] But the relevant point in this context is that, in the final chapter of *Good and Bad Trade*, Hawtrey had already provided a fairly complete statement of the Treasury view he presented 12 years later. Hawtrey did so in considering the proposal of the minority report of the Poor Law Commission of 1909 advocating that government spending on public works be limited to periods of depression to moderate the hardships on the working classes resulting from the business cycle. The essence of his argument appears in a long footnote from which I quote the last two sentences (p. 262):

> The effective demand for all other commodities [aside from Government services] is made up of the incomes of all members of the community (including those in the service of the Government) less the amount paid in taxation, and the cost of production of all these commodities is made up of the incomes of all people not directly or indirectly in the service of the Government. An increase of Government expenditure diminishes the effective demand for commodities, and diminishes correspondingly the number of people employed in producing commodities.

[11] A. C. Pigou (1913) in his review of *Good and Bad Trade* criticized this argument of Hawtrey's and labeled it a demonstrated fallacy, without explanation or citation. It was, then, perhaps not a coincidence that, in his 1925 paper, Hawtrey began with an explicit criticism of Pigou's support for public spending to reduce unemployment.

[12] The key point is that, unless the economy has reached a liquidity trap, monetary policy can increase aggregate demand. Certainly, in the mid- to late 1920s, when Bank Rate set by the Bank of England was rarely less than 5%, there was ample room to reduce Bank Rate to increase aggregate demand. The Bank of England and the Treasury did not favor reducing Bank Rate because it would likely lead to an outflow of gold. As he testified before the Macmillan Committee, Hawtrey believed that the Bank of England could have reduced Bank Rate even if there was an outflow of gold because other central banks would respond with rate cuts of their own. See Chapters 13 and 14.

F. Gibson's Paradox

Anticipating A. W. Gibson's investigation of the relationship between price-level changes and long-term interest rates, Hawtrey noted the puzzling tendency of interest rates to be higher at the price level peak in 1913 than at the price level trough of 1896, dismissing the possibility that differing expectations of long-term movements in the price level could account for observed interest-rate differentials.

In Chapter 17, in discussing the effects of various legislative measures on the business cycle, Hawtrey observed that the shift of many countries in the early 1870s from bimetallic, but de facto, silver standards to the gold standard led to a significant and ongoing increase in the monetary demand for gold, which led to a prolonged period of declining prices until new gold discoveries in the mid-1890s led to nearly two decades of stable or mildly rising prices before the outbreak of World War I in August 1914 caused the gold standard to collapse. Hawtrey believed it unlikely that long-term price-level movements are correctly foreseen. And if the price trend had been foreseen, the decline in interest rates would have occurred early, not late, in the period, just as the declining price trend was replaced by a rising trend in prices.

In noting that the period of falling prices from 1870 to 1896 was associated with falling long-term interest rates while the period from 1896 to 1913, when prices were rising, was associated with rising interest rates, Hawtrey anticipated by ten years the famous empirical observation made by the British economist A. W. Gibson (1923) of the positive correlation between long-term interest rates and the price level, an observation that Keynes (1930, v. 2, p. 198), in attempting to explain the correlation, called the Gibson paradox.

Aside from noting the anomalous correlation between price levels and interest rates, Hawtrey offered a theoretical explanation for the correlation between price levels and interest rates. Rising prices, Hawtrey suggested, subsidize businesses that borrow, enabling them to repay nominal debts previously incurred with money of reduced real value. By increasing the return on capital financed by borrowing, inflation increases the demand for borrowed funds, raising nominal interest rates.

> [T]he price was affected by the experience of investments during the long gold famine when profits had been low for almost a generation, and indeed it may be regarded as the outcome of the experience. In the same way the

> low prices of securities at the present time are the product of the contrary experience, the great output of gold in the last twenty years having been accompanied by inflated profits. (p. 229)

The continuous windfall profits from mild unexpected inflation accruing to businesses that borrowed would tend to encourage further investment by businesses with available funds, but it is not clear why the increased profits would cause increased by borrowing by businesses that were experiencing increasing net cash flows as a result of inflation unless their expectations of future inflation were gradually increasing. That was Irving Fisher's (1930) explanation of Gibson's Paradox. Of course, agreement between Fisher and Hawtrey would not be surprising.

10.4 Financial Crises

Good and Bad Trade is also noteworthy for its account of financial and banking crises, explaining them as the consequence of a cyclical downturn resulting from rising interest rates that cause demand to fall short of expectations, making debts uncollectable, thereby impairing the solvency of both borrowers and lenders. The most vulnerable borrowers are dealers in stocks whose loans from banks are callable.

Among Hawtrey's best-known epigrams is "the inherent instability of credit." Hawtrey begins Chapter 7 ("Origination of Monetary Disturbances in an Isolated Community") with the following deceptively modest introductory paragraph.

> In the last two chapters we have postulated a perfectly arbitrary change in the quantity of legal tender currency in circulation. However closely the consequences traced from such an arbitrary change may correspond with the phenomena we have set out to explain, we have accomplished nothing till we have shown that causes which will lead to those consequences actually occur.... At the present stage, however it is already possible to make a preliminary survey of the causes of fluctuations with the advantage of an artificial simplification of the problem. And at the outset it must be recognized that arbitrary changes in the quantity of legal tender currency in circulation cannot be of much practical importance. Such changes rarely occur. (p. 73)

In other words, Hawtrey is suggesting that the contractionary effects of a reduction, or the expansionary effects of an increase, in "legal tender" or base money are more likely to arise in the real world from changes in the demand for base money than in the supply of base money. Such spontaneous fluctuations in the demand for base money, even if quantitatively small, may have large real effects.

> [W]henever the prevailing rate of profit deviates from the rate of interest charged on loans the discrepancy between them at once tends to be enlarged. If trade is for the moment stable and the market rate of interest is equal to the profit rate, and if we suppose that by any cause the profit rate is slightly increased, there will be an increased demand for loans at the existing market rate. But this increased demand for loans leads to an increase in the aggregate amount of purchasing power, which in turn still further increases the profit rate. This process will continue with ever accelerated force until the bankers intervene to save their reserves by raising the rate of interest up to and above the now enhanced profit rate. A parallel phenomenon occurs when the profit rate, through some chance cause, drops below the market rate; the consequent curtailment of loans and so of purchasing power leads at once to a greater and growing fall in profits, until the bankers intervene by reducing the rate of interest. It appears, therefore, that the equilibrium which the bankers have to maintain in fixing the rate of interest is essentially "unstable," in the sense that if the rate of interest deviates from its proper value by any amount, however small, the deviation will tend to grow greater and greater until steps are taken to correct it. This of itself shows that the money market must be subject to fluctuations. A flag in a steady breeze could theoretically remain in equilibrium if it were spread out perfectly flat in the exact direction of the breeze. But it can be shown mathematically that that position is "unstable," that if the flag deviates from it to any extent, however small, it will tend to deviate further. Consequently the flag flaps. (pp. 76–77)

In addition to fluctuations in the demand for money, Hawtrey considered another class of monetary disturbances: the inability of debtors to repay their obligations to creditors because they have incorrectly forecast the future.

> Credit money is composed of the obligations of bankers, and if a banker cannot meet his obligations the credit money dependent upon him is wholly or partly destroyed. Again, against his obligations the banker holds equivalent assets, together with a margin. These assets are composed chiefly of two items, legal tender currency and loans to traders. The solvency of

> the banker will depend largely on the reality of these assets, and the value of the loans will depend in turn on the solvency of the borrowers. (p. 77)

Thus, the solvency of borrowers hinges on whether their *expectations* of the future will be realized. But those expectations may ultimately be disappointed, in which case the solvency of those holding the liabilities of the borrowers may be threatened or impaired.

> The whole value of the manufacturer's efforts in producing the goods depends upon there being an effective demand for them when they are completed. It is only because the dealer anticipates that this effective demand for them will be forthcoming that he gives the manufacturer the order. The dealer, in fact, is taking the responsibility of saying how £10,000 worth of the productive capacity of the country shall be employed. The manufacturer, in accepting the order, and the banker in discounting the bill, are both endorsing the opinion of the dealer. The whole transaction is based ultimately on an expectation of a future demand, which must be more or less speculative....
>
> Now if a contraction of credit money occurs, the consequent slackening of demand, and fall in the prices of commodities, will lead to a widespread disappointment of dealers' expectations. At such a time the weakest dealers are likely to be impaired. An individual or company in starting a manufacturing business would usually add to the capital they can provide themselves, further sums borrowed in the form of debentures secured on the business and yielding a fixed rate of interest.... But when the general level of prices is falling, the value of the entire business will be falling also, while the debenture and other liabilities, being expressed in money, will remain unchanged.... [D]uring this period of falling prices, the expenses of production resist the downward tendency, and the profits are temporarily diminished and may be entirely obliterated or turned into an actual loss. A weak business cannot bear the strain, and being unable to pay its debenture interest and having no further assets on which to borrow, it will fail. If it is not reconstructed but ceases operations altogether, that will of course contribute to the general diminution of output. Its inability to meet its engagements will at the same time inflict loss on the banks. But at present we are considering credit, and credit depends on the expectation of future solvency. A business which is believed to be weak will have difficulty in borrowing, because bankers fear that it may fail. At a time of contracting trade the probability of any given business failing will be increased. At the same time the probability of any particular venture for which it may desire to borrow resulting in a loss instead of a profit will likewise be increased. Consequently at such a time credit will be impaired,

> but this will be the *consequence*, not the *cause* of the contracting trade. (pp. 78–80)

The solvency of the banker, in turn, depends on the solvency of those businesses to which it has extended credit. An overly optimistic anticipation of future demand must therefore inevitably impair the solvency of the banks.

> We have already seen that the banker's estimate of the proper proportion of his reserve to his liabilities is almost entirely empirical, and that an arbitrary change in the proportion which he thinks fit to maintain between them will carry with it an increase or decrease, as the case may be, in the available amount of purchasing power in the community. If a banker really underestimates the proper amount of reserve, and does not correct his estimate, he may find himself at a moment of strain with his reserve rapidly melting away and no prospect of the process coming to an end before the reserve is exhausted. His natural remedy is to borrow from other banks; but this he can only do if they believe his position to be sound. If they will not lend, he must try to curtail his loans. But if has been lending imprudently, he will find that on his refusing to renew loans the borrowers will in some cases become bankrupt and his money will be lost. It is just when a banker has been lending imprudently that his fellow-bankers will refuse to lend to him, and thus the same mistake cuts him off simultaneously from the two possible remedies. (pp. 81–82)

But the failure of one bank may have wider repercussions, affecting the solvency of other banks as well.

> When a bank fails, there is a cancellation of the whole amount of purchasing power represented by the loans outstanding at the moment of failure. The people who have borrowed from the defunct bank must either borrow from the surviving banks to pay the loans back as they fall due, or they must find the money by economizing their expenditures. The surviving banks cannot increase the aggregate of their loans without any increase in their reserves, and they must take steps to protect their reserves by raising the rate of interest.... In short, the aggregate of bankers' loans having been excessive in comparison with the aggregate of legal tender currency, the former aggregate is diminished as soon as a catastrophe gives practical demonstration of the necessity of such a step. (p. 82)

In a later chapter, Hawtrey returns to the subject of financial crises, providing a detailed discussion of the dynamics of a financial crisis, focusing attention on the banks' advances to dealers in stocks on the stock exchange. New investments in fixed capital, according to Hawtrey, are financed largely out of the pro-cyclical savings of the wealthy. The demand for new investment projects by businesses is also pro-cyclical, depending on the profits expected by businesses when considering the installation of new capital assets, the profit expectations, in turn, depending on current effective demand.

The financing for new long-term investment projects is largely channeled to existing businesses through what Hawtrey calls the investment market, the most important element of which is the stock exchange. The stock exchange functions efficiently only because of specialists whose business it is to hold inventories of various stocks, being prepared to buy those stocks from those wishing to sell them or sell the stocks to those wishing to buy them, at prices that seem at any moment to be market-clearing, i.e., at prices that keep buy and sell orders in rough balance. The specialists, like other traders and middlemen, finance their holdings of inventories by borrowing from banks, using the proceeds from purchases and sales—corresponding to the bid-ask spread—to repay their indebtedness to the banks. Unlike commercial traders and merchants, the turnover of whose inventories is relatively predictable with little chance of large price swings, and who can obtain short-term financing for a fixed term, stock dealers hold inventories that are not very predictable in their price and turnover and therefore can obtain financing only on a day-to-day basis, or "at call." The securities held by the stock dealer serve as collateral for the loan, and banks require the dealer to hold securities with a value exceeding some minimum percentage (margin) of the dealer's indebtedness to the bank.

New investment financed by the issue of stock must ultimately be purchased by savers seeking profitable investment opportunities into which they commit their savings. Existing firms may sometimes finance new projects by issuing new stock, but more often they issue debt or retained earnings to finance investment. Debt financing can be obtained by issuing bonds or preferred stock, or by borrowing from banks. New issues of stock must be underwritten and marketed through middlemen expecting to earn a return on their underwriting or marketing function who must have financing resources sufficient to bear the risk of holding a large stock of securities until they are sold to the public.

Now at a time of expanding trade and growing inflation, when there is a general expectation of high profits and at the same time there is a flood of savings seeking investment, an underwriter's business yields a good profit at very little risk. But at the critical moment when the banks are compelled to intervene to reduce the inflation this is changed….. (pp. 210–211)

[O]f all the borrowers from the banks those who borrow for the purposes of the investment market are the most liable to failure when the period of good trade comes to an end. And as it happens, it is they who are most at the mercy of the banks in times of trouble. For it is their habit to borrow from day to day, and the banks, since they cannot call in loans to traders which will only mature after several weeks or months, are apt to try to reduce an excess of credit money by refusing to lend from day to day. If that happens, the investment market will suddenly have to find the money which the banks want. The total amount of ready money in the hands of the whole investment market will probably be quite small, and, except in so far as they can persuade the banks to wait (in consideration probably of a high rate of interest), they must raise money by selling securities. But there are limits to the amount that can be raised in this way. The demand for investments is very inelastic. The money offered at any time is ordinarily simply the amount of accumulated savings of the community till then uninvested. This total can only be added to by people investing sums which they would otherwise leave as part of their working balances of money, and they cannot be induced to increase their investments very much in this way, however low the price in proportion to the yield of the securities offered. Consequently when the banks curtail the accommodation which they give to the investment market and the investment market tries to raise money by selling securities, the prices of securities may fall heavily without attracting much additional money. Meanwhile the general fall in the prices of securities will undermine the position of the entire investment market, since the value of the assets held against their liabilities to the banks will be depreciated. If the banks insist on payment in such circumstances a multitude of failures on the Stock Exchange and in the investment market must follow. The knowledge of this will deter the banks from making the last turn of the screw if they can help it. But it may be that the banks themselves are acting under dire necessity. If they have let the creation of credit get beyond their control, if they are on the point of running short of the legal tender money necessary to meet the daily demands upon them, they must have no alternative but to insist on payment. When the collapse comes it is not unlikely that some of the banks themselves will be dragged down by it. A bank which has suffered heavy losses may be unable any longer to show an excess of assets over liabilities, and if subjected to heavy demands may be unable to borrow to meet them.

> The calling in of loans from the investment market enables the banks to reduce the excess of credit money rapidly. The failure of one or more banks, by annihilating the credit money based upon their demand liabilities, hastens the process still more. A crisis therefore has the effect of bringing a trade depression into being with striking suddenness....
> It should not escape attention that even in a financial crisis, which is ordinarily regarded as simply a "collapse of credit," credit only plays a secondary part. The shortage of savings, which curtails the demand for investments, and the excess of credit money, which leads the banks to call in loans, are causes at least as prominent as the impairment of credit. And the impairment of credit itself is not a mere capricious loss of confidence, but is a revised estimate of the profits of commercial enterprises in general, which is based on the palpable facts of the market. The wholesale depreciation of securities at such a time is not due to a vague "distrust" but partly to the plain fact that the money values of the assets which they represent are falling and partly to forced sales necessitated by the sudden demand for money.... [T]he crisis dos not *originate* in distrust. Loss of credit in fact is only a symptom. (pp. 212–215)

A more astute and more incisive analysis of the forces creating the frightening downward spiral of the 2008 financial crisis than the generic description of what happens in a crisis provided by Hawtrey nearly a century earlier could not easily be found. The penetrating insightfulness of Hawtrey's description is especially important to take note of inasmuch as Hawtrey, while recognizing that financial crises can play an important role in amplifying the severity of a business-cycle downturn, did not accept that any financial crisis can be understood apart from the context of a cyclical process of which it is but an acute manifestation.

10.5 The Price-Specie-Flow Mechanism

In Chapter 9 of *Good and Bad Trade*, Hawtrey reached what he regarded as the culmination of his theoretical account of the determination of prices, incomes, and exchange rates under a system of national fiat currencies, by then positing that those currencies were all to become convertible into a fixed weight of gold.

After providing a detailed and painstaking account of the process of international adjustment in response to a loss of gold in one country, explaining how the loss of gold would cause interest rates to rise in the country losing gold, thus inducing other countries to lend to the country experiencing losing gold, Hawtrey traced out the repercussions of the disturbance on exchange rates within the limits set by gold import and export points, reflecting the cost of transporting gold and on domestic price levels of the countries experiencing gold flows. Here is how Hawtrey summarized his analysis:

> Gold flows from foreign countries to the area of stringency in response to the high rate of interest, more quickly from the nearer and more slowly from the more distant countries. While this process is at work the rates of interests in foreign countries are raised, more in the nearer and less in the more distant countries. As soon as the bankers' loans have been brought into the proper proportion to the stock of gold, the rate of interest reverts to the profit rate in the area of stringency, but the influx of gold continues from each foreign country until the average level of prices there has so far fallen that its divergence from the average level of prices in the area of stringency is no longer great enough to cover the cost of sending the gold.
>
> So long as any country is actually exporting gold the rate of interest will there be maintained somewhat above the profit rate, so as to diminish the total amount of bankers' loans *pari passu* with the stock of gold.
>
> At the time when the export of gold ceases from any foreign country the rate of exchange in that country on the area of stringency is at the export specie point; and the exchange will remain at this point indefinitely unless some new influence arises to disturb the equilibrium. In fact, the whole economic system will, in the absence of such influence, revert to the stable conditions from which it started. (p. 113)

In subsequent writings, Hawtrey modified his account of the adjustment process in an important respect. I have not identified the first instance in which Hawtrey revised his account of the adjustment process, but, almost twenty years after *Good and Bad Trade*, Hawtrey (1932), Hawtrey explained with exceptional clarity what was wrong with the account of the international adjustment mechanism presented in the earlier work. In the course of an extended historical discussion of how the Bank of England had used its lending rate as an instrument of policy in the nineteenth and early twentieth centuries (a discussion later expanded upon in Hawtrey (1938), Hawtrey quoted the following passage from the First Interim Report of the Cunliffe First Interim Report Committee (1918, paragraphs 4–5) describing the operation of the prewar gold standard. The passage explains how, under the gold standard, the Bank of England, confronting an outflow of gold reserves, could restore an international equilibrium by raising Bank Rate. The explanation in the Cunliffe Report employs the same reasoning embodied in the above quotation from *Good and Bad Trade*.

> The raising of the discount rate had the immediate effect of retaining money here which would otherwise have been remitted abroad, and of attracting remittances from abroad to take advantage of the higher rate, thus checking the outflow of gold and even reversing the stream.
>
> If the adverse conditions of the exchanges was due not merely to seasonal fluctuations but to circumstances tending to create a permanently adverse trade balance, it is obvious that the procedure above described would not have been sufficient. It would have resulted in the creation of a volume of short-dated indebtedness to foreign countries, which would have been in the end disastrous to our credit and the position of London as the financial center of the world. But the raising of the Bank's discount rate and the steps taken to make it effective in the market necessarily led to a general rise of interest rates and a restriction of credit. New enterprises were therefore postponed, and the demand for constructional materials and other capital goods was lessened. The consequent slackening of employment also diminished the demand for consumable goods, while holders of stocks of commodities carried largely with borrowed money, being confronted with an increase in interest charges, if not with actual difficulty in renewing loans, and with the prospect of falling prices, tended to press their goods on a weak market. The result was a decline in general prices in the home market which, by checking imports and stimulating exports, corrected the adverse trade balance which was the primary cause of the difficulty. (Interim Report of the Cunliffe Committee, sects. 10.4-10.5)

Acknowledging that the Cunliffe Report did in some sense reflect the orthodox view of how variations in Bank Rate achieved an international adjustment, Hawtrey took strong issue with the version of the adjustment process outlined in the Cunliffe Report.

> This passage expresses very fairly the principle on which the Bank of England had been regulating credit from 1866 to 1914. They embody the art of central banking as it was understood in the half-century preceding the war. In view of the experience which has been obtained, the progress made in theory and the changes which have occurred since 1914, the principles of the art require reconsideration at the present day.

The Cunliffe Committee's version of the effect of Bank rate upon the trade balance was based on exactly the same Ricardian theory of foreign trade as Horsely Palmer's. It depended on adjustments of the *price level.* But the revolutionary changes in the means of communication during the past hundred years have unified markets to such a degree that for any of the commodities which enter regularly into international trade there is practically a single world market and a single world price. That does not mean absolutely identical prices for the same commodity at different places, but prices differing only by the cost of transport from exporting to the importing centers. Local divergences of prices form this standard are small and casual, and are speedily eliminated so long as markets work freely.

In Ricardo's day, relatively considerable differences of price were possible between distant centers. The merchant could never have up-to-date information at one place of the price quotations at another. When he heard that the price of a commodity at a distant place had been relatively high weeks or months before, he was taking a risk in shipping a cargo thither, because the market might have changed for the worse before the cargo arrived. Under such conditions, it might well be that a *substantial* difference of price level was required to attract goods from one country to another.

Nevertheless it was fallacious to explain the adjustment wholly in terms of the price level. There was, even at that time, an approximation to a world price. When the difference of price level attracted goods from one country to another, the effect was to diminish the difference of price level, and probably after an interval to eliminate it altogether (apart from cost of transport). When that occurred, the importing country was suffering an adverse balance, not on account of an excess price level, but on account of an excess demand at the world price level. Whether there be a difference of price level or not, it is this difference of demand that is the fundamental factor.

In Horsely Palmer's day the accepted theory was that the rate of discount affected the price level because it affected the amount of note issue and therefore the quantity of currency. That did not mean that the whole doctrine depended on the quantity theory of money. All that had to be assumed was that an expansion or contraction of the currency so far tended to cause a rise or fall of the prices could be secured by an appropriate expansion or contraction of the currency. That is a very different thing from saying that the rise or fall of the price level would be exactly proportional to the expansion or contraction of the currency.

But it is not really necessary to introduce the quantity of currency into the analysis at all. What governs demand in any community is the

> consumers' income (the total of all incomes expressed in terms of money) and consumers' outlay (the total of all disbursements out of income, including investment).[13] (pp. 144–145)

Hawtrey's rejection of the PSFM, which he still accepted in *Good and Bad Trade*, is perhaps the only significant theoretical point on which he revised the views articulated in the first of his many publications.

10.6 Conclusion

Hawtrey was not the first economist to offer a monetary theory of the business cycle. In presenting his own version of a monetary theory of the trade cycle in an abstract, theoretical, and deductive exposition, with no citations to the earlier literature, other than two references to Irving Fisher, Hawtrey may have actually made his work appear less original than it was. In reviewing *Good and Bad Trade*, A. C. Pigou, loyal disciple of Marshall and staunch adherent of Marshallian doctrines, praised Hawtrey's systematic and logical development of the material, while finding little novelty in the volume, and chided Hawtrey for not acknowledging earlier works, presumably those of Marshall and his students, in which, Pigou suggested, Hawtrey's ideas had already been stated. Greater care in citing earlier contributions would have allowed Hawtrey to demonstrate the numerous points of originality in his work. But, over a century after its publication, it is not hard to recognize and admire the full extent of Hawtrey's contribution in his first publication in economics.

References

Cain, N. (1982). Hawtrey and multiplier theory. *Australian Economic History Review, 22*, 68–78.

Cassel, G. (1916). The present situation of the foreign exchanges. *Economic Journal, 26*(103), 319–323.

Cassel, G. (1918). Abnormal deviations in international exchanges. *Economic Journal, 28*(112), 413–415.

[13] The final sentence may have been somewhat overstated, but, in the context of a gold standard, in which the quantity of currency is endogenously determined, the relevant point is that the quantity of currency is determined not determining.

Clarke, P. (1988). *The Keynesian revolution in the making 1924–1936*. Clarendon Press.
Corden, W. M. (1985). Exchange-rate protection. In *Protection, growth and trade: Essays in international economics* (Chapter 17). Basil Blackwell.
Cunliffe Committee. (1918). First interim report of the committee on currency and foreign exchanges after the war. In T. E. Gregory (Ed.), *Select statutes, documents and reports relating to British banking, 1832–1928*. Taylor and Francis.
Davis, E. G. (1980). The correspondence between R.G. Hawtrey and J.M. Keynes on the *Treatise*: The genesis of output adjustment models. *Canadian Journal of Economics, 13*, 716–724.
Deutscher, P. (1990). *Ralph Hawtrey and the development of macroeconomics*. University of Michigan Press.
Dimand, R. (1997). Hawtrey and the multiplier. *History of Political Economy, 29*(3), 549–556.
Fisher, I. (1907). *The rate of interest*. Macmillan.
Fisher, I. (1930). *The theory of interest*. Macmillan.
Gibson, A. W. (1923, January). The future course of high class investment values. *The bankers', insurance managers' and agents' Magazine* (15–34).
Glasner, D. (2018). The fisher effect and the financial crisis of 2008. https://ssrn.com/abstract=3247795, https://doi.org/10.2139/ssrn.3247795.
Haberler, G. (1937). *Prosperity and depression*. League of Nations.
Hawtrey, R. G. (1913 [1962]). *Good and bad trade*, 2nd ed. A. M. Constable.
Hawtrey, R. G. (1919). *Currency and credit*. Longmans.
Hawtrey, R. G. (1925). Public expenditure and the demand for Labour. *Economica, 13*(1), 38–48.
Hawtrey, R. G. (1926). *The economic problem*. Longmans.
Hawtrey, R. G. (1932). *The art of central banking*. Longmans.
Hawtrey, R. G. (1938). *A century of bank rate*. Longmans.
Hawtrey, R. G. (1939). *Capital and employment*. Longmans.
Hicks, J. R. (1969). Automatists, Hawtreyans, and Keynesians. *Journal of Money, Credit and Banking, 1*(3), 307–317.
Humphrey, T. M. (1979). The purchasing power parity doctrine. *Federal Reserve Bank of Richmond Economic Review, 65*(3), 3–15.
Keynes, J. M. (1930). *A treatise on money*. Macmillan.
Keynes, J. M. (1936). *The general theory of employment, interest and money*. Macmillan.
Keynes, J. M. (1937). Alternative theories of the rate of interest. *Economic Journal, 47*(2), 241–252.
Mises, L. v. (1913 [1934]). *The theory of money and credit*. Jonathan Cape.
Pigou, A. C. (1913). Review of *good and bad trade. Economic Journal, 23*(92), 580–583.

Schumpeter, J. A. (1954). *The history of economic analysis*. Oxford University Press.
Shackle, G. L. S. (1967). *Years of high theory*. Cambridge University Press.
Thornton, H. (1802 [1939]). *An inquiry into the nature and effects of the paper credit of Great Britain*. George Allen & Unwin.

CHAPTER 11

Hawtrey and Keynes

11.1 Introduction

Like his younger contemporary J.M. Keynes, Ralph George Hawtrey was a Cambridge graduate in mathematics, an Apostle, deeply influenced by the philosophy of G.E. Moore, and associated, though, unlike Keynes, only peripherally, with the Bloomsbury group. Although eventually eclipsing Hawtrey in fame and influence, Keynes more than once acknowledged his intellectual debt to Hawtrey, famously calling Hawtrey his "grandparent in the paths of errancy" (Keynes, 1937, 242).

Born in 1879, Hawtrey graduated from Trinity College, Cambridge, in 1901, a year before Keynes went up to King's College, Cambridge. Both were largely autodidacts in economics. While Keynes was acquainted with Marshall, both as a student and through his father, John Neville Keynes, there is no evidence of personal contact between Hawtrey and Marshall. It is interesting to note that, just as Keynes's 1925 marriage to the Russian ballerina Lydia Lopokova led to his partial estrangement from the Bloomsbury group, Hawtrey's marriage, ten years earlier, to the Hungarian concert pianist Emilia d'Aranyi (a great-niece of the famed violinist Joseph Joachim) elicited a harsh reaction from Virginia Woolf (1976, p. 145) who, writing to Duncan Grant, described Mrs. Hawtrey as "a practically barbaric Pole … with ungoverned passions and the brain

D. Glasner, *Studies in the History of Monetary Theory*, Palgrave Studies in the History of Economic Thought, https://doi.org/10.1007/978-3-030-83426-5_11

of a yellow cockatoo," though she noted—with approval or, perhaps, condescension—the Hawtreys' affectionate manner toward each other.

Upon graduation, Hawtrey entered the British Civil Service. His study of economics seems to have begun when he was preparing for the Civil Service entrance examination. After a brief stint in the Admiralty, Hawtrey began working in the Treasury, becoming the Principal Private Secretary to the Chancellor of the Exchequer, Lloyd George, in 1910, and assisting in drafting the 1911 Budget. His administrative talents having been overshadowed by his scholarly achievements, his wide knowledge of economic theory, history, and of banking and finance,[1] and his exceptional expository talent, Hawtrey was appointed Director of Financial Enquiries Branch of the Treasury in 1919. By then, Hawtrey had published two important books on monetary theory: *Good and Bad Trade* (1913), his first exposition of his own distinctive monetary theory of the business cycle, a theory that for 60 years served as his analytic paradigm, and *Currency and Credit* (1919a), a deeper, more comprehensive, exposition of his theory than the earlier volume, combined with historical and institutional applications of his theoretical apparatus.

Hawtrey remained at the Treasury, with the exception of a stint at Harvard University in the 1928–1929 academic year, until retiring in 1947, when he took a professorship at the Royal Institute of International Affairs. Hawtrey continued to write prolifically until 1971, primarily on British and international monetary policy. Knighted in 1956, Hawtrey died in 1975, still admired, but increasingly neglected by the postwar generation trained after the Keynesian revolution.

The remainder of this chapter focuses on those aspects of Hawtrey's career, both in print and as an adviser to the Treasury, in which he either influenced Keynes or engaged in significant theoretical or policy disputes with Keynes. First, I consider the challenge of post-war monetary reconstruction in which Hawtrey played a key role, planning and guiding the 1922 Genoa Conference to create a framework for restoring the gold standard after World War I. Keynes expressed skepticism about the conference in his *Tract on Monetary Reform*, a volume Hawtrey (1924) reviewed for the *Economic Journal*. The differences between

[1] Hawtrey credited Sir John Bradbury (later Lord Bradbury), his superior at the Treasury, for having taught him much of what he knew about money and finance and about "City wisdom," but Bradbury's instruction was likely more practical and institutional than theoretical.

Keynes and Hawtrey over monetary reconstruction re-emerged in 1925, when Winston Churchill, Chancellor of the Exchequer, pressed to decide whether Britain would rejoin the gold standard at the prewar dollar–sterling parity, solicited advice from a select group of advisers including both Keynes and Hawtrey. About the same time, Hawtrey (1925) published an article articulating what would become known as the "Treasury view," already foreshadowed in *Good and Bad Trade*, that government spending would affect only the composition, not the volume, of total expenditure. Keynes would take increasingly sharp issue with this position over the next few years, culminating in a memorable confrontation at the Macmillan Committee in 1930. Even as they disagreed about the efficacy of fiscal policy as a countercyclical policy tool, Hawtrey, after reading the final proofs of Keynes's *A Treatise on Money* (1930a), provided Keynes with valuable comments and insights, including an early exposition of the multiplier analysis, which may have influenced Keynes as he began writing the *General Theory*. However, a key argument of the *Treatise*—that monetary policy can be effective only by changing the long-term rate of interest—challenged Hawtrey's view that the short-term interest rate—Bank Rate—is the key instrument of monetary policy. Hawtrey responded to Keynes not only in his review of the *Treatise*, but also eight years later in his book *A Century of Bank Rate* (Hawtrey, 1938). Finally, Hawtrey and Keynes engaged in a lengthy correspondence over successive drafts of the *General Theory of Employment, Interest and Money* (Keynes, 1936) sent to Hawtrey by Keynes. Hawtrey's criticisms of the *General Theory* were less warmly received than his comments on the *Treatise*, and Keynes became increasingly frustrated by Hawtrey's resistance to his new ideas. Nevertheless, on the key disputes between Hawtrey and Keynes—whether the equality of savings and investment is an accounting identity or an equilibrium condition, whether liquidity preference provides an alternative to the neoclassical theory of interest, and whether a reduction in nominal wages could, even in theory, reduce unemployment—the weight of professional opinion has subsequently moved in Hawtrey's direction.

11.2 The Genoa Monetary Conference and Reconstruction of the Gold Standard

While at the Treasury during World War I, Hawtrey undertook historical investigations into monetary disorders during wars and political upheavals, publishing articles on the collapse of the assignats in the French

Revolution (Hawtrey, 1918b), and the British suspension of convertibility in 1797 (Hawtrey, 1918a), followed by an article on the gold standard (Hawtrey, 1919b). Asserting that the chief function of a monetary standard is to provide a monetary unit with a stable and predictable value, Hawtrey observed that the nineteenth-century gold standard had discharged that function tolerably well. After the monetary disorders of World War I caused a huge depreciation of gold, it was Hawtrey's view that the goal of economic policy ought to be to restore the gold standard with minimal further disturbance to the value of money. The danger inherent in restoring the gold standard was that a subsequent increase in the monetary demand for gold would cause gold to appreciate. To avoid deflation, central banks would have to cooperate to limit their accumulation of gold reserves. Hawtrey's analysis was widely noted, especially by the Swedish economist Gustav Cassel (Howson, 1985; Chapters 13 and 14).

Hawtrey was a key figure in the Treasury group that organized the Genoa International Monetary Conference to establish a system of international cooperation to restore an international gold standard. Hawtrey and Cassel helped draft recommendations for restoring the gold standard while strictly limiting the use of gold coins, allowing banknotes to be redeemed only in gold bullion, as Ricardo (1816) and Keynes (1913) had proposed, and to encourage central banks to hold foreign-exchange reserves in currencies convertible into gold rather than bullion.

Attending the Genoa Conference as a correspondent for the *Manchester Guardian*, Keynes wrote articles, later included in his *A Tract on Monetary Reform* (Keynes, 1923), criticizing the Genoa Resolutions for recommending international cooperation with no concrete mechanism for securing such cooperation. Keynes argued that, given the size of US gold reserves, the value of gold would be largely controlled by the US Federal Reserve (the Fed). Believing the Fed to be likely to dispose of the huge US hoard of gold, Keynes, unlike Hawtrey, saw inflation as the chief risk of a restored gold standard, and therefore argued that stabilizing the domestic price level should be the goal of British monetary policy.

In reviewing the *Tract*, Hawtrey (1924) disputed Keynes's expectation that the Fed would adopt an inflationary monetary policy under a restored gold standard. Events subsequently confirmed Hawtrey's forecast, and by 1925, Keynes had reversed his position, arguing that domestic deflation, not inflation, would result if Britain re-joined the gold standard.

11.3 Britain's 1925 Return to Gold at the Prewar Sterling–Dollar Parity

In early 1925, sterling having appreciated to within 10% of its prewar parity against the dollar, the Conservative government came under pressure from the Bank of England and financial interests to restore the convertibility of sterling at the prewar parity. Doubting the wisdom of a quick return to gold despite the advice of his closest Treasury advisers, Churchill solicited the views of several monetary experts, including Keynes and Hawtrey. Although not routinely consulted by Churchill, Hawtrey was evidently not unknown to Churchill, who requested that "the learned man should be released from the dungeon … have his chains struck off and the straw brushed from his hair and clothes, and be admitted to the light and warmth of an argument in the Treasury Boardroom" (Grigg 1947, pp. 81–82).

Despite no longer fearing inflation, Keynes remained opposed to a restoration of the gold standard. With unemployment at well over 10%, Keynes now worried that the deflation caused by a further 10% appreciation of sterling against the dollar would exacerbate and prolong high unemployment. Using an analytical framework similar to Keynes's, Hawtrey supported the return to gold, but with an important qualification. Convinced, like Keynes, that deflation must be avoided, Hawtrey urged that, after a return to gold, the Bank of England reduce Bank Rate, believing that the Fed would reduce its own lending rate rather than accept a further influx of gold. Hawtrey argued that the Fed would likely follow the Bank of England in reducing its lending rate, causing a mild increase in US prices, and allowing British and American money wages to converge with no further reduction in British money wages. However, if restoring the prewar parity were to force British money wages to fall, Hawtrey agreed with Keynes that re-joining the gold standard would be a bad bargain for Britain.

Thus, Hawtrey's was a lone voice, everyone else agreeing that deflation would be the necessary consequence of restoring the prewar parity. Supporters viewed the deflation either as a necessary evil, or as the hard cure needed to revive a sick economy; opponents, especially Keynes, judged the cure to be worse than the disease.

11.4 Hawtrey and the "Treasury View"

At about the same time that he advised Churchill to restore sterling to its prewar parity, Hawtrey published perhaps his most famous article, "Public expenditure and the demand for labour" (Hawtrey, 1925). Responding to proposals for additional public-works spending, Hawtrey argued that, if financed either by taxes or borrowing, the added public spending would reduce private spending by an equal amount, changing the composition, not the magnitude, of total spending and employment. Conceding that government spending financed by money creation would increase total spending, Hawtrey maintained that the increase in total spending would be the consequence of monetary expansion, not added public expenditure, describing government spending as "a piece of ritual" enabling politicians to take credit for the increased employment.

Four years later, dismissing proposals, endorsed by Keynes, for increased public-works spending, Churchill relied on what he called the "orthodox Treasury view" that increased government spending would entail an equal reduction in private spending, thereby elevating Hawtrey's previously obscure article to authoritative status. Clarke (1988) recounts how Churchill came to invoke Hawtrey's article as the "orthodox Treasury view" (also see Deutscher, 1990, 19–20, 65–66, 217–219). Churchill, however, did not mention that the author of the "orthodox Treasury view" believed that high unemployment warranted a reduction in Bank Rate.

Hawtrey may be faulted for overlooking that, even without monetary expansion, the increased interest rates associated with increased public borrowing would reduce desired cash holdings, allowing total spending to increase. Nevertheless, this lapse, considered in light of circumstances in 1925, when total spending was constrained by a 5% Bank Rate to encourage an influx of gold and an appreciation of sterling, seems relatively unimportant, Hawtrey's larger point being that cutting Bank Rate would do more than additional public expenditure to increase total spending. Even if reducing Bank Rate caused an outflow of gold, the outflow, or a depreciation of sterling, could be tolerated. Alternatively, other central banks could be induced to follow the Bank of England in cutting interest rates to forestall an outflow of gold (Laidler, 1997).

Unlike nineteenth-century theorists of central banking like Bagehot, Hawtrey believed the primary duty of a central bank was not to ensure the convertibility of the monetary unit into gold, but to preserve its wealth value, that is, stabilizing an index of money wages (Hawtrey, 1932), stability of nominal wages, in Hawtrey's view, being compatible with full employment.

The tension between Keynes and Hawtrey over public spending and restoring the gold standard led to a dramatic confrontation in April 1930, when Hawtrey testified before the Committee on Finance and Industry (the Macmillan Committee) to investigate the causes of depressed trade and high unemployment in Britain. The committee included prominent economists, financiers, former civil servants, and politicians, but Keynes was its dominant figure, relentlessly interrogating witnesses and writing much of its final report. Keynes believed that, given the mistaken restoration of the prewar dollar parity, the Bank of England had no alternative but to defend sterling by raising Bank Rate. To cut Bank Rate, as Hawtrey had been urging since 1925, was no longer, in Keynes's view, a realistic option.

Appearing before the committee, Hawtrey argued that, despite the overvaluation of sterling, the Bank of England could have reduced British unemployment had it dared to cut Bank Rate below the 5% level which it had almost continuously maintained since 1925. Although reducing Bank Rate would have caused an outflow of gold, Hawtrey argued that the gold standard was not worth the game if it could be sustained only at the cost of chronically high unemployment. Since London was still the world's financial center, Hawtrey suggested that, by reducing Bank Rate, the Bank of England could have induced similar reductions by other central banks, mitigating the loss of gold and the threat to the convertibility. Under questioning by Chairman Hugh Pattison Macmillan, Hawtrey denied that gold-standard orthodoxy obligated the Bank of England to raise Bank Rate to ensure convertibility.

> [T]hat kind of orthodoxy is like conventions at bridge; you have to break them when the circumstances call for it. I think that a gold reserve exists to be used … Perhaps once in a century the time comes when you can use your gold reserve for the governing purpose, provided you have the courage to use practically all of it. (Macmillan Committee, 1931, pp. 283–284)

Keynes found an apparent asymmetry in Hawtrey's argument: that an efflux of gold would induce other central banks to expand credit, allowing British prices to converge on a rising, not stable or falling, international price level. Keynes countered that, even if the rest of the world followed Britain in easing credit, it was implausible to expect an easy British policy to raise the international price level more than the internal British price level. A cheap-money policy by the Bank of England would be self-defeating, tending to raise British prices faster than international prices.

Hawtrey responded that only by exporting gold could Britain induce other central banks to change their policy. However, Hawtrey failed to explain a key premise of his reasoning: under a gold standard, movements in domestic prices are not primarily determined by domestic monetary policy. If international prices and wages are less than corresponding British prices and wages, British prices and wages must move toward international levels regardless of the stance of British monetary policy, whose effects are manifested chiefly in the reserve position of the Bank of England. Hawtrey's failure to spell out fully the premises underlying his response to Keynes's questioning led Keynes and the committee to dismiss his position as logically defective.

In charging that it was implausible to expect an easy-money policy by the Bank of England to raise world prices by more than it raised British prices, Keynes neglected to consider that, under the status quo with Bank Rate at 5%, British prices would fall toward the international level. Under Hawtrey's implicit central-bank reaction function, other central banks had no incentive to change their policy, implying no change in the international price level to which the British price level had to adjust. An easy-money policy that allowed an efflux of gold would induce a "sympathetic" easing of policy by other central banks, raising the international price level and thereby reducing deflationary pressure on British prices. The asymmetry identified by Keynes was a property not of Hawtrey's analysis, but of the status quo in which the British price level remained above the international price level.

11.5 Bank Rate as an Instrument of Monetary Policy

Already in *Good and Bad Trade* (1913), Hawtrey had identified Bank Rate as the key policy variable governing the business cycle, the desired holdings of inventories by traders and merchants being highly sensitive to the carrying cost of those inventories. Changes in desired inventories induce corresponding changes in output, in turn causing similar changes in incomes and spending, inducing further changes in traders' desired inventories, and so on. Thus, reducing Bank Rate starts a cumulative expansion of income and output, and increasing Bank Rate starts a contraction. While not disputing Hawtrey's analysis, Keynes questioned its empirical significance, arguing that fluctuations in fixed-capital investment account for most of the cyclical fluctuation in income and employment.

Hicks (1969) suggested that much of Keynes's *Treatise* was a reply to Hawtrey's theory of the cycle. While sharing Hawtrey's view that the business cycle could be managed by a judicious monetary policy, Keynes argued that monetary policy could be effective only if it operated on long-term interest rates. In his review of *The Treatise on Money* (1932, ch. 6), Hawtrey defended his position on the effectiveness of Bank Rate as a policy instrument. Hicks (1969) regarded Hawtrey's 1938 volume, *A Century of Bank Rate*, providing copious evidence from 1844 to 1938 of both the influence of Bank Rate on economic conditions in Britain, and of the lack of correlation between Bank Rate and long-term rates, as a comprehensive response to Keynes's argument in the *Treatise* on the primacy of the long-term interest rate as the crucial instrument of monetary policy.

11.6 Hawtrey's Review of Keynes's Treatise on Money

Although Keynes began writing the *Treatise* in the mid-1920s, it was not until April 1930, just before publication, that he sent Hawtrey proofs, later thanking Hawtrey for his "tremendously useful" criticism (1979, p. 10).[2] However, except for minor changes, Keynes had no time to incorporate Hawtrey's detailed commentary into the final version of the *Treatise*. Hawtrey included his comments on the *Treatise* as part of his written submission to the Macmillan Committee, and published a revision of his comments on the *Treatise* as Chapter 6 of *The Art of Central Banking* (1932).

[2] Keynes did not read some of Hawtrey's comments until after the *Treatise* was published.

Two of Hawtrey's comments are especially noteworthy. First, Hawtrey criticized Keynes's claim that inflation is caused by an excess of investment over saving, as a mere tautology entailed by Keynes's definition of savings and investment.

> [T]he difference between saving and investment is simply another name for the windfall gains or losses or for the difference between prices and costs of output. Throughout the *Treatise*, Mr. Keynes adduces a divergence between saving and investment as the criterion of a departure from monetary equilibrium. But this criterion is nothing more or less than a divergence between prices and costs. Though the criterion ostensibly depends on two economic activities, "investment" and "saving," it depends in reality not on them but on movements of the price level relative to costs. (Hawtrey, 1932, p. 336)

Hawtrey also faulted Keynes for assuming that a monetary disequilibrium would trigger only price, not output, changes. Hawtrey provided an alternative analysis with variations in both output and prices, including an algebraic derivation of the multiplier concept, apparently, as Davis (1980) and Dimand (1997) documented, before Kahn (1931) published his derivation of the multiplier.

Although Hawtrey's formulation of the multiplier may have preceded Kahn's, the timing of their contributions and when they came to Keynes's attention is difficult to ascertain, especially since Keynes was in regular contact with Kahn about the *Treatise*, and, as editor of the *Economic Journal* would certainly have seen Kahn's paper before publication. However, even if Keynes saw Kahn's formulation before Hawtrey's, the almost simultaneous appearance of a similar analysis probably left its mark on Keynes, reinforcing the significance of Kahn's contribution in Keynes's mind (Deutscher, 1990, pp. 103–104).

Hawtrey also corrected Keynes's misinterpretation of his own position on the efficacy of Bank Rate, emphasizing his own belief "that an acceleration or retardation of the creation of credit acts through changes in consumers' income and outlay ... not through changes in the unspent margin" (Hawtrey's term for holdings of cash balances) (Hawtrey, 1932, p. 363), denying that his was, as Keynes had suggested, a quantity-theoretic monetary theory. Rather, Hawtrey believed that the most reliable means for influencing income and expenditure was via Bank Rate, thereby causing businesses and traders to alter desired holdings of unfinished goods and inventories. Those changes, in turn, would lead to changes in output, income and consumer outlay, thereby inducing further changes, and so on.

To identify Hawtrey as "the man who, having stumbled upon [the multiplier], painstakingly suppressed news of its discovery in his subsequent publications" (Clarke, 1988, pp. 242–243) thus betrays a misunderstanding of Hawtrey. A multiplier analysis, implicit in Hawtrey's cycle theory from the outset, was neither stumbled upon nor suppressed. Overlooking the interest-sensitivity of the demand for money, Hawtrey merely maintained that government spending, unsupported by monetary expansion, would be offset by reduced private spending, implying no increase in total spending and, thus, no multiplier effect.

11.7 Hawtrey and the General Theory

Probably because Hawtrey's comments on the *Treatise* had been so helpful, Keynes included Hawtrey among those with whom he shared early drafts of the *General Theory*. A protracted correspondence between Keynes and Hawtrey ensued spanning almost the entire period during which Keynes was writing the *General Theory*, a correspondence that annoyed and frustrated Keynes. "Hawtrey," Keynes wrote to his wife after meeting with Hawtrey in 1933, "was very sweet to the last but quite mad. One can argue with him a long time on a perfectly sane and interesting basis and then, suddenly, one is in a madhouse" (cited in Skidelsky, 1992, 495).

Hardly a month had passed after publication of the *General Theory* in February 1936, before Hawtrey wrote a lengthy memorandum about the *General Theory* to his Treasury colleagues[3] (Hawtrey, 1937a, ch. 7). Hawtrey's review criticized Keynes's claim to have overturned the "classical" theory of interest, in which interest is viewed as the price equating investment with savings. Keynes rejected the idea that adjustment in the interest rate brings the two magnitudes into equality, but not the idea that savings and investment are equal, arguing that aggregate savings and aggregate investment are merely "different aspects of the same thing," both being unconsumed income. By showing that saving and investment are necessarily equal to each other, Keynes believed that he had exposed

[3] The original memorandum as well as many other Treasury memoranda written by Hawtrey may be found in G.C. Peden (1988).

the fallacy underlying the orthodox notion that the rate of interest equilibrates saving and investment. Rejecting the orthodox view that interest is the reward for foregoing consumption, Keynes argued that interest is actually the reward for sacrificing liquidity.

Hawtrey identified the internal contradiction in Keynes's argument: if aggregate investment and aggregate savings are identically equal, then income is no more capable than the interest rate of adjusting to ensure their equality. Echoing his earlier criticism of the fundamental equations in the *Treatise*, Hawtrey ridiculed Keynes's propensity to reason by way of definitions and identities.

> The identity of saving and investment may be compared to the identity of two sides of an account.
>
> Identity so established does not prove anything. The idea that a tendency for saving and investment so defined to become different has to be counteracted by an expansion or contraction of total incomes is an absurdity; such a tendency cannot strain the economic system; it can only strain Keynes's vocabulary. (Hawtrey, 1937a, p. 160)

A year after publishing the *General Theory*, Keynes (1937) defended his liquidity-preference theory of interest. Responding to Hawtrey's criticism of his definition of aggregate investment and aggregate savings as different aspects of the same thing while also using their equality as an equilibrium condition, Keynes (1937, p. 249) compared the identity of investment and savings to the identity of purchases and sales:

> Aggregate saving and aggregate investment … are necessarily equal in the same way in which aggregate purchases of anything on the market are equal to aggregate sales. But this does not mean that "buying" and "selling" are identical terms, and that the laws of supply and demand are meaningless.

Hawtrey rejected Keynes's argument that the necessary equality of savings and investment merely restates the orthodox position, the only novel element of his theory being to identify income rather than interest as the equilibrating variable.

> Old fashioned orthodoxy never held that saving and investment *could not* be unequal; it held that their inequality, when it did occur, was inconsistent with equilibrium. If they are defined as "different aspects of the same thing," how can it possibly be "the level of incomes which ensures equality between saving and investment …? Whatever the level of incomes may be, and however great the disequilibrium, the condition that saving and

investment must be equal is always identically satisfied. (Hawtrey, 1937b, p. 437)

Although Keynes's definition of investment and savings as "different aspects of the same thing" while treating their equality as an equilibrium condition is now generally recognized as problematic, the confusion, as Lipsey (1972) showed, was not a fatal error, Hawtrey being the first, but not the only, author to note Keynes's confusion (e.g., Robertson, 1937; Haberler, 1937). While rejecting Keynes's claim to have shown that liquidity preference, not real factors, determine the rate of interest, Hawtrey failed to see that Keynes, in discussing the liquidity premium in Chapter 13, implicitly recognized the existence of a real rate of return distinct from the liquidity premium. However, Hawtrey did note a similar confusion underlying Keynes's puzzling criticism of the Fisher equation.

11.8 Conclusion

Keynes and Hawtrey had much in common in their upbringing, academic training and interests, and their careers brought them into repeated contact. Despite Keynes's magnetic personality, his social and academic connections, and his gifts as a speaker and writer, Hawtrey, though eventually eclipsed by his younger contemporary, may initially have been the more influential. There were also differences in temperament, Keynes constantly searching for, trying out and discarding new ideas, Hawtrey, throughout his 60-year career, re-stating and refining the same set of basic ideas already set out in his first book. Notwithstanding the tensions in their relationship occasioned by Hawtrey's refusal to give up his prior beliefs and accept the new doctrines of the *General Theory*, Keynes (1937) called Hawtrey, "who had strayed from the fold sooner than I did," my "grandparent in the paths of errancy" (Keynes, 1937, p. 242 n) echoing an earlier tribute (Keynes 1930b, p. 86):

> There are very few writers on monetary subjects from whom one receives more stimulus and useful suggestion … and I think there are few writers on these subjects with whom I personally feel more fundamental sympathy and agreement. The paradox is that in spite of that, I nearly always disagree in detail with what he says! Yet truly and sincerely he is one of the writers who seems to me to be most nearly on the right track!

References

Clarke, P. (1988). *The Keynesian revolution in the making, 1924–1936*. Clarendon.
Davis, E. G. (1980). The correspondence between R.G. Hawtrey and J.M. Keynes on the Treatise: The genesis of output adjustment models. *Canadian Journal of Economics, 13*(4), 716–724.
Deutscher, P. (1990). *Ralph Hawtrey and the development of macroeconomics*. University of Michigan Press.
Dimand, R. (1997). Hawtrey and the multiplier. *History of Political Economy, 29*(3), 549–556.
Grigg, P. J. (1947). *Prejudice and judgement*. Jonathan Cape.
Haberler, G. (1937). *Prosperity and depression*. League of Nations.
Hawtrey, R. G. (1913). *Good and bad trade*. Longmans.
Hawtrey, R. G. (1918a). The bank restriction of 1797. *Economic Journal, 28*(109), 52–65.
Hawtrey, R. G. (1918b). The collapse of the French assignats. *Economic Journal, 28*(111), 300–314.
Hawtrey, R. G. (1919a). *Currency and credit*. Longmans.
Hawtrey, R. G. (1919b). The gold standard. *Economic Journal, 29*(116), 428–442.
Hawtrey, R. G. (1924). Review of A Tract on Monetary Reform by J. M. Keynes. *Economic Journal, 34*(134), 227–235.
Hawtrey, R. G. (1925). Public expenditure and the demand for labour. *Economica, 13*(1), 38–48.
Hawtrey, R. G. (1932). *The art of central banking*. Longmans.
Hawtrey, R. G. (1937). *Capital and employment*. Longmans.
Hawtrey, R. G. (1937). Alternative theories of the rate of interest: Three rejoinders, III. *Economic Journal, 47*(187), 436–443.
Hawtrey, R. G. (1938). *A century of bank rate*. Longmans.
Hicks, J. R. (1969). Automatists, Hawtreyans, and Keynesians. *Journal of Money Credit and Banking, 1*(3), 307–317.
Howson, S. (1985). Hawtrey and the real world. In G. C. Harcourt (Ed.), *Keynes and his contemporaries* (pp. 142–187). Macmillan.
Kahn, R. F. (1931). The relation of home investment to unemployment. *Economic Journal, 41*(2), 173–198.
Keynes, J. M. (1913). *Indian currency and finance*. Royal Economic Society.
Keynes, J. M. (1923). *A tract on monetary reform*. Macmillan.
Keynes, J. M. (1930a). *A Treatise on money* (Vol. 2). Macmillan.
Keynes, J. M. (1930b). Discussion of "money and index numbers" by R. G. Hawtrey. *Journal of the Royal Statistical Society, 93*(1), 86–88.
Keynes, J. M. (1936). *The general theory of employment*. Macmillan.

Keynes, J. M. (1937). Alternative theories of the rate of interest. *Economic Journal, 47*(2), 241–252.
Keynes, J. M. (1979). *The collected writings of John Maynard Keynes* (Vol. XXIX). In D. Moggridge (Ed.). Macmillan for the Royal Economics Society.
Laidler, D. (1997). *Fabricating the Keynesian revolution*. Cambridge University Press.
Lipsey, R. G. (1972). The foundations of the theory of national income: An analysis of some fundamental errors. In M. Peston & B. Corry (Eds.), *Essays in honour of Lord Robbins* (pp. 3–42). Wiedenfeld and Nicholson.
Macmillan Committee. (1931). *Minutes of evidence taken before the committee on finance and industry*. HMSO.
Peden, G. C. (1988). *Keynes and his critics: Treasury responses to the Keynesian revolution 1925–1946*. Oxford University Press.
Ricardo, D. (1816). *Proposals for an economical and secure currency* (2nd ed.). Murray.
Robertson, D. H. (1937). Alternative theories of the rate of interest: Three rejoinders, II. *Economic Journal, 47*(187), 428–436.
Skidelsky, R. (1992). *John Maynard Keynes: The economist as saviour 1920–1937*. Macmillan.
Woolf, V. (1976). *The Question of things happening: The letters of Virginia woolf, 1912–1922* (Vol. 2). In N. Nicholson (Ed.). Hogarth Press.

CHAPTER 12

Where Keynes Went Wrong

12.1 Introduction

Forty-two years after his death, the multifaceted, almost chameleon-like, persona of John Maynard Keynes has not ceased to fascinate us. For years, his family and friends, including his first biographer, Roy Harrod, sought to suppress evidence of his homosexuality, fearing that the revelation might tarnish his reputation and discredit his policy recommendations. Surprisingly, when it finally was revealed, the disclosure only enhanced Keynes's allure. Although the dominance of Keynesian ideas and prescriptions among economists and policymakers has diminished over time, Keynes's position as the most important economist of the twentieth century remains unassailable. Indeed, 1986, which marked the 50th anniversary of his revolutionary book, *The General Theory of Employment, Interest, and Money*, was the occasion for numerous conferences and articles devoted to analyzing and re-analyzing that still controversial volume. Even now, in recent British discussions about inflation and ways of combating it, echoes of Keynes's ideas, pro and con, continue to be heard.

Although the apprehensions that led to the suppression of what certainly was among the most important aspects of Keynes's psychological development now seem exaggerated, I can't help feeling that they were prompted by a sure instinct for preserving the integrity of his ideas. The

D. Glasner, *Studies in the History of Monetary Theory*, Palgrave Studies in the History of Economic Thought, https://doi.org/10.1007/978-3-030-83426-5_12

danger was not that Keynes would be discredited; it was that, in analyzing his ideas, we might fall into the trap of explaining them not as attempts to cope with and solve real problems, both practical and intellectual, but as manifestations of his psycho-sexuality. Precisely because Keynes is such a fascinating figure, the desire to probe ever deeper into his personality may tempt us into believing that, by psychoanalyzing him, we can somehow better understand what he wrote, said, and thought. Insofar as Keynes's family and Roy Harrod helped us to resist that temptation, particularly just after his death, when his work was still being digested, I am inclined to think that they rendered a real service not so much to Keynes's memory and reputation as to the understanding of his thought.

A major biography of Keynes by Robert Skidelsky, of which only the first volume has yet appeared, may have succumbed to this temptation. Unlike Roy Harrod's (1951) discrete and somewhat hagiographic biography, it digs deeply into Keynes's personal life and the relationship between his sexual and intellectual development. How far Skidelsky has succumbed will not be clear until we have before us his account in Volume II of the all-important 1920s and 1930s, when Keynes was intimately involved in both the formulation of economic policy and the debate over that policy, and when his ideas were evolving toward the shape they would take in *The General Theory*.

Skidelsky suggests that this disillusionment and the disdain for conventional morality he acquired at Cambridge, where he was introduced into a culture of homosexuality, prepared Keynes to overturn in *The General Theory* the economic model of rational order that had for so long underlain economic theory and policy. Yet one also gathers from Skidelsky's first volume that Keynes's wartime experience shook his faith in the self-regulating world economy he grew up believing in. Even if Keynes's psychological make-up did affect the development of his ideas about economic theory and policy, I would suggest that we can still learn more about that development from further reflection on the economic conditions that had to be explained by theory and coped with by policy, and how Keynes perceived those conditions, than from studying the inner workings of his psyche.

To account for the development of Keynes's ideas about economics, however, we shall do better to consider the intellectual and practical problems he was trying to solve. The dominant fact confronting him in the 1920s and 1930s, of course, was massive unemployment in Britain, beginning long before the rest of the world sank into the Great Depression.

One explanation attributed high unemployment in Britain to an overvalued pound, caused by Britain's return to the gold standard in 1925. Keynes, himself, had warned that returning to the gold standard would cause unemployment. But the *General Theory* (written after unemployment became an intractable, worldwide problem) ignored the exchange rate, and proposed instead that unemployment depended on aggregate demand.

However, Daniel Benjamin and Levis Kochin (1979), in their investigation of British unemployment in the inter-War period, argued that unusually high British unemployment in the 1920s had little to do with the exchange rate or aggregate demand. Instead, they maintained, it was caused chiefly by the substantial increase in (deflation-adjusted) unemployment benefits during the 1920s. If Benjamin and Kochin are correct, it means that Keynes proposed a revolutionary theory of how an economic system operates to explain, and cure, a problem that was radically different from his perception of it. To see how his possible misreading of economic conditions in the 1920s and 1930s (with which his psychological make-up could not have had much relationship) led Keynes astray, we must first recall conditions in the early 1920s when the world set about reconstructing an international economic order from the wreckage left by the Great War of 1914–1918.

12.2 The Prewar Parity

Among the first casualties of the First World War was the gold standard that had been the pillar of the international monetary system since the early 1870s. Only a few countries formally abrogated the gold standard, but none of the belligerents long tolerated the free convertibility of their currencies into gold and the free export of gold that had been the *sine qua non* of the pre-War gold standard.

Before the War, five French francs were worth slightly less than one dollar. If it cost fewer than five times as many francs to buy wheat in Paris as it cost dollars to buy wheat in Chicago, one could profitably convert dollars into their equivalent in francs and buy the wheat in Paris instead of in Chicago. And if it cost more than five times as many francs to buy wheat in Paris as it cost dollars in Chicago, one could profitably buy wheat in Chicago instead of Paris. Because the same possibility existed for all internationally traded commodities, prices in all gold standard countries could not deviate from a common level. Under the gold standard, therefore, national currencies were little more than different denominations of a common international currency.

The suspension of convertibility, the embargo on gold shipments, and the imposition of exchange controls untied prices measured in national currencies from their gold equivalents. Taking control of their domestic price levels allowed the belligerent countries to use inflation as a method of war finance. Thus, from 1913 to 1919, wholesale prices rose by 100% in the United States, by 150% in Britain, by 230% in France, and by 700% in Germany.

After the economic upheavals of the War and the post-War period, many governments understandably wished to restore the seemingly automatic and stable operation of the pre-War economic order. The desire found practical expression in commitments by those governments to re-establish the international gold standard as soon as possible.

Holding over 40% of the world's gold reserves, the United States emerged from the War as the world's preeminent economic power and was the first to restore convertibility into gold and to permit the free exchange of gold after the effective suppression of gold trading during most of the War. In practice, therefore, going back on the gold standard meant that a country would keep the exchange rate between its currency and the dollar at a fixed parity.

Having inflated more rapidly during the War than the United States, most countries saw their currencies depreciate against the dollar after the lifting of exchange controls. The issue then became whether to stabilize their currencies at the new depreciated exchange rates against the dollar or to try to restore the *status quo ante* by stabilizing at the pre-War parities.

Stabilizing at the old parities was made even more difficult by a severe deflation in the United States in 1920–1921. Wholesale prices fell by about 40% in a little over a year. Rather than allow their currencies to fall further against the dollar, many countries (including Britain) deflated along with (the United States, suffering substantial losses of output and employment as a result.[1]

Despite the depreciation of sterling against the dollar, there was a consensus in Britain for stabilizing at the prewar parity. One reason for

[1] Britain and other countries continued to deflate even after deflation ended in the United States in 1921 as they sought to restore the pre-War currency parity with the dollar.

the consensus was the precedent of 1819–1821, when Britain restored convertibility at the old parity after its suspension during the Napoleonic Wars. Additionally, it reflected a nostalgic desire to restore the pre-War state of affairs, a feeling of moral obligation to repay British war debts in pounds of full value, and a patriotic wish for "the pound to be able to look the dollar in the face."

Economists, ever since Keynes, have not looked kindly at the decision to restore convertibility at the pre-War parity. Yet the seemingly insubstantial justifications for that decision were expressions of an eminently practical consideration: if Britain ever again needed to finance a war by borrowing and printing money, she would be better able to do so if people had confidence that—over the long term, at any rate—the purchasing power of the pound would be stable. Restoring the pound to its prewar parity was a way of building that confidence, and, hence, an investment in Britain's national security. For the British people and their statesmen to have been willing to bear the costs of doing so may indeed have been a misjudgment under the circumstances, but it was not irrational.

Keynes, however, vehemently opposed going back on the gold standard, especially at the pre-War parity. He advocated, instead, stabilizing the internal British price level. In *A Tract on Monetary Reform*, Keynes (1923) stressed the potential conflict between keeping a stable price level and maintaining a fixed exchange rate. Under the gold standard, prices in all countries, measured by their gold equivalents, had to be roughly equal. Thus, prices expressed in any currency would be stable only if prices in terms of gold were stable—that is, if the value of gold in relation to commodities did not change. But if the value of gold did change, prices quoted in gold standard currencies would vary inversely with the value of gold. A country could guarantee the stability of its internal prices, or it could guarantee the stability of an exchange rate; it could not do both.

Since the exchange rate of sterling against the dollar had settled down at about $4.40 in the early 1924, restoring the old parity of $4.86 would necessitate a further deflation, beyond that of 1920–1922, of about 10%. That would cause further losses of output and employment. When the most urgent economic and social priority was the restoration of full employment, Keynes saw no possible justification for incurring the costs of stabilizing at the old parity.

Despite Keynes's arguments against a return to gold, Winston Churchill, then Chancellor of the Exchequer, and Montagu Norman,

Governor of the Bank of England, engineered a resumption of convertibility in April 1925. Keynes (1925 [1931]), venting his frustration at the resumption in his famous essay *The Economic Consequences of Mr. Churchill*, warned of the bleak future facing Britain thanks to an overvalued pound. He directed his formidable powers of invective against the choice of the old parity and against the advice from his experts and from the City that Churchill had relied on.

> If Mr. Churchill had restored gold by fixing the parity lower than the pre-War figure, or if he had waited until our money values were adjusted to the pre-War parity, then these particular arguments would have no force. But in doing what he did in the actual circumstances of last spring, he was just asking for trouble. For he was committing himself to force down money wages and all money values, without any idea how it was to be done. Why did he do such a silly thing?
>
> Partly, perhaps, because he has no instinctive judgment to prevent him from making mistakes; partly because, lacking this instinctive judgment, he was deafened by the clamorous voices of conventional finance; and, most of all, because he was gravely misled by his experts.

And later:

> On grounds of social justice, no case can be made out for reducing the wages of the miners. They are the victims of the economic Juggernaut. They represent in the flesh the 'fundamental adjustments' engineered by the Treasury and the Bank of England to satisfy the impatience of the City fathers to bridge the 'moderate gap' between $4.40 and $4.86. They (and others to follow) are the 'moderate sacrifice' still necessary to ensure the stability of the gold standard. The plight of the coal miners is the first, but not-- unless we are very lucky -- the last of the Economic Consequences of Mr. Churchill.

The next few years seemed to confirm Keynes's warnings. The unsuccessful coal miners' strike and the general strike of 1926 embittered much of the British workforce. Unemployment stayed over 10%, and subsequently the assistance of the Federal Reserve Board and the Bank of France was required on more than one occasion to support the pound.

The Treatise on Money

After losing the battle over the gold standard, Keynes devoted himself to the book, *A Treatise on Money* (Keynes, 1930), that he expected to be his definitive contribution to monetary theory. No short description can adequately summarize this monumental two-volume work—a combination of acute theoretical insight and deep practical and institutional knowledge. But its major theoretical aim was straightforward: to give a new explanation for fluctuations in the price level and economic activity.

After the inflations, hyperinflations, and deflations of the War and its aftermath, the behavior of the price level became the chief theoretical and policy concern of economists. They had always favored stability of the price level—but mainly to secure justice between debtors and creditors. After the War, however, they began to suspect that instability of the price level was the primary cause of the business cycle. If that was so, stabilizing the price level could be the key to preventing cyclical fluctuations in output and employment.

While most theorists viewed changes in the price level from the perspective of the quantity theory of money, in which the stock of money is the strategic variable, Keynes suggested that movements in the price level were caused by differences between total savings and total expenditures on investment. Since decisions to save—to postpone consumption—are made by households, and decisions to invest—to add to productive capacity—by business firms, Keynes saw no necessary reason for the two magnitudes to be equal. But only if they were equal, he argued, would prices be stable. If investment were greater than savings, prices would rise; if less, they would fall.

Despite departing from the quantity theory, Keynes still held to a conventional view of monetary policy in the *Treatise*, insisting that the monetary authority (the Bank of England) could control the price level. Because investment tends to fall and savings to rise with increases in the interest rate, the Bank of England could equalize investment and savings by setting Bank Rate at an appropriate level. The problem with the gold standard, Keynes argued, was that, to defend the exchange rate, the Bank of England had kept Bank Rate so high that savings exceeded investment, thereby causing both deflation and chronic unemployment.

Keynes won widespread acclaim for the *Treatise*. A commanding presence in Britain ever since he published *The Economic Consequences of the*

Peace, Keynes now secured his place as an economic theorist. Nevertheless, he drew sharp criticism on some crucial theoretical issues from his friends D. H. Robertson and R. G. Hawtrey, and his theoretical adversary F. A. Hayek. Robertson, for example, argued that Keynes had so defined savings and investment that his theory differed only semantically from the quantity theory. Also criticizing Keynes for his definitions, Hawtrey noted that, while Keynes assumed that changes in the price level triggered fluctuations in output and employment, his formal model held real output constant while the price level changed. Keynes, therefore, had either to revise his basic assumption about the relationship between the price level and output, or to specify in a formal model just how output depended on the price level. The cumulative effect of the criticisms, including a series of sharply polemical exchanges with Hayek, soon convinced Keynes that his argument in the *Treatise* required substantial revisions.

From Treatise to General Theory

By the time the *Treatise* appeared in 1930, economic conditions were changing radically from those Keynes had written about. Unemployment was no longer just a British problem; it was an international disaster. Until the summer of 1929, the rest of the world, particularly the United States, had been recovering strongly from the Great War and the deflation and depression of 1920–1922. But that summer, the Federal Reserve Board raised its discount rate to check stock-market speculation and an outflow of gold, triggering the onset of deflation in the summer and a stock-market crash in October.

Conditions rapidly worsened in 1930. Unemployment jumped everywhere, even in Britain where it had already been high for almost a decade. The cataclysm intensified in May 1931, when a leading Austrian bank, the Kreditanstalt of Vienna, went bankrupt. Several German banks with a direct interest in the Kreditanstalt soon failed as well.

The growing mistrust of Austrian and German banks led to a banking collapse in those countries. Since many British banks had lent to the bankrupt German banks, the pound came under heavy speculative pressure that summer. With Bank Rate at 4.5%—an extraordinarily high rate in such a deflationary period—the Bank of England chose not to defend the pound by raising Bank Rate further. So, in September 1931, the Bank cut the pound loose from gold.

Early in 1932, Keynes wrote in the preface to the Japanese translation of the *Treatise* that, in response to criticism, he was working on a short book that he expected to complete in a year or two, which would extend and correct the theoretical basis of the *Treatise*. He gave no indication that he yet conceived of the new book as the revolutionary break with orthodox theory that he would later claim *The General Theory* constituted. So what became *The General Theory* seems to have begun simply as a revision of certain theoretical propositions in the *Treatise*. How, then, did *The General Theory* evolve from the *Treatise*?

Much has already been written about this. In the main, it has concentrated on Keynes's strained relationships with colleagues like Dennis Robertson and Ralph Hawtrey, and his close collaboration with a group of young Cambridge economists, especially Richard Kahn, Austen Robinson, Joan Robinson, James Meade, and Piero Sraffa. Kahn, perhaps with an assist from Hawtrey, had in fact invented one of the key concepts in *The General Theory*: the famous "multiplier". Politically, mostly on the Left, "the Cambridge Circus", as they called themselves, perhaps symbolized the break Keynes felt he was making with earlier economic doctrines as his thinking continued to evolve. Robert Skidelsky goes so far as to suggest that a moral sensibility derived from the Cambridge philosopher G. E. Moore, and from his intellectual and sexual relationships with the Bloomsbury group—a sensibility ultimately hostile to and subversive of established order—prompted Keynes, in *The General Theory*, to rebel against the economic model of rational order to which he had earlier adhered.

However, Keynes's susceptibility to the influence of the young Cambridge economists stemmed less from any latent desire to undo the established order than from his loss of confidence in the ability of the old paradigm to explain—and of conventional monetary policy to solve—high unemployment in Britain. Although he had warned that the return to gold would cause deflation which had always been recognized as a source of unemployment. The traditional view was that eventually prices and wages would adjust themselves to the gold parity, and full employment would be restored. In the 1920s, Keynes felt that the (to him) dubious advantages of returning to gold could not justify the loss of employment doing so would cause. But Keynes did not deny that, once deflation brought British wages and prices down to a level corresponding to the old parity, unemployment would, after an unacceptable delay, return to more normal levels. So even he may not have expected that, five years after the return to gold, not only was unemployment not falling, it was rising rapidly.

Keynes's doubts about orthodox theory are evidenced by his willingness, as early as 1929, to advocate heavy spending on public works (Keynes & Henderson, 1929 [1931]), and in 1931 to advocate protection as a stimulus to employment. He did so, to be sure, on the assumption that the gold parity would stay put. Yet, his shift of ground (from adjusting the gold parity to public works and protection) suggests that the idea that there might be causes of unemployment besides an overvalued pound was insinuating itself into his mind, and that he had lost confidence in a purely monetary solution to unemployment.

In November 1931, after Britain left the gold standard, Keynes wrote a memorandum for the Treasury on which the subsequent cheap-money policy was largely based. With England off gold and pursuing a cheap-money policy, Keynes's wavering faith in monetary policy was put to a test. If unemployment had been caused by an overly tight monetary policy dictated by the Ggold standard, it would have been reasonable to expect a sharp recovery to begin once Britain went off gold. But there was no recovery for at least a year.[2] If output and employment had begun to recover in 1932, as he had expected, Keynes, in revising the *Treatise*, might have continued to assume that output and employment were related to changes in the price level. The disappointed hopes of 1932 may have led Keynes to a more fundamental break with orthodoxy than he had contemplated when setting out to revise the *Treatise*.

The break is clearly evident in the mode of analysis of *The General Theory*. It is restricted to a closed economy. The exchange rate, which figured so prominently in the *Tract* and the *Treatise*, has no role in such an economy. Movements in the price level, which drove the business cycle in the *Treatise*, play no causal role in *The General Theory*.

No longer is mass unemployment attributed to a conflict between maintaining a given exchange rate and keeping the price level constant. The problem is more fundamental—rooted in the basic character of a modern economic system. Indeed, the economy is viewed as having no tendency to achieve equilibrium at full employment. No longer, therefore, could the cure for mass unemployment be monetary; it had to be

[2] Another reason for the slow recovery was that Bank Rate was not immediately reduced after convertibility was suspended to prevent further depreciation of the pound against the dollar.

more radical. Direct action by the state was needed to generate enough spending to buy up what available resources could produce. The relationship between stable prices and full employment, on which Keynes had once set so much store, was discarded.

12.3 Unemployment and the Great Depression

Despite the lack of emphasis on the exchange rate in *The General Theory*, many Keynesian and non-Keynesian economists have shared Keynes's early judgment that high unemployment in Britain was related to the restoration of sterling to its pre-War parity of $4.86. The combination of an overvalued pound and rigid wages guaranteed that unemployment in Britain would be high. Subsequently, the Great Depression drove unemployment even higher. Monetarists would say that this is the only explanation needed. But unemployment in Britain remained stubbornly high even after England left the gold standard, taking control of its own monetary policy and price level, in September 1931. This anomaly is precisely what led Keynes from his essential orthodoxy in the *Treatise* to his radicalism in *The General Theory*.

Daniel Benjamin and Levis Kochin (1979) challenged the conventional explanations for unemployment in Britain between the Wars. They maintained that unemployment was unrelated to going back on gold at the pre-War parity, or to the level of aggregate demand, pointing out that, on average, economic growth in the 1920s and 1930s was as rapid as in any comparable period in British history. Yet, in 1938, unemployment was still about 10%—higher than it ever was (with perhaps two exceptions) in the nineteenth century. Benjamin and Kochin attribute this to the scale of unemployment benefits in the 1920s and 1930s.

Unemployment insurance was not introduced in Britain until 1911. At first, coverage was limited to only about 15% of the labor force. But the Unemployment Insurance Act of 1920 raised benefits to compensate for the effects of wartime inflation and extended coverage to most privately employed workers over the age of 16. Only domestics and agricultural workers were excluded. Even though the British price level fell by almost 25% from 1920 through 1922 (falling by perhaps another 8% over the rest of the decade) benefit levels continued to be increased and, perhaps more importantly, eligibility requirements were progressively eased. "By 1931", Benjamin and Kochin observed, "weekly benefits exceeded 50% of average weekly wages, and an adult worker who had made 30 weekly contributions at any time in his working career could draw full benefits for an unlimited period."

Two other features of the system contributed to high unemployment levels. First, benefits were not tied to wages, so lower-paid workers found unemployment a "comparatively attractive" option. Second, after serving an initial waiting period of three to six days of continuous unemployment at some time in their career, workers could obtain benefits for spells of unemployment as short as one day. It was, therefore, not uncommon for workers to arrange with their employers for work-sharing schemes in which workers would work three days a week and collect unemployment benefits for the other three days. Such arrangements were disallowed after World War II. More stringent eligibility requirements for unemployment insurance—until 1966, at any rate—are one important reason why unemployment was so much lower for three decades after World War II than in the inter-War period.[3]

It is not difficult to see why making unemployment benefits more generous and more readily available would raise the rate of unemployment. But, at the time, only two economists (Edwin Cannan of the London School of Economics, and the French economist Jacques Rueff) emphasized the role of unemployment benefits in creating unemployment. This was Edwin Cannan's (1930, pp. 46–47) explanation:

> To throw numbers of your employees out for short intervals to suit your convenience is obviously less likely to create friction, and is therefore more likely to be profitable, when the persons thrown out can draw on a common fund raised by stamp duties on employment and other taxes

[3] An interesting bit of evidence unearthed by Benjamin and Kochin in support of their thesis is that the unemployment rate for juvenile workers was much less than that for adults, with the rate lowest for those 16 and 17 years of age, jumping sharply at 18 and again at 21. This is the reverse of recent experience, in which unemployment rates are higher among young workers than older workers. However, since benefits for single juveniles below 18 only averaged about six shillings and sixpence a week, doubling to thirteen shillings for those over 18, and increasing by another 50% for those over 21, Benjamin and Kochin provide a straightforward explanation for the otherwise anomalous discrepancy in unemployment rates. Since 1966, British unemployment benefits have been raised and eligibility requirements relaxed. By 1986, however, benefits were exceptionally attractive to youngsters. Thus, while the overall unemployment rate had risen to 13%, the unemployment rate for young people is 25% of the national total (The October 1988 figures were 8 and 32%.).

> … [Specifically] in the occupations in which the superiority of employment over unemployment is least, the insurance scheme has reduced the economic pressure which used to make persons grab at every chance of employment. … He [the unemployed worker] takes the alternatives to be, "Take what you can get now, or hold out another week, when something better may turn up"… The magnitude of the turnover of labour… is so great that a very little average delay will make a large addition to the unemployment.

Cannan's intuitive argument could be dismissed, because the quantitative impact of the dole on unemployment was difficult to estimate.[4] To be sure, the increase in unemployment in the Great Depression had been far greater than could be entirely, or even substantially, accounted for by the dole. However, using econometric techniques not available in the 1930s, Benjamin and Kochin calculated that if the 1913 ratio of benefits to wages had been maintained in Great Britain during the 1920s and 1930s, the British unemployment rate would have been 4–7% lower than they had been between 1925 and 1929. Unemployment in Britain would have risen sharply in the Depression, as it did in all countries on the gold standard, even without the dole. But, unless one mentions the dole, it is difficult to explain why, despite the rapid growth of British output after 1932, unemployment did not fall below 10% until 1938.

[4] One who did not reject the idea that the dole was a major source of high unemployment was Winston Churchill (1930), who had drafted the original legislation setting up unemployment insurance. Writing after he had left the Exchequer, Churchill charged that unemployment figures had been inflated, because.

> every case of unemployment, even for short periods, is recorded in the national register, and the benefit is increasingly applied for, even by those not in actual want… as a contribution toward what may be little more than a needed holiday after years of continuous work… . It is significant that after every public holiday—Christmas, Easter, Whitsuntide—there is a very large addition to the unemployment total, which falls off again a few weeks later.

Moreover:

> many British employers have lent themselves to an abuse of the system of unemployment insurance.…They systematically arrange to give their workers just that amount of employment as will enable them to qualify for the benefit.

Increased unemployment benefits also tended to raise British wages. As unemployment became less costly, employers had to improve their wage offers to attract as many workers as they had previously. Since, under the gold standard, British exporters sold at prices determined in international markets, they could not easily raise prices to compensate for rising wages. Thus, rising real wages made it difficult for many British exporters export to remain competitive. High wages raised unemployment in the export industries, and relatively high unemployment benefits reduced the willingness of displaced workers to accept employment elsewhere.

If Britain had followed Keynes's advice and not pegged sterling at $4.86, avoiding the consequent decline in British prices would have prevented the subsequent increase in real unemployment benefits and real wages, thereby allowing at least a modest reduction in unemployment. On this question, Keynes's political instincts about how real wages might be reduced were undoubtedly sound. However, his economic judgment went astray by assuming that unemployment in the 1920s—which often stemmed from rational choices by workers to whom "generous" (in comparison with wages) unemployment benefits had been made available—was mainly involuntary.

Thus, the problem that so vexed Keynes during the 1920s and 1930s, persuading him to abandon economic orthodoxy and his own previous recommendations for stabilizing the price level, may actually have been caused, at least in part, by an unintended increase in unemployment benefits.

12.4 An Unnecessary Revolution

I do not deny that unemployment during the Great Depression was an extraordinary social problem, or that it was involuntary in a sense not true of unemployment in the middle and late 1920s. But neither did it necessitate a revolution in economic theory. The Depression was caused by a rapid and prolonged deflation induced not merely by a collapse of the American banking system—as Friedman and Schwartz (1963) asserted in their *Monetary History of the United States*—but by a worldwide appreciation of gold relative to other commodities. Gold appreciated in the late 1920s and early 1930s, because central banks and individuals were converting their foreign-exchange reserves into gold.

That was a quintessential monetary shock of precisely the kind Keynes wanted to prevent when he advocated stabilizing the price level. Keynes's friend Ralph Hawtrey, in particular, recognized that the Depression was a purely monetary phenomenon—a worldwide deflation that caused by a sudden increase in the demand for gold, which, under the newly re-established gold standard, was manifested in deflation.

Hawtrey did not believe this to be a phenomenon that received economic and monetary theory could not explain. He had been a member of the British delegation to the 1922 International Monetary Conference in Genoa, and it was largely owing to his influence that the Conference adopted several resolutions warning against an appreciation of gold in the event that countries restoring the gold standard substantially increased their demand for gold reserves. The Conference recommended that central banks restrain their demands for gold and, instead, hold reserves in the form of foreign exchange denominated in the major international currencies, the dollar and (after being stabilized) sterling.

Until July 1928, when France formally restored the gold standard, the spirit of the Genoa Resolutions was observed. But once franc was again convertible into gold, the Bank of France began rapidly accumulating gold reserves. The US Federal Reserve Board, already worried by the stock-market boom, did not permit the reduction in its own holdings of gold that might have satisfied the French desire for gold, and, instead, tightened monetary policy, thereby inducing a substantial inflow of gold in 1929. By the second half of 1929, prices began falling. Anticipating deflation after the abandonment of accommodative monetary policy, the stock market collapsed in October.[5]

This was precisely the scenario that Ralph Hawtrey had foreseen, and endeavored to prevent, at the Genoa Conference.[6]

Keynes rejected orthodox theory (and revolutionized economics) in *The General Theory*, because he did not believe it could explain the unemployment created by the Great Depression. The paradox in Keynes's rejection of orthodoxy is that his earlier work suggested a monetary explanation of the Great Depression not unlike that advanced by Hawtrey.

[5] Other shocks were hitting the world economy at the same time, particularly the Smoot-Hawley tariff. This tariff not only undermined world trade—it helped cripple the world financial system by making it more costly for countries indebted to the United States to sell their goods in American markets to earn the dollars they required to repay their debts. Holders of that debt, largely American financial institutions, took heavy losses, and in many instances failed, intensifying the financial collapse of the Depression.

[6] Hawtrey (1932, Chapters 1–2, 1948) provided important accounts of the monetary history of the 1920s and 1930s that can still be read with great profit.

It may be that Keynes rejected that interpretation, because he conflated chronically high British unemployment in the 1920s with the sudden increase in unemployment during the Great Depression, concluding that the worldwide unemployment of the 1930s was an intensified manifestation of the same problem that had caused high unemployment in Britain during the 1920s. That conclusion led him to another: that an entirely new approach to economic theory was needed.

In fact, the specifically British unemployment problem was that relatively high unemployment benefits that were not adjusted for the steep deflation of 1920–1922 induced many workers to accept increased and more frequent periods of unemployment. Unemployment in the Depression, on the other hand, was a product of the worldwide deflation that caused a collapse of business investment, and, because wages fell more slowly than prices, business profits. In principle, if wages fell sufficiently to match the decline in prices, the second source of unemployment would have been eliminated. But merely halting deflation, as Britain did by leaving the gold standard, left wages, in relation to prices, at a level too high to permit full employment.

In the *General Theory*, Keynes insisted that the stimulus to employment from wage reductions would be eroded by matching price reductions. Automatic price adjustments, on this reasoning, could never restore full employment to an economy stuck in depression. But Keynes overlooked the distinction between wage reductions that exceed price reductions and those that compensate for prior price reductions. While the former reductions create windfall profits for business and are "competed away", the latter simply restore profits to normal levels and are not "competed away". (Which, of course, is not to say that economic policy in a depression should promote wage reductions.)

So, in his most important contribution to economic theory, Keynes misunderstood the problem for which he sought to provide both an explanation and a cure. Additionally, the theory he developed to explain a misperceived problem had the unintended effect of undermining the case for stabilizing the price level—of which, in his earlier writings, he had been an outspoken advocate.

In his role as a monetary and financial statesman trying to create an international monetary system following World War II that would avoid the debacle that followed World War I, Keynes was an architect of the Bretton Woods system, under which prices of internationally traded commodities were, on average, nearly stable for 20 years after the end of

World War II. The system was based on the attenuated convertibility of the dollar into gold at a fixed price of $35 an ounce and the maintenance of fixed (but occasionally adjustable) exchange rates of other currencies against the dollar. The dollar became the dominant international currency and was universally acceptable. Indeed, so long as the purchasing power of the dollar remained stable, it was better than gold. Still, the obligation to sell the dollar to other central banks at a fixed price of $35 an ounce provided an important guarantee that the United States would keep prices stable.

The author of *A Tract on Monetary Reform* and *A Treatise on Money* would not have been surprised that a long period of price stability should have also turned out to be an era of perhaps the fastest growth and lowest unemployment that the industrialized world had ever known. But even the loose constraints the Bretton Woods system imposed on the United States eventually proved too confining. During a time of war and social unrest, when the belief (instilled by Keynesian policies) that the business cycle had been tamed was not yet shaken, it was no longer politically possible to tolerate even a temporary increase in unemployment for the sake of price stability. Thus, elevating full employment over price stability as the chief objective of monetary and fiscal policy—one result of Keynes's *intellectual* legacy—ultimately undermined the Bretton Woods system—his *institutional* legacy.

References

Benjamin, D., & Kochin, L. (1979). Searching for an explanation of unemployment in Interwar Britain. *Journal of Political Economy, 87*(3), 441–478.

Cannan, E. (1930). The problem of unemployment. *Economic Journal, 40*(157), 45–55.

Churchill, W. (1930). The abuse of the dole. *Daily Telegraph*, 26–27 March.

Friedman, M., & Schwartz, A. J. (1963). *A monetary history of the United States, 1867–1960*. Princeton University Press.

Harrod, R. (1951). *The life of Keynes*. Macmillan.

Hawtrey, R. G. (1932). *The art of central banking*. Longman, Green and Company.

Hawtrey, R. G. (1948). *The gold standard in theory and practice* (5th ed.). Longman, Green and Company.

Keynes, J. M. (1920). *The economic consequences of the peace*. Macmillan.

Keynes, J. M. (1923). *A tract on monetary reform*. Macmillan.

Keynes, J. M. (1925 [1931]). The economic consequences of Mr. Churchill. In *Essays in persuasion*. Macmillan.
Keynes, J. M. (1930). *A treatise on money* (2 vols.). Macmillan.
Keynes, J. M. (1931). Proposals for a revenue tariff. In *Essays in persuasion*. Macmillan.
Keynes, J. M. (1936). *The general theory of money, interest and employment*. Macmillan.
Keynes, J. M.. & H. D. Henderson. (1929 [1931]). Can Lloyd George do it? In *Essays in persuasion*.
Skidelsky, R. (1983). *John Maynard Keynes, Vol I: Hopes Betrayed , 1883–1920*. Macmillan.

CHAPTER 13

Debt, Deflation, the Great Depression and the Gold Standard (with Ronald W. Batchelder)

13.1 Introduction

This chapter proposes an alternative monetary explanation to the one given by Friedman and Schwartz (1963) of the prolonged deflation in the United States and most of the world during the Great Depression, and to other explanations of that uniquely catastrophic episode in modern economic history. We argue that the monetary contraction of 1929–1933 was the consequence of US adherence to the gold standard and of a sequential and uncoordinated return to gold convertibility by many countries during the 1920s that increased the world monetary demand for gold, thereby causing gold appreciation and a worldwide deflation. We also argue that, owing to the opposition of America's politically powerful, domestic creditor interests to any increase in the dollar-gold parity, the United States maintained its commitment to that fixed parity longer than most other gold-standard countries that abandoned the fixed parities between their currencies and gold. While the role of the gold standard in causing the Great Depression was recognized by several economists at the time, notably Ralph Hawtrey and Gustav Cassel, Friedman and Schwartz incorrectly assumed that the international economy under the gold standard operated in the manner described by the Humean price-specieflow mechanism (PSFM) with national price levels determined by the quantity theory of money.

D. Glasner, *Studies in the History of Monetary Theory*, Palgrave Studies in the History of Economic Thought, https://doi.org/10.1007/978-3-030-83426-5_13

Why the Federal Reserve permitted a dramatic contraction of the money stock between 1929 and 1933 when the Federal Reserve Act of 1913 authorized actions that apparently enabled the Federal Reserve to prevent the contraction remains a puzzle to many economists. The Monetarist explanation of Friedman and Schwartz is that the contraction was caused by the passivity of the Federal Reserve during and after a series of domestic banking panics (late 1930, early 1931, and early 1933), which caused the public to convert bank deposits into currency.

Friedman and Schwartz (1963, pp. 407–419) maintained that although the policies for avoiding a monetary contraction were well-known, the Federal Reserve System had fallen under the control of inept governors whose ineptitude was reinforced by a lack of informed criticism from outside the system. Conceding that the system had performed very well before 1929, they attribute the inept policy after 1929 to a "shift in power within the System and the lack of understanding and experience of those individuals to whom the power shifted" (Id. 411). Until poor health forced his retirement in 1928, Benjamin Strong, governor of the New York Federal Reserve Bank, had dominated monetary policy during the 1920s. Deprived of Strong's wisdom and skillful leadership, the system failed to take the measures that could have averted the catastrophe.[1]

Friedman and Schwartz further argued that the monetary contraction of 1929–1933 caused the Great Depression, assigning ultimate responsibility for the contraction of output and employment to the misguided monetary policy of the Federal Reserve.[2] Friedman and Schwartz proposed their monetary explanation as an alternative to

[1] This view of Strong is based in part upon the earlier work of Chandler (1958). Irving Fisher (1934, p. 151) held a similar view, commenting, "if [Strong] had lived and his policies had been continued, we might have had the stock market crash in a milder form, but after the crash there would not have been the great industrial depression." R. G. Hawtrey (1932, p. 209) also lamented Strong's departure from the Fed and the dire consequences of his departure.

> Under the wise guidance of Governor Benjamin Strong of the New York [Federal Reserve] Bank, they pursued a policy of stabilization which prevented any serious fluctuations of the price level between 1922 and 1929.... It was a disaster for the world that Governor Strong died in the autumn of 1928 and the experiment [in price-level stabilization] came to an end.

[2] Anderson et al. (1988) proposed the alternative thesis that Federal Reserve policy may have been motivated by the desire of large banks to force the failure of smaller banks.

Keynesian interpretations of the Great Depression, which attributed the downturn to a collapse in private spending while dismissing monetary policy as ineffective under such circumstances. In the Keynesian view of the Great Depression, monetary contraction was an effect, not a cause, of the downturn. Supporting the Keynesian view, Temin (1976) challenged the Friedman and Schwartz account of the Depression by arguing that the contraction in the money stock reflected a decrease in money demand caused by the steep decline in income during the period. Temin also pointed to the slight increase in real money balances during the Great Depression as inconsistent with the Friedman and Schwartz interpretation.

The Keynesian-Monetarist debate over the causes of the Great Depression was at bottom an argument about whether government intervention is necessary to stabilize an inherently unstable private sector, or whether government intervention is itself the primary source of instability in a market economy. The Monetarist argument that monetary mismanagement was largely to blame for the prolonged contraction during the Depression was also part of the earlier Austrian explanation of the Great Depression to which Keynes was in large measure responding. The key policy difference between the Austrians and Monetarists is that the Austrians asserted that the error in policy was an overly expansionary monetary policy in the 1920s, particularly in 1927 and 1928,[3] while the Monetarists contend the mistake was an unnecessary policy-induced monetary contraction beginning in 1928 and continuing almost without interruption until 1933.

Not all interpretations of the Great Depression fit easily into the Keynesian or the Monetarist paradigms. According to some, the Great Depression was a historically unique episode that cannot be fully explained within any single theoretical approach. Thus, Kindleberger

[3] The Austrian theory is no longer widely held and concerns us here primarily owing to its influence on the development of macroeconomics. It first displaced the purely monetary theory of the Great Depression of Hawtrey and Cassel with a theory of how monetary policy affects relative prices, leading to misallocations of resources (malinvestments) only to become a casualty of the Keynesian revolution. Many of its early adherents later repudiated it, and even its principal exponent, Hayek, ultimately conceded that, though potentially relevant to other business-cycle episodes, it was not relevant to the conditions in 1929–1933. However, the Austrian opposition to monetary or fiscal stimulus was so fierce that modem Monetarists distinguished their own monetary theory of the Great Depression from the Austrian theory at least as sharply as they did from the Keynesian theory.

(1973) argued that while shifts in spending patterns and monetary mismanagement by the Federal Reserve played a part in the Depression, deflationary trends in commodity prices, the cessation of foreign lending by the United States in the late 1920s, and a lack of international policy coordination all contributed to the magnitude of the catastrophe. Even Irving Fisher (1932), who had developed much of the theoretical foundations of what came to be called Monetarism, adopted an eclectic approach.

Unfortunately, the monetary theory of the Great Depression developed by R. G. Hawtrey (1932, 1933, 1947) and Gustav Cassel (1932, 1936), supported by the empirical studies of George Warren and Frank Pearson (1933), which preceded the Austrian, Keynesian, and Monetarist theories of the Great Depression, fell into undeserved obscurity. As further explained in the next chapter, the Hawtrey-Cassel theory was briefly displaced by the Austrian theory in the early 1930s, so that, by the time of the Keynesian Revolution, it had already been forgotten. This early monetary explanation focused on the deflationary forces inherent in the restoration of the gold standard during the 1920s and specifically on how the actions of the Bank of France and the Federal Reserve in 1928–1929 triggered a deflationary collapse in late 1929.[4]

In presenting their monetary explanation of the Great Depression, Friedman and Schwartz acknowledged the contributions of Clark Warburton (1953) and of previous Chicago monetary theorists, but made no mention of the monetary explanation previously advanced by Hawtrey and Cassel or the empirical work of Warren and Pearson, which supported the Hawtrey-Cassel account. In discussing the background to his approach, Friedman (1970) underscored the difference between his approach and that of Robbins (1934) and others in the Austrian tradition, as if Chicago and Vienna (transplanted to the London School of Economics) produced the only pre-Keynesian monetary explanations of the Great Depression.

[4] Hamilton (1988) emphasized the workings of the gold standard in propagating the Depression. Although implicitly recognizing the importance of the gold market, his focus was primarily on the deflationary implications for monetary policy of countries that were expected to devalue their currencies in terms of gold. While not disagreeing with the substance of Hamilton's analysis, we believe that his analysis is merely one aspect of a more general approach that we are describing.

Although Friedman and Schwartz (1963, pp. 360–361) did attempt to evaluate the role of the gold standard in causing the Depression, they did not specify what hypothesis they were rejecting, ignoring the gold-centric monetary explanation of Hawtrey and Cassel. The discussion of the role of the gold standard in *The Monetary History* involves a simple application of PSFM, and fails to address the essential problem with restoring the international gold standard raised by Hawtrey and Cassel in attributing the Great Depression to the mismanagement of that restoration. The argument of Hawtrey and Cassel was that the increase in the monetary demand for gold resulting from restoration of the international gold standard triggered a decline in the international price level toward the pre-World War I level, about 25% less than the 1929 level. But PSFM can, at most, explain small relative adjustments in the price levels of different countries on the gold standard; it cannot explain the large drop in the price levels of all gold-standard countries during the Great Depression.

The defects in PSFM as an explanation of international price movements were emphasized by Thompson (1974, 1977), who independently restated the essential elements of the Hawtrey-Cassel theory of the Great Depression within a more formal theoretical framework than that used by the McCloskey and Zecher (1976).

We begin by explaining the critical role that restoration of the gold standard played in the monetary contraction and deflation during the Great Depression under the Hawtrey-Cassel-Thompson model of the gold standard. This theory easily incorporates many of the special factors, such as inter-allied war debts, war reparations, and trade conflicts, often cited by Kindleberger and others as independent contributory factors to the Great Depression. In our view, these factors all tended to increase the international monetary demand for gold, exacerbating the inherently deflationary project of restoring an international gold standard. We are therefore led to ask why, under the circumstances of an unprecedented economic catastrophe attributable to the gold standard, the United States remained on the gold standard until April 1933, especially after other countries had begun economic recoveries once they suspended gold convertibility (Warren & Pearson, 1933)? We argue that the explanation lies in the shift of the United States from being a net international debtor to a net creditor and the growing political dominance of US creditor interests that would gain from deflation. Finally, we compare the empirical implications of our approach with those of competing theories of the Great Depression.

13.2 The International Price Level Under the Gold Standard

Before World War I, most industrialized countries were adhering to the gold standard as it had evolved in Britain in the eighteenth and early nineteenth centuries. The essential characteristics of the gold standard were:

(1) the currency unit is legally defined as a fixed weight of gold of specified fineness,
(2) the legally fixed gold parity is maintained by the obligation of the monetary authority to redeem and issue currency for gold in unlimited amounts,
(3) if the monetary authority temporarily suspends convertibility, as may occur during a wartime emergency, the presumption is that convertibility will be restored at the old parity.

The essential characteristics of the gold standard do not include adherence to what were, and still are, referred to as "the rules of the game." Under those "rules," the domestic money stock of a country adhering to the gold standard is supposed to vary proportionately with the gold reserves held by the monetary authority of that country. Although the tight correlation between gold reserves and the total supply of money prescribed by the rules of the game dominates theoretical and popular expositions of the gold standard, such a correlation is neither necessary theoretically nor observed empirically (McCloskey & Zecher, 1976).

If the rules of the game were followed, then the currency stock in a gold-standard country would be primarily determined by the gold holdings of the monetary authority. The benchmark for this system is the behavior of a system in which all money consisted of a gold coinage which could be freely minted or melted down. In principle, a paper currency could be used if the monetary authority issued banknotes (or deposits) fully covered by gold reserves. In tum, the gold reserves of the monetary authority were assumed to be determined by international gold flows resulting from international trade imbalances. Under this gold-reserve version of the international gold standard, the domestic price level in any country is determined according to the relation between the quantity of money and the domestic output of each country, while the quantity of money in each country is determined by the international gold flows that occur whenever the domestic price level in any country is inconsistent with equilibrium in its balance of trade.

The supposed necessity for the rules of the game to be observed follows from the assumption that international monetary equilibrium is maintained by operation of PSFM. Under this view, if a tight correlation between domestic gold reserves and domestic money supplies is not maintained (by the appropriate behavior of the monetary authorities), domestic price levels could diverge considerably for extended periods, eventually either causing a financial crisis or jeopardizing the maintenance of convertibility. But in fact, operation of PSFM is theoretically irrelevant to the maintenance of international monetary equilibrium (Samuelson, 1980) and the observed lack of correlation between gold flows and price-level movements under the gold standard is inconsistent with the implied positive relationship if PSFM had been the mechanism that maintained international monetary equilibrium (McCloskey & Zecher, 1976).

A common equilibrium price level among countries adopting fixed gold parities when there are no restrictions on gold imports or exports obtains without PSFM, because the gold prices of internationally traded commodities are determined in world markets. The prices of these commodities in terms of currencies tied to gold must also be determined simultaneously. Thus, the domestic price level of every gold-standard country, given the currency exchange rates implied by the gold parities of national currencies, is determined by arbitrage, so that, whatever the state of the balance of payments, domestic monetary conditions cannot affect the prices of goods in terms of gold. Perhaps domestic monetary conditions could affect the prices of non-tradable goods, but since international trade tends to equalize the quality-adjusted prices of immobile factors of production, international arbitrage tends to equalize even the prices of non-tradeable goods independently of a balance-of-payments constraint on the domestic monetary authorities (see Chapter 5 and Frenkel & Johnson, 1976).

Since the world stock of gold in the short run is nearly fixed, the combined monetary and non-monetary world demand for gold determines the international value of gold in relation to all other commodities. Because the cost of transporting gold is low compared to its value, the value of gold cannot differ significantly across countries in the absence of controls on the international shipment of gold. But prices for tradable goods are constrained by arbitrage even without gold shipments. The internationally determined value of gold (in relation to all other goods) determines the international price level (in terms of gold). The quantity of convertible paper currency and deposits issued by banks adjusts to the demand for money at the price level consistent with equilibrium in the international gold market (see Chapters 2 and 3, and Thompson, 1974). Only insofar as the gold-reserve accumulations of banks affects the world demand for gold can banks affect the international price level (in terms of gold).

The crucial implication of this convertibility version of the international gold standard is that domestic monetary authorities cannot affect their domestic price levels. What central banks can control is the rate at which they accumulate reserves of gold, or equivalent foreign exchange. For example, suppose monetary authorities in one country adopt a gold-accumulationpolicy. That policy would affect the internal price level of that country only insofar as the increased demand for gold reserves causes gold to appreciate, thereby causing money prices in terms of gold to fall in every gold-standard country. Conversely, gold exports by one country cause domestic inflation only insofar as the reduced demand for gold is sufficient to cause gold to depreciate, thereby causing prices to rise in every gold-standard country. Certainly, no small country adhering to convertibility under the international gold standard can affect its domestic price level.

Under the gold-convertibility version of the gold standard, the role of gold reserves is just to provide a ready inventory from which to satisfy demands for redemption (Black, 2010). The stock of currency in any country need not vary with the gold reserves held by the monetary authority. The automatic regulation of the supply of means of payment operates independently of changes in gold reserves.

Because of national legislation requiring some fraction of monetary liabilities (usually the banknotes issued by central banks) to be "backed" or "covered" by holdings of gold reserves, some correlation may have existed between money stocks and reserves. However, the causal relation was in the opposite direction of that normally assumed. The creation of convertible monetary claims by a bank implies a derived demand for gold reserves to meet any prudential, or legal, reserve requirements. Thus, it is the quantity of money that determines the quantity of reserves, not vice versa.

We conjecture that while there was no operational necessity for legally imposed gold-reserve or cover requirements under a gold-parity system, their existence led to confusion about the difference between the pure logic of the gold standard and its performance under the supposed "rules of the game" in which the quantity of convertible money held by the public was supposed to fluctuate in response to changes in the quantity of gold reserves held by the monetary authority.

An examination of the statutes establishing the US gold standard supports our interpretation of the intended basis for the US gold standard. The procedures the US monetary authorities were to follow in maintaining the gold standard were specified in two important statutes. First, the gold standard Act of 1900 required that "all forms of money issued or coined by the United States shall be maintained at a parity of value with this and it shall be the duty of the Secretary of the Treasury to maintain such parity." The Act required the Treasury to establish and maintain a redemption fund of $150 million in gold coin and bullion. Also, the redemption fund was given a priority claim on all the Treasury's other gold reserves, and, in the event that the redemption fund itself fell below $100 million and the gold reserves of the Treasury were exhausted, the Secretary of the Treasury was required to restore the fund by issuing Treasury bonds payable in gold coin. The issue of gold bonds to obtain gold bullion to maintain convertibility was unlimited; in effect, the entire gold stock of the world served as backing for the US convertibility commitment. The Treasury was also authorized to issue gold certificates upon the presentation of gold coins or bullion to the Treasury.

Second, the Federal Reserve Act of 1913 created the Federal Reserve System and specified its role in maintaining the convertibility of an "elastic" supply. The purpose of the Federal Reserve Act was to provide an elastic currency supply and a means whereby national banks could rediscount commercial paper to obtain currency. The Federal Reserve System was authorized to issue Federal Reserve notes which were to be (a) "receivable by all national and member banks and the Federal reserve banks and for all taxes, customs, and other public dues," and (b) "were to be redeemed in gold on demand at the Treasury Department of the United States, or in gold or lawful money at any Federal reserve bank." The final section of the Federal Reserve Act protected the gold parity of the dollar by stating that nothing in the Federal Reserve Act was to be interpreted as a repeal of the gold-parity provision of the gold standard Act of 1900. These Acts established a mechanism whereby the entire gold stock of the world could be used to discharge a commitment to maintain the convertibility of the US currency.

The requirement that Federal Reserve banks maintain a gold-redemption fund at the Treasury to ensure the redemption of Federal Reserve notes should not be viewed as essential to the US version of a gold standard. In fact, this gold reserve (or cover) requirement, which had tied up a large part of the US gold stock, was overcome in February 1932 by the passage of the Glass-Steagall Act, and was always changed before it became a binding constraint preventing the issue of additional notes.

13.3 Monetary Disorder After World War I and the Restoration of the Gold Standard

The gold standard, as an international institution, was relatively short-lived, lasting only about 35–40 years from the 1870s to the eve of World War I, when the expectation of imminent hostilities caused the countries to renege on their convertibility commitments. The years preceding World War I were a period of unprecedented prosperity and economic growth; although concerns about fluctuations in the value of gold were then common, the period stands out, in retrospect, for the impressive stability of the international price level.

The international gold standard broke down even before the first shots were fired, owing to uncertainty about whether commitments under the gold standard would be honored once hostilities started (Kindleberger, 1984). But another reason also prevented the gold standard from continuing to function: the demands of the belligerent countries for wartime finance were incompatible maintaining the gold standard. To be able to pay for the necessary imports of war materiel, countries mobilized their internal gold coinage, replacing gold coins with paper banknotes and token coins. The accumulated gold was then either exported to pay for needed imports or added to emergency reserves. Although central-bank gold reserves increased sharply during the war, so much of the coined gold was shifted from monetary to non-monetary uses that the value of gold in relation to commodities dropped sharply during the War, as evidenced by the rapid inflation in the US and Sweden, which maintained gold convertibility for much of the War. Because wartime gold inflation reflected a depreciation of gold, sterilizing gold inflows would not have prevented inflation from occurring, it would merely have accelerated the inflow.

Restoring the prewar gold standard presented two especially serious problems:

(1) In the belligerent countries, inflation was even more rapid than in the United States[5] and Sweden, because, the belligerents, having abandoned the gold standard in substance, if not in form. Prices in the belligerent countries reflected domestic monetary conditions not a non-functioning international gold market. In these circumstances, monetary expansion was used as an additional revenue source, amplifying upward pressure on prices.
(2) After the war, support was widespread for restoring the gold standard and convertibility at the prewar parities. But by the end of the war, gold had lost almost half of its prewar value in relation to commodities. Thus, restoring the gold standard at the prewar gold parities would imply a 50% reduction in the value of gold. To make a 50% reduction in the value of gold sustainable, the world demand for gold had to be reduced sufficiently to be consistent with such a reduction in the value of gold relative to other goods. Otherwise, market forces would drive up the value of gold, implying a 50% deflation of prices and wages. For those countries in which prices rose by even more than the value of gold had fallen, the deflationary implications of restoring the prewar gold parity were even more dire.

As early as 1919, R. G. Hawtrey (1919 [1923]) recognized the inherent instability of the postwar international price level and the deflationary danger the world faced in reconstructing an international monetary order based on the gold standard. The problem was sufficiently concerning to occasion an international monetary conference in Genoa in 1922. The Genoa Conference produced no agreements on parity adjustments, but it did lead to a general understanding that central banks ought to moderate their demand for gold reserves as they restored the gold convertibility of their currencies. The conference explicitly endorsed a gold-exchange standard under which countries would join the gold standard not by making their own currencies directly convertible into gold

[5] The United States of course became a belligerent in April 1917, and thereupon also embargoed gold exports.

coin or bullion, but would instead maintain a fixed parity between the currency of each country and all other gold-standard currencies, in particular the dollar, whose convertibility into gold had already been restored (and, presumably, once Britain restored convertibility as expected, pound sterling). Operating in the foreign-exchange markets rather than the gold market, and using dollars or other convertible currencies as reserves, would limit the growth in demand for gold reserves as the international gold standard was restored. (Hawtrey, 1922 [1923]).

The understanding worked reasonably well for most of the decade, and numerous countries rejoined the gold standard. After an immediate postwar inflation followed by a deep deflation from 1920 to 1922, prices remained roughly stable for most of the decade until late 1929, falling only slightly overall in the US from 1923 to 1928. But the potential for deflation was widely recognized and the possibility of a "gold shortage" (i.e., increased demand for gold) and potential deflation was a widely discussed and controversial issue during the 1920s (Nelson, 1991). Gustav Cassel, who closely collaborated with Hawtrey at the Genoa Conference, wrote extensively during the 1920s about the deflationary consequences of restoring the gold standard unless the growth in global monetary demand for gold was limited.[6] (Table 13.1 lists countries that returned to the gold standard during the 1920s either by establishing convertibility into gold or pegging their currencies to the dollar.)

The key fact about the international gold market in the 1920s was that, after importing massive amounts of gold during the war, the United States held about 40% of the world's monetary gold reserves. The US monetary authorities, therefore, had significant control over the value of gold through their conduct of monetary policy. By allowing an outflow of gold, the United States could counteract or neutralize the deflationary pressures inherent in the international monetary system. If US policy instead caused gold imports, deflationary pressures would be intensified.

The uneasy balance of a world economy on the precipice of deflation was first threatened in 1926–1927 by the French stabilization of the franc

[6] Cassel was concerned about two sources of deflation: first that gold production would lag behind the growth of gold demand, causing a long-term secular deflationary trend; second, and of primary concern to Hawtrey, was a substantial increase in gold demand resulting from restoration of the gold standard. That gold production increased more rapidly than Cassel had predicted it would, led critics to dismiss both of his concerns, even though subsequent events confirmed his second, and more immediate, concern.

Table 13.1 The restoration sequence of the international gold standard (1919–1929)

Country	*Date of restoration (or establishment) of gold standard*		*Date of restoration of stability of exchange on New York*	
United States[a]	June	1919		
Lithuania	August	1922	August	1922
Latvia[b]	November	1922	March	1922
Austria*	January	1923	September	1922
Sweden*	April	1924	August	1922
Germany	October	1924	June	1924
Switzerland*	November	1924	November	1924
Netherlands	April	1925	November	1924
United Kingdom	May	1925	May	1925
Australia	May	1925	May	1925
New Zealand	May	1925	May	1925
Union of South Africa	May	1925	May	1925
Hungary*[c]	May	1925	January	1925
Finland*	December	1925	March	1924
Chile*	January	1926	October	1925
Czechoslovakia*	April	1926	February	1923
Canada	July	1926	July	1924
Belgium*	October	1926	October	1926
Bulgaria*	January	1927	January	1924
Denmark	January	1927	March	1926
British India*	March	1927	May	1925
Argentina	August	1927	March	1927
Poland*	October	1927	November	1926
Italy*	December	1927	December	1927
Estonia*	January	1928	November	1924
Norway	May	1928	September	1927
Greece*	May	1928	January	1927
France	June	1928	December	1926
Rurnania*	February	1929	February	1929

*Redemption permitted in gold exchange
[a]Restrictions on export of gold removed
[b]National Bank under obligation to keep its notes at gold par
[c]Stabilized with reference to the British pound, August 1924
Source Mills, *Economic Tendencies in the United States*, p. 319

under the Poincaré national-unity government. After a series of ineffectual governments had permitted a deterioration of the fiscal situation and a loss of confidence in the franc, causing the franc to depreciate to a dollar exchange rate only a tenth of its pre-War parity (from about 20 cents to 2 cents), Poincaré became premier and finance minister in 1926 initiating a series of reforms that led to a rapid doubling of rise in the franc's value relative to the dollar to almost 4 cents in December 1926. The 3.92 cent parity at which the legal value of the stabilized franc was set by agreement between Poincaré and Bank of France Governor Emile Moreau was intended to undervalue the franc, inducing a continuing gold inflow into France, reinforced by a monetary law effectively preventing the creation of domestic francs except in exchange for gold or foreign exchange.

The stabilization took place within the context of the gold-exchange standard, so the initial inflow of foreign-exchange reserves to the Bank of France had negligible deflationary effect. But that changed when the French Parliament restored the legal convertibility of the franc to gold in 1928, imposing strict gold-reserve requirements on the Bank of France, significantly increasing the world demand for gold and intensifying the deflationary pressure on the world economy (Johnson, 1997; Mouré, 1991, 2002).

The usual, and we believe, erroneous presumption is that French real wages had been eroded by the rapid inflation of the previous year, so that the new parity did not restore French real wages to their earlier level. It is not clear from discussions about the behavior of French wages why they responded slowly to purely monetary changes. The slow response raises at least the possibility that real (nonmonetary) factors were reducing French real wages. Under a gold standard, one would normally have expected French prices and wages to adjust rapidly to the international levels dictated by the gold standard and the chosen dollar parity.

A more plausible explanation for the continuing gold inflow was offered by Hawtrey (1932), who observed that the French law stabilizing the exchange rate also limited which assets other than gold that the Bank of France could hold.[7] As the French economy expanded rapidly after the Poincaré economic reforms boosted confidence in the French economy

[7] Hawtrey's assertions about the limitations imposed on the Bank of France in issuing additional banknotes except in exchange for gold or foreign exchange have been confirmed by H. C. Johnson (1997) and K. Mouré (1991, 2002).

triggering a repatriation of assets, the Bank of France could supply the public with the banknotes demanded only by accumulating additional gold or foreign-exchange reserves, but not liabilities of domestic banks. Thus, monetary expansion was possible only insofar as a trade surplus or capital inflow financed the creation of additional francs.[8]

In 1927, economic activity in the United States slowed, creating fears of a recession. The slowdown was counteracted by a loosening of Federal Reserve policy and a reduction of interest rates at the direction of Benjamin Strong. The expansive policy caused an outflow of gold from the United States that helped to meet the growing demand for gold elsewhere in the world. The prompt response by the Federal Reserve to early signs of deflation and recession helped to allay concerns about the deflationary effects of restoring the gold standard.

As fears of deflation receded, optimism about future business conditions increased, fueling the stock market boom of 1927–1929. The Austrian interpretationof this episode is that, instead of allowing natural recessionary forces to cleanse the economy of the inflationary excesses that had built up between 1922 and 1927, the artificial credit expansion induced by Fed policy prolonged the boom beyond its capacity to sustain itself. This interpretation is misguided, yet, despite the general disfavor into which the Austrian explanation of the Great Depression has fallen, it remains influential at least in this respect: it reinforces the popular prejudice against stock-market speculation, suggesting that the added credit created by the Fed to sustain the boom was largely diverted to finance a speculative stock-market boom. That commodity prices remained stable or fell slightly from 1927 to 1929 supposedly masks the inflationary pressures manifested in the stock market until, stock-market prices having risen to unsustainable levels, the stock market collapsed in 1929 when the Federal Reserve could no longer sustain the inflationary boom without breaching the dollar-gold parity.

But even if the stock-market boom could not be justified by expected real increases in earnings, there is no reason to think it was inflationary, and even if the stock-market boom were a speculative bubble, inflationary

[8] The French stabilization, combining currency undervaluation and monetary stringency, provides a textbook example of exchange-rate protectionism described by Max Corden (1985) in a classic essay. While Corden's analysis was undertaken in the context of a monetary authority operating with a flexible exchange rate, the analysis is equally applicable to a fixed-exchange-rate regime or a floating-rate regime.

financing by the Fed had nothing to do with it. Inflationary expectations could have generated an increase in stock prices only if those expectations were reflected in increased earnings forecasts, but not increased discount rates. It is hard to understand what could have caused expectations of inflation to be reflected in earnings forecasts, but not in the discount rates that convert the forecasts into present values (Hawtrey, 1932). Indeed, the stock-market boom itself probably increased the demand to hold money as the volume of stock-market transactions increased rapidly (Field, 1984).[9] Thus, far from being a manifestation of inflation that had to be suppressed by tight money, the stock-market boom would be deflationary unless the money stock expanded to offset the increased demand.

In any event, the Federal Reserve interpreted the stock-market boom in accordance with something like the Austrian view, attempting to counteract it by restricting monetary expansion and raising short-term interest rates in 1928. The tightening coincided with an increasing French demand for gold as the monetary law enacted in June 1928 defining the franc as a fixed weight of gold requiring the Bank to hold gold reserves equal to a minimum of 35% of its sight liabilities (banknotes plus bank-issued transaction deposits). The stable trend in commodity prices broke in the summer of 1929 as the effects of increasing demands for gold began to be felt. Even after the recession had started and deflationary trends were becoming apparent, the stock-market continued rising until the fall, perhaps reflecting a continued expectation that the Federal Reserve, as it had in 1927, would ease monetary policy in time to avert a recession. However, the Federal Reserve was determined to break the stock-market boom, refusing to relent until stock prices crashed.

A full understanding of the deflationary forces affecting the world economy at the outbreak of the Great Depression requires consideration not just of the effects of monetary policy, but also the role of war debts, reparations, and trade policy in unleashing deflation. We address these issues in the following section.

[9] This is the grain of truth in one popular prejudice against stock-market speculation, which holds that speculation in the stock-market diverts capital from productive to unproductive uses and forces up interest rates. Since speculation simply transfers funds from one party to another, there is no net loss of capital available for "productive" investments. However, if the stockmarket boom increases the demand to hold money and the money supply does not respond accordingly, the increased demand to hold money may crowd out some capital spending to support increased demands for liquidity.

13.4 War Debts, Reparations, Tariffs, and the Demand for Gold

Monetary disorder was not the only legacy of World War I. The War also left a huge burden of financial obligations in its wake. The European allies had borrowed vast sums from the United States to finance their war efforts, and the Treaty of Versailles imposed on Germany the obligation to pay heavy reparations to the allies, particularly France.

We need not discuss the controversial question whether the burden imposed on Germany was too great to have been discharged. The relevant question for our purposes is by what means the reparations and war debts could be paid, or, at least, carried forward without causing a default on the obligations. To simplify the discussion, we concentrate on the relationship between the United States and Germany, because many of the other obligations of the allies to the United States were offset by those of Germany to the allies.[10]

The debt to the United States could be extinguished either by a net payment in goods reflected in a German balance-of-trade surplus and a US balance-of-trade deficit, or by a transfer of gold from Germany to the United States. Stretching out the debt would have required the United States, in effect to lend Germany the funds required to service its obligations.

For most of the 1920s, the United States did in fact lend heavily to Germany, thereby lending Germany funds with which to meet its financial obligations to the United States (and its European creditors). US lending was not explicitly for that purpose, but on the consolidated national balance sheets, US lending offset German financial obligations, obviating any real transfer.

Thus, to avoid a transfer, in goods or specie, from Germany to the United States, continued US lending to Germany was necessary. But the sharp tightening of monetary policy by the Federal Reserve in 1928 raised domestic interest rates to near record levels and curtailed lending abroad,

[10] The United States, as a matter of law, always resisted such a comparison, contending that the war debts were commercial obligations in no way comparable to the politically imposed reparations. However, as a final matter, there was obviously a strict correspondence between the two sets of obligations. The total size of German obligations was never precisely determined. However, those obligations were certainly several times the size of the war debts owed the United States. Focusing simply on the US-German relationship is therefore simply a heuristic device.

as foreign borrowers were deterred from seeking funds in US capital markets. An immediate transfer from Germany to the United States could now be avoided only by default. To effect the required transfer in goods, Germany would have had to shift resources from its non-tradable-goods sector to its tradable-goods sector, by reducing spending on, and the relative prices of, non-tradable goods. Thus, Germany began to slide into a recession in 1928.

Then, in 1929, the newly elected Hoover administration reaffirmed the Republican campaign commitment to raise import tariffs, thereby imposing a tax on the goods transfer through which Germany could discharge its financial obligations to the United States. Although the bill to increase tariffs that became the infamous Hawley-Smoot Act was not passed until 1930, the commitment to raise tariffs made it increasingly unlikely that the United States would allow the debts owed it to be discharged by a goods transfer. The only other means by which Germany could discharge its obligations was a gold transfer. Anticipating that its obligations to the United States could be discharged only by transferring gold, Germany took steps to increase its gold holdings to be able to meet its debt obligations. The increased German demand for gold was reflected in a defensive tightening of monetary policy to raise domestic interest rates to reduce spending and to induce an inflow of gold to Germany for eventual remittance to the United States

The connection between Germany's debt obligations and its demand for gold sheds light on the deflationary macroeconomic consequences of the Hawley-Smoot tariff. Given the huge debts owed to the United States, the tariff imposed a deflationary monetary policy on all US debtors as they attempted to accumulate the gold required to service their debt obligations to the United States. But, under the gold standard, the United States was unable to insulate itself from the deflationary effects that its own trade policy was imposing on its debtors.[11]

The United States could have counteracted these macroeconomic pressures with a sufficient easing monetary policy, allowing an outflow of

[11] Viewed from a different perspective, the tariff aimed at transferring wealth from the foreign debtors to the US government by taxing debt payments on debt already fixed in nominal terms. Moreover, deflation from whatever source increased the real value of the fixed nominal debts owed the United States This way of looking at the impact of the tariff will be important for our discussions in Section six.

gold to accommodate the demand of other countries for gold. Monetary expansion would have facilitated the former policy of lending to debtors, enabling them to extend their obligations. But preoccupied with the stock-market boom, US monetary authorities appeared oblivious to the impossible alternatives that were being forced on US debtors by a combination of tight US monetary policy and a protectionist trade policy.

As the prospects that protectionist legislation would pass steadily improved even as tight US monetary policy was being maintained, deflationary signs became increasingly clear and alarming. The panic of October 1929, in our view, was not, as Great Depression historiography often describes it, the breaking of a speculative bubble, but a correct realization that a toxic confluence of monetary and trade policies was leading the world toward a deflationary precipice.

Once the deflation took hold, the nature of the gold standard with a fixed price of gold was such that gold would likely appreciate against weak currencies that were likely to be formally devalued, or allowed to float, relative to gold. A vicious cycle of increasing speculative demand for gold in anticipation of currency devaluation further intensified the deflationary pressures insofar as the devaluation of one currency increased expectations that other currencies would be devalued (Hamilton, 1988).

A uniform devaluation of all currencies against gold might have avoided the speculative increases in gold demand that followed from piecemeal devaluations, but aside from the increase in the speculative demand for gold resulting from these piecemeal devaluations, devaluations that promoted recovery in one country tended to improve, not harm, conditions in other countries. Such devaluations were often condemned as beggar-thy-neighbor policies, but increased expenditure and output in one country were generally beneficial, not harmful, to the trading parties of other countries (Hawtrey, 1933, pp. 154–157).

13.5 The Role of the Federal Reserve System in the Great Depression

Although we, unlike Friedman and Schwartz, have emphasized that the monetary forces that produced the Great Depression were international in origin and scope, we do not deny that the United States played a key role in causing the Depression. Nor, by focusing on events outside the narrow purview of the Federal Reserve, do we mean to minimize the contribution of the Federal Reserve to the catastrophe. As holder of over

40% of the gold reserves held by the world's monetary authorities, the Federal Reserve had ample power to have at least moderated the appreciation of gold and the corresponding price deflation from starting and from continuing as long as it did.

However, for the Federal Reserve to have pursued a serious anti-deflation policy would have required it to violate prevailing views about the obligations of the monetary authorities under the gold standard. A leading precept of orthodox central banking under the gold standard was an obligation to reduce credit availability and interest rates in response to a continuing loss of gold. While this precept may have led to the correct responses under normal conditions, the conditions in the 1920s, when the United States held a huge share of the world's gold reserves and when there were so many other reasons for other countries to increase their gold holdings, were not normal.

For the Federal Reserve to have violated the well-accepted precept would have required considerable statesmanship and courage. Perhaps Friedman and Schwartz as well as Hawtrey, Cassel, and Fisher were correct in speculating that had Benjamin Strong not died in 1928, he would have had the courage and insight to avoid the mistakes made by his successors. But such speculation can lead to no definite conclusion. Hawtrey's characterization of the rules of orthodox central banking in his 1930 testimony to the Macmillan Committee (1931, pp. 283–284) bears repeating in this context.

> [T]hat kind of orthodoxy [restricting credit when gold ebbs away] is like conventions at bridge; you have to break them when the circumstances call for it. I think that a gold reserve exists to be used.... Perhaps once in a century the time comes when you can use your gold reserve for the governing purpose, provided you have the courage to use practically all of it.

Given the policy decisions of the Federal Reserve Board, the United States still could have avoided catastrophe had it abandoned the gold standard, a course eventually followed by Great Britain in September 1931 along with what became known as the sterling bloc, and by Sweden (Jonung, 1981). By abandoning the gold standard, those countries were able to moderate the effects of the Depression and begin recovering a year before the United States did (after President Roosevelt's suspension of the gold standard in April 1933).

Friedman and Schwartz acknowledge that abandoning the gold standard helped Britain and Sweden cushion the impact of the Great Depression. However, they contend, as we understand their argument, that the Depression began in the United States and was transmitted by the gold standard to the nations still on the gold standard. Friedman and Schwartz distinguished between the initial phase of the decline (which they regarded as severe but not unprecedented) from later declines starting in late 1930 with the failure of the Bank of United States. The later shocks, in their view, resulted from banking panics that the Federal Reserve could have prevented or curtailed, but chose not to. It is less clear to what extent they believe the initial deflationary shocks of 1928–1929 originated in the United States.

We view the bank failures as incidental to a deflationary process that would have continued in, more or less, the same fashion even if the United States had a well-developed system of branch banking that would have avoided most of the bank failures that took place (as Canada did). More important to the analysis, the price level was determined in a global setting, and it was the shifts in the demand for gold that primarily determined the behavior of the price level. Bank failures may have had a role in causing people to want to hold gold, which would intensify deflationary pressures. But a decline in the US quantity of money was not, as Friedman and Schwartz argued, the exogenous change to which all other economic variables were adjusting.

As long as the Federal Reserve was constrained by its statutory obligation to maintain the gold standard, it could have stemmed the deflationary tide (after helping to start it in 1928–1929) only by tolerating a massive outflow of gold. A gold outflow large enough to have counteracted the deflation would have been difficult to justify under the traditional, and widely accepted, conception of the gold standard.

An important, and thus far unanswered, question that arises is why the United States was so committed to the gold standard, especially when the attachment of the United States to the gold standard before World War I, particularly in deflationary periods, had been equivocal? We address this question in the following section.

13.6 The Politics of Debt, Deflation, and the Gold Standard

Perhaps the most important immediate effect of unexpected deflation (inflation) is to redistribute wealth from (to) monetary debtors to (from) creditors. Although there are many other reasons to favor or oppose unexpected price-level changes, distributional effects are obviously an important, if not overriding, factor affecting attitudes to such changes. Our thesis is that the political dominance of domestic creditor interests prevented the United States from abandoning the gold standard before 1933. The wealth of creditors was obviously enhanced by deflation, and an expectation that gold would appreciate intensified attachment to the gold standard, at least until debtor insolvency became widespread.

The political dominance of the creditors was manifested by Hoover's pledge to veto any legislation that invalidated the gold-parity provision in the statutes mandating US adherence to the gold standard, and by the inability of the Senate to override a Presidential veto on this issue. It is noteworthy that while most countries attempted to rejoin the gold standard after World War I, only the two major international creditor countries, the United States and Britain, returned at their prewar gold parities. All other countries depreciated the gold content of their currencies, thus writing down the real value of all debts denominated in their currencies.

Changes in the international investment position of the United States also help to explain the strength of the US commitment to the gold standard despite the catastrophic deflation between 1929 and 1933. The United States had shifted from being an international net debtor in 1914 to becoming the largest net creditor in the world by 1919, significantly augmenting its creditor position during the 1920s. The US net creditor position nearly doubled as a percentage of nominal US GDP from 7.6% in 1919 to 14.8% in 1930. From 1919 to 1930, the governmental and private foreign dollar capital issues publicly offered in the United States totaled $12.1 billion (*Handbook on American Underwriting of Foreign Securities*, 1930, pp. 10–11). The foreign debts owed the United States were payable in fixed nominal amounts of US dollars. For 1929, Warren and Pearson (1933, p. 237) estimated total public and private debts in the United States to be $203 billion, while US national wealth was estimated at $362 billion. Total debts were thus equal to 56% of national wealth.

US net investment abroad totaled approximately $15 billion, or roughly 7.5% of the total US creditor-debtor position.

According to Warren and Pearson (1933, p. 360), most outstanding debts in the United States in 1929 had been contracted during the period 1922–1929 when the price level was 50% above the prewar price level. In contrasting the situation in the United States in 1929 to earlier panics, Warren (in testimony before the United States Senate Seventy-Second Congress, May 12, 1932, p. 63) argued that the panics of 1815, 1865, and 1920 were not similar to the 1929 episode, because each of the earlier panics followed a relatively short period of high prices in which most public and private debts were not generally expressed in terms of the higher price levels of the short periods preceding the panics.

While the net external creditor position of the United States grew substantially during the 1930s, the real wealth transfer from the US foreign-net-creditor position during the Great Depression was small, especially in comparison with the country's loss of output in the Depression. It is possible that the credit expansion during the 1920s was predicated upon the ability of creditor interests to defend the gold standard, and that expectations were formed on that presumption. US creditor interests would have had to develop significant political power compared to their economic position in the country. The significant growth of the United States as an international creditor country was concentrated in large US banks, and it was the large banks that were the chief defenders of the gold standard during the Great Depression.

Several attempts were made in the 1920s and early 1930s to eliminate or repeal the statutory provisions for maintaining the convertibility of the dollar into gold. Such legislation was first introduced in the House of Representatives in 1922 after the 1920–1921 Depression; the last attempt was in May 1932 when the House passed the Goldsborough bill described in the next paragraph. In each instance, the legislation was introduced as an amendment to the Federal Reserve Act of 1913, directing the Federal Reserve to conduct its monetary policy to stabilize the value of the dollar rather than maintain the legal gold parity. For our purposes, what makes this series of failed attempts to abandon the gold standard interesting is the transparent political power of domestic creditor interests to block enactment of the legislation. The debates show that the participants clearly understood how the gold standard operated, and that many participants identified the quantity theory of money as relevant to a different system from (and, for some, a more desirable system than) the gold standard.

In early 1932, legislation to amend the Federal Reserve Act was introduced by Representative T. Alan Goldsborough to force the United States to abandon the fixed convertibility of the dollar into gold by directing the Federal Reserve System to take actions to raise the wholesale commodity price level as fast as possible to the average level prevailing between 1921 and 1929. With gold appreciating, the Federal Reserve could either maintain the gold parity of the dollar or raise the dollar price level of goods, but not both. After passing the House with 289 in favor and just 60 opposed on May 2, 1932, the Goldsborough bill died in the Senate Committee on Banking and Currency. The final section of the bill, stating that any other "acts and parts of acts inconsistent with this act are hereby repealed," was especially controversial. This provision would have forced the United States to abandon the gold parity of the dollar, because maintaining the dollar-gold parity would not have allowed the wholesale price level to rise back to its 1926 level.

Opposition to the Goldsborough bill was led by Senator Carter Glass, the co-author and chief architect of the Federal Reserve Act (the Glass-Owen bill). The Goldsborough bill was never reported from the Senate Committee on Banking and Currency for consideration by the Senate because of a threatened veto by President Hoover, and the lack of sufficient support in the Senate to override his veto. In fact, the essential provisions of the Glass-Steagall Act had originally been introduced as part of the Goldsborough bill. It was alleged that Senator Glass had copied those provisions in a separate bill to limit the appeal of the Goldsborough bill and then to separately defeat the price-stabilization provisions that would have been incompatible with maintaining the gold content of the dollar. For our purposes, the significance of the Goldsborough bill is, first, that the House and Senate hearings and debates reveal that the central issue about maintaining the gold standard was protecting US creditor interests, and, second, that its defeat is attributable to the political dominance of US creditors.

Representative Goldsborough had first introduced a purchasingpower-stabilization bill in 1922, after the 1920–1921 Depression in which the US wholesale price level fell by 50%. The stated purpose of the bill was to protect the economy from price-level fluctuations and the redistribution of wealth between debtors and creditors. The original bill sought to stabilize the purchasing power of the dollar by varying the amount of gold that would convertible into the dollar, an idea that Goldsborough took from Irving Fisher. In 1926 and 1928, Representative James G. Strong, the Chairman of the House Banking and Currency Committee, introduced bills directing the Federal Reserve System to stabilize the purchasing power of the dollar. In fact, the original draft of the Federal Reserve Act had directed the Federal Reserve System to use its powers to promote a stable price level. Senator Glass was responsible for removing the stabilization provision, adding the final section of the Act which restated the gold-parity provision and the grant of unlimited authority to the Treasury to issue bonds to finance gold purchases if needed to maintain the gold parity.

In discussing the Goldsborough bill, Irving Fisher (1932, pp. 149–152), attributed opposition to the Goldsborough bill to fears that the United States would be forced off the gold standard leading to inflation. He expressed amazement that, in 1932, when the problem was rapid deflation, opponents of the bill were warning of inflation. In a similar vein, Ralph Hawtrey (1938, p. 145) famously compared inflation fears during the Great Depression to crying "fire, fire!" in Noah's Flood.

Responding to an amendment by Senator Glass in the Senate Banking and Currency Committee that Glass himself had described as an attempt to defeat the bill, Goldsborough, in a speech to the House on June 8, 1932, expressed frustration that his bill could be defeated by a relatively small group of powerful opponents. He complained that, after the bill was passed by the House, "the administration came out in advance and said that if the Senate passed the bill and it was put up to the executive he would veto it." He continued, "I will call your attention to the fact that the Democratic Party does not control the Senate, and call your attention to the further fact that if this stabilization legislation had the support of the administration it would pass the Senate without five dissenting votes." Goldsborough attributed the opposition to his bill by the Hoover administration to the banks: "It has been impossible for me, in the very serious, prolonged, and trying study I have made of this matter, to disassociate the action of the great bankers of this country from the point of view of the executive branch of this Government" (*Congressional Record*-House June 8, 1932, pp. H123454-5).

13.7 Evaluating the Evidence on the Great Depression

The reasons for believing that monetary sources predominated are powerful. First, we know of no episode of severe deflation that was not caused by monetary forces. Second, the severity and longevity of the Depression in various countries was closely related to the nature of the monetary regime. Countries on the gold standard suffered most, and no country recovered before leaving the gold standard. Countries like Britain and Sweden and later the United States began to recover very soon after abandoning the gold standard.

China, which was on a silver standard, at first escaped the ravages of the Depression. However, the subsequent silver-purchase policy adopted by the United States to raise silver prices at the behest of domestic silver interests after 1933 inflicted a severe deflation on China from 1933 onwards (Kindleberger, 1973). This episode is particularly noteworthy, because it demonstrates that shifts in the international supply of, or demand for, a precious metal used as a monetary standard can cause inflation or deflation in countries without first altering the domestic quantity of money.

During the Great Depression, the Spanish peseta was inconvertible into gold with a flexible exchange rate into gold-standard currencies. Choudri and Kochin (1980) presented evidence showing that Spain was only mildly affected by the Depression and attributed the relatively mild effect to Spain's flexible-exchange-rate monetary regime.

Few economists deny that monetary factors played some role in the Depression. Most critics of a monetary explanation are content to assert that monetary forces could not have been the whole story, that the Depression was too complex a phenomenon to have resulted from a single causal relationship (Hughes, 1984, Kindleberger, 1973). Temin (1976, 1981) has argued that the changes in the money stock documented by Friedman and Schwartz (1963) were purely passive responses to a decline in income and prices that occurred for other reasons. His argument rests on the failure of interest rates to rise, as they would have been expected to within a standard IS-LM framework in response to an excess demand for money, and on the fact that the real quantity of money rose rather than declined between 1929 and 1933. He also noted that the reduction in the nominal quantity of money in 1929 and 1930 was relatively small, so that it is difficult to believe that a small downward adjustment in the money growth path of the previous two years could have produced the cataclysmic downturn of 1929–1930.[12]

It should be noted that Temin's criticisms apply only to the quantity-theoretic explanation of Friedman and Schwartz, but not to the Hawtrey-Cassel-Thompson theory of the value of money convertible into gold. The causality from the quantity of money to nominal income underlying the Friedman-Schwartz explanation is reversed in Hawtrey-Cassel-Thompson explanation. Changes in the international value of gold determine the international price level with no immediate effect on national money stocks. The monetary aggregates on which Friedman and Schwartz focused are not the source of the exogenous monetary shock that triggered the Great Depression. Only after the initial shock to the international price level caused by gold appreciation was there an endogenous response by national money stocks to the changes in the international price level.[13]

Moreover, the argument that a decline in the quantity of money should have led to rising nominal interest rates is valid only if expectations of worsening deflation were not depressing nominal interest rates. Our interpretation of events after World War I suggests that the risk of deflationwas widely recognized and that the events of 1928–1929 were widely understood at the time to have increased those risks (Nelson, 1991, Jalil & Rua, 2016).[14]

[12] In subsequent work Temin (1989), Eichengreen (1992) and Bernanke (2000) have recognized the role of the gold standard in causing and propagating the Great Depression. Friedman (1991) himself eventually acknowledged that he had underestimated the role of France in causing the Great Depression. However, neither Temin, Eichengreen, Bernanke, nor Friedman, adequately acknowledged the contributions of Hawtrey and Cassel in providing advance warning of the deflationary risk created by an uncoordinated and unmanaged restoration of the gold standard. Nor did they articulate the basic theoretical model of the gold standard as clearly as Hawtrey and Cassel themselves had done. More recently, in explaining the role of the gold standard in the Great Depression, Mouré (1991, 2002), Johnson (1997), Irwin (2012, 2014), and Sumner (2015) have appropriately acknowledged the early contributions of Hawtrey and Cassel and their claims to historical priority. Eichengreen in a personal communication has graciously acknowledged the priority of Hawtrey and Cassel.

[13] See Chapter 3, pp. 31–37, for a discussion of how the inflation following the Australian gold discoveries could have caused changes in national money supplies rather than, as it usually assumed, vice versa.

[14] Gordon and Wilcox (1981, pp. 54–58) dismiss a purely monetary explanation of the 1929–1930 downturn precisely because they contend that a shift in price-level expectations

It might be objected in reply that if deflation had been widely expected, then the increase in unemployment and the decline in output associated with the deflation are difficult to explain, because workers should have then been willing to accept wage reductions sufficient to allow them to retain employment. While possibly correct under sufficiently restrictive assumptions, the practical significance of the point, given inevitable uncertainty about future price and wages, is questionable.[15] Many workers may not have been forecasting deflation and therefore resisted the cuts in wages that might have prevented unemployment from rising as rapidly as it did. Furthermore, as long as employers expected greater deflation than workers did, expected deflationwould still have a net contractionary effect, the wage cuts acceptable to workers being less than those required by employers to maintain output. Finally, even if workers and employers were correctly anticipating deflation on average, rapid expected deflation implies that the return to holding money exceeds the return to holding real capital, so that investment in new capital goods ceases until enough existing capital wears out to raise the expected return to holding capital goods as high as the expected return to holding money.[16] The cessation of investment implies the shutdown of capital-goods industries and requires workers employed in those industries to find employment elsewhere. A sectoral shift of that magnitude cannot fail to have a large negative effect on output and employment.

in 1929 is "inexplicable" given the previous eight years of relative price-level stability. Given the disparity between the prewar price level measured in gold and the obvious increase in the world demand for gold caused by French monetary policy, the United States shift toward protectionism, and the policy tightening by the Federal Reserve to counter stock-market speculation when a sharp easing of policy was necessary to offset the other factors, that shift does not seem to us inexplicable, at all. As we have already pointed out, the dangerous potential for deflation under a restored gold standard was already identified in 1919 by Hawtrey (1919 [1923], p. 56) and was widely enough understood to have prompted the international conference at Genoa in 1922 to avoid that outcome. That deflation was avoided until 1929 does not mean that people ceased be concerned about it.

[15] Moreover, on a priori grounds there is more reason to expect bond traders to devote resources to predicting the future price level than to expect workers to do so. Thus, we might expect participants in the bond markets to predict inflation or deflation more accurately than we should expect workers to.

[16] See Glasner (2018) for a further development of this argument and its application to the 2008–2009 financial crisis and its aftermath.

The high anticipated return to holding money easily accounts for the increase in the real quantity of money, quite apart from the well-confirmed cyclical tendency of velocity to decline in a downturn. Nor is the direction of change in the real value of the money stock in the Great Depression a test of the Hawtrey-Cassel-Thompson theory of the Great Depression. We see no reason to assume that the stock of money in the United States was persistently less than the amount that the public wanted to hold. The decline in the price level was generated by an excess demand for gold, not by an excess demand for deposits or for currency.

Temin's contention that the Great Depression was caused by an unexplained reduction in consumption spending is difficult to evaluate systematically, because the fall in consumption cannot be derived from a more general model. Similar fluctuations in consumption do not seem to have had as powerful an impact on output as Temin asserts it did after 1929, so not only the cause, but the effect, of the posited change remain unexplained (Gandolfi & Lothian, 1977).

Kindleberger (1973) enumerated a variety of factors contributing to the Great Depression. Commodity prices were under downward pressure because of increased output. Meanwhile, the United States closed off its markets to those commodities, increasing pressures on commodity prices elsewhere, forcing primary producers to default on their loans, in turn forcing countries dependent upon primary commodities for income to devalue their currencies to avoid internal price deflation. We disagree with little of Kindleberger's argument, which actually increases the theoretical coherence and explanatory power of our argument; most of the factors he discussed can be interpreted as factors tending to increase the demand for gold and to reinforce deflationary trends. But Kindleberger largely ignored the inherently deflationary monetary conditions of the 1920s, and his discussion of the monetary forces behind the Depression did not go beyond dismissing bank runs as the crucial element in the Great Depression. Kindleberger also ignored any theory of an international price level, introducing international considerations only insofar as he asserted that the series of devaluations to which the Great Depression gave rise were on balance deflationary.[17]

[17] While we agree with Eichengreen and Sachs (1985) that devaluations were on balance helpful, we do not believe their stimulative impact came from the profits enjoyed by the devaluing central banks with which they could then finance a more expansive

In arguing that US bank runs rather than international monetary conditions were the crucial exogenous monetary shock that precipitated the acceleration of the decline in 1931, Friedman and Schwartz (1963, pp. 360–361) rely on the fact that the United States was importing gold between 1929 and 1932. If the monetary shock had been outside the United States, they assert, the United States should have been exporting, rather than importing, gold. An inflow of gold into the United States indicates that the United States was the source of the monetary disturbance.

But in focusing on the inflow of gold into the United States, Friedman and Schwartz overlooked an even greater inflow of gold into France at the same time. From December 1928 to December 1929, the United States imported $154 million of gold, and France imported $389 million. From December 1929 to December 1930, the United States imported $325 million of gold, and France imported $467 million (Cassel, 1936, p. 60).[18] Thus, by their own criterion, France was an even greater source of deflationary pressure than the United States. Moreover, as Fremling (1985, p. 1183) pointed out, the increase in US gold holdings during the Great Depression was proportionately less than the growth in total world reserves of gold, so the test for identifying the source of the shock to the international economy was not appropriately constructed (see Chapter 14, Section seven).

In our view, however, the fault of the United States government was that, holding 40% of international gold reserves, the United States could easily have accommodated the increasing French demand for gold. Instead, US monetary policy attracted a gold inflow exactly when a gold outflow to the rest of the world was required.

Nor do international gold flows capture the extent of increased monetary demand for gold. With a fixed stock of gold, redistributions of gold among countries occurred in response to changes in their relative demands for gold. Changes in relative demands tell us nothing about what was happening to the absolute demand for gold, which is what determines the world price level under the gold standard. We maintain that it was increasing rapidly. However much it increased,

policy. Rather, as Hawtrey (1933) argued, devaluation had an immediate impact in raising nominal prices in comparison with prevailing prices measured in terms of gold.

[18] See also Chapter 14, Table 14.1 for different, but not inconsistent estimates drawn from Johnson (1997).

a uniform increase in gold demand would cause no redistribution of existing stocks.[19] Focusing exclusively on changes in gold holdings misses an important part of the larger story.

A more appropriate measure of the increase in the demand for gold is the increase in the percentage of world gold held as central-bank assets. In his study of the interwar gold standard, Ragnar Nurske (1944) showed the enormous increase in the share of world gold held as monetary reserves during the Depression. Nurske calculated the reserves held by 24 central banks, not including the Federal Reserve. Between 1928 and 1932, the gold holdings of the banks increased by nearly $2.4 billion while their holdings of foreign exchange fell by $2 billion. That shift in demand from financial instruments to holdings of gold reflected the serious deflationary pressure exerted by national monetary authorities other than the Federal Reserve during the Great Depression.

Other attempts to test the role of the gold standard in causing the Great Depression (Meltzer, 1976 [1981]; Gordon & Wilcox, 1981) suffer from a similar preoccupation with the operation of PSFM. Gordon and Wilcox rightly dismissed Meltzer's argument that PSFM had an important role in propagating the Depression by noting that the mechanism implies a relative shift in expenditure patterns, not the absolute shift required to explain the monumental impact of the Great Depression. But having made that observation, Gordon and Wilcox, without even noticing the Hawtrey-Cassel-Thompson explanation, incorrectly concluded that they had thereby disposed of the question whether the gold standard led to the Great Depression.

Finally, the importance of bank failures seems diminished when one observes that, while no other country experienced bank failures on the scale of those in the United States, the Great Depression was not more severe in the United States than in a number of other countries. Adherence to the gold standard seems to be a better predictor of the seriousness of the Great Depression in any country than the number of bank failures in the country, a fact supporting our contention that the attempt to restore the gold standard and the resulting increase in the monetary demand for gold was the main cause of the Great Depression.

[19] This assertion is not strictly correct, inasmuch as a proportional increase the demand of all central banks for gold reserves would, by raising the real value of gold, induce gold inflows to the central banks that otherwise would have been devoted to non-monetary uses. In addition, the increased demand of central banks for gold reserves would induce an increased flow of newly produced gold into central-bank vaults.

13.8 Conclusion

It may be that the attempt to restore the gold standard was not inevitably destined to produce the subsequent catastrophic deflation and economic contraction. As we have argued, the attempts of most central banks to accumulate gold reserves, the proximate cause of deflation, were not required by the theory or practice of the gold standard. However, the international experience in trying to revive the gold standard after World War I surely justifies the overwhelming reluctance of the public and of almost all economists to consider seriously proposals to re-establish the gold standard.

References

Anderson, G. M., Shughart-II, W. F., & Tollison, R. D. (1988). A public choice theory of the great contraction. *Public Choice, 59*(4), 3–23.
Bernanke, B. (2000). *Essays on the great depression*. Princeton University Press.
Black, F. (2010). A gold standard with double feedback and near zero reserves. In *Business Cycles and Equilibrium* (updated ed.), (pp. 129–134). John Wiley and Sons.
Brown, W. A. (1940). *The International gold standard reinterpreted, 1914–1934* (Vol. 2, no. 37), NBER.
Cassel, G. (1932). *Crisis in the World's monetary system*. The Clarendon Press.
Cassel, G. (1936). *The downfall of the gold standard*. The Clarendon Press.
Chandler, L. V. (1958). *Benjamin strong, central banker*. Brookings.
Choudhri, E. U., & Kochin, L. A. (1980). The exchange rate and the international transmission of the business cycle disturbances. *Journal of Money, Credit, and Banking, 12*(4), 565–574.
Congressional Record. (1932, May 2). *72nd Congress* (Vol. 75, Part 9). U.S. Government Printing Office.
Corden, W. M. (1985). Exchange rate protection. In *Protection, growth and trade: Essays in international economics* (pp. 271–287). Basil Blackwell.
Eichengreen, B., & Sachs, J. (1985). Exchange rates and economic recovery in the 1930s. *Journal of Economic History, 45*(4), 925–946.
Eichengreen, B. (1992). *Golden fetters*. Oxford University Press.
Field, A. J. (1984). Asset exchanges and the transactions demand for money, 1919–1929. *American Economic Review, 74*(3), 43–59.
Fisher, I. (1932). *Booms and depressions*. Adelphi Co.
Fisher, I. (1934, January). Discussions by Professor Irving Fisher. *The Annals of the American Academy of political and social science* (pp. 150–51).

Frenkel, J. A., & Johnson, H. G. (1976). The monetary approach to the balance of payments: Essential concepts and historical origins. In J. A. Frenkel & H. G. Johnson (Eds.), *The monetary approach to the balance of payments* (pp. 21–45). George Allen and Unwin.
Friedman, M. (1970). Comments on the critics. In R. J. Gordon (Ed.), *Milton Friedman's monetary framework* (pp. 132–185). The University of Chicago Press.
Friedman, M. (1991). *Preface in Èmil Moreau, The golden franc: Memoirs of a Governor of the bank of France: The stabilization of the Franc*. Westview Press.
Friedman, M., & Schwartz, A. J. (1963). *A monetary history of the United States, 1867–1960*. Princeton University Press.
Fremling, G. (1985). Did the United States transmit the great depression to the rest of the World? *American Economic Review, 75*(4), 1181–1185.
Gandolfi, A. E., & Lothian, J. R. (1977). Did monetary forces cause the great depression: A review essay. *Journal of Money, Credit and Banking, 9*(4), 679–691.
Glasner, D. (1989). *Free banking and monetary Reform*. Cambridge University Press.
Glasner, D. (2018). The Fisher effect and the financial crisis of 2008 (Mercatus Research Paper). *SSRN:* https://doi.org/10.2139/ssrn.3247795
Gordon, R. J., & Wilcox, J. A. (1981). Monetarist interpretations of the great depression: An interpretation and critique. In K. Brunner (Ed.), *The Great depression revisited* (pp. 49–107). Martinus Nijhoff.
Hamilton, J. D. (1988). The role of the international gold standard in propagating the great depression. *Contemporary Policy Issues, 6*(2), 67–89.
Hawtrey, R. G. (1919 [1923]). The gold standard. *Economic Journal, 29*(116), 428–442, In *Monetary reconstruction* (pp. 48–65). Longmans, Green and Co.
Hawtrey, R. G. (1922 [1923]). The Genoa resolutions on currency. *Economic Journal, 32*(127), 290–304, In *Monetary reconstruction* (pp. 131–147). Longmans, Green and Co.
Hawtrey, R. G. (1932). *The art of central banking*. Longmans, Green, and Co.
Hawtrey, R. G. (1933). *Trade depression: The way out* (2d ed.). Longmans, Green, and Co.
Hawtrey, R. G. (1938). *A century of bank rate*. Longmans.
Hawtrey, R. G. (1947). *The gold standard in theory and practice* (5th ed.). Longmans, Green, and Co.
Hughes, J. R. T. (1984). Stagnation without 'flation: The 1930s again. In B. N. Siegel (Ed.), *Money in crisis* (pp. 137–156). Ballinger.
Irwin, D. A. (2012). The French gold sink and the great deflation of 1929–32. *Cato Papers on Public Policy, 2*, 3–41.

Irwin, D. A. (2014). Who anticipated the great depression? Gustav Cassel versus Keynes and Hayek on the Interwar Gold Standard. *Journal of Money, Credit and Banking, 46*(1), 197–228.

Jalil, A. J., & Rua, G. (2016). Inflation expectations and recovery in Spring 1933. *Explorations in Economic History, 62*(4), 26–50.

Johnson, H. C. (1997). *Gold, France, and the great depression*. Yale University Press.

Jonung, L. (1981). The depression in Sweden and the United States: A comparison of causes and politics. In K. Brunner (Ed.) *The great depression revisited*. Martinus Nijhoff.

Kindleberger, C. P. (1973). *The World in depression, 1929–39*. University of California Press.

Kindleberger, C. P. (1984). *A Financial history of Western Europe*. George Allen and Unwin.

Macmillan Committee on Finance and Industry. (1931). *Minutes of evidence*. H.M.S.O.

McCloskey, D. N., & Zecher, J. R. (1976). How the Gold Standard worked, 1880–1913. In J. A. Frenkel & H. G. Johnson (Eds.), *The Monetary approach to the balance of payments* (pp. 357–385). George Allen and Unwin.

Meltzer, A. H. (1976). Monetary and other explanations of the start of the great depression. *Journal of Monetary Economics, 2*(4), 455–473.

Meltzer, A. H. (1981). Comments on 'Monetarist interpretations of the great depression.' In K. Brunner (Ed.), *The great depression revisited* (pp. 148–164). Martinus Nijhoff.

Mills, F. C. (1932). *Economic tendencies in the United States*. NBER, Number 21.

Mouré, K. (1991). *Managing the franc Poincaré*. Cambridge University Press.

Mouré, K. (2002). *The Gold Standard illusion: France, the bank of France, and the international gold standard 1914–1939*. Oxford University Press.

Nelson, D. B. (1991). Was the deflation of 1929–1930 anticipated? The monetary regime as viewed by the business press. *Research in Economic History, 13*, 1–65.

Nurske, R. (1944). *International currency experience, lessons of the Interwar Period*. League of Nations.

Robbins, L. (1934). *The great depression*. Macmillan.

Samuelson, P. A. (1980). A corrected version of Hume's equilibrating mechanisms for International Trade. In J. S. Chipman & C. P. Kindleberger (Eds.), *Flexible exchange rates and the balance of payments* (pp. 141–158). North Holland.

Sumner, S. (2015). *The midas paradox*. Independent institute.

Temin, P. (1976). *Did Monetary forces cause the great depression?* Norton.

Temin, P. (1981). Notes on the causes of the great depression. In K. Brunner (Ed.), *The great depression revisited* (pp. 108–124). Martinus Nijhoff.

Temin, P. (1989). *Lessons of the great depression*. MIT Press.

Thompson, E. A. (1974). The theory of money and income consistent with orthodox value theory. In G. Horwich & P. A. Samuelson (Eds.), *Trade, stability, and macroeconomics* (pp. 427–453). Academic Press.

Thompson, E. A. (1977). A reformulation of macroeconomic theory (Discussion Paper number 91), UCLA Department of Economics.

United States Senate Seventy-Second Congress. (1932) (May 12, 13, and 18). First Session, on H.R. 11499, S. 4429. Restoring and maintaining the average purchasing power of the dollar: Hearings before the committee on banking and currency. United States Senate.

United States Statutes at Large. December 1889 to March 1901, Vol. XXX. Government Printing Office, 1901.

Warburton, C. (1953). *Depression, inflation and monetary policy: Selected papers*. Johns Hopkins University Press.

Warren, G. F., & Pearson, F. A. (1933). *Prices*. John Wiley and Sons.

CHAPTER 14

Pre-Keynesian Monetary Theories of the Great Depression: Whatever Happened to Hawtrey and Cassel? (with Ronald W. Batchelder)

14.1 Introduction

Ralph Hawtrey and Gustav Cassel, both internationally renowned business-cycle theorists (Haberler, 1937; Schumpeter, 1954), were among the most influential economists of the 1920s and 1930s. Immediately after World War I, when many governments were seeking to reconstruct the international gold standard that collapsed with the outbreak of war, Hawtrey (1919 [1923]) and Cassel (1920, 1921) both warned that restoring the gold standard without international cooperation to restrict the monetary demand for gold would cause a deflationary crisis.

The advice of Hawtrey and Cassel, later embodied in the resolutions of the 1922 international monetary conference in Genoa,[1] was that countries should restore the gold standard, while holding their monetary

[1] Black (1977: 380–381), in his memorialization of Hawtrey, observed that Hawtrey, as Director of Financial Enquiries at the British Treasury, drafted the British proposals for the Genoa Conference, working closely with Montagu Norman, Governor of the Bank of England. As a member of the British Delegation to Genoa, Hawtrey's "participation in framing the resolutions on monetary policy and central banking that were largely adopted by the Conference was perhaps the highest point of his influence in economic policy-making." The Genoa Resolutions embodied Hawtrey's view of "the most important guidelines in international economic cooperation." Hawtrey was convinced that the goal of stabilizing the purchasing power of gold could be accomplished only through cooperation among central banks.

D. Glasner, *Studies in the History of Monetary Theory*, Palgrave Studies in the History of Economic Thought,
https://doi.org/10.1007/978-3-030-83426-5_14

reserves in the form of gold-based foreign exchange (i.e., dollars and, after its convertibility into gold was restored, pound sterling) and without reintroducing circulating gold coins. By adopting the Genoa Resolutions in 1922, participating countries made a non-binding pledge to pursue the goal of monetary reconstruction by establishing an international *gold-exchange standard* such as recommended by Hawtrey (1922b [1923]) and Cassel.

However, as the pace of countries rejoining the gold standard quickened after Germany (1924) and Britain (1925) restored the gold standard, and especially when France, having stabilized the franc in 1926, enacted legislation in 1928 restoring full convertibility and requiring a 35% gold cover on the note issues of the Bank of France, the international monetary demand for gold began increasing significantly in 1928. To accumulate gold, many countries, especially France, began converting dollar- or sterling-denominated foreign-exchange reserves into gold. For the United States, having accumulated enormous gold reserves during World War I through 1924, the resulting modest drain on its gold reserves was of little consequence. But for Britain, having only just restored sterling to its prewar parity, and still facing a further relative deflation of about 10% to restore rough purchasing-power parity with the US dollar, demands to convert sterling-denominated foreign exchange into gold increased deflationary pressure on an economy still struggling to regain international competitiveness.

In 1927, the Federal Reserve System, under the leadership of Benjamin Strong, governor of the New York Federal Reserve Bank, in line with the views of Hawtrey and Cassel, reduced its discount rate from 4 to 3.5%, allowing an outflow of gold from New York to augment the less than ample gold reserves of the Bank of England, thereby easing deflationary pressures on Britain, and the world economy. Following the rate cut, stock prices rose sharply. But rising stock prices were widely viewed not as a vote of confidence in the Fed's action, but as a sign that monetary policy was fueling speculation, eliciting criticism from business leaders, the financial press, politicians, and officials of the Coolidge Administration, especially Secretary of Commerce Herbert Hoover. Stock prices continued rising even after Strong raised the discount rate back to 4%. Despite calls for another rate hike, Strong kept the discount rate at 4% until forced by ill health to relinquish his duties. Strong's deputy William

Harrison acceded to the demands to quell the stock-market boom,[2] raising the discount rate to 5% in August 1928. Then, in August 1929, with stock prices still climbing upward, Harrison raised the rate to 6%.

Hawtrey and Cassel had both urged the Fed to accommodate the growing monetary demand for gold, after France rejoined the gold standard, by not reversing a gold outflow that had started in 1927. But, by raising interest rates in 1928 and 1929, the Fed induced an inflow of cash and gold from abroad to New York, just as French demand for gold began increasing rapidly after enactment of the 1928 monetary law restoring convertibility of the franc into gold, while the creation of additional francs was prohibited except in exchange for gold or gold-backed foreign exchange. Rapidly increasing world demand for gold raised the value of gold, which, under a gold standard, meant falling money prices. Commodity prices began tumbling in the summer of 1929, and the stock market crashed in October, triggering an accelerating decline in the general price level and a contraction in output and employment. The Great Depression had begun.

Although the scenario played itself out, almost exactly as Hawtrey and Cassel had anticipated, confirming their warnings that restoring the gold standard without limiting the international demand for gold could trigger a deflationary debacle, Hawtrey and Cassel earned little recognition or even acknowledgment—then or thereafter—for anticipating the Great Depression and explaining the mechanism by which it was triggered and propagated.

What accounts for the neglect of the Hawtrey-Cassel explanationof the Depression? An obvious answer is that it was forgotten in the wake of the Keynesian Revolution. However, the *General Theory* and the Keynesian Revolution did not arrive until 1936, when the Hawtrey-Cassel explanation of the Great Depressionhad already been largely neglected and forgotten. Perhaps the disregard of the Hawtrey-Cassel explanation is attributable to a presumption at the time (a presumption also evident since the financial crisis of 2008) that the low interest rates after the 1929

[2] Perversely, Montagu Norman, governor of the Bank of England, added his voice to the chorus clamoring for a rate hike to counter stock-market speculation. Norman felt that Wall Street speculation was sucking capital from around the world into the US stock market, so that the gold reserves of the Bank of England were more endangered by rising stock prices than by rising interest rates. What Norman failed to understand was that the mechanism by which rising interest rates would check stock-market speculation was a deflationary downturn whose consequences Norman never imagined.

crash proved the impotence of monetary policy. Indeed, such was the view not just of Keynes, but of F. A. Hayek, his chief theoretical adversary in the early 1930s, who, despite blaming the crash on a supposedly easy-money policy before 1929, denied that easy money could promote recovery.

The mystery of why the Hawtrey-Cassel explanation of the Great Depressionwas forgotten is further deepened when one considers that Milton Friedman, in a largely successful campaign to promote his monetary explanation of the Great Depression never cited or referred to the pre-Keynesian monetary explanation of Hawtrey and Cassel. It is therefore worth asking, why, despite correctly anticipating the consequences of policies they warned against, the Hawtrey-Cassel explanation failed to influence contemporary discussions of the Great Depression, and why, despite anticipating key elements of the later Monetarist explanation of the Great Depression, nevertheless remained in obscurity for at least a quarter century until Glasner (1989) and Mouré (1991) first drew attention to their contribution.[3]

In this chapter, we explain why the essentially correct explanation of how trying to reconstruct the prewar gold standard in the 1920s caused the Great Depression was replaced by an incorrect, non-monetary Keynesian theory, and how the Monetarist explanation of the Great Depression that displaced the Keynesian theory was, in every respect, inferior to the

[3] Indeed, Glasner (1989), Temin (1989) Eichengreen (1992) and Bernanke(2000), Johnson (1997) and Mouré (1991, 2002) and most recently by Irwin (2012, 2014) Sumner (2015) subsequently offered explanations of the Great Depression which, in their emphasis on the role of the gold standard, and the role of the gold accumulation by the Bank of France, after 1928 largely restated the arguments made over 60 years earlier by Hawtrey and Cassel. The gold-standard explanation of the Great Depression has been widely accepted, but the fact that the explanation was largely anticipated in the work of Hawtrey and Cassel in the 1920s and 1930s has gone largely unnoticed, except by Glasner (1989), Mouré, Irwin (2012, 2014), Johnson (1997), and Sumner (2015). See Glasner (2019). We note that Irwin (2014, 201 n. 4) suggests that Hawtrey was less direct than Cassel in warning that unless the monetary demand for gold was restrained, the restoration of the gold standard would likely lead to a deflationary crisis, is unsupported by any citations from Hawtrey. As a public figure, Cassel may have been more outspoken and polemical than Hawtrey in such warnings, but Hawtrey was unequivocal in his analysis of the deflationary danger (Robertson, 1923). While Hawtrey minimized the deflationary danger of inadequate gold production that greatly concerned Cassel, his skepticism about Cassel's concern seems, rather, a point in his favor. Hawtrey's straightforward rejection of PSFM may be another reason for awarding him a slightly higher grade than Cassel on purely analytical grounds.

pre-Keynesian monetary explanation offered by Hawtrey and Cassel more than four decades earlier.

Since the first version of this chapter was written about 30 years ago, the views of the economics profession about the causes of the Great Depression have changed dramatically. A turning point was Temin (1989) who identified the gold standard as critical to an explanation of that catastrophe. While his account was important and insightful, he viewed the gold standard largely as a set of presuppositions about the appropriate, and very limited, role of monetary and fiscal policy—what Temin called the gold-standard mentality. Missing from Temin's account was an analysis of the shock that caused the downturn or the mechanism that transmitted the shock—precisely what Hawtrey and Cassel had provided.

Temin's work was soon followed by Eichengreen (1992) who filled in much of what Temin left out about the nature of the shock that caused the Great Depression and its transmission by the gold standard. While Eichengreen (1992, p. 13 n. 17) did mention works by Hawtrey and Cassel bearing on the gold standard and the Great Depression, he did not acknowledge their prior explanation of the Great Depression in terms of the gold standard, stating that although Hawtrey had criticized the policies of the Federal Reserve and the Bank of England, he had not considered the role of the Bank of France, overlooking Hawtrey's explicit criticisms of the Bank of France, especially Hawtrey (1932, ch. 1; 1933).[4] Subsequently, Bernanke (2000), further elaborating on the earlier contributions of Temin and Eichengreen, documented the role of the gold standard in both causing and transmitting the Great Depression, without mentioning either Hawtrey or Cassel.

Thus, three eminent economists, in widely acclaimed and cited works on the Great Depression between 1989 and 2000, rediscovered—more or less unknowingly—the key elements of the Hawtrey-Cassel explanation of the Great Depression, while overlooking the prior path-breaking work. Moreover, in doing so, Eichengreen, and especially Bernanke, minimized the conceptual differences between their gold-standard explanation

[4] See Glasner (2019). Eichengreen's original contributions to our understanding of the Great Depression and many other aspects of international monetary history fully justify the high esteem in which we, and the rest of our profession, hold him. We are happy to report that before Glasner (2019) noted Eichengreen's failure to acknowledge Hawtrey's priority in explaining the causes of the Great Depression, Eichengreen graciously acknowledged that he had overlooked Hawtrey's criticisms of the Bank of France.

(anticipated by Hawtrey and Cassel) of the Great Depression and the bank-failure explanation of Friedman and Schwartz (1963). The critical difference between the two explanations is that, in the gold-standard explanation, the initial shock was a sudden (but not unforeseen) increase in the demand for gold subjecting a precariously restored international gold standard to an almost immediate worldwide deflationary downturn, while, in the bank-failure explanation, the initial shock—waves of bank failures that the Federal Reserve chose not to prevent—was unrelated to the gold standard, except insofar as the shock was transmitted from the US to the rest of the world by PSFM.[5,6]

A more recent discussion of Hawtrey's role in economic policy-making also requires attention. Mattei (2018) subjects Hawtrey to critical scrutiny for his role, as Director of Financial Studies and sole economic theorist in the British Treasury, in formulating the orthodox monetary and fiscal policies that emerged from the Treasury after World War I. Largely tangential to our focus on Hawtrey's explanation of the Great Depression, we need not comment in detail on Mattei's treatment of Hawtrey. However, her characterization of Hawtrey as an orthodox supporter of the gold standard who regarded inflation as the overriding danger to be avoided and the gold standard as an essential bulwark against inflation seems one-sided, overlooking Hawtrey's deep concerns about deflation in general and especially the dangerous deflationary forces potentially let loose by restoration of the gold standard, while consistently (albeit unsuccessfully) supporting reductions in Bank Rateto counter deflationary tendencies and to promote employment. Although Hawtrey (1925) did indeed articulate the "Treasury view," his reasoning followed from the premise that Bank Rate was the only instrument necessary to control total spending and employment.

[5] Friedman (1991) himself, belatedly, acknowledged that the account of the Great Depression in the *Monetary History* did not adequately take into account the role of the Bank of France in precipitating the Great Depression, but, while doing so, he betrayed his failure to grasp the nature of the shock and the mechanism by which it was propagated. See Chapter 13.

[6] Respect for the priority of ideas also requires us to acknowledge our own indebtedness to two seminal papers on macroeconomic theory by Earl Thompson (1974, 1977), which brought the theoretical insights on which the original Hawtrey-Cassel explanation was based to our attention. Writing long after the Hawtrey-Cassel explanation had been forgotten, Thompson independently identified increased gold demand after World War I as the proximate cause of the Great Depression.

We begin our inquiry in Sect. 14.2 by summarizing the Hawtrey-Cassel theory of international price adjustment under the classical gold standard. The theory of international adjustment under the gold standard has been beset by confusion arising from two opposing traditions: a quantity-theoretic tradition derived from David Hume, which inspired the Currency School and the 1844 Bank Charter Act, and an alternative tradition derived from Adam Smith, within which the Hawtrey-Cassel theory can be easily understood, which inspired the Banking School that opposed the Bank Charter Act. Section 14.3 recounts the common, but independently formulated, views of Hawtrey and Cassel about the reconstituted postwar gold standard. In Sect. 14.4, we detail the characteristics of the regime change associated with the postwar gold standard, a change resulting from the postwar emergence of the United States as primary creditor nation, holding of 40% of the world's monetary gold reserves. Section 14.5 describes the onset of the Depression and its close correspondence to the scenario about which Hawtrey and Cassel had previously warned. In Sect. 14.6, we explore the reasons for the subsequent neglect of the Hawtrey-Cassel explanation, contrasting Hawtrey's views with those of his leading theoretical competitors in Britain: Keynes and Hayek. In Sect. 14.7, we suggest why both Keynesians and Monetarists ignored the earlier Hawtrey-Cassel explanation of the Great Depression. We conclude in Sect. 14.8.

14.2 Hawtrey and Cassel on the Theory of International Prices Under the Prewar Gold Standard

The standard textbook theory of international price adjustment under the gold standard is derived from David Hume's (1752 [2006]) famous thought experiment supposing the annihilation of four-fifths of the monetary gold in Great Britain. According to Hume, the response to the reduced British gold stock would be a proportionate reduction in British prices, causing British exports to increase and imports to decrease until Britain's gold stock was replenished (and British prices were raised) via balance-of-trade surpluses. Hume's account of international adjustment became known as the price-specie-flow mechanism (PSFM).

Although Hume's analysis became orthodoxy, not all economists agreed. Hume's friend Adam Smith, for example, ignored it in the *Wealth of Nations* (1937) despite having summarized it in his *Lectures* (1978).[7] David Ricardo, Henry Thornton, and other classical theorists associated with the Banking School also rejected PSFM in whole or in part (Chapters 2–7).

What caused dissenters to reject the Humean PSFM was their denial that prices in each country connected by trade and a common monetary unit to other countries are determined by the quantity of the common monetary unit in each country. Adherents of PSFM believed that local price levels are linked only by a long-run tendency operating through gold flows, local price levels diverging in the short from the long-run equilibrium level. Following Hume (1752 [2006], 67–68), quantity theorists believed that banks, unless subject to quantitative restraint, would overissue their liabilities. The export of gold would eventually check the expansion, but only with a lag, while national price levels diverged from equilibrium levels. A century later, the Currency School relied on PSFM and Hume's banking theory in proposing monetary reforms resulting in the 1844 Bank Charter Act. Believing that the response to international gold movements under a mixed currency (banknotes and gold circulating at par) should mimic the PSFM, the Currency School maintained that additional banknotes should be issued only by the Bank of England at the official gold price of sterling.[8]

The Banking School dissented, maintaining that arbitrage constrains the spatial variation in the value of gold without international monetary equilibrium. International gold movements were, therefore, typically

[7] The omission was characterized by Viner (1937) as one of the great mysteries in the history of economics. However, subsequent studies by Girton and Roper (1978), Humphrey (1981), Laidler (1981), Glasner (1989) and Bloomfield (1975 [1994]) have explained Smith's omission as an implicit dissent from PSFM. See also Chapters 2–4, and six. Ahiakpor (2004) has argued that Smith actually did accept the Humean theory, see Chapter 6, fn 1.

[8] The Currency School implicitly assumed an unchanging monetary demand for gold reserves, so that gold inflows or outflows would never increase or decrease the stock of gold reserves without also affecting the amount of currency in "circulation." The Banking School (e.g., Fullarton, 1845) argued that the existence of "hoards" of idle reserves would frustrate the operation of the Bank Charter Act. The implicit assumption of a fixed demand for money was a recurring lapse in the monetary discussions of the classical economists, even though they recognized, in other contexts (e.g., discussions of specific events like a financial crisis), that special circumstances could cause sudden changes in the demand for cash or liquidity (Chapters 5 and 7).

caused not by price-level differences forcing exchange rates to the gold-export or import points, but by local changes in the distribution of gold demand. Rejecting Hume's view that banks overissue liabilities, the Banking School (Fullarton, 1845) argued that banks, subject to the law of reflux, cannot systematically keep excess bank liabilities in circulation.

Later in the nineteenth-century, British monetary orthodoxy, reflecting the Currency School legacy of the Bank Charter Act tempered by some Banking School doctrines, developed policy rules ("the rules of the game") for national monetary authorities under a gold standard. Because gold flows were viewed as a sign of domestic price-level disequilibrium, monetary authorities were urged to respond to gold flows by raising (reducing) domestic interest rates, causing domestic prices to fall (rise), thereby hastening the equilibration of the domestic price level.

The orthodox view misunderstood how the gold standard worked, mistakenly identifying the gold standard with a set of "rules of the game" essential for its proper functioning (Chapter 7). Fortunately, the "rules of the game," prescribing the wrong responses by domestic monetary authorities to gold movements, were honored mostly in the breach not the observance (Bloomfield, 1959; McCloskey & Zecher, 1976).

This misunderstanding of the gold standard and the rules by which it was governed led to a mischaracterization of the necessary and sufficient conditions for its functioning.[9] Orthodox defenders of the French monetary legislation requiring the Bank of France to hold gold reserves equal to at least 35% of its outstanding note denied that a gold-exchange standard without circulating gold coins and with "unbacked" convertible banknotes was a true gold standard.[10]

But, as we understand it, the gold standard functions if and only if the issuer of a monetary unit credibly commits to convert the unit on demand into a fixed weight of gold or into another monetary unit convertible

[9] See Friedman (1961) for an extreme case of such a misunderstanding and mischaracterization and Glasner (2014) for a contrary view.

[10] The Monetary Law of June 25, 1928 (Moreau, 1991, 559): Articles 2 and 3 specified the gold content of the franc and set the rules for convertibility by the Bank of France; Article 4 specified the reserve in gold ingots and coin equal to no less than 35% of the total sum of the bearer banknotes in circulation and the current credit accounts of its depositors, and abrogated previous legal restrictions fixing the maximum sum of Bank of France notes in circulation. The stabilization legislation was drafted by the French Finance Ministry in cooperation with the Bank of France and passed the Senate and Chamber of Deputies with huge majorities.

into a fixed weight of gold. How much gold circulates or is held as reserves is immaterial to whether the gold standard is operating. Ambiguity about whether it is operating arises only insofar as doubts exist about whether the commitment will be discharged. This ambiguity is logically distinct from a legal reserve requirement, because only reserves not legally required are available to discharge the commitment (Black, 2010).

Hawtrey and Cassel departed from gold-standard orthodoxy. Although both argued that the free movement of gold ensured international commodity-price equalization in terms of gold, Hawtrey and Cassel gave somewhat different accounts of the mechanism that maintained a common international price level. In discussing the monetary and price adjustment process under a gold standard, Cassel (1932, 1–7) distinguished between different variants of a gold standard. Agreeing that a metallic currency in which only gold coins serve as means of payment would operate as described by PSFM, Cassel recognized that, once the gold standard covered most of the world, and uncovered banknotes and bank deposits were created, the automatic adjustment of the quantity of money described by PSFM no longer applied. Under the new circumstances, the goal of national monetary policy was to ensure the gold parity of its currency (which could be done with minimal gold reserves) by maintaining exchange-rate parity with other gold currencies.[11]

More closely aligned than Cassel with the Smithian monetary tradition, Hawtrey argued that commodity arbitrage ensured that the gold prices of commodities cannot differ by more than transport costs, so that price-level changes in gold-standard countries are positively correlated with each other, and uncorrelated with gold flows.[12] Relying on an arbitrage

[11] While recognizing the limitations of PSFM as a description of international adjustment under the gold standard, Cassel overlooked the inconsistency of PSFM, which implies national prices levels are negatively correlated, with the law of one price, which implies that national price levels are positively correlated.

[12] Early on, Hawtrey (1913, 180) noticed that gold movements frequently occurred even when exchange rates were within the gold points.

> It is sometimes found that gold is sent to a place where the exchanges are still far from the specie point... This is particularly the case with the Bank of France, which can defend its gold from attack under a rampart of overvalued five-franc pieces, but which is unwilling to push its use of this defense so far as to drive its notes to a discount. But quite apart from this resource it can choose its own moment for sending gold to London... and the knowledge that it will do so prevents other people from speculating in the export of gold....This advantage in controlling gold

model,[13] Hawtrey argued that market forces equalize commodities prices regardless of local monetary conditions.[14] Like Smith (Laidler, 1981) and the Banking School (Chapter 7), Hawtrey anticipated the monetary approach to the balance of payments, in which international monetary adjustment proceeds under the gold standard without relative price-level changes (Frenkel & Johnson, 1976; Samuelson 1980).[15]

While accepting PSFM in theory, Cassel, in his applied work, emphasized that national price levels would correspond to the international equilibrium level, a condition he famously called purchasing-power parity (PPP). Cassel differed from orthodox quantity theorists in linking the long-run trend in the international price level to the growth rate of the world gold stock rather than to the total quantity of money. In one study (1924), he suggested that the secular variation in the price level from 1850 to 1910 reflected changes in the gold stock relative to total output, calculating that a 3.1% annual increase in the gold stock would stabilize the international price level.[16]

> movements is open to any central bank which possesses the only large stock of gold to be found in the country in which it is situated, and consequently in practice the theory of the specie points is often found to be quite at fault.

Ricardo (1810) actually made a similar observation a century earlier. See Chapter 6.

[13] "The revolutionary changes in the means of communication," wrote Hawtrey (1932, 144), have unified markets to such a degree that... there is practically a single world market and a single world price.... It was fallacious to explain the adjustment wholly in terms of the price level. There was even at that [Ricardo's] time, an approximation to a world price."

[14] "The gold standard," wrote Hawtrey (1919, 430), "in fact, gave uniformity to the monetary unit, not only in time, but in space too. A trader could with confidence exchange a credit in his own country, not only for a future credit in the same place, but for a credit, present or future, in almost any other part of the world. In peacetime the portability of gold is such that, unless there are legal restrictions on its movement, its value can only differ very slightly in different places at the same time, and its world value remained steady enough from year to year for it to be accepted without reservation as the basis of financial contracts extending far into the future." Writing in the next issue of the *Economic Journal*, Cassel (1920, 40) stated that his "... views coincide, I think, pretty nearly with those set forth by Mr. Hawtrey in his very able and instructive article on 'The Gold Standard.'"

[15] In their introduction and historical account of the origins of the monetary approach, Frenkel and Johnson (1976) quote Hawtrey six times, more than any other author.

[16] Warren and Pearson (1933, 76–87) also estimated that a 3.1% annual increase in the monetary stocks of gold was necessary to maintain stable prices.

The legal gold-reserve requirements typically imposed by gold-standard countries on banknotes served mainly to immobilize much of the world gold stock, causing gold appreciation and deflation of prices measured in gold. Legal reserve requirements reinforced the textbook ("rules of the game") version of gold-standard operation, but the idea that causation runs from the amount of reserves to the amount of money, rather than the other way around, has no theoretical basis. As we shall see, Hawtrey and Cassel both identified such regulations, particularly those imposed by the French monetary law reestablishing the gold standard, as a major source of unnecessary demand for gold and deflationary pressure as countries restored the gold standard.

14.3 Hawtrey and Cassel on the Postwar Gold Standard

The classical gold standard governed international monetary arrangements for hardly forty years before collapsing at the start of World War I.[17] Suspending their commitments to maintain convertibility, the belligerents could use their domestic gold stocks to finance imports for the war effort. The demonetization of gold reduced the monetary demand for gold, significantly reducing its value. The depreciation was such that some neutral countries stopped *buying* gold at the official price to avoid domestic inflation. Before declaring war in 1917, the United States maintained the official parity, tolerating domestic inflation. However, the fiscal demands of the war led the United States to export gold to finance its own imports, and, like other belligerents, to prohibit unauthorized gold exports by private individuals.

A further consequence of gold depreciation was a reduced incentive to find and extract gold. Gold production during and after the war fell sharply from prewar levels, adding to deflationary pressures that later overwhelmed the world economy.

The prestige of the gold standard, perhaps owing to a nostalgic retrospective view, meant that there were few opponents to restoring the gold standard after the war. However, the wartime and postwar economic

[17] The modern gold standard first arose in England early in the eighteenth century, with other countries eventually imitating and linking to the English system. The international gold standard can be dated to the early 1870s, when most of the leading commercial countries of the world had adopted the gold standard.

and political upheavals made restoring the gold standard, in its prewar form, more problematic than was generally recognized. The perilous deflationary implications of restoring the gold standard if the monetary demand for gold was allowed to increase to prewar levels were immediately understood by Hawtrey. "We have already observed," Hawtrey (1919 [1923], 56) wrote:

> that the displacement of vast quantities of gold from circulation in Europe has greatly depressed the world value of gold in relation to commodities. Suppose that in a few years' time the gold standard is restored to practically universal use. If the former currency systems are revived, and with them the old demands for gold, both for circulation in coin and for reserves against note issues, the value of gold in terms of commodities will go up. In proportion as it goes up, the difficulty of regaining or maintaining the gold standard is accentuated. In other words, if the countries which are striving to recover the gold standard compete with one another for the existing supply of gold, they will drive up the world value of gold, and will find themselves burdened with a much more severe task of deflation than they ever anticipated.

Writing soon thereafter in the same journal, Cassel reiterated the same points. "The decrease in the monetary demand for gold," Cassel warned (1920, 39).

> in comparison with the more and more abundant supply of paper money has brought the value of gold down to about half its pre-War level, with the consequence that, as seen in the United States, the prices of commodities in gold have risen to about double what they were before the war. Though this enhancement of prices has certainly been a most injurious process, the inverse process of bringing prices down again to their old level would probably be still more disastrous.

What concerned Hawtrey and Cassel was not deflation in individual countries rejoining the gold standard at parities overvalued relative to those chosen by other countries; overvaluation could be problematic for one country, but would not be destabilizing for the international system. What Hawtrey and Cassel feared was that the countries restoring the gold standard without regard for the resulting increased monetary demand for gold would cause substantial gold appreciation. The reduced monetary demand for gold during and immediately after World War I having caused gold depreciation, increased monetary demand for gold back to prewar levels under a restored gold standard could cause potentially catastrophic gold appreciation and price deflation, back to prewar levels.

Hawtrey and Cassel therefore urged that, as countries restored the gold standard, they take cooperative measures to limit increases in their demand for gold.[18] At the 1922 Genoa Conference, Cassel unsuccessfully proposed terminating the circulation of gold coins. However, when Britain returned to the gold standardin 1925, the gold coinage was eliminated, and the convertibility of paper was into bullion, not coin.

Hawtrey and Cassel attached equal importance to encouraging central banks not to increase their gold reserves as they restored the gold standard, proposing a gold-exchange standard, in which central banks would hold reserves in the form of the convertible liabilities of the leading gold-standard countries (i.e., the United States and, after it restored convertibility, Britain) rather than gold. Doing so would prevent increases in the demand to hold gold reserves, thereby avoiding deflationary increases in the monetary demand for gold.[19]

The support of Hawtrey and Cassel for restoring the gold standard was therefore strictly conditional on an expectation that increased international monetary demand for gold would be limited by international cooperation. When consulted by Churchill in 1925 about restoring convertibility at the prewar parity, Hawtrey recommended doing so, but only on the condition that deflation be avoided, which, unlike Keynes, he felt was possible if international cooperation were forthcoming.[20]

On only one issue did Cassel and Hawtrey hold substantially different views. Cassel (1920, 40) criticized Hawtrey (1919 [1923]) for not being concerned about falling gold production caused by the wartime depreciation of gold. Reduced gold production, Cassel argued, would exacerbate the deflationary consequences of restoring the gold standard. Hawtrey

[18] Cassel also provided a restatement of the purchasing-power parity doctrine that could act as a guide for countries seeking to reestablish convertibility at new inflation-adjusted parities, thereby avoiding deflation and minimizing the effect of setting currency parities.

[19] After World War II, the IMF was instituted as a means by which to avoid such increases in the monetary demand for gold.

[20] See Moggridge (1972). Mattei's (2018) suggestion that deflation was a secondary concern of Hawtrey's is inconsistent with his explicit warnings about worldwide deflation resulting from an unmanaged restoration of the gold standard and his unceasing recommendations for reductions in Bank Rate after the 1920–1922 deflation.

(Royal Institute of International Affairs, 1932, 76) believed that future supply-and-demand conditions were too uncertain to predict, it being reasonable to imagine that gold would appreciate or depreciate over the next twenty years. Hawtrey believed that Cassel's deflation forecast overlooked the tendency of credit instruments to replace gold in mediating transactions, allowing gold to be shifted to non-monetary uses. To provide long-term price stability, the gold standard required a mechanism to accommodate excess demands for, or absorb excess supplies of, gold.

14.4 The Transformation of the Gold-Standard Monetary Regime Advocated by Hawtrey and Cassel

Aside from its extreme vulnerability to deflation, Hawtrey and Cassel emphasized another difference between the prewar and postwar versions of the gold standard: the dominance of the United States. US dominance had three causes: first, gold shipments by the Allies to pay for US exports during and immediately after the war. By 1920, US gold reserves accounted for nearly 40% of total world gold reserves, more than double its prewar holdings. Second, US exports were also financed by debts incurred to the United States, making the United States the leading creditor nation. Third, US gold reserves were concentrated within the newly created Federal Reserve System; no longer the outcome of independent decisions by US banks, the quantity of US gold reserves was now determined by the Federal Reserve.

Thus, after the war, US monetary authorities exercised unprecedented control over the value of gold. As the leading international creditor nation, the United States, by demanding repayment in gold, could significantly add to the global demand for gold, causing gold appreciation even beyond that implied by an uncoordinated gold standard restoration.[21] But given its enormous holdings of gold, the United States, by allowing or inducing a sufficient gold outflow, could reduce the real value of gold, causing international inflation. In contrast to the prewar gold standard,

[21] See Chapter 13 for a discussion of how U.S. protectionism in the form of the Hawley-Smoot tariff, combined with a tightening of monetary policy to counter stock-market speculation, caused increased gold demand as the U.S. closed off or taxed exports to the U.S., thereby increasing the cost borne by debtors in repaying their debts unless they could repay their debts in gold.

when monetary authorities could assume that the international price level was beyond their control, the world price level under a restored gold standard would depend largely on the decisions of the US monetary authorities (Hawtrey, 1922a [1923]).

Recognizing the new economic environment in which a restored gold standard would function, both Hawtrey and Cassel urged US monetary authorities to commit to price-level stabilization. Foreseeing the potential cumulative buildup of deflationary pressure as countries resumed the convertibility of their currencies into gold, Hawtrey and Cassel recommended international cooperation to avoid or limit increases in the monetary demand for gold. And given the size of its gold reserves, they recognized that the United States had a unique responsibility to tolerate gold outflows to accommodate increasing demands for gold reserves as countries rejoined the gold standard.

Although Hawtrey and Cassel gave the earliest and most complete theoretical accounts of the deflationary dangers inherent in restoring the gold standard, the underlying analysis was broadly shared by other leading theorists. Keynes (1923) argued that restoring the gold standard was probably deflationary in the short run, but likely inflationary in the long run. The potential instability in the value of gold led Keynes (1923) to oppose restoring the gold standard, proposing instead the stabilization of domestic price levels by national monetary authorities, leaving it to exchange-rate adjustments to achieve international monetary equilibrium.

Similarly, Irving Fisher (1913, 1920) recognized that fluctuations in the value of gold could cause either inflation or deflation, and proposed counteracting such fluctuations with offsetting changes in the gold content of the dollar, a proposal incompatible with the emerging role of the dollar as the dominant international currency (Cassel, 1920, 42–43). Ludwig von Mises (1924 [1934], 392–93) also recognized, to obvious dismay, that, given its huge postwar gold holdings, the value of gold was primarily determined by Federal Reserve policy, while Dennis Robertson (1928) simply noted the transformation of the prewar gold standard into a dollar standard tied to gold. "It would be misleading to say," wrote Robertson (1928, 67),

> that in America the value of money is being kept equal to the value of a defined weight of gold: but it is true even there that the value of money and the value of a defined weight of gold are being kept equal to one

another. We are not therefore forced into the inconveniently paradoxical statement that America is not on a gold standard. Nevertheless, it is arguable that a truer impression of the state of the world's monetary affairs would be given by saying that America is on an arbitrary standard, while the rest of the world has climbed back painfully on to a dollar standard.

Thus, Hawtrey and Cassel occupied a middle ground between orthodox advocates of a "rules of the game" gold standard that had not really existed before World War I and advocates of managed money such as Keynes and Fisher who, preferring domestic-price-level stabilization to an international currency, opposed restoring the gold standard in any form. However, Hawtrey and Cassel believed that the international price level in terms of gold could be stabilized, enabling the world to enjoy the benefit of a single international currency.

While holding a middle ground on policy, Hawtrey and Cassel were analytically closer to Keynes, Fisher, and others favoring price-level stabilization" than to "orthodox" proponents of the gold standard. Among those advocating restoration of the gold standard in its prewar form were a group of economists who were developing the Austrian theory of the business cycle, notably Ludwig von Mises, F. A. Hayek, Gottfried Haberler (1932), and Lionel Robbins (1934). The Austrians (e.g., Hayek, 1932 [1984], 119–120) criticized Hawtrey and Cassel for advocating a managed gold standard rather than the orthodox version.[22] According to the Austrians, by not forcing domestic money stocks to contract as gold was exported, a managed gold standard would cause an unsustainable excess of investment over voluntary savings, triggering an investment boom followed, when banks raised interest rates and restricted credit, by a bust. The Austrians would play a brief, but pivotal, role in the debates following the 1929 downturn and deflation.

14.5 The Onset of the Great Depression

Although Hawtrey and Cassel were among the leading monetary economists of the 1920s, their influence on policy, after the Genoa Conference, is hard to document. After causing the 1920–1921 depression[23] to counter postwar inflation, the Fed seemed to follow a policy

[22] See Chapter 16 for a detailed examination of Hayek's views on the gold standard during the Great Depression.

[23] The depression started in 1920 when the Federal Reserve raised its discount rate to 7%. The depression ended in the U.S. in 1921 when the Fed cut its discount rate after

consistent with the price-level-stabilization advocated by Hawtrey, Cassel, and others. However, given the deflationary pressure on Britain after restoring sterling convertibility at the prewar parity, Hawtrey favored a mildly inflationary policy by the US. Hawtrey's support for restoring the prewar dollar-sterling parity had been conditioned on an assumption that Britain could avoid a deflationary policy with the aid of mild US inflation. He consistently advocated reducing Bank Rate below the 5% level where, to his frustration, it remained almost continuously until the Bank of England, fearing a gold outflow, began raising Bank rate up to 6.5% in 1929.[24]

The writings and opinions of Hawtrey and Cassel were mentioned in the internal documents and correspondence of both Benjamin Strong and Montague Norman, especially in the early 1920s in connection with the Genoa Conference and later in 1927–1928 as the Bank of France began its rapid accumulation of gold. Strong had early reservations about the Genoa Resolutions, and his disapproval the gold-exchange standard and the Genoa Resolutions to economize on gold holdings intensified. In 1928, despite the concerns of Montague Norman and others about an impending gold shortagecaused by French gold accumulation and demands by the Bank of France on London to convert foreign exchange into gold, Strong declined to intervene on the side of the Bank of England, expressing doubts about the Genoa Resolutions and the idea of a gold-exchange standard, rejected advice by interlocutors to limit the monetary demand for gold in accord with the Genoa Resolutions.[25]

a deflation of about 25%. In Britain and other countries seeking to restore the prewar parities of their currencies against the dollar, high interest rates were maintained after the Fed cut its interest rate until 1922 so that their currencies would appreciate toward their prewar parities against the dollar. In Britain and other countries, the depression did not end until 1922.

[24] In his history of the restoration of sterling to gold at the old parity, D. E. Moggridge (1972) provided incidental information on the extent of Hawtrey's role in the decision. Alan Gaukroger (2008) in an unpublished doctoral dissertation sheds light on Hawtrey's role in Churchill's decision, but it is unclear whether Hawtrey's qualified support for restoring the prewar parity was decisive. In his testimony to the Macmillan Committee, Hawtrey argued that Britain might have induced further easing by the Federal Reserve by a preemptive reduction in Bank Rate.

[25] See Glasner (2015) for a discussion of Strong's negative views about the gold-exchange standard, the Genoa Conference and his skepticism toward Cassel's warnings about an imminent deflationary gold shortage in 1928. In his correspondence, Strong frequently expressed disdain for Cassel while the tone of his references to Hawtrey, with

In 1927, the hopes of Hawtrey and Cassel that the British restoration of the prewar dollar-sterling parity would be accommodated by Federal Reserve policy, thereby obviating further British deflation, seemed to be fulfilled. They applauded the Fed's reduction of the discount rate from 4 to 3.5% to counteract an incipient downturn. That rate cut set off a two-year stock-market rally. Despite the success of the policy, orthodox supporters of the gold standard, especially the Austrians, and even the monetary authorities, interpreted the stock-market boom as a sign of a gathering inflationary boom, an interpretation later disputed by both Hawtrey (1932, 41–83) and Cassel (1932).[26]

One of Strong's last decisions at the Fed, in February 1928, was to raise the discount rate back to 4%. In August 1928, while Strong, already in failing health, was convalescing, his deputy, George Harrison, raised the discount rate to 5% expressly to curb rising stock prices. That increase having failed to halt the stock-market boom, Harrison, who succeeded Strong after his death in October, raised the discount rate to 6% in August 1929 just after economic conditions had clearly started deteriorating.

Meanwhile, in France, after a series of weak and unstable governments had allowed the franc to depreciate from its prewar parity of 20 cents to about 2 cents in July 1926, a national-unity government was formed by Raymond Poincaré. Implementing reforms to stabilize the franc, Poincaré succeeded in restoring confidence, thereby inducing capital repatriation and further franc appreciation on the foreign exchanges. Although the franc had risen above 4 cents in the exchanges, to increase French exports and induce further foreign-exchange inflows, the government fixed the new parity at 3.92 cents.

The monetary law reinstating the gold standard enacted in June 1928 required the Bank of France to hold gold reserves equal to at least 35%

one exception, was mildly favorable. However, Carl Snyder his economic and statistical advisor at the New York Fed clearly remarked on the close agreement between Hawtrey and Cassel on the need to avoid deflation as the gold standard was restored. However, Allyn Young of Harvard, an academic advisor of Strong's, was deeply influenced by Hawtrey (Laidler, 1993) and may have served as a conduit to Strong for Hawtrey's policy recommendations, despite Strong's growing antipathy to the gold-exchange standard and the Genoa Resolutions. Unfortunately, Young died in 1929 a few months after Strong.

26 Hawtrey (1932, Chapter 2) denied that the rise in stock prices had been unjustified under the circumstances; Cassel conceded that the boom could have been fueled by speculative excesses, but denied that speculation was caused by monetary expansion.

of its outstanding sight liabilities (Eichengreen, 1986 [1990]; Hawtrey, 1932, 1–40). The law required the Bank of France to convert sufficient foreign-exchange reserves to satisfy the gold-reserve requirement. By 1932, the gold holdings of the Bank of France were nearly 60% of its note issues. The law having been drafted with the cooperation of the Bank of France and enacted with the support of the Bank, it cannot be assumed that the Bank unwillingly took the actions that caused gold accumulation.[27]

Thus, by the end of 1928, international monetary conditions were tightening as both France and the United States began importing gold from the rest of the world. Viewing these developments as a deflation portent, Hawtrey and Cassel urged the French and the US monetaryauthorities to reverse their policies. Their warnings of deflation and international financial collapse were already well known and had been discussed in the business and financial press (Nelson, 1991).[28]

After the stock-market crash, Hawtrey and Cassel condemned tight US monetary policy, pleading for monetary easing to reverse the gold inflow into the United States to counteract powerful deflationary pressures. When it became clear that the United States and other gold-standard countries would not ease monetary policy to reverse gold appreciation, Hawtrey and Cassel recommended suspending gold convertibility to avoid further deflation and reverse the deflation that had already occurred, welcoming Britain's departure from gold in September 1931. Cassel also played an important role in the Swedish suspension of the gold standard a week later and its adoption of a price-level target (Jonung, 1981).

Although Hawtrey (1913, 1919) and Cassel (1924) had already developed their own differing theories of business cycles, they agreed that

[27] After the war, the Bank of France and the Finance Ministry had become intertwined, with the Finance Ministry having a virtually unlimited ability to monetize debt issues. Èmile Moreau, Governor of the Bank of France at the time, supported a compromise to guarantee the Bank's independence. According to his published notes, Moreau (1991) had two central objectives: (1) to reestablish the convertibility of the franc into gold and (2) to establish the independence of the Bank of France from the Finance Ministry. In short, to gain independence, the Bank of France supported the gold-reserve requirement as an accommodation.

[28] See Glasner (2015) for evidence that similar warnings had been personally communicated to Strong by Montague Norman and others from November 1927 until May 1928, only to be rebuffed. Whether subsequent events would have caused him to reverse his view can only be the subject of speculation.

the 1929 downturn was not a typical business-cycle episode (Haberler, 1937, 73). They viewed the Great Depression as a special case caused by a purely deflationary shock resulting from the misguided monetary policies of the world's central banks, chiefly the Federal Reserve and the Bank of France.[29]

The abandonment of the gold standard by Great Britain, Sweden, and other countries in late 1931 allowed them to avoid the continuing downturn suffered by the United States and other countries remaining on the gold standard.[30] A severe banking crisis, triggered by fears that the newly elected President Roosevelt would take the United States off gold, started in early 1933. Upon taking office, Roosevelt declared a national bank holiday and suspended gold convertibility. In April, the administration allowed the dollar to depreciate against gold, igniting the fastest four-month expansion of industrial production in American history (a 56% increase from April through July), spurred by a 14% increase in wholesale prices, while the Dow Jones Industrial average doubled (Hawtrey, 1933).[31] Dollar depreciation ended in July, just as the newly enacted National Industrial Recovery Act forced nominal wages to rise 20%, dramatically slowing the recovery until the NIRA was ruled unconstitutional in 1935 (Sumner, 2015).

Despite the confirmation provided by these events to the Hawtrey-Cassel explanation of the Great Depression, their explanation was almost immediately forgotten or ignored by subsequent economists, including those later espousing alternative monetary explanations of the Depression. In the next two sections, we suggest some possible explanations for this puzzling gap in the historiography of the Great Depression and the history of monetary theory.

[29] Hawtrey also criticized the Bank of England for cautiously husbanding its gold reserves, arguing that the Bank of England could have altered the dominant mindset of the central bankers by adopting an aggressively expansionary policy. See Deutscher (1990, 84).

[30] Indeed, a recovery did not begin while any country remained on the gold standard.

[31] Although delayed, the U.S. recovery was initially far stronger than recoveries elsewhere. Eggertsson (2008) and Jalil and Rua (2016) attribute the exceptional strength of the initial recovery in the U.S. to the explicit goal of FDR to restore the U.S. price level to its 1926 level while in other countries the purpose of suspending the gold standard was merely to avoid further deflation. Eggertsson also credits the fiscal stimulus provided by FDR's New Deal spending policies, though as a percentage of GDP, the fiscal deficit in FDR's first term was quite small.

14.6 The Austrian Challenge and the Keynesian Revolution

Although the 1929 downturn and the downward spiral into the Great Depression are consistent with the warnings Hawtrey and Cassel had offered almost a decade earlier, there were others claiming that events had vindicated their predictions. The Austrian economists Ludwig von Mises and F. A. Hayek, for example, had warned that the Fed's credit easing in 1927 would only postpone an inevitable downturn, causing it to be deeper and more damaging than it would otherwise have been.

Unlike Hawtrey and Cassel, the Austrians considered the 1929 downturn a typical business-cycle downturn, unique only in the deliberate use of monetary policy to prolong a boom. Because easing credit in 1927 exacerbated the subsequent downturn, the Hawtrey-Cassel advice to ease monetary policy after the crash would have made matters worse by treating a disease with a remedy that was its cause.

Though the timing may be coincidental, the influence of Hawtrey and Cassel on monetary policy seems to have declined after 1927 as that of the Austrian analysis increased. Surprisingly, the deflationary implications of the Austrian theory attracted a large following, including policy makers, individuals repulsed by the greed, speculation, and financial excesses of the 1920s, and powerful creditor interests with a stake in deflation (Temin, 1989, also see Chapter 13).[32]

The Austrian theory achieved a breakthrough in 1931, when Hayek, invited by Lionel Robbins, gave four lectures on monetary and business-cycle theory at the London School of Economics. Impressive in their scholarly and analytical depth, the lectures caused a sensation among British economists, earning Hayek a position at LSE and publication of his lectures as *Prices and Production* (Hayek, 1931b).[33]

[32] The popularity of Austrian business-cycle theory may now seem less surprising than when this sentence was first written (1991). Austrian business-cycle theory has enjoyed an impressive revival, especially among committed libertarians and conservatives opposed on principal to government intervention in the economy. But even among academic economists, the Austrian theory has attracted renewed attention and interest.

[33] According to Schumpeter (1954, 1120), *Prices and Production* "met with a sweeping success that has never been equaled by any strictly theoretical book that failed to make amends for its rigors by including plans and policy recommendations or to make contact in other ways with its readers' loves or hates. A strong critical reaction followed that, at first, but served to underline the success, and then the profession turned away to

That Hayek made fundamental contributions to the understanding of intertemporal equilibria and disequilibria in monetary economies, contributions for which he won the Nobel Prize, is indisputable. However, as the economic crisis worsened in the early 1930s, it became clear to most economists, including many who were deeply influenced by Hayek at LSE, like J. R. Hicks, Abba Lerner, Nicholas Kaldor, G. L. S. Shackle, and, eventually, Robbins himself, that Hayek's policy recommendation to allow deflation to run its course[34] were indefensible.[35]

Hayek's lectures were followed by heated exchanges between Hayek and Keynes (1931) occasioned by Hayek's (1931b) critical review of Keynes (1930), followed by a withering review by Sraffa (1932) of *Prices and Production* (See Chapter 15). The controversies riveted the attention of British (and other Anglophone) economists in the early 1930s, perhaps further distracting attention from the Hawtrey-Cassel explanation of the Great Depression.

On the central policy question of deflation versus reflation, Hawtrey and Keynes, despite earlier clashes over the resumption of gold convertibility at the prewar parity and the efficacy of public expenditure in reducing unemployment (Hawtrey, 1925), were allies. Both

other leaders and other interests. The social psychology of this is an interesting matter for study."

[34] It should be noted that Hayek did later acknowledge that deflation is an inappropriate policy after a downturn, distinguishing between a business-cycle downturn, which could be self-correcting and a "secondary deflation," which, without a monetary expansion, can trigger a cumulative contraction. The distinction was not inconsistent with Hayek's idea of a neutral monetary policy, as it would imply stabilizing total nominal expenditure or aggregate demand. But that implication of Hayek's analysis was overlooked or ignored, by Hayek himself and by Robbins (1934) in applying Hayek's analysis to the Great Depression, a book Robbins later disavowed. See White (2008), and Chapters 15 and 16.

[35] Another example of Hayek's wrong-headedness was his defense of gold accumulation by the Bank of France. Despite acknowledging the plausibility of the gold-hoarding charge, Hayek (1932 [1991], 125) defended the policy.

> France did pursue an extremely cautious foreign policy after the franc stabilized at a level which considerably undervalued it with respect to its domestic purchasing power, and prevented an expansion of credit proportional to the amount of gold coming in. Nevertheless, France did not prevent her monetary circulation from increasing by the very same amount as that of the gold inflow – and this alone is necessary for the gold standard to function.

See Chapters 7 and 16 for critiques of Hayek's defense of the Bank of France.

had supported Britain's departure from gold in 1931 (though in Keynes's case, only after the fact).[36]

In the early 1930s, Keynes, though still sympathetic to Hawtrey's position that the Depression had been caused by a deflationary monetary policy, became skeptical of a monetary remedy. He had articulated his own variations on this theme in his *Treatise on Money* (1930). But after telling criticisms of its theoretical apparatus, Keynes began working in 1932 to revise that apparatus, eventually transforming it into *The General Theory* (1936) (See Chapter 12). In his earlier approach, the price level, exchange rate, and interest rate were the critical determinants of economic activity, attributing deflation and high unemployment to an overvalued exchange rate that, at the existing money-wage level, required the interest rate to be set above the level consistent with full employment. In the *General Theory*, Keynes shifted his focus to aggregate spending, arguing that the monetary authority, even with no exchange-rate constraint, might be unable to restore full employment by cutting interest rates.

Instead of attributing high unemployment to monetary mismanagement, as he and Hawtrey had previously, Keynes viewed high unemployment as characteristic of modern economies regardless of monetary policy or the exchange rate.[37] Keynes's argument in the *General Theory* that monetary expansion could not achieve full employment made no sense in the open-economy model of the *Tract* or the *Treatise*; monetary expansion and currency depreciation in one country would be expansionary, increasing the competitiveness of its tradable-goods sector but also increasing total domestic spending, causing imports to increase. Currency depreciation in one country would not cause offsetting losses in others. In Hawtrey's (1933) view, competitive devaluations were indeed a way out of depression.

From the perspective of Hawtrey and Cassel, the Keynesian Revolution, despite its important theoretical insights, was unnecessary. They

[36] Keynes sharply questioned Hawtrey when Hawtrey testified at the Macmillan Committee in 1930 and argued in favor of a policy of monetary ease. By that point, Keynes was advocating fiscal rather than monetary policy to stimulate employment, and Keynes challenged Hawtrey's argument that monetary easing by Britain would increase output and employment. On Keynes's misunderstanding of Hawtrey's argument, see Chapter 11.

[37] For an attempt to explain why Keynes wound up shifting his theoretical position in the *General Theory* more drastically than he at first intended, see Chapter 11.

viewed the Great Depression as abnormal, a special case in which world-wide deflation was caused by avoidable policy errors committed while restoring the gold standard.[38] A purely monetary explanation, which, until the early 1930s, Keynes had not disputed, was capable of accounting for the catastrophe.

However, such was its success that the *General Theory* eclipsed not only the Austrian theory, whose rapid rise was followed by an equally rapid decline, but all other monetary theories as well. For almost a generation after the *General Theory* appeared, pre-Keynesian monetary theories were ignored.[39] The only explanation of the Great Depression taken seriously was the Keynesian story of a sudden, unexplained, collapse in investment spending in 1929. Initially overshadowed by the brief Austrian ascendancy, the Hawtrey-Cassel explanation was pushed further out of sight by the Keynesian Revolution.

Perhaps another factor contributing to loss of interest in the Hawtrey-Cassel explanation of the Depression was its association with the work of Warren and Pearson (1933), who, like Hawtrey and Cassel, argued that the Depression had been caused by gold appreciation relative to commodities. Their scholarly work, notable for the diligent collection and presentation of price data, had considerable merit, providing a coherent account of the forces that brought about the Depression. However, as a Presidential advisor, Warren's advocacy of manipulating the official US price of gold to promote recovery was scorned by many economists.

After suspending convertibility in March 1933, Roosevelt, following Warren's advice, began increasing the official gold price. Warren believed that, by increasing the price of gold, the government could reflate the general price level to its pre-Depression level. As long as gold remained a monetary standard in terms of which exchange rates were reckoned, increasing the dollar price of gold meant dollar depreciation against currencies with unchanged gold prices, raising commodity prices in dollars, as occurred from April to July 1933 when a 40% rise in the dollar

[38] For example, Hawtrey (1932, 301–302), Cassel (1932). Also see Haberler (1937, 73): "Like Mr. Hawtrey, [Cassel] believes that "the economic development of post-war times has been so strikingly dominated by great monetary disturbances that trade cycles of the earlier kind are no longer applicable."

[39] An exception to this statement is the League of Nations study (1944) primarily written by Ragnar Nurkse, whose emphasis on the extent to which central banks redeemed foreign-exchange reserves for gold, reflected the influence of Hawtrey and Cassel.

price of gold was associated with a 15% rise in the wholesale price index.[40] Nevertheless, the episode, marked by FDR's obsession with manipulating the dollar price of gold, was ridiculed, causing the reputations of Warren and Pearson, and perhaps, by association, those of Hawtrey and Cassel as well, to be maligned.

14.7 The Monetarist Counterrevolution

While the Austrian challenge was rather easily surmounted, the Keynesian Revolution faced a more formidable rival a quarter century later with the rise of the Monetarist counterrevolution. The empirical studies of the effects of money and monetary policy by Milton Friedman, his students and followers, rehabilitated the idea that monetary policy had significant macroeconomic effects. Friedman and Schwartz (1963) advanced a seemingly remarkable claim that the chief cause of the Great Depression had been a series of policy mistakes by the Federal Reserve. Although Hawtrey and Cassel had also implicated the Federal Reserve in their explanation of the Great Depression, they were unmentioned by Friedman and Schwartz or by other Monetarists.[41]

The chief difference between the Monetarist and the Hawtrey-Cassel explanations of the Great Depressionis that Monetarists posited a monetary shock (bank failures) specific to the United States as the primary, if not sole, cause of the Depression, while Hawtrey and Cassel considered the Depression a global phenomenon reflecting a rapidly increasing international demand for gold, bank failures being merely an incidental and aggravating symptom, specific to the United States, of a more general monetary disorder.

[40] Sumner (2015) has argued persuasively that Roosevelt's gold price policy did serve to alter expectations about the future price of gold, thereby affecting price-level expectations, which under the monetary arrangements at that time were still linked to the price of gold even though a gold standard was not in effect. More recently Eggertsson (2008) and Jalil and Rua (2016) have provided striking evidence that the dollar devaluation after the suspension of gold payments in March 1933 boosted price-level expectations, thereby stimulating aggregate spending, output and employment, suggesting that FDR's gold-price manipulation may well have promoted the recovery.

[41] Meltzer (2003) did mention Hawtrey, but the references largely perfunctory and entirely unrelated to his (and Cassel's) explanation of the Great Depression. In earlier writings on the origins of the Great Depression, Meltzer (1976, 1981) mentioned neither Hawtrey nor Cassel, and his reasoning in discussing the role of the gold standard was limited to what is implied by the PSFM.

Arguing that the Great Depression originated in the United States following a typical business-cycle downturn, Friedman and Schwartz (1963) attributed the depth of the downturn not to the unexplained initial shock, but to the contraction of the US money stock caused by the bank failures. Dismissing any causal role for the gold standard in the Depression, Friedman and Schwartz (359–360) acknowledged only its role in propagating, via PSFM, an exogenous, policy-driven, contraction of the US money stock to other gold-standard countries. According to Friedman and Schwartz, the monetary contraction was the cause, and deflation the effect.

But the causation posited by Friedman and Schwartz is the opposite of the true causation. Under the gold standard, deflation (i.e., gold appreciation) was the cause and the decline in the quantity of money the effect. Deflation in an international gold standard is not a local phenomenon originating in any single country; it occurs simultaneously in all gold-standard countries.

To be sure, the banking collapse in the United States exacerbated the catastrophe. But the collapse was the localized effect of a more general cause: deflation. Without deflation, neither the unexplained 1929 downturn nor the subsequent banking collapse would have occurred. Nor was an investment boom in the most advanced and most productive economy in the world unsustainable as posited, with no evidence of unsustainability other than the subsequent economic collapse, by the Austrian malinvestment hypothesis.

Friedman and Schwartz based their assertion that the monetary disturbance that caused the Great Depression occurred in the United States on the observation that, from 1929 to 1931, gold flowed into, not out of, the United States. Had the disturbance occurred elsewhere, they argued, gold would have flowed out of, not into, the United States.

Table 14.1 shows the half-year changes in United States, French, and world gold reserves starting in June 1928, when the French monetary law reestablishing the gold standard was enacted.

In the three-and-a-half years from June 1928 (when gold convertibility of the franc was restored) to December 1931, gold inflows into France exceeded gold inflows into the United States. The total gold inflow into France during the June 1928 to December 1931 period was $1.563 billion compared to only $319 billion into the United States.

However, much of the difference in the totals stems from the gold outflow from the United States into France in the second half of 1931,

Table 14.1 Gold Reserves in US, France, and the world (June 1928–December 1931)

Date	*World Reserves*	*US Reserves*	*US Share (percent)*	*French Reserves*	*French Share (percent)*
June 1928	9,749	3,732	38.3	1,136	11.7
December 1928	10,057	3,746	37.2	1,254	12.4
2nd half 1928 change	312	14	-1.1	118	0.7
June 1929	10,126	3,956	39.1	1,436	14.2
1st half 1929 change	69	210	1.9	182	1.8
December 1929	10,336	3,900	37.7	1,633	15.8
2nd half 1929 change	210	−56	−1.4	197	1.6
June 1930	10,671	4,178	39.2	1,727	16.2
1st half 1930 change	335	278	1.5	94	0.4
December 1930	10,944	4,225	38.7	2,100	19.2
2nd half 1930 change	273	47	−0.5	373	3.0
June 1931	11,264	4593	40.8	2,212	19.6
1st half 1931 change	320	368	2.1	112	0.4
December 1931	11,323	4,051	35.8	2,699	23.8
2nd half 1931 change	59	−542	−5.0	487	4.2
June 1928–December 1931 change	1,574	319	−2.5	1,563	12.1

Source Johnson (1997)

reflecting fears of a possible US devaluation or suspension of convertibility after Great Britain and other countries suspended the gold standard in September 1931 (Hamilton, 2012). From June 1928 through June 1931, the total gold inflow into the United States was $861 billion and the total gold inflow into France was $1.076 billion, the US share of total reserves increasing from 38.3 to 40.8%, while the total French share increased from 11.7% to 19.6%.[42]

[42] By far, the largest six-month increase in U.S. gold reserves was in the January–June 1931 period coinciding with the two waves of bank failures at the end of 1930

In the first half of 1931, when the first two waves of US bank fail-uresoccurred, the increase in US gold reserves exceeded the increase in world gold reserves. The shift by the public from holding bank deposits to holding currency increased reserve requirements, an increase reflected in the gold reserves held by the United States. The increased US demand for gold likely exacerbated the deflationary pressures affecting all gold-standard countries, perhaps contributing to the failure of the Credit-Anstalt in May 1931 that intensified the European crisis that helped force Britain off the gold standard in September.

The combined increase in US and French gold reserves was $1.937 billion compared to an increase of only $1.515 billion in total world reserves, indicating that the United States and France were drawing reserves either from other central banks or from privately held gold stocks. Clearly, both the United States and France were exerting powerful deflationary pressure on the world economy, before and during the downward spiral of the Great Depression.[43]

Deflationary forces were operating directly on prices before the quantity of money adjusted to the decline in prices. In some countries, the adjustment of the quantity of money was relatively smooth; in the United States, it was exceptionally painful, but, not even in the United States, was it the source of the disturbance. Hawtrey and Cassel understood that; Friedman did not.

In explaining the sources of his interest in monetary theory and the role of monetary policy, Friedman (1970) pointedly distinguished between the monetary tradition from which his work emerged and the dominant tradition in London *circa* 1930, citing Robbins's (1934) Austrian-deflationist book on the Great Depression, while ignoring Hawtrey and Cassel. Friedman linked his work to the Chicago oral tradition, citing a lecture by Jacob Viner (1933) as foreshadowing his own explanation of the Great Depression, attributing the loss of interest

and in March 1931 causing a substantial shift from deposits to currency, which required an increase in gold reserves owing to the higher ratio of required gold reserves against currency than against bank deposits.

[43] Fremling (1985) noted that, even during the 1929–1931 period, the U.S. share of world gold reserves actually declined. However, her calculation includes the extraordinary outflow of gold from the U.S. in the second half of 1931. The U.S. share of global gold reserves rose from June 1928 to June 1931.

in monetary theory and policy by the wider profession to the deflationism of LSE monetary economists. Friedman went on to suggest that the anti-deflationism of the Chicago monetary tradition immunized it against the broader reaction against monetary theory and policy that the Austro-London pro-deflation bias provoked against monetary theory and policy.

Though perhaps superficially plausible, Friedman's argument ignores, as he did throughout a half-century of scholarship and research, the contributions of Hawtrey and Cassel and especially their explanation of the Great Depression. Unfortunately, Friedman's outsized influence on economists trained after the Keynesian Revolution distracted their attention from contributions outside the crude Keynesian-Monetarist dichotomy that shaped his approach to monetary economics.

Eclectics like Hawtrey and Cassel were neither natural sources of authority, nor obvious ideological foils for Friedman to focus upon. Already forgotten, providing neither convenient targets, nor ideological support, Hawtrey and Cassel, were easily, and conveniently, overlooked or ignored.

14.8 Conclusion

Despite the oblivion into which the Hawtrey-Cassel explanation of the Great Depressionfell, time was on their side. Increased interest in the international dimensions of the Great Depression and in the role of the gold standard so evident in the writings of Hawtrey and Cassel before and during the Great Depression has marked many works on the subject in the last three decades. Although the posthumous reputations of Hawtrey and Cassel have not yet been restored to the front rank of economic theorists among whom they were once counted, our early confidence that this line of historical inquiry would prove fruitful has already been vindicated.

References

Ahiakpor, J. (2004). *Classical macroeconomics: Some modern variations and distortions*. Routledge.
Bernanke, B. (2000). *Essays on the great depression*. Princeton University Press.
Black, F. (2010). *Business cycles and equilibrium* (updated ed.). John Wiley.
Black, R. D. C. (1977). Ralph George Hawtrey 1879–1975. *Proceedings of the British Academy, 63*, 363–397.

Bloomfield, A. I. (1959). *Monetary policy under the international gold standard, 1890–1914*. Federal Reserve Bank of New York.
Bloomfield, A. I. (1975 [1994]). Adam Smith and the theory of international trade. In A. S. Skinner & T. Wilson (Eds.), *Essays on Adam Smith*. Clarendon Press.
Brown, W. A., Jr. (1940) *The international gold standard reinterpreted, 1914–1934* (2 vols). National Bureau of Economic Research.
Cassel, G. (1920). Further observations on the world's monetary problem. *Economic Journal, 30*(117), 39–44.
Cassel, G. (1921). *The world's monetary problems: Two memoranda*. E. P. Dutton.
Cassel, G. (1924). *The theory of social economy* (J. McCabe, Trans.). Harcourt.
Cassel, G. (1928). The rate of interest, the bank rate, and the stabilization of prices. *Quarterly Journal of Economics, 42*(4), 511–529.
Cassel, G. (1932). *Memorandum of dissent*. In League of Nations (1932).
Deutscher, P. (1990). *R. G. Hawtrey and the development of macroeconomics*. University of Michigan Press.
Eichengreen, B. (1986 [1990]). The Bank of France and the sterilization of gold, 1926–1932. *Explorations in Economic History, 23*(1), 56–84. In Eichengreen *Elusive stability: Essays in the history of international finance, 1919–1939* (pp. 83–112). Cambridge University Press.
Eichengreen, B. (1992). *Golden fetters*. Cambridge University Press.
Eichengreen, B., & Temin, P. (2000). The gold standard and the great depression". *Contemporary European History, 9*(2), 183–207.
Eggertsson, G. (2008). Great expectations and the end of the great depression. *American Economic Review, 98*(4), 1576–1616.
Fausten, D. (1979). The Humean origin of the contemporary monetary approach to the balance of payments. *Quarterly Journal of Economics., 93*(4), 655–673.
Ferrell, R. H. (1952). *Peace in their time: The origins of the Kellogg-Briand pact*. Yale University Press.
Fetter, F. W. (1965). *The evolution of British monetary orthodoxy, 1797–1875*. Harvard University Press.
Fisher, I. (1913). *The purchasing power of money*. Macmillan.
Fisher, I. (1920). *Stabilizing the dollar*. Macmillan.
Flanders, M. J. (1990). *International monetary economics, 1870–1960*. Cambridge University Press.
Fremling, G. (1985). Did the United States transmit the great depression to the rest of the world? *American Economic Review, 75*(4), 1181–1185.
Frenkel, J. A., & Johnson, H. G. (1976). The monetary approach to the balance of payments: Essential concepts and historical origins. In J. A. Frenkel & H. G. Johnson (Eds.), *The monetary approach to the balance of payments* (pp. 21–45). G. Allen and Unwin.

Friedman, M. (1961). Real and pseudo gold standards. *Journal of Law and Economics, 4*(2), 66–79.

Friedman, M. (1970). Comments on the critics. In R. J. Gordon (Ed.), *Milton Friedman's monetary framework* (pp. 132–185). University of Chicago Press.

Friedman, M. (1991). Preface. In *The Golden franc, memoirs of a Governor of the Bank of France: The Stabilization of the franc (1926–1928)* (S. D. Stoller & T. C. Roberts, Trans.). Westfield Press.

Friedman, M., & Schwartz, A. J. (1963). *A monetary history of the United States, 1867–1960*. Princeton University Press.

Fullarton, J. (1845). *On the regulation of currencies* (2nd ed.). John Murray.

Girton, L., & Roper, D. (1978). J. Laurence Laughlin and the quantity theory of money. *Journal of Political Economy., 88*(3), 599–625.

Glasner, D. (1989). *Free banking and monetary reform*. Cambridge University Press.

Glasner, D. (2014). Real and pseudo gold standards: Could Friedman tell the difference? In *Uneasy money*. https://uneasymoney.com/2014/08/27/real-and-pseudo-gold-standards-could-friedman-tell-the-difference/.

Glasner, D. (2015). The great, but misguided, Benjamin Strong goes astray in 1928. In *Uneasy money*. https://uneasymoney.com/2015/06/24/the-great-but-misguided-benjamin-strong-goes-astray-in-1928/.

Glasner, D. (2019). Friedman and Schwarts, Eichengreen and Temin, Hawtrey and Cassel. In *Uneasy money*. https://uneasymoney.com/2019/01/23/friedman-and-schwartz-eichengreen-and-temin-hawtrey-and-cassel/.

Gaukroger, A. (2008). *The director of financial enquiries: A study of the treasury career of R. G. Hawtrey (1919–1939)*. Doctoral Thesis, University of Huddersfield.

Haberler, G. (1932). Money and the business cycle. In Q. Wright (Ed.), *Gold and monetary stabilization* (pp. 7–20). University of Chicago Press.

Haberler, G. (1937). *Prosperity and depression*. League of Nations.

Hamilton, J. D. (1987). Monetary factors in the great depression. *Journal of Monetary Economics, 19*, 145–169.

Hamilton, J. D. (1988). The role of the international gold standard in propagating the great depression. *Contemporary Policy Issues, 6*(2), 67–89.

Hamilton, J. D. (2012). *Comment on Irwin* (2012).

Hawtrey, R. G. (1913). *Good and bad trade*. Constable and Company.

Hawtrey, R. G. (1919). *Currency and credit*. Longmans, Green, and Co.

Hawtrey, R. G. (1919 [1923]). The gold standard. *Economic Journal, 29*(116), 428–42. Reprinted in Hawtrey, *Monetary reconstruction* (pp. 48–65). Longmans, Green, and Co.

Hawtrey, R.G. (1922a [1923]). The Federal Reserve System of the United States. *Journal of the Royal Statistical Society, 85*(2), 224–269. Reprinted in Hawtrey, *Monetary Reconstruction* (pp. 93–130). Longmans, Green, and Co.

Hawtrey, R. G. (1922b [1923]). The Genoa resolutions on currency. *Economic Journal, 32*(127), 290–304. Reprinted in Hawtrey, *Monetary Reconstruction* (pp. 131–47). Longmans, Green, and Co.
Hawtrey, R. G. (1925, March). Public expenditure and the demand for labour. *Economica, 13*, 38–48.
Hawtrey, R. G. (1932). *The art of central banking*. Longmans, Green, and Co.
Hawtrey, R. G. (1933). *Trade depression and the way out* (2nd ed.). Longmans, Green, and Co.
Hawtrey, R. G. (1947). *The gold standard in theory and practice* (5th ed.). Longmans, Green, and Co.
Hayek, F. A. (1931a). Reflections on the pure theory of money of Mr. J. M. Keynes. *Economica, 33*, 270–295.
Hayek, F. A. (1931b). *Prices and production*. G. Routledge and Sons.
Hayek, F. A. (1932 [1984]). The fate of the gold standard. Translated from German and reprinted in R. McCloughry (Ed.), F. A. Hayek, *Money, Capital, and Fluctuations: Early Essays* (pp. 118–35). University of Chicago Press.
Hayek, F. A. (1937). *Monetary nationalism and international stability*. Longmans, Green and Company.
Hume, D. (1752 [2006]). Of the balance of trade. In E. Rotwein (Ed.), *Economic writings of David Hume* (pp. 60–77). Routledge.
Humphrey, T. R. (1981). Adam Smith and the monetary approach to the balance of payments. *Federal Reserve Bank of Richmond Economic Review, 67*(6), 3–10.
Irwin, D. A. (2012). The French Gold Sink and the great deflation of 1929–32. *Cato Papers on Public Policy, 2*, 3–41.
Irwin, D. A. (2014). Who anticipated the great depression? Gustav Cassel versus Keynes and Hayek on the interwar gold standard. *Journal of Money, Credit and Banking, 46*(1), 197–228.
Jalil, A. J., & Rua, G. (2016). Inflation expectations and recovery in Spring 1933. *Explorations in Economic History, 62*(4), 26–50.
Johnson, H. C. (1997). *Gold, France, and the great depression, 1919–1932*. Yale University Press.
Jonung, L. (1981). The depression in Sweden and the United States: A comparison of causes and policies. In K. Brunner (Ed.), *The great depression revisited* (pp. 286–315). Martinus Nijhoff.
Keynes, J. M. (1923). *A tract on monetary reform*. Macmillan and Company.
Keynes, J. M. (1930). *A treatise on money*. 2 vols. Macmillan and Company.
Keynes, J. M. (1931). The pure theory of money: A reply to Dr. Hayek. *Economica, 34*, 387–397.
Keynes, J. M. (1936). *The general theory of employment, interest, and money*. Macmillan.

Laidler, D. (1981). Adam Smith as a monetary economist. *Canadian Journal of Economics, 14*(2), 185–200.
Laidler, D. (1988). British monetary orthodoxy in the 1870s. *Oxford Economic Papers, 40*(1), 74–109.
Laidler, D. (1993). Hawtrey, Harvard, and the origins of the Chicago tradition. *Journal of Political Economy, 101*(6), 1068–1103.
League of Nations. (1932). *Report of the gold delegation of the financial committee*. League of Nations.
League of Nations (Ragnar Nurkse, et al). (1944). *International currency experience: Lessons of the interwar period*. League of Nations.
Machlup, F. (1931). *The stock market, credit, and capital formation*. W. Hodge.
Mattei, C. E. (2018). Hawtrey, austerity, and the 'treasury view', 1918 to 1925. *Journal of the History of Economic Thought, 40*(4), 471–492.
McCloskey, D. N., & Zecher, J. R. (1976). How the gold standard worked, 1880–1913. In J. A. Frenkel & H. G. Johnson (Eds.), *The monetary approach to the balance of payments* (pp. 357–385). George Allen and Unwin.
Meltzer, A. H. (1976). Monetary and other explanations of the start of the great depression. *Journal of Monetary Economics, 2*(4), 455–473.
Meltzer, A. H. (1981). Comments on 'monetarist interpretations of the great depression.' In K. Brunner (Ed.), *The Great Depression Revisited* (pp. 148–164). Martinus Nijhoff.
Meltzer, A. H. (2003). *A history of the federal reserve, vol. 1: 1913–1951.* University of Chicago Press.
Mises, L. (1924 [1934]). *The theory of money and credit* (2nd ed.). Jonathan Cape.
Moggridge, D. E. (1972). *British monetary policy, 1924–1931: The norman conquest of $4.86*. Cambridge University Press.
Moreau, E. (1991). *The golden Franc, memoirs of a Governor of the Bank of France: The Stabilization of the Franc (1926–1928)* (S. D. Stoller & T. C. Roberts, Trans.). Westfield Press.
Mouré, K. (1991). *Managing the Franc Poincaré*. Cambridge University Press.
Mouré, K. (2002). *The gold standard illusion: France, the Bank of France, and the International Gold Standard, 1914–1939*. Oxford University Press.
Nelson, D. B. (1991). Was the deflation of 1929–1930 anticipated? The monetary regime as viewed by the business press. *Research in Economic History., 13*, 1–65.
Pigou, A. C. (1920). *Memorandum on credit, currency, and exchange fluctuations*. League of Nations (Submitted to the Brussels International Financial Conference 1920).
Pigou, A. C. (1941). *The political economy of war*. Macmillan.
Ricardo, D. (1810 [1951]). *The high price of bullion: A proof of the depreciation of bank notes*. John Murray.

Robertson, D. H. (1923). Review of Hawtrey (1923) in *Economic Journal, 33*(130), 204–207.
Robertson, D. H. (1928). *Money* (2d ed.). Cambridge University Press.
Robbins, L. C. (1934). *The great depression*. Macmillan.
Royal Institute of International Affairs. (1932). *The international gold problem: Collected papers*. Oxford University Press.
Samuelson, P. A. (1980). A corrected version of Hume's equilibrating mechanisms for international Trade. In J. S. Chipman & C. P. Kindleberger (Eds.), *Flexible exchange rates and the balance of payments* (pp. 141–158). North Holland.
Schumpeter, J. A. (1954). *History of economic analysis*. Oxford University Press.
Selgin, G. (1988). *The theory of free banking: Money supply under competitive note issue*. Rowman and Littlefield.
Smith, A. (1937). *The wealth of nations* (E. Cannan, Ed.). Modern Library.
Sraffa, P. (1932). Dr. Hayek on money and capital. *Economic Journal, 42*(165), 42–53.
Sumner, S. (2015). *The midas paradox: Financial markets, government policy shocks, and the great depression*. Independent Institute.
Temin, P. (1989). *Lessons from the great depression*. MIT Press.
Thompson, E. A. (1974). The theory of money and income consistent with orthodox value theory. In G. Horwich & P. A. Samuelson (Eds.), *Trade, stability, and macroeconomics* (pp. 427–453). Academic Press.
Thompson, E. A. (1977). *A reformulation of macroeconomic theory*.
Thompson, E. A., & Hickson, C. R. (2000). *Ideology and the evolution of vital institutions: Guilds, the gold standard, and modern international cooperation*. Kluwer.
Viner, J. (1933). *Balanced deflation, inflation, or more depression*. University of Minnesota Press.
Viner, J. (1937). *Studies in the theory of international trade*. Harper and Brothers.
Warren, G. F., & Pearson, F. A. (1933). *Prices*. John Wiley & Sons.
White, L. H. (1984). *Free banking in Britain: Theory, experience, and debate, 1800–1845*. Cambridge University Press.
White, L. H. (2008). Did Hayek and Robbins deepen the great depression? *Journal of Money, Credit and Banking, 40*(4), 751–68.

CHAPTER 15

The Sraffa-Hayek Debate on the Natural Rate of Interest (with Paul Zimmerman)

15.1 Introduction

The pivotal role of Piero Sraffa's (1932a) review of F. A. Hayek's *Prices and Production* (1931b) in turning professional opinion against Hayek's business-cycle theory, clearing the ground for the subsequent Keynesian ascendency, is well known to historians of economics.[1] Sraffa's criticism of Hayek's restatement and elaboration of Mises's (1912 [1934]) business-cycle theory, and his failure to respond effectively, reinforced the impression that Sraffa had exposed critical flaws in Hayek's theory.[2]

Hayek's goal was to show that the business cycle could be avoided if monetary disturbances were eliminated and that those disturbances could be avoided by a neutral-money policy in which the monetary authority sets the interest rate on bank loans equal to the "natural" rate of interest. Sraffa's attack on Hayek was two-pronged, criticizing both the idea of a neutral-money policy to stabilize or dampen the business cycle and the

[1] See, e.g., Lawlor and Horn's (1992, n. 3) discussion of Lachmann's recollection of the Hayek-Sraffa debate (stating in part: "What is particularly interesting about Lachmann's account... is his view that Sraffa's review was a critical factor in Hayek's fall from stature as an economic theorist in the 1930s").

[2] The Sraffa-Hayek exchange has been reviewed extensively, e.g., by Kurz and Salvadori (2003), Kurz (2003), and Desai (1995).

D. Glasner, *Studies in the History of Monetary Theory*, Palgrave Studies in the History of Economic Thought, https://doi.org/10.1007/978-3-030-83426-5_15

coherence of the underlying concept of a natural rate of interest.[3] Our attention in this chapter is on Sraffa's second criticism: that the concept of a "natural rate of interest"—at least Hayek's version of it—is incoherent. According to Sraffa, Hayek's conception of the natural rate of interest—the rate of interest determined solely by real forces in a pure barter equilibrium—is incoherent, because multiple commodity (or own) rates of interest exist in a growing barter economy with savings and investment, none of them having a special claim to be *the* natural rate of interest. If no single commodity rate can be identified as *the* natural rate to serve as the criterion for monetary policy, Hayek's proposal for a neutral-money policy based on *the* natural-rate collapses.

To show that no commodity rate of interest in a barter economy can be identified as *the* natural rate, Sraffa explained that, in a barter economy in which loans cannot be executed in monetary terms, all loans would be denominated in terms of specific commodities, with a corresponding "own rate" of interest defined for each commodity (Lawlor and Horn, p. 392).[4] Thus, the rate at which any commodity could be "borrowed" today and repaid in the future would define the own rate for that commodity.

Sraffa analogized such transactions to a cotton spinner that borrows money to buy spot cotton at the current price and then to sell forward at the current forward, in effect borrowing cotton now and contracting for future repayment. The ratio of the forward price to the spot price of cotton would determine the cotton own rate over the term of the loan. Transactions equivalent to such commodity loans can be executed in any economy with forward and spot commodity markets. Arbitrage would ensure that the own rate for commodity loans would exactly correspond to the ratio of the forward and spot prices of that commodity in terms of money (or any numeraire).

While Sraffa acknowledged that, in a static equilibrium, characterized by unchanging prices over time, own rates for all commodities would be equal, he denied that the equality would be preserved in a

[3] Note that Hayek (1931b) referred to the natural rate as the "equilibrium" rate of interest. For Hayek, the terms appear to have synonymous; however, his use of the terms in his reply to Sraffa is problematic. See below Sect. 15.6.

[4] While Sraffa first developed the notion of the own rate, he did not call it that. Rather, as discussed later, "own rate" is the term that Keynes used for that concept in the General Theory.

growing economy with changing relative prices. In a growing economy, the resulting multiplicityof own rates renders the notion of a unique natural rate of interest defined by pure barter relationships incoherent. And only a growing, capital-using, economy is susceptible to the kind of business-cycle analyzed by Hayek. Because deviations from the uniform equilibrium rate of interest can occur even in a barter economy, Hayek's assignment of blame for business cycles to the introduction of bank-supplied credit money was misplaced. But, even more problematically, the very notion of a unique natural rate of interest when there could be multiple commodity rates of interest was incoherent, there being no basis on which to select any of those commodity rates as *the* natural rate of interest.

> [I]n times of expansion and production ... there is no such thing as an equilibrium (or unique) natural rate of interest, so that the money rate can neither be equal to, nor lower than it: the 'natural' rate of interest on producer's goods, the demand for which has relatively increased, is higher than the 'natural' rate on consumers' goods, the demand for which has relatively fallen. (Sraffa, 1932a, 51)

Facing this challenge to the coherence of the key concept of his theory, Hayek (1932) offered a seemingly ineffective defense easily dismissed by Sraffa. Hayek's weak response provided the grounds for other economists to dismiss a theory both counterintuitive and uncongenial to their policy preferences, but whose logic had initially seemed persuasive.

Our thesis is that Hayek's notion of a unique natural rate is not, as Sraffa charged, incoherent. Hayek's understanding of the uniqueness of the natural rate is also consistent with Fisher's (1896) prior discussion and supported by Keynes (1936) himself, deploying by name Sraffa's own-rate analysis, in Chapter 17 of the *General Theory*, to show that individual own rates converge on an equilibrium rate of return adjusted for the real-service yield of the asset, expected appreciation, and the cost of storage.[5] That equilibrium net rate of return corresponds to the natural

[5] Majewski (1988) and Mongiovi (1990) discuss the influence of Sraffa's work on the development of Chapter 17 in the *General Theory*. An extensive subsequent literature on the relationship between Sraffa's analysis of the commodity rate and Keynes's adaptation of that analysis in Chapter 17 has developed. See Grieve (2015) and Nardi (2015) and citations therein. We found Grieve's discussion especially useful and would agree with his

rate identified by Hayek. The correspondence between Keynes's treatment of own rates and Hayek's understanding of a unique natural rate of interest, originally noted by Lachmann (1956), deepens the puzzle about Hayek's ineffectual response to the charge of incoherence brought against him by Sraffa.

To avoid misunderstanding, let us make clear what we are, and what we are not, asserting. Sraffa made two arguments against Hayek: First, business cycles could result from causes other than nominal interest-rate reductions by banks below the natural rate, and rate reductions could occur without necessarily triggering a business-cycle downturn; second, and more fundamentally, the notion of a natural rate of interest, though perhaps defensible in the sense in which Wicksell used it, was, in Hayek's sense, incoherent.

We take issue only with the second criticism. We maintain that, even in a barter system, the variation among own rates is constrained by arbitrage, so that, as Keynes (1936, Chapter 17) argued, borrowers and lenders would be indifferent between borrowing and lending in terms of one commodity rate or another. Nevertheless, readers of earlier drafts of this chapter have noted that Sraffa disagreed with Keynes's treatment of own rates in and his conclusion that borrowers and lenders would be indifferent between loans whatever the commodity in which they were denominated. Perhaps so.[6] But we need not show that Sraffa would necessarily have accepted an argument by Hayek that the net advantages

resolution of the apparent inconsistencies between Keynes's discussion and Sraffa's discussion. Grieve notes that while Sraffa couched his analysis in the rate paid by borrowers, Keynes's analysis focused on the expected rate of return to asset holders. Thus, the difference between them can be reduced to a difference in perspective, not substance. We therefore agree with Grieve that Sraffa's criticisms of Chapter 17 were terminological rather than substantive.

[6] There are two levels of ambiguity. The first is whether Sraffa disagreed with Keynes's substantive argument as some have alleged, or whether his disagreement was merely terminological. See Grieve (2015) and additional references cited therein. The second is whether if Sraffa disagreed with Keynes on substance, Sraffa was right and Keynes was wrong. But even if the latter, there is no evidence to our knowledge that Sraffa thought that Keynes's position was incoherent. Indeed, Sraffa argued that in Chapter 17 Keynes was inconsistent with Fisher's own-rate analysis; if the disagreement was substantive, Sraffa was siding with Fisher against Keynes. In Sect. 15.4, we restate Sraffa's argument in Fisherian terms, but the argument of Sect. 15.6 establishes that the Hayek'snatural-rate concept was consistent with Fisher's distinction between real and nominal rates and Keynes's argument in Chapter 17.

of borrowing and lending under barter would be equalized in whichever commodity loans were denominated. Sraffa did not argue that Hayek's analysis was wrong, but that it was incoherent. We show that Hayek could have explained that there is, under his understanding of a barter economy, an equilibrium real own rate and that the various nominal own rates are equilibrium own rates, so that borrowers and lenders are indifferent between borrowing and lending at any of the nominal own rates corresponding to each commodity. Sraffa might have rejected that argument if Hayek had made it, but there is nothing senseless or incoherent about it.

This chapter proceeds as follows. Section 15.2 discusses the historical background of Sraffa's review. Section 15.3 summarizes Sraffa's critique and Hayek's response. In Sect. 15.4, noting the formal equivalence between Sraffa's treatment of own rates, and Fisher's (1896) distinction between real and nominal rates, we restate Sraffa's own-rate analysisin Fisherian terms. In Sect. 15.5, Hayek's ineffectual response to Sraffa's criticism is discussed. In Sect. 15.6, we argue that Hayek's assertion of a unique natural rate is conceptually supported by Keynes's (1936, Chapter 17) discussion of own rates and, after appropriate adjustments, their necessary equality in equilibrium. However, establishing that Hayek's position about a unique natural rate was not incoherent does not mean that the natural rate provides an operational, much less a useful, criterion for banking and monetary policy. Section 15.7 offers concluding remarks including thoughts about why Hayek did not consider alternatives to the natural-rate criterion, alternatives that would have been more consistent with his theoretical approach and more useful than the conceptually coherent, but unobservable, natural-rate criterion.

15.2 Background Leading Up to the Debate

Perhaps the key analytical concept developed by Hayek in his early work on monetary theory and business cycles was the idea of an intertemporal equilibrium. Before Hayek, the idea of equilibrium was confined to a stationary state in which economic agents continue doing what they have been doing. Equilibrium represents an end state in which all adjustments to a set of initial conditions have been fully worked out. Seeking to generalize this narrow concept to make it applicable to the study of business cycles in which he was engaged, Hayek defined equilibrium not in terms of the stationarity of objective or measurable magnitudes, but as the mutual consistency of the decentralized, subjectively optimal, plans of economic agents.[7] The potential consistency of these plans may be conceived of even if economic magnitudes fluctuate, as long as fluctuations are correctly foreseen.

The meaning of correct foresight in this context relates to the need for agents making plans about future production and consumption to either know or anticipate future prices. Insofar as forward markets for planned future transactions are unavailable, agents must formulate plans based not on observed, but expected, prices, plans being optimized conditional on expectations of future prices. When actual prices differ from what they had been expected to be, optimized plans are likely to be changed, but the revision of plans after unexpected price changes is itself likely to induce further price changes, so a sequence of revisions of once-optimal plans in response to unanticipated price changes need not lead to a new equilibrium in which price expectations are correct and plans are optimized and mutually consistent (Radner, 1987).

The congruence of expectations is not guaranteed by a priori assumptions about the predictive power of agents; it is merely assumed that agents at a particular moment share common price expectations, so that, conditional on those expectations, the individually formulated plans will be mutually consistent. Hayektherefore distinguished between correct foresight and the more commonly used term "perfect foresight," with its connotation of superhuman knowledge and predictive powers.[8] The assumption of correct foresight does not exclude the possibility, indeed the inevitability, that new information falsifying previous price expectations will become available (see Chapter 17). Intertemporal

[7] Hayek (1937) provided a definitive statement of his conception of intertemporal equilibrium, with a subsequent restatement provided in Hayek (1941). But Hayek's (1928 [1984]) first statement of the concept was published nearly a decade earlier.

[8] Hayek (1937) explains that the equilibrium concept can be weakened so that even correct foresight is not necessary. All that is required is that the individual expectations of economic agents be consistent so that they could be validated by some possible future contingency. The resulting plans would then constitute an equilibrium relative to the information possessed by the agents at a given moment. Even if the expectations are eventually disappointed, the plans formulated were in equilibrium with respect to each other in the sense that they were mutually consistent and could have been realized had the expected state of the world been realized.

equilibriumrequires merely contingently correct anticipation, not perfect foresight of, future prices.[9]

Starting from a state of intertemporal equilibrium, Hayek traced the disturbing influence of money on the intertemporal structure of price relationships, and hence, on the intertemporal structure of production. An equilibrium structure of intertemporal prices corresponds to the Wicksellian natural rate matching the rates of intertemporal substitution in production and consumption, thereby determining the optimal length or roundaboutness of production processes via the choice among production processes of varying degrees of capital intensity and roundaboutness. Insofar as banks provide entrepreneurs with financing for investment projects without utilizing the voluntary savings of households, the equilibrium reconciliation of intertemporal plans to produce and consume is disturbed, implying the deviation of future prices from the prices that were expected, thereby requiring the eventual revision of the pre-existing network of mutually consistent plans.

Hayek posited a credit expansion induced by banks setting their lending rate[10] below the natural rate as the initiating monetary disturbance that starts the cycle. As a consequence, the prices of investment goods would rise relative to consumption goods, reflecting increased entrepreneurial demand for investment given the reduced interest rates charged by banks on loans. The resulting adoption of overly roundabout production processes (termed by Hayek "malinvestments") by entrepreneurs borrowing at below-equilibrium interest rates would restrict the output of consumption goods, causing their prices to rise as well, tending to reduce consumption spending overall, a phenomenon described by Hayek as forced savings. Corresponding to "overinvestment" induced by a below-natural rate of interest, household consumption would be restricted by the increased relative prices of current

[9] By defining correct foresight as a contingent outcome rather than as an essential property of economic agents, Hayek elegantly avoided the problems confounding Oscar Morgenstern (1935 [1976]) in his discussion of the meaning of equilibrium. See Chapter 17.

[10] The bank rate of interest, sometimes referred to as the "actual," "money," or "market" interest rate, is the rate banks charge borrowers of credit for financing capital investment.

consumption goods reflecting the shift of output from consumption to investment goods.[11]

For Hayek, monetarily-induced lengthening of the capital structure is the key factor generating the business cycle, the price-level effect on which Wicksell (1898 [1936]) and Keynes (1930) had focused, being of secondary importance. Hayek argued that, because monetarily induced lengthening of the capital structure is unsustainable, the crisis, or upper-turning point of a cycle, occurs when the inconsistencies between intertemporal plans occasioned by monetary expansion cause disappointment of expectations, making some plans prohibitively costly to execute, triggering a cascade of plan revisions and disappointments, and a state of general economic discoordination. The unraveling of plans constitutes the downturn and the contraction phase of the cycle.

The implied policy message for banks and especially central banks is to keep the market rate of interest equal to the natural rate corresponding to a state of intertemporal equilibrium. Hayek maintained that such an interest-rate policy would neutralize the distorting effect of money, eliminating distortions in the capital structure induced by monetary expansion.[12] As discussed further in Sect. 15.6, the problem is the unobservability of the natural rate, which renders Hayek's policy recommendation non-operational.

15.3 Sraffa's Critique

Hayek developed these ideas in a series of publications in the late 1920s and early 1930s, including most notably his 1931 lectures at the London School of Economics, subsequently published as *Prices and Production* (1931b), and his review (1931a) of Keynes's *Treatiseon Money*, exposing

[11] Our short outline of the argument of *Prices and Production* should not be construed to mean that Hayek viewed the business cycle as an equilibrium phenomenon. Intertemporal equilibrium provides a benchmark of comparison against which the disturbances introduced by credit expansion are analyzed. Deviations from an equilibrium path create countervailing forces rendering the initial deviations unsustainable, leading to a potentially unstable adjustment toward a new equilibrium path. The cycle reflects a time path away from, and back to, an equilibrium path. The natural-rate criterion was intended to avoid deviations from intertemporal equilibrium induced by monetary forces.

[12] That is, with the rate of interest held at the natural rate, a monetary expansion by banks to finance investments in excess of voluntary savings, a state of affairs that could not obtain in a barter equilibrium, would not occur.

conceptual problems in its analytical framework. Stung by Hayek's criticisms, Keynes (1931) issued an ill-natured response, quickly shifting from a reply to Hayek's criticisms to an attack on Hayek and *Prices and Production*, a response deplored even by Keynes's admiring biographer Roy Harrod (1951).

Perhaps realizing that his reply to Hayek had misfired, Keynes, then editor of the *Economic Journal*, enlisted the formidable Piero Sraffa to write a review of *Prices and Production*. It is hard to imagine that Sraffa would have written a negative review on order, but it can be assumed that Keynes was not displeased with the review Sraffa submitted.

Sraffa's first criticism was to conjecture that the capital distortion identified by Hayek was caused not by an increased quantity of money, but by a change in its *distribution* (Sraffa, 1932a, 48–49). Sraffa also suggested that it was possible that the accumulation of capital associated with forced saving was not, as Hayek supposed, unsustainable[13]; the augmented capital stock financed by monetary expansion might well drive the natural rate of interest down to the level of the reduced money rate, an outcome whose possibility von Mises (1912 [1934]) himself had conceded.

Our concern in this chapter is with Sraffa's second criticism of Hayek: the incoherence of the natural rate of interest as defined by Hayek. Sraffa observed that in a barter economy borrowing and lending would take place not in terms of a non-existent medium of exchange, but in terms of specific commodities. For any commodity in terms of which a loan might be contracted, an own rate of interest for borrowing and repayment in terms of that commodity could be defined. That own rate of interest would correspond to the ratio of the forward and spot prices of that commodity (Sraffa, 1932a, 50–51).[14] Sraffa used the ratio of forward to spot prices as a heuristic device to engage the intuition of readers rather than an actual description of how loans would be made. Even so, the constraint of forward prices, reflecting expectations of the future that would constrain the own rates agreed upon in a barter setting, even absent forward markets, cannot be ignored in reasoning about the

[13] The meaning of "unsustainable" in Austrian business-cycle is both vague and problematic.

[14] As noted by Hagemann (2008) and discussed further below, the concept of an own rate of interest can be traced back to Fisher (1896). Fisher's concept was adopted by Sraffa and then by Keynes.

behavior of own rates in a barter economy. And Hayek would surely have been entitled to posit their existence in framing a reply to Sraffa.

The ratio of the forward to the spot prices of any commodity being market-determined, Sraffa argued that, in some circumstances, those ratios would not be equalized across commodities. If so, Hayek's claim that it is the operation of the banking system that causes the market interest rate to diverge from the natural rate is meaningless, because no single own rate of interest toward which all other own rates would gravitate could be identified. If there are different own rates for different commodities, then none of them is uniquely natural, so deviations of the market rate from the natural rate cannot be attributed, as Hayek did, to operation of the banking system.

It will be instructive to follow the own-rate analysis Sraffa uses against Hayek, his argument being more complicated than a bare assertion that the distinct own rates for individual commodities may be unequal. After quoting Hayek's assertion that, in a money economy, the money rate of interest may diverge from the equilibrium (natural) rate, Sraffa observed:

> An essential confusion, which appears clearly from [Hayek's] statement, is the belief that the divergence of rates is a characteristic of a money economy: and the confusion is implied in the very terminology adopted, which identifies the "actual" with the "money" rate, and the "equilibrium" with the "natural" rate. If money did not exist, and loans were made in terms of all sorts of commodities, there would be a single rate which satisfies the conditions of equilibrium, but there might be at any one moment as many "natural" rates of interest as there are commodities, though they would not be "equilibrium" rates. The "arbitrary" action of the banks is by no means a necessary condition for the divergence; if loans were made in wheat and farmers (or for that matter the weather) "arbitrarily changed" the quantity of wheat produced, the actual rate of interest on loans in terms of wheat would diverge from the rate on other commodities and there would be no single equilibrium rate. (Sraffa, 1932a, 49)

Sraffa correctly observes that, owing to a change in demand or supply, particular own rates might deviate from their (static) equilibrium values. However, such deviations are not, as Sraffa suggested, analogous to the deviations from equilibrium associated with a monetary disturbance, the deviations toward which Hayek directed his attention. Deviations from equilibrium caused by fluctuations in the supply of real commodities would not persist; market forces would operate immediately to restore an equilibrium with all own rates again equalized, a tendency not mentioned by Sraffa, though two paragraphs later Sraffa acknowledged that, in equilibrium, all own rates must be equal.

> In equilibrium the spot and forward prices coincide, for cotton as for any other commodity; and all the "natural" or commodity rates are equal to one another, and to the money rate. But if, for any reason, the supply and the demand for a commodity are not in equilibrium (i.e. its market price exceeds or falls short of its cost of production), its spot and forward prices diverge, and the "natural" rate of interest on that commodity diverges from the "natural" rates on other commodities. (Sraffa, 1932a, 50)

Perhaps thinking of a stationary equilibrium in which prices do not change rather than the intertemporal equilibrium analyzed by Hayek, Sraffa, positing a change in demand, traced the effect of the change in demand on the relationship between spot and forward prices.

> Suppose there is a change in the distribution of demand between various commodities; immediately some will rise in price, and others will fall; the market will expect that, after a certain time, the supply of the former will increase, and the supply of the latter fall, and accordingly the forward price, for the date on which equilibrium is expected to be restored, will be below the spot price in the case of the former and above it in the case of the latter; in other words, the rate of interest on the former will be higher than on the latter. (Id.)

Inferring from the shift in demand and consequent price adjustment that own rates of interest need not be equalized, Sraffa argued that a unique natural rate does not exist. But Sraffa overlooked that the divergence in own rates in his example might be accounted for by anticipated changes in the prices of individual commodities. Thus, the alleged divergence of own rates to which Sraffa drew attention could be understood as reflecting Fisher's (1896) distinction between the real and the nominal rate of interest. What Sraffa called a multiplicity of own rates might be viewed as a multiplicity of nominal own rates reflecting the expected appreciation or depreciation of those commodities for which demand was increasing or decreasing. Given those expectations, borrowers and lenders would be indifferent between contracting loans at own rates corresponding to either commodity. If Sraffa's example exposed a flaw in the theory of interest, the flaw is not only Hayek's; it is also Irving Fisher's. Sraffa's thought experiment did not show that the natural rate, expressed as a real rate (adjusted for expected price changes) is not unique.

Sraffa further observed that Hayek could have avoided the problem of a non-unique natural rate by adopting Wicksell's definition of a price level as an appropriately weighted average of the money prices of individual commodities. By extension, Hayek could then have defined the natural rate as a weighted average of the own rates of individual commodities (Sraffa, 1932a, 51). But that option, as Sraffa (1932b, 251) noted, had been foreclosed to Hayek by his rejection of statistical price levels in his review of Keynes's *Treatiseon Money*.[15] The observation is correct, but Sraffa overstated its significance, overlooking the distinction between the unique (real) natural rate and the multiplicity of nominal rates consistent with the unique natural rate, depending on expected appreciation or depreciation of the commodity whose (nominal) own rate is being determined. Defining the natural rate in terms of a constant price level pins down a nominal rate; the real rate was already pinned down by Fisher's analysis.

15.4 Deconstructing Sraffa's Critique

It may be helpful, using Fisherian terminology, to restate our argument about the uniqueness of the *real* own rate of interest under Sraffian barter conditions. Consider a barter economy with two commodities, tomatoes and cucumbers, whose prices are expressed in terms of a third commodity, say, onions serving as the numeraire. We begin with an initial equilibrium, expressing own rates of interest for tomatoes and cucumbers, as follows:

$$(1 + i_t) = (1 + r_t) \text{ x } \left({}^{f_t}/_{s_t}\right)$$ [16]

$$(1 + i_c) = (1 + r_c) \text{ x } \left({}^{f_c}/_{s_c}\right)$$

where i_t and r_t are the nominal and real own rates of interest for loans in terms of tomatoes and f_t and s_t are the forward and spot prices for

[15] See Hayek (1931a).

[16] In Fisher (1896), the ratio of the forward price to the spot price is expressed as (1 + *a*), where "*a*" denotes the expected rate of appreciation in the price of the commodity, i.e., the ratio of the forward to the spot price.

tomatoes expressed in terms of the numeraire, onions. Similarly, i_c and r_c are the nominal and real own rates of interest for loans in terms of cucumbers and f_c and s_c are the forward and spot prices for cucumbers in terms of onions.

In a static equilibrium with unchanging prices, spot and forward prices are the same, so the above equations reduce to the following:

$$i_t = r_t$$

$$i_c = r_c$$

If borrowers and lenders are indifferent between borrowing or lending in terms of one commodity or another, then the real own rates are equal, i.e., $r_t = r_c$. The equality of real rates established by arbitrage implies that $i_t = i_c$.

Thus, in static equilibrium all real and nominal own rates are equal, and a unique natural rate of interest is well-defined. However, Sraffa argued that a deviation from static equilibrium, causing a temporary increase in the price of one commodity, say tomatoes, and a decrease in the price of another, say cucumbers, would be expected to be temporary, causing the spot and forward prices of the commodities to diverge, and, therefore, the real own rates of the two commodities to diverge. From the inequality between two or more own rates, Sraffa concluded that Hayek's conception of the natural rate of interest is incoherent.

Sraffa's argument for the multiplicity of own rates hinged on an argument that borrowers and lenders would expect the future price of tomatoes to fall and the future price of cucumbers to rise. But given that expectation, borrowers would prefer to borrow from lenders offering to lend in terms of cucumbers and lenders would prefer to lend in terms of tomatoes. Competition between borrowers to borrow and lenders to lend would constrain the terms at which borrowers and lenders were making loans to adjust until, at the margin, borrowers and lenders, given their expectations of the appreciation of cucumbers and depreciation of tomatoes, were indifferent between borrowing and lending in terms of either commodity. The tomato own rate on loans would have to be sufficiently greater than the cucumber own rate to compensate for the expected difference between the expected rates of appreciation of two commodities.

The argument can be restated formally by assuming that forward prices for tomatoes and cucumbers are posted in forward prices, but the tendency toward elimination of differential incentives to borrow or lend in terms of either commodity exists even without observable forward prices. The assumption of explicit forward prices shows the outcome to which incentives to profit from expected differences in the prices of tomatoes and cucumbers lead, by converting speculative profit opportunities into arbitrage opportunities. The consequent indifference between borrowing and lending in terms of either commodity undermines Sraffa's argument that there is a multiplicityof own rates.

Consider the sort of case posited by Sraffa: a shift in demand between tomatoes and cucumbers raising the spot price of cucumbers and lowering that of tomatoes. Sraffa asserted that the deviation from long-term equilibrium would be temporary, implicitly assuming constant long-run costs for both commodities (Arrow & Starret, 1973). Given that deviations of the prices of cucumbers and tomatoes from their long-run equilibrium values are only temporary, the forward and spot prices for both commodities would no longer be equal, forward cucumber prices being below and forward tomato prices above their spot values.

The following relationships must hold after a demand shift causes tomato and cucumber spot prices to diverge from long-run equilibrium values:

$$(1 + i_t^*) = (1 + r_t^*) \text{ x } \left({}^{f_t}/_{s_t^*}\right)$$

$$(1 + i_c^*) = (1 + r_c^*) \text{ x } \left({}^{f_c}/_{s_c^*}\right)$$

where starred variables represent post-demand-shift values. Because the shift in demand raises the spot price of cucumbers and reduces the spot price of tomatoes, while leaving forward prices unchanged, we have.

$$\left({}^{f_t}/_{s_t^*}\right) > \left({}^{f_t}/_{s_t}\right)$$

$$\left({}^{f_c}/_{s_c^*}\right) < \left({}^{f_c}/_{s_c}\right)$$

Since $(f_t/s_t) = (f_c/s_c)$, it follows that $\left({}^{f_t}/_{s_t^*}\right) > \left({}^{f_c}/_{s_c^*}\right)$. From this inequality, Sraffa inferred that, after a temporary disturbance of a static equilibrium, not all own rates of interest are equal, so that there is no natural rate. But Sraffa overlooked the arbitrage constraint on real own rates. When fully effective, the arbitrage constraint ensures that $r_t^* = r_c^*$. If that equality holds, given the forward prices of cucumbers and tomatoes, borrowers and lenders would be indifferent between contracting loans in terms of cucumbers or tomatoes.

Let $r^*{}_t = r^*{}_c = r^*$. Thus, a unique real own rate of interest can be identified after the demand shift posited by Sraffa, namely r^*, and it can also be defined as the natural rate of interest. Hayek's conception of the natural rate therefore is not incoherent; it is consistent with Fisher's distinction between the real and nominal rates of interest, corresponding to the real own rate, whose existence is ensured by the arbitrage constraint. Sraffa's critique of Hayek was ultimately a critique of Fisher's distinction between real and nominal rates; the critique of Fisher was not explicit, only implied.

Such a critique might have taken either of two forms. First, it might deny that the concept of a real rate of interest is coherent. After all, loans are contracted in terms of nominal, not real rates. But Sraffa, himself, acknowledged that, given expectations of differential rates of appreciation, nominal rates adjust to reflect differences in expected appreciation. The adjustment to expected appreciation is evidence that real rates matter. Second, it might deny that the unique real rate that existed before the hypothesized demand shift equals the unique real rate, r^*, that obtains after the demand shift. If the unique real rate is not invariant to demand shifts, then Sraffa's critique would only have been conjectural, not absolute. We shall have more to say about this question below in Sect. 15.6.

15.5 Hayek's Response

Hayek's (1932) response to Sraffa seemed ineffectual, appearing to concede Sraffa's point that multiple own rates of interest are possible in a barter economy. While conceding the point, Hayek denied that the concession compromised his position, thereby appearing to ignore, or not even to grasp, how damaging the concession was for his position.

> I think it would be truer to say that ... there would be *no single rate* which, applied to all commodities, would satisfy the conditions of equilibrium rates, but there might, at any moment, be as many "natural" rates of interest as there are commodities, *all* of which would be *equilibrium*

> rates; and which would all be the combined result of the factors affecting the present and future supply of the individual commodities, and of the factors usually regarded as determining the rate of interest. (Hayek, 1932, emphasis in original)

Without elaboration, Hayek simply withdrew behind an evasive statement ("The inter-relation between these different rates of interest is far too complicated to allow of detailed discussion within the compass of this reply"), suggesting that he was incapable of framing a counterargument to Sraffa's attack. The previous two sections have shown that the inter-relation between the different rates of interest was less complicated than Hayek suggested.

From his terse commentary about multiple natural rates, Hayek shifted to a discussion of the related, though possibly second-order, issue of whether the effects following from any one natural (own) rate of interest in a barter economy being "out of equilibrium" would be comparable to the effects arising in a monetary economy when the money rate diverged from the natural rate.[17] Silent on how to implement his policy rule in a monetary economy with multiple natural rates, Hayek left unanswered Sraffa's criticism that, in the ideal barter economy serving as his conceptual benchmark, a multiplicity of natural rates is possible, with none having a claim to serve as the criterion for a neutral monetary policy.

Sraffa's (1932b, p. 251) rejoinder chided Hayek for conceding the existence of multiple natural rates without responding to his substantive criticism:

> Dr. Hayek now acknowledges the multiplicity of the "natural" rates, but he has nothing more to say on this specific point than that they "all would be equilibrium rates." The only meaning (if it be a meaning) I can attach to this is that his maxim of policy now requires that the money rate should be equal to all these divergent natural rates.

In other words, Hayek's new position on the natural rate was either unresponsive or nonsensical.

[17] Hayek (1932, p. 246) maintains that the latter, but (in general) not the former, will lead to disequilibrium outcomes ("I certainly believe that it is possible in this case to change 'artificially' the rate of interest in a sense in which this... cannot be said of any commodity").

But Hayek'sresponse may be interpreted more charitably than Sraffa did; it could be interpreted in a way that is at least suggestive of our criticism of Sraffa's own-rate analysis and of Lachmann's (1956) argument that, even under barter, arbitrage would force the distinct own rates to converge on a common equilibrium value, with due allowance for differences in real service yields, expected appreciation, and storage costs.

We digress briefly to note a terminological ambiguity. We showed in the previous section that the existence of a unique real own rate follows immediately from the existence of forward markets providing a tight arbitrage constraint. Even without forward markets, a tendency toward a unique real own rate follows from the expectations of future price changes that Sraffa himself invoked to establish the existence of multiple own rates. The arbitrage constraint operating even without the existence of an intertemporal equilibrium, Lachmann's argument for a unique real own rate holds even without a full intertemporal equilibrium.[18]

Having himself previously (1928 [1984]) argued that anticipated price changes are not inconsistent with intertemporal equilibrium, Hayek did not deny the divergence of nominal own rates of interest. His response was problematic in not distinguishing between the unique real own rate embedded in divergent nominal own rates constrained by arbitrage and divergent anticipated rates of commodity appreciation.

But such a response would have required Hayek to enlarge his conception of what constitutes a neutral-money policy. This was a concession he was unable or unprepared to make. He would have had to acknowledge that multiple rates of monetary expansion are consistent with a neutral-money policy provided that price expectations are correct. But Hayek's conception of a neutral monetary policy did not allow him to do so.

15.6 Keynes to the Rescue?

Given Keynes's stake in refuting Hayek's analysis in *Prices andProduction*, his selection of Sraffa to write a review of *Prices and Production*, and his adoption in Chapter 17 of the *General Theory* of Sraffa's own-rate analysis, it is remarkable that Chapter 17 actually provided the analytical tools with which Hayek could have responded to Sraffa's criticism of his

[18] See F. M. Fisher (1983) who used the arbitrage constraint as an alternative to tâtonnement in proving the stability of a general equilibrium.

conception of the natural rate of interest.[19] This curiosum went unnoticed for over twenty years until Lachmann (1956), Hayek's student at LSE, but also an admirer of Keynes, relied on Chapter 17 to explain that, even in a barter system, the *expected* return (including the pecuniary and non-pecuniary yields plus price appreciation, net of storage costs) tend to be equalized for all assets held from period to period. Three decades later, commenting on his earlier defense of Hayek and Lachmann (1986, 238; first emphasis added) wrote:

> If there is a multiplicity of commodity rates, it is evidently possible for the money rate of interest to be lower than some but higher than others. What, then, becomes of monetary equilibrium? …
>
> It is not difficult, however, to close this particular breach in the Austrian rampart. In a barter economy with free competition *commodity arbitrage would tend to establish an overall equilibrium rate of interest*. Otherwise, if the wheat rate were the highest and the barley rate the lowest of interest rates, it would become profitable to borrow in barely and lend in wheat. Inter-market arbitrage will tend to establish an overall equilibrium in the loan market such that, in terms of a third commodity serving as *numéraire*, say, steel, it is no more profitable to lend in wheat than in barley.

Lachmann (id.) went on to conjecture what arbitrage activity implies for the *expected* own rates of return in intertemporal equilibrium:

> This does not mean that actual own-rates must all be equal, but that the disparities are exactly offset by disparities between forward prices. The case is exactly parallel to the way in which international arbitrage produces equilibrium in the international money market, where differences in local interest rates are offset by disparities in forward rates. In overall equilibrium, it must be impossible to make gains by "switching" commodities as in currencies.

[19] Fisher (1896) had already provided the basic framework for Keynes's analysis, earlier exploited by Keynes (1923) in his analysis of covered interest arbitrage. Chapter 17 generalized the framework to encompass liquidity preference, providing a theory of the interaction between the demand for money and the yield on assets held from period to period. Although he claimed too much for his liquidity preference theory, his analysis of liquidity preference and liquidity premium remains foundational for the theory of asset valuation and interest-rate determination.

Thus, while own rates in intertemporal equilibriummay differ, the differences are subject to the condition that the expected returns from holding every asset must be equalized, any divergence of expected returns triggering readjustments of asset valuations. Lachmann argued that the weakness of the natural-rate concept is not that it pertains to a barter, rather than a monetary, economy, but that it can be defined uniquely only in the context of full intertemporal equilibrium, which, Lachmann believed, rendered it useless as a policy criterion.

But Lachmann conceded too much, because, in the presence of forward markets, the arbitrage constraint operates without intertemporal equilibrium. Sraffa, himself, related the divergence of own rates to the ratios between forward and spot prices in commodity markets, because own rates are constrained by those ratios.[20]

While Keynes adopted Sraffa's own-rate analysis and rejected the natural-rate concept, which he had expounded upon in the *Treatise*, his reasons for doing so differed from Sraffa's:

> In my *Treatise on Money* I defined what purported to be a unique rate of interest, which I called the *natural rate* of interest—namely, the rate of interest which ... preserved equality between the rate of saving ... and the rate of investment ... I had, however, overlooked the fact that in any given society there is, on this definition, a *different* natural rate of interest for each hypothetical level of employment. And, similarly, for every rate of interest there is a level of employment for which the rate is the "natural" rate, in the sense that the system will be in equilibrium with that rate of interest and that level of employment. Thus it was a mistake to speak of *the* natural rate of interest or to suggest that the above definition would yield a unique value for the rate of interest irrespective of the level of employment. (Keynes, 1936, 242) (emphasis in original)

Thus, for Keynes, "non-uniqueness" of the natural rate refers not to a multiplicity of own rates, but to the possibility that different natural rates of interest hold in different equilibrium states *corresponding to differing levels of employment*. That is to say, while there is a particular natural rate corresponding to the full-employment equilibrium, there may be different

[20] Murphy (2010), though a devoté of Austrian business-cycle theory, defends Sraffa's criticism of Hayek's use of the natural rate of interest, rejecting Lachmann's defense that there is a tendency even in a pure barter economy for equality among own rates, as Keynes explained in Chapter 17. The problem with Murphy's discussion is that he mistakenly believes that there is real significance to the choice of the numeraire in terms of which prices are quoted.

"natural" rates corresponding to equilibria at less than full employment. Thus, for any level of employment, the real own rates of interest would all converge to the same "unique" rate corresponding to a particular level of equilibrium employment. As we noted in discussing Sraffa's argument against a unique own rate of interest, it is entirely possible for the unique real own rate to change after a shift in demand.[21]

This view of multiple natural rates is different from Sraffa's criticism of Hayek's conception of the natural rate, which concerned differing own rates of interest across commodities and assets held from period to period, a possibility Keynes dismissed in Chapter 17. No divergence between real own rates would be observed if expectations of differential returns caused asset prices to change.[22] Even if (nominal) *gross* own rates of return differ across commodities held from period to period, anticipated *net* real rates of return across these assets must be equalized; otherwise, profits are being foregone. Taking money as the standard measure of value, Keynes (1936, 227; emphasis added) made this very point:

> To determine the relationships between the expected returns on different assets *which are consistent with equilibrium*... let the expected percentage appreciation (or depreciation) of houses be a_1 and of wheat $a_2.q_1$, $-c_2$, and l_3 we have called the own-rates of interest of houses, wheat and money in terms of themselves as the standard of value... with this notation it is easy to see that the demand of wealth owners will be directed at houses, to wheat or to money according as $a_1 + q_1$, $a_2 - c_2$, or l_3 is greatest.

This realization in turn leads Keynes (pp. 227–228; first emphasis added) to the following unambiguous conclusion:

> Thus *in equilibrium* the demand-prices of houses and wheat in terms of money will be such that there is nothing to choose in the way of advantage between the alternatives, *i.e.*, $a_1 + q_1$, $a_2 - c_2$, and l_3 will be *equal*.

[21] See Glasner (2018) for a criticism of the implicit assumption that the real interest rate in the Fisher equation is unique. The assumption is clearly untenable when expected inflation falls at zero lower bound. In such cases the nominal rate, being bound from below the Fisher equation can only be satisfied by an increase in the real rate.

[22] And if there are reasons to believe that the adjustment of "disequilibrium" natural (own) rates would be sticky, one will not find them laid out in the *General Theory*.

Of course, there are reasons why such a result might not hold, e.g., informational imperfections discussed by Grossman and Stiglitz (1980), butSraffa was not implicitly relying on such notions in his review of Hayek.

Viewed in this light, it may be possible, as we suggested in the previous section, to construe Hayek's seemingly ineffectual response to Sraffa in a more favorable light than has been customary. His apparent concession that own rates might indeed be different may have been no more than an acknowledgment that differences in service flows or storage costs or expected appreciation could account for differences in *nominal* own rates. However, for equilibrium to obtain, such differences would be such as to equalize the net expected *real* returns from holding different assets. But if Hayek had fully grasped the distinction, he ought to have articulated the difference less cryptically than he did. So, while we cannot be confident that Hayekperceived the gist of Keynes's argument, there may be reason to reconsider the received view that Hayek's response to Sraffa was ineffectual.

15.7 Conclusion

Although we have argued that Sraffa's criticism of Hayek's business-cycle theory and his criterion for a neutral-money policy was less damaging than it seemed to subsequent commentators, we make no claim to have rehabilitated Hayek's cycle theory or his natural-rate criterion. We claim only that Sraffa's charge that Hayek'sconception of the natural rate of interest is incoherent was not proven, because the natural rate referenced by Hayek was simply the unique Fisherian *real* rate of interest of which Keynes himself provided a generalized exposition in Chapter 17 of the *General Theory*.

It may be worth mentioning that the Fisherian basis of Keynes's own-rate analysis in Chapter 17, on which Keynes (1923) had previously relied in his theory of covered interest-rate arbitrage, is difficult to reconcile with Keynes's (1936, 142) strident criticism of the Fisher equation relating the nominal rate of interest to the real rate plus expected inflation. Presumably, Keynes directed his criticism at the implicit assumption in the Fisher equation that the real rate is independent of expected inflation. However, the reasoning behind Keynes's attack on the Fisher equation remains difficult to grasp and seems, at least superficially, at odds with his own-rate discussion in Chapter 17.[23]

In fact, the source of intertemporal disequilibrium identified by Hayek—equality between the market rate and the natural rate of interest—could not serve as a criterion for neutral money, because neutral money could be achieved at any nominal rate of interest if price expectations are aligned with the nominal rate of interest set by the monetary authority. Hayek, one of the originators of the concept of intertemporal equilibrium, was equipped to grasp that point, but failed to transcend a reflexive attachment to the notion of a unique nominal natural rate.

But even within his limitations, Hayek was groping for an alternative to equality between the nominal interest rate and a nominal natural rate as the criterion for neutral money. Hayek (1931b, Chapter 4) introduced an alternative criterion of neutral money: a constant stream of spending (MV). If the quantity of money were adjusted to keep total spending constant, changes in the money stock (M) would just offset changes in the demand to hold money $\left(\frac{1}{V}\right)$. Under such circumstances, Hayek felt that money would have no disturbing effect on economic activity. Excess cash would not drive up prices, nor would a deficiency of cash drive them down. Prices would adjust only to changes in productivity implying corresponding changes in cost. Unlike the equality between the nominal interest rate and a supposedly unique nominal natural rate, the constant-total-spending criterion was at least defined in terms of an observable magnitude.

To Hayek's discredit, and later regret, and despite the reasons he himself had advanced for constant MV as a policy criterion, he relentlessly advocated deflationary policies to counter the Great Depression (See Chapter 16).[24] Had he followed the implications of his own analysis, Hayek would have supported reflation during the Great Depression to restore MV to its pre-crash level and would have been allied with, rather

[23] The reconciliation would presumably focus on the distinction between the relation between different nominal rates at a point in time, reflecting different rates of expected depreciation at that time of different assets, and how an exogenous change in expected appreciation would change the previous relationship between the nominal and the real rates.

[24] On Hayek's conflicting policy positions during the Great Depression, see White (2008).

than opposed to, Keynes and other supporters, like Hawtrey, Cassel, and Fisher, of monetary easing to promote recovery from the Great Depression. Exactly why Hayek chose to advocate policies inconsistent with his own theoretical position is a question that ought to engage Hayek scholars for some time to come.

References

Arrow, K. J., & Starrett, D. A. (1973). *Cost- and demand-theoretical approaches to the theory of price determination.* In Carl Menger and the Austrian school of economics, J. R. Hicks and W. Weber (eds.), 129–48. Clarendon Press.

Desai, M. (1995). The task of monetary theory: The Hayek-Sraffa debate in a modern perspective. *Macroeconomics and monetary theory: The selected essays of Meghnad Desai* (pp. 39–60). Edward Elgar.

Fisher, F. M. (1983). *The disequilibrium foundations of general equilibrium.* Cambridge University Press.

Fisher, I. (1896). *Appreciation and interest.* Macmillan.

Glasner, D. (2018). *The fisher equation at the financial crisis of 2018.* Mercatus Center

Grieve, R. H. (2015). Keynes and Sraffa on own-rates: A present-day misunderstanding. *Contributions to Political Economy, 34*, 1–16.

Grossman, H., & Stiglitz, J. E. (1980). On the impossibility of informationally efficient markets. *American Economic Review, 70*(3), 393–408.

Hagemann, H. (2008). Interest, own rate of. *International Encyclopedia of the Social Sciences.*

Harrod, R. (1951). *A life of John Maynard Keynes.* Harcourt, Brace.

Hayek, F. A. (1928 [1984]). The intertemporal equilibrium system of prices and the movements of the monetary value, translated from German and reprinted in R. McCloughry (Ed.), F. A. Hayek, *Money, capital, and fluctuations: Early essays* (pp. 28–74). University of Chicago Press.

Hayek, F. A. (1931a). Reflections on the pure theory of money of Mr. J. M. Keynes. *Economica, 11*(33), 270–295.

Hayek, F. A. (1931b). *Prices and production.* G. Routledge and Sons.

Hayek, F. A. (1932). Money and capital: A reply. *Economic Journal, 42*(2), 237–249.

Hayek, F. A. (1937). Economics and knowledge. *Economica, N.S., 4*(13), 33–54.

Hayek, F. A. (1941). *The pure theory of capital.* University of Chicago Press.

Keynes, J. M. (1923). *A tract on monetary reform.* Macmillan.

Keynes, J. M. (1930). *A treatise on money.* 2 vols. Macmillan.

Keynes, J. M. (1931). The pure theory of money: A reply to Dr. Hayek. *Economica, 11*(34), 387–397.

Keynes, J. M. (1936). *The general theory of employment, income and money*. Macmillan.
Kurz, H. D. (2003). The Hayek-Keynes-Sraffa controversy reconsidered. In H. D. Kurz & N. Salvadori (Eds.), *The legacy of Piero Sraffa* (Vol. 1, pp. 257–447). Edward Elgar.
Kurz, H. D. (2011). Keynes, Sraffa and the latter's secret skepticism. In B. Bateman, T. Hirai, & M. C. Marcuzzo (Eds.), *The return to Keynes* (pp. 184–204). Belknap Press.
Kurz, H. D., & Salvadoi, N. (2003). Introduction. In H. D. Kurz & N. Salvadori (Eds.), *The legacy of Piero Sraffa* (Vol. 1, pp. xvii–xx). Edward Elgar.
Lachmann, L. M. (1956). *Capital and its structure*. Bell & Sons.
Lachmann, L. M. (1986). Austrian economics under fire: The Hayek-Sraffa duel in retrospect. In *Expectations and the meaning of institutions* (pp. 141–158).
Lawlor, M. S., & Horn, B. L. (1992). Notes on the Sraffa-Hayek exchange. *Review of Political Economy, 10*(3), 317–340.
Majewski, R. (1988). The Hayek challenge and the origins of chapter 17 of Keynes' *General Theory*. In H. Hagemann & O. Steiger (Eds.), *Keynes' General Theory nach funfzing Jahren* (pp. 99–112). Duncker und Humblot.
Mises, L. v. (1912 [1934]). *The theory of money and credit*. Jonathan Cape.
Mongiovi, G. (1990). Keynes, Hayek and Sraffa: On the origins of chapter 17 of *The General Theory*. *Economie Appliquée, 43* (2), 131–56.
Morgenstern, O. (1935 [1976]). Perfect foresight and economic equilibrium. In A. Schotter (Ed.), *Selected economic writings of Oscar Morgenstern* (pp. 169–183). New York University Press.
Murphy, R. P. (2010, September 16–19). *Multiple interest rates and Austrian business cycle theory*. Paper presented to Liberty Fund Conference "Symposium on Business Cycles and the New Economic Reality," San Diego, CA. Available at http://consultingbyrpm.com/uploads/Multiple%20Interest%20Rates%20and%20ABCT.pdf.
Nardi, N. (2015). Sraff and Keynes on the concept of *commodity* rates of interest. *Contributions to Political Economy, 34*, 17–30.
Panico, C. (1988). Sraffa on money and banking. *Cambridge Journal of Economics, 12*(1), 7–28.
Radner, R. (1987). Uncertainty and general equilibrium. In J. Eatwell, M. Milgate, & P. Newman (Eds.), *The New Palgrave Dictionary of Economics*. Macmillan.
Schumpeter, J. A. (1954). *The history of economic analysis*. Oxford University Press.
Sraffa, P. (1932a). Dr. Hayek on money and capital. *Economic Journal, 42*(1), 42–53.
Sraffa, P. (1932b). A rejoinder. *Economic Journal, 42*(2), 249–251.

White, L. H. (2008). Did Hayek and Robbins deepen the great depression? *Journal of Money Credit and Banking, 40*(4), 561–578.

Wicksell, K. (1898 [1936]) *Interest and prices*. Royal Economic Society (Macmillan).

CHAPTER 16

Hayek, Deflation, Gold and Nihilism

Few economists ever experienced as rapid a rise to stardom as F. A. Hayek did after arriving in London in January 1931 to deliver a series of four lectures on the theory of industrial fluctuations at the London School of Economics. The Great Depression having started over a year earlier, British economists were desperately seeking new insights into the unfolding and deteriorating economic catastrophe. The subject on which Hayek was to expound was of more than academic interest; it was of the most urgent economic, political and social, import.

Only 31 years old, Hayek, director of the Austrian Institute of Business Cycle Research, had never held an academic position.[1] He had received his doctorate in law from the University of Vienna in 1924, but had written a doctoral thesis in economic theory under Friedrich von Wieser, a founding father of the Austrian School of Economics. Upon graduation, Hayek spent over a year in the United States doing research on business cycles, establishing relationships with such leading American experts on business cycles as W. C. Mitchell and Warren Persons, while also undertaking an exhaustive study of the English literature on the monetary

[1] The position was secured for Hayek by his mentor, Ludwig von Mises, who was secretary of the Vienna Chamber of Commerce, one of the sponsoring institutions of the Institute.

D. Glasner, *Studies in the History of Monetary Theory*,
Palgrave Studies in the History of Economic Thought,
https://doi.org/10.1007/978-3-030-83426-5_16

history of the eighteenth and nineteenth centuries and the, mostly British, monetary doctrines of that period.

Even without an academic position, Hayek's productivity upon returning to Vienna was impressive. Aside from writing a monthly digest of statistical reports, financial news, and analysis of business conditions for the Institute, Hayek published several important theoretical papers, gaining a reputation as a young economist of great promise. Moreover, Hayek's immersion in the English monetary literature and his sojourn in the United States gave him an excellent command of English, so that when, in the summer of 1930, he received an invitation from William Beveridge, Director of the London School of Economics, at the suggestion of Lionel Robbins, who had been greatly impressed by Hayek's earlier papers, especially Hayek (1929 [1931]), to deliver a series of lectures on business-cycle theory. A secure academic position for a young economist, even one as talented as Hayek, was then hard to come by in Austria or Germany. Perhaps sensing that, if successful, the lectures might result in the offer of a position at LSE, Hayek eagerly accepted the invitation, dropping his other research efforts in order to compose in English the four lectures he would have to present only a few months later (Howson, 2011; Klausinger, 2013).

Upon arriving in England in January 1931, Hayek actually went first to Cambridge to give a lecture, a condensed version of the four LSE lectures. Hayek was not feeling well when he came to Cambridge to face an unsympathetic, if not hostile, audience, and the lecture was not a success. However, despite, or perhaps because of, his inauspicious debut at Cambridge, Hayek's performance at LSE turned out to be an immediate sensation. In his *History of Economic Analysis*, Joseph Schumpeter (1954, 1120), who, although an Austrian with a background in economics similar to Hayek's, was neither a personal friend nor an ideological ally of Hayek's, wrote that Hayek's theory

> on being presented to the Anglo-American community of economists, met with a sweeping success that has never been equaled by any strictly theoretical book that failed to make amends for its rigors by including plans and policy recommendations or to make contact in other ways with its readers loves or hates. A strong critical reaction followed that, at first, but served to underline the success, and then the profession turned away to other leaders and interests.

The remarkable success of Hayek's lectures led Beveridge, quite on his own, to offer Hayek a one-year visiting appointment at LS, even though Beveridge was sympathetic neither to Hayek's abstract theoretical approach nor to his non-interventionist policy prescriptions. Upon being informed by Beveridge of his desire to make Hayek an offer, Robbins was both surprised and delighted. Having accepted the visiting appointment, Hayek was back in London in time for 1931–1932 academic year. The visiting appointment led to the offer of a permanent position, the Tooke Chair in Economics and Statistics, which Hayek accepted, remaining in that position until 1950.

The lectures provided a masterful survey of business-cycle theory from a Continental perspective unfamiliar to his British audience, including a lucid summary of the Austrian capital-theoretic approach to business-cycle theory and of the equilibrium price relationships necessary for economic stability, an explanation of how those equilibrium price relationships are disturbed by monetary disturbances giving rise to cyclical effects, with comments on the appropriate policies for avoiding or minimizing such disturbances. The goal of monetary policy should be to set the money interest rate equal to the hypothetical equilibrium interest rate determined by strictly real factors. The only policy implication that Hayek could extract from this rarified analysis was that monetary policy should aim not to stabilize the price level as recommended by such distinguished monetary theorists as Alfred Marshall and Knut Wicksell, but to stabilize total spending or total money income.

This objective would be achieved, Hayek argued, only if injections of new money preserved the equilibrium relationship between savings and investment, investments being financed entirely by voluntary savings, not by money newly created for that purpose. Insofar as new investment projects were financed by newly created money, the additional expenditure thereby financed would entail a deviation from the real equilibriumthat would obtain in a barter economy or in one in which money had no distortionary effect. The interest rate corresponding to that real equilibrium was called by Hayek, following Wicksell, the natural (or equilibrium) rate of interest.

What Wicksell's analysis of the natural rate had missed was that, in a progressive economy with real investment financed out of voluntary saving, the increasing output of goods and services over time implies generally falling prices as the increasing productivity of factors of production allows output to be produced at progressively falling cost. A stable price level would require ongoing increases in the quantity of money to keep output prices from falling, the new money being used to finance additional investment over and above voluntary saving, thereby causing the economy to deviate from its equilibrium time path by inducing investment that would not otherwise have been undertaken.

But according to Hayek, Wicksell failed to see that, in a progressive economy with real investment financed by voluntary saving, the increasing output of goods and services over time implies generally falling prices as the increasing productivity of factors of production progressively reduces costs of production. A stable price level would require ongoing increases in the quantity of money, the new money going to finance additional investment over and above voluntary saving, thereby causing a deviation from the equilibrium time path of the economy.

Hayek's argument identified monetary expansion of any sort that moderated or reversed the natural tendency of prices to fall in a progressive expanding economy, as a disturbing and distorting impulse that causes business-cycle fluctuations. Although he did not offer a detailed account of the origins of the Great Depression in his lectures, Hayek's diagnosis of the causes of the Great Depression, made explicit in other writings, was clear: monetary expansion by the Federal ReserveSystem during the 1920s, especially in 1927, to keep the US price level stable and to moderate deflationary pressure on Britain, sterling having been overvalued at the prewar dollar-sterling parity when gold convertibility was restored in March 1925, distorted relative prices and the capital structure. When distortions become unsustainable, unprofitable investment projects would be liquidated, thereby freeing up resources for redeployment in more productive activities. Why the Depression was continuing to deepen rather than recover more than a year after the downturn had started, was a different, and possibly even more perplexing, question.

As explained in the previous chapter, Hayek's argument that it is not possible to attain the real equilibriumcorresponding to that of a pure barter economy in a monetary economy unless all investment is financed out of savings with no money being created to finance investment depends on the assumption that money is non-interest-bearing and that the rate of inflation is not correctly foreseen. Such an economy, according to Hayek, would have the property that the rate of deflation equals the rate of increase in factor productivity. But if money does bear competitive interest, and if inflation is correctly foreseen, the economy can attain its real equilibriumat any correctly foreseen rate of inflation—provided that the rate of deflation is not greater than the real rate of interest.

Despite warning of the dangers of price-level stabilization as the goal of monetary policy, Hayek was reluctant to advance an alternative policy goal or criterion beyond the general maxim that policy should avoid any distorting effect on the economic system. But this abstract precept is not easily translated into an operational policy.

So Hayek's assumption that the real equilibriumrequires a rate of deflation equal to the rate of increase in factor productivity was unfounded, reflecting a failure to understand that, when prices levels and rates of inflation are correctly anticipated, the real equilibrium of the economy is independent of the price levels in different time periods and of rates of inflation between time periods.[2] If inflation is correctly foreseen, nominal wages will rise commensurately with inflation and real wages with productivity increases, so that the increase in nominal money supplied by banks will not induce, or finance, investment beyond voluntary savings. Hayek's argument reflected his failure to work through the full implications of his equilibrium method. As Hayek (1937a) would later explain, disequilibrium is the result not of money creation by banks, but of mistaken expectations about the future, a point already made, but less clearly articulated, by Hayek (1928 [1984]).

The simplest implementation of Hayek's objective would be to hold the quantity of money constant. But such a policy, as Hayek acknowledged, was beset with both practical and conceptual difficulties. Under a gold standard, which, as we shall see, Hayek favored in the early 1930s, the relevant area within which to keep the quantity of money constant would be the entire world (or, more precisely, the set of countries linked to the gold standard). But national differences between the currency systems linked to the gold standard would make it practically impossible to coordinate those national systems to keep some aggregate measure of the quantity of money convertible into gold constant. Aside from that

[2] Hayek (1934) actually understood the point in a different context noting in his reply to a review of *Prices and Production* by Hansen and Tout (1933) that a steady rate of monetary expansion would cease to have any effect on the capital structure of an economy once the public came to expect that rate of monetary expansion to persist over time, thereby anticipating by over 30 years Friedman's (1968) argument that the long-run Phillips Curve is vertical.

problem, Hayek also recognized that fluctuations in the demand to hold money (the reciprocal of the velocity of circulation) produce monetary disturbances analogous to variations in the quantity of money, so that the relevant policy objective was not a constant quantity of money, but a quantity of money that changed proportionately (inversely) with the demand to hold money (velocity of circulation).

Thus, Hayek's argument mistakenly identified monetary expansion of any sort that moderated or reversed what Hayek considered the natural tendency of prices to fall in a progressively expanding economy, as the disturbing and distorting impulse responsible for business-cycle fluctuations. Although he did not offer a detailed account of the origins of the Great Depression, Hayek's diagnosis of the causes of the Great Depression, made explicit in various other writings (e.g. Hayek, 1934), was clear: monetary expansion by the Federal Reserveduring the 1920s—especially in 1927—to keep the US price level from falling and to moderate deflationary pressure on Britain (sterling having been overvalued at the prewar dollar-sterling parity when Britain restored gold convertibility in March 1925) distorted relative prices and the capital structure. When distortions eventually become unsustainable, unprofitable investment projects would be liquidated, supposedly freeing those resources to be re-employed in more productive activities. Why the Depression continued to deepen rather than recover more than a year after the downturn had started, was another question, left largely unanswered except to cast blame on various government interventions obstructing free-market price adjustment.

Despite warning of the dangers of price-level-stabilization policies, Hayek was reluctant to advance an alternative policy goal or criterion beyond the general maxim that policy should avoid any disturbing or distorting effect—in particular monetary expansion—on the economic system. But Hayek was unwilling or unable to translate this abstract precept into a definite policy norm.

Hayek therefore suggested that the appropriate criterion for the neutrality of money might be to hold total spending (or alternatively total factor income) constant. With constant total spending, neither an increase nor a decrease in the amount of money the public desired to hold would lead to disequilibrium. This was a compelling argument for constant total spending as the goal of policy, but Hayek was unwilling to adopt it as a practical guide for monetary policy.

In the final paragraph of his final LSE lecture, Hayek (1931) made his most explicit, though still equivocal, policy recommendation.

> [T]he only practical maxim for monetary policy to be derived from our considerations is probably … that the simple fact of an increase of production and trade forms no justification for an expansion of credit, and that—save in an acute crisis—bankers need not be afraid to harm production by overcaution. … It is probably an illusion to suppose that we shall ever be able entirely to eliminate industrial fluctuations by means of monetary policy. The most we may hope for is that the growing information of the public may make it easier for central banks both to follow a cautious policy during the upward swing of the cycle, and so to mitigate the following depression, and to resist the well-meaning but dangerous proposals to fight depression by "a little inflation."

Thus, Hayek concluded his series of lectures by implicitly rejecting his own idea of neutral money as a policy criterion, warning instead against the "well-meaning but dangerous proposals to fight depression by 'a little inflation.'" The only sensible interpretation of Hayek's counsel of "resistance" is an icy expression of indifference to falling nominal spending in a deep depression.

Lawrence White (2008) has defended Hayek against the charge that his policy advice in the depression was liquidationist, encouraging policy makers to take a "hands-off" approach to the unfolding economic catastrophe. In making this argument, White relied on Hayek's neutral-money concept as well as Hayek's decades-later disavowals of his early pro-deflation policy advice. However, White omitted any mention of Hayek's explicit rejection of neutral money as a policy normat the conclusion of his LSE lectures. White also disputed the characterization of Hayek's policy stance as "liquidationist," arguing that Hayek supported liquidationnot for its own sake, but only as a means to reallocate resources from lower- to higher-valued uses. Although that is certainly a correct characterization of Hayek's intent, White failed to establish that any of the other liquidationists he mentions favored liquidation as an end and not, like Hayek, as a means to improve resource allocation as an anti-depression strategy.

Hayek's policy stance in the early 1930s was characterized by David Laidler (1999) as a skepticism bordering on nihilism in opposing any monetary- or fiscal-policy responses to mitigate the suffering caused by the Depression. White's efforts at rehabilitation notwithstanding, Laidler's characterization seems to be on the mark. The perplexing and disturbing question raised by Hayek's policy stance in the early 1930s is why, given the availability of his neutral-money criterion as a justification for favoring at least a mildly inflationary (or reflationary) policy to promote economic recovery from the Depression, did Hayek remain, until about 1935 at any rate, implacably opposed to expansionary monetary policies? Hayek's later disavowals of his early position actually provide some insight into his reasoning in the early 1930s, but to understand the reasons for his advocating a policy inconsistent with his own theoretical understanding of the situation for which he was offering policy advice, it is necessary to understand the intellectual and doctrinal background that set the boundaries on the policies Hayek was prepared to entertain. I am going to argue that the ultimate source of that intellectual and doctrinal background was David Hume (1752 [2006]) and that Hume's influence was indirectly transmitted to Hayek by his mentor Ludwig von Mises.

My goal in the remainder of this chapter is to explain the internal conflicts that led to Hayek's self-contradictory and inconsistent policy advice, showing how certain received doctrines to which Hayek was intellectually committed were in tension with his own innovations in monetary theory. Thus, the advice that Hayek was offering in 1931 and 1932, when the Great Depression was already at, or near, bottom, reflected pre-existing policy commitments whose irreconcilability with his own theory were still unresolved. The policy advice Hayek was explicitly offering in 1931 and 1932 belie the idea, based on his neutral-money criterion embraced only later as a policy guide, that Hayek was not encouraging a policy of passivity in the face of deflation and depression.

16.1 Hayek's Lament for the Gold Standard

In February 1932, Hayek (1932 [1984]) published an article in German "Der Schicksal der Goldwahrung" (The Fate of the Gold Standard) occasioned by the decision of Great Britain during the financial crisis of the previous September to let the pound float rather than remain on the gold standard and tolerate further deflation. Britain having given birth to the gold standard in the early eighteenth century and promoted its widespread adoption as an international standard in the second half of the nineteenth century, its abandonment by Britain was, despite her diminished international position after World War I, a profound shock to the international financial system and to the many and influential supporters of the gold standard. Whether the gold standard would survive as an international financial and monetary system, a contingency that had hardly been considered before Britain went off gold, suddenly became an open question, and Hayek, deeply disturbed by the suspension, doubted that the gold standard would survive. The bitter tone of Hayek's lament for the gold standard and his disdain for Britain's departure from gold are highlighted in his opening sentence:

> There has been much talk about the breakdown of the gold standard, particularly in Britain where, to the astonishment of every foreign observer, the abandonment of the gold standard was very widely welcomed as a release from an irksome constraint.

Amazingly, Hayek dares to suggest that a 10% decline of real income in less than two years and a near doubling of the 1929 unemployment rate of 8 percent, which had been over 10% for most the 1920s, was an annoyance, not a catastrophe. Hayek further argued that problems wrongly attributed to the gold standard were caused by the policy of price-level stabilization that governments and monetary authorities had been urged to set as their goal rather than restore the prewar gold standard as it used to operate under the rubric of the "rules of the game."

The stabilizationists, of whom Hayek so heartily disapproved were Irving Fisher, Gustav Cassel, Ralph Hawtrey, and, especially, J. M. Keynes. Fisher and Keynes favored stabilizing national price levels, with currency exchange rates fluctuating as needed to reflect local changes in the terms of trade between countries, while Cassel and Hawtrey favored price-level stabilization in the context of a restored international gold standard with national central banks cooperating to manage their demands for gold to prevent the widespread and nearly simultaneous restoration of the gold standard from greatly increasing the demand for gold, driving up its real value, thereby causing a deflationary downturn in output and employment.

Failing to address, perhaps even oblivious to, the danger of an increasing monetary demand for gold as countries rejoined the gold standard, Hayek dismissed the idea of central-bank cooperation as an attempt to circumvent the "rules of game" by which the prewar gold standard had operated. Conceding that British prices were falling compared to prices in other gold-standard countries, Hayek nevertheless maintained that Britain was violating the rules of the game by not reducing its "overall circulation."

> In diametric opposition to the basic concept of the gold standard, the gold which was draining away was constantly being compensated for by bank

> loans, so that the overall circulation was kept stable at a time when it would have had to diminish if a genuine gold standard had existed. (p. 122)

Hayek's statement is factually false, the gold holdings of the Bank of England having increased year over year in 1926 (convertibility having been restored in March 1925), 1927, and 1928. Although gold holdings in 1929, fell to a level slightly below the 1926 level, they remained above the 1925 level. But the only essential requirement of a gold standard is that gold be convertible on demand into a fixed weight of gold, which clearly had been the case with the dollar/sterling exchange rate having been tightly fixed from 1925 to 1929.

Because Hayek's comments on the gold standard betray a quite comprehensive misunderstanding of how the gold standard worked, it will be worthwhile to explore the sources of that misunderstanding. The key sources, as I suggested above, were David Hume's (1752 [2006]) account of international monetary adjustment, the application of Hume's account by the British Currency School, and Ludwig von Mises's application of the Currency School doctrine in developing his own theory of business cycles used by Hayek as the starting point for his own theory.

16.2 Humean Misunderstandings of the Gold Standard[3]

Hayek's misunderstandings of the gold standard were not his own; they were largely derived from the quantity-theoretic tradition originating in David Hume's celebrated 1752 essay "On the Balance of Trade." Hume's essay was a brilliant refutation of the idea that countries could accumulate gold without limit, arguing that increased imports of gold would raise prices in the importing country thereby reducing the international competitiveness of their products and discouraging further imports of gold. The essay was a wonderful refutation of the economic fallacy underlying the eighteenth-century Mercantilist ideology, but Hume's argument had two shortcomings of its own.

First, deeply hostile toward banks, which he regarded as inflationary engines of financial disorder, Hume assumed that payments for domestic and international exchanges were made using gold when in fact, even in

[3] The argument in this section draws on previous discussions of the Hume and the Currency and Banking Schools in Chapters 2, 3, 6, and 7.

the middle of the eighteenth century, trade was being carried domestically and internationally using credit instruments (banknotes, deposits, and bills of exchange) that largely obviated gold shipments to finance international trade. So the actual adjustment mechanism when Hume wrote was already considerably more sophisticated than the one Hume described. Second, Hume's argument presumed that the equilibration of prices was achieved by way of international gold shipments, with gold being shipped from countries with high prices to countries with low prices, which was not wrong, but in framing that argument, Hume mistakenly assumed that prices within any country fluctuated in proportion to the amount of gold "circulating" in the country. But the assumption that differences between local price levels are integral to the international adjustment mechanism—hence the standard description of the Humean equilibrating mechanism as the price-specie-flow mechanism (PSFM)—is inconsistent with the operation of arbitrage that prevents prices between any two locations from diverging by more than the cost of transportation between those locations. Hume's naïve assumptions about the international adjustment mechanism were thus factually incorrect and theoretically flawed.

Despite its shortcomings, the Humean PSFM has long held an almost canonical status—Samuelson (1980) being an important exception—in the literature on international trade and finance. Because of that near-canonical status, many of Hume's successors concluded that the appropriate way to fill in the theoretical gap in PSFM, under a mixed system of gold and privately created bank money convertible into gold, was to create institutional arrangements ensuring that the international adjustment mechanism would operate under a mixed-convertible-currency system in just the way that Hume described the operation of a pure gold system. The validity of this approach to filling the gap in PSFM was a key point in dispute between the Currency and Banking Schools in the middle of the nineteenth century.

Believing, like Hume, that banks are inherently predisposed to inflationary overissue, the Currency School argued that international monetary adjustment required the quantity of banknotes to be constrained to change by exactly as much as the amount of gold flowing into or out of the country, just as if all currency were gold: the Currency Principle. Their position, codified in Peel's Bank Charter Act of 1844, superimposed a quantity rule upon Britain's already operational gold standard in the form of a 100% marginal gold-reserve requirement on the creation of banknotes beyond a £14-million unbacked fiduciary issue allowed to the

Bank of England and a cap on the existing note issues of the country banks. Arguing that excess issues of convertible banknotes would be returned to the banks issuing them, the Banking School opposed the Bank Charter Actas an unnecessary and potentially destabilizing restraint on the ability of banks to respond to the public's demand for liquidity.

Proving unworkable in practice, the rigid quantitative constraints of the Bank Charter had to be suspended periodically to avoid or alleviate financial crises. Nevertheless, the general idea that an inflow of gold into a country on the gold standard requires an increase in the quantity of bank money while an outflow of gold from a country on the gold standard requires a decrease in the quantity of bank money gained wide acceptance as a general—but non-binding—precept, one of the "rules of the game" that the monetary authorities were supposed to follow under the gold standard.

The misunderstanding underlying this view of the gold standard is that the direction of causality runs from reserves to bank money (either banknotes or bank deposits) rather than the other way around. Under a gold standard, gold reserves are held because banks want, or are required, to hold reserves when creating banknotes or deposits. But the ability to make loans profitably depends on the existence of a demand to hold the banknotes or the deposits being created. Without such a demand, borrowing banknotes or deposits created by banks would be pointless.

The Humean analysis of the international adjustment mechanism characteristically began with the assumption of a negative shock to the quantity of gold in a single country followed by an immediate reduction in prices in that country alone, triggering an adjustment toward a new equilibrium in which prices in a country with a reduced gold stock increasing the competitiveness of its tradable products in international markets. Eventually enough gold would be imported into the country with a reduced gold stock to raise prices there back to the level elsewhere.

This version of the international adjustment mechanism is problematic for at least two reasons. First, because prices in the country with a reduced gold stock are constrained by prices elsewhere, the reduction in prices in the home market could not be proportional to the reduction in the local gold stock. The price effects of the reduction in the gold stock would be diffused over the entire world, not confined to the country in which gold had disappeared.

The second problem is less a mistake in economic logic than a misjudgment of which potential shocks are most likely to disturb international monetary equilibrium. The Humean analysis began with a thought experiment in which 80 percent of Britain's gold stock somehow vanished into thin air. While understanding that such an event was of no practical concern, Hume and the Currency School, believing in the inherently inflationary tendencies of banks, were concerned about a different kind of supply shock: increasing amounts of banknotes raising prices in Britain compared to other countries, thereby causing an efflux of gold from Britain.

The implicit assumption of the Currency School was that strictly limiting the nominal quantity of money would prevent the overissue of banknotes, the most likely source of monetary shocks, thereby allowing the automatic operation of PSFM to maintain international monetary equilibrium. While shifts in the terms of trade or differences in the rate of productivity growth could occasionally lead to trade imbalances, those imbalances would be gradually resolved if a redistribution of gold reserves led to corresponding changes in national money stocks and, as a result, in price levels. Balance-of-payments disequilibria were thus attributed either to monetary or political mismanagement, or to shifts in the terms of trade and differential rates of productivity growth.

With a few exceptions, the idea that, under the gold standard, fluctuations in the balance of payments and in the direction of gold flows actually monetary conditions was not well understood until the late 1960s and early 1970s when Harry Johnson and his colleagues and students began developing what came to be known as the monetary approach to the balance of payments. Johnson's key conceptual insight was to view the balance of payments as a mechanism by which a country could dispose of an excess supply of domestic money through a balance-of-payments deficit or satisfy an excess demand for money through a balance-of-payments surplus.

This perspective on the balance of payments implies that, at least as a first approximation—and a very good approximation for a small open economy—the quantity of money in any country tied to an international gold standard equals the quantity of money demanded in that country at the international price level implied by the gold standard. If the domestic monetary system supplies the amount of money demanded, the balance of payments will be in equilibrium with no gold flowing into (or out of) the country. However, if the domestic monetary system supplies less than the amount of money demanded, the deficiency is supplied by way of an export surplus that induces an inflow of foreign exchange or gold to be converted into the domestic cash balances needed to satisfy domestic liquidity demands.

So the most basic maxim of the "rules of the game:" that monetary authorities should respond to inflows (outflows) of gold by expanding (contracting) their domestic money stocks, and thereby raising (reducing) their domestic price levels, was completely backwards. An inflow of gold does not mean that the quantity of money in the country receiving the inflow has to be increased as a result, because the inflow of gold may have been the means by which the domestic money stock was increased to match the existing domestic demand to hold money. However, if the domestic demand to hold money is being satisfied by way of gold imports, it is likely more economical to satisfy the demand by domestic credit creation than by gold imports achieved by way of an export surplus.

The relevant questions are thus (1) why the domestic monetary system is not supplying the amount of money demanded without the gold inflow, (2) whether the influx of gold reserves held by the monetary authority provides a benefit greater than would have otherwise accrued if the additional gold had not flowed into the vaults of the monetary authority, and (3) what consequences gold accumulation by the monetary authority might have for the international value of gold, a question with implications not limited to the country accumulating gold but affecting all countries on the gold standard. Without understanding the cause of an inflow or outflow of gold, no inference can be drawn about the appropriate policy response.

A further implication of the monetary approach to the balance of payments is that the concept of sterilization, which is said to occur when a country accumulates gold, but, contrary to "the rules of the game," does not allow the quantity of domestic money to increase accordingly is incoherent. The concept of sterilization presumes that the monetary authority can control the domestic money stock under a gold standard or a fixed-exchange regime, but the monetary authority has no more power to control the quantity of money within a country on the gold standard than the naval forces of a country have to control the tides. What is misidentified as sterilizationis really not a failure to expand the domestic money stock, but an accumulation of gold or foreign-exchange reserves caused by a failure of the monetary authority to satisfy the local demand for cash balances, thereby forcing the local demand for cash to be satisfied by curtailing imports and increasing exports sufficiently to import gold or other foreign exchange to be converted into domestic money.

Such a policy by the monetary authority potentially harms other countries, either by driving up the value of gold, and imposing deflation on other countries, or by depressing the real exchange rate of the country accumulating foreign-exchange reserves, thereby subsidizing the country's tradable-good sector; a policy Corden (1985) called exchange-rate protection.

16.3 Hayekian Fallacies about the Interwar Gold Standard

Following Hume, the Currency School, and his mentor Ludwig von Mises, in attributing to the banking system in a country on the gold standard the power to raise local prices by overissue of banknotes or of deposits, Hayek blamed the inflationary tendencies that he perceived under the gold standard in the 1920s after Britain's restoration of convertibility at the prewar parity in 1925 to insufficient adherence to the "rules of the game," by Britain and America. While criticizing the British decision to restore the prewar parity, Hayek argued that, having chosen an overvalued parity, the British were obligated by rules of the gold standard to pursue a deflationary monetary policy to bring the British price level into equality with the international gold price level, rather than attempt to maintain the prewar parity without deflation.

As indicated above, Hayek's understanding of British policy was factually wrong, the British price level actually did fall after 1925 reflecting the gradual approach of the British price level to common international price level in terms of gold. The decline in British prices was, to a first approximation, dictated not by British monetary policy, but by the prevailing dollar/sterling parity and the forces of arbitrage tending to equalize prices of tradable commodities. What British monetary policy could control was the accumulation of British reserves of gold and other forms of foreign exchange. Contrary to Hayek's assertions, British gold reserves actually increased in each year from 1926 to 1928 over the previous year. Here is how Hayek (1932 [1984]) described the situation facing Britain after restoring the prewar parity:

> If the gold standard were to be permanently adhered to by Britain, the deflation would therefore have to continue until the British domestic price level had also reached an equilibrium with the rest of the world. The British, however, wanted less than anything to do this, and the new ideas

> of stabilizing prices and the economy as the aim of monetary policy were welcomed as justifying deviation from the orthodox rules of monetary policy.

What Hayek failed to understand is that the United States, with 40% of the world's gold reserves, could powerfully influence the value of gold by allowing a substantial outflow of gold to other countries. That is what the US did in 1927–1928, thereby easing deflationary pressure on the international price level, reflected in a modest increase in the US price level even as the British price level continued to fall slightly. As long as sterling was pegged to the dollar at the prewar parity, the Bank of England had no power to control its internal price level. Any easing of deflationary pressure on Britain was possible only insofar as the Federal Reserve was willing to allow an efflux of gold to raise, if only slightly, the world price level in terms of gold. For price-level stabilization to occur, the US had to take deliberate policy steps to achieve it. But what Hayek failed to acknowledge, though the point had been made explicitly by Keynes (1923) and Robertson (1928) and by Mises (1924 [1934]) that, given its huge share of the world's monetary gold reserves, the international value of gold was necessarily determined—one way or the other—by the policy choices of the Federal Reserve.

The orthodox rules of the gold standard invoked by Hayek, even if, for argument's sake, their existence is stipulated, could never have applied to a situation in which a single country had the power, by its own policy choices, to alter the real value of gold, a comparable concentration of the world's gold reserves in the hands of a single country never previously having existed. On the one hand, Hayek condemned Britain for choosing to restore prewar dollar/sterling parity, because it required Britain to accept deflation, while on the other hand, he condemned the United States for using its control over the real value of gold to mitigate the deflationary effect of the prewar dollar/sterling parity.

> The attempt ... to ... avoid the inevitable fall in the [British] level of prices would not have been relatively successful for so long if it had not met with sympathetic co-operation and efforts along the same lines in the United States because of the supremacy there of the concept of stabilization. The ... fall in cost which occurred in America should have led, if it had not been compensated for by an enormous expansion of credit, to a corresponding fall in prices. On the one hand, this fall in prices would not have harmed production in any way, since it would merely have resulted from

> the fall in costs, and on the other hand, it would have forced the ultimately unavoidable reduction in costs in Europe by absorbing Europe's gold. That such a fall in prices corresponding to the reduction in costs can take place without any detriment to production was clearly demonstrated by developments in the United States between 1925 and 1927, when there was a boom despite continuously falling prices.

Hayek correctly observes that, by stabilizing the value of gold, or even allowing it to fall slightly, the US eased deflationary pressures on Britain, of which easing Hayek clearly expresses his disapproval. Hayek's premise is that, because American productivity was increasing so rapidly, it would have been possible for output prices in America to fall by as much as the increase in productivity, so that, with constant nominal income and spending, real output would have increased. Hayek then asserts that such a policy in the US could have been replicated in Europe even if productivity was not rising as rapidly in Europe as in the US, without "harm[ing] production in any way, because it would have forced the ultimately unavoidable reduction in costs in Europe by absorbing Europe's gold."

Hayek's assertion is noteworthy on two levels. First, he asserts that international prices of tradable good would be driven down to match the American costs of production, which are the lowest in the world owing to the fastest increases in productivity in the world. According to Hayek, prices in Europe would be driven down to match American prices by a deflation caused by the inflow of gold from the rest of the world to the United States associated with America's export surplus. Hayek here betrays Humean confusion about how prices are determined under the gold standard, because the prices of tradables are equalized by arbitrage regardless of the direction of gold flows. But if all output prices are just high enough to cover only American costs with constant nominal incomes, then countries in which productivity is increasing less rapidly than in the US would be able to cover their costs of production only if nominal income, and presumably nominal wages, were falling. Thus, the policy implicitly favored by Hayek was one in which nominal income in every gold-standard country except the United States (where it would be stable) was falling, so that aggregate nominal income in all gold standard countries combined would be falling.

Moreover, even from the narrow perspective of "the orthodox rules of the gold standard," it made no sense for Hayek to argue that the adjustment to gold flows should be borne entirely by every country other than the one with fastest rate of productivity growth; Hayek was clearly arguing that the burden of adjustment to gold flows into the United States ought to be borne by cost deflation in countries losing gold rather than by the one country—the US—gaining gold. Finally, it should be observed that Hayek clearly manifests the obliviousness of the Humean PSFM to the demand for money and the derived demand for gold, whose importance was not brought into explicit focus by economists, with a few notable exceptions like R. G. Hawtrey, until the advent of the monetary approach to the balance of payments.

16.4 Hayek and the Bank of France

In his lament for the gold standard, Hayek addressed charges that gold accumulation by the US and the Bank of France between 1928 and 1931 had been responsible for Britain's economic difficulties and ultimately for her departure from the gold standard. His defense of the US is straightforward, arguing that it would have been against her own self-interest for the US to adopt an even more inflationary policy than it had adopted in the 1920s just to ease deflationary pressure on Britain.[4] Oblivious to the role of the US in determining the international price level, Hayek did not mention that by easing monetary policy and allowing an efflux of gold in 1927 and the first part of 1928, the Fed, accommodated the growing monetary demand for gold as countries were rejoining the gold standard. By reversing the efflux later in 1928 when it began tightening monetary policy just as the world monetary demand for gold, especially in France, began increasing rapidly, the Fed joined the Bank of France in causing gold appreciation and deflation.

Here is what Hayek (1932 [1984]) had to say about the policy of the Bank of France

[4] Of course, the defense that the US policy served US self-interest could hardly be persuasive if the US policy contributed to the worldwide downturn that started in 1929 owing, at least in part to US monetary policy. US interests were obviously not served by the Great Depression.

> The accusation that France systematically hoarded gold seems at first sight to be ... correct. France did pursue an extremely cautious foreign policy after the franc stabilized at a level which considerably undervalued it with respect to its domestic purchasing power, and prevented an expansion of credit proportional to the amount of gold coming in. Nevertheless, France did not prevent her monetary circulation from increasing by the very same amount as that of the gold inflow – and this alone is necessary for the gold standard to function.

Hayek is again repeating a fundamental error by assuming that, having stabilized the franc in 1926 and restored gold convertibility in 1928, France could control the quantity of money in circulation or its price level. Preventing her monetary circulation from increasing by as much as the gold inflow was not an option; gold flowed in, precisely because that was the only means, under the monetary policy followed by the Bank of France, whereby the French public could increase their holdings of cash by as much as they desired. The franc having been pegged to the dollar in 1926 at $0.0392/franc, the French monetary authorities could not control the French price level; commodity arbitrage required commodity prices quoted in francs to equal commodity prices quoted in dollars at the fixed dollar/franc parity. The equalization was not perfect, because not all commodities enter into international trade, and because there are differences between similar products sold in different countries that preclude complete price equalization. But the divergence between national price levels under a gold standard was strictly limited.

Hayek's assertion betrays a basic misunderstanding of what "is necessary for the gold standard to function." All that was necessary was to maintain the fixed parity between the dollar and the franc; operation of the gold standard did not require the Bank of France to achieve any particular ratio between changes in the quantity of francs and changes the gold reserves of the Bank of France. That ratio was chosen by the Bank of France, not dictated by the requirements of the gold standard. Hayek seems to have assumed that the inflow of gold into France was determined by forces independent of French monetary conditions. But the reality was otherwise. By preventing the quantity of money in France from increasing except through the importation of gold, the Bank of France transformed any increase in the French demand for money into an equivalent increase in French (and, hence, the world's) demand for gold, thereby driving up the value of gold. That increase in the world demand for gold was an immediate, though not the only, source of the deflation that produced the Great Depression, a fact that escaped Hayek's grasp until 1935 (Caton, 2020; Hayek, 1935).

Hayek's misunderstanding of how the gold standard operated, derived from his naïve acceptance of the Humean PSFM as it had been transmitted by way of the British Currency School and Ludwig von Mises, either blinded Hayek to the deflationary implications of the gold accumulation policy of the Bank of France, or caused him to welcome those implications. His citation of both Cassel and Hawtrey in his paper on the gold standard would indicate that he had at least been exposed to their arguments about the deflationary implications of gold accumulation by central banks. But Hayek's disdainful tone toward those unwilling to tolerate deflation in his 1932 defense of the gold standard and of the radically deflationary policy of the Bank of France shows that, even in 1932, Hayek fully supported a policy of rapid deflation.[5]

16.5 Hayek on Primary and Secondary Deflation

Further evidence of Hayek's insouciance about deflation is provided by Klausinger (2013) in his introduction to volume VII of Hayek's *Collected Works* containing his early writings (mostly from the 1920s and 1930s) about business-cycle theory. Klausinger discusses at length Hayek's views about deflation, and, in particular, the distinction between what Hayek called "primary" and "secondary" deflations.

In Hayek's explanation of the downturn, a crisis or cyclical upper-turning point occurs when banks, having financed an artificial lengthening of the structure of production, are unwilling to continue supplying the necessary financing for projects still in progress. Because the artificially lengthened structure of production cannot be sustained by voluntary savings, the withdrawal or substantial curtailment of bank financing

[5] J. L. Caton (2020) documents that in essay in the *Economist*, Hayek (1935) acknowledged that the demand of central banks for gold reserves was in fact a source of instability in the value of gold and that, without some mechanism of international cooperation to limit the monetary demand for gold sufficiently to preserve a stable value of gold, restoring the widely abandoned gold standard could lead to renewed deflation. Thus, by 1935, Hayek seems to have accepted the Cassel-Hawtreyview that international cooperation was necessary to ensure that a gold standard would be consistent with international price stability, precisely the view that he had criticized so harshly in his 1932 essay on the gold standard.

leads to the failure or collapse of the business firms and expansion projects dependent on a continued flow of financing to carry on. The amount of required financing exceeds what is forthcoming from voluntary savings, so that it can only be maintained by progressively larger injections of funds financed by newly created bank credit. When banks reach the limits of their capacity to sustain the financing, and cut back their lending, borrowers, cut off from bank financing, are compelled to scale back, or cease, operations. The loss of financing requires the distress sale of unsold inventories and assets, triggering an immediate deflation. This initial liquidation process serves to free up capital and resources for redeployment in less "capitalistic" modes of production.

The turning point is associated with collapsing asset prices and distress sales of inventories, which constitute the primary deflation. After the initial shock, the downward pressure on prices may dissipate, allowing a recovery to start on a solid footing. However, the collapse in asset prices and the distress sales of inventory might become cumulative if the initial contraction extendsing beyond those firms that had undertaken capital expansion and been implicated in lengthening the capital structure of the economy. Largely independent of the disproportionalities that triggered the initial downturn, the contagion of business failures throughout the economy constitutes the secondary phase of deflation and depression. The secondary deflation serving little or no remedial purpose, Haberler (1937) and Röpke (1932 [1936]) argued that monetary expansion to counteract it was both necessary and appropriate.

Despite conceding that there is a meaningful distinction between a primary and secondary deflation that might justify monetary expansion to counteract the latter, Hayek remained opposed to monetary expansion during the depths of the Great Depression. Moreover, as discussed above, his own neutral-money criterion implied monetary expansion to stabilize nominal spending and income. The inconsistency between Hayek's use of the neutral-money criterion as both an analytical tool and as a justification for deflation in periods of increasing output and employment and his disregard of that criterion when arguing for deflation while output and employment were decreasing is palpable.

Addressing Hayek's pro-deflationary stance in the 1930s, White (2008) absolved Hayek from responsibility for the policy errors of the 1930s on the grounds that the Federal Reserve Board and the Hoover Administration had been influenced not by Hayek, but by a different strand of pro-deflationary thinking, further pointing out that Hayek's own theory of monetary policy, had he followed it consistently, would have led him to support monetary expansion during the 1930s to prevent any decline in aggregate spending. White may well be correct in denying that Hayek's pro-deflation policy stance influenced policy makers, but Hayek's policy advice was what it was: consistently pro-deflation.

Why did Hayek offer policy advice so blatantly contradicted by his own neutral-money criterion? White suggests that Hayek viewed deflation as potentially beneficial if it would break the rigidities obstructing adjustments in relative prices. It was the lack of relative-price adjustments that, in Hayek's view, caused the depression.

Hayek (1933 [1939], 175–176) expressed this view as follows:

> The analysis of the crisis shows that, once an excessive increase of the capital structure has proved insupportable and has led to a crisis, profitability of production can be restored only by considerable changes in relative prices, reductions of certain stocks, and transfers of the means of production to other uses. In connection with these changes, liquidationsof firms in a purely financial sense of the word may be inevitable, and their postponement may possibly delay the process of liquidation in the first, more general sense; but this is a separate and special phenomenon which in recent discussions has been stressed rather excessively at the expense of the more fundamental changes in prices, stocks, etc.

Hayek distinguishes between two possible interpretations of liquidation, noting that widespread financial bankruptcy is not necessary for liquidation in the economic sense.[6] Continuing with the following argument about rigidities, he wrote:

[6] White uses this distinction to absolve Hayek from the charge liquidationism, providing intellectual support for the liquidationist policies supposedly pursued by Andrew Mellon, Secretary of the Treasury. Following Eichengreen (1992), White suggests that insofar as the liquidationist position enjoyed any intellectual support, that support was derived from supporters of the real-bills doctrine in the Federal Reserve such as Adolph Miller, a former academic economist, and a member of the Fed Board of Governors. Eichengreen and White are probably correct in identifying the Fed as the source of liquidationist sentiment that was influencing administration and Fed policy. And White is also correct in noting that Hayek was a critic of the real-bills doctrine. However, disagreement about the real-bills doctrine does not establish any substantive difference between the liquidationist position of Miller and of his associates on the Fed and the liquidationist position espoused by Hayek in 1933. Presumably, Miller et al. were not unaware of the distinction between bankruptcy and liquidationin the economic sense; White provides no evidence that Miller et al. did not understand that distinction.

> A theoretical problem of great importance which needs to be elucidated in this connection is the significance, for this process of liquidation, of the rigidity of prices and wages, which since the great war has undoubtedly become very considerable. There can be little question that these rigidities tend to delay the process of adaptation and that this will cause a "secondary" deflation which at first will intensify the depression but ultimately will help to overcome those rigidities. (Id., p. 176)
>
> The main problems in this connection, on which opinions are still diametrically opposed, are, firstly, whether this process of deflation is merely an evil which has to be combated, or whether it does not serve a necessary function in breaking these rigidities, and, secondly, whether the persistence of these deflationary tendencies proves that the fundamental maladjustment of prices still exists, or whether, once that process of deflation has gathered momentum, it may not continue long after it has served its initial function. (Id.)

Two observations are relevant here. First, Hayek seems to be suggesting that the cause of the secondary deflation was the rigidity of prices and wages that presumably frustrated the rapid reabsorption of unemployed resources into new productive employment. That is certainly a possibility, but Hayek provided no theoretical argument that price and wage flexibility would ensure a rapid restoration of full employment. Indeed, as Hayek (1937a) later recognized, in a world with an incomplete set of markets, market forces do not, even in theory, necessarily move an economy toward an equilibrium state.

The intuitively appealing notion that a free-market system necessarily self-adjusts is an extrapolation from Marshallian partial-equilibrium analysis in which the disequilibrium of a single market is analyzed under the assumption that all other markets remain in equilibrium. The assumption of approximate macroeconomic equilibrium is a necessary precondition for the partial-equilibrium analysis to show that a single (relatively small) market reverts to equilibrium after a disturbance. In the general case, in which multiple markets are simultaneously disturbed from an initial equilibrium, it cannot be shown that price adjustments based on excess demands in individual markets lead to the restoration of equilibrium. Thus, Hayek's assertion that the cause of secondary deflation and the intensification of the depression was the rigidity of wages and prices was mere conjecture, as was his prediction that intensified deflation would help to overcome the rigidities.

Unable to demonstrate that deflation was not exacerbating economic conditions, Hayek justified tolerating further deflation, as White acknowledged, in the hope that it would break the "rigidities" preventing the relative-price adjustments that he felt were necessary for recovery. Lacking a solid basis in economic theory,[7] Hayek's prediction that deflation would break rigidities in relative-price adjustment invites evaluation in ideological terms. Conceding that monetary expansion might increase employment, Hayek may have been disturbed by the prospect that an expansionary monetary policy would be credited for having led to recovery, thereby increasing the chances that inflationary policies would be adopted under less extreme conditions. Hayek's support for deflation appears in retrospect to have been a means to accomplish a political end—breaking politically imposed and supported rigidities in prices—rather than a dispassionate economic analysis.

16.6 Deflation and Nihilism

My hypothesis that Hayek's support for deflation reflected a political strategy rather than an unbiased assessment of the economic situation in the early 1930s is supported by Hayek's own recollections four decades after the fact. As White pointed out, Hayek himself not only changed his views about deflation; he expressed regret for not having forcefully opposed deflation during the Great Depression. In 1975, in remarks at the American Enterprise Institute where his old friend Gottfried Haberler was then a resident fellow, Hayek explicitly renounced his earlier position, as he had done previously (Hayek, 1960).

> I am the last to deny – or rather, I am today the last to deny – that, in these circumstances, monetary counteractions, deliberate attempts to maintain the money stream, are appropriate.

[7] However, I am unaware of evidence that Hayek in 1933 understood the full implications of the argument of his 1937 paper acknowledging that there is no market mechanism for achieving equilibrium when, given the lack of a complete set of markets, independent plans are coordinated only insofar as economic agents share identical expectations. Unless there is a market mechanism by which expectations are reconciled—and Hayek acknowledged the lack of such a mechanism—price and wage flexibility does not ensure a tendency toward equilibrium. At most, Hayek conceded, there is an observed, but not theoretically established, empirical tendency toward equilibrium, a tendency hardly in evidence in 1933.

> I probably ought to add a word of explanation: I have to admit that I took a different attitude forty years ago, at the beginning of the Great Depression. At that time I believed that a process of deflation of some short duration might break the rigidity of wages which I thought was incompatible with a functioning economy. Perhaps I should have even then understood that this possibility no longer existed. . . . I would no longer maintain, as I did in the early '30s, that for this reason, and for this reason only, a short period of deflation might be desirable. Today I believe that deflation has no recognizable function whatever, and that there is no justification for supporting or permitting a process of deflation. (Hayek, 1975, 5)

Responding to Haberler's repetition of his old question about "secondary deflation," Hayek went on to elaborate:

> The moment there is any sign that the total income stream may actually shrink, I should certainly not only try everything in my power to prevent it from dwindling, but I should announce beforehand that I would do so in the event the problem arose...
>
> You ask whether I have changed my opinion about combating secondary deflation. I do not have to change my theoretical views. As I explained before, I have always thought that deflation had no economic function; but I did once believe, and no longer do, that it was desirable because it could break the growing rigidity of wage rates. Even at that time I regarded this view as a political consideration; I did not think that deflation improved the adjustment mechanism of the market. (Id., pp. 12–13)

I am not sure that Hayek's characterization of his early views is accurate. Although Hayek may indeed have believed that a short period of deflation would be enough to break the rigidities that he found so troublesome, he never spoke out against deflation, even as late as 1933 more than two years the start of deflation. But on the key point, Hayek was perfectly candid: "I regarded this view as a political consideration."

Such a rationale, I am sorry to say, reminds me of Lenin's famous saying that you can't make an omelet without breaking eggs. In other words, to achieve a desired political outcome, Hayek was prepared to support policies that he had—or should have had—good reason to believe would increase the suffering of great numbers of people. I don't accuse Hayek of malevolence, but the political and moral calculation that led him to such a conclusion is troubling, both morally and pragmatically.

David Laidler (1999) described Hayek's policy stance in the 1930s as extreme pessimism verging on nihilism. It is hard to argue that, in supportingdeflation as a means to accomplish a political end, Hayek did not cross the line separating pessimism from nihilism.

16.7 Conclusion

Hayek first achieved international celebrity as a young man in his early thirties. His ideas and values, largely inherited from the Viennese environment into which he was born, raised and educated, were still evolving. Hayek had begun studying economics holding the fashionably socialist views he had absorbed in his childhood. Even his instruction in economics at the University of Vienna under Friedrich von Wieser, one of the illustrious figures of the Austrian School, had not fundamentally changed his socialist leanings. It was only after his subsequent encounter with the ideas of Ludwig von Mises subjecting him to what he later called a kind of intellectual shock treatment that his economic and political worldview was fundamentally transformed.

Not one to just take ideas over from someone else, Hayek's indebtedness and deference to Mises did not prevent him from working out the ideas that he had taken from Mises for himself. That was, especially the case in the way Hayek in a long series of publications from the late 1920s to the early 1940s, built up his own theories of capital and business cycles from the outlines that Mises had previously marked out. As Caldwell (2005) amply demonstrates, Hayek parted company from Mises on a variety of theoretical, philosophical issues over the course of his career, e.g., shifting from the extreme methodological apriorism of Mises to the falsificationism of Popper, from Mises's pure time-preference theory of interest to the Fisherian time-preference cum productivity theory of interest, and from the dogmatic laissez-faire liberalism and the intransigent opposition to all forms of the welfare state espoused by Mises in *Human Action* to more flexible articulation of liberal principles combined with a measured acceptance of welfare-state programs in *The Road to Serfdom* and *The Constitution of Liberty*.

But in the early 1930s, as the Great Depression was spiraling downward, the intellectual journey of self-definition on which Hayek had embarked was still in its early stages, and much of what Hayek had to say was still largely an echo of what he had heard from Mises during their years together in Vienna. Gradually, the Misesian baggage—the adulation of the gold standard, the welcoming of deflation, the blanket rejection of any government intervention and of the welfare state in all its forms—were discarded. Other early disciples of von Mises, like Haberler and Fritz Machlup, also left their youthful Misesian orthodoxy behind after leaving Vienna. But in the early 1930s, Hayek was still reading from Mises's script. To what extent he succeeded in freeing himself from Mises's overbearing influenceis perhaps a question that Hayek scholars are likely to continue exploring in the future.

References

Caldwell, B. M. (2005). *Hayek's challenge: An intellectual biography of F. A. Hayek*. University of Chicago Press.

Caton, J. L. (2020). The evolution of Hayek's thought on gold and monetary standards. *Southern Economic Journal, 87*(1), 386–405.

Corden, W. M. (1985). Exchange-rate protection. *Protection, growth and trade: Essays in international economics* (pp. 271–288). Basil Blackwell.

Eichengreen, B. (1992). *Golden fetters*. Oxford University Press.

Friedman, M. (1968). The role of monetary policy. *American Economic Review, 58*(1), 1–17.

Haberler, G. (1937). *Prosperity and depression*. League of Nations.

Hansen, A. H., & Tout, H. (1933). Annual survey of business cycle theory: Investment and saving in business cycle theory. *Econometrica, 1*(2), 119–147.

Hayek, F. A. (1928 [1984]). The intertemporal price equilibrium and movements in the value of money. In R. McCloughry (Ed.), *Money, capital and fluctuations: Early essays* (pp. 171–215). University of Chicago Press.

Hayek, F. A. (1929 [1931] May). The paradox of savings. *Economica, 32*, 125–169.

Hayek, F. A. (1931). *Prices and production*. Routledge and Kegan Paul.

Hayek, F. A. (1932 [1984]). The fate of the gold standard. In R. McCloughry (Ed.), *Money, capital and fluctuations: Early essays* (pp. 118–135). University of Chicago Press.

Hayek, F. A. (1933 [1939]). The present state and immediate prospects of the study of industrial fluctuations. In *Profits, interest and investment* (pp. 171–182). Routledge.

Hayek, F. A. (1934). Capital and industrial fluctuations. *Econometrica, 2*(2), 152–167.

Hayek, F.A. (1935, May 11). A regulated gold standard. *Economist*, pp. 1077–1078.

Hayek, F.A. (1937a). Economics and knowledge. *Economica, n.s., 4*(1), 33–54.

Hayek, F. A. (1937b). *Monetary nationalism and international stability*. Longmans Green and Company.
Hayek, F. A. (1944). *The road to serfdom*. University of Chicago Press.
Hayek, F. A. (1960). *The constitution of liberty*. University of Chicago Press.
Hayek, F. A. (1975). *A discussion with Friedrich A. von Hayek: Held at the American Enterprise Institute on April 9, 1975*. Washington: American Enterprise Institute.
Howson, S. (2011). *Lionel Robbins*. Cambridge University Press.
Hume, D. (1752 [2006]). Of the balance of trade. In E. Rotwein (Ed.), *Hume's writings on economics* (pp. 60–77). Routledge.
Keynes, J. M. (1923). *A tract on monetary reform*. Macmillan.
Klausinger, H. (2013). Introduction. *Business cycles* II. Vol. VII of *The Collected Works of F. A. Hayek*. University of Chicago Press.
Laidler, D. (1999). *Fabricating the Keynesian revolution*. Cambridge University Press.
Mises, L. v. (1924 [1934]). *The theory of money and credit*. Jonathan Cape.
Robertson, D. H. (1928). *Money*, 2nd ed. Cambridge.
Röpke, W. (1932 [1936]). *Crises and cycles*. Hodge.
Samuelson, P. A. (1980). A corrected version of Hume's equilibrating mechanisms for international trade. In J. S. Chipman & C. P. Kindleberger (Eds.), *Flexible exchange rates and the balance of payments* (pp. 141–158). North-Holland.
Schumpeter, J. A. (1954). *The history of economic analysis*. Oxford University Press.
White, L. H. (2008). Did Hayek and Robbins Deepen the Great Depression? *Journal of Money, Credit and Banking, 40*(4), 751–768.

CHAPTER 17

Hayek, Hicks, Radner, and Four Equilibrium Concepts: Intertemporal, Sequential, Temporary, and Rational-Expectations

17.1 The Concept of Intertemporal Equilibrium

Equilibrium is an essential concept in economics. While also essential in other sciences, and probably imported into economics from physics (Canard, 1801), equilibrium has a distinct meaning in economics that cannot be derived from its meaning in physics. The dissonance between the physical and economic meanings of equilibrium occasioned a long process of explication and clarification, before the concept and its essential role in economic theory came into clear focus.

Applying the physical meaning of equilibrium, the classical economists regarded an economic system in equilibrium as analogous to a physical system at rest, movement being either absent or repetitive. But what does it mean for an economic system to be at rest? The classical answer was that quantities and prices of goods produced, exchanged, and consumed would not change. If the amount supplied equals the amount demanded in each market, and if no exogenous change (e.g., in population, technology, tastes, etc.) disturbs the system, there would be no reason for prices or quantities to change. But because of a large, and causally important, subset of economic activity—saving and investment—is predicated on the assumption that prices and quantities do change, the notion of an economic system at rest seemed unrealistic.

D. Glasner, *Studies in the History of Monetary Theory*, Palgrave Studies in the History of Economic Thought, https://doi.org/10.1007/978-3-030-83426-5_17

Thus, in the works of classical economists, equilibrium was not an achievable state, but simply an end-state toward which economic processes, if allowed to operate without disturbance, were tending. This, not very satisfactory, equilibrium concept of a system at rest was undermined when the neoclassical pioneers, Jevons, Menger and Walras introduced the idea of optimizing decisions by rational agents. The notion of optimality, later formalized by Pareto, provided the analytical key to transforming the earlier classical equilibrium concept into a more robust and fruitful concept.

If each economic agent (household or business firm) is viewed as making optimal decisions, based on given preferences, and subject to constraints imposed by capacities, endowments, technologies, and the legal system, the equilibrium of an economy can be understood as a state of affairs in which the optimal decisions of each agent are both consistent with, and, directly or indirectly, contingent upon those of all other agents; the decisions of all buyers of how much to buy must be consistent with the decisions of all sellers of how much to sell. Like pieces in a jigsaw puzzle, decisions must fit in with all other decisions. If one decision is suboptimal, none of the decisions contingent upon that decision can be optimal.[1]

The idea of an equilibrium as a set of independently conceived, mutually consistent, optimal decisions was latent in the earlier notions of equilibrium, but it could not be coherently articulated without a formal concept of optimality.[2] The concept of an optimal plan allowed a uniquely economic idea of equilibrium to be formulated, not in terms of stationarity, but in terms of mutually consistent optimal plans.

But an optimal plan may encompass not just actions at a moment in time, it may encompass a sequence of actions taken over an interval of time. Indeed, the idea of an optimal plan at least implies a future different from the present. So, once grasped, the idea of equilibrium as the mutual consistency of optimal plans, it became possible to extend the idea to

[1] Individual agents can optimize their plans conditional on the suboptimal plans of other agents, but plans conditional on the suboptimal plans of other agents will not be socially optimal. For example, a chess player may choose an optimal strategy based on expected moves of his opponent. If both players are optimizing, the game must end in a draw. Note the analogy to the theory of second-best (Lipsey & Lancaster, 1956).

[2] An anonymous referee observes that the idea of optimality was in some sense already implicit in Smith (1937), but perhaps first formalized by Pareto (1906 [2014]), though Wicksteed (1910) may also have some claim to priority.

encompass change and development over time. But a lengthy process of intellectual reflection was required before change and development could be incorporated into an equilibrium framework, allowing time to have significance beyond merely assigning the label "time" to one of the axes in in an n-dimensional vector space.

This paper examines the process by which the concept of equilibrium was transformed from a timeless or static concept into an intertemporal one by focusing on the pathbreaking contribution of F. A. Hayek and its relation to subsequent developments of the idea of intertemporal equilibrium. While the idea of intertemporal equilibrium was articulated more or less contemporaneously with Hayek (1928 [1984]) by Lindahl (1929 [1939]) and Myrdal (1927), all three justly sharing credit for priority, in this paper I am especially interested in Hayek's subsequent 1937 paper, clarifying the distinction between perfect and correct foresight. Confusion about the meaning and interpretation of foresight led to Morgenstern's (1935 [1976]) attack on the idea of equilibrium. Hayek's, 1937 paper, apparently responding to Morgenstern's attack, provided a deep understanding of what is, and what is not, entailed by the concept of intertemporal equilibrium as the consistency of optimal plans extending through time.

Beyond explaining Hayek's articulation of intertemporal equilibrium, I examine four noteworthy, derivative versions of the intertemporal equilibrium in light of Hayek's articulation: (1) the modern version of a perfect-foresight intertemporal equilibrium embodied in the canonical complete-markets Arrow-Debreu-McKenzie (ADM) model, (2) Radner's modern incomplete-markets version of Hayek's intertemporal equilibrium as an equilibrium of plans, prices, and price expectations, (3) Hicks's incomplete-markets temporary equilibrium, and (4) Lucas's incomplete-markets rational-expectations equilibrium.

Before discussing these versions of intertemporal equilibrium, I summarize in Sect. 17.2 Hayek's 1937 contribution, clarifying the necessary conditions for the existence of an intertemporal equilibrium. In Sect. 17.3, I elaborate on Hayek's distinction between perfect foresight and contingently correct foresight in response to Morgenstern's attack on equilibrium and the assumption of perfect foresight. In Sect. 17.4, I consider Radner's incomplete-markets generalization of the ADM model, which captures Hayek's understanding of a correct-foresight intertemporal equilibrium. But in proving the existence of an equilibrium of plans, prices and price expectations, Radner departed from Hayek's philosophically parsimonious view of rationality and knowledge.

In Sect. 17.5, I explore how Hicks's concept of temporary equilibrium, inspired by Hayek, though later credited by Hicks (1965) to Lindahl (1929 [1939]), provides a bridge connecting the hypothetical equilibrium of correct expectations and consistency of plans with the messy real world of disappointed expectations and revised and abandoned plans. The advantage of the temporary-equilibrium approach is to provide the conceptual tools for understanding how financial crises occur and how they may be propagated and amplified into economic depressions, thereby enabling the kind of business-cycle model that Hayek had tried to create. But while Hicks omitted mention of Hayek's insights in articulating the temporary-equilibrium approach, Hayek, for his part, dismissed the temporary-equilibrium approach, failing to grasp its potential as a modeling strategy by which to adapt the equilibrium method to the expectational inconsistency among agents that characterizes disequilibrium.[3]

Finally, in Sect. 17.6, I discuss rational expectations in macroeconomic models, mainly to point out that it assumes away the problem of expectational convergence and plan consistency with which Hayek, Hicks, Radner and others who developed the idea of intertemporal equilibrium were so deeply concerned. Rational expectations thereby became the means by which the complete-markets, virtual-perfect-foresight ADM model could be transformed into a workable macroeconomic model, even though the ADM model is fundamentally unequipped, and unsuited, to analyze macroeconomic fluctuations. I conclude in Sect. 17.7.

17.2 Hayek and Intertemporal Equilibrium

Because current goods and services, and, otherwise identical, future goods and services can be treated as economically distinct, defining the conditions for an intertemporal equilibrium is formally almost equivalent to defining the conditions for a static equilibrium. Just as the conditions for a static equilibrium may be stated in terms of equalities between the

[3] I refer to "expectational inconsistency" among agents rather than "expectational error" to emphasize that inconsistent expectations are a sufficient condition for disequilibrium while "incorrect expectations" held by all agents could be equilibrium expectations in a possible (though not actual) state of the world.

marginal rates of substitution between goods and their corresponding price ratios, the conditions for an intertemporal equilibrium could be stated in terms of equalities between the marginal rates of intertemporal substitution and their corresponding intertemporal price ratios.

Bliss (1975) has explained with clarity and insight that the rate of interest is a relationship implicit in the structure of an intertemporal general-equilibrium price vector, but the key point was already made by Fisher (1896, 1907). In the following passage, Fisher (1907, 6–7) explains that the interest rate is not determined in a partial-equilibrium analysis of the market for loanable funds, but as a general-equilibrium phenomenon:

> If a modern business man is asked what determines the rate of interest, he may ... answer, "the supply and demand of loanable money." But "supply and demand" is a phrase which has been too often into service to cover up difficult problems. Even economists have been prone to employ it to describe economic causation which they could not unravel. ... It is true that every ratio of exchange is due to the resultant of causes operating on the buyer and seller, and we may classify these as "demand" and supply." But this fact does not relieve us of the necessity of examining specifically the two sets of causes, including utility in its effect on demand, and cost in its effect on supply. Consequently, when we say that the rate of interest is due to the supply and demand of "capital" or of "money" or of "loans," we are very far from having an adequate explanation. It is true that when merchants seek to discount bills at a bank in large numbers and for large amounts, the rate of interest will tend to be low. But we must inquire for what purposes and from what causes merchants thus apply to a bank for the discount of loans and others supply the bank with the funds to be loaned. The real problem is: What causes make the demand for loans and what causes make the supply? This question is not answered by the summary "supply and demand" theory. The explanation is not simply that those who have little capital demand them. In fact, the contrary is often the case.

Where Fisher's formulation fell short of Hayek's is in not explicitly recognizing that intertemporal equilibrium hinges on a consistency of plans contingent on equilibrium current prices and expected future prices. However, in a minimally realistic intertemporal model, unlike a static model or the quasi-static ADM model, marginal rates of substitution cannot be equated with ratios of known actual prices. Instead, marginal rates of substitution in a true intertemporal model must be equated either with ratios of *unknown expected* prices to known actual prices or with ratios of *unknown expected* prices to other *unknown expected* prices. It follows that, unless all economic agents have the same expectations of the future prices in terms of which they formulate their optimal plans, their plans cannot be mutually consistent.

The formal identity between the necessary conditions for a static equilibrium and the necessary conditions for an intertemporal equilibrium is preserved in the ADM model with a complete set of forward markets covering all contingent events. However, that formal identity cannot be maintained without a complete set of markets, because agents cannot optimize relying on their *common knowledge* of actual prices unless they all have access to all current and forward prices when choosing their optimal plans. With incomplete forward markets, agents must optimize relying on expected, but unknown, future prices.

With complete forward and contingent markets, the resulting intertemporal equilibrium presupposes that all economic decisions are made *before* production and consumption begin. The passage of time is conceptual, and all decisions are pre-programmed. The unrealism of the ADM paradigm is impressive, rendering money and asset markets superfluous. Though intertemporal in the sense that actual production and consumption are presumed to occur in a sequence of distinct time periods, all decisions are made irrevocably in advance.

Although Hayek (1937) provided the first English articulation of the concept of intertemporal equilibrium, it was from Hicks (1939) that the concept became widely known. Hicks distinguished between a full dynamic equilibrium in which expectations are correct and a temporary equilibrium in which expectations may be incorrect while current prices adjust to clear current (spot) markets.[4] Despite generally acknowledging

[4] Flow demands and flow supplies need not be equal, but accumulation or decumulation of stocks is voluntary in the sense that, given the future price expectations of stock holders, stock holdings increase or decrease by the amounts desired. See Hicks (1983, 232).

> What makes the difference is that on the flexprice method it is insisted that the producer will only accumulate stocks if he thinks that the price he will be able to get, by selling them in some future period, will be better (in spite of the costs of holding) than what he could get by selling now; so in this sense the accumulation is *voluntary*. If the behaviour of all markets is interpreted in this manner, the

Hayek's contribution to the ideas presented, Hicks did not acknowledge Hayek's, or any author's, contribution to the idea of intertemporal equilibrium.[5]

Although the ADM model is now considered the canonical version of an intertemporal equilibrium model, the assumption of complete forward and contingent markets upon which it rests attenuate its status as an intertemporal model. At time zero, not only does trading for all future time periods take place, contingent trading also occurs for all future time periods. Just as identical goods traded at distinct prices for delivery at distinct times and places, identical goods can be distinguished under different states of the world (an ice-cream cone on July 4, 2022 in Washington DC at 2 p.m. only if the temperature is above 90 degrees). Given complete state-contingent markets and the known probabilities of the contingent events, an equilibrium price vector for the complete set of markets would result in optimal trades reallocating the risks associated with future contingencies, thereby allowing optimal resource-allocation across space, time, and states of the world.

The assumptions of the ADM model are intended to replace what was called a perfect-foresight equilibrium, in which agents can foresee the future. But the alternative assumptions of the ADM model—that agents across all future time periods gather at time zero to trade at an equilibrium price vector covering all time periods and all possible states of the world, for which states they assign accurate probabilities—hardly seem less extreme than that of perfect foresight.

The seminal work of Radner (1972, 1979, 1982) in relaxing the extreme assumptions of the ADM model, puts Hayek's contribution to the understanding of the necessary conditions for an intertemporal equilibrium into sharp relief. At an informal level, Hayek had addressed the same problem that Radner, possessing analytical tools unavailable to Hayek, did: under what conditions could agents, lacking both perfect

system is regarded as being *in equilibrium* all the time.... The flexprice method is a *temporary equilibrium* method.

[5] Milgate (1979) drew attention to Hayek's key role in developing the idea of intertemporal equilibrium in terms of the consistency of decentralized optimal plans and to document Hayek's claim to priority in introducing the concept to economists. See Currie and Steedman (1989) for an illuminating and insightful comparison of the evolution of Hayek's and Lindahl's understanding of intertemporal equilibrium between 1928 and 1939.

foresight and complete markets, reach a state of intertemporal equilibrium? Without complete forward and state-contingent markets, an intertemporal equilibrium is not determined in advance; it unfolds as time passes. Outcomes are anticipated, not predetermined.

Rediscovering Hayek's insight, Radner described intertemporal equilibrium under uncertainty as an equilibrium of plans, prices, and price expectations (EPPPE). Even if it exists, the Radner equilibrium differs from an ADM equilibrium, because, with incomplete markets, agents are subject to unavoidable uncertainty. The distinction between ex ante and ex post, absent from the ADM equilibrium, is inherent in the Radner equilibrium.

Additionally, because trading in the ADM model occurs before "time" starts, neither the holding of an asset used only as a medium of exchange nor the existence of a liquidity premium can be rationalized.[6] In early writings on business cycles, Hayek (1929 [1933]) seemed to grasp this point, questioning whether the holding of money could be explained in a model of full equilibrium, and observing that the identity of aggregate demand and aggregate supply characteristic of a barter economy is broken when money is held and used as a medium of exchange. The shift from a barter to a money economy implies that Say's Law can be violated, and that cumulative deviations from an equilibrium time-path may occur.

Hayek never realized his early hopes that the Walrasian equilibrium method could accommodate the existence of money, uncertainty, and other features of the real world, bringing the analytical rigor of the equilibrium method and the optimality principle to bear on the study of economic fluctuations. Although that research program required resources beyond those then at Hayek's, or perhaps anyone else's, disposal, it would be unfair to fault Hayek for perceiving and framing a problem he could not solve. But nearly at the end of Hayek's intensive engagement with business-cycle theory, Hicks (1939) introduced the concept of temporary equilibrium as an alternative approach to studying economic fluctuations. Recognizing the key point that full intertemporal equilibrium requires that agents base their plans upon correctly foreseen future prices, Hicks suggested restricting the assumption of equilibrium and market-clearing to the current period while allowing agents to base

[6] Patinkin (1965) avoided the problem of explaining why money is held in general equilibrium with an ad hoc assumption real money balances are an argument in household utility functions.

their plans to purchase and sell in the current period on diverging, and therefore incorrect, expectations of future prices. Hayek (1941), however, dismissed the idea of temporary equilibrium.

Moreover, the holding of an asset as a medium of exchange and the provision by financial intermediaries of credit instruments that serve as media of exchange can be rationalized in a temporary-equilibrium framework (Bliss, 1976). In temporary equilibrium, not only can the private supply of a medium of exchange be modeled, but the systemic breakdowns and financial crises have an obvious and straightforward explanation along lines explained by Hawtrey (1913) as the result of the divergent expectations held by agents and financial intermediaries. Extreme divergences of actual from expected prices may preclude the existence of a temporary equilibrium. Perfect price flexibility cannot lead to an equilibrium that does not exist.

In a general-equilibrium framework with incomplete markets, price expectations, like spot prices, are equilibrating variables, in the sense that an equilibrium exists only for a subset of vectors of prices *and* expected prices.[7] Although we have a partial-equilibrium theory of how spot prices may tend to reach their equilibrium values, we have no comparable theory for expected-price equilibration. The rational-expectations postulate *imposes* expected-price equilibration as a methodological axion implied by rational optimizing behavior rather deriving correct expectations of future prices from more basic assumptions about rational conduct in a theory of market interactions. The macroeconomic significance of the methodologically imposed rational-expectations axiom is thus equivalent to the assumption of perfect foresight.

17.3 Correct Versus Perfect Foresight in Intertemporal Equilibrium

I have suggested that Hayek's conceptual breakthrough was to view equilibrium not as a stationary state, but as a state in which decentralized plans are both individually optimal and mutually consistent, so that the individual plans could, potentially, be executed simultaneously without revision or regret.

[7] Under certain conditions, there may be expected prices that are self-fulfilling and give rise to sunspot equilibria or rational bubbles (Cass and Shell 1983). Such equilibria require a convergence of individual expectations.

In an intertemporal context, optimal plans cannot be formulated on the basis of just those prices at which transactions are currently executed; the relevant set of prices must include the future prices at which planned future transactions will be executed. Because even decisions about current transactions depend on the anticipated prices at which future transactions occur, future prices affect both current and future demands and supplies. So the concept of intertemporal equilibrium requires generalizing the notion of equilibrium as a vector of all currently observed prices of goods and services into a multi-period context, so that the equilibrium price vector includes both the prices of goods currently traded and the prices of goods that agents plan to buy or sell in the future.

But without a complete set of forward markets, the future prices on which plans are formulated are not known, only anticipated. And unless each individual plan is formulated on the basis of the same vector of anticipated prices, those individually optimal plans may well not be executed without revision, because at least some of those plans, having been based on incorrectly expected future prices, will turn out to be sub-optimal relative to the actual price vector.

The recognition that the mutual consistency of optimal plans requires individuals to anticipate the future prices upon which their optimal choices are conditioned suggests that an intertemporal equilibrium cannot be attained unless individual agents are endowed with extraordinary capacities of foresight. This reasoning led Oskar Morgenstern (1935 [1976]) to launch an attack on the concept of equilibrium owing to its reliance on the self-contradictory, assumption of perfect foresight.

> The impossibly high claims … attributed to the intellectual efficiency of the economic subject immediately indicate that there are included in this equilibrium system not ordinary men, but rather … exactly equal demi-gods, in case the claim of complete foresight is fulfilled. If this is the case, there is, of course, nothing more to be done. If "full" or "perfect" foresight is to provide the basis of the theory of equilibrium in the strictly specified sense, and in the meaning obviously intended by the economic authors, then, a completely meaningless assumption is being considered. If limitations are introduced in such a way that the perfection of foresight is not reached, then these limitations are to be stated very precisely. They would have to be so narrowly drawn that the fundamental aim of producing ostensibly full rationality of the system by means of high, de facto unlimited, foresight, would be lost. For the theoretical economist, there is no way out of this dilemma.

Continuing in this vein, Morgenstern reinforced his argument against perfect foresight by invoking an example that reappeared in the famous work on game theory by von Neumann and Morgenstern (1944, 177).

> Sherlock Holmes, pursued by his opponent, Moriarty, leaves London for Dover. The train stops at a station on the way, and he alights there rather than traveling on to Dover. He has seen Moriarty at the railway station, recognizes that he is very clever and expects that Moriarty will take a faster special train in order to catch him in Dover. Holmes' anticipation turns out to be correct. But what if Moriarty had been still more clever, had estimated Holmes' mental abilities better and had foreseen his actions accordingly? Then, obviously, he would have traveled to the intermediate station. Holmes, again, would have had to calculate that, and he himself would have decided to go on to Dover. Whereupon, Moriarty would again have "reacted" differently. Because of so much thinking they might not have been able to act at all or the intellectually weaker of the two would have surrendered to the other in the Victoria Station, since the whole flight would have become unnecessary. Examples of this kind can be drawn from everywhere. However, chess, strategy, etc. presuppose expert knowledge, which encumbers the example unnecessarily.
>
> One may be easily convinced that here lies an insoluble paradox. And the situation is not improved, but, rather, greatly aggravated if we assume that more than two individuals--as, for example, is the case with exchange--are brought together into a position, which would correspond to the one brought forward here. Always, there is exhibited an endless chain of reciprocally conjectural reactions and counter-reactions. This chain can never be broken by an act of knowledge but always only through an arbitrary act--a resolution. This resolution, again, would have to be foreseen by the two or more persons concerned. The paradox still remains no matter how one attempts to twist or turn things around. Unlimited foresight and economic equilibrium are thus irreconcilable with one another. But can equilibrium really take place with a faulty, heterogeneous foresight, however, it may be disposed? This is the question which arises at once when an answer is sought. One can even say this: has foresight been truly introduced at all into the consideration of equilibrium, or, rather, does not the theorem of equilibrium generally stand in no proven connection with the assumptions about foresight, so that a false assumption is being considered?

Zappia (1999) suggests that Morgenstern's attack on intertemporal equilibrium and perfect foresight prompted Hayek's (1937) articulation of the idea. Hayek's insight was that an intertemporal equilibrium is not the causal result of correct foresight. Rather, correct foresight is a defining property of "intertemporal equilibrium." Morgenstern's error was to mistake a tautological statement about what must be true if intertemporal equilibrium obtains for a statement about what causes a state of intertemporal equilibrium to be reached. As Hayek (pp. 41–42) put it:

> Correct foresight is then not, as it has sometimes been misunderstood, a precondition which must exist in order that equilibrium may be arrived at. It is rather the defining characteristic of a state of equilibrium. Nor need foresight for this purpose be perfect in the sense that it need extend into the indefinite future, or that everybody must foresee everything correctly. We should rather say that equilibrium will last so long as the anticipations prove correct, and that they need to be correct only on those points which are relevant for the decisions of the individuals.

It is worth noting that, under a probabilistic interpretation of the interaction between Holmes and Moriarty, there could be equilibrium mixed strategies in a repeated Holmes-Moriarty game. But if the interaction is a unique non-repeatable event, the correct interpretation of the interaction is not that correct foresight is impossible, but that the game has no equilibrium solution.[8] It is therefore precisely the non-existence of an equilibrium that renders correct foresight a logical impossibility. It is the existence of an equilibrium that makes correct foresight possible, not perfect foresight that makes equilibrium possible.

17.4 Radner on the Equilibrium of Plans, Prices, and Price Expectations

In this section, I discuss Radner's treatment of an equilibrium of plans, prices, and price expectations (EPPPE) and its relationship to Hayek's conception of intertemporal equilibrium.

Although it does not appear that Radner was influenced by Hayek, Radner's conception of EPPPE can be viewed as a technically sophisticated version of Hayek's conception of an intertemporal equilibrium as a state in which agents, independently formulating their optimal plans based

[8] Alternatively, as Koppl and Rosser (2002) argued, even if there is a mixed (probabilistic) strategy that could be considered an equilibrium solution of a non-repeated game, the equilibrium mixed probabilistic solution could not necessarily be found in a finite number of iterations owing to the reflexive nature of the problem.

on observed current prices and conditional on expected future prices, can execute their plans as intended. While currently observed prices are treated as common knowledge, expected future prices are conjectures, based partly on common, and partly on private, knowledge, as well as on the subjective methods used to form expectations of future prices.

The mutual consistency of the optimal plans of agents turns out to be equivalent to the condition that all agents observe the same current prices—their common knowledge—and make the same forecasts of the future prices upon which they rely in formulating their optimal plans. Even if their forecasts of future prices are not realized, until those forecasts are changed or disappointed, their plans remain mutually consistent and, relative to the information on which those plans were chosen, optimal. The failure of equilibrium to be realized is attributable to new information that renders once optimal plans sub-optimal. But until new information becomes available, the mutual consistency of optimal plans signifies, at least momentarily, an equilibrium state.

The EPPPE, being an equilibrium characterized by a vector of observed current, and expected future, prices, differs fundamentally from the ADM equilibrium in which equilibrium prices over all future time periods become common knowledge before trading starts. Furthermore, under the assumptions of the ADM model, the equilibrium is Pareto-optimal, and any Pareto-optimum allocation, by a suitable redistribution of initial endowments, could be achieved as a general equilibrium (two welfare theorems). These results do not generally hold for EPPPE, because, unlike ADM agents, EPPPE agents can acquire additional information over time, not only passively, but by devoting resources to produce or acquire information.

Devoting resources to obtaining information results in two inefficiencies: first, by creating non-convexities (owing to start-up costs in information-gathering activities) inconsistent with the uniform prices characteristic of the ADM equilibrium; second, by creating incentives to devote resources to acquire information whose value derives from trading with those without the information (Hirshleifer, 1971). But the salient macroeconomic distinction between the EPPPE and the ADM equilibria is the fragility of EPPPE. Unlike the ADM equilibrium, established once and forever at time zero, the EPPPE, even if achieved, is momentary and subject to revision or disequilibrium as new information induces changes in current or expected future prices, requiring agents to revise, or replace, formerly optimal plans.

In the EPPPE, time is not, as it is in the ADM model, a mere appendage (Bliss, 1976, p. 187). EPPPE therefore accounts for phenomena, practices, and institutions excluded from the ADM model, e.g., stock markets in which ownership shares of firms, capitalizing the expected future income streams generated by those firms, are traded, and a medium of exchange supplied by banks. Each agent in the ADM model faces, at time zero, an intertemporal budget constraint over periods from 1 to *n*. Given that constraint, Walras's Law holds across all time periods, all agents transacting at the same *n*-period price vector. The solvency and the integrity of all parties to all transactions being assured through the trading process at time zero, a loan default is impossible, and all agents can trade income between time periods at the same intertemporal price ratios. All transactions being costlessly and irrevocably executed at time zero, holding or supplying a medium of exchange cannot be rationalized.

Moreover, an equilibrium vector of all future prices having been announced at time zero, each agent knows that optimal plans conditioned on those prices will be executed exactly as initially formulated. The future income streams from each firm being known in advance, a market for trading shares of firms would be redundant.

The ADM equilibrium describes a process different from Radner's EPPPE, because, in EPPPE, agents cannot assume that their current plans will remain so, even if those plans are at any time both optimal and mutually consistent with those of all other agents. Unlike the ADM equilibrium, EPPPE does not exclude the possibility that new or updated information will upset an existing equilibrium, rendering formerly optimal plans sub-optimal and incompatible.

Because momentarily equilibrium plans may eventually require revision, agents must consider the solvency of counterparties. The potential for insolvency allows financial intermediaries (aka banks) to offer their debt, generally considered more reliable than that of other agents, in exchange for the debt of non-banks seeking to finance purchases of consumption or investment goods. Many agents therefore exchange their own debt for generally accepted bank debt with fixed face value. Moreover, as new information becomes available, agents may undertake speculative trades of commodities or assets. Such assets include shares of firms, and agents may revise their valuations of shares as they revise their expectations of future prices.[9]

I discuss the special role of banks at length in the following section on temporary equilibrium.

But one point deserves immediate attention: in the EPPPE, if agents hold differing expectations of future prices, Walras's Law may be violated. The standard proof of Walras's Law assumes that the market price for any commodity (defined by location and time period) is the same price in all transactions. But in the EPPPE, in which only current, not future, prices are observed, plans are formulated based on expected future prices. If agents hold different price expectations for the same commodity, then some of those expectations must be disappointed. Agents, whose plans were conditioned on overly optimistic price expectations, may find themselves unable to discharge commitments to buy (or future commitments to repay debts financing present purchase) leading to the violation of Walras's Law (see Chapter 9).

Finally, a word about Radner's terminology. Radner (1987, 312) writes:

> A trader's expectations concern both future environmental events and future prices. Regarding expectations about future environmental events, there is no conceptual problem. According to the Expected Utility Hypothesis, each trader is characterized by a subjective probability measure on the set of complete histories of the environment. Since, by definition, the evolution of the environment is exogenous, a trader's conditional probability of a future event, given the information to date, is well-defined.
>
> It is not so obvious how to proceed with regard to trader's expectations about future prices. I shall contrast two possible approaches. In the first, which I shall call the perfect foresight approach, let us assume that the behaviour of traders is such as to determine, for each complete history of the environment, a unique corresponding sequence of price system[s]...
>
> Thus, the perfect foresight approach implies that, in equilibrium, traders have common price expectation functions. These price expectation functions indicate, for each date-event pair, what the equilibrium price system would be in the corresponding market at that date-event pair. ... [I]t follows that, in equilibrium the traders would have strategies (plans) such that if these strategies were carried out, the markets would be cleared at

[9] As noted above, the possibility of an equilibrium bubble cannot be ruled out, though the definition of a "speculative bubble" may be tricky.

> each date-event pair. Call such plans *consistent*. A set of common price expectations and corresponding consistent plans is called an *equilibrium of plans, prices, and price expectations*.

My only reservation about Radner's formulation concerns the definition of equilibrium in terms of the assumed capacity of traders to predict prices rather than the correctness of those expectations. Why traders can predict future prices correctly is irrelevant for the definition of EPPPE. When agents' price expectations are momentarily in accord, it is irrelevant whether expectations are in accord because agents share the correct model of the economy, or because, they randomly formed matching expectations of future prices.

Nevertheless, by pursuing the idea that agents have their own models of how the economy works, Radner modified the perfect-foresight approach in which all relevant information is held in common. In such cases, by observing that prices differ from what had been expected, agents may be able to draw corresponding inferences about their environment.

> The situation in which traders enter the market with different non-price information presents an opportunity for agents to learn about the environment from prices, since current prices reflect, in a possibly complicated manner, the non-price information signals received by the various agents. To take an extreme example, the "inside information" of a trader in a securities market may lead him to bid up the price to a level higher than it otherwise would have been. … [A]n astute market observer might be able to infer that an insider has obtained some favourable information, just by careful observation of the price movement. (p. 313)

The ability to infer non-price information from otherwise inexplicable movements in prices suggested to Radner a particular concept of rational-expectations equilibrium.

> [E]conomic agents have the opportunity to revise their individual models in the light of observations and published data. Hence, there is a feedback from the true relationship to the individual models. An equilibrium of this system, in which the individual models are identical with the true model, is called a rational-expectations equilibrium. This concept of equilibrium is more subtle, of course, than the ordinary concept of equilibrium of supply and demand. In a rational-expectations equilibrium, not only are prices determined so as to equate supply and demand, but individual economic

> agents correctly perceive the true relationship between the non-price information received by the market participants and the resulting equilibrium market prices. (p. 313)

While an interesting line of theoretical inquiry, Radner's concept does not capture the Hayek's (1937) distinction between the necessary conditions for an intertemporal equilibrium to obtain and the assumptions that entail satisfaction of those conditions. If all agents formulate their optimal plans based on the same vector of current and expected future prices, those optimal plans are potentially consistent and will be successfully executed without revision if the underlying common knowledge upon which their plans were conditioned proves to have been correct. How it happened that they arrived at identical expectations—by luck, chance or supernatural powers of foresight—is irrelevant to the definition of equilibrium.

At any rate, Radner properly recognized that to be a useful tool of positive analysis, equilibrium theory had to be revised to relax the necessary conditions for equilibrium to obtain. And although EPPPE accommodates a richer set of activities and institutions than the ADM (virtual perfect-foresight) equilibrium, Radner argued for a further relaxation of the assumptions to allow incorrect future price expectations to be accommodated within an equilibrium analytical framework.

> Although it is capable of describing a richer set of institutions and behavior than is the Arrow-Debreu model, the perfect-foresight approach is contrary to the spirit of much of competitive market theory in that it postulates that individual traders must be able to forecast ... the equilibrium prices that will prevail in the future under all alternative states of the environment. ...[T]his approach ... seems to require of the traders a capacity for imagination and computation far beyond what is realistic. ...
>
> These last considerations lead us in a different direction, which I shall call the bounded rationality approach. This approach ... expresses itself in terms of various retreats from the hypothesis of "fully rational" behavior by traders. ... An example of the bounded rationality approach is the theory of temporary equilibrium. (pp. 313–314)

Irrespective of the "rationality" or computational powers of agents, the key issue is whether agents share identical expectations of future prices. If expectations are in accord, a momentary equilibrium of plans, prices, and price expectations, though not guaranteed, is possible. When expectations diverge, a temporary equilibrium may not even exist, and what kind of the dynamic path(s) is (are) associated with diverging expectations is unclear. In the next section, I discuss the characteristics and implications of a temporary-equilibrium approach for macroeconomics.

17.5 Hayek, Hicks, and Temporary Equilibrium

What defines an intertemporal equilibrium is that agents share the same—correct—expectations of future prices over their planning horizons. In such an equilibrium, the optimizing plans of the agents are at least momentarily consistent, because, given those expectations, none of the agents would change its optimal plan unless price expectations change or are disappointed.

A natural generalization of the intertemporal equilibrium concept is for agents to hold different price expectations reflecting differences in information or the processing of information. But given informational differences, agents' subjectively optimal plans will be inconsistent and incapable of simultaneous implementation without revision. Unfortunately, this generalization seems incompatible with the sequential equilibrium of optimal plans, prices and price expectations conceived by Hayek and elaborated by Radner. As Radner recognized in the passage quoted at the end of the previous section, relaxing the assumption that agents have correct expectations about future prices means a retreat from the assumption of full rationality, full rationality requiring that each agent optimize subject to the optimal plans of all other agents.

The question arises how the absence of an equilibrium in which agents are executing optimal plans can be reconciled with the intuitive notion of market clearing, routinely applied to markets for assets, for current delivery, and for services. If those markets are in equilibrium, in the sense that prices adjust to equate the quantities demanded and supplied, how can the inconsistency of the optimizing plans of agents be reconciled with market-clearing equilibrium?

Hicks (1939) was the first to analyze this intermediate situation, which in one sense is, and in another is not, an equilibrium. Agents' divergent price expectations on the basis of which they formulate optimal plans makes the disappointment of at least some of those expectations inevitable, with at least some agents being unable to execute their plans as originally formulated.

In his early writings, Hayek suggested analyzing business cycles as deviations from an equilibrium path. The problem Hayek struggled with was that equilibrium analysis can characterize the equilibrium path of an economy, but not a non-equilibrium path, corresponding to attempts by agents to implement incompatible plans that must be revised or replaced. When the optimality (aka rationality) postulate is inapplicable, standard equilibrium methods become analytically suspect.

Hayek (1929 [1933], 1931) attributed cumulative cyclical deviations from an equilibrium path to the lagged effects of monetary expansion, which cause an unsustainable, investment-driven increase of output and employment followed by a disappointment of expectations leading to a cumulative decrease in output and employment. But Hayek's use of equilibrium analysis to explain business-cycle fluctuations was unsuccessful, and his monetary theory of the cycle remained inconsistent with standard equilibrium analysis.

In temporary equilibrium, all spot prices adjust to clear markets for assets and for current delivery. If future prices don't match current expectations, agents will revise or replace plans that were based on incorrect expectations. Hayek (1941, pp. 44–45) mentioned temporary equilibrium as an alternative to the Walrasian intertemporal equilibrium, only to dismiss it. His cursory comments on temporary equilibrium mark the conclusion to Hayek's unsuccessful efforts to fashion a coherent business-cycle theory in a Walrasian general-equilibrium framework. Yet, Hicksian temporary equilibrium might have provided Hayek with an alternative framework within which to analyze the divergent expectations that lead first to an expansion and then, as expectations adjust, trigger a downturn and, with a variable lag, a recovery.[10]

How could a temporary-equilibrium method have enabled Hayek to describe the conditions for a cumulative monetary disequilibrium? I make no attempt to outline a specifically Hayekian theory of monetary disequilibrium, though others may find such an endeavor worthwhile. My focus

[10] Keynes (1936) also sought to provide a vehicle whereby equilibrium analysis could be made applicable to a disequilibrium phenomenon. But instead of pursuing an intertemporal equilibrium approach, Keynes reverted to a single-period multiplier analysis with appendages like the explicitly forward-looking marginal efficiency of capital but remained in the background of his one-period equilibrium model. See Laidler (1998) for insightful discussion of these issues.

is on monetary effects without attending to the capital-theoretic analysis on which Hayek, in my view, laid undue stress.

As noted above, agents are aware that their price expectations may not be implemented as planned, recognizing that their plans may require revision or replacement. Agents also recognize that, given such uncertainty, not all debt instruments are equally reliable. The understanding that debt instruments—promises to make future payments—must be assessed makes specializing in debt assessment by financial intermediaries profitable.

A particular kind of financial intermediary—banks—is of special interest. After assessing the debt instruments offered by non-banks, the bank selects those instruments that it considers sufficiently reliable to be accepted in exchange for the bank's instruments. Non-banks do not generally accept the instruments of non-banks on terms as favorable as those offered by banks. In return for non-bank instruments, the bank issues borrowers a corresponding amount of its own instruments, which, because the bank promises to redeem those instruments for the numeraire commodity on demand at a fixed pre-specified rate, are generally accepted at face value. Banks' debt instruments therefore serve as a medium of exchange, enabling non-banks to make expenditures they might not otherwise have made.

In assessing a prospective borrower's creditworthiness, a bank makes two judgments. First, is the income-earning capacity of the borrower sufficient to make the repayments to which the borrower commits himself? Second, if the borrower is unable to meet its repayment obligations, does the borrower post sufficient collateral to allow the debt to be recovered? In making those judgments, the bank must assess both the future income of the borrower and the future value of the collateral.

In a temporary equilibrium, agents hold differing price expectations, so that they are vulnerable if they have incurred future obligations conditioned on expected prices higher than realized prices. If they hold assets of sufficient value, they may still be able to meet their obligations by selling assets. Besides selling assets, they may have to reduce expenditures, thereby reducing the incomes of other agents below their expectations. Many agents will prefer to finance current obligations by borrowing and repaying on a fixed schedule to distress liquidation of assets, but only prospective borrowers able to show creditworthiness, which, in turn, depends on prices and expected prices, will be able to borrow.

Agents whose optimistic price expectations have been disappointed, whether they are able to borrow or must liquidate assets, will revise previous plans, primarily by reducing expenditures. The disappointment of some agents' expectations becomes cumulative when the disappointment of their optimistic expectations is not offset by the better-than-expected results of other agents (Hawtrey, 1913, 210–214).

If the disappointment of optimistic price expectations is of sufficient magnitude, or if the disappointment is systematic, for example, prices falling generally below what they had been expected to be, a systemic contractionary process may start (Fisher, 1933). If so, instead of revising their plans, some agents may choose, or may be forced, to abandon them entirely. In general, beyond some threshold level of disappointment, previously optimal plans will be abandoned rather than revised, whether by firms that cease to produce or by workers that become unemployed.

When agents whose price expectations have been disappointed respond with marginal revisions of existing plans rather than scrapping them or replacing them with new ones, a temporary equilibrium with disappointed expectations may still exist, and price adjustments in the markets for current delivery may achieve a temporary equilibrium with markets for current delivery clearing notwithstanding that agents hold divergent expectations of future prices. A suboptimal temporary equilibrium is inferior to the allocation that would have resulted had all agents correctly anticipated future prices, but, given a history of incorrect price expectations and misallocations of capital assets, labor, and other factors of production, the sub-optimal temporary equilibrium may be the best currently feasible outcome.[11]

But even the existence of a temporary equilibrium cannot be taken for granted. If actual prices differ from what they were expected to be, sufficiently large deviations of actual from expected prices in markets for current delivery may imply discontinuous changes in the excess demands of agents (Bliss, 1976, 199–201). When the price of a product falls below some threshold, one or more firms producing that product will cease producing it, either shutting down or switching to the production of another. Moreover, below some threshold price for a product, firms producing the product may be forced into bankruptcy and households with ownership shares in the firm may also become bankrupt, especially if households anticipating high prices borrowed on that expectation and are unable to repay their loans at current prices. The implied discontinuities in

[11] Of course, even if a price vector consistent with temporary equilibrium exists, there is no assurance that the temporary-equilibrium price vector will be arrived at.

excess demand functions make it difficult to apply the standard fixed-point theorems normally used to demonstrate the existence of equilibrium.[12]

If ownership shares in a firm forced to cease production are held by households that have predicated their consumption plans on prior borrowing and current repayment obligations, those households may be unable to fulfill their obligations once those firms stop paying dividends and share prices plummet. The net worth of banks holding debts incurred by firms or households that borrowers cannot service may be reduced sufficiently to impair the creditworthiness of the banks, potentially leading to a systemic breakdown of the payment system and a sudden contraction in the privately supplied medium of exchange. Such systemic crises and breakdowns are not excluded by a temporary-equilibrium model if realized prices diverge sufficiently from the prices agents had expected and whose consumption and production plans had been conditioned on those expectations.

From the perspective of macroeconomic and business-cycle theory, the introduction of banks that supply a medium of exchange while intermediating between ultimate borrowers and ultimate lenders seems a promising way to think about how an economy may, in some circumstance, operate at or near a temporary equilibrium, but, under other circumstances, may break down. This approach captures the potential for monetary disruptions caused by the lending and money-creating activities of private banks—a central concern of Hayek—while providing a rationale for the money-creating operations of private banks, which, in Hayek's business-cycle writings, seemed, on balance, destabilizing.

In the real world, economies sometimes appear to function, from a high-level macroeconomic perspective, reasonably well with low unemployment, increasing per capita output, and stable prices. At other times, economies do not function well, with high unemployment, negative growth, and with high rates of inflation or deflation. Sometimes,

[12] Depending on what assumptions are made about limited liability and bankruptcy, the fluctuations in wealth resulting from unexpected price changes will be reflected entirely in the potentially negative wealth of shareholders if there is no limited liability, or, if there is limited liability, in creditors holding non-performing debit. "[I]t seems plain that the history of the economy may make it impossible to guarantee the continuity properties of the various functions and correspondences and this is bad for existence proofs" (Arrow & Hahn, 1971, 354). Also see (Ravagnani, 1989) for a discussion of the problem of reconciling the expectational differences of households owning the firm with the investment and production plans chosen by the firm.

economies are beset with financial crises in which there is contagious insolvency, affecting many formerly solvent firms, with credit becoming unavailable. A macroeconomic model should be able to account in some way for the diversity of observed macroeconomic experience, and specify, if only in general terms, the conditions that lead to stability or instability.

The temporary-equilibrium paradigm offers such a theoretical account: the degree of congruence between actual prices and the prices that had been expected by agents. When price expectations are reasonably accurate, the economy is able to function at or near a temporary equilibrium. When expectations diverge greatly, or are disappointed by unexpected changes, a temporary equilibrium may not exist, and even if it does, the equilibrium may not reached. Price adjustments in current markets may be incapable of restoring equilibrium inasmuch as expectations of future prices must also adjust to equilibrate the economy, there being no market mechanism that causes price expectations to adjust in a way that is consistent with restoration of equilibrium.

This insight is consistent with and elucidates Leijonhufvud's (1973 [1981]) idea of a corridor within which an economy normally tends to stay close to an equilibrium path. However, if the economy drifts, or is shocked away, from its equilibrium time path, the kinds of discontinuities described above may overwhelm whatever stabilizing forces had previously been keeping the economy within the corridor.

17.6 Hayek, Radner, and Rational Expectations

In this section, I focus on a particular kind of intertemporal equilibrium: rational-expectations equilibrium. It is noteworthy that in his discussions of intertemporal equilibrium, Radner assigns a meaning to the term "rational-expectations equilibrium" different from that normally associated with the term, defining it as the equilibrium that results if agents can draw inferences about the beliefs of other agents upon observing prices that differ from what had been expected. Attributing the differences between observed and expected prices to the information of better-informed agents, they revise their own expectations to correspond to the implied information justifying observed prices.[13]

[13] At least one historical episode in which unknown—indeed secret—information was inferred from publicly available price data has been documented. In 1954, Armen Alchian inferred the chemicals used to make the just developed hydrogen bomb by identifying

Radner also showed that if less-informed agents can infer from the deviation of observed from expected prices the information used by more-informed agents to cause actual prices to deviate from their expectations, those inferences do not necessarily cause a convergence on correct price expectations. The interaction between expectational revisions and price changes need not lead to correct expectations even in the absence of further new information.[14] Radner's result actually supports Hayek's insight that, although expectations are equilibrating variables, there is no economic mechanism that leads expectations toward their equilibrium values.[15] Unlike the mechanism whereby current prices rise (fall) in response to excess demands (supplies), no corresponding feedback mechanism operates on price expectations inconsistent with equilibrium. If price expectations are brought into correspondence with what the future holds, it comes about through their own more or less well-informed conjectures, not by automatic responses to market signals.

Although Radner's conception of rational expectations differs from the more commonly used meaning of the term, his conception clarifies the narrow sense in which the rational-expectations assumption has a role to play in macroeconomics. In this narrow sense, the following rational-expectations assumption is a property of any macroeconomic model: if agents in a model hold price expectations equal to the predicted prices of the model, those expectations will be realized. That is, equilibrium price expectations must be self-fulfilling. If equilibrium price expectations are not self-fulfilling, the model is internally inconsistent and flawed.

companies whose stock prices had risen too much to be otherwise explained. Then consulting at the Rand Corporation, Alchian wrote a paper for Rand listing the chemicals used to make the hydrogen bomb. When word of the paper reached the Pentagon, the paper was confiscated, at the behest of the Defense Department, from Alchian and destroyed. Newhard (2014) recounts the incident and reconstructs Alchian's event study.

[14] Such interactions give rise to the indeterminacy exemplified by the Holmes-Moriarty interaction discussed above. See Koppl and Rosser (2002).

[15] See Hayek (1937, 47).

> For any one individual, constancy of the data does in no way mean constancy of all the facts independent of himself, since, of course, only the tastes and not the actions of other people can in this sense be constant. As all those other people will change their decisions as they gain experience about the external facts and about other people's actions, there is no reason why these processes of successive changes should ever come to an end.

But there is a difference between saying (a) that a model should have the property that correct expectations are self-fulfilling and saying (b) that agents in the model understand how the model works, and, based on their knowledge of the model, form expectations of the equilibrium predicted by the model.

Rational expectations in the first sense is a minimal consistency property of an economic model; in the latter sense it is an empirical hypothesis. But a macroeconomic model is not ipso facto a theory of how expectations are formed. One can assert rational expectations as a hypothesis, but it remains an empirical statement that may, or may not, be true, not an axiomatic truism or a methodological imperative. The nearly sacrosanct status of the rational-expectations postulate in modern macroeconomics is supported not by empirical evidence, but by methodological tyrannizing and a reductive insistence on microfoundations.

Hayek (1937) explained that correct expectations are logically implied by the concept of an equilibrium of mutually consistent plans extending through time. But he also understood that correct expectations are not normally descriptive of reality and that we lack a theoretical explanation of any mechanism whereby correct expectations become commonly shared, merely alluding to the empirical observation—perhaps not the most realistic description of reality in 1937—of a tendency for markets to move toward equilibrium, so that there is a tendency toward expectational accuracy over time.

It is noteworthy that, when Muth (1961) introduced the idea of rational expectations, it was in the context of a partial-equilibrium model in which the rational expectation in the model is the equilibrium price of the model. Muth used rational expectation of the equilibrium price as an empirical hypothesis with which to challenge the cobweb-cycle model in which producers decide how much to produce in the next period before learning the future price of what they produce. With a one-period time lag between production decisions and realized output, basing production decisions on the currently observed price of output implies an alternating sequence of high and low prices, high prices in one period inducing increased output in the next period, driving prices down, then leading to low output and high prices in the third period, and so on.

Muth argued that rational producers would not respond to price signals in such a way that their expectations were consistently mistaken period after period as the model suggested. Muth conjectured that the rational-expectations assumption would predict observed prices more accurately than the unit-elastic-expectations assumption of the cobweb model. In Muth's hands, rational expectations was a testable hypothesis about expectation-formation.[16]

Although originally proposed as a testable theoretical innovation, when applied in macroeconomics, the rational-expectations assumption has been almost completely insulated from empirical testing. When subjected to serious testing by Carlaw and Lipsey (2012), rational-expectations models failed to generate better predictions than macro-models using other expectational assumptions. Instead, rational expectations has been treated as an axiom supposedly required by a spurious methodological imperative that all macroeconomic models be "microfounded."

The imperative stems from a reductionist impulse that is no more than a question-begging exercise. A macro-theory (e.g., chemistry or psychology) cannot be reduced to a more basic theory (physics or neuroscience) by methodological fiat; the reduction must be derived in detail, accounting for previously unknown or unrecognized relationships and interactions, not by radical simplifications that abstract from, or assume away, those relationships (Popper & Eccles, 1977, 14–21), or in macroeconomics by mere hand-waving.

In an autobiographical account of his development as an economist, Lucas (1995) credited the first four chapters of Samuelson (1947), covering the basic ideas of optimization, equilibrium, and comparative statics, for teaching him the "standards for when an economic question had been properly posed and when it had been answered." Samuelson's explication of the method of comparative-statics thus became Lucas's ideal of rigorous theorizing based on equilibrium and optimization.

But Lucas and other advocates of rational-expectations methodology misunderstood the role of the comparative-statics method. The comparative-statics method isolates the pure theoretical effect of a parameter change under a *ceteris-paribus* assumption. Such an effect can be derived by comparing two equilibria (before and after the parameter change) under the assumption of a unique and locally stable equilibrium.

The refutable theorems of microeconomics derived from rigorously applying the comparative-statics method depend on the assumption

[16] While Muth found empirical support for rational expectations in microeconomic applications, as the lag between production decisions and realized output lengthens, the volatility of the price and output cycles seems to increase. See Rosen et al. (1994).

that all markets but the one under analysis are in equilibrium.[17] It has become an axiom of modern macroeconmoics that macroeconomic analysis that does not rest on microfoundations—equilibrium and optimization—is unworthy of serious attention. But the refutable theorems constituting the empirical content of microeconomics could not be derived without macrofoundations, i.e., a locally stable general equilibrium. The comparative-statics method, though appropriate for partial-equilibrium microeconomic analysis, is inappropriate for most macroeconomic problems, which are concerned with a failure to achieve, or even to approximate, the locally stable equilibrium state presumed by the comparative-statics method (Fisher, 1983, 15–16).

Modern macroeconomics now offers an array of models simplified sufficiently to be solvable using dynamic-optimization techniques. Dynamic optimization by individual agents—the microfoundations of modern macro—makes sense only in the context of a full intertemporal equilibrium with correct expectations. But it is just the possibility that intertemporal equilibrium may not obtain that makes macroeconomics interesting and relevant. As Lavington (1922, 24) so acutely observed, "the inactivity of all is the cause of the inactivity of each."

But the confusion besetting the macroeconomic application of rational expectations runs deeper. The original empirical application of the rational-expectations hypothesis by Muth was to a single market populated by well-informed specialists presumed to have well-founded expectations, implicitly conditioned on a stable macroeconomic environment, of future prices. Under unstable macroeconomic conditions, the accumulated knowledge and experience of market participants would not necessarily enable specialists and traders to form accurate expectations of future prices even in those markets about which they are knowledgeable.

Thus, the plausibility of rational expectations as an assumption about the formation of price expectations is sensitive to the context in which expectations are being formed: expectations about a single market in isolation or expectations about the evolution of a vector of relative prices and

[17] An anonymous referee argues that comparative-statics does not assume that all markets but the one under analysis are in equilibrium, just that total income, input prices, and the prices of other products don't change. While I suppose it is possible to imagine a situation in which the absence of equilibrium in markets other than one under analysis is compatible with no violation of the *ceteris-paribus* assumption, the assumption seems implausible if not almost certain to be violated.

their overall level. It is one thing to assume that some agents have expert knowledge about future prices in a narrow set of particular markets; it is quite another to assume that they have knowledge sufficient to forecast the course of all future prices and in particular to understand the subtle interactions between prices in one market and the apparently unrelated prices in another market. Partial-equilibrium analysis abstracts from those interactions, but general equilibrium analysis and macroeconomics cannot make such abstractions.

It is often subtle interactions that allow the kinds of informational inferences made by Alchian (Newhard, 2014) to be drawn from differences between expected and observed prices. Expert traders are likely to be able to predict future prices when the assumptions of partial-equilibrium analysis are satisfied and the effects of interactions with other markets can be safely disregarded.[18] But the comprehensive knowledge required to anticipate a broad range of prices in unrelated markets is knowledge that would only be possessed by an omniscient central planner.

The key error of the rational-expectations methodology is that rational expectations somehow cause or bring about an intertemporal equilibrium. It is certainly a fact that people strive to use all available information to anticipate what may happen in the future, and any bit of new information will be rapidly assessed and processed, possibly causing previously held price expectations to be revised. But that does not mean that the continuous gathering, evaluation and processing of new information causes a convergence on correct expectations of future prices. Indeed, Radner proved that, even under strong assumptions, ongoing information revision based on the observed differences between expected and actual prices need not lead to an equilibrium.

There is no causal relationship between rational expectations and equilibrium. Rational expectations are a property of equilibrium. The term "rational-expectations equilibrium" is a truism. Expectations can be rational in macroeconomics only in an equilibrium state. Outside of equilibhrium, expectations cannot be "rational." Failing to grasp that point, Morgenstern mistakenly argued that the Holmes-Moriarty interaction shows that equilibrium is a nonsensical concept; all he showed was

[18] This is somewhat of an overstatement. Clearly close markets for close substitutes and complements will figure into the expectations of expert traders. However, as more distant markets and broader macroeconomic forces begin to impinge on specific markets, the ability of expert traders to forecast future prices is impaired.

that in the single unrepeatable game played by Holmes and Moriarty, there is no equilibrium outcome.

To think about rational expectations as if it is what results in equilibrium is a category error, akin to thinking that a triangle is caused by having angles that add up to 180 degrees. That the angles of a triangle add up to 180 degrees doesn't cause the triangle; it is a property of being a triangle.

Modern macroeconomic models are typically so highlyaggregated that the extreme nature of the rational-expectations assumption is concealed. To treat all output as a single good (which involves treating the single output as both a consumption good and a productive asset generating a flow of productive services) imposes the assumption that the only relative price that can change is the real wage, so that only one future relative price is unknown. That assumption dispenses with the problem of incorrect expectations except for two variables: the future price level and the future productivity of labor.

Having eliminated complexity from their models, modern macroeconomists, purporting to solve microfounded macromodels, assume that there are just two variables about which agents must form their rational expectations. The simplified expectational requirements for achieving a microfounded equilibrium belie the claim to have achieved anything of the sort.

17.7 Conclusion

Four score and four years after Hayek explained how challenging the notion of intertemporal equilibrium really is and the difficulties inherent in explaining any empirical tendency toward intertemporal equilibrium, modern macroeconomics now denies that all those difficulties even exist. Many macroeconomists feel proud of what modern macroeconomics has achieved, but there is reason to think that the path trod by Hayek, Hicks, and Radner could have led macroeconomics in a more fruitful direction than the one on which it has been led by Lucas and his associates.

References

Arrow, K. J., & Hahn, F. H. (1971). *General Competitive Analysis*. Holden-Day.
Bliss, C. J. (1975). *Capital theory and the distribution of income*. North Holland.

Bliss, C. J. (1976). Capital theory in the short run. In M. Brown, K. Sato, & P. Zarembka (Eds.), *Essays in modern capital theory* (pp. 187–201). North-Holland.
Canard, N.-F. (1801). *Principes d'Économie politique*. Chez F. Buisson.
Carlaw, K., & Lipsey, R. G. (2012). Does history matter? Empirical analysis of the evolutionary versus the stationary equilibrium views of the economy. *Journal of Evolutionary Economics, 22*(4), 735–766.
Cass, D., & Shell, K. (1983). Do sunspots matter? *Journal of Political Economy, 91*(2), 193–227.
Currie, M., & Steedman, I. (1989). Agonising over equilibrium: Hayek and Lindahl. *Quaderni Di Storia Dell'economia Politica, 7*(1), 75–99.
Fisher, F. M. (1983). *Disequilibrium foundations of equilibrium economics*. Cambridge University Press.
Fisher, I. (1896). *Appreciation and interest*. Macmillan.
Fisher, I. (1907). *The rate of interest*. Macmillan.
Fisher, I. (1933). The debt-deflation theory of great depressions. *Econometrica, 1*(3), 337–57.
Hawtrey, R. G. (1913). *Good and bad trade*. Constable.
Hayek, F. A. (1928 [1984]). Intertemporal price equilibrium and movements in the value of money. In R. McCloughry (Ed.), *Money, capital and fluctuations: Early essays* (pp. 171–215). Routledge.
Hayek, F. A. (1929 [1933]). *Monetary theory and the trade cycle*. Jonathan Cape.
Hayek, F. A. (1931). *Prices and production*. Routledge and Kegan Paul.
Hayek, F. A. (1937). Economics and knowledge. *Economica New Series, 4*(13), 33–54.
Hayek, F. A. (1941). *The pure theory of capital*. University of Chicago Press.
Hicks, J. R. (1939). *Value and capital*. Oxford University Press.
Hicks, J. R. (1965). *Capital and growth*. Oxford University Press.
Hicks, J. R. (1983). *Classics and moderns*, vol. 3 of *Collected essays on economic theory*. Harvard University Press.
Hirshleifer, J. (1971). The private and social value of information and the incentive to reward to inventive activity. *American Economic Review, 61*(4), 561–574.
Keynes, J. M. (1936). *The general theory of employment, interest, and money*. Macmillan.
Koppl, R., & Rosser, B. (2002). All that I have to say has already crossed your mind. *Metroeconomica, 53*(4), 339–360.
Laidler, D. (1998). *Fabricating the Keynesian revolution*. Cambridge University Press.
Lavington, F. (1922). *The trade cycle: An account of the causes producing rhythmical changes in the activity of business*. P.S. King.

Leijonhufvud, A. (1973 [1981]). Effective demand failures. In *Information and coordination* (pp. 103–129). Oxford University Press.
Lindahl, E. (1929 [1939]). The place of capital in the theory of price. In *Studies in the theory of money and capital*. George, Allen & Unwin.
Lindahl, E. (1930 [1939]). The rate of interest and the price level. In *Studies in the theory of money and capital*. George, Allen & Unwin.
Lipsey, R. G., & Lancaster, K. (1956). The general theory of second best. *Review of Economic Studies, 24*(1), 11–32.
Milgate, M. (1979). On the origin of the notion of intertemporal equilibrium. *Economica New Series, 46*(181), 1–10.
Morgenstern, O. (1935 [1976]). Perfect foresight and economic equilibrium. In A. Schotter (Ed.), *Selected writings of Oskar Morgenstern* (pp. 169–183). Princeton University Press.
Muth, J. (1961). Rational expectations and the theory of price movements. *Econometrica, 29*(3), 315–335.
Myrdal, G. (1927). *Prisbildningsproblemet och Foranderligheten* (Price Formation and the Change Factor). Almqvist & Wicksell.
Neumann, J. v., & Morgenstern, O. (1944). *The theory of games and economic behavior*. Princeton University Press.
Newhard, J. (2014). The stock market speaks: How Dr. Alchian learned to build the bomb. *Journal of Corporate Finance, 27*, 116–132.
Pareto, V. (1906 [2014]). *Manual of political economy*. Oxford University Press.
Patinkin, D. (1965). *Money, interest, and prices: An integration of monetary and value theory* (2nd ed.). Harper and Row.
Popper, K. R., & Eccles, J. C. (1977). *The self and its brain*. Springer International.
Radner, R. (1972). Existence of equilibrium of plans, prices, and price expectations. *Econometrica, 40*(2), 289–303.
Radner, R. (1979). Rational expectations equilibrium: Generic existence and the information revealed by prices. *Econometrica, 47*(3), 655–678.
Radner, R. (1982). Equilibrium under uncertainty. In K. J. Arrow & M. Intriligator (Eds.), *Handbook of mathematical economics* (pp. 923–1006). North-Holland.
Radner, R. (1987). Uncertainty and equilibrium. In J. Eatwell, M. Milgate, & P. Newman (Eds.), *New Palgrave dictionary of economics*. Macmillan.
Ravagnani, F. (1989). On conflicting expectations in temporary equilibrium models. *Political economy: Studies in the surplus approach, 5*(1), 13–36.
Rosen, S., Murphy, K. M., & Scheinkman, J. (1994). Cattle cycles. *Journal of Political Economy, 102*(3), 468–492.
Samuelson, P. J. (1947). *The foundations of economic analysis*. Harvard University Press.
Smith, A. (1937). *The wealth of nations*. Modern Library.

Wicksteed, P. H. (1910). *The common sense of political economy*. Macmillan.
Zappia, C. (1999). The assumption of perfect foresight in Hayek's theory of knowledge. *Revue D'economique Politique, 109*(6), 833–846.

Index

D. Glasner, *Studies in the History of Monetary Theory*, Palgrave Studies in the History of Economic Thought,
https://doi.org/10.1007/978-3-030-83426-5

B

C

J

K

Y

Z

www.ingramcontent.com/pod-product-compliance
Ingram Content Group UK Ltd.
Pitfield, Milton Keynes, MK11 3LW, UK
UKHW041120071026
15587UKWH00009B/9
* 9 7 8 3 0 3 0 8 3 4 2 5 8 *